6

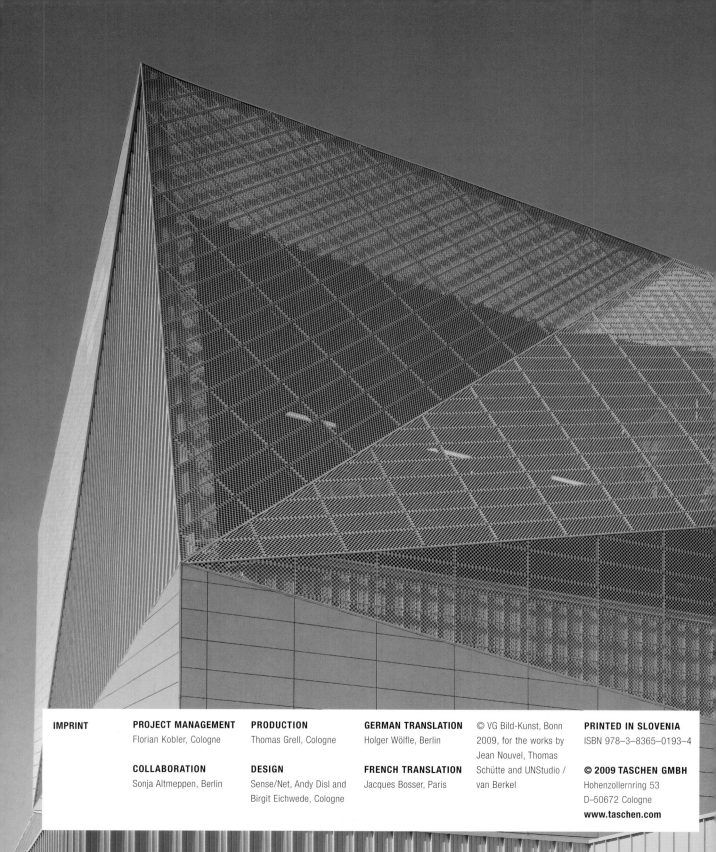

IMPRINT

PROJECT MANAGEMENT
Florian Kobler, Cologne

COLLABORATION
Sonja Altmeppen, Berlin

PRODUCTION
Thomas Grell, Cologne

DESIGN
Sense/Net, Andy Disl and
Birgit Eichwede, Cologne

GERMAN TRANSLATION
Holger Wölfle, Berlin

FRENCH TRANSLATION
Jacques Bosser, Paris

© VG Bild-Kunst, Bonn
2009, for the works by
Jean Nouvel, Thomas
Schütte and UNStudio /
van Berkel

PRINTED IN SLOVENIA
ISBN 978–3–8365–0193–4

© 2009 TASCHEN GMBH
Hohenzollernring 53
D–50672 Cologne
www.taschen.com

ARCHITECTURE NOW!

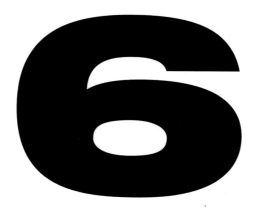

Architektur heute / L'architecture d'aujourd'hui
Philip Jodidio

TASCHEN

HONG KONG KÖLN LONDON LOS ANGELES MADRID PARIS TOKYO

CONTENTS

CONTENTS

INTRODUCTION

ARCHITECTURE IS ALIVE

The architecture of this moment is nothing if not varied and inventive. The extravagant blobs that were born of the first generation of computer design have all but disappeared, while computers have nonetheless made their inroads in a more far-reaching way. Even buildings that appear to be rectilinear or Modernist in their inspiration are now full of details and elements that could not have existed before 3D modeling and CNC (computer numerical control) milling became common. This edition of *Architecture Now!* features buildings ranging in size from Terunobu Fujimori's tiny (6.07 m^2) Teahouse Tetsu to Norman Foster's gigantic Crystal Island project in Moscow (1.1 million m^2), and this is no accident. Without any *parti pris*, this book attempts to give a useful overview of what is happening right now in architecture, be it of thoroughly traditional inspiration, or at the very edge of current thinking. What is the spirit of this moment, and how does architecture reflect the creativity as the first decade of the 21st century draws to a close? The eminent sociologist Zygmunt Bauman imagines the condition of modern society in terms that may well be applicable to contemporary architecture when he speaks of "liquid modernity." "Living in a 'liquid' modern world breaks down into three conditions. We need to act under the condition of first: uncertainty; second: under the condition of continuous risk which we try to calculate but which in principle is not fully calculable, as there are always surprises; and third: we need to act under the condition of shifting trust. A common trend that was trustworthy today may become condemned and rejected tomorrow. This is not only true in the field of work but everywhere. The food that you are recommended by doctors as healthy today will be proclaimed as carcinogenic tomorrow. If you look into glossy weeklies or glossy attachments of daily newspapers, you will see that virtually every week there is a column which informs you about the latest fashions, not only dressing fashions, but fashions of behavior, of decorating your house, of the fashionable celebrities which you must be informed about, and so on, columns which inform you what is 'on.' But next to it is a column that informs you what is out and what you should be ashamed of yourself if you still follow it."[1]

THE BOYS IN BEIJING

Contemporary architecture has often sought the state of liquid modernity as a virtue. PTW's monumental Watercube (National Swimming Center for the 2008 Beijing Olympic Games, page 404) is a solid square block of a building wearing a most ephemeral dress—skin made of ETFE (Ethylene Tetrafluoroethylene) pillows with a "random, organic appearance" based on the natural formation of soap bubbles. Few images conjure up the ephemeral better than soap bubbles, and yet the liquidity of architecture must surely have its limits. Architecture takes time to design and build, can cost a great deal, and most often serves a specific purpose—conditions that run counter to the "uncertainty" sought by some architects with such alacrity. The pursuit of fashion can, of course, make itself felt in such monumental buildings as the Watercube, the neighboring Main Stadium for the 2008 Olympic Games (Herzog & de Meuron, page 222), or the double Koolhaas/OMA CCTV tower. Intended to give contemporary Beijing the iconic architectural presences that it has conspicuously lacked until now, these structures pose the question of just where architecture is going as China, India, and the Arabian Gulf build at breakneck speed. The *Financial Times* pointedly questioned the architecture of the Olympic Games in December 2007: "In Beijing, the world's greatest architects have virtually given up on the idea of the city. This is modernism minus utopia, and with no context—physical, topographical, political, theoretical or urban. The

1

simple, single image is everything. Any of these buildings could have been built anywhere else. Beijing is becoming a realization of the most superficial aspects of a contemporary design culture obsessed with the gesture and the icon, with the cleverness and complexity of its own structure. This is architecture as stage set for the Olympics, for a regime determined to demonstrate its modernity and its emerging economic and cultural power. Radical architecture has let itself be used for spectacle and propaganda. Cities are made of buildings but great buildings are not enough to make cities."[2]

Quoting this article does not represent an acceptance of its substance, but rather acknowledges the variety of emotions and opinions elicited by the most spectacular expressions of contemporary architecture. It may look good, but what does it represent in terms of the inevitable compromises that go with any large project? It is said that Norman Foster once tried to explain to Chinese clients that the reliance of their country on bicycles was an ecological plus, something that they should strive to perpetuate. He was told in no uncertain terms that China aspired not to bicycles but to cars and jets. There is a powerful trend toward iconic architecture driven by vast amounts of money spread across the globe in new patterns from Mumbai to Dubai and on to Shanghai. One can criticize such trends, but contemporary architects are not so much agents of political protest as they are the creators of useful objects. Like everyone else, they seek to make a living and to leave their mark.

This book includes three iconic structures designed for the 2008 Beijing Olympic Games, but also the Ullens Center for Contemporary Art (UCCA, 2006–07, page 546), a remake of a 1950s factory by the Frenchman Jean-Michel Wilmotte (with MADA s.p.a.m.). The UCCA shows that the slash-and-burn demolition favored by local authorities is not the only way to make Beijing the kind of cosmopolitan center that many dream of. It also provides a counterpoint to the "superficial gestures" excoriated by the *Financial Times*. Even in a burgeoning capital like Beijing, it may not be possible to generalize about the directions of contemporary architecture.

The *Architecture Now!* series has also made frequent reference to works that can best be described as being situated at the frontier between art and architecture, or between architecture and design. This edition is no exception, with the decidedly "un-monumental" 2007 Serpentine Gallery Pavilion in London designed by the artist Olafur Eliasson and Snøhetta principal Kjetil Thorsen (page 138). Eliasson appears again with his *New York City Waterfalls*—installations that question the rapport of the city with its rivers (2008, page 134). Another artist, the German Anselm Kiefer, occupied the Grand Palais in Paris in the late spring and early summer of 2007 with an installation (*Sternenfall*, or Falling Stars, **2/3**) that owes much to architecture, or perhaps, more precisely, to ruins. "What you see is despair," says Kiefer. "I am completely desperate because I cannot explain why I am here. It's more than mourning, it's despair. But to survive, you build, you create illusions."[3] A questioning of the reasons for existence might well seem contrary to the "liquid modernity" defined by Bauman, but the point is precisely that architecture, the art of the built environment, expressed in its myriad forms, can either confirm or negate most theories of modernity. Solid enough to withstand the test of time, it is the object of ceaseless efforts to dissolve its substance practically into thin air. The March 11 Memorial in Madrid (Spain, 2005–07, page 164) by FAM Arquitectura, a ring of glass over a blue subterranean room, comments on a tragedy, again, curiously enough, inscribed on a membrane fashioned with EFTE, a sort of transparent Teflon, there, but hardly there. Like the wounds of some and the heartache of others, architecture here assumes an evanescent yet lasting tribute to an event that played out in a few moments of death and destruction.

2   3

2 + 3
Anselm Kiefer, Sternenfall, *Grand Palais, Paris, France, 2007*

FROM THE SHOCK OF THE OLD TO THE CHARMS OF THE METAVERSE

Perhaps because buildings take so long to build as compared to the quick creative cycle of artists, for example, or, rather, because they engage so much money, architecture has a curious rhythm, not quite like that of other "sociological" manifestations of fashion. The Young Turks who burst onto the scene with theories and forms that astonish go on to build, but so many years later their innovations seem to be relics of the past. Thus, the "Deconstructivist Architecture" show at New York's Museum of Modern Art (1988), curated by Philip Johnson, showed mostly unbuilt work by Frank O. Gehry, Daniel Libeskind, Rem Koolhaas, Peter Eisenman, Zaha Hadid, Bernard Tschumi, and Coop Himmelb(l)au. Today, looking at the BMW Welt (2001–07, page 124) in Munich by Coop Himmelb(l)au, their Akron Art Museum in Ohio (2001–07, page 114), or Libeskind's Royal Ontario Museum Extension (Toronto, Canada, 2002–07, page 314), one could be forgiven for assuming that the MoMA show was particularly prescient, revealing trends that would only take form 20 years later. "Deconstructivist architecture," wrote Mark Wigley, associate curator of the MoMA show, "does not constitute an avant-garde. Rather, it exposes the unfamiliar hidden within the traditional. It is the shock of the old."[4] The aesthetics and forms of contemporary architecture are surely not only determined by the age of architects. Steven Holl, for example, was born in 1947, just one year after Daniel Libeskind, and yet he has taken an independent, artistic approach to his designs. Holl's extension for the Nelson-Atkins Museum of Art (Bloch Building, Kansas City, Missouri, 2002–07, page 240) was the winner of a 2008 American Institute of Architects Honor Award. The jury commented, "The expansion of the Nelson-Atkins Museum of Art fuses architecture with landscape to create an experiential architecture that unfolds for visitors as it is perceived through each individual's movement through space and time." The luminous boxes that form the new building take an approach to surface, light, and space that is not the product of a "school" like Deconstructivism, but today this architecture may seem much more contemporary than fractured forms first publicized in the late 1980s.

Tadao Ando, born in 1941, is five years older than Libeskind, and has taken a route that is clearly anchored in the history of modern architecture, beginning with Le Corbusier. Yet Ando, like Steven Holl, has an artistic approach to his work that has allowed him to evolve and to create such surprising buildings as 21_21 Design Sight in Tokyo (Japan, 2004–07, page 76). Part of the ambitious Tokyo Midtown complex built on the site of the former Self-Defense Agency, 21_21 Design Sight does include a number of the concrete walls for which Ando is known, but its essential, visible structure is a folded metal roof that brings to mind the pleats of the fashion designer Issey Miyake, who was also involved in this project. A reduced, geometric vocabulary does seem to allow for a more "timeless" building than fractured complexity, but the general public may have more difficulty dating ideas than those who live in the world of contemporary architecture.

A number of important figures have influenced modern and contemporary architecture more through their drawings than through their built work. This trend can easily be dated back to Antonio Sant'Elia (1888–1916), Hugh Ferriss (1889–1962), or more recently John Hejduk (1929–2000), Peter Eisenman, and Zaha Hadid. Both Eisenman and Hadid have, of course, made the transition to more active building, but their reputations were established on the basis of theory and drawings much more than on their built work, until a fairly recent date. Computer imagery has, of course, facilitated the task of architects, who have the ability to imagine new worlds without making use of concrete and glass. It might be interesting to note that an architect who was a Chief Designer and Project Partner at Coop Himmelb(l)au for over 10 years, in charge of both the Akron Art Museum in Ohio and BMW Welt in Munich, has since struck out on his own, creating astonishing competition designs that seem to take the complex forms of the late 20th century one large leap forward. Tom Wiscombe created his own firm, EMERGENT, in 1999 and worked recently on two projects published in this volume, the National Library of the Czech Republic (Prague, Czech Republic, 2006–07, page 150) and the Shenzhen Museum of Contemporary Art (Shenzhen, China, 2007, page 144). Wiscombe's seductive imagery for these unbuilt projects may blend the powerful angles of Coop Himmelb(l)au with the kind of computer technology from which "blobs" first emerged, but he puts forth a thoroughly contemporary vision that could well be very influential in years to come.

While Wiscombe has considerable experience in translating computer-driven ideas into built form, others seem to have accepted the idea that some of today's architecture will never be built in the real world. Worldwide press attention has been focused on the Web site "Second Life" (www.secondlife.com) that has been described as a "metaverse"—which is to say a fully immersive 3D virtual space in which players interact (as avatars) with each other socially and economically. One architect featured in *Architecture Now! 6*, Scope Cleaver, can only be described as being virtual himself, since he declines to give any "real-world" information about himself. Rather, he writes that he "entered 'Second Life' in January 2006," as though he might well not have existed at all before that date. Scope Cleaver has designed a large number of virtual buildings in "Second Life" that can readily be visited. His Princeton University Gallery of the Arts (2007, page 460) is part of a rather extensive effort by the prestigious university to project itself into "Second Life." The University owns seven *sims* (65 536 m^2 regions) in "Second Life," administered by Princeton's Office of Information Technologies, Academic Services. Scope Cleaver has emerged as a principal designer of structures that may well play a "real-world" role in broadening the horizons of education. Although he is clearly not bound by the usual rules of architecture, Scope Cleaver creates his structures without relying on external CAD tools, preferring to use only elements that can be found within "Second Life." As he says, "Second Life" buildings involve "fantastic shapes that push the limits of virtual building while retaining realistic structural components." Though fashion certainly plays some role in the success of a site like "Second Life," its 20 million registered users (many inactive) are an indication of the potential for similar virtual environments that may well take a place in the future development of architecture.

THE WAYS OF THE LORD

Though surely not as great a source of significant contemporary architecture as cultural institutions, places of worship, in one form or another, continue to generate invention and cutting-edge design. The reuse of places of religion for other purposes sometimes poses the problem of deconsecration, with the reticence some users may have when asked to dine or party in a former church. One of the more successful of such recent initiatives is the Selexyz Dominicanen Bookstore (Maastricht, The Netherlands, 2005–07, page 352) by the architects Merkx+Girod working within the former Dominican church of Maastricht, built in the 13th century. Though the building had not in fact been used as a church since the French occupation that began in 1794, the architecture retained its decidedly ecclesiastical, even Gothic appearance. The designers won a prestigious Dutch award for this project in 2007, the Lensvelt de Architect Interior Prize. The jury's comment on their work deserves to be cited: "In Maastricht, Merkx+Girod Architecten have created a contemporary bookshop in a former Dominican

4
Merkx+Girod Architecten, Selexyz Dominicanen Bookstore, Maastricht, The Netherlands, 2005–07

5
Jensen & Skodvin Arkitektkontor, Tautra Maria Convent, Tautra Island, Norway, 2004–06

4   5

church, preserving the unique landmark setting. The church has been restored to its former glory and the utilities equipment has been housed in the extended cellar. In order to preserve the character of the church while achieving the desired commercial square footage, the architects erected a two-story structure in black steel on one side, where the books are kept. Keeping the shop arrangement on the other side low created a clear and decipherable shop. The jury was very impressed by these spatial solutions, as well as by the gorgeous lighting plan. The combination of book complex and church interior was deemed particularly successful."

A number of other buildings designed intentionally as places of worship are included in this edition of *Architecture Now!*. The Our Lady of the Conception Chapel (Recife, Pernambuco, Brazil, 2004–06, page 340) by the noted architect Paulo Mendes da Rocha was built within the walls of a 19th-century ruin on the grounds of the Brennand Ceramics factory, 16 kilometers from the city of Recife. Mendes da Rocha, winner of the 2006 Pritzker Prize, is known for his powerful concrete shapes, and yet here he has devoted himself to the restoration of old brick walls, while still covering the new structure with a concrete slab roof. The very weight and solidity of his architecture embrace and transform the existing ruin, modulating light, along with transparency and obvious mass to ends that are specifically religious. The very thought that contemporary architecture is unable to evoke spirituality can be put aside with a building such as the Brennand chapel.

Far from the style and fame of an architect such as Mendes da Rocha, contemporary designers show a consistent and inventive dedication to church or chapel spaces, as witnessed by the French architect Marc Rolinet, who recently completed the Chapel of the Deaconesses of Reuilly (Versailles, France, 2004–07, page 430). Working with a limited budget, but for clients who were open to his ideas, Rolinet has blended a modern and transparent envelope with an inner volume cloaked in wood. The boat-like form of the chapel itself brings to mind Christian symbolism—the boat of Saint Peter, or the words of Christ, "Follow me, and I will make you fishers of men" (Matthew 4:19; Mark 1:17). A devout Protestant, Rolinet has given a simple and modern form to his faith that suits the Deaconesses of Reuilly. This is not the sort of building that will draw worldwide attention, but it is nonetheless worthy of note.

Much more in the media spotlight, albeit somewhat against his own will, the Swiss architect Peter Zumthor has emerged from a rather long period of little construction to sign at least two interesting and important buildings—the Kolumba Art Museum in Cologne (Germany, 2003–07, page 566) and, not far away, the much smaller St. Niklaus von Flüe Chapel (Mechernich-Wachendorf, Germany, 2003–07, page 560). With seminal buildings such as his Thermal Baths in Vals, Switzerland (completed in 1996), Zumthor showed a strong attachment to the roots of Swiss history, and this chapel, dedicated to the patron saint of his country (St. Nicholas of Flüe, 1417–87, also known as Brother Klaus), can be seen as a further expression of his willful evocation of his heritage. With its extremely simple exterior form, and unusual interior shaped by spruce formwork burned at the end of the construction process, the chapel is also the product of essentially local labor, eschewing the kind of sophisticated multinational computer-driven spectacles favored by many architects who are as well known as Zumthor.

Another modest, yet powerful, piece of religious architecture is the Tautra Maria Convent by Jensen & Skodvin (Tautra Island, Norway, 2004–06, page 280) made for 18 Cistercian nuns. Much as the Deaconesses of Reuilly in France, these nuns played an active role in the development of the architecture, and are cited by the architects as being responsible for the landscape design. Relatively simple in its architectural expression, the Convent rose not far from the ruins of a Cistercian Monastery founded on the Island of Tautra 800 years ago. By care-

6
Peter Zumthor, St. Niklaus von Flüe Chapel, Mechernich-Wachendorf, Germany, 2003–07

7
Peter Zumthor, Kolumba Art Museum of the Archdiocese of Cologne, Cologne, Germany, 2003–07

6

7

fully examining the daily routines of the nuns, the architects managed to devise simple, economical solutions to their needs, while bringing forward unexpected ideas such as the refectory, where the nuns are all aligned on the same side of the table ("like Leonardo da Vinci's *Last Supper*," according to the architects), looking out at the countryside. The remote location of this convent, but also its dedication to simplicity combined with an openness to an architecture that does not imitate the past, allows it to generate a sense of spirituality that does not depend on any cliché about religious architecture. It is modern but respectful of its function in the best sense of the terms.

BURN BABY BURN

Perhaps inspired most by contemporary art that has long since assumed the beauty of the ephemeral, architecture, too, has accepted and even sought out the virtues of the temporary. Naturally, burgeoning new cities, perhaps first amongst them Los Angeles, gave rise to admittedly short-lived buildings that had no pretense to the kind of permanence to which architecture long aspired. In previous editions of the *Architecture Now!* series, works of art have figured prominently. Volume 3 had an image of Olafur Eliasson's *Weather Project* (Turbine Hall, Tate Modern, London, UK, October 16, 2003–March 21, 2004) on its cover. The relation between an architecture-related work of art and some obviously ephemeral buildings is not a negligible aspect of the evolution of contemporary architecture. Ideas that emerge at the border between art and architecture often go on to influence more durable types of buildings in a substantive, or sometimes only aesthetic, way. Arne Quinze is neither an architect nor really a pure artist. Rather, he is a self-educated designer of some importance. His elaborate installation for the 2006 Burning Man Festival, *Uchronia: Message out of the Future* (Black Rock City, Black Rock Desert, Nevada, page 412), was intended from the first to be burnt to the ground after a week of festivities. A movie and a book chronicling the construction (and destruction) of the open pavilion is the only remaining trace of its existence. Some may liken *Uchronia* to an art event as opposed to an architectural realization, but its function as a dance or party locale clearly places it in the realm of buildings. The collective nature of its realization and its meandering, almost organic structure make *Uchronia* aesthetically interesting, and, indeed, Arne Quinze has since built a less fleeting version of this design in Brussels.

Shipping containers have enjoyed something of an architectural fashion in recent years with such striking (temporary) realizations as Shigeru Ban's Bianimale Nomadic Museum (Pier 54, New York, New York, 2005). The Brazilian architects Bernardes + Jacobsen used such containers to create the location of the TIM Festival 2007 in Rio de Janeiro (Rio de Janeiro, Brazil, page 108). Using no less than 250 six- and 12-meter-long containers, they created the essential structures for a popular music festival that lasts only two nights. Shipping containers were standardized as of 1956, based on the ideas of the American Malcom McLean, and have become a frequent fixture of a contemporary architecture that has admitted it can (or should) be ephemeral. The TIM Festival is a case in point of the need for rather substantial architectural elements that can be easily moved into place and removed just as readily. In this instance, it is more the realm of industrial design and transportation that shapes architecture, but just as art can play this role, so, too, it seems, can more practically oriented disciplines.

Works of art often verge on the architectural, just as some architects aspire to the status conferred to their less down-to-earth friends in the art world. The German artist Thomas Schütte has shown a frequent interest in architectural forms in his varied production. One of his

8
Renzo Piano, The New York Times
Building, New York, New York, USA,
2005–07

9
Renzo Piano, Los Angeles County
Museum of Art, Los Angeles,
California, USA, 2006–08

8

9

most recent works, an installation for the so-called Fourth Plinth in London's Trafalgar Square (*Model for a Hotel*, 2007–08, page 456) is in reality nothing more than a stack of skewed, colored glass plates, and yet its appearance, varying considerably depending on the angle of view, poses interesting questions about how architecture can go about better dissolving its sometimes too heavy presence. From some angles, Schütte's work almost disappears, a result that many architects have sought to no avail. But then again, art does not obey the same rules as architecture in most instances—a rule that certainly applies to the Fourth Plinth installation. What can be admitted readily is that architecture has sought out a cross-fertilization that can be found in art, design, or even industrial applications, as the use of shipping containers shows. The openness demonstrated by this fact allows architecture to evolve in sometimes unexpected directions, and sometimes to break free of the gravity that so weighs down many "traditional" buildings. Though few buildings are meant to be incinerated like Arne Quinze's *Uchronia*, the escape from the rules of architectural permanence implied by the work of Quinze does have an almost immediate bearing on what contemporary architecture can do.

FEET IN THE SAND, HEAD IN THE STARS

Although it may be fashionable to affirm that "globalization" is greatly reducing the variety of contemporary architecture, the fact remains that different cities, and indeed different climates, impose varying approaches, even if the fundamental methods and materials of architects are often quite similar. The skyscraper culture of a city like New York imposes limits, both in terms of potential use and because of the rather complex zoning restrictions that may apply, according to the sites concerned. Two of architecture's "star" designers have been called to Manhattan to work on towers that may, in their own way, each redefine some of the stylistic conventions that have long applied to the city. Renzo Piano completed the New York Times Building near Times Square in New York in 2007 (page 394), marking an improvement in the quality of the architecture in the immediate area. Piano's 52-story, 228-meter-high tower is occupied on the lower 28 floors by the newspaper, and on the upper 24 by real estate and law firms. The core of the design, the newsroom of the daily, occupies three floors, grouped around an internal garden planted with 15-meter-tall paper birch trees, ferns, and moss. This garden, and its trees, which are, after all, the source of the paper used by *The New York Times* in a metaphorical and even a literal sense, together with the willful transparency imposed by the architect, demonstrate the Italian's ability to deliver a quality design that does not necessarily meet with the expectations that one might have had of the co-designer (with Richard Rogers) of the Centre Pompidou in Paris (1977). Since the basic form of a Manhattan tower is imposed by the city's grid and the high cost of land, Piano has used the subtlety for which he is known to create an American building with a European sensibility.

While Piano may well have left his radical instincts behind some time after the completion of the Centre Pompidou, it can be said that Jean Nouvel has remained something of an irritant in the ranks of well-known architects. His buildings retain their ability to surprise and even to upset. The new Tour de Verre (New York, New York, 2007–12, **10/11**), designed by the French architect with the developer Hines, will change the very profile of mid-town Manhattan, rising 75 stories next to the Museum of Modern Art. *The New York Times*, which has long been something of an arbiter of taste in the city, wrote of the project in glowing terms, "A new 75-story tower designed by the architect Jean

10 + 11
Jean Nouvel, Tour de Verre, New York,
New York, USA, 2007–12

10

11

Nouvel for a site next to the Museum of Modern Art in Midtown promises to be the most exhilarating addition to the skyline in a generation. Its faceted exterior, tapering to a series of crystalline peaks, suggests an atavistic preoccupation with celestial heights. It brings to mind John Ruskin's praise for the irrationality of Gothic architecture: 'It not only dared, but delighted in, the infringement of every servile principle.'" Nouvel's tower is clearly more audacious than the recent additions to the Museum of Modern Art signed by the Japanese architect Yoshio Taniguchi, a fact that led *The New York Times* to make a rather unfavorable comparison between the two projects. Nouvel's Tour de Verre is also slated to add new space to the Museum, and the paper commented, "The additional gallery space is a chance for MoMA to rethink many of these spaces, by reordering the sequence of its permanent collection, for example, or considering how it might re-situate the contemporary galleries in the new tower and gain more space for architecture shows in the old. But to embark on such an ambitious undertaking the museum would first have to acknowledge that its Taniguchi-designed complex has posed new challenges. In short, it would have to embrace a fearlessness that it hasn't shown in decades. MoMA would do well to take a cue from Ruskin, who wrote that great art, whether expressed in 'words, colors or stones, does not say the same thing over and over again.'"[5]

Whether because of zoning restrictions or simple conservative thinking, New York has not proven to be the most inventive city when it comes to contemporary architecture. Manhattan as a whole might be considered a quintessentially modern urban area, and yet its bits and pieces seem to date more from the 1930s than from the new century. Other cities, such as Dubai in the United Arab Emirates, are rising at a hectic speed and hope to become new centers in their own right, for business of course, but also for architecture. Until recently, Dubai has relied on large Western architectural practices with little imagination, but that situation is fast changing with such famous names as Zaha Hadid now signing major projects. Sitting on the Arabian Gulf, just next to the great deserts of Saudi Arabia, Dubai must cope with a series of complicated circumstances that make it physically different from New York, for example. With a population made up largely of expatriates and summer temperatures that can soar to about 50° centigrade, this is not really a place for walking about, enjoying the urban scenery. People move in cars and seem astonished to see anyone other than workers from Bangladesh exposed to the afternoon sun. Cities like Los Angeles long ago developed a car-based urban culture, but in Dubai it is a matter as much of climate as of distance. The Saudi developer Adel al Mojil has sought, through a high-level competition including such architects as Ryue Nishizawa and Kazuyo Sejima, to pose the question of just what kind of person might want to use the enormous complex he plans to build at the limit of the new Business Bay area in Dubai. Calling his project "The Edge" (Dubai, UAE, 2008–, page 418), Al Mojil asks what the needs of the "knowledge worker" of the future may be. Positing the emergence of Dubai as a real world financial center and not simply an oil-fueled mirage, The Edge is to be a 350 000-square-meter, 600-million-euro colossus of a project including offices, hotels, residences, retail—in short everything needed for a "knowledge worker" to live, eat, and sleep the few months he or she may remain in the United Arab Emirates. This is surely not the scheme imagined by Renzo Piano when he designed the New York Times Building, a pure office facility. Nouvel's Tour de Verre will have hotel and apartment space, as well as galleries for the Museum of Modern Art and offices, but residents would by no means be encouraged to live their entire life within its walls. The inventive Spanish firm RCR was selected to build The Edge after the 2007 competition. Their mirage-like series of towers rising from a "floating carpet" platform is aesthetically interesting and quite new in its conception. Although the project may evolve somewhat before

12

12
Savioz Meyer Fabrizzi Architectes,
Hôtel de la Poste, Sierre, Switzerland,
2006–07

actual construction, RCR's proposal will remain a first step along the path to designing a very large building specifically meant for a place like Dubai. Climate, more than local culture, really seems to be the driving force behind the development of such practically self-contained complexes, but The Edge is big enough to be a sort of city unto itself, no longer bound by the more traditional constraints of urban life. In one of his recent pamphlets called "The Gulf," Rem Koolhaas (OMA) writes, "Eventually, the Gulf will reinvent the public and the private: the potential of infrastructure to promote the whole rather than favor fragmentation; the use and abuse of landscape—golf or the environment?; the coexistence of many cultures in a new authenticity rather than a Western Modernist default; experiences instead of Experience—city or resort?"

DESIGNER BED AND BREAKFAST

Just as cultural institutions have provided a good deal of the work for inventive architects over past years, the hotel business, increasingly interested in design, perhaps inspired by the spate of Schrager-Starck projects in the 1990s, has also employed numerous well-known architects in the hope of drawing in a chic, moneyed clientele. This phenomenon has spread beyond world cities such as New York and Berlin and now concerns less well-known destinations like Zuoz in the Engadine region of Switzerland. Though it is a beautiful medieval town, Zuoz is a few kilometers from St. Moritz and its glamorous resort life. The Hotel Castell is situated just above the old town at an altitude of 1900 meters. The Swiss art collector and artist Ruedi Bechtler bought the original building, built as a fashionable "Kurhotel" in 1912–13 by Nicolaus Hartmann, in the mid-1990s. The architect Gabrielle Hächler and the noted Swiss artist Pipilotti Rist designed their first project in the hotel, the Red Bar, inaugurated in 1998. Beginning in 2000, the Amsterdam architects UNStudio came on board and designed a new building with 14 luxury apartments (2003–04, page 502). Within the old building, they added a colorful hamam in the east wing basement, and redesigned about half of the hotel's 60 rooms in a style typical of their work. The local architect Hans-Jörg Ruch redid the other rooms, while the Japanese artist Tadashi Kawamata added a wooden terrace and walkway leading to a sauna on the grounds of the hotel. Completed recently by the construction of a cylindrical *Skyspace* by artist James Turrell, the Castell is in a sense typical of many "designer hotels" across the world, but, in this instance, the high quality of the different architectural and artistic interventions is particularly notable.

Two mountain passes and about 300 kilometers away, though still in Switzerland, the Hôtel de la Poste in Sierre (2006–07, **12**) by the young architects Savioz Meyer Fabrizzi does not have the kind of world-class art seen in the Castell, but it shows just how far the idea of the designer, or in this case architect, hotel has come. Working with a rectilinear mid-18th-century building, the architects dared to make the exterior bright orange and to paint the name of the hotel in large letters on its side façade. Situated in front of a small park that runs behind the neighboring city hall toward the railway station, the Hôtel de la Poste now has a sinuous glass dining room to the rear. The architects also redesigned the hotel rooms, using a different type of wood for each of the 15 suites and naming the rooms after the wood used. Photos of the trees concerned figure on the ceiling of each room, giving a "green" tinge to this otherwise traditional old structure.

Legorreta + Legorreta, architects based in Mexico City, completed the renovation of a former water bottling factory in Puebla, Mexico, creating La Purificadora Boutique Hotel in 2007 (page 308). Like their less famous colleagues in Sierre, the Mexicans renovated the existing

13
UNStudio, Hotel Castell, Zuoz,
Switzerland, 2001–04

13

19th-century structure while retaining many of its more colorful or picturesque features. The local stone walls of the original single-story structure were kept, while the architects added three floors with masonry walls, a bar-lounge on the roof, and a 30-meter-long swimming pool with glass walls. The architects reused the wooden beams of the original water plant, employed specially made ceramic tiles that recall local cladding materials, and local onyx. Though Ricardo Legorreta is known for using saturated color schemes that bring to mind those of Luis Barragán, in the case of this hotel, it is the palette of materials, both new and old, that is allowed to fill the space without many strong colors aside from the bright purple seen in the furniture.

DOING IT RIGHT

Much contemporary architecture of quality is created with a compromise at its heart, since money, sometimes a great deal of it, is necessary to make an outstanding or innovative building. The architecture that most people live with is quite ordinary, or in any case fundamentally repetitive and boxlike. The poor, or those dispossessed by natural disasters or wars, obviously do not benefit much from the brilliant designs of today's top architects. Naturally there are exceptions to this rule, and architects who have made a point of creating affordable or easily built lodgings that serve those who are most in need. The Japanese architect Shigeru Ban is one of these. Though he, too, has his share of wealthy clients, Ban has created temporary housing in India, Turkey, and Rwanda (for UNHCR). His most recent initiative of this nature, the Post-Tsunami Rehabilitation Houses (Kirinda, Hambantota, Sri Lanka, 2005–07, page 98), aimed to create a total of 50 houses for victims of the December 26, 2004, tsunami. At an approximate cost of $13 000 per house, these 71-square-meter residences are made of local rubber tree wood and compressed earth blocks. Comfortable and carefully studied to meet the requirements of local culture, the Kirinda houses may be an exception that proves the rule that famous architects do not work for the poor, but the case is surely notable enough to figure in this volume.

Shigeru Ban is also participating in the Make It Right initiative in New Orleans (Louisiana, 2007–, page 530). In this instance, the actor Brad Pitt and the architects Graft are leading an effort to rebuild affordable architect-designed houses in the Lower Ninth Ward of the city, devastated by Hurricane Katrina. With such participants as Kieran Timberlake, Morphosis, David Adjaye, and MVRDV, Make It Right surely has a higher profile than Ban's Kirinda project, and may well have a political message. In "the richest country in the world," it can certainly be considered shocking that some of America's poorest people should remain homeless through long periods marked essentially by bureaucratic ineptitude, evidenced up to the highest levels of the government. Strictly observed from the perspective of contemporary architecture, it is interesting of course to see what "star" architects can do with the $150 000 budget allotted per residence. Ban's Kirinda houses make no pretense to employ the sophisticated vocabulary for which the architect became known—rather, they are a strict, coherent effort to bring relief to those in need, using ecologically responsible methods and materials. The conditions for participants to be selected for Make It Right demonstrate that the organizers had taken into account a series of factors that may rarely come together in the high-flying world of cutting-edge architecture:

– Prior interest or involvement in New Orleans, preferably post-Katrina and/or experience with disaster relief;

14

- Familiarity and interest in sustainability;
- Experience with residential and multifamily housing;
- Proven to be skilled innovators of low-budget projects;
- Experience dealing with structures that have to successfully address water-based or low-lying environment(s);
- And, of course, deep respect for design quality.

The actor Brad Pitt and his partner Angelina Jolie have shown their commitment to worthy causes through the Jolie-Pitt Foundation, which has recently donated substantial funds to help Sudanese refugees affected by the Darfur crisis, and given to such charities as Global Action for Children or Médecins sans Frontières. The fact that their help is so desperately needed in the midst of the United States, and that so many important architects have agreed to donate their services to the Make It Right initiative, says a great deal about the state of America, and perhaps also something rather more positive about contemporary architecture.

MEDIEVAL TOWERS AND TEA IN THE TREES

The title *Architecture Now!* surely implies an interest in recent developments, and indeed many of the projects featured in this book are aesthetically or technically at the cutting edge of today's art of building. It should be noted in passing that a good number of the projects published here have to do with creating a rapport between existing structures and new additions or uses. The Our Lady of the Conception Chapel by Paulo Mendes da Rocha in Brazil and the Ullens Center by Jean-Michel Wilmotte in Beijing are examples of this type of symbiosis, or confrontation if one prefers, between the past and the present. Renovation of existing structures will continue to be a significant element in the evolution of contemporary architecture, if only for basic, economic reasons. It often costs less to renovate a structure than to build anew. The expanding notion of which buildings should or should not be considered historically interesting or significant also plays a role in the rise of renovation as a large part of contemporary architecture. Neither the neo-Bauhaus factory renovated by Wilmotte in Beijing nor the old water bottling plant turned into a chic hotel in Puebla by Legorreta might have qualified 20 years ago as being worth redoing, yet their space and materials give a richness to the completed projects that could not have been produced with purely contemporary elements.

The presence of the past suffuses even the most contemporary architecture. That past may be historical and linked to a specific site, as is the case in the Bergen-Belsen Documentation and Information Center by KSP Engel und Zimmermann (Celle, Germany, 2005–07, page 156) or LIN's renovation of part of the Saint-Nazaire Submarine Base (France, 2005–07, page 320), or it might be an evocation of even more distant memories, as seen in Holzer Kobler's Arche Nebra building (Wangen, Germany, 2005–07, page 250), inspired by a Bronze Age disk found nearby. It is clear that in some countries the exploration of the more distant past and its cultural and architectural implications can come to the fore in unexpected ways. Switzerland, a small country with a very long history, has recently produced such architects as Peter Zumthor, who is clearly inspired by the Alps, their culture, and even their stone. Less well-known than Zumthor, but equally steeped in his country's history, Hans-Jörg Ruch, who works essentially in the Engadine Valley near St. Moritz, was educated partly in the United States. His restoration of the 14th-century Chesa Madalena in Zuoz (Switzerland, 2001–02, page 438) that permitted the discovery of a medieval tower

15
Valerio Olgiati, Atelier Bardill,
Scharans, Switzerland, 2006–07

15

walled up in the old farm building is remarkable in its combination of respect for the past and openness to the present. The Chesa Madalena is now a contemporary art gallery showing works by Richard Long or Balthasar Burkhard without any contradiction. Especially in "old" cultures like those of Europe or parts of Asia, the awareness of the past and a respect for its lessons have surely risen greatly in recent years. Architects like Ruch are both the confirmation of this trend and instigators in their own right of a new sensibility that can accommodate the past and present simultaneously.

Another Swiss architect, Valerio Olgiati, has taken a somewhat more radical approach to the construction of an artist's atelier, in the heart of the old village of Scharans (Atelier Bardill, 2006–07, page 382). In the place of an old wooden barn, he has erected a red poured-in-place concrete structure that assumes the profile of the farm structure, while opening its heart to the sky with an oval courtyard. Though the use of almost blank concrete walls might be considered shocking in this context, it is a fact that the new structure has captured the austerity of the original architecture of this Swiss mountain village. Olgiati made his concrete red because the village demanded that the new structure have the same color as the old one. Thus, in the process of respecting a request formulated for historic preservation reasons, he has made a thoroughly modern building, with an internal courtyard worthy of James Turrell's *Skyspaces*.

Terunobu Fujimori is a Professor at the University of Tokyo specialized in the history of Western-style buildings erected in Japan from the Meiji period (1868–1912) onwards. He is particularly knowledgeable about the emergence of modern architecture through the work of such figures as Le Corbusier, Mies van der Rohe, and Gropius, and yet when he himself began to build, he created very unexpected buildings that seem deeply rooted in the past. Fujimori writes, "From my first project, I have tried to adopt the following two rules as a design policy:

1) The building should not resemble anyone else's building, past or present, or any style that has developed since the Bronze Age;

2) Natural materials should be used on parts of the building that are visible, and at times plants should be incorporated in the building, so as to harmonize the building with nature."[6]

Though the very desire to design structures that resemble no other might be seen as pretentious, Fujimori remains as modest as his 6.07-square-meter Teahouse Tetsu built in the grounds of a museum in Japan (Kiyoharu Shirakaba Museum, Nakamaru, Hokuto City, Yamanashi, 2005, page 174). He compares it to a "house for a midget from a fairytale," but also makes reference to some of the most important cultural symbols of Japan, like Sen no Rikyu (1522–91, the historical figure who had the most profound influence on the Japanese tea ceremony), in describing the project. Made for observing cherry blossom in the area, Teahouse Tetsu also finds its purpose in the most deeply felt Japanese customs and traditions, from the tea ceremony to the annual *sakura* (cherry blossom) frenzy that grips the country. Like the "fairytale midget" evoked by the architect, this tiny project is an object of humor, but it is also the product of ancient traditions. It is "displaced" in an intellectual sense, somewhat like Olgiati's Atelier in Scharans. Nothing is as it seems here, and that is a fact that makes Fujimori's surprising work fundamentally contemporary. It is about the condition of architecture as much as it is rooted in the more or less distant past. In the case of another of his projects, the Too-High Teahouse (Miyagawa Takabe, Chino City, Nagano, 2003), Fujimori writes, "In the distance is the house where Toyo Ito grew up. Even though the two of us grew up in the same area and during the same period, what we create is completely opposite. The relationship between human beings and their environments is not simple and straightforward."[7]

16

SUNFLOWERS AND STARS

It is not an accident that this brief tour around the premises of *Architecture Now! 6* ends with Kirinda, Make It Right, and the smallest building in the book, the Teahouse Tetsu. The attention of the press is often focused on the most expensive and visible works of contemporary architecture, such as 2008's star attractions in Beijing. Those buildings, the Main Olympic Stadium and the nearby Watercube, are featured here, as is the spectacular BMW Welt by Coop Himmelb(l)au, but it seems clear that a consciousness of other reasons for architecture to exist has emerged and been expressed with humor by unexpected figures such as Terunobu Fujimori. Fujimori is interested in what he calls an "architecture of humanity" not related so much to Japanese tradition as to the earth itself. It might seem logical that stars of contemporary architecture should align themselves with the firmament of Hollywood, as appears to have happened with Make It Right in New Orleans, but designing homes for people who have none is a far different exercise from creating playgrounds for millionaires. Contemporary architecture, despite its rather durable nature (at least as compared to the latest issue of *Vanity Fair*), often ignores the fundamentals of existence, searching for a glamorous effect, an eye-catching surprise. The fact that an artist of the significance of Anselm Kiefer feels that his ideas can best be expressed through the forms of architecture is an interesting comment on the state of things—his vision is one of ruins, of post-Apocalyptic sunflowers, growing out of shattered concrete and fallen stars. Contemporary art has long seemed to be searching for itself, reaching out for a soul lost in the transition from the figure to splash of paint, or more recently the video installation. Might it be that contemporary architecture in its full variety comes closest to expressing hope, fears, excesses, and triumphs, of crystallizing the moment? The "liquid modernity" in all its splendid commercial superficiality evoked by Zygmunt Bauman is surely present in this book, but so too is the weighty concrete of Bergen-Belsen or the ethereal monument to March 11 in front of Atocha Station. And if shipping containers gathered together for a two-day music festival in Rio, or 150 kilometers of wooden planks burning in the Nevada desert, are part of the equation, then let them burn. And what of an architect who exists only in "Second Life," designing virtual buildings for a real university? At the other extreme, restoring a 14th-century building in Zuoz, Switzerland, must also be seen as an integral part of the process and evolution of contemporary architecture. If there is an affirmation here, it is that understanding architecture means not excluding the past or even the most ephemeral expressions of the present. The contemporary architecture seen in this book spans across history and hopes, from places of religion to places of sport and commerce, from the largest building in the world to one of the smallest. Architecture is alive.

Philip Jodidio, Grimentz, 2008

16 + 17
PTW Architects, The Watercube,
National Swimming Center, Beijing,
China, 2003–08

17

1   Zygmunt Bauman, "Value Dilemmas as a Challenge in the Practice and Concepts of Supervision and Coaching," ANSE-conference, May 7, 2004, Leiden, The Nether-
     lands. Born in 1925, Dr. Zygmunt Bauman, Emeritus Professor of Sociology at the University of Leeds, is one of the best-known sociologists and philosophers in the
     world through publications such as *Liquid Modernity* (2000). He was awarded the European Amalfi Prize for Sociology and Social Sciences in 1989 and 1990, and
     the Theodor W. Adorno Award by the City of Frankfurt in 1998.
2   Edwin Heathcote, "Modernism Minus Utopia," *The Financial Times*, December 29, 2007.
3   Alan Riding, "An Artist Sets Up House(s) at the Grand Palais," *The New York Times*, May 31, 2007.
4   Mark Wigley, in *Deconstructivist Architecture*, The Museum of Modern Art, New York, 1988.
5   Nicolai Ouroussoff, "Next to MoMA, Reaching for the Stars," *The New York Times*, November 15, 2007.
6   Terunobu Fujimori, *Fujimori Terunobu Architecture*, Toto Shuppan, Tokyo, 2007.
7   Ibid.

EINLEITUNG

DIE ARCHITEKTUR LEBT

Die Architektur der Gegenwart zeichnet sich vor allem durch ihre Vielfalt und Originalität aus. Zwar trifft man kaum noch auf jene „Blob-Architektur", die mit der ersten Generation von computergesteuertem Entwerfen entstanden ist, der allumfassende Einsatz von Computern ist indes ganz selbstverständlich geworden. Selbst Gebäude, die sich augenscheinlich an klaren geometrischen oder klassisch-modernen Formen orientieren, stecken heute voll von Details und Elementen, die es vor der Verbreitung von 3-D-Modeling und CNC-Fräsen nicht hätte geben können. In dieser Ausgabe von *Architecture Now!* werden Gebäude verschiedenster Dimensionen vorgestellt, von Terunobu Fujimoris 6,07 m^2 großem Teehaus Tetsu in Japan bis hin zu Norman Fosters gigantischem Moskauer Projekt Crystal Island mit einer Gesamtnutzfläche von 1,1 Millionen m^2 — und dies ist kein Zufall: Die folgenden Seiten sollen einen Überblick über den aktuellen Stand des Architekturgeschehens geben — ganz unvoreingenommen und unabhängig davon, ob es sich im Einzelnen mehr in eine bewusst traditionelle Richtung bewegt oder allerneueste Entwicklungen abbildet. Welcher Geist herrscht gegenwärtig, wie und inwiefern spiegelt Architektur die Kreativität der verklingenden ersten Dekade des 21. Jahrhunderts? Der bedeutende Soziologe Zygmunt Bauman fasst den Zustand der modernen Gesellschaft mit dem Stichwort der „flüchtigen Moderne" in eine Begrifflichkeit, die sich auch treffend auf die zeitgenössische Architektur anwenden lässt. „Das Leben in einer ‚flüchtigen' modernen Welt ist von drei Faktoren gekennzeichnet: Zum Ersten ist unser Handeln zwangsläufig von Unsicherheit bestimmt, zum Zweiten von einem beständigen Risiko, das wir zu berechnen suchen, das aber im Prinzip nicht zu berechnen ist, da immer wieder Überraschungen auftauchen, und zum Dritten davon, dass sich unser Vertrauen auf bestimmte Dinge zwangsläufig wandelt. Ein allgemeiner Trend, der heute noch vertrauenswürdig erscheint, kann morgen schon in Verruf geraten und für ungültig erklärt werden. Das gilt nicht nur in Bezug auf die Arbeit, sondern überall. Was Ärzte heute zur gesunden Ernährung empfehlen, kann morgen schon als krebserregend gelten. Wirft man einen Blick in Illustrierte oder in die bunten Beilagen von Tageszeitungen, trifft man praktisch jede Woche auf Kolumnen, die einen über die neuesten Trends auf dem Laufenden halten, nicht nur zu modischer Kleidung, sondern auch dazu, wie man sich allgemein zu benehmen hat, wie man seine vier Wände einrichten soll, über welche Prominenten man Bescheid wissen muss und so weiter — Kolumnen also, die einen darüber informieren, was gerade ‚in' ist. Direkt daneben findet sich allerdings eine Kolumne, die einem erklärt, was ‚out' ist und welcher Trend einem peinlich sein sollte, falls man ihm immer noch anhängt."[1]

DIE JUNGS IN PEKING

Die zeitgenössische Architektur sieht den Zustand flüchtiger Modernität häufig als erstrebenswert an. Das Nationale Schwimmzentrum für die Olympischen Spiele 2008 in Peking, der monumentale Watercube des Architekturbüros PTW (S. 404), ist ein Gebäude in Form eines massiven Quaders, der in ein äußerst flüchtig wirkendes Gewand gehüllt ist — in eine Haut aus ETFE-Kissen (Ethylen-Tetrafluorethylen), deren Anordnung nach dem natürlichen Vorbild von Seifenblasen „zufällig und organisch anmutet". Es dürfte nicht viele Bilder geben, die Kurzlebigkeit treffender beschwören als Seifenblasen, obwohl die Flüchtigkeit von Architektur natürlich ihre Grenzen hat. Um Architektur zu schaffen, braucht es Zeit und mitunter sehr viel Geld, und außerdem soll sie zumeist einem speziellen Zweck dienen — Voraussetzungen, die der von vielen Architekten mit großem Eifer angestrebten „Unbestimmtheit" entgegenstehen. Das Bestreben, auf der Höhe der Zeit zu sein, ist bei

18
Coop Himmelb(l)au, BMW Welt,
Munich, Germany, 2001–07

19
Coop Himmelb(l)au, Akron Art
Museum, Akron, Ohio, USA, 2001–07

18

19

Monumentalbauwerken wie dem Watercube, dem benachbarten Hauptstadion für die Olympischen Spiele 2008 von Herzog & de Meuron (S. 222) oder dem Doppelturm für die chinesische Fernsehgesellschaft CCTV von Rem Koolhaas und seinem Office for Metropolitan Architecture (OMA) wohl nicht zu verkennen. Diese Bauwerke, die mit ihrer zeichenhaften Architektur dem neuen Peking jene Ausstrahlung verschaffen sollen, die der Stadt bislang offenkundig fehlte, werfen jedoch die Frage auf, welche Richtung die Architektur einschlägt, die in China, Indien und am Persischen Golf in so halsbrecherischem Tempo entsteht. Die *Financial Times* ging im Dezember 2007 mit der Architektur der Olympischen Spiele hart ins Gericht: „In Peking haben sich die bedeutendsten Architekten der Welt von der Idee der Stadt weitestgehend verabschiedet. Man trifft auf eine Moderne ohne Utopie und ohne jeden Kontext – in ihrer physischen Beschaffenheit wie in topografischer, politischer, theoretischer oder städtebaulicher Hinsicht. Das einfache, einzelne Bild ist alles. Jedes dieser Gebäude hätte auch irgendwo anders gebaut sein können. Peking wird zu einem Ort, an dem sich die oberflächlichsten Aspekte einer zeitgenössischen Designkultur realisieren, die allein von äußerlichem Ausdruck und Symbolwirkung sowie der Raffiniertheit und Komplexität ihrer eigenen Strukturen besessen ist. Es ist eine reine Schauarchitektur für die Olympischen Spiele – und für ein Regime, das seine Modernität und seine wachsende ökonomische und kulturelle Macht demonstrieren will. Radikale Architektur hat sich für Spektakel und Propaganda benutzen lassen. Städte bestehen aus Bauwerken, aber großartige Bauwerke allein machen noch keine Stadt aus."[2]

Unabhängig davon, ob man der Kritik dieses Artikels zustimmt oder nicht, gibt er zumindest einen Hinweis auf die Bandbreite der Emotionen und Meinungen, die die besonders spektakulären Erscheinungsformen der zeitgenössischen Architektur hervorrufen. Sie sehen vielleicht ansprechend aus, wie aber steht es mit den unvermeidlichen Kompromissen, die stets mit solchen Großprojekten einhergehen? Norman Foster soll einmal versucht haben, seinen chinesischen Auftraggebern zu erklären, dass die große Bedeutung von Fahrrädern für ihr Land ein ökologisches Plus darstelle, das es zu bewahren lohne. Man entgegnete ihm unmissverständlich, dass China es nicht auf Fahrräder abgesehen habe, sondern auf Autos und Flugzeuge. Es gibt einen mächtigen Trend hin zu einer zeichenhaften Architektur, angetrieben von riesigen Geldmengen, die sich in neuer Art und Weise von Mumbai über Dubai bis nach Shanghai über den ganzen Globus verteilen. Man kann solche Entwicklungen kritisieren, aber zeitgenössische Architekten sind weniger Vertreter eines politischen Protests als vielmehr Schöpfer nützlicher Objekte. So wie jeder andere versuchen sie, ihr Auskommen zu finden und ein Zeichen zu hinterlassen.

Das vorliegende Buch stellt drei zeichenhafte, für die Olympischen Spiele 2008 in Peking entworfene Bauwerke vor, aber auch das Ullens Center for Contemporary Art (UCCA, 2006–07, S. 546), ein von dem Franzosen Jean-Michel Wilmotte entworfener und von MADA s.p.a.m. ausgeführter Umbau einer Fabrik aus den 1950er-Jahren. Das UCCA zeigt, dass die von den lokalen Behörden bevorzugte kompromisslose Abrissstrategie nicht der einzige Weg ist, um Peking zu jenem kosmopolitischen Zentrum zu machen, von dem viele träumen. Zudem bildet das UCCA einen Kontrapunkt zu den von der *Financial Times* missbilligten „oberflächlichen Ausdrucksformen". Selbst in einer boomenden Hauptstadt wie Peking lassen sich kaum allgemeine Aussagen darüber treffen, in welche Richtungen die zeitgenössische Architektur sich bewegt.

In den bisherigen Ausgaben von *Architecture Now!* fanden immer auch solche Arbeiten Erwähnung, die im Grenzbereich zwischen Kunst und Architektur oder zwischen Architektur und Design anzusiedeln sind. So auch im vorliegenden Band, angefangen mit dem betont

20

20
*Steven Holl, The Nelson-Atkins Muse-
um of Art, Bloch Building, Kansas
City, Missouri, USA, 2002–07*

„unmonumentalen" Serpentine Gallery Pavilion in London (2007, S. 138), dessen Entwurf von dem Künstler Olafur Eliasson und Kjetil Thorsen, einem der Gründer des Architekturbüros Snøhetta, stammt. Ein zweiter Eintrag widmet sich Eliassons Installation „New York City Waterfalls" (2008, S. 134), die die besondere Verbundenheit der Stadt mit ihren Flüssen thematisiert. Als weiterer Künstler bespielte Anselm Kiefer mit seiner Installation „Sternenfall" (**2/3**) von Ende Mai bis Anfang Juli 2007 den Grand Palais in Paris und nimmt damit in der Architektur – oder vielleicht besser in ihren Ruinen – eine herausragende Rolle ein. „Was man hier sieht, ist Verzweiflung", so Kiefer, „ich bin absolut verzweifelt, weil ich nicht erklären kann, warum ich existiere. Es ist mehr als Trauer, es ist Verzweiflung. Um aber zu überleben, errichtet man Bauwerke, man erschafft Illusionen."[3] Nach den Gründen für unsere Existenz zu fragen, mag als das Gegenteil der von Bauman apostrophierten „flüchtigen Moderne" erscheinen, doch genau das ist der Punkt: Architektur, die Kunst der gebauten Umwelt, kann in ihren unendlich vielen Erscheinungsformen die meisten Theorien zur Moderne ebenso gut bestätigen wie widerlegen. Einerseits so solide, dass sie längste Zeiträume überdauert, ist sie andererseits beständiges Objekt von Versuchen, ihre Substanz geradezu in Luft aufzulösen. Etwa das von dem Architekturstudio FAM entworfene Denkmal für die Opfer des Terroranschlags vom 11. März 2004 in Madrid (2005–07, S. 164), ein gläserner, runder Körper über einem blau gehaltenen unterirdischen Raum. An die Tragödie erinnert es mithilfe einer beschrifteten Membran, die – interessanterweise wiederum aus ETFE, einer Art transparentem Teflon, hergestellt – so durchsichtig ist, dass man sie kaum wahrnimmt. Fast unsichtbar und doch immer gegenwärtig, so wie die Wunden und Schmerzen der direkt und indirekt Betroffenen, verkörpert Architektur hier das Andenken an ein Ereignis, das binnen weniger Augenblicke Tod und Zerstörung brachte.

VOM SCHOCK DES ALTEN ZUM CHARME DES METAVERSUMS

Die Architektur folgt einem seltsamen Rhythmus, der sich recht deutlich vom Rhythmus anderer „soziologischer" Erscheinungsformen von Moden unterscheidet – vielleicht weil die Entstehung von Bauwerken sich so lange hinzieht (verglichen etwa mit den kurzen Produktionszyklen von Künstlern) bzw. weil so viel Geld involviert ist. Die jungen Wilden, die mit aufregenden neuen Theorien und Formen die Bühne stürmen, bauen auch Jahre später noch, doch wirken ihre einstigen Innovationen dann wie Relikte aus der Vergangenheit. So zeigte die 1988 von Philip Johnson kuratierte Ausstellung „Deconstructivist Architecture" am New Yorker Museum of Modern Art vorwiegend nicht realisierte Arbeiten von Frank O. Gehry, Daniel Libeskind, Rem Koolhaas, Peter Eisenman, Zaha Hadid, Bernard Tschumi und Coop Himmelb(l)au. Schaut man sich heute die Münchener BMW Welt (2001–07, S. 124) von Coop Himmelb(l)au oder ihr Akron Art Museum in Ohio (2001–07, S. 114) oder Libeskinds Erweiterungsbau für das Royal Ontario Museum (2002–07, S. 314) an, darf man mit Verlaub sagen, dass die MoMA-Ausstellung ausgesprochen vorausahnend gewesen ist und Entwicklungen aufgezeigt hat, die erst 20 Jahre später Gestalt annahmen. „Dekonstruktivistische Architektur", schrieb Mark Wigley, Mitkurator der Ausstellung, „stellt keine Avantgarde dar. Vielmehr enthüllt sie das Unbekannte, das im Traditionellen verborgen liegt. Es ist das Alte, was schockiert."[4] Ganz bestimmt aber haben Ästhetik und Gestalt zeitgenössischer Architektur nicht nur mit dem Lebensalter ihrer Schöpfer zu tun. Steven Holl beispielsweise wurde 1947 geboren, nur ein Jahr nach Daniel Libeskind, aber der künstlerische Stil seiner Entwürfe ist ein ganz anderer. Für seinen Erweiterungsbau des Nelson-Atkins Museums of Art (Bloch Building, Kansas City, Missouri, 2002–07, S. 240) gewann Holl 2008 einen der Ehrenpreise des American Institute of Archi-

21
Tadao Ando, 21_21 Design Sight,
Tokyo Midtown, Minato-ku, Tokyo,
Japan, 2004–07

21

tects. In ihrer Begründung schrieb die Jury: „Die Erweiterung des Nelson-Atkins Museum of Art verbindet Architektur und Landschaft zu einer Erlebnisarchitektur, die sich den Besuchern mit jeder einzelnen Bewegung durch Raum und Zeit eröffnet." Die leuchtenden Kästen, die den neuen Museumsbau bilden, setzen sich auf eine Weise mit Oberfläche, Licht und Raum auseinander, die nicht das Ergebnis einer „Schule" wie der Dekonstruktivismus ist, dennoch wirkt diese Architektur heute womöglich weitaus zeitgenössischer als die zersplitterten Formen, die erstmals in den späten 1980er-Jahren der Öffentlichkeit präsentiert wurden.

Tadao Ando, geboren 1941 und damit fünf Jahre älter als Libeskind, hat einen Weg eingeschlagen, dessen Ausgangspunkt eng mit der mit Le Corbusier beginnenden Geschichte der modernen Architektur verbunden ist. Aber wie bei Steven Holl zeigt sich auch in Andos Arbeit ein künstlerischer Ansatz, der es ihm erlaubt, sich immer weiter zu entwickeln und so ungewöhnliche Gebäude wie das 21_21 Design Sight in Tokio (2004–07, S. 76) zu entwerfen. Das als Teil des großangelegten Gebäudekomplexes Tokyo Midtown auf dem Gelände der ehemaligen Verteidigungsbehörde errichtete 21_21 Design Sight besitzt mehrere der für Ando typischen Betonwände. Was an der Konstruktion jedoch vor allem ins Auge fällt, ist das gefaltete Metalldach, das an die Faltenmode des ebenfalls an dem Projekt beteiligten Designers Issey Miyake erinnert. Eine reduzierte, klassisch geometrische Formensprache scheint zwar besser geeignet als eine komplexe, vielschichtige, um ein Gebäude „zeitlos" erscheinen zu lassen. Dem breiten Publikum mag es allerdings schwerer fallen, solche Erscheinungsformen zeitlich einzuordnen, als denen, die sich tagtäglich mit zeitgenössischer Architektur befassen.

Viele wichtige Protagonisten haben die moderne und die zeitgenössische Architektur stärker durch ihre Zeichnungen beeinflusst als durch ihre realisierten Arbeiten. Diese Tendenz lässt sich zurückverfolgen bis zu Antonio Sant'Elia (1888–1916) und Hugh Ferriss (1889–1962) und findet sich in der jüngeren Vergangenheit bei John Hejduk (1929–2000), Peter Eisenman oder Zaha Hadid. Freilich setzen inzwischen sowohl Hadid als auch Eisenman zahlreiche ihrer Entwürfe tatsächlich um, ihr Ruf gründete jedoch bis vor nicht allzu langer Zeit weit stärker auf ihren theoretischen Überlegungen und ihren Zeichnungen als auf ausgeführten Arbeiten. Natürlich haben Computervisualisierungen die Aufgaben des Architekten erleichtert, der nun die Möglichkeit hat, sich neue Welten auszudenken, ohne sie gleich in Stahl und Glas zu bauen. Interessant ist in diesem Zusammenhang der Hinweis auf Tom Wiscombe, der nach über zehn Jahren als Chefdesigner und Projektpartner für Coop Himmelb(l)au und verantwortlich für das Akron Art Museum in Ohio oder für die BMW Welt in München nun in eigenem Namen arbeitet und erstaunliche Wettbewerbsbeiträge kreiert, die die komplexen Formen des ausgehenden 20. Jahrhunderts noch ein großes Stück weiterzuführen scheinen. Mit seiner 1999 gegründeten Firma EMERGENT arbeitete Wiscombe zuletzt u. a. an zwei Projekten, die im vorliegenden Band vorgestellt werden, zum einen für die Tschechische Nationalbibliothek in Prag (2006–07, S. 150), zum anderen für das Museum für zeitgenössische Kunst in Shenzhen (China, 2007, S. 144). Das verführerische Bildmaterial zu diesen unrealisierten Projekten lässt sich auffassen als eine Verschmelzung der in den Arbeiten von Coop Himmelb(l)au anzutreffenden dynamischen Kanten und jener Computertechnologie, der die „Blob-Architektur" entsprang, wobei Wiscombe höchst zeitgemäße Visionen vorstellt, die in den kommenden Jahren von großem Einfluss sein könnten.

Während Wiscombe praktische Erfahrungen vorweisen kann, was die Realisierung computergenerierter Entwürfe angeht, scheinen andere sich mit der Idee zu begnügen, dass ein Teil der heutigen Architektur niemals in der Realität existieren wird. Weltweit große Medien-

22
Marc Rolinet, Chapel of the Diaco-
nesses of Reuilly, Versailles, France,
2004–07

23
Paolo Mendes da Rocha, Our Lady
of the Conception Chapel, Recife,
Pernambuco, Brazil, 2004–06

aufmerksamkeit hat die Webseite „Second Life" (www.secondlife.com) gefunden, die gerne als „Metaversum" bezeichnet wird. Gemeint ist damit ein vollständig ausgebildeter dreidimensionaler virtueller Raum, in dem die Mitspieler (so genannte Avatare) sozial und ökonomisch interagieren. Einen der in dieser Ausgabe von *Architecture Now!* vorgestellten Architekten, Scope Cleaver, kann man nicht anders denn als virtuell bezeichnen, da er die Preisgabe jeglicher Informationen über seine Existenz in der realen Welt verweigert. Stattdessen gibt er an, dass er „seit Januar 2006 Mitglied bei ‚Second Life'" ist, so als hätte es ihn vor diesem Datum gar nicht gegeben. Cleaver hat eine große Anzahl virtueller Bauwerke in „Second Life" entworfen, die man leicht besuchen kann. Seine Princeton University Gallery of the Arts (2007, S. 460) ist Bestandteil eines recht umfangreichen Versuchs der angesehenen Universität, sich selbst in „Second Life" hineinzuprojizieren. Princeton besitzt in „Second Life" sieben *sims* Land (65 536 m^2), die von der Abteilung Academic Services des Office of Information Technologies der Universität verwaltet werden. Cleaver hat sich zu einem führenden Designer von Konstruktionen entwickelt, die auch in der „realen Welt" eine Rolle spielen könnten, etwa zur Unterrichtsvertiefung im Architekturstudium. Obgleich Cleaver natürlich nicht an die normalerweise für Architektur geltenden Regeln gebunden ist, entwirft er seine Bauwerke ohne Zuhilfenahme von CAD-Programmen, sondern bevorzugt Elemente, die direkt in „Second Life" vorzufinden sind. Wie Cleaver erläutert, böten die Gebäude in „Second Life" „fantastische Formen, die sämtliche Möglichkeiten des virtuellen Bauens ausschöpfen, gleichzeitig aber realistische Konstruktionskomponenten beibehalten". Wenngleich der Erfolg von „Second Life" wohl auch damit zu tun hat, was gerade in Mode ist, sind seine 20 Millionen registrierten Nutzer (viele nicht aktiv) doch ein Hinweis auf das Potenzial für ähnliche virtuelle Umgebungen, die für die künftige Entwicklung der Architektur durchaus von Bedeutung sein könnten.

DIE WEGE DES HERRN

Gotteshäuser spielen als Bauaufgabe für bedeutende zeitgenössische Architektur sicherlich eine weniger große Rolle als Kulturinstitutionen, sind aber in der einen oder anderen Form nach wie vor Gegenstand innovativer Gestaltung. Die Umnutzung religiöser Bauten wirft zuweilen das Problem der Profanierung auf, einhergehend mit einer möglichen Befangenheit, die manche Gäste gegenüber dem Speisen oder Feiern in einem einstigen Kirchengebäude empfinden könnten. Eine der gelungeneren Initiativen dieser Art aus jüngerer Zeit ist die Buchhandlung Selexyz Dominicanen (Maastricht, Niederlande, 2005–07, S. 352) des Architekturbüros Merkx+Girod, untergebracht in einer ehemaligen Dominikanerkirche, deren Baubeginn auf das 13. Jahrhundert datiert wird. Obwohl das Gebäude seit 1794, dem Beginn der damaligen französischen Besatzung, nicht mehr als Kirche genutzt wurde, besitzt es noch immer einen sakralen, gotischen Charakter. 2007 erhielten die Designer für ihre Umgestaltung den angesehenen niederländischen Lensvelt de Architect Interieurprijs. Der Begründungstext der Jury verdient zitiert zu werden: „Das Architekturbüro Merkx+Girod hat in Maastricht eine zeitgemäße Buchhandlung in einer früheren Dominikanerkirche eingerichtet und dabei die besondere Eigenart des Ortes erhalten. Die frühere Pracht der Kirche wurde wiederhergestellt, die Ausstattungsgegenstände fanden einen neuen Platz im geräumigen Kellerbereich. Um den Charakter der Kirche zu bewahren und gleichzeitig eine Verkaufsfläche von der gewünschten Größe zu erhalten, errichteten die Architekten auf einer Seite des Kirchenraums eine zweistöckige Konstruktion aus schwarzem Stahl, in der die Bücher Platz finden. Auf der anderen Raumseite wurden niedrigere Einrichtungsstücke so angeordnet, dass

22

23

sich ein klar gegliederter und übersichtlicher Ladenbereich ergibt. Die Jury war von den räumlichen Lösungen wie von dem ansprechenden Beleuchtungskonzept sehr angetan. Die Verbindung von Buchbereich und Kircheninterieur wurde als ausgesprochen gelungen beurteilt."

Auch eine Reihe von Gebäuden, die als Kirchen gebaut wurden, findet sich in dieser Ausgabe von *Architecture Now!*. Bei seinem Entwurf für die Capela de Nossa Senhora da Conceição (Recife, Pernambuco, Brasilien, 2004–06, S. 340) bezog der renommierte Architekt Paulo Mendes da Rocha die Wände einer Ruinenanlage aus dem 19. Jahrhundert mit ein, die sich auf dem Gelände der Keramikfabrik Brennand befindet, 16 km von Recife entfernt. Mendes da Rocha, der 2006 den Pritzker-Preis erhielt, ist für seine robusten Betonformen bekannt; hier allerdings konzentrierte er sich auf die Restaurierung alter Ziegelwände. Nur auf ein Flachdach aus Beton hat er nicht verzichtet. Mendes da Rochas schwere, solide Architektur schließt die alten Ruinenwände vollständig in sich ein und verleiht ihnen durch das Zusammenspiel von gedämpftem Licht, freien Durchblicken und augenscheinlicher Massivität eine ganz spezielle religiöse Aura. Die Vorstellung, zeitgenössische Architektur sei nicht in der Lage, eine spirituelle Atmosphäre zu schaffen, lässt sich mit einem Gebäude wie der Brennand-Kapelle umstandslos widerlegen.

Auch zeitgenössische Architekten, deren Stil und Berühmtheit weit von einem Mendes da Rocha entfernt sind, widmen sich nach wie vor und mit Einfallsreichtum dem Entwerfen von Kirchen oder Kapellen. So etwa der französische Architekt Marc Rolinet, der unlängst die Kapelle der Diakonissen von Reuilly (Versailles, 2004–07, S. 430) fertiggestellt hat. Mit nur geringem Budget, aber in Zusammenarbeit mit Auftraggebern, die sich für seine Ideen aufgeschlossen zeigten, kombinierte Rolinet eine durchsichtige moderne Hülle mit einem darin befindlichen, holzummantelten Raumkörper. Die wie ein Boot geformte Kapelle erinnert an christliche Symbolik – an das Boot des Petrus oder die Worte Jesu „Kommt her, folgt mir nach! Ich werde Euch zu Menschenfischern machen" (Matthäus 4,19; Markus 1,17). Der gläubige Protestant Rolinet hat seinen Glauben in eine schlichte, moderne Form überführt, die mit den Diakonissen von Reuilly harmoniert. Obschon dieses Gebäude keine weltweite Aufmerksamkeit erregt – bemerkenswert ist es allemal.

Weit stärker im medialen Scheinwerferlicht, allerdings immer ein wenig gegen seinen Willen, steht der Schweizer Architekt Peter Zumthor. Nach einer längeren Phase, in der er nur wenig entwarf, übernahm der Schweizer die Entwürfe für gleich zwei interessante und bedeutsame Bauwerke: zum einen für das Diözesanmuseum Kolumba in Köln (2003–07, S. 566) und zum anderen, im nahen Kreis Euskirchen, für die weitaus kleinere Bruder-Klaus-Kapelle (Mechernich-Wachendorf, 2003–07, S. 560). Die enge Verbundenheit zu seiner Heimat hat Zumthor schon mit zukunftsweisenden Bauwerken wie seiner Therme im schweizerischen Vals (fertiggestellt 1996) gezeigt; die dem Schweizer Schutzpatron Niklaus von Flüe (1417–87) gewidmete Kapelle in Mechernich-Wachendorf lässt sich erneut als eine bewusste Beschwörung seiner Herkunft auffassen. Der Kapellenbau mit seinem ausgesprochen schlichten Äußeren und einem ungewöhnlichen Interieur, das mittels einer nach Bauausführung verbrannten Fichtenholzschalung ausgeformt wurde, ist vor allem das Ergebnis lokaler Kräfte – im Gegensatz zu jenen aufwendigen multinationalen und über Computernetzwerke entstandenen Spektakeln, wie sie bei vielen Architekten von ähnlicher Reputation wie Zumthor beliebt sind.

Ein anderer zurückhaltender, aber um nichts weniger eindrucksvoller Beitrag zur religiösen Architektur ist das Marienkloster Tautra auf der gleichnamigen norwegischen Insel (2004–06, S. 280), von dem Architekturbüro Jensen & Skodvin für 18 Zisterzienserinnen entworfen.

Ähnlich wie die Diakonissen von Reuilly haben hier die Ordensschwestern aktiv an der Planung der Anlage mitgewirkt und waren außerdem, wie die Architekten hervorheben, für die Landschaftsgestaltung verantwortlich. Das Nonnenkloster, das sich durch einen schlichten architektonischen Ausdruck auszeichnet, wurde unweit der Ruinen eines 800 Jahre zuvor errichteten Zisterzienserklosters gebaut. Um den Bedürfnissen der künftigen Bewohnerinnen mit einfachen und wirtschaftlichen Lösungen gerecht zu werden, machten sich die Architekten ein genaues Bild von dem Tagesablauf der Nonnen. Zusätzlich warteten sie mit überraschenden Gestaltungsideen wie dem Refektorium auf, an dessen Tafel alle Schwestern auf einer Seite nebeneinander sitzen („wie in Leonardo da Vincis ‚Letztem Abendmahl'", so die Architekten) und in die Landschaft hinausschauen können. Die Abgelegenheit des Konvents, aber auch seine Verpflichtung zur Einfachheit, gepaart mit einer aufgeschlossenen Haltung gegenüber einer Architektur, die nicht die Vergangenheit imitiert, ließen eine spirituelle Atmosphäre entstehen, die sich nicht auf die bekannten Klischees religiöser Architektur stützt. Das Kloster erfüllt seine Funktion so würdevoll wie es modern ist.

BURN BABY BURN

Vielleicht ist es vor allem dem Vorbild der zeitgenössischen Kunst, die sich schon lange mit der Schönheit des Vergänglichen befasst, zu verdanken, dass auch die Architektur die besondere Wirkung des Temporären inzwischen nicht nur anerkennt, sondern sogar sucht. Natürlich hat auch durch boomende Städte, Los Angeles vielleicht allen voran, die Zahl kurzlebiger Gebäude zugenommen, die keinen Anspruch auf jene Art von Beständigkeit erheben, an der Architekten lange Zeit gelegen war. In den vorangegangenen Ausgaben von *Architecture Now!* haben künstlerische Arbeiten stets einen prominenten Platz eingenommen; Band 3 beispielsweise zeigte auf dem Cover eine Abbildung von Olafur Eliassons „Weather Project" (Turbinenhalle, Tate Modern, London, 16. Oktober 2003 bis 21. März 2004). Das Verhältnis zwischen Kunstwerken mit Architekturbezug und Bauwerken, die nur für kurze Zeit bestehen sollen, ist kein unwesentlicher Aspekt in der Entwicklung der zeitgenössischen Architektur. Oft haben Ideen, die im Grenzbereich von Kunst und Architektur entstehen, einen anhaltenden substanziellen – oder manchmal auch nur ästhetischen – Einfluss auf langlebigere Gebäudetypen. Der Belgier Arne Quinze ist als Autodidakt eigentlich weder Architekt noch reiner Künstler, sondern eher – ein nicht unbedeutender – Designer. Seine kunstvolle Installation „Uchronia: Message out of the Future" (Black Rock City, Black Rock Desert, Nevada, S. 412) für das Burning Man Festival 2006 war von vornherein dazu bestimmt, zum Abschluss des Festivals niedergebrannt zu werden. Ein Film und ein Buch, die die Errichtung (und die Zerstörung) des offenen Pavillons dokumentieren, sind die einzigen Zeugnisse seiner Existenz. Der eine oder andere wird „Uchronia" vielleicht als ein reines Kunstevent und deshalb nicht als eine architektonische Konstruktion beurteilen, angesichts ihrer Funktion als Party-Location ist die Installation jedoch eindeutig den Gebäuden zuzurechnen. Ästhetisch interessant ist an „Uchronia" neben seiner gewundenen, fast organischen Struktur auch die Tatsache, dass es im Kollektiv aufgebaut wurde – im Übrigen hat Arne Quinze in Brüssel eine weniger flüchtige Version des Entwurfs angefertigt.

In den vergangenen Jahren ist es zu einer Art Mode geworden, Bauwerke aus Schiffscontainern zu errichten, darunter so bestechende (temporäre) Ergebnisse wie Shigeru Bans Bianimale Nomadic Museum (Pier 54, New York, 2005). Die brasilianischen Architekten Bernardes + Jacobsen nutzten die Frachtbehälter, um das Gelände für das TIM Festival 2007 in Rio de Janeiro (S. 108) zu gestalten. Mit nicht weniger als 250 Containern von 6 und 12 m Länge schufen sie alle wesentlichen Bauten für ein Popmusikfestival, das nur zwei Tage lang dauerte. Stan-

24
*Olafur Eliasson, 2007 Serpentine
Gallery Pavilion, Kensington Gardens,
London, UK, 2007*

24

dardisierte Frachtcontainer, wie sie seit 1956 nach der Idee des Amerikaners Malcom McLean gebaut werden, sind zum festen Bestandteil einer Gegenwartsarchitektur geworden, die es sich mittlerweile erlaubt (oder es sogar als Qualität ansieht), vergänglich zu sein. Das TIM Festival ist ein typisches Beispiel für den Bedarf an wenigen architektonischen Grundelementen, die sich leicht an einem Ort auf- und ebenso bequem wieder abbauen lassen. Es muss also nicht nur die Kunst sein – auch praktischer orientierte Disziplinen können die Form der Architektur bestimmen, so wie hier Industriedesign und Gütertransportwesen.

So wie Kunstwerke sich nicht selten dem Architektonischen annähern, streben auch manche Architekten nach jenem Status, der ihren weniger praktisch veranlagten Freunden aus der Kunstwelt zukommt. Ein Künstler wiederum, der sich in seinen diversen Arbeiten schon häufiger mit architektonischen Formen auseinandergesetzt hat, ist der Deutsche Thomas Schütte. Eine seiner jüngsten Arbeiten, eine „Model for a Hotel" (2007–08, S. 456) betitelte Installation für die so genannte Fourth Plinth (den vierten Sockel) auf dem Londoner Trafalgar Square ist eigentlich nichts anderes als ein schräg abgestufter Stapel farbiger Glasscheiben. Dennoch wirft das Objekt, dessen Aussehen sich je nach Betrachtungswinkel erheblich verändern kann, die interessante Frage auf, inwiefern Architektur sich von ihrer manchmal zu wuchtigen Erscheinung lösen könnte. Aus bestimmten Perspektiven verschwindet Schüttes Arbeit beinahe, ein Effekt, um den sich schon viele Architekten erfolglos bemüht haben. Indes gehorcht die Kunst in den meisten Fällen nicht denselben Regeln wie die Architektur – ein Grundsatz, der zumindest für die Installation der Fourth Plinth gelten dürfte. In jedem Fall aber kann man behaupten, dass die Architektur auf eine gegenseitige Befruchtung aus ist, für die sie ihren jeweiligen Gegenpart in der Kunst, im Design oder sogar, wie die Verwendung von Schiffscontainern zeigt, im industriellen Bereich findet. Die darin zum Ausdruck kommende Aufgeschlossenheit gestattet es ihr, sich in zuweilen unerwartete Richtungen zu entwickeln und sich manchmal auch von jener Schwere zu befreien, die auf so vielen „traditionellen" Gebäuden lastet. Auch wenn die allerwenigsten Bauwerke zu demselben Zweck wie Arne Quinzes „Uchronia" entstanden sind – nämlich niedergebrannt zu werden –, ist die seiner Arbeit implizite Befreiung vom Regelfall architektonischer Beständigkeit doch ein deutlicher Verweis darauf, was in der zeitgenössischen Architektur alles möglich ist.

DIE FÜSSE IM SAND, DEN KOPF IN DEN WOLKEN

Es wird zwar gerne behauptet, die Globalisierung bringe die Architektur der Gegenwart um ihre Vielfalt, dennoch bleibt die Tatsache bestehen, dass unterschiedliche Städte und natürlich unterschiedliche klimatische Verhältnisse unterschiedliche Anforderungen stellen, auch wenn sich die grundsätzlichen Arbeitsweisen von Architekten und die verwendeten Materialien häufig sehr ähneln. Die Hochhauskultur einer Stadt wie New York bringt bestimmte Einschränkungen mit sich, sowohl hinsichtlich der Nutzungsmöglichkeiten als auch aufgrund der reichlich komplizierten Abstandsbestimmungen, die für ein Baugrundstück gelten können. Vor einiger Zeit sind zwei als „Stardesigner" geltende Architekten nach Manhattan eingeladen worden, um an Türmen zu arbeiten, die, auf je eigene Weise, einige der in der Stadt lange Zeit vorherrschenden stilistischen Konventionen neu definieren könnten. 2007 wurde unweit des Times Square Renzo Pianos New York Times Building (S. 394) eröffnet, das einen neuen architektonischen Standard für seine unmittelbare Umgebung markiert. Die unteren 28 Etagen von Pianos 52-geschossigem und 228 m hohem Wolkenkratzer werden von der namengebenden Tageszeitung genutzt, die oberen 24 von Immobilienun-

25   26

ternehmen und Anwaltskanzleien. Das Herzstück des Entwurfs, die Redaktion der *New York Times,* umfasst drei Geschosse, die um einen innenliegenden Garten herum angeordnet sind, der mit 15 m hohen Weißbirken sowie Farnen und Mosen bepflanzt ist. Der Garten mit seinen Bäumen – die im metaphorischen und hier sogar in einem buchstäblichen Sinn einen Grundbestandteil des Zeitungspapiers bilden – und die vom Architekten bewusst gewählte Transparenz demonstrieren die Begabung des Italieners, einen Entwurf vorzulegen, der nicht unbedingt dem entspricht, was man von dem Erschaffer des Centre Pompidou (1977 in Zusammenarbeit im Richard Rogers entstanden) erwartet hätte. Da in New York die Grundform eines Gebäudes durch das Rastersystem der Stadt und die hohen Grundstückskosten vorgegeben ist, hat Piano mit der ihm eigenen Finesse ein amerikanisches Gebäude von europäischer Sinnlichkeit erschaffen.

Während Piano nach dem Bau des Centre Pompidou durchaus an Radikalität eingebüßt hat, kann man von Jean Nouvel sagen, dass er im Kreise der großen Architekten nach wie vor ein etwas irritierendes Element verkörpert. Noch immer sind seine Gebäude geeignet, Überraschung oder sogar Verärgerung hervorzurufen. Sein Tour de Verre (New York, 2007–12, **10/11**), den der französische Architekt in Zusammenarbeit mit dem Projektentwickler Hines entworfen hat und der sich direkt neben dem Museum of Modern Art auf 75 Stockwerken in die Höhe erheben wird, wird dem Profil von Midtown Manhattan einen ganz neuen Zug verleihen. Die *New York Times*, lange Zeit eine Art Geschmacksrichter für die Stadt, zeigte sich von dem Projekt glühend begeistert: „Das neue 75-geschossige Hochhaus, das der Architekt Jean Nouvel für ein Nachbargrundstück des Museum of Modern Art im Zentrum von Manhattan entworfen hat, verspricht, die aufregendste Ergänzung der Skyline seit vielen Jahren zu werden. Sein facettiertes, sich zu mehreren Spitzen verjüngendes Äußeres lässt mit seiner atavistischen Begeisterung für himmlische Höhen an John Ruskins Lobrede auf das Irrationale in der gotischen Architektur denken: ‚Sie unterstand sich nicht nur, sondern fand sogar Vergnügen daran, sich gegen jede Form von Unterwürfigkeit zu stellen.'" Nouvels Bau ist deutlich kühner als die jüngsten Erweiterungen des Museum of Modern Art von Yoshio Taniguchi, eine Tatsache, die die *New York Times* zu einem Vergleich veranlasste, der für die Arbeit des japanischen Architekten ziemlich unvorteilhaft ausfiel. Nouvels Tour de Verre ist u. a. dafür vorgesehen, neue Ausstellungsflächen für das Museum bereitzustellen, wozu die Zeitung schrieb: „Die zusätzliche Ausstellungsfläche bietet dem MoMA die Gelegenheit, die Nutzung eines großen Teils seiner Räumlichkeiten zu überdenken und beispielsweise den Aufbau seiner ständigen Ausstellung zu verändern oder zu überlegen, ob man nicht die Räume für zeitgenössische Kunst in das neue Hochhaus verlegen und so im alten Teil mehr Platz für Architekturausstellungen gewinnen könnte. Um ein solch ehrgeiziges Unternehmen anzugehen, müsste sich das Museum allerdings zuerst einmal eingestehen, dass der von Taniguchi entworfene Bereich neue Schwierigkeiten mit sich gebracht hat. Kurz gesagt, müsste das MoMA eine Courage beweisen, die es seit Jahrzehnten nicht mehr gezeigt hat. Das Museum täte gut daran, einen Hinweis Ruskins zu beherzigen, welcher schrieb, dass große Kunst, ob sie sich nun in ‚Worten, Farben oder Stein' ausdrückt, ‚nicht bloß immer und immer wieder dasselbe erzählt'."[5]

Wenn es um zeitgenössische Architektur geht, hat New York – mag es an Abstandsbestimmungen oder schlicht an einer konservativen Einstellung liegen – sich nicht gerade als die innovativste Stadt erwiesen. Manhattan mag in seiner Gesamtheit als ein Paradebeispiel für ein modernes Stadtgebiet gelten, aber seine einzelnen Teile scheinen eher aus den 1930er-Jahren als aus dem neuen Jahrhundert zu stammen. Andere Städte, etwa Dubai in den Vereinigten Arabischen Emiraten, schießen mit atemberaubender Geschwindigkeit in die Höhe, geknüpft an

25 + 26
Zaha Hadid, Nordpark Cable Railway,
Innsbruck, Austria, 2004–07

die Hoffnung, eigenständige neue Zentren zu werden – sowohl natürlich für das Wirtschaftsleben als auch für die Architektur. Bis vor Kurzem hat Dubai auf große westliche Architekturbüros gesetzt, die sich weniger durch Einfallsreichtum hervortaten, doch die Situation hat sich rasch verändert und mittlerweile entwerfen berühmte Architekten wie Zaha Hadid Großprojekte. Angesichts seiner Lage am Arabischen Golf, direkt bei den riesigen Wüsten der Arabischen Halbinsel, sieht sich Dubai mit einer Reihe komplizierter äußerer Umstände konfrontiert, die nicht mit denen einer Stadt wie New York zu vergleichen sind. Mit einer Bevölkerung, die überwiegend nicht aus Einheimischen besteht, und Sommertemperaturen von bis zu 50° Celsius ist Dubai eigentlich nicht der Ort, an dem man herumflaniert und die urbane Szenerie genießt. Die Bewohner bewegen sich mit dem Auto umher und sind erstaunt, wenn sie jemand anderen als Arbeiter aus Bangladesch in der prallen Sonne sehen. Städte wie Los Angeles haben schon vor langer Zeit eine urbane Kultur entwickelt, die ganz auf dem Auto basiert; in Dubai ist dies nicht nur eine Frage der Entfernungen, sondern auch des Klimas. Bei einem von dem saudischen Projektentwickler Adel al Mojil ausgeschriebenen Wettbewerb, zu dessen hochkarätig besetztem Teilnehmerfeld Architekten wie Ryue Nishizawa und Kazuyo Sejima gehörten, ging es um die Frage, welcher Art von Nutzern die riesige Anlage dienen könnte, deren Bau al Mojil in Dubai am Rand eines neuen Areals namens Business Bay plant. Al Mojil, der sein Projekt „The Edge" (Dubai, VAE, seit 2008, S. 418) nennt, wollte wissen, wie die Bedürfnisse des „Wissensarbeiters" der Zukunft aussehen könnten. Davon ausgehend, dass Dubai mehr ist als eine aus dem Ölreichtum entstandene Fata Morgana und sich vielmehr zu einem wichtigen Finanzzentrum der Welt entwickeln wird, soll „The Edge" ein 350 000 m² großes Riesenprojekt mit Gesamtkosten in Höhe von 600 Millionen Euro werden, zu dem Büros, Hotels, Wohnungen und Geschäfte gehören – kurz: alles, was ein Wissensarbeiter zum Leben, Essen und Schlafen während der Monate benötigt, die er in den Vereinigten Arabischen Emiraten verbringt. Dieses Schema deckt sich wohl kaum mit dem, woran Renzo Piano bei seinem Entwurf für das New York Times Building, ein reines Bürogebäude, gedacht hat. Jean Nouvels Tour de Verre wiederum sieht zwar auch Bereiche für Hotelbetrieb und Apartments sowie für Ausstellungsräume des Museum of Modern Art und Büros vor, jedoch sollen hier die Nutzer ganz gewiss nicht dazu ermuntert werden, ihr gesamtes Leben in diesen Räumlichkeiten zu verbringen. Für den Bau von „The Edge" wurde nach dem Wettbewerb im Jahr 2007 die innovative spanische Firma RCR ausgewählt. Ihr Hochhausensemble folgt einer ganz neuartigen Konzeption und ist von einem besonderen ästhetischen Reiz – wie eine Fata Morgana erhebt es sich über einer Plattform, die wiederum an einen fliegenden Teppich denken lässt. Bis zu seiner tatsächlichen Realisierung wird sich das Projekt vielleicht noch in einigen Punkten weiterentwickeln, Grundlage bleibt aber der Vorschlag von RCR für den Entwurf eines Großkomplexes, der speziell auf einen Ort wie Dubai abgestimmt ist. Die treibende Kraft hinter der Entwicklung derartiger, praktisch in sich geschlossener Gebäudekomplexe scheint weniger die lokale Kultur als vielmehr das Klima zu sein, wobei „The Edge" sogar so groß ist, dass es eine Art Stadt für sich bildet, auf die die traditionellen Beschränkungen einer Stadt nicht mehr zutreffen. Rem Koolhaas (OMA) schreibt in einer seiner jüngsten Publikationen mit dem Titel „The Gulf": „Letztlich werden am Golf die Begriffe des Öffentlichen und des Privaten neu definiert: Infrastrukturpotenziale zur Förderung des Ganzen statt Fragmentierung; Nutzung und Fehlnutzung des Landschaftsraums – Golfspielen oder Umwelt?; Koexistenz vieler Kulturen im Rahmen einer neuen Authentizität statt westlich-moderner Versäumnisse; Erleben statt Erfahrung – Stadt oder Resort?"

27
Legorreta + Legorreta, La Purificadora Boutique Hotel, Puebla, Mexico,
2006–07

ÜBERNACHTUNG MIT FRÜHSTÜCK IM DESIGNERAMBIENTE

Nicht nur Kultureinrichtungen stellten in den vergangenen Jahren eine breite Auftraggeberschaft für kreative Architekten dar. Auch das Hotelgewerbe mit seinem wachsenden Interesse an Design – angeregt vielleicht durch die gemeinsamen Projekte von Ian Schrager und Philippe Starck in den 1990er-Jahren – nahm zahlreiche bekannte Architekten in seinen Dienst, in der Hoffnung, eine schicke und betuchte Klientel anzuziehen. Dieses Phänomen beschränkt sich nicht auf Weltstädte wie New York oder Berlin. Es betrifft mittlerweile auch weniger bekannte Orte, z. B. die reizvolle mittelalterliche Gemeinde Zuoz im Schweizer Engadin, rund 20 km vom glamourösen Touristenziel St. Moritz entfernt. Oberhalb des Ortes befindet sich auf einer Höhe von 1900 m das Hotel Castell. Mitte der 1990er-Jahre kaufte der Schweizer Künstler und Sammler Ruedi Bechtler das 1912/13 von Nicolaus Hartmann als mondänes Kurhotel errichtete Gebäude. Ebendort wurde 1998 die „Rote Bar" eröffnet, das erste Projekt der Architektin Gabrielle Hächler und der bekannten Schweizer Künstlerin Pipilotti Rist für das Hotel. Im Jahr 2000 kam das Amsterdamer Architekturbüro UNStudio dazu und entwarf ein zusätzliches Gebäude mit 14 Luxusapartments (2003–04, S. 502). Im alten Haupthaus bauten sie ins Untergeschoss des Ostflügels einen farbenfrohen Hamam ein und gestalteten rund die Hälfte der 60 Hotelzimmer in einem für sie typischen Stil um. Die übrigen Räume überarbeitete der Engadiner Architekt Hans-Jörg Ruch, während der japanische Künstler Tadashi Kawamata eine hölzerne Terrasse nebst Steg beisteuerte, über den man zu der ebenfalls auf dem Grundstück befindlichen Sauna gelangt. Den Abschluss bildete unlängst ein runder, so genannter Skyspace (ein Raum zur gemeinsamen Himmelsbetrachtung) des Künstlers James Turrell. Eigentlich ist das Hotel Castell nicht untypisch für zahlreiche „Designerhotels", wie man sie auf der ganzen Welt antrifft, doch in diesem Fall sind der hohe Anspruch und die Vielfalt der architektonischen und künstlerischen Beiträge besonders bemerkenswert.

Zwei Bergpässe und rund 300 km entfernt – aber immer noch in der Schweiz – trifft man in dem Ort Sierre auf das Hôtel de la Poste (2006–07, **12**) der jungen Schweizer Architektengemeinschaft Savioz Meyer Fabrizzi. Es hat zwar nicht die Weltklassekunst des Hotel Castell zu bieten, führt aber vor Augen, wie weit sich die Idee des Designer- bzw. – wie in diesem Fall – des Architektenhotels inzwischen fortentwickelt hat. Die Architekten hatten die Chuzpe, ein schlichtes, viereckiges Gebäude aus der Mitte des 18. Jahrhunderts in einem leuchtenden Orangeton anzustreichen und den Namen des Hotels in großen Lettern auf die Fassadenkanten zu malen. Außerdem erhielt das Hotel auf seiner Rückseite einen gläsernen, geschwungenen Speiseraum, der in einen kleinen Park hinausragt, der zwischen der Rückseite des angrenzenden Rathauses und dem Bahnhof verläuft. Auch die 15 Zimmer wurden von den Architekten neu gestaltet. Dazu verwendeten sie die entsprechende Anzahl verschiedener Holzarten, die den Suiten nun ihren jeweiligen Namen geben. An den Decken sind Fotografien von den jeweiligen Baumsorten angebracht, die dem alten Gebäude einen „grünen Touch" verleihen.

Die in Mexiko-Stadt ansässigen Architekten Legorreta + Legorreta schlossen 2007 ihren Komplettumbau einer ehemaligen Anlage zur Flaschenabfüllung im mexikanischen Puebla ab, in der sich jetzt das Boutique-Hotel La Purificadora befindet (S. 308). Ähnlich wie seine weniger berühmten Kollegen im schweizerischen Sierre bewahrte das Architektenteam bei seiner Erneuerung viele der farbenfroheren oder pittoreskeren Elemente des aus dem 19. Jahrhundert stammenden Baus. So wurden die mit Steinen aus der Umgebung errichteten Mauern der ursprünglich eingeschossigen Anlage beibehalten, ergänzt um drei weitere Geschosse mit gemauerten Wänden, eine Bar-Lounge auf dem

27

Dach und einen 30 m langen, von gläsernen Wänden eingefassten Swimmingpool. Ferner griffen die Architekten auf die originalen hölzernen Tragbalken der früheren Abfüllanlage zurück und fügten speziell angefertigte, für die Gegend typische Keramikfliesen sowie ebenfalls aus der Nähe stammenden Onyx neu hinzu. Während Ricardo Legorreta sonst für seine Vorliebe für kräftige Farbschemata bekannt ist, die an die Arbeiten von Luis Barragán erinnern, sind die Räume des Boutique-Hotels – abgesehen vom satten Violett der Sitzgarnituren – weniger von ihrer Farbigkeit bestimmt als von der Materialpalette aus Alt und Neu.

MACH'S RICHTIG

Ein nicht geringer Anteil anspruchsvoller zeitgenössischer Architektur kommt unter wesentlichen Kompromissen zustande, da die Entstehung eines ungewöhnlichen oder innovativen Bauwerks immer auch eine Kostenfrage ist, bei der es mitunter um Unsummen geht. Die meisten Menschen leben mit einer Architektur, die ziemlich durchschnittlich ist oder zumindest immer gleich aussieht und wenig Platz bietet. Mittellose oder solche, die durch Krieg oder Naturkatastrophen um Haus und Habe gekommen sind, haben erst recht nicht viel von den großartigen Entwürfen heutiger Toparchitekten. Natürlich gibt es Ausnahmen von dieser Regel, Architekten, denen es ein Anliegen ist, kostengünstige oder leicht zu errichtende Unterkünfte für Notleidende zu entwerfen. Einer von ihnen ist der japanische Architekt Shigeru Ban. Zwar ist auch Ban häufig für wohlhabende Auftraggeber tätig, was ihn aber nicht davon abhält, in Indien, Ruanda oder der Türkei Behelfsbauten für das UN-Flüchtlingshilfswerk zu entwerfen. Seine jüngste Initiative dieser Art für den Wiederaufbau nach der Tsunami-Katastrophe vom 26. Dezember 2004 (Kirinda, Hambantota, Sri Lanka, 2005–07, S. 98) sah insgesamt 50 Wohnhäuser für die Opfer des Unglücks vor. Die 71 m² großen Bauten kosteten rund 13 000 Dollar pro Einheit und wurden aus Gummibaumholz und Blöcken aus gepresster Erde errichtet. Diese Häuser, nicht nur komfortabel, sondern auch mit Rücksicht auf die kulturellen Gegebenheiten der Gegend konzipiert, mögen eine Ausnahme von der Regel sein, nach der berühmte Architekten nicht für Arme arbeiten – umso mehr ein Grund, das Projekt im vorliegenden Band aufzuführen.

Shigeru Ban ist ebenfalls beteiligt an der Initiative „Make It Right" für die Stadt New Orleans (Louisiana, seit 2007, S. 530). Das Projekt des Schirmherrn Brad Pitt hat sich zum Ziel gesetzt, in dem von dem Hurrikan Katrina verwüsteten Stadtbezirk Lower Ninth Ward unter Federführung des Architekturbüros Graft neue kostengünstige Häuser aufzubauen, deren Entwürfe von renommierten Architekten stammen. Angesichts weiterer Beteiligter wie Kieran Timberlake, Morphosis, David Adjaye oder MVRDV findet „Make It Right" sicherlich mehr Aufmerksamkeit als Bans Kirinda-Projekt, zumal auch die politische Botschaft kaum zu übersehen ist. Man darf es wohl als schockierend bezeichnen, dass im „reichsten Land der Welt" einige der ärmsten Bewohner über einen langen Zeitraum zur Obdachlosigkeit verurteilt sind wegen verwaltungstechnischer Unzulänglichkeiten, die bis in die höchsten Regierungsebenen reichen. Rein aus der Perspektive der Gegenwartsarchitektur ist es natürlich interessant zu sehen, was sich ein „Stararchitekt" mit einem Budget von 150 000 Dollar pro Hauseinheit einfallen lässt. Bans Häuser in Kirinda erheben nicht den Anspruch auf jene ausgeklügelte Formensprache, für die er bekannt geworden ist – vielmehr präsentieren sie sich als eine strenge, zielgerichtete Unternehmung, um den in Not Geratenen zu helfen und zwar unter Einsatz ökologisch verantwortbarer Methoden und Materialien. Die an die Architekten gestellten Teilnahmebedingungen für „Make It Right" zeigen, dass die Organisatoren eine Reihe von Faktoren berücksichtigten, die in der prätentiösen Welt avancierter Architektur wohl selten zusammentreffen.

28

28
Holzer Kobler Architekturen, Arche Nebra Visitors' Center, Wangen, Germany, 2005–07

So sollten die Teilnehmer

– ein schon bestehendes Interesse an oder Engagement in New Orleans, vorzugsweise aus der Zeit nach dem Hurrikan Katrina, und/oder Erfahrung im Bereich der Katastrophenhilfe vorweisen können,

– mit nachhaltigem Bauen vertraut sein,

– Erfahrung im Bau von Mehrfamilienunterkünften haben,

– Erfahrung mit gering budgetierten Projekten vorweisen können,

– Erfahrung mit dem Bauen in Gewässernähe oder auf Wasserspiegelniveau haben

– und natürlich hohen Wert auf anspruchsvolles Design legen.

Um sich für gute Zwecke zu engagieren, haben der Schauspieler Brad Pitt und seine Lebensgefährtin Angelina Jolie die Jolie-Pitt-Stiftung ins Leben gerufen, die unlängst beachtliche Mittel bereitgestellt hat, um den von der Darfur-Krise betroffenen sudanesischen Flüchtlingen zu helfen; daneben unterstützt das Paar wohltätige Organisationen wie Global Action for Children oder Ärzte ohne Grenzen. Dass eine solche Unterstützung in den Vereinigten Staaten dringend nötig ist und dass zahlreiche Architekten sich bereit erklärt haben, ohne Honorar für „Make It Right" zu arbeiten, sagt auf jeden Fall einiges über den Zustand der USA aus – aber vielleicht noch etwas anderes, Positiveres, über die zeitgenössische Architektur.

TÜRME AUS DEM MITTELALTER UND TEE IN DEN BÄUMEN

Wie der Titel *Architecture Now!* besagt, geht es in dieser Reihe natürlich um aktuelle Entwicklungen. Dementsprechend nehmen viele der präsentierten Projekte in ästhetischer oder technischer Hinsicht eine Vorreiterrolle ein. Bei einem großen Teil geht es außerdem darum, eine enge Verbindung zwischen bereits bestehenden Bauwerken und neu Hinzugefügtem oder neuen Nutzungsarten herzustellen. Die Brennand-Kapelle von Paulo Mendes da Rocha in Brasilien oder das Ullens Center von Jean-Michel Wilmotte in Peking sind Beispiele für diese Art der Symbiose oder der – falls der Begriff treffender erscheint – Konfrontation von Altem und Neuem. Die Um- und Neugestaltung bestehender Bauten wird auch weiterhin ein wesentliches Element in der Entwicklung der zeitgenössischen Architektur sein, sei es auch nur aus ökonomischen Gründen. Oftmals kostet es weniger, ein altes Bauwerk zu renovieren, als ganz neu zu bauen. Eine weitere Rolle für den großen Anteil von Instandsetzungen in der zeitgenössischen Architektur spielt die zunehmende Diskussion der Frage, welche Gebäude von historischem Interesse oder Wert sind und welche nicht. Vor 20 Jahren hätten sich womöglich weder die von Wilmotte renovierte Fabrik im Neobauhausstil in Peking noch die Abfüllanlage in Puebla, aus der Legorreta + Legorreta ein schickes Hotel gemacht haben, für eine Neugestaltung qualifiziert. Dabei gewinnen diese Projekte erst durch die zuvor schon vorhandenen Räume und Materialien eine Intensität, die allein mit neuen Elementen gar nicht zu erzielen gewesen wäre.

Selbst in der aktuellsten Architektur macht sich die Gegenwart der Vergangenheit bemerkbar. Diese Vergangenheit kann mit konkreten historischen Ereignissen und Orten verknüpft sein, wie beim Dokumentations- und Informationszentrum Bergen-Belsen von KSP Engel und Zimmermann (Kreis Celle, 2005–07, S. 156) oder der von LIN ausgeführten Neugestaltung eines U-Boot-Bunkerteilstücks im französischen

29

Saint-Nazaire (2005–07, S. 320). Sie kann aber auch noch fernere Zeiten beschwören, wie das Besucherzentrum Arche Nebra von Holzer Kobler (Wangen, Deutschland, 2005–07, S. 250) am Fundort der so genannten Himmelsscheibe von Nebra aus der Bronzezeit. Es liegt auf der Hand, dass in manchen Ländern die Erforschung der ferneren Vergangenheit und ihrer kulturellen und architektonischen Zusammenhänge ungewöhnliche Formen annehmen kann. Die Schweiz, ein kleines Land mit einer reichen Geschichte, hat in jüngerer Zeit Architekten wie Peter Zumthor hervorgebracht, für den die Alpen, die alpenländische Kultur und selbst das Gestein der Berge wichtige Inspirationsquellen sind. Weniger bekannt als Zumthor, aber ebenso intensiv mit der Geschichte seines Landes befasst, ist der Architekt Hans-Jörg Ruch, der einen Teil seiner Ausbildung in den Vereinigten Staaten genossen hat und heute vornehmlich in der Nähe von St. Moritz im Engadin arbeitet. Seine Restaurierung der aus dem 14. Jahrhundert stammenden Chesa Madalena in Zuoz (Schweiz, 2001–02, S. 438), bei der ein aus dem Mittelalter stammender Wohnturm innerhalb des alten Bauernhauses freigelegt werden konnte, stellt eine bemerkenswerte Kombination aus Respekt gegenüber der Vergangenheit und Aufgeschlossenheit gegenüber der Gegenwart dar. Heute beherbergt die Chesa Madalena eine Kunstgalerie, in der so verschiedene Künstler wie Richard Long oder Balthasar Burkhard ausgestellt werden. Speziell in „alten" Kulturen, den Kulturen Europas und Teilen Asiens, hat das Bewusstsein von der Vergangenheit und der Respekt vor ihren Lehren in den vergangenen Jahren stark zugenommen. Architekten wie Ruch sind Teil dieser Entwicklung, aber zugleich auch eigenständige Stifter einer neuen Sensibilität, die Vergangenheit und Gegenwart in Einklang zu bringen weiß.

Einen etwas radikaleren Ansatz zeigt der Architekt Valerio Olgiati, ebenfalls Schweizer, bei seiner Gestaltung des Künstlerateliers Bardill im Herzen des alten Schweizer Dörfchens Scharans (2006–07, S. 382). Wo zuvor ein alter Holzstall stand, errichtete Olgiati eine Konstruktion aus rotem Ortbeton in der gleichen Form des früheren Bauwerks, allerdings mit einem ovalen Innenhof, der sich zum Himmel öffnet. Weitgehend schmucklose Betonwände aufzustellen, mag zunächst als unpassend für die Umgebung erscheinen, tatsächlich aber fügt sich das neue Gebäude anstandslos in die Schlichtheit der ursprünglichen Architektur des Schweizer Dorfes ein. Den roten Betonanstrich wählte Olgiati, da vonseiten des Dorfes verlangt war, dass das neue Gebäude den gleichen Farbton wie das alte haben müsse. Während Olgiati also einerseits den Auflagen zur Wahrung des historischen Dorfbildes nachkam, schuf er zugleich ein durch und durch modernes Bauwerk, dessen Innenhof den „Skyspaces" von James Turrell ebenbürtig ist.

Terunobu Fujimori ist Lehrstuhlinhaber an der Universität Tokio und spezialisiert auf die Geschichte der im westlichen Stil in Japan seit der Meiji-Zeit (1868–1912) errichteten Gebäude. Er ist auch ein ausgewiesener Kenner der frühen modernen Architektur, die sich mit Namen wie Le Corbusier, Mies van der Rohe und Walter Gropius verbindet, und als er selbst anfing zu bauen, schuf er überraschende Bauten, deren Wurzeln tief in der Vergangenheit zu liegen scheinen. Dazu schreibt Fujimori: „Seit meinem ersten Projekt versuche ich, mich an die folgenden beiden Grundsätze zu halten: 1) Das Gebäude sollte keinem Bauwerk eines anderen Architekten, ob aus Vergangenheit oder Gegenwart, und keinem seit der Bronzezeit entstandenen Stil ähneln; 2) an sichtbaren Gebäudeteilen sollen natürliche Materialien verwendet sowie gelegentlich Pflanzen in das Gebäude einbezogen werden, damit es mit der Natur harmoniert."[6]

Der Anspruch, Bauwerke ohne jede Ähnlichkeit mit anderen zu entwerfen, mag anmaßend erscheinen, doch der Architekt bleibt ebenso bescheiden wie sein 6,07 m^2 großes Teehaus Tetsu auf dem Gelände des Museums Kiyoharu Shirakaba (Nakamaru, Hokuto, Yamanashi,

30

30
FAM Arquitectura, March 11 Memorial
for the Victims, Madrid, Spain,
2005–07

2005, S. 174). Fujimori vergleicht es mit einem „Zwergenhaus aus einem Märchen", verweist aber bei seiner Projektbeschreibung auch auf für Japan so wichtige kulturelle Symbole wie die historische Figur von Sen no Rikyu (1522–91), der den denkbar größten Einfluss auf die japanische Teezeremonie hatte. So angelegt, dass man ringsumher die Kirschbäume überschauen kann, steht das Teehaus Tetsu im Dienst emotional tief verankerter japanischer Bräuche und Traditionen, eben von der Teezeremonie bis zur „sakura", der Kirschblüte, die das Land alljährlich in ihren Bann schlägt. So wie der von seinem Erbauer angeführte „Märchenzwerg" hat das gesamte Minibauwerk viel mit Humor zu tun, aber es ist auch ein Produkt althergebrachter Traditionen. Ähnlich wie Olgiatis Atelier in Scharans hat es etwas – im intellektuellen Sinn – „Schräges" an sich. Nichts ist an ihm so, wie es scheint – aber genau das ist es, was Fujimoris außergewöhnliche Arbeiten so zeitgenössisch macht. So sehr sie den gegenwärtigen Zustand der Architektur thematisieren, so sehr sind sie in einer mehr oder weniger fernen Vergangenheit verwurzelt. Mit Bezug auf eines seiner anderen Projekte, das Teehaus Takasugi-an (Miyagawa Takabe, Chino City, Nagano, 2003) schreibt Fujimori: „Nicht weit entfernt steht das Haus, in dem Toyo Ito aufgewachsen ist. Obwohl wir beide zur gleichen Zeit in der gleichen Gegend groß geworden sind, sind unsere Arbeiten grundverschieden. Zwischen Menschen und ihren jeweiligen Umgebungen besteht keine einfache, logische Verbindung."[7]

SONNENBLUMEN UND STERNE

Es ist kein Zufall, dass unsere kurze Inhaltsübersicht zu *Architecture Now! 6* mit Kirinda, „Make It Right" und dem kleinsten Gebäude des Buchs, dem Teehaus Tetsu abschließt. In den Medien finden die teuersten und auffälligsten Arbeiten der Gegenwartsarchitektur die meiste Aufmerksamkeit, wie im Jahr 2008 die großen Attraktionen in Peking. Diese Gebäude, das Hauptstadion der Olympischen Spiele und der benachbarte Watercube, aber auch die spektakuläre BMW Welt von Coop Himmelb(l)au, sollen hier nicht fehlen. Daneben scheint sich jedoch ein deutliches Bewusstsein dafür entwickelt zu haben, dass es noch andere Existenzgründe für Architektur gibt, ein Bewusstsein, das ungewöhnliche Protagonisten wie Terunobu Fujimori auf humorvolle Weise zum Ausdruck bringen. Fujimoris Interesse gilt einer – wie er es nennt – „Architektur der Menschlichkeit", weniger bezogen auf die japanische Tradition als auf die gesamte Erde. Auch erscheint es durchaus logisch, wenn sich die Stars der zeitgenössischen Architektur denen des Firmaments von Hollywood anschließen, so wie bei „Make It Right" in New Orleans, wobei das Entwerfen von Häusern für Menschen, die ohne Obdach sind, eine ganz andere Herausforderung ist als Tummelplätze für Millionäre zu bauen. Allerdings verkennt die zeitgenössische Architektur – ungeachtet ihres verhältnismäßig langlebigen Charakters (zumindest im Vergleich zu einer Ausgabe von *Vanity Fair*) – auf ihrer Suche nach prachtvollen Effekten und ins Auge springenden Überraschungen nicht selten die Grundbedingungen unserer Existenz. Die Tatsache, dass ein Künstler vom Rang eines Anselm Kiefer das Gefühl hat, seine Ideen am besten durch architektonische Formen zum Ausdruck bringen zu können, stellt einen interessanten Kommentar zur Lage der Dinge dar – Kiefers Vision ist eine, in der es um Ruinen, um postapokalyptische, aus geborstenem Beton hervorsprießende Sonnenblumen und gefallene Sterne geht. Die zeitgenössische Kunst scheint schon seit Langem auf der Suche nach sich selbst zu sein, auf der Suche nach einer Seele, die im Übergang vom Figürlichen hin zum Farbklecks bzw. in noch jüngerer Zeit der Videoinstallation verlorengegangen ist. Ist es vielleicht die zeitgenössische Architektur in ihrer großen Vielfalt, die dem Ausdruck von Hoffnung, Ängsten, Exzessen und Triumphen, dem

Festhalten des Moments am nächsten kommt? Natürlich wird auf den folgenden Seiten die von Zygmunt Bauman apostrophierte „flüchtige Moderne" in all ihrer fabelhaften kommerziellen Oberflächlichkeit berücksichtigt, aber eben auch die schwere Betonarchitektur in Bergen-Belsen oder das ätherische Mahnmal für den 11. März 2004 vor dem Bahnhof Atocha in Madrid. Und wenn Schiffscontainer, die für ein zweitägiges Musikfestival in Rio zusammengebaut werden, mit zu der Gleichung gehören, oder Holzbalken von insgesamt 150 km Länge, die in der Wüste von Nevada verbrannt werden – dann sollen sie eben brennen. Oder wie steht es mit einem Architekten, der ausschließlich in „Second Life" existiert und der virtuelle Gebäude für eine reale Universität entwirft? Genauso ist das entgegengesetzte Extrem, die Restaurierung eines Bauwerks aus dem 14. Jahrhundert im schweizerischen Zuoz, als integraler Bestandteil der Fortentwicklung zeitgenössischer Architektur zu begreifen. Wenn denn an dieser Stelle für irgendetwas Partei ergriffen werden soll, dann dafür, dass Architektur zu verstehen heißt, weder ihre Vergangenheit auszuschließen noch ihre kurzlebigsten Erscheinungsformen in der Gegenwart. Die auf den folgenden Seiten vorgestellte Gegenwartsarchitektur umspannt die verschiedensten historischen Epochen und Hoffnungen, von religiösen Orten über Sportstätten hin zu Geschäftsbauten, vom größten Gebäude der Welt bis zu einem ihrer kleinsten. Die Architektur lebt.

Philip Jodidio, Grimentz, 2008

1   Bauman, Zygmunt, „Value Dilemmas as a Challenge in the Practice and Concepts of Supervision and Coaching", ANSE-Konferenz, 7. Mai 2004, Leiden, Niederlande. Zygmunt Bauman, geboren 1925, ist emeritierter Professor der Universität von Leeds und zählt mit Publikationen wie *Liquid Modernity* (2000) zu den weltweit bekanntesten Soziologen und Philosophen. 1989 und 1990 erhielt er den Europäischen Amalfi-Preis für Soziologie und Sozialwissenschaften, 1998 den Theodor-W.-Adorno-Preis der Stadt Frankfurt.
2   Heathcote, Edwin, „Modernism Minus Utopia", in: *The Financial Times* vom 29. Dezember 2007.
3   Riding, Alan, „An Artist Sets Up House(s) at the Grand Palais", in: *The New York Times* vom 31. Mai 2007.
4   Wigley, Mark, in: *Deconstructivist Architecture*, Museum of Modern Art, New York 1988.
5   Ouroussoff, Nicolai, „Next to MoMA, Reaching for the Stars", in: *The New York Times* vom 15. November 2007.
6   Fujimori, Terunobu, *Fujimori Terunobu Architecture*, Toto Shuppan, Tokio 2007.
7   Ebd.

INTRODUCTION

UNE ARCHITECTURE VIVANTE !

La diversité et l'inventivité caractérisent l'architecture de notre époque. Les *blobs* extravagants nés de la première génération des essais de conception assistée par ordinateur ont pratiquement tous disparu, mais l'informatique n'en a pas moins poursuivi son chemin d'une façon beaucoup plus intégrée. Même des bâtiments qui paraissent rectilignes ou d'inspiration moderniste débordent maintenant de détails et d'éléments qui n'auraient pu exister sans la modélisation en trois dimensions et la fabrication assistée par ordinateur devenues courantes. Cette édition d'*Architecture Now !* présente des réalisations qui vont de la taille de la minuscule maison de thé Tetsu (6,07 m^2) de Terunobu Fujimori au gigantesque projet de Crystal Island signé par Norman Foster à Moscou (1,1 million de m^2), et ce n'est pas par hasard. Sans parti pris, cet ouvrage tente d'offrir un panorama utile de ce qui se produit en ce moment même dans le monde de l'architecture, de l'inspiration traditionnelle à l'avant-garde la plus extrême. Quel est l'esprit de notre temps et comment l'architecture reflète-t-elle sa créativité alors que la première décennie du XXIe siècle touche déjà à sa fin ? L'éminent sociologue Zygmunt Bauman analyse l'état de la société moderne en des termes qui pourraient bien s'appliquer à l'architecture contemporaine lorsqu'il parle de « modernité liquide ». « Vivre dans un monde moderne »liquide« dépend de trois conditions. Nous agissons d'abord en fonction de la première, l'incertitude, puis sous l'influence de la seconde, un risque continu que nous essayons de calculer, mais qui n'est, en principe, pas totalement calculable, puisque l'on peut toujours être confronté à des surprises. La troisième condition est que nous devons agir dans le cadre d'une confiance évolutive. Une tendance qui semble sans problème aujourd'hui peut être condamnée et rejetée demain. Ce n'est pas seulement vrai dans le domaine du travail, mais partout. Les aliments qui vous sont recommandés par votre médecin comme particulièrement sains aujourd'hui seront proclamés cancérigènes demain. Si vous feuilletez les magazines sur papier glacé ou les suppléments des quotidiens, vous trouvez pratiquement chaque semaine une rubrique qui vous informe sur les dernières tendances non seulement des vêtements, mais aussi des comportements, de la décoration de la maison ou de la vie des célébrités que vous devez connaître. Et ainsi de suite, des rubriques vous dictent ce qui est »in«. Mais, juste à côté, un autre article vous montre ce qui n'est plus à la mode, et dont vous devriez avoir honte… si vous en êtes encore là. »[1]

LES HOMMES DE PÉKIN

L'architecture contemporaine a souvent fait de la recherche de cette « modernité liquide » une vertu. Le monumental Watercube (Cube d'eau, Centre national de natation pour les jeux Olympiques de Pékin 2008, page 404) de PTW est un bloc massif gainé d'un habit des plus éphémères : une peau en coussins d'ETFE (Tetrafluoroéthylène d'éthylène) à « l'aspect organique et aléatoire » inspirée de la formation des bulles de savon. Peu d'images évoquent mieux le caractère éphémère que ces bulles, et cependant la liquidité de l'architecture doit certainement connaître des limites. L'architecture prend du temps à concevoir et à construire. Elle peut être coûteuse, et sert la plupart du temps une raison spécifique – ces conditions vont contre « l'incertitude » pensée par certains architectes avec tant d'empressement. La recherche de la mode peut, bien sûr, s'imposer dans des bâtiments aussi monumentaux que le Watercube, le stade principal des Jeux 2008 par Herzog & de Meuron (page 222) ou la double tour CCTV de Koolhaas/OMA. Voulues et conçues pour donner au Pékin contemporain la présence architecturale iconique dont elle manquait, ces structures posent le problème suivant : où va l'architecture en Chine, en Inde et dans le Golfe persique

31
Herzog & de Meuron, National Stadium, Main Stadium for the 2008 Olympic Games, Beijing, China, 2003–08

où l'on construit à vitesse précipitée. Le *Financial Times* en décembre 2007 s'interrogeait sur l'architecture des jeux Olympiques : « À Pékin, les plus grands architectes du monde ont pratiquement abandonné toute réflexion sur la ville. C'est du modernisme moins l'utopie et sans le contexte qu'il soit physique, topographique, politique, théorique ou urbain. Tout tient dans une image simple et unique. Chacun de ces immeubles aurait pu être construit n'importe où dans le monde. Pékin devient l'incarnation des aspects les plus superficiels d'une culture contemporaine du design, obsédée par le geste et l'icône, l'intelligence et la complexité de ses structures. C'est de l'architecture de scène pour le spectacle des Jeux, pour un régime déterminé à démontrer sa modernité et à illustrer l'émergence de sa puissance économique et culturelle. L'architecture radicale s'est prêtée à ce spectacle et à cette propagande. Les villes sont faites de bâtiments, mais de grands bâtiments ne suffisent pas à faire une ville. »[2]

Citer cet article ne signifie pas l'approuver dans sa substance, mais plutôt montrer la variété des émotions et des opinions suscitées par les expressions les plus spectaculaires de l'architecture contemporaine. L'idée peut paraître intéressante, mais tient-elle compte des inévitables compromis inhérents à tout grand projet ? On raconte qu'un jour Norman Foster avait tenté d'expliquer à des clients chinois que l'importance du vélo dans leur pays était un avantage écologique, et qu'ils devaient s'efforcer de le conserver. On lui répondit dans les termes les plus clairs que la Chine aspirait non pas à la bicyclette mais à la voiture et aux jets. Une puissante tendance en faveur d'une architecture iconique est apparue. Elle se nourrit des énormes disponibilités financières actuelles que l'on trouve en ce moment de Mumbai à Dubaï jusqu'à Shanghai. On peut critiquer ces tendances, mais les architectes d'aujourd'hui ne sont pas tant des agents de contestation politique que des constructeurs d'objets utiles. Comme tout un chacun, ils cherchent à faire travailler leur agence et à laisser leur marque.

Ce livre contient trois réalisations iconiques spécifiquement conçues pour les jeux Olympiques de Pékin 2008, mais également l'Ullens Center for Contemporary Art (UCCA, 2006–07, page 546), réhabilitation des bâtiments d'une usine des années 1950 par le Français Jean-Michel Wilmotte (avec MADA s.p.a.m.). Ce dernier projet montre que les démolitions brutales pratiquées par les autorités locales ne sont pas la seule voie possible pour faire de Pékin le centre cosmopolite dont beaucoup rêvent. Il apporte un contrepoint aux « gestes superficiels » montrés du doigt par le *Financial Times*. Même dans une capitale en pleine effervescence comme Pékin, il n'est pas possible de généraliser sur le devenir de l'architecture contemporaine.

La série *Architecture Now !* a fait fréquemment référence à des réalisations qui pourraient au mieux se situer à la frontière entre l'art et l'architecture, ou à celle établie entre l'architecture et le design. Cette édition n'y fait pas exception avec le très certainement « non monumental » pavillon de la Serpentine Gallery 2007 à Londres, conçu par l'artiste Olafur Eliasson et le principal responsable de Snøhetta, Kjetil Thorsen (page 138). Eliasson est à nouveau présent à travers ses *New York City Waterfalls*, des installations qui interrogent sur le rapport entre la ville et ses fleuves (2008, page 134). Un autre artiste encore, l'Allemand Anselm Kiefer, a occupé le Grand Palais à Paris à la fin du printemps et au début de l'été 2007, avec une installation (*Sternenfall*, Pluie d'étoiles, **2/3**) qui doit beaucoup à l'architecture ou plus précisément, à ses ruines. « Ce que vous voyez là est le désespoir, dit Kiefer, je suis complètement désespéré parce que je ne peux pas m'expliquer pourquoi je suis ici. C'est plus qu'un deuil, c'est un désespoir. Mais pour survivre, vous construisez, vous créez des illusions. »[3] Ces questions sur les raisons de notre existence pourraient sembler opposées à la « modernité liquide » de Bauman, mais l'argument est précisément que

32

l'architecture – l'art de l'environnement construit –, exprimé dans sa myriade de formes, peut soit confirmer soit nier la plupart des théories de la modernité. Assez résistante au temps, elle fait l'objet d'efforts infinis pour dissoudre pratiquement sa substance. Le mémorial du 11 mars à Madrid (Espagne, 2005–07, page 164) par les architectes FAM, simple anneau de verre, au-dessus d'une salle souterraine bleue, est un commentaire sur une tragédie dont les noms des victimes sont assez curieusement inscrits sur une membrane en ETFE. Ils sont présent, mais quasiment invisibles. L'architecture rend ici un hommage évanescent, mais durable, à un événement de mort et de destruction qui n'a duré qu'un bref instant.

DU CHOC DE L'ANCIEN AUX CHARMES DU METAVERSE

C'est sans doute parce que les chantiers sont si longs à mener à bien, si on les compare au cycle créatif rapide de l'artiste, par exemple, ou parce qu'ils nécessitent tant d'investissements, que l'architecture suit un rythme assez spécial par rapport à d'autres manifestations « sociologiques » de la mode. Les jeunes Turcs qui surgissent bardés de théories et de formes provocantes nous étonnent, mais lorsqu'ils commencent enfin à passer à la réalisation, leurs innovations font figure de reliques. Ainsi l'exposition « Architecture déconstructiviste », organisée au Museum of Modern Art de New York par Philip Johnson en 1988, présentait essentiellement des œuvres non réalisées de Frank O. Gehry, Daniel Libeskind, Rem Koolhaas, Peter Eisenman, Zaha Hadid, Bernard Tschumi et Coop Himmelb(l)au. Aujourd'hui lorsque l'on regarde le BMW Welt (2001–07, page 124) de Coop Himmelb(l)au à Munich, leur Akron Art Museum dans l'Ohio (2001–07, page 114) ou l'extension par Libeskind du Royal Ontario Museum (Toronto, Canada, 2002–07, page 314), on ne peut que saluer la prescience du MoMA d'avoir révélé une tendance qui ne se matérialiserait réellement que vingt ans plus tard. « L'architecture déconstructiviste, écrivait Mark Wigley, commissaire associé pour l'exposition du MoMA, ne constitue pas une avant-garde. Elle met plutôt en évidence le non-familier caché dans le traditionnel. C'est le choc de l'ancien. »[4] L'esthétique et les formes de l'architecture contemporaine ne sont certainement pas uniquement déterminées par l'âge des architectes. Steven Holl, par exemple, est né en 1947, juste un an après Daniel Libeskind, et a cependant emprunté une voie autre, de nature plus artistique. Son extension du Nelson-Atkins Museum of Art (Bloch Building, Kansas City, Missouri, 2002–07, page 240) a remporté en 2008 le Prix d'honneur de l'American Institute of Architects accompagné de ce commentaire du jury : « L'extension du Nelson-Atkins Museum of Art fusionne l'architecture et le paysage pour créer une architecture expérimentale qui se déploie devant le visiteur qui la perçoit au cours de chacun de ses déplacements dans le temps et l'espace. » Les boîtes lumineuses qui forment ce nouveau bâtiment empruntent une approche de la surface, de la lumière et de l'espace qui n'est pas celle d'une école comme le déconstructivisme et, aujourd'hui, cette architecture peut sembler beaucoup plus contemporaine que les formes fracturées annoncées à la fin des années 1980.

Tadao Ando, né en 1941, est plus âgé de cinq ans que Libeskind et a emprunté une voie clairement ancrée dans une architecture moderne issue de Le Corbusier. Néanmoins, comme Holl, il possède une approche artistique qui lui permet d'évoluer et de créer des bâtiments aussi surprenants que le 21_21 Design Sight à Tokyo (Japon, 2004–07, page 76). Élément de l'ambitieux complexe de Tokyo Midtown érigé sur le site de l'ancienne Agence de défense, 21_21 Design Sight fait appel à ces murs de bétons qui ont fait la célébrité de l'architecte, mais sa structure de base, et très visible, est néanmoins un toit en métal qui évoque les plis du créateur de mode Issey Miyake, d'ailleurs

35
Bernardes + Jacobsen Arquitetura,
TIM Festival 2007, Rio de Janeiro,
Rio de Janeiro, Brazil, 2007

Les conteneurs de transport ont connu une sorte de mode en architecture au cours de ces dernières années comme on l'a vu dans certaines réalisations surprenantes (temporaires) dont le Bianimale Nomadic Museum de Shigeru Ban (quai 54, New York, 2005). Les architectes brésiliens Bernardes + Jacobsen s'en sont servi pour le site du festival TIM 2007 à Rio de Janeiro (Brésil, page 108). Avec pas moins de 250 conteneurs de six et 12 mètres de long, ils ont créé les structures nécessaires à un festival de musique populaire qui ne durait que deux nuits. Ce type de caisse de transport, standardisé en 1956 à la suite des propositions de l'Américain Malcom McLean, réapparait régulièrement dans une architecture contemporaine qui a admis qu'elle pouvait (ou devait) jouer l'éphémère. Le festival TIM est un exemple du besoin existant d'éléments architecturaux d'assez grandes dimensions montables et démontables rapidement. Ici, c'est davantage le design industriel et le transport qui ont donné forme à l'architecture. Si l'art peut jouer ce rôle, des disciplines plus concrètes peuvent également s'y prêter.

Les œuvres d'art se trouvent souvent aux limites de l'architecture, et certains architectes aspirent au statut de leurs amis plasticiens. L'artiste allemand Thomas Schütte a fréquemment montré son intérêt pour la forme architecturale dans sa production très diverse. L'une des ses œuvres les plus récentes, une installation pour la Fourth Plinth à Trafalgar Square (Londres, *Model for a Hotel*, 2007–08, page 456) n'est en réalité rien de plus qu'un empilement évasé de plaques de verre de couleur, mais son aspect varie énormément selon la perspective du spectateur, ce qui pose d'intéressantes questions sur la façon dont l'architecture peut dissoudre une présence parfois trop lourde. Sous certains angles, l'œuvre disparaît pratiquement, résultat que beaucoup d'architectes ont recherché sans y arriver. Mais là encore, l'art n'obéit pas aux mêmes règles que l'architecture à de nombreux égards, ce que l'on peut constater dans cette installation. Mais l'on peut aisément admettre que l'architecture est en recherche d'une fertilisation croisée avec l'art, le design ou même des applications industrielles, comme dans le cas des conteneurs. L'ouverture manifestée par cette tendance lui permet d'évoluer vers des directions parfois inattendues, et, à l'occasion, de rompre avec ce poids qui « plombe » tant de bâtiments traditionnels. Bien que peu de constructions soient conçues pour être incinérées comme l'*Uchronia* d'Arne Quinze, cette fuite devant les grandes règles de la permanence architecturale qu'implique ce travail n'est pas sans répercussion immédiate sur ce que peut faire l'architecture contemporaine.

LES PIEDS DANS LE SABLE, LA TÊTE DANS LES ÉTOILES

S'il est peut-être très à la mode d'affirmer que la « globalisation » réduit de beaucoup la variété de l'architecture d'aujourd'hui, il reste que les différences entre les villes et encore plus les climats imposent des approches variées, même si les méthodes et les matériaux des architectes sont pratiquement les mêmes. La culture du gratte-ciel d'une ville comme New York connaît ses limites, aussi bien en termes d'utilisation potentielle que des restrictions complexes de la réglementation urbanistique. Deux « stars » de la création ont été appelées à Manhattan pour travailler sur des projets qui, à leur façon, redéfinissent certaines conventions stylistiques new-yorkaises bien installées. Renzo Piano a achevé le New York Times Building, près de Times Square, en 2007 (page 394), tour qui manifeste l'amélioration de la qualité architecturale de ce quartier. Les 28 premiers étages de cet immeuble de 52 niveaux et 228 mètres de haut sont occupés par le journal, autour d'un jardin intérieur plantés de fougères, de mousses et de bouleaux de 15 mètres de haut, arbres qui sont après tout à l'origine du papier utilisé par le grand quotidien au sens métaphorique. La transparence voulue par l'architecte, démontre la capacité de celui-ci à offrir

Allemagne, 2003–07, page 566), et, non loin de là, le projet beaucoup plus petit de la chapelle St. Niklaus von Flüe (Mechernich-Wachendorf, Allemagne, 2003–07, page 560). Dans ses constructions phares comme ses thermes de Vals en Suisse (achevés en 1996), Zumthor a montré un fort attachement aux racines de l'histoire helvétique, et cette chapelle dédiée au saint patron du pays (St. Niklaus von Flüe, 1417–87, également connu sous le nom de frère Klaus) peut être considérée comme une nouvelle expression de ce patrimoine. De forme extérieure très simple, et dotée d'un curieux intérieur bardé de coffrages d'épicéa brûlés en fin du chantier, la chapelle est également le produit de l'artisanat local et a échappé aux effets de spectacle des projets assistés par ordinateur si appréciés d'autres architectes tout aussi réputés que Zumthor.

Une autre réalisation modeste mais forte est le couvent Tautra Maria par Jensen & Skodvin (île de Tautra, Norvège, 2004–06, page 280), édifié pour 18 sœurs cisterciennes. En grande partie comme les Diaconesses de Reuilly, ces sœurs ont joué un rôle actif dans la mise au point du projet architectural et sont citées par l'architecte en tant que responsables des aménagements paysagers. Relativement simple dans son expression, le couvent se dresse non loin des ruines d'un monastère cistercien fondé sur cette île huit siècles plus tôt. Grâce à une étude approfondie du rituel quotidien des religieuses, les architectes ont trouvé des solutions simples et économiques tout en proposant des idées inattendues comme pour le réfectoire dans lequel les nonnes sont alignées du même côté de la table (comme dans la *Cène* de Léonard de Vinci, selon l'agence), le regard tourné vers le paysage. La situation isolée de ce couvent, mais aussi le choix de la simplicité combinée avec une ouverture à une architecture qui n'imite pas le passé, génère un sentiment de spiritualité éloigné des clichés sur l'architecture sacrée. Il est moderne mais respecte sa fonction au meilleur sens du terme.

BURN BABY BURN

Inspirée peut-être et surtout par l'art contemporain qui depuis longtemps nous fait apprécier la beauté de l'éphémère, l'architecture accepte elle aussi, et même recherche, les vertus du temporaire. Les cités en plein développement, dont sans doute Los Angeles la première, ont donné naissance à des constructions à la durée de vie limitée qui ne prétendaient pas au type de permanence auquel l'architecture avait longtemps aspiré. Dans de précédentes éditions de la série *Architecture Now !,* des œuvres d'art ont déjà occupé une place importante. Le volume 3 présentait même en couverture une image du *Weather Project* d'Olafur Eliasson (Turbine Hall, Tate Modern, Londres, 16 octobre 2003 – 21 mars 2004). La relation entre une œuvre d'art proche de l'architecture et certaines constructions d'évidence éphémères n'est pas à négliger dans l'évolution de l'architecture contemporaine. Des idées qui sont apparues aux frontières de l'art et de l'architecture finissent parfois par influencer des types plus durables, d'une façon tantôt substantielle, tantôt simplement esthétique. Arne Quinze n'est ni un architecte ni un pur artiste, mais plutôt un concepteur autodidacte d'une certaine importance. Son installation complexe pour le Burning Man Festival 2006, *Uchronia : Message out of the Future* (Black Rock City, Black Rock Desert, Nevada, page 412) devait dès l'origine être brûlée après une semaine de festivités. Un film et un livre qui retracent la construction et la destruction de ce pavillon ouvert sont les seules traces restantes de son existence. Certains peuvent comparer *Uchronia* à un événement artistique, mais sa fonction de salle de danse et de fête le place clairement dans le domaine du bâti. La nature collective de sa construction et sa structure ondulante, presque organique, lui confèrent un réel intérêt esthétique. Arne Quinze en a déjà édifié une version moins éthérée à Bruxelles.

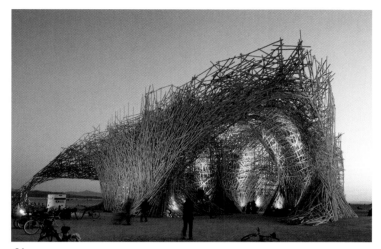

34

LES VOIES DU SEIGNEUR

Bien qu'ils n'influent pas aussi fortement l'architecture contemporaine que les institutions culturelles, les lieux de culte, sous une forme ou une autre, ne cessent de susciter l'inventivité et les projets avant-gardistes. La réutilisation de bâtiments religieux pour d'autres fonctions pose parfois le problème de la désacralisation et les réticences de certains de se rendre à une réception mondaine dans une ancienne église. L'une de ces initiatives récentes les plus réussies est la librairie Selexyz Dominicanen (Maastricht, Pays-Bas, 2005–07, page 352) des architectes Merkx+Girod qui sont intervenus sur l'intérieur de l'ancienne église des Dominicains de la ville, édifiée au 13e siècle. Bien que le bâtiment n'ait pas servi depuis l'occupation française en 1794, il avait conservé son style résolument ecclésial et même gothique. Les concepteurs ont remporté une prestigieuse distinction néerlandaise pour ce projet en 2007, le prix d'intérieur Lensvelt de Architect. Les commentaires du jury méritent d'être cités : « À Maastricht, Merkx+Girod Architecten ont créé une librairie contemporaine dans une ancienne église de Dominicains, préservant son cadre monumental exceptionnel. L'église a été restaurée à son ancienne gloire et les équipements techniques logés dans la crypte agrandie. Afin de préserver le caractère du lieu tout en obtenant la surface commerciale souhaitée, les architectes ont érigé sur un côté une structure de deux niveaux en acier noirci, où les livres sont conservés. L'aménagement de la boutique elle-même se trouve de l'autre côté au niveau inférieur, ce qui rend l'endroit lisible et déchiffrable. Le jury a été très impressionné par ces solutions spatiales, ainsi que par le superbe éclairage. La combinaison d'une vraie librairie et d'un intérieur d'église a été jugée particulièrement réussie. »

Un certain nombre de réalisations conçues pour êtres des lieux de culte ont été retenues pour cette édition. La chapelle de Notre-Dame de-la-Conception (Recife, Pernambuco, Brésil, 2004–06, page 340) par le célèbre architecte Paulo Mendes da Rocha a été édifiée dans les murs d'une ruine du XIXe siècle sur les terrains de l'usine de céramique Brennand à 16 kilomètres de Recife. Mendes da Rocha, Pritzker Prize 2006, est connu pour ses puissantes formes en béton, mais il a dû ici s'adapter à la restauration de vieux murs de brique tout en recouvrant l'ensemble d'une dalle de béton. Le poids et la massivité de cette architecture s'emparent et transforment la ruine existante, modulent la lumière, jouent sur la transparence et les volumes pour répondre aux nécessités du culte. L'idée que l'architecture contemporaine serait incapable d'évoquer la spiritualité tombe d'elle-même devant cette chapelle.

Loin du style et de la notoriété d'un architecte comme Mendes da Rocha, les concepteurs contemporains montrent un intérêt inventif pour les églises et les chapelles, comme le prouve l'architecte français Marc Rolinet, qui a récemment achevé la chapelle des Diaconesses de Reuilly (Versailles, France, 2004–07, page 430). Dans le cadre d'un budget limité, mais pour des clients ouverts à ses idées, Rolinet a associé une enveloppe moderne et transparente à un volume intérieur gainé de bois. La forme de bateau de la chapelle évoque le symbolisme chrétien (la barque de saint Pierre ou les paroles du Christ : « Venez à ma suite, et je vous ferai pêcheurs d'hommes » Mathieu 4:19 ; Marc 1:17). Protestant pratiquant, Rolinet a donné une forme simple et moderne à sa foi, ce qui a plus aux Diaconesses de Reuilly. Même si cette réalisation n'a pas attiré l'attention de la presse mondiale, il s'agit néanmoins d'une œuvre de valeur.

L'architecte suisse Peter Zumthor, beaucoup plus exposé à l'éclairage médiatique — même si parfois un peu contre sa volonté, est sorti d'une période assez longue de relatif silence pour signer au moins deux réalisations importantes : le musée d'Art Kolumba (Cologne,

également impliqué dans ce projet. Ce vocabulaire réduit et géométrique permet sans doute d'imaginer des constructions plus «intemporelles» que la complexité fractale, mais le grand public a davantage de difficultés à dater ces idées que les milieux de l'architecture contemporaine.

Un certain nombre d'intervenants importants ont davantage influencé l'architecture moderne et contemporaine par leurs dessins que par leurs travaux construits. Cette tendance remonte aisément jusqu'à Antonio Sant'Elia (1888–1916), Hugh Ferriss (1889–1962) ou plus récemment John Hejduk (1929–2000), Peter Eisenman et Zaha Hadid. Ces deux derniers ont bien sûr accompli leur transition et sont devenus des constructeurs actifs, mais leur réputation s'est établie sur des éléments théoriques, des plans et des dessins plutôt que sur leurs réalisations, et ce jusqu'à une date assez récente. L'image numérique de synthèse a facilité la tâche des architectes qui peuvent maintenant imaginer des univers nouveaux sans même toucher au béton et à l'acier. Il est intéressant de noter qu'un architecte qui fut longtemps concepteur principal et chargé de projet chez Coop Himmelb(l)au pendant plus de dix ans, responsable à la fois du Akron Art Museum et du BMW Welt, a pris son indépendance et proposé des projets de concours qui portent encore plus loin l'audace formelle de la fin du XXᵉ siècle. Tom Wiscombe a créé sa propre agence, EMERGENT en 1999 et a récemment travaillé sur deux projets publiés dans ce volume, la Bibliothèque nationale de la République tchèque (Prague, 2006–07, page 150) et le musée d'Art contemporain de Shenzen (Shenzen, Chine, 2007, page 144). L'imagerie séduisante de ces projets non réalisés associe l'angularité puissante de Coop Himmelb(l)au à une technologie informatique d'où naquirent les premiers *blobs*, mais avec une vision profondément contemporaine qui pourrait devenir très influente dans les années à venir.

Si Wiscombe possède une expérience considérable de la translation des idées de l'informatique à la forme construite, d'autres semblent avoir accepté l'idée qu'une partie de la conception architecturale actuelle ne se matérialisera jamais dans le monde réel. La presse du monde entier s'est concentrée récemment sur le site Internet «Second Life» (www.secondlife.com) décrit comme un «metaverse», ce qui signifie espace virtuel en 3D dans lequel s'immerger totalement et où les intervenants (en tant qu'avatars) se rencontrent et interagissent sur le plan aussi bien social qu'économique. Un architecte, présenté dans *Architecture Now! 6*, Scope Cleaver, est pratiquement virtuel lui-même puisqu'il refuse de fournir toute information «du monde réel» sur lui. Il préfère dire être «entré dans »Second Life« en janvier 2006», comme s'il n'avait jamais existé avant cette date. Il a conçu un grand nombre de constructions virtuelles pour «Second Life» qui sont déjà visitables. Sa galerie d'art réalisée pour l'université de Princeton (2007, page 460) fait partie d'un effort marqué de cette prestigieuse institution pour se projeter dans ce monde nouveau. Elle possède sept *sims* (zones de 65 536 m²) sur «Second Life» administrées par les services académiques du Bureau des technologies de l'information. Scope Cleaver est ainsi devenu l'un des principaux concepteurs de structures qui pourraient bien avoir à jouer un rôle «dans le monde réel» si on leur ouvre les horizons de l'éducation. Bien qu'il ne se sente à l'évidence pas lié par les règles habituelles de l'architecture, il crée ses projets sans s'appuyer sur des ressources de CAD externes, préférant les éléments trouvables sur le site. Il précise: «Les constructions sur »Second Life« permettent des formes fantastiques qui repoussent les limites des constructions virtuelles, tout en conservant des composants structurels réalistes.» Si la mode joue certainement un rôle dans le succès d'un site de ce genre, ses 20 millions d'utilisateurs enregistrés (beaucoup sont inactifs) donnent une indication sur le potentiel d'environnements virtuels similaires qui pourraient bien trouver leur place dans de futurs développements de l'architecture.

35

une qualité qui ne correspond peut-être pas à l'image attendue du co-auteur (avec Richard Rogers) du Centre Pompidou (1977). Comme la forme basique des tours de Manhattan est imposée par la trame urbaine et le coût pharamineux des terrains, le subtil Piano a créé un immeuble américain de sensibilité européenne.

Si l'on peut dire de l'architecte génois qu'il a sans doute mis de côté sa radicalité peu après l'achèvement du Centre Pompidou, Jean Nouvel reste toujours un élément irritant au sein du petit groupe des grands praticiens internationaux. Ses réalisations ne lassent pas de surprendre et même de fâcher. La future Tour de Verre (New York, 2007–12, **10/11**) de 75 niveaux, adjacente au Museum of Modern Art, conçue par l'architecte français pour le promoteur Hines, modifiera le profil du Midtown de Manhattan. Le *New York Times*, qui est depuis longtemps l'un des arbitres du goût dans la grande cité, a parlé de ce projet en termes extasiés : « Une nouvelle tour de 75 niveaux, conçue par l'architecte Jean Nouvel pour un terrain voisin du Museum of Modern Art dans Midtown, promet d'être le plus enthousiasmant enrichissement du panorama urbain de Manhattan depuis une génération. Son extérieur facetté, effilé en une série de pics cristallins, suggère l'ambition atavique de conquête des altitudes célestes. » On pense à l'admiration de John Ruskin pour l'irrationalité de l'architecture gothique : « Elle n'osait pas seulement, mais se plaisait à infirmer tout principe servile. » Il est clair que la tour de Nouvel est plus audacieuse que les récentes extensions du Museum of Modern Art de l'architecte japonais Yoshio Taniguchi, ce qui a conduit le *New York Times* à dresser une comparaison assez critique entre les deux projets. La Tour de Verre offrant également de nouveaux espaces au musée, le journal commentait : « Ces galeries supplémentaires sont une chance pour le MoMA de repenser une grande partie de son organisation, de réordonnancer la séquence de la collection permanente, par exemple, ou d'étudier comment redistribuer les galeries contemporaines dans la nouvelle tour et gagner de la place pour les expositions sur l'architecture dans l'ancien bâtiment. Mais pour se lancer dans une entreprise aussi ambitieuse, il devrait d'abord reconnaître que le complexe conçu par Taniguchi lui a posé de nouveaux problèmes. En bref, il devrait faire preuve d'une intrépidité dont il n'a guère témoigné depuis des décennies. Le MoMA serait bien inspiré de regarder du côté de Ruskin qui écrivait que le grand art, qu'il s'exprime en »mots, couleurs ou pierres, ne se répète pas sans cesse«. »[5]

Que ce soit à cause de sa réglementation de zonage ou d'un pur conservatisme, New York ne s'est pas montrée la ville la plus créative dans le domaine de l'architecture contemporaine. Manhattan peut être considéré dans l'ensemble comme un quartier essentiellement moderne, mais beaucoup de ses immeubles semblent dater davantage des années 1930 que de notre siècle. D'autres villes, comme Dubaï dans les Émirats arabes unis, se développent à un rythme frénétique et espèrent devenir de grands centres urbains, dans le secteur des affaires bien sûr, mais aussi dans celui de l'architecture. Jusqu'à récemment, on y faisait appel à de grandes agences occidentales sans beaucoup d'imagination, situation qui évolue rapidement, comme le montre l'arrivée de noms aussi fameux que Zaha Hadid qui y signe d'importants projets. Sur le Golfe persique, en bordure du grand désert d'Arabie, l'émirat doit s'adapter à une série de circonstances complexes qui en font un site très différent de New York, par exemple. En grande partie habité par des populations expatriées, vivant sous des températures qui peuvent s'élever à 50°, ce n'est certainement pas un endroit où profiter du spectacle de la rue. On s'y déplace en voiture et l'on semble étonné de voir des piétons s'exposer au soleil de l'après-midi, qui ne soient pas des travailleurs du Bangladesh. Les villes comme Los Angeles ont depuis longtemps développé une culture de l'automobile, mais à Dubaï il s'agit autant d'un problème de climat que de distance. Le promoteur

36

saoudien Adel al Mojil, a cherché à travers un concours en trois étapes, dont la liste de participants comprenait des architectes comme Ryue Nishizawa et Kazuyo Sejima, à poser la question de quel type d'utilisateur pourrait être attiré par l'énorme complexe qu'il projette d'édifier à la limite du nouveau quartier de Business Bay. Baptisant son projet « The Edge » (Dubaï, EAU, 2008–, page 418). Positionnant Dubaï comme un grand centre financier mondial, et non plus seulement comme un mirage gavé d'or noir, The Edge sera un quartier de 350 000 m^2 et coûtera 600 millions d'euros. Il comprendra des bureaux, des hôtels, des appartements, des commerces, tout ce dont un « travailleur de la connaissance » peut avoir besoin pour vivre, manger et dormir les quelques mois de son séjour dans les Émirats arabes. Ce n'est certainement pas le schéma auquel pensait Piano lorsqu'il a conçu le New York Times Building, pur immeuble de bureaux. La Tour de Verre de Nouvel regroupera un hôtel et des appartements ainsi que des bureaux et des galeries pour le MoMA, mais ses résidents ne seront certainement pas encouragés à y passer intégralement leur vie. C'est la très créative agence espagnole RCR qui a été sélectionnée pour construire The Edge après les appels d'offre de 2007. Cette série de tours qui font penser à un mirage s'élevant au-dessus d'un podium en « tapis volant » est esthétiquement intéressante et assez neuve dans sa conception. Bien que le projet puisse encore évoluer avant le début du chantier, la proposition de RCR restera un premier pas pour un modèle de très grand immeuble spécifiquement conçu pour des sites comme celui de Dubaï. Le climat, plus que la culture locale, semble réellement être le moteur du développement de ces complexes autarciques, mais « The Edge » sera suffisamment vaste pour être comparé à une ville en soi, sans être restreint par les contraintes urbaines habituelles. Dans un de ses récents ouvrages, intitulé *The Gulf*, Rem Koolhaas (OMA) écrit : « En fin de compte, le Golfe réinventera la notion de public et de privé : le potentiel d'une infrastructure à promouvoir un tout plutôt qu'à favoriser une fragmentation ; l'usage et l'abus du paysage (golf ou environnement) ; la coexistence de nombreuses cultures dans une authenticité nouvelle plutôt qu'une solution occidentale moderniste par défaut, des expériences au lieu de l'Expérience – ville ou complexe ? »

CHAMBRES D'HÔTES DE DESIGNER

De même que les institutions culturelles ont beaucoup fait travailler des architectes inventifs au cours de ces dernières années, l'hôtellerie, de plus en plus intéressée par le design et peut-être inspirée par l'avalanche de projets Schrager/Starck des années 1990, a fait appel à de nombreux architectes célèbres dans le but d'attirer une clientèle chic et aisée. Ce phénomène, né dans des villes mondiales comme New York ou Berlin, concerne maintenant des destinations moins connues dont Zuoz en Suisse. Cette superbe petite cité médiévale se trouve en Engadine à quelques kilomètres du luxueux St. Moritz. L'Hotel Castell est situé juste au-dessus de la vieille ville, à une altitude de 1900 mètres. Le collectionneur d'art et artiste suisse Ruedi Bechtler a acheté cet élégant hôtel de cure édifié en 1912–13 par Nicolaus Hartmann, au milieu des années 1990. L'architecte Gabrielle Hächler et la célèbre artiste suisse Pipilotti Rist ont conçu le premier projet de transformation de l'établissement, le « Bar Rouge », inauguré en 1998. Au début de l'an 2000, les architectes Amstellodamois UNStudio ont été hélés à bord et ont conçu un nouveau bâtiment de 14 appartements de luxe (2003–04, page 502). Dans l'ancienne structure, ils ont créé un hammam dans le sous-sol de l'aile orientale et rénové à peu près la moitié des 60 chambres existantes dans leur style personnel. Un architecte de la région, Hans-Jörg Ruch, a rénové les autres chambres et l'artiste japonais Tadashi Kawamata ajouté une terrasse en bois et une passerelle

36
*Shigeru Ban, Post-Tsunami Rehabili-
tation Houses, Kirinda, Hambantota,
Sri Lanka, 2005–07*

qui conduit à un sauna aménagé à l'extérieur. Récemment achevé avec la construction d'un *Skyspace* cylindrique de l'artiste américain James Turrell, le Castell est typique des nombreux « designer hotels » apparus dans le monde, mais le haut niveau des interventions architecturales et artistiques dont il a bénéficié en fait un cas particulièrement remarquable.

Deux cols de montagne et 300 kilomètres plus loin, mais toujours en Suisse, l'Hôtel de la Poste à Sierre (2006–07, **12**) des jeunes architectes Savioz Meyer Fabrizzi n'affiche pas les interventions artistiques de niveau international du Castell, mais montre à quel point l'idée de *designer* – ou plutôt ici – d'*architect hotel* a pu se développer. Travaillant sur un bâtiment du milieu du XVIIIe siècle, ils ont osé peindre la façade en orange vif et inscrire le nom de l'hôtel en énormes lettres sur un côté. Situé sur un petit parc qui va de derrière l'hôtel de ville voisin jusqu'à la gare, l'Hôtel de la Poste possède maintenant une vaste salle à manger de forme sinusoïdale sur l'arrière. Les architectes ont rénové les chambres en utilisant un bois différent pour chacune des 15 suites qui en ont pris le nom. Les photos des arbres utilisés sont reproduites au plafond de chaque chambre et donnent un aspect « vert » à ce bâtiment assez traditionnel.

En 2007, Legorreta + Legorreta, architectes de Mexico, ont transformé une ancienne usine d'embouteillage d'eau à Puebla, au Mexique, pour en faire La Purificadora Boutique Hotel (page 308). Tout comme leurs moins célèbres confrères de Sierre, ils ont rénové ce bâtiment du XIXe siècle en conservant un grand nombre de ses caractéristiques pittoresques. Les murs en pierre de la construction originelle sur un seul niveau ont été conservés, mais supportent maintenant trois étages de maçonnerie, un bar-lounge sur le toit et une piscine de 30 mètres de long à parois de verre. On a utilisé des poutres de bois de l'ancienne usine, des carreaux de céramique spécialement dessinés pour rappeler les matériaux locaux et de l'onyx de la région. Bien que Ricardo Legorreta soit connu pour ses couleurs saturées qui rappellent Luis Barragán, c'est ici la palette des matériaux, aussi bien nouveaux qu'anciens, qui remplit cet espace sans couleurs fortes, en dehors du pourpre éclatant du mobilier.

DOING IT RIGHT

Une grande partie de l'architecture contemporaine de qualité ne peut échapper aux compromis, puisque l'argent – parfois en énorme quantité – reste nécessaire pour réaliser un projet remarquable ou innovant. L'architecture dans laquelle vivent la plupart des habitants de cette planète est assez ordinaire, ou pour le moins répétitive dans sa déclinaison du concept de boîte. Les plus démunis, ou les victimes de désastres naturels ne bénéficient pas, bien entendu, des conceptions brillantes des grands architectes d'aujourd'hui. Cette règle connaît cependant quelques exceptions et certains praticiens se sont fait un point d'honneur de créer des logements accessibles ou faciles à construire. Shigeru Ban est de ceux-ci. Bien qu'il ait un bon portefeuille de riches clients, il a également créé des habitats temporaires en Inde, Turquie et Rwanda (pour le UNHCR). Sa plus récente initiative de cette nature, les maisons de réhabilitation post-tsunami (Kirinda, Hambantota, Sri Lanka, 2005–07, page 98), était un projet de 50 maisons destinées aux victimes de la catastrophe du 26 décembre 2004. Pour un coût d'environ 13 000 dollars par unité, ces logements de 71 m² sont en bois de caoutchoutier local et parpaings de terre compressée. Confortables, bien étudiées pour répondre au mode de vie local, ces maisons sont une exception à l'élitisme des grands architectes et méritent de figurer dans ce volume.

Shigeru Ban participe également à l'initiative Make it Right qui se déroule à la Nouvelle-Orléans (Louisiane, 2007, page 530). Ici, l'acteur Brad Pitt et les architectes de Graft ont lancé une action pour construire des maisons bien conçues à de prix accessibles dans le Lower Ninth Ward, un quartier de la ville dévasté par l'ouragan Katrina. Grâce à des participants comme Kieran Timberlake, Morphosis, David Adjaye et MVRDV, cette opération plus médiatisée que le projet pour Kirinda de Ban, présente peut-être aussi un message politique. Dans « le plus riche pays du monde », il est choquant que certains des Américains les plus pauvres restent sans toit, pendant de longues périodes, du fait de l'incapacité de l'administration jusqu'aux plus hauts niveaux de l'État. Sur le plan le plus strict de l'architecture contemporaine, il est intéressant de voir ce que des architectes « stars » peuvent faire avec les 150 000 dollars alloués par résidence. Les maisons de Kirinda de Ban ne prétendent pas utiliser le vocabulaire sophistiqué de leur créateur, mais sont un effort cohérent pour soutenir des personnes dans le besoin, à l'aide de méthodes et des matériaux du développement durable. Les conditions imposées aux participants de Make it Right montrent que les organisateurs ont pris en compte une série de facteurs rarement réunis dans le monde assez éloigné des contraintes habituelles de l'architecture d'avant-garde :

– Intérêt pour, ou implication en faveur de la ville de la Nouvelle-Orléans, de préférence après Katrina et/ou expériences dans des opérations de secours après une catastrophe.
– Familiarité avec le développement durable.
– Expérience des logements résidentiels et multifamiliaux.
– Preuve d'une compétence en innovations à budget réduit.
– Expérience de constructions conçues avec succès dans des environnements de terrains gorgés d'eau ou sous le niveau des eaux.
– Attachement à la qualité de conception.

L'acteur Brad Pitt et Angelina Jolie ont prouvé leur engagement en faveur de causes humanitaires à travers la Jolie-Pitt Foundation qui a récemment accordé des dons substantiels pour aider les réfugiés soudanais affectés par la crise du Darfour, des organisations comme Global Action for Children ou Médecins sans frontières. Que leur aide soit si désespérément attendue aux États-Unis même et que tant de grands architectes aient accepté d'offrir leurs services à l'initiative de Make it Right en dit beaucoup sur l'état de l'Amérique et peut-être aussi – en plus positif – sur celui de l'architecture contemporaine.

TOURS MÉDIÉVALES ET THÉ DANS LES ARBRES

Le titre d'*Architecture Now !* implique par nature un intérêt pour les développements les plus récents et beaucoup des projets figurant dans cet ouvrage sont esthétiquement et techniquement à l'avant-garde de l'art de construire. Il faut noter en passant que bon nombre des projets publiés ici traitent du rapport entre des constructions existantes et de nouvelles extensions ou usages. La chapelle Brennand de Paulo Mendes da Rocha au Brésil et le Ullens Center de Jean-Michel Wilmotte à Pékin sont des exemples de ce type de symbiose, ou de confrontation si l'on préfère, entre le passé et le présent. La rénovation de structures existantes continuera à jouer un rôle significatif dans l'évolution de l'architecture contemporaine, ne serait-ce que pour des raisons économiques de base. Il est souvent moins coûteux de rénover un bâti-

37
LIN Finn Geipel + Giulia Andi, Alvéole 14, Submarine Base Rehabilitation, Quartier Ville Port, Saint-Nazaire, France, 2005–07

37

ment que d'en construire un nouveau. La notion de plus en plus large de l'intérêt historique de bâtiments anciens joue également un rôle dans ce développement des chantiers de rénovation. Ni l'usine néo-Bauhaus rénovée par Wilmotte à Pékin, ni la vieille usine d'embouteillage d'eau transformée en hôtel chic à Puebla par Legorreta + Legorreta n'auraient sans doute été jugées dignes d'être rénovées 20 ans plus tôt, et pourtant leurs volumes et leurs matériaux confèrent au projet achevé une richesse que n'auraient pu apporter des éléments strictement contemporains.

La présence du passé pénètre même l'architecture la plus contemporaine. Ce passé peut être historique et lié à la spécificité d'un site, comme c'est le cas pour le centre de documentation et d'information de Bergen-Belsen par KSP Engel et Zimmermann (Celle, Allemagne, 2005–07, page 156) ou la rénovation par LIN d'une partie de la base sous-marine de Saint-Nazaire (France, 2005–07, page 320), ou encore n'être que l'évocation de souvenirs encore plus lointains, comme le centre d'acceuil des visiteurs Arche Nebra de Holzer Kobler (Wangen, Allemagne, 2005–07, page 250), inspiré par un disque datant de l'âge de bronze trouvé à proximité. Il est sûr que, dans certains pays, l'exploration du passé et de ses implications culturelles et architecturales peut devenir d'actualité de façon inattendue. La Suisse, petit pays à la très longue histoire, a donné naissance à des architectes comme Peter Zumthor, inspiré par les Alpes, leur culture et même leur pierre. Moins connu, mais tout aussi enraciné dans l'histoire de son pays, Hans-Jörg Ruch, qui travaille essentiellement dans la vallée d'Engadine près de St. Moritz, a été en partie formé aux États-Unis. Sa restauration de la Chesa Madalena à Zuoz (Suisse, 2001–02, page 438) a permis de redécouvrir une tour médiévale emmurée dans les vieux bâtiments de la ferme. Ce travail est remarquable par sa combinaison de respect du passé et d'ouverture au présent. La Chesa Madalena est aujourd'hui une galerie d'art contemporain qui présente des œuvres de Richard Long ou de Balthasar Burkhard, sans que l'on sente aucune contradiction avec les lieux. La conscience du passé et le respect de ses leçons se sont sûrement beaucoup accrus au cours de ces dernières années, en particulier dans les cultures « anciennes » comme celles de l'Europe ou de parties de l'Asie. Des architectes comme Ruch sont à la fois la confirmation de cette tendance et les pionniers d'une nouvelle sensibilité qui sait faire vivre ensemble le passé et le présent.

Un autre architecte suisse, Valerio Olgiati, a emprunté une approche nettement plus radicale pour construire un atelier d'artiste au cœur du vieux village de Scharans (Atelier Bardill, 2006–07, page 382). À la place d'une ancienne grange en bois, il a érigé une construction en béton coulé en place teinté en rouge qui reprend le profil d'une structure de ferme, mais s'ouvre vers le ciel par le biais d'une cour ovale. Si les murs aveugles en béton peuvent choquer dans ce contexte, la nouvelle structure a su capter l'austérité de l'architecture d'origine de ce village de montagne. Olgiati a utilisé le rouge parce que le village voulait que le nouveau bâtiment soit de la même couleur que l'ancien. Ainsi, en respectant une demande conservationniste, il a réalisé un projet réellement actuel et une cour intérieure qui rappelle les *Skyspaces* de James Turrell.

Terunobu Fujimori est professeur à l'université de Tokyo, spécialisé dans l'histoire des constructions de style occidental érigées au Japon à partir de l'ère Meiji (1868–1912). Il est particulièrement versé dans l'apparition de l'architecture moderne au Japon à travers les interventions de créateurs comme Le Corbusier, Mies van der Rohe et Walter Gropius, mais a aussi commencé à construire lui-même des projets très inattendus, qui paraissent profondément enracinés dans le passé. Il écrit : « De mon premier projet, j'ai essayé d'adopter les deux

38

38
Terunobu Fujimori, Chashitsu Tetsu
(Teahouse Tetsu), Kiyoharu Shirakaba
Museum, Nakamaru, Hokuto City,
Yamanashi, Japan, 2005

règles suivantes en tant que chartre de conception : 1) Le bâtiment ne doit pas ressembler à un autre quel qu'il soit, passé ou présent, ni évoquer aucun des styles apparus depuis l'âge de bronze. 2) Des matériaux naturels doivent être utilisés sur les parties visibles du bâtiment et, parfois des plantes doivent être intégrées, pour harmoniser le projet avec la nature. »[6]

Même si ce souhait de créer des constructions qui ne ressemblent à aucune autre peut sembler prétentieux, Fujimori reste aussi modeste que sa maison de thé Tetsu construite sur le domaine d'un musée (Musée Kiyoharu Shirakaba, Nakamaru, Hokuto, Yamanashi, 2005, page 174). Il le compare à une « maison pour un nain de conte de fée », mais fait également référence à certaines des grandes icônes culturelles du Japon comme Sen no Rikyu (1522–91), personnage historique qui a exercé une très profonde influence sur la cérémonie du thé au Japon. Construite pour admirer le fleurissement des cerisiers, cette maison de thé trouve également sa justification dans les coutumes et traditions japonaises les plus ressenties, de la cérémonie du thé à la frénésie annuelle du *sakura* (les cerisiers en fleurs) qui s'empare du pays. À l'instar de son « nain de conte de fée », ce petit projet est un acte d'humour, mais également le produit d'anciennes traditions. Il est « déplacé » au sens intellectuel, un peu comme l'atelier d'Olgiati à Scharans. Rien n'est comme il paraît, ce qui rend le surprenant travail de Fujimori fondamentalement contemporain. Il parle des conditions de l'architecture autant que de son enracinement dans un passé plus ou moins lointain. Dans un autre de ses projets, la maison de thé Too-High (Miyagawa Takabe, Chino, Nagano, 2003) Fujimori commente : « Non loin se trouve la maison où Toyo Ito est né. Même si nous avons tous deux grandi dans le même quartier et à la même période, ce que nous créons est opposé. La relation entre les êtres humains et leur environnement n'est ni simple ni directe. »[7]

LES TOURNESOLS ET LES ÉTOILES

Ce n'est pas par hasard que ce bref panorama se termine par Kirinda, Make It Right et la plus petite construction de ce livre, la maison de thé Tetsu. L'attention de la presse se concentre souvent sur les réalisations architecturales les plus visibles et les plus coûteuses, comme ce qui se passe aujourd'hui à Pékin. Ces projets, comme le stade olympique principal et le Watercube voisin sont illustrés ici, de même que le spectaculaire BMW Welt de Coop Himmelb(l)au, mais il semble qu'une conscience nouvelle d'autres raisons de l'existence de l'architecture apparaissent et sont exprimées avec humour par des créateurs inattendus comme Terunobu Fujimori. Il s'intéresse à ce qu'il appelle une « architecture d'humanité » qui n'est pas tant reliée à la tradition japonaise qu'à la nature elle-même. Il peut sembler logique que les « stars » de l'architecture contemporaine se comparent à celles d'Hollywood, dont celles de l'initiative Make It Right à la Nouvelle-Orléans, mais concevoir des maisons pour ceux qui n'en ont pas est un exercice très différent de la création de terrains de jeux pour milliardaires. L'architecture contemporaine, malgré sa nature plutôt durable (du moins si on le compare à la durée de vie d'un numéro de *Vanity Fair*) ignore souvent les fondamentaux de l'existence et recherche les effets surprenants, les paillettes. Le fait qu'un artiste de l'importance d'Anselm Kiefer ressente que ses idées peuvent trouver un terrain d'expression idéal dans les formes architecturales laisse un commentaire intéressant sur l'état des choses – sa vision est celle de ruines, de tournesols post-apocalyptiques poussant à travers le béton brisé et les étoiles filantes. L'art contemporain a longtemps paru se chercher, en quête d'une âme perdue lors du passage de la figure à la projection de peinture, ou plus récemment à l'installation vidéo. Il se pourrait que l'architecture contemporaine dans toute sa variété soit plus en position d'exprimer l'espoir, les peurs, les excès, les triomphes, les cristallisations du moment. La « modernité liquide », dans sa splendide et commerciale superficialité évoquée par Zygmunt Bauman, est certainement présente dans ce livre, mais on y trouve aussi le lourd béton de Bergen-Belsen ou la structure légère du monument de la gare d'Atocha commémorant les attentats du 11 mars 2004. Si des conteneurs de bateau réunis pour deux jours de fête à Rio ou 150 kilomètres de planches brûlant dans le désert du Nevada font partie de l'équation, pourquoi pas ? Que penser d'un architecte qui n'existe que dans « Second Life », mais y conçoit des immeubles virtuels pour une université bien réelle ? À l'autre extrême, restaurer un bâtiment du XIVe siècle à Zuoz (Suisse) fait aussi partie intégrante du processus et de l'évolution de l'architecture contemporaine. Si l'on peut affirmer quelque chose, c'est bien que la compréhension de l'architecture ne veut dire ni exclure le passé ni même les expressions les plus éphémères du présent. L'architecture contemporaine présentée dans cet ouvrage traverse l'histoire et ses espoirs, des lieux de culte aux lieux de sport et de commerce, de la plus grande construction du monde à l'une des plus petites. L'architecture est bien vivante !

Philip Jodidio, Grimentz, 2008

1   Zygmunt Bauman, « Value Dilemmas as a Challenge in the Practice and Concepts of Supervision and Coaching, » ANSE Conference, 7 mai 2004, Leyden, Pays-Bas. Né en 1925, le Dr. Bauman, professeur émérite de sociologie à l'université de Leeds, est l'un des sociologue et philosophe les plus célèbres au monde pour des publications comme *Liquid Modernity* (2000). Il a reçu le prix européen Amalfi de sociologie et de sciences sociales en 1989 et 1990 ainsi que le Theodor W. Adorno Award de la ville de Francfort en 1998.
2   Edwin Heathcote, « Modernism Minus Utopia », *The Financial Times*, 29 décembre 2007.
3   Alan Riding, « An Artist Sets Up House(s) at the Grand Palais », *The New York Times*, 31 mai 2007.
4   Mark Wigley, in *Deconstructivist Architecture*, The Museum of Modern Art, New York, 1988.
5   Nicolai Ouroussoff, « Next to MoMA, Reaching for the Stars », *The New York Times*, 15 novembre 2007.
6   Terunobu Fujimori, *Fujimori Terunobu Architecture*, Toto Shuppan, Tokyo, 2007.
7   Ibid.

3DELUXE TRANSDISCIPLINARY DESIGN

3deluxe transdisciplinary design
Schwalbacher Str. 74 / 65183 Wiesbaden / Germany
Tel: +49 611 95 22 05-0 / Fax: +49 611 95 22 05-22
E-mail: info@3deluxe.de / Web: www.3deluxe.de

3DELUXE is a team of 40 people from the fields of architecture, interior design, art, graphic design, media, and product design. The firm was created in 1992 in Wiesbaden by communication designers Andreas and Stephan Lauhoff and designers Nikolaus Schweiger and Dieter Brell. Since 1999, system modern GmbH, headed by Peter Seipp, has been responsible for the development, production, and management of 3deluxe's common projects. Andreas Lauhoff was born in Ingelheim am Rhein in 1966. He studied communication design at the Wiesbaden University of Applied Sciences (1985–92). He participated in the creation of 3deluxe in 1992, before obtaining a Master's degree from Saint Martins College of Art and Design (London, 1996–98). Andreas Lauhoff's twin brother Stephan studied communication design in Wiesbaden (1986–92), before co-founding 3deluxe in 1992. Andreas and Stephan Lauhoff are the heads of 3deluxe graphics and 3deluxe motion. Dieter Brell was born in Frankfurt in 1960. He has been the head of 3deluxe in/exterior since the mid-1990s. Peter Seipp, born in 1957 in Marburg, studied industrial engineering at the Technische Universität in Darmstadt (1976–83). He created the firm system modern GmbH in 1999 and is presently its head. Aside from the Leonardo Glass Cube (Bad Driburg, 2004–07, published here), 3deluxe has completed the Cocoon Club with its two restaurants in Frankfurt (2004); the design and scenography for the closing ceremony of the 2006 FIFA World Cup in Berlin. Current work includes a theater, lounge, and bar at the Palazzo Hotel and Casino Resort in Las Vegas (Nevada, 2008); and the Hydropolis underwater hotel resort (Dubai, UAE, 2008).

Der Name **3DELUXE** steht für ein interdisziplinäres Team von 40 Personen aus den Bereichen Architektur, Innenarchitektur, Kunst, Medien-, Grafik- und Produktdesign. Das Unternehmen entstand 1992 in Wiesbaden als Gemeinschaftsprojekt der Kommunikationsdesigner Andreas und Stephan Lauhoff sowie der Designer Nikolaus Schweiger und Dieter Brell. Seit 1999 ist die von Peter Seipp geführte system modern GmbH verantwortlich für Entwicklung und Produktion sowie Management der Gemeinschaftsprojekte von 3deluxe. Andreas Lauhoff, geboren 1966 in Ingelheim am Rhein, studierte Kommunikationsdesign an der Fachhochschule Wiesbaden (1985–92). Nach der Gründung von 3deluxe im Jahr 1992 erwarb er seinen Masterabschluss am Saint Martins College of Art and Design (London, 1996–98). Andreas Lauhoffs Zwillingsbruder Stephan studierte vor der Entstehung von 3deluxe ebenfalls Kommunikationsdesign in Wiesbaden (1986–92). Gemeinsam leiten die Lauhoffs den Projektbereich 3deluxe graphics, daneben sind sie mitverantwortlich für 3deluxe motion. Dieter Brell wurde 1960 in Frankfurt am Main geboren. Seit Mitte der 1990er-Jahre leitet er die Projektabteilung 3deluxe in/exterior. Peter Seipp, 1957 in Marburg geboren, studierte von 1976 bis 1983 Wirtschaftsingenieurwesen an der Technischen Universität Darmstadt und gründete 1999 die system modern GmbH, die er heute führt. Neben dem hier vorgestellten Leonardo Glass Cube (Bad Driburg, 2004–07) übernahm 3deluxe Projekte wie die Gestaltung des Frankfurter Cocoon-Clubs mit zwei Restaurants (2004), Eventdesign für die Fußball-Weltmeisterschaft in Berlin 2006 – u. a. Bauten und Szenografie der Abschlussfeier. Derzeit arbeitet 3deluxe u. a. an einem Theater, einer Lounge und einer Bar für das Hotel-Casino Palazzo in Las Vegas (Nevada, 2008) sowie für das Unterwasserhotel Hydropolis in Dubai (VAE, 2008).

3DELUXE est une équipe de 40 personnes intervenant dans les domaines de l'architecture, de l'architecture intérieure, de l'art, du graphisme, des médias et du design produit. L'agence a été créée en 1992 à Wiesbaden par les graphistes en communication Andreas et Stephan Lauhoff et les designers Nikolaus Schweiger et Dieter Brell. Depuis 1999, la société system modern GmbH, dirigée par Peter Seipp, est chargée du développement, de la production et de la gestion des projets communs de 3deluxe. Andreas Lauhoff, né à Ingelheim am Rhein en 1966, a étudié le graphisme en communication à l'université des Sciences appliquées de Wiesbaden (1985–92). Il a créé l'agence 3deluxe avant d'obtenir son Master au Saint Martins College of Art and Design (Londres, 1996–98). Stephan Lauhoff, le frère jumeau d'Andreas, a étudié le graphisme en communication à Wiesbaden (1986–92) avant de participer à la création de l'agence. Les deux frères dirigent ensemble 3deluxe graphics ainsi que 3deluxe motion. Dieter Brell, né à Francfort en 1960, est responsable de 3deluxe in/exterior design depuis le milieu des années 1990. Peter Seipp, né à Marburg en 1957, a étudié l'ingénierie industrielle à la Technische Universität de Darmstadt (1976–83) et a créé system modern GmbH en 1999 dont il est actuellement le directeur. En dehors du Leonardo Glass Cube (Bad Driburg, 2004–07, publié ici), 3deluxe est intervenu sur le Cocoon Club avec ses deux restaurants à Francfort (2004) et la conception et la scénographie de la cérémonie de clôture de la Coupe du monde de football de la FIFA à Berlin en 2006. L'agence travaille actuellement sur un projet de théâtre, salon et bar pour le Palazzo Hotel and Casino Resort à Las Vegas (Nevada, 2008) et sur celui de l'Hydropolis Underwater Hotel Resort (Dubaï, EAU, 2008).

LEONARDO GLASS CUBE

Bad Driburg, Germany, 2004–07

Floor area: 1200 m². Client: Leonardo/Glaskoch B. Koch Jr. GmbH.
Cost: €8 million

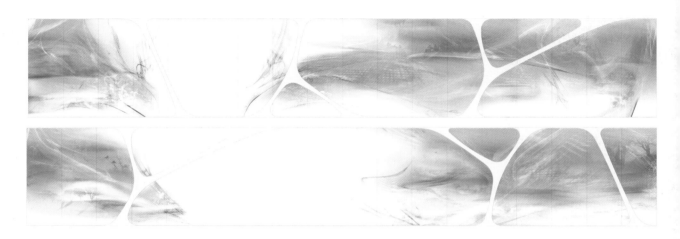

This exhibition pavilion with conference rooms is the first permanent building completed by 3deluxe. A consistent effort has been made to combine the firm's areas of competence—architecture, interior and graphic design, and landscape architecture—to create a "complex aesthetic entity." An open floor plan allows for maximum flexibility, and the building manifests a "willful" connection to its natural surroundings. As the designers say, "This aspect allows for a reinterpretation of one of 3deluxe's essential leitmotifs: the staged overlaying of real and virtual elements with the intention of changing both the space and the observer's patterns of perception." Images of the design and surrounding countryside were used to create a large-scale digital image (6 x 96 m) that was printed on PVB (Polyvinyl butyral) foil in 48 segments and then laminated onto the glass panels of the façades. The external cubelike shell inscribed in a square floor plan is contrasted with a freeform volume inside the building, with a curving white wall containing an exhibition space. Organically shaped white structures called "Genetics" connect the separate zones of the building, penetrating the freeform interior volume. The main exhibition area is located below grade, but is visible from the entrance. 3D computer models and CNC milling were used for the design of the walls, and six-meter-high frameless panes of laminated safety glass emphasize transparency. Given that the structure was designed for the Westphalia glass company Glaskoch, which distributes products under the name Leonardo, this solution was particularly apt. The exterior paths, made from 187 cast, white concrete elements, and landscaping are clearly related to the innovative structure itself.

Der Leonardo Glass Cube, ein Ausstellungspavillon mit angeschlossenen Konferenzräumen, ist das erste nichttemporäre Gebäude, das 3deluxe realisiert hat. Die Unternehmensfelder Architektur, Innengestaltung, Grafikdesign und Landschaftsgestaltung wurden in einem schlüssigen Gesamtkonzept gebündelt, um eine „komplexe ästhetische Einheit" zu schaffen. Die offene Grundrissgestaltung bietet ein Maximum an Nutzungsmöglichkeiten, zugleich zeichnet sich das Gebäude durch die gezielte Einbindung in seine natürliche Umgebung aus. „Hierin", so die Designer, „kommt eines der wesentlichen Leitmotive von 3deluxe zur Anwendung: eine inszenierte Überlagerung realer und virtueller Elemente, die ebenso den Raum wie die Wahrnehmungsmuster des Betrachters verändern soll." Unter Verwendung von Aufnahmen sowohl der Architektur selbst als auch der umgebenden Landschaft wurde ein großformatiges Digitalbild (6 x 96 m) angefertigt, das auf eine 48-teilige PVB-Folie (Polyvinylbutyral) gedruckt und anschließend auf die Glasscheiben der Fassade auflaminiert wurde. In die äußere kubische Hülle auf einem quadratischen Grundriss wurde als Kontrast eine Freiform eingestellt, deren geschwungene weiße Wandflächen einen Ausstellungsraum umschließen. Diese Freiform durchziehen organisch geformte Gebilde, von den Designern als „Genetics" bezeichnet, die die verschiedenen Gebäudezonen miteinander verbinden. Der Hauptausstellungsbereich liegt unter der Erde, ist aber vom Eingang aus einzusehen. Der Entwurf wurde mithilfe von 3-D-Modellen und CNC-Fräsen erstellt; 6 m hohe, rahmenlose Scheiben aus laminiertem Sicherheitsglas sorgen für seine besondere Transparenz. Dieses Erscheinungsbild ist umso sinnfälliger, da das Gebäude im Auftrag der westfälischen Firma Glaskoch entstanden ist, die unter dem Namen Leonardo Glasprodukte vertreibt. Die Gestaltung des Außenbereichs mit seinen Wegen aus 187 weißen Gussbetonelementen steht in direkter Wechselbeziehung mit dem innovativen Gebäude.

Ce pavillon d'exposition doté de salles de conférences est le premier bâtiment à caractère permanent réalisé par l'agence. Un effort particulier a été mené pour associer les secteurs de compétence du groupe « architecture, décoration, graphisme et aménagement paysager », afin de créer une « entité esthétique complexe ». Le plan au sol ouvert apporte le maximum de souplesse et le bâtiment est en liaison avec son environnement naturel. Comme le précisent ses créateurs : « Cet aspect permet une réinterprétation de thèmes essentiels pour 3deluxe : une mise en scène stratifiée d'éléments réels et virtuels pour modifier l'espace et les modes de perception du spectateur. » Des photos du projet et de son cadre champêtre ont servi à créer une image numérique de grandes dimensions (6 x 96 m) qui a été imprimée sur un film de PVB (polyvinyle de butyral) en 48 parties et laminées sur les panneaux de verre des façades. La coquille extérieure en forme de cube, qui s'inscrit dans un plan au sol carré, contraste avec le volume intérieur de forme libre. Un mur incurvé délimite un espace d'exposition. Des éléments organiques appelés « Genetics » relient les diverses zones du bâtiment. Le principal espace d'exposition se trouve en sous-sol, mais reste visible de l'entrée. Des modèles 3D et des techniques de commande numérique par ordinateur (CNC) ont été utilisés pour la conception des murs et des panneaux de six mètres de haut non encadrés, en verre de sécurité laminé mettent en valeur le concept de transparence. Cette solution est proche du client, la société verrière Glaskoch qui distribue ses produits sous le nom de Leonardo. Les cheminements extérieurs composés de 187 éléments de béton blanc ainsi que les aménagements paysagers ont été traités dans l'esprit du bâtiment.

The organic appearance is consistently applied to the building's exterior façades and to the interior.

Außen wie innen zeichnet sich das Gebäude durch ein durchweg organisches Erscheinungsbild aus.

L'aspect organique du bâtiment se retrouve constamment sur les façades et à l'intérieur.

The plan shows the continuity of the landscape design vis-à-vis the interior elements, where continuous curves are the rule.

Der Grundriss lässt erkennen, wie sich die Landschaftsgestaltung in den von Rundungen bestimmten Innenräumen fortsetzt.

Le plan montre la continuité de l'esprit de la conception des aménagements paysagers et des éléments intérieurs, où règne la ligne courbe.

3LHD ARCHITECTS

3LHD Architects
N. Božidarevića 13/4
HR 10000 Zagreb
Croatia

Tel: +385 1 232 02 00
Fax: +385 1 232 01 00
E-mail: info@3lhd.com
Web: www.3lhd.com

3LHD is a multidisciplinary architectural practice based in Zagreb, Croatia, focused on integrating architecture, urban planning, design, and art. The firm's partners are Saša Begović, born in 1967 in Bjelovar; Marko Dabrović, born in 1969 in Dubrovnik; Tatjana Grozdanić, born in 1968 in Zagreb; and Silvije Novak, born in 1971 in Rijeka. The four partners are all graduates of the Architectural Faculty of the University of Zagreb, Croatia. Some of their most important designs are projects such as the Memorial Bridge (Rijeka, 1997–2001); the Croatian Pavilion at Expo '05 (Aichi, Japan, 2004–05); the Sports Hall Bale (Bale-Valle, Croatia, 2005–06, published here); Riva Waterfront (Split, 2005–07); the Hotel Lone (Rovinj, 2006–), all in Croatia, unless stated otherwise; and recently a project for the Eastern European Cultural Center in Xi'an (China, 2006). They were selected to design the Croatian Pavilion for Expo '08 in Zaragoza, Spain, and they are also working on spatial planning and development for the shoreline of Bale, Croatia.

3LHD ist eine interdisziplinär ausgerichtete Architektengemeinschaft mit Sitz im kroatischen Zagreb, die sich auf integrative Gesamtkonzepte aus Architektur, Stadtplanung, Design und Kunst spezialisiert hat. Das Büro besteht aus den Partnern Saša Begović, geboren 1967 in Bjelovar, Marko Dabrović, geboren 1969 in Dubrovnik, Tatjana Grozdanić, geboren 1968 in Zagreb, und Silvije Novak, geboren 1971 in Rijeka. Alle vier sind Absolventen der Fakultät für Architektur an der Universität Zagreb. Zu ihren wichtigsten Projekten gehören die Entwürfe für die Most Hrvatskih Branitelja, die Erinnerungsbrücke, in Rijeka (Kroatien, 1997–2001), der kroatische Pavillon für die Expo '05 in Aichi (Japan, 2004–05), die Sporthalle in Bale (Bale/Valle, Kroatien, 2005–06, hier vorgestellt), die Hafenpromenade von Split (Kroatien, 2005–07), das seit 2006 im Bau befindliche Hotel Lone im kroatischen Rovinj sowie ein Projekt für das Osteuropäische Kulturzentrum in Xi'an (China, 2006). Ferner wurde 3LHD für die Gestaltung des kroatischen Pavillons zur Expo '08 im spanischen Saragossa ausgewählt, daneben ist das Büro verantwortlich für die Raumplanung und Entwicklung des Uferbereichs in dem istrischen Städtchen Bale.

3LHD est une agence d'architecture multidisciplinaire basée à Zagreb, Croatie, qui intègre des services d'architecture, d'urbanisme, de design et création artistique. Les associés sont Saša Begović, né en 1967 à Bjelovar, Marko Dabrović, né en 1969 à Dubrovnik, Tatjana Grozdanić, née en 1968 à Zagreb et Silvije Novak, née en 1971 à Rijeka. Tous quatre sont diplômés de la faculté d'architecture de l'université de Zagreb. Parmi leurs projets les plus importants : le pont du Souvenir (Rijeka, Croatie, 1997–2001) ; le Pavillon croate à l'Expo '05 (Aichi, Japon, 2004–05) ; une salle de sports à Bale (Bale-Valle, Croatie, 2005–06, publiée ici) ; le front de mer de Riva (Split, Croatie, 2005–07) ; l'Hôtel Lone (Rovinj, Croatie, 2006–), et récemment un projet pour le Centre culturel de l'Europe de l'Est à Xian (Chine, 2006). Ils ont été sélectionnés pour concevoir le Pavillon croate à l'Expo '08 à Saragosse en Espagne, et travaillent actuellement sur un plan d'urbanisme et de développement pour la côte de Bale en Croatie.

SPORTS HALL BALE
Bale-Valle, Croatia, 2005–06

Site area: 3660 m². Floor area: 1108 m². Client: Bale Municipality.
Cost: € 900 000. Project Team: Saša Begović, Marko Dabrović, Tatjana Grozdanić,
Silvije Novak, Ljerka Vučić, Marin Mikelić

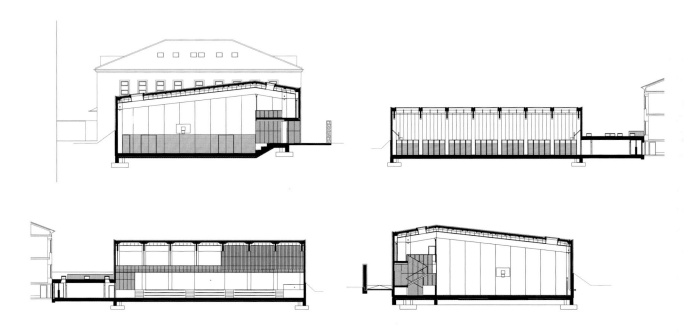

Bale, or Valle d'Istria in Italian, is a small town on the peninsula of Istria on the Adriatic Sea with a population of about 1000 people. The new sports hall designed by 3LHD is adjacent to an old school. Due to the small size of the village, where the new building is the second-largest structure after the church, it will also be used as a public facility for social gatherings. A basketball court and additional facilities including a fitness center and a sauna defined the size of the building. Locker rooms were planned as an extension to the school. A traditional local drystone wall was used as a template for the cladding, and a traditional stone hut, known as a *kazun*, inspired the basic structural pattern. A rapid schedule, allowing only 11 months from design to construction, made it necessary to use prefabricated elements for the load-bearing structure and façade. The architects conclude that the integration of the Sports Hall into the environment "has been achieved by minimizing its size, blending with the landscape and using local stone materials for façade surfacing, which gives this modern building the appearance of a traditional house."

Bale (italienisch Valle d'Istria) ist eine kleine, auf der Halbinsel Istrien an der Adriaküste gelegene Gemeinde mit rund 1000 Einwohnern. Die von 3LHD entworfene Sporthalle ist ein Erweiterungsbau zu einem älteren Schulgebäude. Aufgrund der Überschaubarkeit des Städtchens – das neue Gebäude ist das zweitgrößte Bauwerk nach der Kirche –, wird die Sporthalle auch als öffentlicher Raum für gesellschaftliche Anlässe genutzt. Ein Basketballplatz und weitere Einrichtungen wie ein Fitnesscenter und eine Sauna gaben die Größe des Baus vor. Die Umkleideräume stellen die Verbindung zwischen Halle und Schulgebäude her. Als Vorbild für die Außenverkleidung der Halle diente ein in der Gegend traditionell zum Bauen verwendeter Bruchstein, dessen Gefüge sich an typische alte Steinhütten, so genannte Kažuni, anlehnt. Da das gesamte Projekt innerhalb von nur elf Monaten realisiert werden sollte, griffen die Architekten für Tragwerk und Fassade auf Fertigbauteile zurück. Wie die Architekten erklären, ließ sich die Sporthalle gelungen in die Umgebung einbinden, „indem wir ihre Größe im Rahmen hielten und sie mit der Landschaft in Einklang brachten. Durch die Verwendung eines für die Gegend typischen Steins zur Verkleidung der Fassade erhielt das moderne Gebäude das Erscheinungbild eines traditionellen Hauses."

Bale, ou Valle d'Istria en italien, est une petite ville de 1000 habitants de la péninsule d'Istrie au bord de l'Adriatique. La nouvelle salle de sports conçue par 3LHD jouxte une école ancienne. Le nouveau bâtiment sera le second plus grand du village après l'église, et servira aussi de salle de réunions. Il comprend un terrain de basket, une salle de gymnastique et un sauna. Les vestiaires sont une extension de l'école. Les murs ont été parés de pierre sèche selon une tradition locale tandis que la hutte de pierre traditionnelle de la région, ou *kazun*, a inspiré la structure. Les délais très courts imposés au chantier – 11 mois – ont conduit à utiliser des formules préfabriquées pour les éléments porteurs structurels et de façade. Pour les architectes, l'intégration de cette salle de sport dans son environnement « a été obtenue en minimisant sa taille, en se fondant dans le paysage et en se servant de pierre locale en façade, ce qui donne à cette construction moderne l'aspect d'une maison traditionnelle ».

The stone-clad volume of the new building forms an almost continuous block when seen from certain angles—while lifting up to reveal glazed openings elsewhere.

Aus bestimmten Perspektiven wirkt der mit Naturstein verkleidete Baukörper wie ein weitgehend massiver Block, und doch kommen unter der hochgezogenen Verkleidung verglaste Öffnungen zum Vorschein.

Vu sous certains angles, le volume du nouveau bâtiment habillé de pierre forme un bloc presque continu, qui se soulève par instant pour laisser la place à des ouvertures vitrées.

The partially glazed ground level gives the impression that the more massive stone volume is cantilevered over an almost open space.

Durch die Teilverglasung im unteren Bereich wirkt es, als krage der robuste, steinverkleidete Bauteil über einem fast ganz offenen Zwischenraum aus.

Le rez-de-chaussée, en partie vitré, donne l'impression que ce massif volume de pierre est suspendu en porte-à-faux au-dessus d'un espace quasiment ouvert.

The architects provided the image below of a Croatian stone hut that served as inspiration for the Sports Hall.

Die Architekten liefern das Bild einer jener kroatischen Steinhütten, die als Inspiration für die Sporthalle gedient haben.

Les architectes ont fourni l'image, ci-dessous, d'une hutte de pierre typique de l'architecture vernaculaire croate, qui a inspiré la salle de sports.

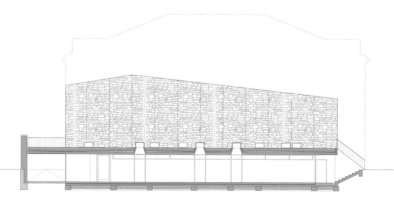

Interior spaces are functional and relatively straightforward as a floor plan and further photos demonstrate.

Die Aufnahmen und der Grundriss zeigen die funktionale und relativ schlichte Gestaltung der Innenräume.

Le plan au sol et les photographies montrent la fonctionnalité et la simplicité des espaces intérieurs.

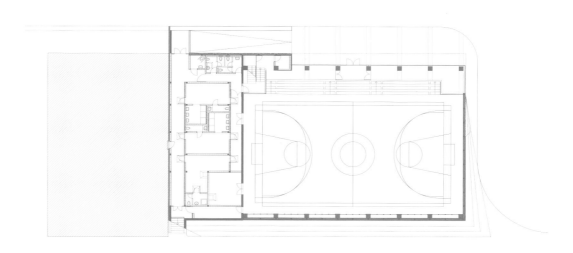

ADJAYE/ASSOCIATES

Adjaye/Associates, 23–28 Penn Street
London N1 5DL / UK

Tel: +44 20 77 39 49 69 / Fax: +44 20 77 39 34 84
E-mail: info@adjaye.com / Web: www.adjaye.com

David Adjaye was born in 1966 in Dar es Salaam, Tanzania. He studied at the Royal College of Art in London (M.Arch, 1993), and worked in the offices of David Chipperfield and Eduardo Souto de Moura, before creating his own firm, **ADJAYE/ASSOCIATES**, in London in 2000. He has been widely recognized as one of the leading architects of his generation in the United Kingdom, in part because of the talks he has given in various locations such as the Architectural Association, the Royal College of Art, and Cambridge University, as well as Harvard, Cornell, and the Universidad de Luisdad in Lisbon. He was also the co-presenter of the BBC's six-part series on modern architecture "Dreamspaces." His Idea Store library in East London was selected by Deyan Sudjic for the exhibition highlighting "100 Projects that are Changing the World" at the 8th Venice Biennale of Architecture in 2002. His office employs a staff of 35, and some of his key works are: a house extension (St. John's Wood, 1998); the studio/home for Chris Ofili (1999); the SHADA Pavilion (2000, with artist Henna Nadeem); the Siefert Penthouse (2001); the Elektra House (2001); and a studio/gallery/home for Tim Noble and Sue Webster (2002), all in London. Recent work includes the T-B A21 Pavilion with artist Olafur Eliasson (Venice, 2005); the Nobel Peace Center (Oslo, Norway, 2002–05); the Bernie Grant Performing Arts Center (London, 2001–06); the Stephen Lawrence Center (London, 2004–06); a visual arts building for Iniva and Autograph ABP at Rivington Place (London, 2003–07); and the Museum of Contemporary Art/Denver (Denver, Colorado, 2004–07, published here).

David Adjaye, geboren 1966 im tansanischen Daressalam, studierte am Londoner Royal College of Art, wo er 1993 seinen Master of Architecture erwarb. Er arbeitete u. a. in den Büros von David Chipperfield und Eduardo Souto de Moura, ehe er im Jahr 2000 in London seine eigene Firma **ADJAYE/ASSOCIATES** gründete, die heute 35 Mitarbeiter beschäftigt. Adjaye gilt als einer der führenden britischen Architekten seiner Generation. Sein internationaler Ruf verdankt sich auch seinen Vorträgen an Institutionen wie der Architectural Association und dem Royal College of Art in London sowie an den Universitäten Cambridge, Harvard, Cornell und der Universidad de Luisdad in Lissabon. Daneben übernahm Adjaye die Rolle des Komoderators für die sechsteilige BBC-Serie „Dreamspaces" über moderne Architektur. Seine „Idea Store" genannte Bibliothek in Ost-London wurde von Deyan Sudjic im Rahmen der 8. Architekturbiennale in Venedig 2002 bei der Ausstellung „100 Projekte, die die Welt verändern" vorgestellt. Zu Adjayes zentralen Arbeiten gehören ein Hausanbau in St. John's Wood (1998), eine Atelierwohnung für Chris Ofili (1999), der gemeinsam mit der Künstlerin Henna Nadeem realisierte SHADA Pavillon (2000), das Siefert Penthouse (2001), das Elektra House (2001) und eine Kombination aus Atelier, Galerie und Wohnraum für Tim Noble und Sue Webster (2002), alle in London. Projekte jüngeren Datums sind der T-B A21 Pavillon (in Zusammenarbeit mit Olafur Eliasson, Venedig, 2005), das Nobel-Friedenszentrum in Oslo (Norwegen, 2002–05), das Bernie Grant Performing Arts Centre (London, 2001–06), das Stephen Lawrence Centre (London, 2004–06), ein Haus für visuelle Kunst für Iniva (Institute of International Visual Arts) und Autograph ABP am Rivington Place (London, 2003–07) sowie das hier vorgestellte Museum of Contemporary Art in Denver (Colorado, 2004–07).

David Adjaye, né en 1966 à Dar es Salaam, Tanzanie, a étudié au Royal College of Art à Londres (M. Arch, 1993), et travaillé chez David Chipperfield et Eduardo Souto de Moura, avant de créer l'agence **ADJAYE/ASSOCIATES** à Londres en 2000. Il est reconnu comme l'un des plus brillants architectes de sa génération au Royaume-Uni, en partie du fait des conférences qu'il a données à l'Architectural Association, au Royal College of Art et à la Cambridge University, mais aussi à Harvard, à Cornell et à l'Universidad de Luisdad à Lisbonne. Il a aussi été coprésentateur d'une série télévisée de la BBC sur l'architecture moderne *Dreamspaces*. Sa bibliothèque Idea Store dans l'Est londonien a été sélectionnée par Deyan Sudjic pour l'exposition « 100 Projets qui changent le monde » à la 8e Biennale d'architecture de Venise en 2002. Son agence emploie 35 collaborateurs. Parmi ses réalisations les plus notables : l'extension d'une maison (St. John's Wood, 1998) ; le studio-maison de Chris Ofili (1999) ; le pavillon SHADA (2000, avec l'artiste Henna Nadeem) ; la Siefert Penthouse (2001) ; la maison Elektra (2001) et un studio-galerie-résidence pour Tim Noble et Sue Webster (2002), le tout à Londres. Plus récemment, il a réalisé le pavillon T-B A21 avec l'artiste Olafur Eliasson (Venise, 2005) ; le Centre Nobel pour la Paix (Oslo, Norvège, 2002–05) ; le Bernie Grant Performing Arts Center (Londres, 2001–06) ; le centre Stephen Lawrence (Londres, 2004–06) ; un bâtiment pour les arts plastiques pour Iniva et Autograph ABP à Rivington Place (Londres, 2003–07) et le musée d'Art contemporain à Denver (Denver, Colorado, 2004–07, publié ici).

MUSEUM OF CONTEMPORARY ART/DENVER

Denver, Colorado, USA, 2004–07

Total floor area: 2320 m². Client: Museum of Contemporary Art/Denver.
Cost: not disclosed. Project Director: Joe Franchina.
Architect of Record: Davis Partnership

This is the first public commission of Adjaye/Associates in the United States. Located on a prominent site, the new museum is at the corner of 15th and Delgany Street. The structure is due to be the first LEED (Leadership in Energy and Environmental Design) Gold-certified museum, thanks to its low-energy consumption, greenhouse gas emissions, and use of environmentally appropriate raw materials. The new building includes 1858 square meters of exhibition, education and lecture spaces, a bookshop, and a roof garden for outdoor art. The announced intention of the building is that it should "support rather than define the museum's mission." The architect has chosen to employ "a limited number of monochromes and textures" because of the "kunsthalle" or temporary-exhibition function to which most of the building is put. With respect to its immediate architectural environment, the structure has four stories in its main volume. As the architects explain, "In order to establish a visual relationship with the traffic moving in and out of the downtown area, the northeast façade is set at a slight angle to 15th Street. The southeastern corner of the building has been pulled forward so that it's visible from the metro station on Delgany Street." Thanks to its sincere modesty and its environmental credentials, the Museum of Contemporary Art/Denver participates in the emergence of a new generation of cultural facilities in the United States, perhaps less flamboyant but more responsible than its predecessors.

Das neue Museum für zeitgenössische Kunst in Denver war der erste Auftrag, den Adjaye/Associates in den USA von öffentlicher Seite erhielten. Aufgrund seines geringen Energieverbrauchs, des geringen Treibhausgasausstoßes und der Verwendung umweltgerechter Materialien war es der erste Museumsbau, der für eine LEED-Auszeichnung (Leadership in Energy and Environmental Design) in der Kategorie Gold vorgesehen war. Prominent platziert an der Delgany Street, Ecke 15th Street, besitzt das Gebäude eine Gesamtnutzfläche von 1858 m² mit Ausstellungs-, Seminar- und Vortragsräumen sowie einem Buchladen und einem Dachgarten für Außeninstallationen. Der Entwurf orientiert sich an dem ausdrücklichen Ziel, „dem Museumsauftrag entgegenzukommen, statt ihn einzugrenzen." Da der größte Teil des Gebäudes als Kunsthalle für temporäre Ausstellungen fungieren soll, entschied sich der Architekt, „eine begrenzte Farb- und Materialauswahl" zu verwenden. Mit Rücksicht auf die Architektur der umliegenden Gebäude ist der Hauptkörper des Museums auf vier Geschosse beschränkt. Ferner erläutern Adjaye/Associates: „Um eine visuelle Beziehung zu dem vorbeifließenden Zentrumsverkehr herzustellen, wurde die Nordostfassade in einem leichten Winkel zur 15th Street hin verschoben. Die nach Südosten weisende Ecke des Gebäudes wurde nach vorne gezogen, so dass sie von der Metrostation auf der Delgany Street aus zu sehen ist." Angesichts seiner zurückhaltenden Erscheinung und der vorbildlichen Umweltverträglichkeit ist das Museum of Contemporary Art/Denver in eine Reihe zu stellen mit einer neuen Generation von amerikanischen Kultureinrichtungen, die vielleicht weniger extravagant als ihre Vorgänger, dafür aber verantwortungsbewusster auftreten.

Il s'agit de la première commande américaine reçue par Adjaye/Associates. Ce nouveau musée se trouve sur un site très en vue, à l'angle de 15th Street et Delgany Street. Il est le premier musée certifié Or LEED (Leadership in Energy and Environnemental Design), pour sa faible consommation énergétique, son bas niveau d'émissions de gaz à effet de serre et son utilisation de matériaux bruts écologiques. Il comprend 1858 m² de salles pour expositions, conférences et activités éducatives, une librairie et un jardin sur le toit pour exposer des sculptures. L'intention affichée était que ce bâtiment « soutienne plutôt que définisse la mission du musée ». L'architecte a choisi d'utiliser « un nombre limité de couleurs et de textures » pour s'adapter à la fonction d'accueil d'expositions temporaires du Kunsthalle. Le musée, respectant son environnement architectural immédiat, ne compte que quatre niveaux dans sa partie principale. « Afin de créer une relation visuelle avec la circulation qui le longe, la façade nord-est est légèrement inclinée par rapport à la 15th Street. L'angle sud-est a été poussé en avant pour être visible de la station de métro de Delgany Street », a expliqué l'architecte. Grâce à sa modestie, sa sincérité et sa valeur environnementale, ce musée participe à l'émergence d'une nouvelle génération d'équipements culturels aux États-Unis, peut-être moins flamboyants, mais plus responsables que leurs prédécesseurs.

The LEED Gold certification granted to the museum proves that its environmental design is in harmony with its modest, yet fully modern, appearance.

Die LEED-Auszeichnung in Gold für das Museum beweist, dass eine umweltbewusste Gestaltung zu einem zurückhaltenden und doch durchweg modernen Erscheinungsbild passt.

L'aspect modeste mais authentiquement moderne du musée s'accorde à sa conception environnementale, garantie par sa certification LEED Or.

The building's vertical panels are shifted from one row to the next, giving a rather dynamic appearance to the exterior façades.

Durch die von Reihe zu Reihe verschobenen, vertikalen Felder erhalten die Außenfassaden des Gebäudes ein sehr dynamisches Aussehen.

Le décalage des rangées de panneaux de verre verticaux assure une présence assez dynamique aux façades.

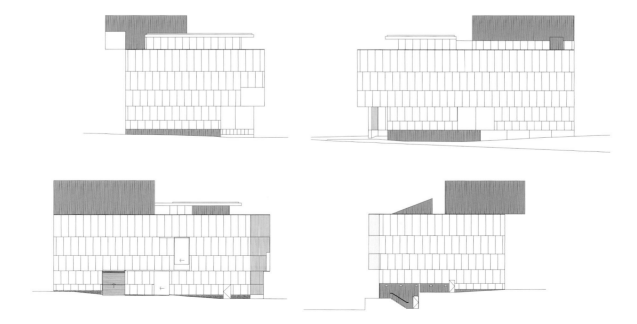

Interior spaces confirm the impression of modesty generated by the exterior of the building. Though not specifically minimalist, the spaces convey an impression of simplicity that does not deny their architectural interest.

In den Innenräumen bestätigt sich der Eindruck der Bescheidenheit, den bereits die Außenseite des Gebäudes vermittelt. In den Räumen zeigt sich eine Einfachheit von besonderem architektonischem Reiz, ohne dabei direkt minimalistisch zu sein.

Les espaces intérieurs confirment la modestie exprimé par l'extérieur du bâtiment. Bien qu'ils ne soient pas spécifiquement minimalistes, ils donnent une impression de simplicité qui n'enlève rien à leur intérêt architectural.

AI WEI WEI/FAKE DESIGN

Ai Wei Wei/FAKE Design
Caochangdi 258
Chaoyang District
Beijing 100015
China

Tel/Fax: +86 10 8456 4194
E-mail: nobody@vip.sina.com / Web: blog.sina.com.cn/aiweiwei

The artist-architect **AI WEI WEI** was born in 1957 in Beijing, the son of the well-known Chinese poet Ai Qing. In 1978, after a 20-year period during which his family was banished from the capital for political reasons, Ai Wei Wei returned to Beijing to study at the Film Institute. He went to New York in 1981 and studied at the Parson's School of Design. He returned to China in 1994 and opened his studio in Beijing in 1999. This 500-square-meter home-studio, with a 1300-square-meter courtyard made of brick, was his first widely published work. It was built with the help of local workers. In 2000, he organized Shanghai's first independent art biennale under the evocative title "Fuck Off." His firm, FAKE Design, currently employs four architects, four designers, two photographers, and five assistants and interns, and works on landscape and interior design as well as on architecture and art projects. Their design philosophy is: "Make it simple." They participated with Herzog & de Meuron in the 2003 competition for the Beijing Stadium intended for the 2008 Olympic Games. Ai Wei Wei is the coordinator and a participant in the Jinhua Architecture Park, inaugurated in 2007. Other recent work includes the Gowhere Restaurant, a renovation and construction project (2004); 9 Boxes-Taihe Complex (2004); the Photofactory (Caochangdi, 2007); 241 Art Corridor (2007); and Red No. 1, all in Beijing, as well as the installation *Template* realized for Documenta 12 (Kassel, Germany, 2007, published here). Current work includes the Lijing Studio (Yunnan); the Undercover Villa in Ordos (Inner Mongolia); and the curating of the Ordos100 project, all in China.

Der Künstler und Architekt **AI WEI WEI** wurde 1957 in Peking als Sohn des bekannten Dichters Ai Qing geboren. Im Jahr 1978, nachdem seine Familie 20 Jahre lang aus politischen Gründen aus der chinesischen Hauptstadt verbannt gewesen war, kehrte Ai Wei Wei nach Peking zurück, um ein Studium am dortigen Filminstitut aufzunehmen. 1981 ging Ai Wei Wei nach New York, wo er an der Parson's School of Design studierte, um 1994 nach China zurückzukehren und 1999 in Peking ein Atelier zu eröffnen. Diese mithilfe lokaler Arbeitskräfte gebaute Kombination aus Wohnhaus und Atelier, mit 500 m^2 Innenfläche und einem 1300 m^2 großen Hof aus Ziegeln, war Ai Wei Weis erste vielbeachtete Arbeit. Im Jahr 2000 organisierte er die erste unabhängige Kunstbiennale Shanghais unter dem provozierenden Titel „Fuck Off". Seine Firma FAKE Design beschäftigt derzeit vier Architekten, vier Designer, zwei Fotografen sowie fünf Assistenten und Praktikanten. Die Philosophie des Unternehmens, das sich mit Architektur, Innenarchitektur, Landschaftsgestaltung und Kunstprojekten beschäftigt, lautet: Mach es einfach. 2003 beteiligte FAKE Design sich gemeinsam mit Herzog & de Meuron an dem Wettbewerb für den Entwurf des Nationalstadions für die Olympischen Spiele 2008 in Peking. Zusätzlich zu einem eigenen Beitrag übernahm Ai Wei Wei die Koordinierung des 2007 eröffneten Jinhua-Architekturparks. Weitere Projekte jüngeren Datums sind das Gowhere-Restaurant in Peking, entstanden durch die Renovierung und Erweiterung eines älteren Gebäudes (2004), die Wohnanlage 9 Boxes-Taihe (Peking, 2004), die Photofactory im Pekinger Stadtteil Cao Chang Di (2007), der 241 Art Corridor (Peking, 2007) und das Red No. 1 (Peking). Für die documenta 12 realisierte Ai Wei Wei die nachfolgend vorgestellte Installation „Template" (Kassel, 2007). Gegenwärtig werden in China das Studio Lijing (Yunnan), die Undercover Villa in Ordos (Innere Mongolei) und das Projekt Ordos100 realisiert.

L'artiste architecte **AI WEI WEI**, né en 1957 à Pékin, est le fils du célèbre poète Ai Qing. En 1978, après 20 années de bannissement de sa famille pour des raisons politiques, il revint à Pékin pour étudier à l'Institut du cinéma. Il part pour New York en 1981 et étudie à la Parson's School of Design. Il rentre en Chine en 1994 et ouvre son studio à Pékin en 1999. Cet atelier-habitation de 500 m^2 construit avec l'aide d'artisans locaux dans une cour de brique de 1300 m^2 est sa première réalisation publiée. En 2000, il organise la première biennale d'art indépendante de Shanghai sous le titre évocateur de « Fuck Off ». Son agence, FAKE Design, emploie actuellement quatre architectes, quatre designers, deux photographes et cinq assistants et stagiaires. Elle intervient dans les domaines de l'architecture, l'architecture intérieure, le paysagisme et l'art. Sa philosophie de conception se résume à « Faire simple ». Elle a participé avec Herzog & de Meuron au concours de 2003 pour le stade olympique de Pékin. Ai Wei Wei est le coordinateur et l'un des participants au projet du Jinhua Architecture Park, inauguré en 2007. Parmi ses autres travaux récents : le restaurant Gowhere, projet de rénovation et construction (2004) ; le complexe 9 Boxes-Taihe (2004) ; la Photofactory (Caochangdi, 2007) ; le 241 Art Corridor (2007) et Red No. 1, tous à Pékin, ainsi que l'installation *Template* réalisée pour la Documenta 12 (Kassel, Allemagne, 2007, publiée ici). Il travaille actuellement en Chine sur les projets du studio Lijing (Yunnan), de la villa Undercover à Ordos (Mongolie-Intérieure) et le commissariat du projet Ordos100.

TEMPLATE

Documenta 12, Kassel, Germany, 2007

Dimensions: 720 x 1200 x 850 cm (before collapsing);
422 x 1106 x 875 cm (after collapsing)

Made of wooden doors and windows from demolished Ming and Qing Dynasty houses (1368–1911), *Template* might more easily be described as a work of art than a piece of architecture, and yet it employed elements derived from houses in a distinctly architectural form. Built in front of the "Crystal Palace," a temporary acrylic greenhouse designed by the French architects Lacaton & Vassal, the "architecture of *Template*," according to Ai Wei Wei, "is comprised of late Ming and Qing Dynasty wooden windows and doors which, joined together in five layers per side, form an open vertical structure having an eight-pointed base. In spite of its large size, from afar the installation conveys the illusion of being something foldable, like a gigantic three-dimensional paper cutout. Where the external framework is massive and regular, the internal part of each wall made out of windows and doors is shaped according to the volume of a hypothetical traditional Chinese temple, giving the impression that the whole wooden construction was assembled around a building that has later been removed." The artist goes on further to explain the connection of this work to architecture: "The windows and doors I employed used to belong to [...] houses located in the Shanxi area of northern China, where entire old towns have been pulled down. We bought the fragments from different quarters, and these are probably the last pieces of that civilization. I like to use these leftovers as part of... not a sentiment, but evidence of our past activity. I like to carry these pieces into a completely contemporary context and I think it works well. It really is a mixed, troubled, questioning context, and a protest for its own identity. To me, the temple itself, you know I'm not religious, means a station where you can think about the past and the future; it's a void space. The selected area, not the material temple itself, tells you that the real physical temple is not there, but constructed through the leftovers of the past." At the end of June 2007, the structure, which had been intended to stand until the closure of the Documenta on September 23, collapsed during a storm. Ai Wei Wei said, "It's better than before; now the power of nature is in evidence, and art only becomes beautiful through this kind of emotion."[1]

[1] Quotes from www.artnet.de/magazine/usa/features/colonnello08–10–07.asp, accessed on January 30, 2008.

Ai Wei Weis Documentabeitrag „Template", zusammengesetzt aus Holztüren und -fenstern, die aus Abrisshäusern aus der Ming- und Qing-Dynastie (1368–1911) stammen, erweckt zunächst eher den Eindruck eines Kunstwerks als den einer architektonischen Arbeit; trotzdem bilden die früheren Wohnhauselemente eine eindeutig architektonische Form. Ai Wei Wei selbst erklärt zu seiner Installation, die vor dem temporären „Kristallpalast" – dem in Gewächshausbauweise errichteten Aue-Pavillon der französischen Architekten Lacaton & Vassal – aufgestellt wurde: „Die hölzernen Türen und Fenster aus der späten Ming- und der Qing-Dynastie, die die Architektur von ‚Template' ausmachen, sind auf jeder Seite in fünf Schichten übereinandermontiert und bilden eine offene vertikale Struktur mit einer achteckigen Basis. Trotz ihrer beachtlichen Größe erweckt die Installation aus der Ferne betrachtet den Eindruck, dass man sie so zusammenfalten könnte, als sei sie ein riesiger dreidimensionaler Papierschnitt. Während die Außenseite des Gebildes massiv und regelmäßig ist, ist der innere Teil der ganz aus Türen und Fenstern bestehenden Wände in der vermeintlichen Form eines traditionellen chinesischen Tempels ausgespart, so dass der Eindruck entsteht, die gesamte hölzerne Konstruktion sei um ein anderes Gebäude herum angelegt worden, das später entfernt wurde." Die Verbindung seiner abstrakt zur Architektur erläutert der Künstler wie folgt: „Die Fenster und Türen, die ich verwendet habe, gehörten früher zu [...] Häusern in der Provinz Shanxi in Nordchina, wo man alte Städte komplett abgerissen hat. Die Fragmente, die wir gekauft haben, stammen aus verschiedenen Vierteln und sind vermutlich die letzten Relikte dieser Zivilisation. Diese Überreste möchte ich benutzen als Teil ... nicht einer besonderen Sentimentalität, sondern als Zeugnis dessen, was wir früher getan haben. Ich möchte sie in einen ganz zeitgenössischen Kontext stellen und ich finde, das funktioniert recht gut. Natürlich ist es ein unübersichtlicher, schwieriger Kontext, der auch Fragen aufwirft – und ein Protest für eine eigene Identität. Für mich, der ich ja selbst nicht religiös bin, ist der Tempel ein Ort, an dem man über die Vergangenheit und die Zukunft nachdenken kann; es ist ein leerer Raum. Der ausgewählte Bereich – kein materieller Tempel als solcher – zeigt an, dass hier der konkrete Tempel nicht real vorhanden ist, sondern durch die Überreste der Vergangenheit konstruiert wird." Ende Juni 2007 fiel das Gebilde, das der Planung nach bis zum Abschluss der documenta am 23. September hätte stehenbleiben sollen, durch einen Sturm in sich zusammen, wozu Ai Wei Wei erklärte: „Es ist jetzt besser als vorher – die Macht der Natur tritt in Erscheinung und nur durch diese Form der Emotion kommt die Kunst zu ihrer Schönheit."[1]

[1] Zitate aus: www.artnet.de/magazine/usa/features/colonnello08–10–07.asp, 30. Januar 2008.

Réalisée à partir de portes et de fenêtres de maisons démolies des dynasties Ming et Qing (1368–1911), *Template* est peut-être plus une œuvre d'art qu'une réalisation architecturale, mais elle emploie des éléments de maisons dans une forme à l'évidence architecturée. Édifiée devant le « Crystal Palace », serre temporaire en acrylique conçue par les Français Lacaton & Vassal, « l'architecture de *Template*, selon Ai Wei Wei, se compose de fenêtres et de portes en bois des anciennes dynasties Ming et Qing, réunies en cinq strates par côté pour former une structure verticale sur une base octogonale. Malgré ses importantes dimensions, l'installation vue de loin donne l'impression d'être repliable, tel un gigantesque découpage en papier. Alors que le cadre externe est plein et régulier, chaque paroi interne est composée de portes et de fenêtres rappelant le volume d'un hypothétique temple chinois ancien, donnant l'impression que cette construction en bois a été assemblée autour d'un bâtiment supprimé à un certain moment. » L'artiste éclaire également le lien de cette œuvre avec l'architecture : « Les fenêtres et les portes employées appartenaient à [...] des maisons de la région du Shanxi dans le Nord de la Chine où des villes anciennes ont été démolies. Nous avons acheté ces fragments en différents endroits et ce sont probablement les dernières traces de cette civilisation. J'ai aimé les remonter dans un contexte contemporain entièrement différent et je pense que la proposition fonctionne bien. C'est un contexte de questionnements mêlés et troublés et la protestation d'une identité. Pour moi qui ne suis pas croyant, le temple est un lieu où chacun peut penser au passé et au futur. C'est un espace vide. La zone choisie, pas le temple matériel lui-même, vous enseigne que le vrai temple n'est pas là, mais construit avec les vestiges du passé. » À la fin du mois de juin 2007, la structure qui devait durer jusqu'à la clôture de la Documenta, le 23 septembre, s'est effondrée lors d'une tempête. Pour Ai Wei Wei : « C'est mieux qu'avant, maintenant la puissance de la nature est mise en évidence et l'art ne devient vraiment magnifique qu'à travers ce type d'émotion. »[1]

[1] Citations extraites de www.artnet.de/magazine/usa/features/colonnello08–10–07.asp, 30 janvier 2008.

Photographed before (top right) and after its collapse in a storm at the end of June 2007, Ai Wei Wei's Template assumes two different forms, both of which remain valid for the artist.

Ai Wei Weis Kunstwerk vor (rechts oben) und nach seiner Zerstörung durch einen Sturm im Juni 2007 – beide Zustandsformen erklärte der Künstler für gültig.

Photographiée avant (à droite, en haut) et après son effondrement lors d'une tempête fin juin 2007, l'œuvre d'Ai Wei Wei s'est présentée sous deux formes très différentes.

TADAO ANDO

Tadao Ando Architect & Associates
Osaka / Japan

Born in Osaka in 1941, **TADAO ANDO** was self-educated as an architect, largely through his travels in the United States, Europe, and Africa (1962–69). He founded Tadao Ando Architect & Associates in Osaka in 1969. He has received the Alvar Aalto Medal, Finnish Association of Architects (1985); the Medaille d'or, French Academy of Architecture (1989); the 1992 Carlsberg Prize; and the 1995 Pritzker Prize. He has taught at Yale (1987), Columbia (1988), and Harvard (1990). Notable buildings include: Rokko Housing (Kobe, 1983–93); Church on the Water (Hokkaido, 1988); Japan Pavilion Expo '92 (Seville, Spain, 1992); Forest of Tombs Museum (Kumamoto, 1992); and the Suntory Museum (Osaka, 1994), all in Japan unless stated otherwise. Recent work includes the Awaji Yumebutai (Awajishima, Hyogo, Japan, 1997–2000); the Pulitzer Foundation for the Arts (St. Louis, Missouri, 1997–2000); and the Modern Art Museum of Fort Worth (Texas, 1999–2002). He completed the Chichu Art Museum on the Island of Naoshima in the Inland Sea, in 2003, part of the continuing project that led him to create the Benesse House museum and hotel there beginning in the early 1990s. He is currently working on the Punta della Dogana for François Pinault (Venice, Italy, 2007–). Other recent work, aside from 21_21 Design Sight (Tokyo, 2004–07, published here), includes the Omotesando Hills complex (Tokyo, 2006). Tadao Ando is working on an expansion of the Clark Art Institute (Williamstown, Massachusetts); the Abu Dhabi Maritime Museum (Abu Dhabi, UAE, 2006–); and a house for the designer Tom Ford near Santa Fe, New Mexico.

TADAO ANDO, geboren 1941 in Osaka, kam als Autodidakt zum Architektenberuf, angeregt vor allem durch seine Reisen durch die USA, Europa und Afrika zwischen 1962 und 1969. 1969 gründete er in Osaka das Büro Tadao Ando Architect & Associates. Ando erhielt neben anderen Auszeichnungen die Alvar-Aalto-Medaille des Finnischen Architektenverbands (1985), die Medaille d'or der Académie française d'Architecture (1989), den dänischen Carlsberg-Architekturpreis (1992) und den Pritzker-Preis (1995). Lehraufträge führten ihn an die Universitäten Yale (1987), Columbia (1988) und Harvard (1990). Herausragende Bauten Andos sind u. a. die Rokko-Wohnanlage in Kobe (Japan, 1983–93), die Kirche auf dem Wasser (Hokkaido, Japan, 1988), das Museum im Gräberwald von Kumamoto (1992), der japanische Pavillon zur Expo '92 in Sevilla (Spanien, 1992) und das Suntory Museum in Osaka (Japan, 1994). In jüngerer Zeit entstanden etwa das Awaji Yumebutai (Awajishima, Hyogo, Japan, 1997–2000), das neue Museum für die Pulitzer Foundation for the Arts (St. Louis, Missouri, 1997–2000) und das Modern Art Museum of Fort Worth (Texas, 1999–2002). 2003 schloss Ando die Arbeiten an dem auf der Insel Naoshima in der Seto-Inlandsee gelegenen Chichu-Kunstmuseum ab. Das Museum ist Teil eines fortlaufenden Projekts, für das Ando ebendort in den frühen 1990er-Jahren das Benesse-Haus, ein Museum mit angeschlossenem Hotel, entworfen hatte. Seit 2007 entsteht für François Pinault in Venedig die Punta della Dogana. Ferner errichtete er in jüngerer Zeit, neben dem hier vorgestellten 21_21 Design Sight (Tokio, 2004–07), eine Wohnanlage in den Hügeln von Omotesando (Tokio, 2006). Gegenwärtig in Arbeit sind ein Erweiterungsbau für das Clark Art Institute (Williamstown, Massachusetts), das Meeresmuseum von Abu Dhabi (VAE, seit 2006) und ein Wohnhaus für den Modedesigner Tom Ford in der Nähe von Santa Fe im US-Bundesstaat New Mexico.

Né à Osaka en 1941, **TADAO ANDO** est un architecte autodidacte formé en grande partie par ses voyages aux États-Unis, en Europe et en Afrique (1962–69). Il fonde Tadao Ando Architect & Associates à Osaka en 1969. Parmi ses prix et distinctions : l'Alvar Aalto Medal de l'Association finlandaise des architectes (1985), la médaille d'or de l'Académie d'architecture (Paris, 1989), le Carlsberg Prize (1992), et le Pritzker Prize (1995). Il a enseigné à Yale (1987), Columbia (1988) et Harvard (1990). Il a notamment réalisé : les immeubles d'appartements Rokko (Kobé, Japon, 1983–93) ; l'église sur l'eau (Hokkaido, Japon, 1988) ; le Pavillon japonais d'Expo '92 (Séville, Espagne, 1992) ; le musée de la Forêt des tombes (Kumamoto, Japon, 1992) et le musée Suntory (Osaka, Japon, 1994). Plus récemment, il a conçu le Awaji Yumebutai (Awajishima, Hyogo, Japon, 1997–2000) ; la Pulitzer Foundation for the Arts (St. Louis, Missouri, 1997–2000); le Modern Art Museum de Fort Worth (Texas, 1999–2002). En 2003, il a achevé le musée d'Art Chichu sur l'île de Naoshima en Mer Intérieure, dans le cadre d'un projet à long terme pour lequel il avait déjà conçu le musée et l'hôtel de la maison Benesse au début des années 1990. Il travaille actuellement sur la rénovation de la Punta della Dogana (« la Pointe de la douane ») pour François Pinault (Venise, 2007–). Ses interventions récentes comprennent, en dehors de 21–21 Design Sight (Tokyo, 2004–07, publié ici), le complexe Omotesando Hills (Tokyo, 2006), une extension du Clark Art Institute (Williamstown, Massachusetts) ; le Musée maritime d'Abu Dhabi (Abu Dhabi, EAU, 2006–) et une maison pour le créateur Tom Ford près de Santa Fe au Nouveau Mexique.

21_21 DESIGN SIGHT

Minato-ku, Tokyo, Japan, 2004–07

Site area: 2653 m². Floor area: 1932 m². Client: Mitsui Fudosan Co. Ltd., and five other companies.
Cost: not disclosed. Team: Tadao Ando Architect & Associates and Nikken Sekkei

This very attractive project is an integral part of the ambitious 10-hectare Tokyo Midtown development, near the city's Roppongi district. Nikken Sekkei developed the site of the former Self-Defense Agency of Japan, Tokyo Midtown, along the lines of a Skidmore, Owings & Merrill master plan. The complex includes approximately 550 000 square meters of office, residential, retail, and hotel space, and yet 50 percent of the site is open or green space. It is in this green area, to the rear of the site, that Tadao Ando designed 21_21 Design Sight, an innovative museum imagined by the clothing designer Issey Miyake "to create a new place of culture in Japan for 'design' in a broad sense—exploring new points of view and ways of thinking, expressing surprise and emotion, and communicating these feelings to society." Seeking to maintain the continuity of the landscaping master plan by EDAW, Ando placed one floor of the new building below grade. As the architect says, the building's roof is "made of two larger and smaller sheets of steel folded as they slope down toward the ground. This concept is based on 'a piece of cloth,' the origin of Issey Miyake's creations. Inside a simple form composed of this 'sheet of steel' a folded space develops suitable for freely creating designs." Two lower-level gallery spaces respectively measuring 133 square meters and 443 square meters, both of which have five-meter-high ceilings, form the heart of the design with small café and bookshop spaces on the ground floor.

Dieses ausgesprochen reizvolle Projekt ist eingebunden in eine ehrgeizige, 10 ha große Anlage im Tokioter Zentrum unweit des Bezirks Roppongi. Die Entwicklung des Geländes, auf dem die ehemalige japanische Verteidigungsbehörde ihren Sitz hatte, übernahm das Büro Nikken Sekkei im Rahmen eines von Skidmore, Owings & Merrill konzipierten Bebauungsplans. Während der Komplex eine Nutzfläche von rund 550 000 m² für Büros, Wohnbauten, Einzelhandel und Hotelgewerbe umfasst, ist das Gelände zu 50 % offen oder begrünt. Das im hinteren Bereich des Parkareals liegende 21_21 Design Sight präsentiert sich als ein innovatives Museum und wurde von Ando nach Ideen des Modedesigners Issey Miyake entworfen. Es soll „eine neue japanische Kulturinstitution für einen weitgefassten Begriff von ,Design' sein – in der neue Perspektiven und Denkweisen erkundet werden, Überraschendes und Aufregendes entsteht und diese Eindrücke der Öffentlichkeit vermittelt werden". Um der Einheitlichkeit der von EDAW entwickelten Landschaftsplanung entgegenzukommen, verlegte Ando eines der Geschosse des neuen Gebäudes unter die Erde. Das Dach der Konstruktion besteht, so der Architekt, „aus zwei größeren und zwei kleineren gefalteten Stahlflächen, die sich bis zum Boden neigen. Das Konzept orientiert sich an ,einem Stück Stoff', dem Ausgangsunkt von Miyakes Kreationen. Im Innern der einfachen, aus einem ,Stück Stahl' zusammengesetzten Form entsteht ein gefalteter Raum, der gut zur kreativen Designarbeit passt." Zwei Ausstellungsräume im Untergeschoss, mit Grundflächen von 133 und 443 m² sowie 5 m hohen Decken, bilden zusammen mit einem kleinen Café und einem Buchladen im Erdgeschoss das Herzstück des Entwurfs.

Ce très séduisant projet fait partie intégrante d'un ambitieux programme de rénovation de 10 ha du centre de Tokyo, près du quartier de Roppongi. Nikken Sekkei a repris le site de l'ancienne Agence japonaise de défense dans le cadre d'un plan directeur établi par Skidmore, Owings & Merrill. Le complexe comprend environ 550 000 m² de bureaux, appartements, commerces et hôtels, mais 50 % du terrain restent consacrés aux espaces verts. C'est dans cette zone de verdure, à l'arrière du site, que Tadao Ando a conçu 21_21 Design Sight, nouveau type de musée imaginé par le couturier Issey Miyake « pour créer un nouveau lieu de culture au Japon pour le *design* au sens large, explorant de nouveaux points de vue et manières de penser, exprimant la surprise et l'émotion et communiquant ces sentiments à la société ». Pour maintenir la continuité du traitement paysager de EDAW, Ando a creusé un des niveaux en sous-sol. L'architecte précise que : « [le toit] est fait de deux feuilles d'acier de dimensions différentes pliées dans leur pente vers le sol. Ce concept est issu d'une »pièce de vêtement« de Miyake. À l'intérieur, la forme simple délimitée par cette »feuille d'acier« produit un espace adaptable à toutes sortes de projets. » Les deux galeries en sous-sol, respectivement de 133 et 443 m², à plafonds de cinq mètres de haut, forment le cœur du bâtiment, accompagnées d'un petit café et d'une librairie en rez-de-chaussée.

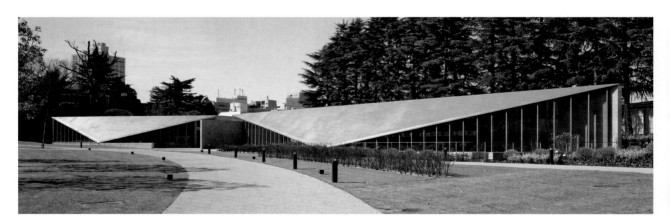

The folded metal roof of the building and its partial insertion into the landscape give it a more modest appearance than Ando's more frequent striking concrete designs.

Mit seinem bis zum Boden geneigten und in die Parklandschaft integrierten Metalldach zeigt das Gebäude eine zurückhaltendere Erscheinung als die robusten Betonentwürfe, für die Ando ansonsten bekannt ist.

Le toit en métal plié et son insertion partielle dans le paysage donnent à ce bâtiment une allure plus modeste que la plupart des réalisations en béton que l'on retrouve fréquemment dans l'œuvre d'Ando.

Seen against the Tokyo skyline, 21_21
Design Sight is embedded into a
large green area designed by the US
firm EDAW.

Das 21_21 Design Sight, hier vor der
Skyline von Tokio, fügt sich in eine
von der US-amerikanischen Firma
EDAW gestaltete Grünanlage ein.

Vu sur le fond du panorama de Tokyo :
le 21_21 Design Sight s'insère
dans un vaste espace vert conçu
par l'agence américaine EDAW.

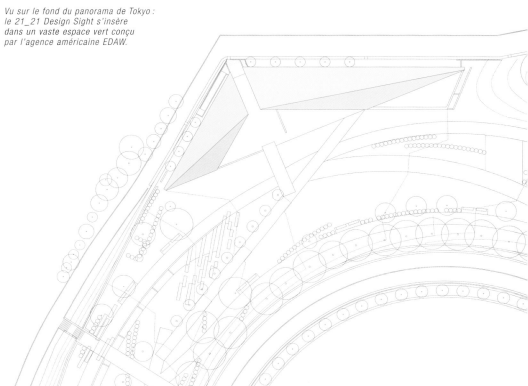

Concrete is present in the walls of the building. Ando slices the volumes into the earth, bringing natural light below grade and allowing visitors to feel removed from their urban setting.

Deutlich sichtbar ist der Beton der Wände. Ando hat die Baukörper so in die Erde eingelassen und mit natürlichem Licht erhellt, dass man sich als Besucher abseits der Stadt wähnt.

Le béton est quand même présent dans les murs du bâtiment. Ando a partiellement enfoncé ses volumes dans le terrain et amené l'éclairage naturel jusque dans les sous-sols. Le visiteur se sent bien loin du contexte urbain.

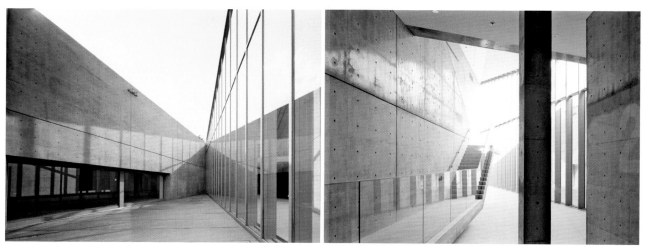

The gallery spaces vary from a court-yard open to the sky to relatively closed, rectangular volumes, well-suited to a variety of different types of exhibitions on design.

Die Präsentationsräume reichen von einem himmelwärts geöffneten Innenhof bis zu relativ geschlossenen rechteckigen Räumen, die speziell für verschiedene Arten von Designausstellungen ausgelegt sind.

Les espaces d'expositions se composent aussi bien d'une cour ouverte sur le ciel que de volumes rectangulaires relativement fermés, facilement adaptables à divers types d'expositions sur le design.

ALEJANDRO ARAVENA

Alejandro Aravena Arquitectos
El Comendador 1916
Providencia, Santiago
Chile

Tel: +56 2 354 7726
Fax: +56 2 354 7749
E-mail: info@elementalchile.cl
Web: www.alejandroaravena.com, www.elementalchile.cl

ALEJANDRO ARAVENA graduated as an architect from the Universidad Católica de Chile (UC) in 1992. He studied history and theory at the Istituto Universitario di Architettura di Venezia (Italy, 1992–93). Aravena was a Visiting Professor at Harvard University (2000–05) and has been a Professor at the UC since 1994. He created Alejandro Aravena Arquitectos in 1994. Since 2006, he has been the Elemental Copec Professor at UC and Executive Director of Elemental, described as a "Do Tank affiliated with the Pontificia Universidad Católica de Chile and Copec, its focus is the design and implementation of urban projects of social interest and public impact." His professional work includes the Mathematics (1998–99), Medical (2002–04), and Architecture (2004) Schools at UC (Santiago); the Pirihueico Lake House (2003–04); Quinta Monroy Social Housing (Iquique, 2003–04, 15th Santiago Biennale Grand Prix); and the Siamese Towers at UC (Santiago, 2003–06, published here), all in Chile. In 2006, he was chosen as the architect for the new facilities of Saint Edward's University in Austin, Texas.

ALEJANDRO ARAVENA schloss 1992 sein Architekturstudium an der Universidad Católica de Chile (UC) in Santiago ab und vertiefte seine Ausbildung anschließend in den Bereichen Architekturtheorie und -geschichte am Instituto Universitario di Architettura di Venezia (Italien, 1992–93). Seit 1994 ist Aravena Lehrstuhlinhaber an der UC, 2004/05 war er Gastprofessor an der Harvard University. 1994 gründete er die Firma Alejandro Aravena Arquitectos. Seit 2006 ist er Geschäftsführer von Elemental, einer Einrichtung, die in Zusammenarbeit mit der Energiefirma Copec und der Pontificia Universidad Católica de Chile entstand und sich als einen an die UC angeschlossenen „Dotank" bezeichnet, der „sich mit der Gestaltung und Durchführung von sozialpolitisch verantwortungsbewussten und öffentlichkeitswirksamen Stadtentwicklungsprojekten befasst". Zu Aravenas Arbeiten als Architekt gehören die Fakultäten für Mathematik (1998–99), Medizin (2002–04) und Architektur (2004) der UC in Santiago, ein Haus am Pirihueico-See (Chile, 2003–04), die Sozialwohnungsanlage Quinta Monroy in Iquique (Chile, 2003–04, ausgezeichnet mit dem Großen Preis der 15. Biennale von Santiago) und die hier vorgestellten „Siamesischen Zwillingstürme" der UC (Santiago, 2003–06). 2006 wurde Aravena als Architekt für die neuen Universitätsbauten der Saint Edward's University im texanischen Austin ausgewählt.

ALEJANDRO ARAVENA est diplômé d'architecture de l'Universidad Católica (UC) du Chili (1992). Il a également étudié l'histoire et la théorie de l'architecture à l'Istituto Universitario di Architettura di Venezia (Italie, 1992–93). Il a été professeur invité à Harvard University (2000–05) et enseigne à l'UC du Chili depuis 1994. Il a créé l'agence Alejandro Aravena Arquitectos en 1994. Depuis 2006, il est professeur Elemental Copec à l'UC et directeur exécutif d'Elemental, un « *Do tank* dépendant de la Pontificia Universidad Católica du Chili et de Copec, ayant pour objet la conception et la mise en œuvre de projets urbains d'intérêt public à impact social ». Parmi ses réalisations figurent les collèges de Mathématiques (1998–99), de Médecine (2002–04), et d'Architecture (2004) à UC (Santiago) ; la maison du lac de Pirihueico (2003–04) ; les logements sociaux de la Quinta Monroy (Iquique, 2003–04, Grand Prix de la 15e Biennale de Santiago) et les tours siamoises de UC (Santiago, 2003–06, publiées ici), le tout au Chili. En 2006, il a été choisi pour concevoir les nouvelles installations de l'université de Saint Edward à Austin, Texas.

CENTRO TECNOLÓGICO

Universidad Católica, San Joaquin Campus, Santiago, Chile, 2003–06

Floor area: 4628 m². Client: Pontificia Universidad Católica de Chile. Cost: $3.5 million.
Team: Alejandro Aravena, Charles Murray, Alfonso Montero, Ricardo Torrejón,
Emilio de la Cerda (collaborator)

A sketch by the architect shows concern for the air currents and cladding with respect to sun conditions. Opposite, the images show the building's unusual skewed design.

Die Zeichnung macht nachvollziehbar, welche Überlegungen der Architekt angesichts der Sonneneinstrahlung zu Luftzirkulation und Gebäudeverkleidung angestellt hat. Die Abbildungen auf der rechten Seite zeigen die ungewöhnliche, schiefe Konstruktion des Gebäudes.

Un croquis de l'architecte illustre la circulation de l'air et le parement des façades adaptés en fonction des déplacements du soleil. À droite, les images de cet immeuble étonnant aux volumes inclinés.

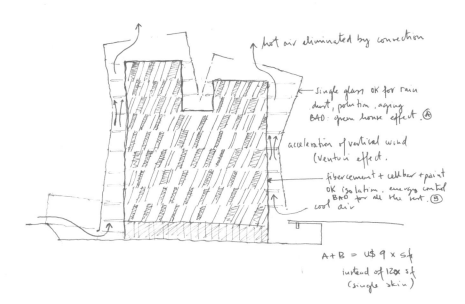

Most frequently known as the "Siamese Towers" because it appears to be joined together and yet divided in two, this structure was designed to house computer equipment and laboratories for the Universidad Católica San Joaquin campus, as well as classroom space for 500 students. The architect rightly underlines the low, $700-per-square-meter construction cost. The nine-story building divides itself in two above the seventh floor, and despite its crocked appearance, the design allows only for rectilinear, untilted internal spaces. The glass-clad concrete structure is a clear testimony for the new and vibrant architecture rising in Latin America, often against all odds, as might have been the case here with an administration that wanted an inexpensive glass tower, but instead gained an architectural landmark. As the architect puts it, "We were asked to build a glass tower to host everything that had to do with computers in the university. We saw three problems in this: the computers, the glass, and the tower." The architects feel that computers alienate people and sought to create convivial spaces for interaction. Their problem with glass was that they did not have a budget for a curtain wall, so they opted for a single glass skin over an internal structure of fiber-cement, the two separated by air. The space between the two volumes acts as a perimeter chimney, allowing hot air to leave the system and avoiding a "greenhouse" effect. Strips of aluminum with slightly different colors differentiate the volumes and give this unique "Siamese" building its visual identity.

Dieses aufgrund seiner Form – zusammengewachsen und doch getrennt – häufig als „Siamesischer Zwillingsturm" bezeichnete Gebäude dient der Unterbringung von EDV-Anlagen und Werkstätten des San-Joaquin-Campus der Universidad Católica und bietet zudem Seminarräume für insgesamt 500 Studenten. Die Baukosten betrugen nur 700 $ pro m², wie der Architekt zu Recht hervorhebt. Ab dem siebten Geschoss teilt sich das neungeschossige Gebäude in zwei Hälften und obwohl der Entwurf etwas verdreht aussieht, ist keiner der Innenräume schief oder zueinander verschoben. Die glasumhüllte Betonkonstruktion ist ein klares Bekenntnis zu einer neuen, aufregenden Architektur, wie sie sich in Lateinamerika seit einiger Zeit bemerkbar macht – und zwar nicht selten trotz widriger Umstände, wie sie auch hier auftraten, weil die Universitätsverwaltung eigentlich ein kostengünstiges Glashochhaus gewünscht hatte. Bekommen hat sie stattdessen ein architektonisches Wahrzeichen. Oder wie der Architekt es ausdrückt: „Wir waren gebeten worden, ein gläsernes Hochhaus zu bauen, in dem alles untergebracht werden sollte, was in der Universität mit Computern zu tun hat. Dabei sahen wir drei Probleme: die Computer, das Glas und das Hochhaus." Die Architekten gingen von der Überlegung aus, dass Computer die Menschen einander entfremden, weshalb sie Räume schaffen wollten, in denen man gerne zusammenkommt. Der Freiraum zwischen den beiden Gebäudeeinheiten fungiert als eine Art Außenkamin, durch den aufgeheizte Luft abziehen kann, so dass ein „Treibhauseffekt" vermieden wird. Farblich leicht unterschiedliche Aluminiumstreifen verleihen den Gebäudeteilen einen jeweils eigenen Zug und dem ungewöhnlichen „Siamesischen Zwillingsgebäude" seine besondere visuelle Identität.

Surnommées les « Tours siamoises », cet ensemble regroupe les équipements informatiques et les laboratoires de l'Universidad Católica du campus de San Joaquin et des salles de cours pour 500 étudiants. Le coût de construction de 700 dollars au m² est particulièrement faible. L'immeuble de neuf niveaux se divise en deux à partir du sixième étage mais, malgré cet écartement, conserve des volumes intérieurs rectilignes réguliers. Cette construction en béton habillée de verre est un témoignage de l'intérêt porté à une architecture vibrante et actuelle qui émerge en Amérique latine, souvent contre toute attente. C'est le cas de cette administration qui ne souhaitait qu'une tour de verre peu coûteuse, et qui bénéficie aujourd'hui d'un véritable monument. Comme l'explique l'architecte : « On nous avait demandé de construire une tour de verre pour réunir toute l'informatique de l'université. Nous avons identifié trois problèmes : les ordinateurs, le verre et la tour. » L'agence a cherché à créer des espaces conviviaux. Le budget alloué ne permettant pas un mur-rideau, elle a opté pour une simple peau de verre posée sur une structure interne en fibrociment, séparée par une couche d'air. L'espace entre les deux volumes fonctionne comme une cheminée périphérique qui permet la ventilation naturelle et atténue l'effet de serre. Des bandeaux d'aluminium de couleurs légèrement différentes différencient les volumes et confèrent à cet bâtiment « siamois » une identité originale.

The apparently skewed design of the
"Siamese Towers" actually reveals a
relatively simple floor plan (below).
The angled roofs of the building seem
to bend in homage to the distant
mountains.

*Trotz des deutlich erkennbaren
verschobenen Aufrisses des „Siamesischen Zwillingsturms" sind die
Grundrisse (unten) recht gewöhnlich.
Die abgeschrägten Dächer scheinen
sich respektvoll vor der Bergkulisse
zu verneigen.*

*La forme apparemment inclinée des
tours siamoises dissimule en fait
un plan au sol relativement simple
(ci-dessous). Les toitures semblent
se courber pour saluer les montagnes
dans le lointain.*

Despite the relatively low budget of the building, Aravena has taken care to give something of the spirit of the architecture to the interiors, as can be seen in the openings and light-fixture designs.

Ungeachtet des relativ niedrigen Budgets hat Aravena Wert darauf gelegt, den Geist seiner Außenarchitektur auch im Inneren walten zu lassen, etwa bei den Gebäudeöffnungen oder dem Design der Raumbeleuchtungen.

Malgré un budget de construction relativement faible, Aravena s'est efforcé d'insuffler un peu de l'esprit de son architecture dans les espaces intérieurs, comme le montrent certaines ouvertures ou les systèmes d'éclairage.

Large, irregular glazed surfaces seen in the image below allow for natural light to enter, while also offering a view of the region.

Große, in unregelmäßigen Formen verglaste Oberflächen wie in der Abbildung unten lassen natürliches Licht ins Gebäude und eröffnen zudem den Ausblick aufs Umland.

De vastes plans vitrés de surface irrégulière, comme ci-dessous, laissent entrer la lumière naturelle à l'intérieur, en offrant des perspectives sur la région environnante.

ARGE GRAZIOLI KRISCHANITZ

Alfred Grazioli and Adolf Krischanitz
ARGE Grazioli Krischanitz GmbH, Zurich
Quellenstr. 27
8005 Zurich
Switzerland

Tel: +41 44 274 80 70
Fax: +41 44 274 80 71
E-mail: wien@krischanitzundfrank.com
buero@graziolimuthesius.de
Web: www.krischanitz.at

ADOLF KRISCHANITZ was born in 1946 in Schwarzach/Pongau, Austria. During his studies of architecture at the University of Vienna, he co-founded "Missing Link" with Angela Hareiter and Otto Kapfinger. From 1991 to 1995, Krischanitz was the President of the Secession in Vienna. He has acted as a Visiting Professor and teacher in Vienna, Munich, Karlsruhe, and Berlin, and, since 1992, he has been a Professor of Design and Urban Renewal at the University of the Arts in Berlin. Since 2001, Krischanitz has worked in cooperation with Alfred Grazioli on several projects. **ALFRED GRAZIOLI** was born in Basel, Switzerland, in 1940. He studied architecture at the Hochschule für Gestaltung in Ulm and at the École d'Architecture of the University of Geneva (EAUG). He has worked as an assistant at the ETH in Zurich and the EPFL in Lausanne, and, since 1972, he has been a Professor at the University of the Arts in Berlin. He created the Office of Architecture, Urban Design and Interior Design with Wieka Muthesius. He has worked with Adolf Krischanitz in Zurich and Berlin, and lives in Berlin and Rome.

ADOLF KRISCHANITZ wurde 1946 im österreichischen Schwarzach im Pongau geboren. Noch während seines Architekturstudiums an der Universität Wien gründete er gemeinsam mit Angela Hareiter und Otto Kapfinger die Arbeitsgemeinschaft „Missing Link". Von 1991 bis 1995 war Krischanitz Präsident der Wiener Sezession. Als Gastprofessor und Dozent war er in Wien, München, Karlsruhe und Berlin tätig, seit 1992 ist er Professor für Entwerfen und Stadterneuerung an der heutigen Universität der Künste Berlin. Seit 2001 sind mehrere Projekte in Zusammenarbeit mit Alfred Grazioli entstanden. **ALFRED GRAZIOLI**, geboren 1940 in Basel, studierte an der Hochschule für Gestaltung Ulm sowie an der Architekturschule der Universität Genf (EAUG). Grazioli arbeitete als Assistent an der ETH Zürich sowie der EPFL Lausanne und lehrt seit 1972 an der heutigen Universität der Künste Berlin. Gemeinsam mit Wieka Muthesius hat er ein Büro für Architektur, Innengestaltung und Städtebau. Mit Adolf Krischanitz hat Grazioli in Zürich und Berlin zusammengearbeitet. Er lebt in Berlin und Rom.

ADOLF KRISCHANITZ est né en 1946 à Schwarzach au Pongau, Autriche. Au cours de ses études d'architecture à l'université de Vienne, il fonde « Missing Link » avec Angela Hareiter et Otto Kapfinger. De 1991 à 1995, il préside la Secession à Vienne. Après avoir été professeur invité et enseignant à Vienne, Munich, Karlsruhe et Berlin, il est depuis 1992 Professeur de conception et de rénovation urbaine à l'Université des Arts de Berlin. Depuis 2001, il a travaillé en collaboration avec Alfred Grazioli sur plusieurs projets. **ALFRED GRAZIOLI**, né à Bâle, Suisse, en 1940, a étudié l'architecture à la Hochschule für Gestaltung d'Ulm et à l'École d'architecture de l'université de Genève (EAUG). Il a été assistant à l'ETH à Zurich et à l'EPFL à Lausanne, et, depuis 1972, est professeur à l'Université des Arts de Berlin. Il a créé l'agence Office of Architecture, Urban Design and Interior Design avec Wieka Muthesius, et a travaillé avec Adolf Krischanitz à Zurich et Berlin. Il vit à Berlin et Rome.

MUSEUM RIETBERG EXTENSION

Zurich, Switzerland, 2004–06

Floor area: 5350 m². Client: Office for Building Construction, City of Zurich.
Cost: € 29 million. Team: Wieka Muthesius, Birgit Frank, Ralf Wilkening (competition);
and for the realization, Elke Eichmann (Project Leader),
Thomas Künzle, Jay Thalmann, Dimitri Kaden, Naomi Hajnos, Simone Wiestner. Artwork: Helmut Federle

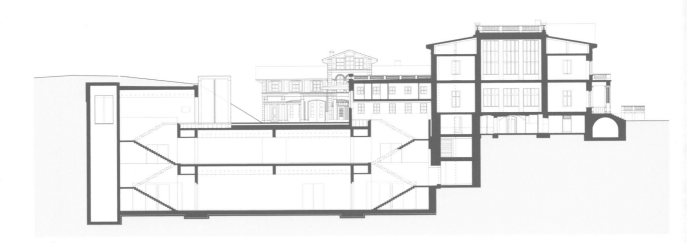

The Rietberg Museum in Zurich has a long and rich history. Otto and Mathilde Wesendonck built the Villa Wesendonck on the site in 1857. Friendly with Richard Wagner, they gave the German composer refuge in Zurich in 1849 in a half-timber house next to their house, today called the Villa Schönberg. The Rieter family from Winterthur, after whom the present museum and park are named, then occupied the property. In 1949, the citizens of Zurich decided that the Villa Wesendonck should be turned into a museum for the collection of Baron Eduard von der Heydt, which was to be donated to the city. The Museum Rietberg of the City of Zurich opened in 1952 and is the only art museum for non-European cultures in Switzerland, housing an internationally renowned collection of Asian, African, and ancient Native American art. The insufficient size of the Villa Wesendonck made enlargement of the Rietberg essential, and Grazioli and Krischanitz won the competition held in 2002 on the basis of their essentially underground proposal, which left the villa and park largely intact. Construction required digging more than 12 meters into the hillside near the villa and resulted in a greatly increased exhibition area. The architects describe the glass entrance, the main external trace of their work, as a "shining green lampion." A concrete relief work by Helmut Federle marks the rear of the foyer. A double oak staircase, linked above to the Villa Wesendonck, descends from the foyer to the underground exhibition spaces. A temporary-exhibition gallery with higher ceilings is located below the permanent-collection areas.

Das Gelände des Museums Rietberg in Zürich kann auf eine lange und bewegte Geschichte zurückblicken. 1857 hatten Otto und Mathilde Wesendonck dort ihre Villa Wesendonck errichten lassen – jene Wesendoncks, die 1849 dem aus Deutschland geflohenen Richard Wagner ihre Gastfreundschaft und eine Unterkunft in einem neben ihrer eigenen Villa gelegenen Fachwerkhaus, heute die Villa Schönberg, anboten. 1871 wurde das Anwesen von der Industriellenfamilie Rieter aus Winterthur übernommen, nach der das heutige Museum und der Park ihre Namen erhielten. Im Jahr 1949 entschieden die Züricher Bürger, dass die Villa Wesendonck in ein Museum umgewandelt werden und eine Sammlung aufnehmen sollte, die die Stadt von Baron Eduard von der Heydt als Schenkung erhalten hatte. Das 1952 eröffnete städtische Museum Rietberg ist das einzige Schweizer Museum für die Kunst außereuropäischer Kulturen und besitzt eine international angesehene Sammlung asiatischer, afrikanischer, amerikanischer und ozeanischer Kunst. Aufgrund der zu knappen Ausstellungsfläche wurde 2002 ein Architekturwettbewerb für eine Museumserweiterung ausgeschrieben, den Alfred Grazioli und Adolf Krischanitz für sich entschieden. Ihr Vorschlag sah vor allem unterirdische Erweiterungsmaßnahmen vor, die Villa wie Park weitgehend unbeeinträchtigt ließen. Dazu wurde der Boden des Geländes neben der Villa 12 m tief ausgehoben, wodurch sich eine immense Vergrößerung der Gesamtausstellungsfläche erzielen ließ. Den gläsernen Eingang, die einzige von außen sichtbare Spur ihrer Arbeit, beschreiben die Architekten als einen „glänzenden grünen Lampion". Die hintere Foyerwand schmückt ein Betonrelief von Helmut Federle. Zwei Eichenholztreppen, deren eine die Verbindung zur Villa Wesendonck herstellt, führen in die unterirdischen Ausstellungsräume. Unterhalb der Ebene, die die ständige Sammlung beherbergt, befindet sich ein Saal mit niedrigerer Decke für temporäre Ausstellungen.

Le musée Rietberg à Zurich possède une longue et riche histoire. Otto et Mathilde Wesendonck avaient fait construire leur villa sur ce site en 1857. Amis de Richard Wagner, ils offrirent au compositeur en 1849 l'hospitalité dans une maison à colombage à proximité de leur résidence, la villa Schönberg. La famille Rieter, de Winterthur, qui a donné son nom au musée et au parc actuels, acquirent par la suite la propriété. En 1949, la ville de Zurich décida que la villa Wesendonck devait être transformée en musée pour accueillir les collections du baron Eduard von der Heydt, dont elle venait d'hériter. Le musée Rietberg de la ville de Zurich a ouvert en 1952 et reste le seul consacré aux cultures non européennes en Suisse. Il abrite une collection renommée d'arts asiatique, africain et précolombien. Les dimensions insuffisantes de la villa nécessitaient un agrandissement qui fut l'objet d'un concours en 2002, remporté par Grazioli et Krischanitz sur la base d'une proposition essentiellement en sous-sol, qui ne touchait pratiquement pas la villa ni le parc. Il a fallu creuser sur plus de 12 mètres de profondeur le flanc de la colline près de la maison pour créer des espaces d'expositions beaucoup plus généreux que les anciens. Les architectes présentent l'entrée en verre, principale manifestation extérieure de leur intervention comme « un lampion vert étincelant ». Un bas-relief en béton réalisé par Helmut Federle marque le fond du hall d'accueil d'où descend un double escalier en chêne, qui relie les nouvelles salles à la villa. Un espace pour expositions temporaires à plafonds surélevés a été installé au-dessous des collections permanentes.

The green glass design (Ludwig + Weiler, Augsburg) is a characteristic feature of the visible parts of the Rietberg Extension, justifying the architect's reference to it as a "green lampion."

Grünes Glas (Ludwig + Weiler, Augsburg) ist das herausragende Merkmal der von außen sichtbaren Abschnitte der Erweiterung des Museums und lässt die Architekten zu Recht von einem „grünen Lampion" sprechen.

Le verre de teinte verte (Ludwig + Weiler, Augsburg) est l'une des caractéristiques marquantes des parties visibles de l'extension du musée Rietberg, et explique l'allusion des architectes à un « lampion vert ».

The relative emptiness of the entrance area, together with its interesting floor, ceiling, and wall finishes, gives the impression of a precious box—an entrance area but also a preparation for the works on display beyond.

Die verhältnismäßig leere Eingangs-halle wirkt im Zusammenspiel mit der reizvollen Gestaltung von Boden, Wänden und Decke wie ein Schmuck-kasten – so dass der Eingangsbereich bereits einen Vorgeschmack auf die zu erwartenden Kunstwerke bietet.

Le vide relatif de la zone d'entrée et les finitions intéressantes du sol, du plafond et des murs donnent une impression de coffre précieux : c'est une entrée, mais qui joue en même temps le rôle d'une introduction aux œuvres présentées plus loin.

SHIGERU BAN

Shigeru Ban Architects
5–2–4 Matsubara
Setagaya-ku
Tokyo 156–0043
Japan

Tel: +81 3 3324 6760 / Fax: +81 3 3324 6789
E-mail: tokyo@shigerubanarchitects.com / Web: www.shigerubanarchitects.com

Born in 1957 in Tokyo, **SHIGERU BAN** studied at SCI-Arc from 1977 to 1980. He attended the Cooper Union School of Architecture, where he studied under John Hejduk (1980–82). He worked in the office of Arata Isozaki (1982–83), before founding his own firm in Tokyo in 1985. His work includes numerous exhibition designs (Alvar Aalto show at the Axis Gallery, Tokyo, 1986). His buildings include the Odawara Pavilion (Kanagawa, 1990); the Paper Gallery (Tokyo, 1994); the Paper House (Lake Yamanaka, 1995); and the Paper Church (Takatori, Hyogo, 1995), all in Japan. He has also designed ephemeral structures such as his Paper Refugee Shelter made with plastic sheets and paper tubes for the United Nations High Commissioner for Refugees (UNHCR). He designed the Japanese Pavilion at Expo 2000 in Hanover. He installed his Paper Temporary Studio on top of the Centre Georges Pompidou in Paris to work on the new Pompidou Center in Metz (France, 2004–09). Other recent work includes the Nicolas G. Hayek Center (Tokyo, 2005–07); and the Takatori Church (Kobe, Hyogo, 2005–07), both in Japan; and the disaster relief Post-Tsunami Rehabilitation Houses (Kirinda, Hambantota, Sri Lanka, 2005–07, published here). Current work includes a small museum of Canal History in Pouilly-en-Auxois (France); the Schwartz Residence (Sharon, Connecticut); the Forest Park Pavilion, Bamboo Gridshell-02 (St. Louis, Missouri); Mul(ti)houses (Mulhouse, France); the Sagaponac House, Furniture House-05 (Long Island, New York); and the Hanegi Forest Annex (Setagaya, Tokyo).

SHIGERU BAN, geboren 1957 in Tokio, studierte von 1977 bis 1980 am Southern California Institute of Architecture und von 1980 bis 1982 bei John Hejduk an der Cooper Union School of Architecture in New York. Im Anschluss arbeitete er bis 1983 im Büro von Arata Isozaki, 1985 gründete er in Tokio seine eigene Firma. Shigeru Ban gestaltete zahlreiche Ausstellungen, so die 1986 in der Galerie Axis in Tokio gezeigte Alvar-Aalto-Schau. Zu seinen in Japan realisierten Bauten gehören der Odawara-Pavillon (Kanagawa, 1990), die Paper Gallery in Tokio (1994), das Paper House am Yamanaka-See (1995) und die Paper Church in Takatori, Hyogo (1995). Ferner umfasst seine Werkliste temporäre Bauten, etwa die für den Hohen Flüchtlingskommissar der Vereinten Nationen (UNHCR) entworfenen Behelfsbauten aus Pappröhren und Plastikfolie, den japanischen Pavillon für die Expo 2000 in Hannover oder das Paper Temporary Studio auf dem Dach des Pariser Centre Georges Pompidou, in dem das neue Centre Pompidou in Metz geplant wird (Frankreich, 2004–09). Weitere Projekte aus jüngerer Zeit sind das Nicolas G. Hayek Center in Tokio (Japan, 2005–07), die Takatori-Kirche in Kobe, Hyogo (Japan, 2005–07), sowie die hier vorgestellten Wohnhäuser für die Tsunami-Opfer in Kirinda (Hambantota, Sri Lanka, 2005–07). Gegenwärtig arbeitet Ban an einem kleinen Museum für die Geschichte des Kanalbaus im französischen Pouilly-en-Auxois, dem Haus Schwartz in Sharon, Connecticut, einem Bamboo Gridshell-022 genannten Pavillon im Forest Park von St. Louis, Missouri, den Mul(ti)houses im französischen Mulhouse, dem Haus Sagaponac oder Furniture House-05 auf Long Island, New York, sowie einem Anbau im Hanegi-Park in Setagaya, Tokio.

Né en 1957 à Tokyo, **SHIGERU BAN** a étudié à SCI-Arc de 1977 à 1980 et à la Cooper Union School of Architecture, auprès de John Hejduk (1980–82). Il a travaillé dans l'agence d'Arata Isozaki (1982–83), avant de fonder sa propre agence à Tokyo en 1985. Son œuvre comprend de nombreuses installations d'expositions (Alvar Aalto Show à la galerie Axis, Tokyo, 1986) et des bâtiments comme le pavillon Odawara (Kanagawa, 1990) ; la Paper Gallery (Tokyo, 1994) ; la Paper House (Lake Yamanaka, 1995) et la Paper Church (Takatori, Hyogo, 1995), tous au Japon. Il a également conçu des structures éphémères comme son Abri en papier pour réfugiés, fait de films plastiques et de tubes de papier, pour le Haut-Commissariat des Nations Unies pour les Réfugiés (HCR). Il a dessiné le Pavillon japonais pour Expo 2000 à Hanovre. Son atelier de papier temporaire a été installé au sommet du Centre Georges-Pompidou à Paris comme annexe de son agence pour le nouveau Centre Pompidou à Metz (France, 2004–09). Parmi d'autres réalisations récentes : le Nicolas G. Hayek Center (Tokyo, 2005–07) ; l'église de Takatori (Kobe, Hyogo, 2005–07), tous deux au Japon, et les maisons de reconstruction post-tsunami (Kirinda, Hambantota, Sri Lanka, 2005–07, publiées ici). Actuellement, il travaille sur un projet de petit musée sur l'histoire d'un canal à Pouilly-en-Auxois (France) ; la résidence Schwartz (Sharon, Connecticut) ; le pavillon Forest Park, Bamboo Gridshell-02 (St. Louis, Missouri) ; Mul(ti)houses (Mulhouse, France) ; Sagaponac House, Furniture House-05 (Long Island, New York) et l'annexe de la Forêt d'Hanegi (Setagaya, Tokyo).

POST-TSUNAMI REHABILITATION HOUSES

Kirinda, Hambantota, Sri Lanka, 2005–07

Floor area: each house 71 m². Client: Colliers Kirinda Trust.
Cost per house: $13 000; total project cost: $1 million. Associate Architect: Philip Weeraratne/PWA architects.
General Contractor: Duminda Builders. Structural Design: J. D Pooranampillai

The earthquake of December 26, 2004, that unleashed a catastrophic tsunami killed an estimated 38 000 people in Sri Lanka. With a history dating back in local legend to the 2nd century B.C., Kirinda is a small port on the south coast of Sri Lanka, about 270 kilometers from Colombo. A one-million-dollar charity program was initiated by the real-estate group Colliers International to rebuild Kirinda after the earthquake, and Shiguru Ban Architects donated their time and efforts to this project. Made of compressed earth blocks and wood, a total of 50 houses, of which 36 had been completed by April 30, 2006, are planned. Intended to be environmentally friendly and sizeable enough to be comfortable, the houses made of natural materials stay cool within even when outside temperatures are very high. Furniture units made of local rubber tree wood are also part of the designs. Shigeru Ban had already designed disaster-relief housing as demonstrated by his Paper Log House-Turkey (northwestern Turkey, 1989); Paper Log House-India (Gujarat, India, 2001); and earlier Paper Emergency Shelter for UNHCR (Rwanda, 1999), although in this instance emphasis was placed on locally available, inexpensive materials rather than Ban's favorite paper tube elements.

Bei der am 26. Dezember 2004 durch ein Seebeben ausgelösten Tsunami-Katastrophe kamen in Sri Lanka schätzungsweise 38 000 Menschen ums Leben. Schwer betroffen war auch die kleine Hafenstadt Kirinda an der Südküste der Insel, rund 270 km von Colombo entfernt, deren Geschichte der lokalen Legende nach bis in das 2. Jahrhundert v. Chr. zurückreicht. Nach dem Unglück rief die Immobiliengruppe Colliers International ein mit 1 Million Dollar ausgestattetes Hilfsprogramm für den Wiederaufbau Kirindas ins Leben, dem Shigeru Ban Architects ihre unentgeltliche Unterstützung zusagten. Insgesamt wurden 50 Häuser aus Holz und Blöcken aus gepresster Erde geplant, von denen am 30. April 2006 insgesamt 36 Einheiten fertiggestellt waren. Es wurde darauf geachtet, dass die Bauten nicht nur umweltverträglich sind und ausreichenden Platz bieten, sondern die Räume auch bei sehr hohen Außentemperaturen kühl bleiben. Möbeleinbauten – aus Gummibaumholz – waren in den Entwürfen bereits mit berücksichtigt. Schon bei früheren Anlässen hatte Shigeru Ban mit Unterkünften einen Beitrag zur Katastrophenhilfe geleistet: etwa mit seinen Papierblockhäusern, die 1989 in der Nordwesttürkei und 2001 im indischen Gujarat errichtet wurden, oder 1999 mit den Papiernotunterkünften in Ruanda für den UNHCR, wobei hier kostengünstigere Materialien als die von Ban gerne verwendeten Papphöhren zum Einsatz kamen.

Le tremblement de terre du 26 décembre 2004 qui déclencha un tsunami catastrophique tua environ 38 000 personnes au Sri Lanka. Fondé, selon la légende locale, au IIe siècle av. J.-C., le petit port de Kirinda se trouve sur la côte sud, à 270 km environ de Colombo. Un programme caritatif d'un million de dollars a été lancé par le groupe immobilier Colliers International pour reconstruire la ville de Kirinda après le séisme et Shigeru Ban Architects a fait présent de son temps et de ses efforts. Réalisées en briques de terre compressée et en bois, 50 maisons, dont 36 étaient achevées en avril 2006, sont prévues. Respectant l'environnement et de taille suffisante pour apporter un confort correct, elles sont donc réalisées avec des matériaux naturels qui restent frais malgré les températures extérieures élevées. Les meubles en caoutchoutier, un bois local, font également partie du projet. Shigeru Ban s'était déjà intéressé aux logements de secours avec sa Maison en bûches en papier (Turquie du Nord-Ouest, 1989), sa maison Paper Log (Gujarat, Inde, 2001), et même auparavant avec ses abris d'urgence en papier pour le UNHCR (Rwanda, 1999), bien que cette fois, l'accent ait été mis sur des matériaux locaux disponibles et bon marché plutôt que sur des tubes en papier.

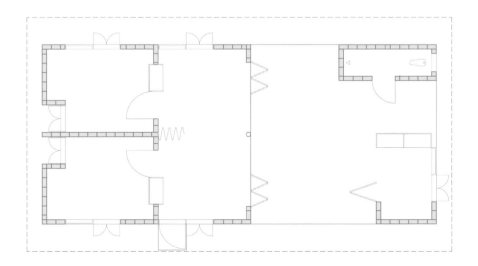

The floor plan of the houses is deliberately simple, but demonstrates a study of local living habits as well as the appropriate technology and construction methods used.

Die Raumaufteilung der Häuser ist bewusst einfach gehalten, lässt aber auch erkennen, dass Rücksicht auf lokale Lebensgewohnheiten genommen und angemessene Technologien und Bauweisen angewendet wurden.

Le plan au sol des maisons est forcément très simple, mais témoigne de l'étude des habitudes de vie des habitants et de la pertinence des technologies et méthodes de construction employées.

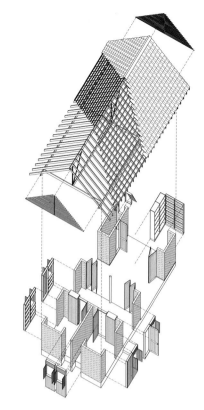

The houses can be left largely open, and, as the site plan above shows, they are disposed in a village-like pattern that also increases their acceptability for local populations.

Die Häuser lassen sich weit öffnen und sind zudem, wie der Lageplan (oben) zeigt, wie in einem Dorf ange-ordnet, damit sich die Einheimischen leichter mit ihnen anfreunden können.

Les maisons peuvent être laissées largement ouvertes et, comme le montre le plan ci-dessus, sont regroupées en village, ce qui facilite leur acceptation par la population.

BARKOW LEIBINGER ARCHITEKTEN

Barkow Leibinger Architekten
Schillerstr. 94
10625 Berlin
Germany

Tel: +49 30 31 57 12-0
Fax: +49 30 31 57 12-29
E-mail: info@barkowleibinger.com
Web: www.barkowleibinger.com

REGINE LEIBINGER was born in 1963 in Stuttgart, Germany. She studied architecture in Berlin (Diploma, Technische Universität, 1989) and at Harvard University (M.Arch, 1990). She created a joint office with **FRANK BARKOW** in 1993. She has been a Visiting Professor at the Architectural Association (AA) in London (Unit Master, 1997–98), Cornell University, and Harvard University, and, since 2006, a Professor for Building Construction and Design at the Technische Universität in Berlin. Frank Barkow was born in 1957 in Kansas City, Missouri, USA, and studied architecture at Montana State University (B.Arch, 1982) and Harvard University (M.Arch, 1990). He has been a Visiting Professor at the AA in London (Unit Master, 1995–98), Cornell University, Harvard University, and at the State Academy of Art and Design in Stuttgart. Their recent work includes Pavilions for Research and Production (Grüsch, Switzerland, 2001–04); the Trutec Building (Seoul, Korea, 2005–06, published here); a house in Berlin-Karlshorst (2007); a Gatehouse (Ditzingen, Stuttgart, 2007); and a Campus Restaurant (also at Ditzingen, Stuttgart, 2008), the latter three in Germany.

REGINE LEIBINGER, geboren 1963 in Stuttgart, studierte Architektur an der Technischen Universität Berlin (Diplom 1989) und an der Harvard University (Master of Architecture 1990). 1993 gründete sie mit **FRANK BARKOW** ein Gemeinschaftsbüro in Berlin. Leibinger war Gastprofessorin an der Architectural Association (AA) in London (Unit Master, 1997–98) sowie an den Universitäten Cornell und Harvard, seit 2006 ist sie Professorin für Baukonstruktion und Entwerfen an der TU Berlin. Der 1957 in Kansas City in den USA geborene Frank Barkow erwarb 1982 seinen Bachelor of Architecture an der Montana State University und 1990 seinen Master of Architecture an der Harvard University. Wie Leibinger war Barkow Gastprofessor an der AA in London (Unit Master, 1995–98) und an den Universitäten Cornell und Harvard, außerdem lehrte er an der Staatlichen Akademie der Bildenden Künste Stuttgart. Zu ihren jüngeren Projekten gehören zwei Forschungs- und Produktionspavillons für eine Maschinenfabrik im schweizerischen Grüsch (2001–04), das hier vorgestellte Trutec-Gebäude in Seoul (Korea, 2005–06), ein Wohnhaus in Berlin-Karlshorst (2007) sowie ein Pförtnerhaus und ein Betriebsrestaurant in Ditzingen bei Stuttgart (2008).

REGINE LEIBINGER, née en 1963 à Stuttgart, Allemagne, a étudié l'architecture à Berlin (diplômée de la Technische Universität, 1989) et à Harvard University (M. Arch, 1990). Elle a créé son agence en association avec **FRANK BARKOW** en 1993. Elle a été professeur invité à l'Architectural Association (AA) de Londres (Unit Master, 1997–98), Cornell University et Harvard University, et, depuis 2006, elle est professeur de conception et de construction à la Technische Universität de Berlin. Frank Barkow, né in 1957 à Kansas City, USA, a étudié l'architecture à Montana State University (B. Arch, 1982) et Harvard University (M. Arch, 1990). Il a été professeur invité à l'AA de Londres (Unit Master, 1995–98), Cornell University, Harvard University et à l'Académie d'art et de design de Stuttgart. Parmi leurs récents travaux : pavillons pour la recherche et la production (Grüsch, Suisse, 2001–04) ; le Trutec Building (Séoul, Corée, 2005–06, publié ici) ; une maison à Berlin-Karlshorst (2007) ; un pavillon d'entrée (Ditzingen, Stuttgart, 2007) et un restaurant de campus (également à Ditzingen, Stuttgart, 2008).

TRUTEC BUILDING

Seoul, Korea, 2005–06

Floor area: 20 000 m² (including parking area). Height: 55 m. Client: TKR Sang-Am Ltd., Seoul, Korea.
Cost: not disclosed. Team: Martina Bauer (Project Architect), Matthias Graf von Ballestrem, Markus Bonauer, Michael Schmidt,
Elke Sparmann, Jan-Olivier Kunze. Local Architect: Chang-Jo Architects, Seoul.
Façades: Arup Façade Engineering, Alutek Ltd., Seoul, Korea

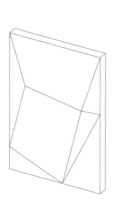

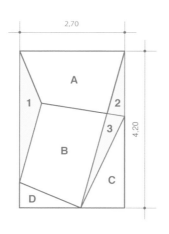

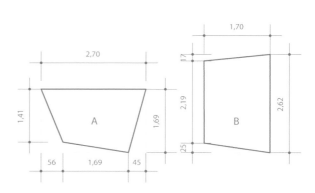

The Trutec won a 2008 AIA Honor Award for Architecture. The citation for the Award read in part, "This 11-story building situated over a five-level underground parking structure is clad in a mirrored fractal glass articulated into a series of crystalline-formed bays projecting 20 centimeters. This pattern refracts light and images, rendering the façade as a fragmented and abstract surface." European CNC digital milling technology was used to cut and assemble the three-dimensional window frames. Despite the complexity of the façade, it proved possible to resolve the design with two essential window types, reducing costs. According to the architects, the so-called Digital Media City, where the project is located, is a place "where site, history, or methods may be irrelevant, transitional or appropriated from other places… With an urban master plan for an office and residential quarter (DMC), in the beginning of realization there was little to respond to beyond local zoning and code regulations." The "mirrored fractal glass articulated into a series of crystalline-formed bays projecting 20 centimeters" is certainly one of the most outstanding features of the structure, which otherwise corresponds to office-building standards. The architects decided to displace the office core from the center of the structure to the eastern corner, cladding that volume with dark zinc shingles on the exterior. This decision allows for large column-free office floors. The ground floor is a double-height space for German high-tech machine tools, while a 12th-floor roof garden is conceived as an "open-air courtyard."

Das Trutec-Gebäude erhielt einen der 2008 vergebenen Honor Awards des American Institute of Architects. In einem Auszug aus der Begründung heißt es: „Das elfgeschossige Gebäude, angelegt über fünf unterirdischen Parkebenen, ist mit Versatzstücken aus Spiegelglas verkleidet, die zu Feldern mit kristallartiger Oberfläche angeordnet 20 cm weit aus der Konstruktion hervorragen. In dieser Anordnung brechen sich Licht und Spiegelungen und machen die Fassade zu einer abstrakten, kaleidoskopartigen Oberfläche." Um die dreidimensionalen Fensterrahmen zurechtzuschneiden und zusammenzufügen, wurden digital gesteuerte CNC-Fräsen europäischer Fertigung verwendet. Trotz der komplexen Fassadenstruktur gelang es, den Entwurf mit nur zwei Fenstergrundtypen umzusetzen und auf diese Weise die Kosten gering zu halten. Wie die Architekten erklären, ist die so genannte Digital Media City, der Standort ihres Projekts, ein Ort, „an dem der Bezug zum Umfeld, historische Zusammenhänge oder auch die Bauweise kaum eine Rolle spielen oder nur vorläufig feststanden oder von anderen Orten übernommen waren […] Da nur der Generalbebauungsplan für das Büro- und Wohnviertel DMC vorlag, gab es abgesehen von den Abstandsbestimmungen und rechtlichen Vorschriften wenig, was man in die Planungen hätte einbeziehen können." Die kristallartig verspiegelte Fassade, deren Einzelfelder aus den Außenseiten hervorragen, ist sicherlich eines der hervorstechendsten Merkmale dieses Gebäudes, das ansonsten die in Bürohäusern üblichen Standards bietet. Allerdings entschieden sich die Architekten, den Versorgungs- und Erschließungskern nicht in der Mitte, sondern in der östlichen Ecke des Baukörpers anzulegen, wo die Fassade mit dunklen Zinkplatten verkleidet ist. Auf diese Weise entstanden weitläufige, stützenfreie Büroetagen. Im Erdgeschoss mit doppelter Geschosshöhe sind Hightech-Fertigungsanlagen made in Germany untergebracht, im zwölften Stockwerk stößt man auf einen als Dachgarten gestalteten offenen Innenhof.

Le Trutec a remporté le Honor Award for Architecture 2008 de l'AIA qui l'a présenté de la façon suivante : « Cet immeuble de 11 niveaux au-dessus d'une structure de cinq niveaux en sous-sol est habillé de verre fractal poli miroir, articulé en une série de travées de formes cristallines se projetant vers l'avant de 20 centimètres. Cette disposition réfracte la lumière et les images, ce qui transforme la façade en une surface abstraite fragmentée. » Une technologie européenne de fabrication pilotée par ordinateur (CNC) a été utilisée pour les cadres de fenêtres tridimensionnels. Il a été possible de s'en tenir à deux types de fenêtres de base pour réduire les coûts. Selon les architectes, la Digital Media City, dans laquelle est implantée cette réalisation est un lieu « où le site, l'histoire ou les méthodes peuvent être transitoires, décalées ou appropriées à d'autres expériences. Le plan directeur pour un quartier résidentiel et de bureaux (DMC) étant déjà établi, au début, il n'y avait que peu d'opportunités d'aller au-delà des réglementations locales de zonage et de codes. » Cette façade est certainement l'un des traits les plus remarquables de cette réalisation qui répond par ailleurs aux standards des immeubles de bureaux. Les architectes ont décidé de déplacer le noyau de bureaux du centre de la structure vers l'angle est et d'habiller ce volume de shingles de zinc gris foncé sur sa face extérieure. Ceci a permis d'obtenir de vastes niveaux sans colonnes. Le rez-de-chaussée est un volume double hauteur qui sert à l'exposition de machines-outils allemandes de haute technologie. Sur le toit, un jardin fait office de « cour en plein air ».

The three-dimensional effects of the glazed façade lend the building a character that changes according to natural or artificial lighting conditions.

Durch die je nach Tageslicht oder Innenbeleuchtung wechselnden drei-dimensionalen Effekte auf der Glas-fassade verändert sich beständig der Charakter des Gebäudes.

Les effets tridimensionnels de la façade de verre donnent à l'immeuble un caractère certain, qui change avec l'éclairage naturel ou artificiel.

The full-height glazed interior spaces clearly echo the variety introduced in the exterior of the building, animating it and giving life to office areas.

Die deckenhoch verglasten Innenräume nehmen die Erscheinungsvielfalt der Außenfassaden auf und geben den Büros eine lebendige Atmosphäre.

Les volumes intérieurs vitrés toute hauteur font écho à la dynamique des façades et contribuent à l'animation des espaces de travail.

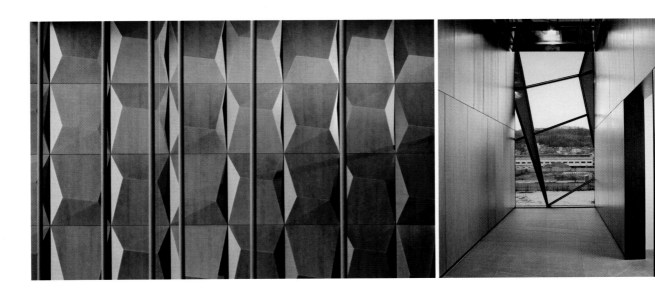

*A suspended interior stairway pro-
longs the theme of lightness and play
on space already orchestrated by the
external façades.*

*Eine schwebende Innentreppe setzt
das von den Außenfassaden aufgenommene Thema der Leichtigkeit
und des Spiels mit dem Raum fort.*

*Un escalier intérieur suspendu
reprend le thème de la légèreté
et du jeu des volumes orchestré sur
les façades externes.*

BERNARDES + JACOBSEN ARQUITETURA

Bernardes + Jacobsen Arquitetura
Rua Corcovado 250, Jardim Botânico
22460-050 Rio de Janeiro, RJ
Brazil

Tel/Fax: +55 21 2512 7743
E-mail: bjrj@bja.com.br
Web: www.bja.com.br

Thiago Bernardes was born in Rio de Janeiro in 1974. The office of **BERNARDES + JACOBSEN** was created in 1980 by his father, Claudio Bernardes, and Paulo Jacobsen, pioneers of a new type of residential architecture based on an effort to combine contemporary design and Brazilian culture. Thiago Bernardes worked in his father's office from 1991 to 1996, when he left to create his own firm, working on more than 30 residential projects between that date and 2001. With the death of his father, Thiago Bernardes reintegrated the firm and began to work with Paulo Jacobsen, who was born in 1954 in Rio de Janeiro. Jacobsen had studied photography in London, before graduating from the Bennett Methodist Institute in 1979. The office of Bernardes + Jacobsen currently employs approximately 50 people in Rio de Janeiro and São Paulo, and they work on roughly 40 projects per year. Some of their significant projects include the Gerdau Headquarters (Porto Alegre, 2005); the Villa Isabela (Henriksberg, Finland, 2005); the Hotel Leblon (Rio de Janeiro, 2005); the FW House (Guaruja, 2005); and the MPM Agency Main Office (São Paulo, 2006), all in Brazil unless stated otherwise. As well as the TIM Festival 2007 (Rio de Janeiro, 2007, published here), current work includes the Boa Vista Houses (São Paulo, 2007); Eco Resort Houses (Bahia, 2007), both in Brazil; the St. James Villa (St. James Island, Virgin Islands, 2007); and a number of residential projects.

Thiago Bernardes wurde 1974 in Rio de Janeiro geboren. Das Büro **BERNARDES + JACOBSEN** wurde 1980 von seinem Vater, Claudio Bernardes, und Paulo Jacobsen gegründet. Bernardes und Jacobsen gelten als Pioniere für einen neuen Typus von Wohnarchitektur, der darauf abzielt, zeitgenössisches Design und brasilianische Kultur miteinander zu kombinieren. Von 1992 bis 1996 arbeitete Thiago Bernardes in der Firma seines Vaters, um anschließend sein eigenes Büro zu gründen, das in den Jahren bis 2001 mehr als 30 Wohnhausprojekte umgesetzt hat. Nach dem Tod seines Vaters integrierte Thiago sein Büro in die väterliche Firma und begann seinerseits, mit dem 1954 in Rio de Janeiro geborenen Paulo Jacobsen zusammenzuarbeiten. Jacobsen hatte zunächst in London Fotografie studiert, ehe er am Instituto Metodista Bennett ein Studium aufnahm, das er 1979 abschloss. Das Büro Bernardes + Jacobsen beschäftigt derzeit rund 50 Mitarbeiter in Rio de Janeiro und São Paulo und arbeitet pro Jahr an etwa 40 verschiedenen Projekten. Zu ihren bedeutenden Arbeiten gehören der Hauptsitz des Gerdau-Konzerns in Porto Alegre (Brasilien, 2005), die Villa Isabela im finnischen Henriksberg (2005), das Hotel Leblon in Rio de Janeiro (Brasilien, 2005), das FW Haus in Guaruja (Brasilien, 2005) und das Hauptbüro der Agentur MPM in São Paulo (Brasilien, 2006). Jüngste Projekte neben den hier vorgestellten Bauten für das TIM Festival 2007 in Rio de Janeiro sind die Condomínios Boa Vista (São Paulo, Brasilien, 2007), Unterkünfte im Eco Resort (Bahia, Brasilien, 2007), die Villa St. James (St. James Island, Jungferninseln, 2007) sowie eine Reihe weiterer Wohnhausprojekte.

Thiago Bernardes est né à Rio de Janeiro en 1974. L'agence **BERNARDES + JACOBSEN** a été créée en 1980 par son père, Claudio Bernardes, et Paulo Jacobsen, pionniers d'un nouveau type d'architecture résidentielle reposant sur une volonté d'associer une conception d'esprit contemporain à la culture brésilienne. Thiago Bernardes a travaillé dans l'agence de son père de 1991 à 1996, puis a fondé sa propre structure, intervenant sur plus de 30 projets résidentiels de cette date à 2001. Après le décès de son père, il a réintégré l'agence et commencé à collaborer avec Paulo Jacobsen, né en 1954 à Rio de Janeiro. Jacobsen avait étudié la photographie à Londres, avant d'être diplômé du Bennett Methodist Institute en 1979. Bernardes + Jacobsen emploie actuellement une cinquantaine de personnes à Rio et São Paulo, qui travaillent sur une quarantaine de projets environ chaque année. Parmi leurs réalisations les plus significatives : le siège de Gerdau (Porto Alegre, 2005) ; la villa Isabela (Henriksberg, Finlande, 2005) ; l'Hotel Leblon (Rio de Janeiro, 2005) ; la maison FW (Guaruja, 2005) et le siège de l'agence MPM (São Paulo, 2006). Avec le TIM Festival 2007 (Rio de Janeiro, 2007, publié ici), ils ont récemment achevé les maisons Boa Vista (São Paulo, 2007) ; les maisons Eco Resort (Bahia, 2007) ; la villa St. James (St. James Island, Îles Vierges, 2007), et un certain nombre de projets résidentiels.

TIM FESTIVAL 2007
Rio de Janeiro, Rio de Janeiro, Brazil, 2007

*Floor area: 40 000 m². Client: TIM Festival.
Cost: not disclosed*

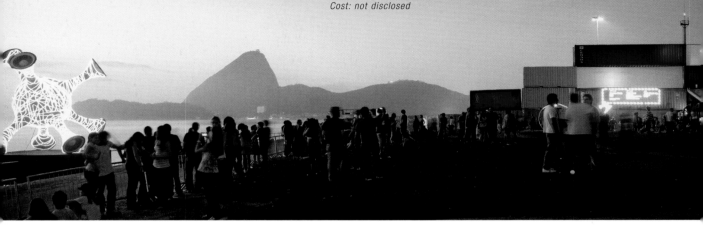

Overlooking the spectacular Bay of Guanabara, the festival buildings play on color and lights to animate the outdoor space.

Die Festivalbauten vor dem Panorama der eindrucksvollen Bucht von Guanabara beleben mit ihrem Farb- und Lichtspiel das Gelände.

Dominant la spectaculaire baie de Guanabara, les bâtiments du festival jouent sur la couleur et la lumière pour animer l'espace extérieur.

The architects were asked to design four tents that would shelter stages during a two-night music festival (October 26 and 27, 2007) that hosted such well-known singers as Cat Power, Feist, and Antony and the Johnsons. These modules were to have different sizes and be able to host rock, jazz, and electronic music at the same place. Although the architects found the limited budget, low cost, and short construction period daunting, they were attracted to a site at the tip of Roberto Burle Marx's Attero do Flamengo that offers views of the Bay of Guanabara, the famous Sugerloaf and the symbol of Rio, the Cristo Redentor sculpture. A series of more than 250 six- and 12-meter-long containers were assembled in one week, essentially in the form of a large wall. Some were used for restrooms, snack bars, and so on. For the rest of the wall, containers were selected by color, nationality, and their worn looks. Twelve-meter containers were used as doorways, signaling access to the stages, entries, and exits of the event. In the form of a large, sinuous curve, open to the sea, the highest part of the wall hid the 15-meter-high tents used for concerts. Spaces between the containers were used for video projections and stages for performances set at different levels. The facilities were assembled beginning on September 16, 2007, and had been fully dismantled by November 18. More than 23 000 people attended the two nights of concerts.

Anlässlich eines für den 26. und 27. Oktober 2007 geplanten Musikfestivals erhielten Bernardes + Jacobsen den Auftrag, vier Bühnenzelte für die Auftritte von Popgrößen wie Cat Power, Feist und Antony and the Johnsons zu entwerfen. Die Spielstätten sollten unterschiedliche Größen haben und die Möglichkeit bieten, sowohl Rock als auch Jazz oder elektronische Musik aufzuführen. Zwar mussten die Architekten mit einem erschreckend bescheidenen Budget und ebenso wenig Zeit auskommen, dafür waren sie fasziniert von dem Festivalstandort – am Rand des Attero do Flamengo von Roberto Burle Marx, von dem aus man die Guanabara-Bucht, den berühmten Zuckerhut und das Symbol von Rio, die Christussskulptur, überblickt. Innerhalb von einer Woche besorgten Bernardes + Jacobsen 250 Container von 6 und 12 m Länge, deren größerer Teil – sortiert nach Farbe, Herkunft und Abnutzungsgrad – zu einer großen Wand zusammengesetzt wurde. Einige der Container übernahmen die Funktion von Snackbars oder Toilettenräumen usw. Die großen Container dienten als Ein- und Ausgänge für das Veranstaltungsgelände und als Durchgänge zu den Bühnen. Hinter dem höchsten Teil der Wand, die sich in einem langen, geschwungenen Bogen zum Meer hin öffnete, standen 15 m hohe Konzertzelte. Zwischen einigen Containern wurden in unterschiedlicher Höhe Zwischenräume freigelassen, in denen Videoprojektionen und Performances zu sehen waren. Der Aufbau der Bauten begann am 16. September 2007, am 18. November war alles wieder komplett abgebaut. Mehr als 23 000 Besucher erlebten die beiden Konzertnächte.

La demande du client portait sur la conception de quatre tentes qui abriteraient des scènes pour un festival de musique durant deux nuits (les 26 et 17 octobre 2007) qui devait accueillir des chanteurs aussi connus que Cat Power, Feist ou Antony and the Johnsons. Ces modules de différentes tailles devaient pouvoir s'adapter à des groupes de rock, de jazz et de musique électronique. Si les architectes jugèrent le budget bien limité et les délais de construction très brefs, ils furent séduits par le site à la pointe du jardin Attero do Flamengo du paysagiste Roberto Burle Marx et des vues sur la baie de Guanabara, le célèbre Pain de Sucre et la statue du Christ rédempteur, symbole de Rio. Un ensemble de plus de 250 conteneurs de transport de six et douze mètres a été assemblé sur place en une semaine pour former une sorte de grand mur. Certains servaient de bars, d'autres de toilettes, etc. Sur le reste du mur, les conteneurs étaient disposés selon leurs couleurs, leur origine ou leur état. Des conteneurs de 12 mètres servirent de portes, signalant l'accès aux scènes, les entrées et les sorties. La partie supérieure du mur en courbe cachait les tentes de 15 mètres de haut utilisées pour les concerts. Des espaces aménagés entre ces éléments servaient d'écrans pour des projections vidéo ou de petites scènes à différents niveaux. Le montage avait commencé le 16 septembre 2007, et le démontage s'est achevé le 18 novembre. Plus de 23 000 personnes ont assisté aux deux nuits de concerts.

COOP HIMMELB(L)AU

Coop Himmelb(l)au
Wolf D. Prix / W. Dreibholz & Partner ZT GmbH
Spengergasse 37 / 1050 Vienna / Austria
Tel: +43 1 546 60 / Fax: +43 1 546 60-600
E-mail: office@coop-himmelblau.at / Web: www.coop-himmelblau.at

Wolf D. Prix, Helmut Swiczinsky, and Michael Holzer founded **COOP HIMMELB(L)AU** in 1968 in Vienna, Austria. Wolf D. Prix was born in 1942 in Vienna and educated at the Technische Universität, Vienna, at SCI-Arc, and at the Architectural Association (AA), London. Since 1993, he has been a Professor of Architecture at the University of Applied Arts in Vienna. From 1999 to 2003 he was Dean of Architecture, Industrial Design, Product Design, Fashion Design, and Stage Design at the same university. Helmut Swiczinsky, born in 1944 in Poznan, Poland, was raised in Vienna and educated at the Technische Universität, Vienna, and at the AA, London. He retired from the firm in 2006. Michael Holzer left the team in 1971. Wolfdieter Dreibholz, born in Vienna in 1941, received a degree in engineering and architecture from the Technische Universität in Vienna in 1966. He became CEO of Coop Himmelb(l)au Wolf D. Prix/W. Dreibholz & Partner ZT GmbH in 2004. Completed projects of the group include the east pavilion of the Groninger Museum (Groningen, The Netherlands, 1993–94); the UFA Cinema Center (Dresden, Germany, 1993–98); the SEG Apartment Tower (Vienna, Austria, 1994-98); and the Forum Arteplage for Expo '02 (Biel, Switzerland, 1999–2002), as well as the Academy of Fine Arts (Munich, Germany, 1992/2002–2005). Recent work includes BMW Welt (Munich, Germany, 2001–07, published here) and the Akron Art Museum (Akron, Ohio, 2001–07, published here). The office is currently working on the Central Los Angeles Area High School #9 for the Visual and Performing Arts (Los Angeles, 2002–08); the Musée des Confluences (Lyon, France, 2001–10); the European Central Bank (Frankfurt, Germany, 2003–11); and the Busan Cinema Center (Busan, South Korea, 2005–11).

COOP HIMMELB(L)AU wurde 1968 von Wolf D. Prix, Helmut Swiczinsky und Michael Holzer in Wien gegründet. Wolf D. Prix, geboren 1942 in Wien, studierte an der Technischen Universität Wien, am Southern California Institute of Architecture und an der Architectural Association (AA) in London. Seit 1993 ist er Professor für Architektur an der Universität für Angewandte Kunst Wien, an der er von 1999 bis 2003 das Amt des Studiendekans für die Fachbereiche Architektur, Industrial Design, Produktgestaltung, Mode und Bühnengestaltung bekleidete. Der 1944 in Posen, dem heute polnischen Poznan, geborene Helmut Swiczinsky wuchs in Wien auf und studierte an der dortigen Technischen Universität sowie an der AA in London; 2006 zog er sich aus dem Büro Coop Himmelb(l)au zurück. Michael Holzer verließ das Team 1971. Wolfdieter Dreibholz, geboren 1941 in Wien, erwarb 1966 sein Ingenieursdiplom mit Schwerpunkt Architektur an der Technischen Universität Wien. 2004 wurde er Geschäftsführer der Coop Himmelb(l)au Wolf D. Prix/W. Dreibholz & Partner ZT GmbH. Zu den realisierten Projekten des Büros gehören der Ostpavillon des Groninger Museums (Groningen, Niederlande, 1993–94), den UFA-Kinopalast in Dresden (1993–98), der SEG-Wohnturm in Wien (1994–98) und das Forum Arteplage für die Expo '02 im schweizerischen Biel (1999–2002). Aus jüngerer Zeit stammen die Akademie der bildenden Künste München (1992/2002–05), die hier vorgestellte BMW Welt in München (2001–07) und das ebenfalls hier präsentierte Akron Art Museum (Akron, Ohio, 2001–07). Zurzeit arbeitet das Büro an der Central Los Angeles Area High School #9 (einer Schule mit Schwerpunkt bildende und darstellende Kunst) in Los Angeles (2002–08), dem Musée des Confluences in Lyon (2001–10), dem Neubau für die Europäische Zentralbank in Frankfurt (2003–11) und Busan Cinema Center in Südkorea (2005–11).

Wolf D. Prix, Helmut Swiczinsky et Michael Holzer ont fondé **COOP HIMMELB(L)AU** à Vienne (Autriche) en 1968. Wolf D. Prix est né à Vienne en 1942 et a étudié à la Technische Universität de Vienne, au Southern Califonia Institute of Architecture (SCI-Arc) et à l'Architectural Association de Londres (AA). Il est professeur d'architecture à l'université des Arts appliqués de Vienne. De 1999 à 2003, il a été doyen d'architecture, de design industriel, design produit, mode et scénographie de la même université. Helmut Swiczinsky est né en 1944 à Poznan, Pologne, mais a été élevé à Vienne et a étudié à la Technische Universität de cette ville ainsi qu'à l'AA de Londres. Il a quitté l'agence en 2006. Michael Holzer a quitté l'équipe en 1971. Wolfdieter Dreibholz, né à Vienne en 1941, est diplômé d'ingénierie et d'architecture à la Technische Universität de Vienne (1966). Il a pris la direction de la Coop Himmelb(l)au Wolf D. Prix/ W. Dreibholz & Partner ZT GmbH. Parmi les réalisations du groupe : le pavillon est du musée de Groningue (Pays-Bas, 1993–94) ; le complexe de salles de cinéma UFA (Dresde, Allemagne, 1993–98) ; la tour d'appartements SEG (Vienne, Autriche, 1994–98) et le Forum Arteplage pour Expo '02 (Biel, Suisse, 1999-2002). Ils ont récemment construit l'Académie des Beaux-Arts (Munich, Allemagne, 1992/2002–05) ; BMW Welt (Munich, Allemagne, 2001–07, publié ici) et l'Akron Art Museum (Akron, Ohio, 2001–07, publié ici). Actuellement, ils travaillent sur la Central Los Angeles Area High School #9 for the Visual and Performing Arts (Los Angeles, Californie, 2002–08) ; le projet du Musée des Confluences (Lyon, France, 2001–10) ; la Banque Centrale Européenne (Francfort, Allemagne, 2003–11) et un complexe de salles de cinéma à Busan (Corée du Sud, 2005–11).

AKRON ART MUSEUM

Akron, Ohio, USA, 2001–07

Site area: 8370 m². Floor area: 6045 m². Client: Akron Art Museum. Cost: $20 million.
Principal in Charge: Wolf D. Prix. Project Partner: Michael Volk. Project Architect: Angus Schoenberger.
Design Team: Wolf D. Prix (principal), Tom Wiscombe, Mona Marbach. Project Team: Florian Pfeifer, Mona Bayr, Marcelo Bernardi, Philip Vogt,
Dan Narita, Lorenz Bürgi, Daniela Kobel, Mohamed Fezazi, Robert Haranza, Dionicio Valdez. Executive Architect: Westlake, Reed,
Leskosky, Cleveland, Ohio. Partner in Charge: Ron Reed. Project Director: Rich Keilmann

Winners of a 2001 competition for this project, the architects state: "The concept of museums has changed radically since the cabinet of curiosities ("Wunderkammer") of Rudolf II and Ferdinand II in the 16th century. The museum of today is no longer conceived only as an institution for the storage and display of knowledge, it is an urban concept. The museum of the future is a three-dimensional sign in the city that exhibits the content of our visual world. Museums are no longer only exhibition spaces to display diverse forms of digital and analog visual information, but they also function as spaces that cater to urban experiences." The design of the new building is divided into three parts, called the Crystal, the Gallery Box, and the Roof Cloud. The entrance and orientation space between the new and old buildings is the Crystal. Great care has been taken to design the Crystal in an environmentally responsible way, notably directing climate control to areas where people congregate. The Gallery Box has poured-in-place concrete floors with an efficient radiant heating system and is relatively column free and "flexible." As the architects conclude, "The Roof Cloud, which hovers above the building, creates a blurred envelope for the museum because of its sheer mass and materiality. It encloses interior space, provides shade for exterior spaces, and operates as a horizontal landmark in the city."

Zum vorliegenden Projekt, mit dem sie 2001 den Wettbewerb für einen Erweiterungsbau des Akron Art Museum gewannen, erklären Coop Himmelb(l)au: „Seit den im 16. Jahrhundert von Rudolf II. und Ferdinand II. eingerichteten Kunst- und Wunderkammern haben sich die Vorstellungen davon, was ein Museum ausmacht, von Grund auf geändert. Ist das Museum von heute kein bloßer Ort des Wissens mehr, sondern ein städtisches Konzept – so stellt das Museum der Zukunft ein dreidimensionales urbanes Zeichen dar, das die Inhalte unserer Bilderwelt kommuniziert. Es ist kein bloßer Schauraum mehr, in dem auf verschiedenste Weise digitale und analoge visuelle Informationen geboten werden, sondern ein auf urbanes Erleben ausgerichteter Ort." Der Entwurf für das neue Gebäude besteht aus drei verschiedenen Teilen: dem „Kristall", der „Galerienbox" und der „Dachwolke". Besondere Aufmerksamkeit wurde auf eine umweltbewusste Gestaltung gelegt. Bei dem Kristall, der den Übergangs- und Orientierungsbereich zwischen dem alten und dem neuen Gebäude bildet, lassen sich einzelne Aufenthaltszonen durch ein ausgeklügeltes Klimatisierungssystem gezielt beheizen oder kühlen. Die Galerienbox zeichnet sich durch Ortbetonbodenplatten aus, in die ein effizientes Radiatorensystem eingebaut wurde, und ist aufgrund nur weniger Säulen flexibel nutzbar. „Die über dem Gebäude schwebende ‚Dachwolke'", so die Architekten, „schafft dank ihrer Masse und Materialität eine verschwommene Hülle für das Museum. Sie umschließt den Innenraum, beschattet verschiedene Außenräume und fungiert als ein horizontales Wahrzeichen der Stadt."

Ce projet avait remporté un concours organisé en 2001. Selon les architectes: «Le concept de musée a radicalement changé depuis les Wunderkammer de Rudolf II et Ferdinand II au XVIe siècle. Le musée d'aujourd'hui n'est plus conçu seulement comme une institution pour conserver et exposer les connaissances, c'est un concept urbain. Le musée du futur est un signe tridimensionnel dans la ville qui expose le contenu de notre monde plastique. Les musées ne sont plus seulement des espaces d'expositions destinés à présenter différentes formes d'information visuelle analogique ou numérisée, mais fonctionnent également comme des espaces qui nourrissent l'expérience urbaine.» Le nouveau bâtiment est divisé en trois parties: le Cristal, la Boîte-Galerie et le Nuage sur le toit. L'entrée et l'espace d'accueil et d'orientation entre le nouveau bâtiment et l'ancien passent par le Cristal. Une grande attention a été portée au respect des contraintes environnementales, en orientant notamment la climatisation sur les zones où se retrouvent les visiteurs. La Boîte-Galerie aux différents niveaux en béton possède un chauffage radiant efficace et se présente comme un espace «souple», pratiquement sans colonnes. L'agence conclut: «Le Nuage sur le toit, qui surplombe l'immeuble, crée par sa masse et sa matérialité une enveloppe floue. Il enferme un volume, apporte de l'ombre à l'extérieur et fonctionne comme un signal pour la ville.»

The cantilevered, tilted volumes of the building give it a dynamic appearance that recalls earlier work by the firm, here updated and adapted to the circumstances of the site.

Die auskragenden und geneigten Gebäudeteile verleihen dem Museum eine dynamische Wirkung, die an frühere Arbeiten der Architekten erinnert, hier freilich auf neuestem Stand und an die Erfordernisse des Grundstücks angepasst.

Inclinés et en porte-à-faux, les volumes du musée lui confèrent une apparence dynamique qui rappelle certaines réalisations antérieures de l'agence, ici actualisées et adaptées aux contraintes du lieu.

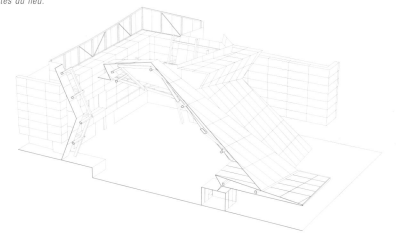

Seen at night and during the day,
the main structure seems to float
above its base, glowing from within
after dark.

Tags wie nachts scheint der Hauptkörper des Gebäudes über seiner
Basis zu schweben, die nach Einbruch
der Dunkelheit von innen heraus
leuchtet.

De nuit comme de jour, la structure
principale semble flotter au-dessus
de sa base, éclairée de l'intérieur
à la tombée de la nuit.

Like wings hovering over the older building of the museum, the spectacular shape of the museum is compared to that of an airliner or the Goodyear Blimp in the drawings below.

Wie Flügel schweben über dem älteren Museumsteil die Ausläufer des Neubaus, dessen spektakuläre Form man mit der eines Flugzeugs oder Luftschiffs vergleichen könnte, wie in den Zeichnungen unten zu sehen.

Se déployant comme des ailes au-dessus de l'ancien bâtiment, les formes spectaculaires du musée rappellent celles d'un avion de ligne ou du dirigeable Goodyear, montrées dans les dessins ci-dessous.

230 f

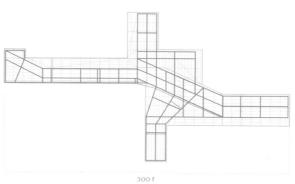

300 f

192 f

An angled concrete volume contrasts with the glass and metal superstructure of the building. Ample natural light floods these public spaces.

Ein verwinkelter Betonkörper bildet einen Kontrast zur Überbaukonstruktion aus Stahl und Glas. Die Besucherbereiche werden von natürlichem Licht durchflutet.

Un volume incliné en béton contraste avec la structure de métal et de verre du bâtiment. La lumière naturelle inonde ces espaces publics.

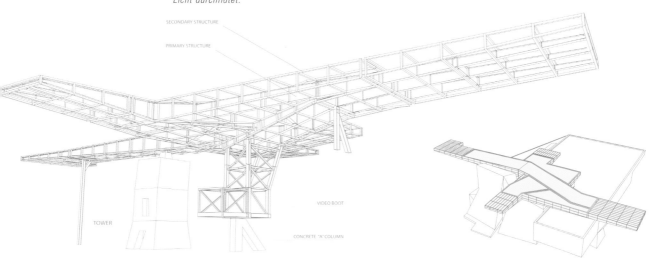

SECONDARY STRUCTURE

PRIMARY STRUCTURE

TOWER

VIDEO BOOT

CONCRETE "A" COLUMN

The cantilever effects seen in the exterior volumes are here echoed in the interior, allowing visitors to see the space from a number of different angles.

Auch im Gebäudeinneren finden sich auskragende Elemente, von denen aus die Besucher den Raum aus verschiedensten Perspektiven betrachten können.

Les effets de porte-à-faux remarqués dans les volumes extérieurs se retrouvent en écho à l'intérieur, permettant aux visiteurs de percevoir l'espace sous différents angles.

BMW WELT

Munich, Germany, 2001–07

Site area: 25 000 m². Floor area: 73 000 m² (excluding ramps). Client: BMW AG. Cost: over € 100 million.
Principal in Charge: Wolf D. Prix. Project Architect: Paul Kath.
Design Team: Wolf D. Prix (principal), Tom Wiscombe, Paul Kath, Waltraut Hohenender, Mona Marbach.
Partial Project Architects: Günther Weber, Penelope Rüttimann, Renate Weissenböck, Mona Marbach, Verena Perius

This building consists of seven floors: three above grade and four below. The underground area (44 500 m²) exceeds the space above grade (28 500 m²). The architects won a 2001 competition and began planning in November of 2001. Construction started in August 2003 and the building was inaugurated on October 20, 2007. Some 850 000 visitors per year are expected. The design is made up of five thematic blocks: Hall, Premiere, Forum, Tower, and Double Cone. Mechanical apparatus for ventilation was minimized in this gathering space. A natural air supply is generated by thermal currents. The Premiere area, open to the Hall, is devoted to the delivery of 40 cars per hour or 250 per day. The Forum is an event area for up to 1200 people in either a theater or a conference room. The Tower is for gastronomic functions, while the Double Cone is an event or exhibition space. The structure is supported by just 11 columns plus the elevator shafts, requiring close collaboration in the planning phase between the architects, structural engineers, and facility services. This structure, one of the most ambitious to be completed by the architects, was described by Wolf D. Prix in these terms: "The concept behind the design envisions a hybrid building representing a mixture of urban elements. Not an exhibition hall, not an information and communication center, not a museum, but instead all of these things, along a passage organized under one roof, and horizontally and vertically layered. A conjoining of urban marketplace and stage for presentations."

Die BMW Welt besteht aus sieben Geschossen, drei davon – insgesamt 44 500 m² – über der Erde, die übrigen vier mit insgesamt 28 500 m² unterirdisch. Nach dem Wettbewerbsentscheid für ihren Entwurf 2001 begannen die Architekten im November des Jahres mit der Bauplanung. Baubeginn war im August 2003, eröffnet wurde das Gebäude am 20. Oktober 2007. Es wird mit einer jährlichen Besucherzahl von rund 850 000 gerechnet. Der Entwurf setzt sich aus fünf thematischen Blöcken zusammen: Halle, Premiere, Forum, Turm und Doppelkegel. Auf mechanische Klimatisierung wurde weitgehend verzichtet, die Frischluftversorgung erfolgt auf thermischem Weg. Der zur Halle hin geöffnete Premiere-Bereich ist auf die Auslieferung von 40 Autos pro Stunde, insgesamt 250 Einheiten täglich, ausgelegt. Das Forum bietet, wahlweise als Vortragssaal oder Konferenzraum, Platz für Veranstaltungen mit bis zu 1200 Teilnehmern. Im Turm sind Gastronomiebereiche untergebracht, der Doppelkegel dient als Event- und Ausstellungsareal. Die gesamte Konstruktion wird von nur elf Stützen sowie den Aufzugsschächten getragen, was in der Planungsphase eine enge Zusammenarbeit von Architekten, Statikern und Gebäudetechnikern erforderlich machte. Wolf D. Prix beschrieb das Bauwerk, eines der anspruchsvollsten Projekte seines Büros, mit den Worten: „Das Konzept des Entwurfs sieht ein hybrides Gebäude vor, das eine Mischung aus urbanen Elementen darstellt. Nicht eine Ausstellungshalle, nicht ein Informations- und Kommunikationszentrum, nicht ein Museum: sondern alles zusammen, entlang einer Passage unter einem Dach organisiert und horizontal und vertikal geschichtet. Eine Verschränkung von urbanem Marktplatz und einer Bühne für Präsentation."

Ce vaste bâtiment compte sept niveaux, dont quatre en sous-sol. La partie souterraine de 44 500 m² est plus importante que la partie extérieure (28 500 m²). Après avoir remporté le concours en 2001, les architectes en ont commencé la programmation détaillée dès novembre de la même année. Le chantier a débuté en 2003 et l'inauguration s'est déroulée le 20 octobre 2007. Quelque 850 000 visiteurs sont attendus chaque année. Le projet se compose de cinq blocs thématiques : Hall, Premiere, Forum, Tour et Double Cône. La ventilation artificielle a été minimisée. La fourniture d'air naturel est assurée par les courants thermiques. La zone Premiere, ouverte sur le Hall, est consacrée à la livraison de 40 voitures par heure ou 250 par jour. Le Forum est un espace pour recevoir des événements, équipé d'un amphithéâtre de 1200 places. La Tour est réservée à la restauration. Le Double Cône est lui aussi prévu pour accueillir des événements ou des expositions. La structure est soutenue par 11 colonnes et les cages des escaliers mécaniques, ce qui a demandé une coopération étroite entre l'agence, les ingénieurs structurels et les bureaux d'études. Ce projet, l'un de plus ambitieux jamais réalisés par Coop Himmelb(l)au, a été décrit en ces termes par Wolf D. Prix : « Le concept majeur est celui d'un bâtiment hybride composé d'un mélange d'éléments urbains. Ce n'est pas un hall d'exposition, ni un centre d'information et de communication, ni un musée, mais un long passage organisé en strates verticales et horizontales sous un même toit. Un lieu commercial urbain qui est en même temps une scène. »

Contrasting glass and metal cladding, the spiraling tower of the complex evokes movement and the sense of excitement sought by the car manufacturer in its products.

Der sich in die Höhe schraubende Doppelkegel mit den kontrastierenden Glas- und Metallverkleidungen verkörpert eine ebensolche Dynamik und Spannung, wie sie der Autobauer bei seinen Produkten anstrebt.

Par ses habillages de verre et de métal contrastés, la tour en spirale du complexe évoque le mouvement, et provoque le sentiment d'excitation recherché par le constructeur automobile dans ses produits.

Seen at night, the twisting volume of the tower is emblematic of the entire complex, conveying a sense of frozen movement.

Nachts erweckt der verdrehte Turm als Sinnbild der gesamten Anlage den Eindruck einer eingefrorenen Bewegung.

Vu la nuit, le volume tors de la tour est l'emblème du complexe tout entier. Il exprime une sorte de mouvement gelé dans l'espace.

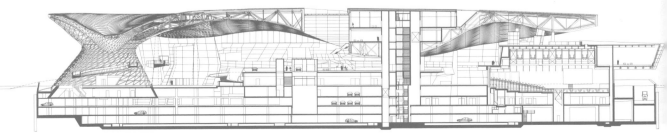

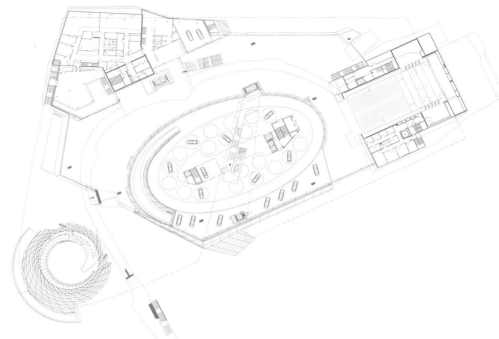

Seen in plan, the building contrasts relatively basic geometric forms with the visible complexity of its elevations or sections.

Den im Grundriss erkennbaren, relativ einfachen geometrischen Grundformen des Gebäudes stehen deutlich komplexere Aufrisse bzw. Schnitte gegenüber.

Vu en plan, le bâtiment fait contraster ses formes géométriques relativement basiques et la complexité visible de ses élévations et de ses coupes.

Sky bridges and volumes that penetrate each other in unexpected ways
contribute to the overall impression
of innovation and excitement that
characterizes BMW Welt.

Freischwebende Brücken und Gebäudeteile, die sich überraschend
durchdringen, tragen zu dem von
Innovation und Dynamik bestimmten
Gesamteindruck der BMW Welt bei.

Des coursives suspendues et des
volumes qui s'interpènètrent de façon
surprenante contribuent à donner une
impression générale d'innovation et
de passion pour l'automobile.

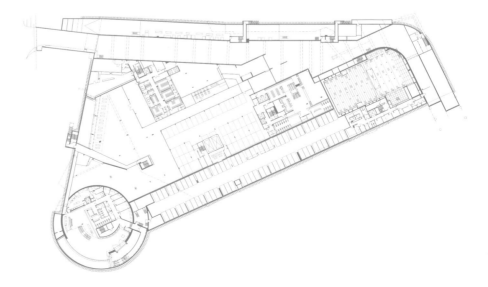

Interior spaces, intended for the display of automobiles, continue the theme of sweeping movement defined by the exterior curves and regenerated within in the images visible here like variations on a theme.

In den Vorführhallen für die Wagen setzen sich die von den äußeren Gebäuderundungen vorgegebenen schwungvollen Bewegungen fort wie die Variationen zu einem Thema.

Dans ces images, les volumes intérieurs conçus pour la présentation des voitures, reprennent les amples mouvements définis par les courbes des façades extérieures, telles des variations sur un même thème.

Where daunting architectural complexity could be a hindrance to the building's function, here, there is an almost airy lightness in the forms that sweep over the display areas.

Steht architektonische Komplexität oftmals der Funktionalität eines Gebäudes entgegen, sorgen die Formen hier für eine besondere Leichtigkeit der Vorführbereiche.

Alors que cette complexité architecturale aurait pu aller à l'encontre de la fonction du bâtiment, on est frappé par la légèreté presque aérienne des formes dans les zones d'exposition.

The powerful spiral forms of the tower impart a sensation of perpetual movement to the architecture, bringing forth thoughts of the shapes of nature, in storms or whirlpools, for example.

Die dynamischen Spiralformen des Doppelkegels sorgen für eine konstante Bewegung in der Gebäudearchitektur und lassen an Formen aus der Natur denken, etwa an Wirbelstürme oder Strudel.

La puissante spirale de la tour crée la sensation d'une architecture en mouvement perpétuel, et rappelle certaines formes de la nature comme par exemple les tempêtes ou les tourbillons.

OLAFUR ELIASSON

Studio Olafur Eliasson
Christinenstr. 18/19, Haus 2 / 10119 Berlin / Germany
E-mail: studio@olafureliasson.net / Web: www.olafureliasson.net

OLAFUR ELIASSON was born in 1967 in Copenhagen, Denmark, of Icelandic parents. He attended the Royal Danish Academy of Fine Arts in Copenhagen (1989–95). Early in his career he moved to Germany, establishing Studio Olafur Eliasson in Berlin. Eliasson lives and works in Copenhagen and Berlin, and Studio Olafur Eliasson is an experimental laboratory based in Berlin. It functions as an interdisciplinary space, generating dialogues between art and its surroundings. Eliasson has participated in numerous exhibitions and his work is included in collections ranging from the Solomon R. Guggenheim Museum, New York; the Museum of Contemporary Art, Los Angeles; the Deste Foundation, Athens; to the Tate Modern, London. He has had solo exhibitions at the Kunsthaus Bregenz, the Musée d'Art Moderne de la Ville de Paris and the ZKM in Karlsruhe, and represented Denmark in the 2003 Venice Biennale. More recent solo exhibitions include "Your Tempo: Olafur Eliasson," and "Take Your Time: Olafur Eliasson," both at the San Francisco Museum of Modern Art (San Francisco, California, 2007–08). His installations feature elements appropriated from nature—billowing steam evoking a water geyser, rainbows, fog-filled rooms, or water, as in *The New York City Waterfalls* (New York, New York, 2008, published here). By introducing "natural" phenomena, such as water, mist, or light, into an artificial setting, the artist encourages viewers to reflect on their perception of the physical world. This moment of perception, when viewers pause to consider what they are experiencing, has been described by Eliasson as "seeing yourself sensing." For the Icelandic National Concert and Conference Center in Reykjavik the artist has created the outer shell. The building, to be finished in 2009, is in collaboration with Henning Larsen Architects.

OLAFUR ELIASSON, geboren 1967 in Kopenhagen als Sohn isländischer Eltern, besuchte ebendort von 1989 bis 1995 die Königlich Dänische Kunstakademie. Noch zu Beginn seines Schaffens zog Eliasson nach Berlin, wo er das Studio Olafur Eliasson gründete, das sich als experimentelles Labor versteht. Der Künstler lebt und arbeitet heute in Kopenhagen und Berlin. Als interdisziplinärer Raum setzt es Dialoge zwischen Kunst und ihrer Umgebung in Gang. Eliasson hat an zahlreichen Ausstellungen teilgenommen, seine Arbeiten sind in den Sammlungen namhafter Museen vom Solomon R. Guggenheim Museum in New York oder dem Museum of Contemporary Art in Los Angeles über die Deste Foundation in Athen bis hin zur Londoner Tate Modern vertreten. Das Kunsthaus Bregenz, das Musée d'Art Moderne de la Ville de Paris und das ZKM Karlsruhe veranstalteten Einzelausstellungen. 2003 nahm Eliasson als Vertreter Dänemarks an der Biennale von Venedig teil. In jüngerer Zeit fanden am San Francisco Museum of Modern Art in Kalifornien die Soloschauen „Your Tempo: Olafur Eliasson" und „Take Your Time: Olafur Eliasson" statt (2007–08). In Eliassons Installationen geht es um die Aneignung von Elementen, die man aus der Natur kennt – Dampfschwaden, die an einen Geysir erinnern, Regenbögen, nebelgefüllte Räume oder schlicht Wasser, wie bei den hier vorgestellten „New York City Waterfalls" (New York, 2008). Indem er „natürliche" Phänomene wie Wasser, Nebel oder Licht in einen künstlichen Rahmen stellt, lädt der Künstler die Betrachter dazu ein, über ihre Wahrnehmung der physischen Welt nachzudenken. Das daraus resultierende Wahrnehmungsmoment – wenn ein Betrachter innehält und darüber nachdenkt, was er gerade erlebt – hat Eliasson als „seeing yourself sensing" (etwa: sich beim Wahrnehmen zusehen) – bezeichnet. Für das isländische Nationale Konzert- und Konferenzzentrum in Reykjavik hat der Künstler die äußere Hülle entworfen. Das Veranstaltungsgebäude, das 2009 vollendet sein soll, entstand in Zusammenarbeit mit dem Architekturbüro Henning Larsen.

OLAFUR ELIASSON est né en 1967 à Copenhague, Danemark, de parents islandais. Il a étudié à l'Académie royale des arts à Copenhague (1989–95). Très tôt dans sa carrière, il s'est installé en Allemagne où il a créé son atelier à Berlin, le Studio Olafur Eliasson, laboratoire expérimental et espace interdisciplinaire qui pratique un dialogue entre l'art et l'environnement. L'artiste vit actuellement a Copenhague et Berlin. Eliasson a participé à de nombreuses expositions et ses œuvres font partie de grandes collections allant du Solomon R. Guggenheim Museum de New York, au Museum of Contemporary Art de Los Angeles, de la fondation Deste à Athènes à la Tate Modern à Londres. Il a été l'objet d'expositions personnelles à la Kunsthaus Bregenz, au musée d'Art moderne de la Ville de Paris et au ZKM de Karlsruhe, et a représenté le Danemark à la Biennale de Venise en 2003. Plus récemment, il a organisé deux expositions au San Francisco Museum of Modern Art (San Francisco, Californie, 2007–08) : « Your Tempo : Olafur Eliasson » et « Take Your Time : Olafur Eliasson ». Ses installations utilisent des éléments tirés de la nature : de la vapeur évoquant un geyser, des arcs-en-ciel, des salles remplies de brouillard ou d'eau comme dans les *New York City Waterfalls* (New York, 2008, publiées ici). En introduisant « des phénomènes naturels comme l'eau, le brouillard ou la lumière dans un cadre artificiel, l'artiste encourage les spectateurs à réfléchir sur leur perception du monde physique ». Ce moment de perception, lorsque le spectateur s'arrête pour comprendre ce qu'il est en train d'expérimenter, est décrit par Eliasson comme « se voir en train de ressentir ». Pour le Centre national islandais de concerts et de conférences à Reykjavik l'artiste a créé la coque extérieure. Le bâtiment, achevé en 2009, est réalisé en collaboration avec Henning Larsen Architects.

THE NEW YORK CITY WATERFALLS

New York, New York, USA, June 26–October 13, 2008

Height: 30 to 40 m. Presented by the Public Art Fund, in collaboration with the City of New York.
Cost: $15 million

Announced on January 26, 2008, by Michael Bloomberg, the Mayor of New York, *The New York City Waterfalls* were described by Susan K. Freedman, the President of the Public Art Fund, a non-profit organization that commissioned the installation, as "the most ambitious project the Public Art Fund has ever undertaken and, I dare say, the city has ever seen." The four Waterfalls were located in the East River—one on the Brooklyn anchorage under Brooklyn Bridge, another between Piers 4 and 5 in Brooklyn, one in Lower Manhattan at Pier 35, and one on Governors Island. The 30- to 40-meter-high installations, consisting of scaffolding, pumps that will send more than 132 000 liters of water a minute down each structure, and hoses, are related to Eliasson's previous works: *Waterfall* 1998, *Reversed waterfall* 1998, and *Waterfall* 2004. Officials of the City of New York estimated that more than 85 000 tourists were drawn to visit between mid-July and mid-October only because of the installation. Private funding included a contribution by Bloomberg LP, an information services company belonging to the Mayor.

Am 26. Januar 2008 gab der New Yorker Bürgermeister Michael Bloomberg die Umsetzung von Olafur Eliassons Projektidee zu *The New York City Waterfalls* bekannt. Susan K. Freedman, die Präsidentin des gemeinnützigen Public Art Fund, beschreibt die von ihrer Organisation in Auftrag gegebene Installation als „das ehrgeizigste Projekt, das der Public Art Fund jemals in Angriff genommen hat, und, so möchte ich behaupten, sogar das ehrgeizigste, das die Stadt New York jemals gesehen hat." Die vier Wasserfälle wurden direkt im East River installiert – einer am Ankerpfeiler unter der Brooklyn Bridge, einer zwischen den Piers 4 und 5 in Brooklyn, einer in Lower Manhattan am Pier 35 und einer bei Governors Island. Mit seinen 30 bis 40 m hohen, aus Gerüsten, Schläuchen und Pumpen bestehenden Installationen, die mehr als 132 000 l Wasser pro Minute in den Fluss stürzen lassen, nimmt Eliasson den Faden früherer Arbeiten, *Waterfall* 1998, *Reversed waterfall* 1998 und *Waterfall* 2004, auf. Vertreter der Stadt New York rechneten im Vorfeld damit, dass die Installationen von Mitte Juli bis Mitte Oktober mehr als 85 000 zusätzliche Besucher anziehen würden. Zu den privaten Sponsoren des Projekts gehört auch das vom derzeitigen Bürgermeister gegründete Nachrichtenunternehmen Bloomberg L. P.

Annoncées le 26 janvier 2008 par Michael Bloomberg, maire de New York, *The New York City Waterfalls* ont été décrites par Susan K. Freedman, présidente du Public Art Fund, organisme à but non lucratif commanditaire de l'installation, comme « le plus ambitieux projet que le Public Art Fund ait jamais financé… et même que la ville ait jamais vu ». Ces quatre cascades sont situées dans l'East River : la première au mouillage de Brooklyn, sous le pont, la seconde entre les jetées 4 et 5 à Brooklyn, la troisième dans le bas-Manhattan, sur la jetée 35, et la dernière sur Governors Island. Ces installations de 30 à 40 mètres de haut sont constituées d'éléments d'échafaudage, de tuyaux et de pompes qui projettent plus de 132 000 litres d'eau par minute. Elles sont inspirées d'œuvres antérieures de l'artiste : *Waterfall* 1998, *Reversed Waterfall* 1998 et *Waterfall* 2004. La ville de New York a estimé à plus de 85 000 le nombre de touristes venus entre la mi-juillet et la mi-octobre découvrir ces installations. Le financement privé a bénéficié d'une contribution de Bloomberg LP, une société de services d'information propriété du maire.

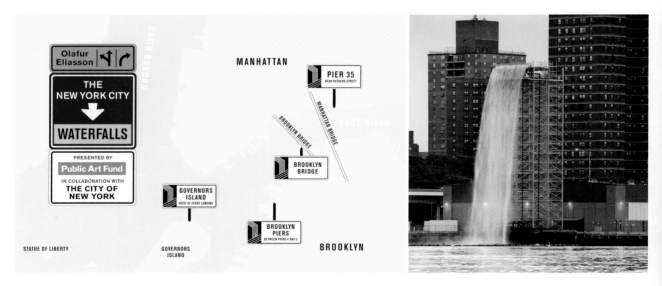

Eliasson's waterfalls have been created in four different locations in New York. The idea of a waterfall descending from the sky elicits the rapport between art and nature seen in earlier works by the artist.

Die Abbildungen zeigen Eliassons Wasserfälle, die an vier verschiedenen Standorten in New York installiert wurden. Der Wasserfall, der sich aus dem Himmel ergießt, hebt auf ein enges Verhältnis zwischen Kunst und Natur ab.

Les cascades d'Eliasson, aménagées dans quatre lieux new-yorkais différents, sont présentées ici en images. L'idée de cascade tombant du ciel éclaire le rapport entre l'art et la nature.

SERPENTINE GALLERY PAVILION 2007

Kensington Gardens, London, UK, 2007

Floor area: 500 m². Height: 15 m.
Cost: not disclosed. Design: Olafur Eliasson, Kjetil Thorsen

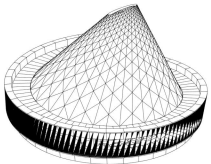

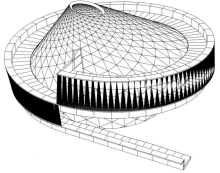

The essential pattern developed by the structure is that of a rising spiral—quite unusual in these circumstances, the form gives an impression that it could rise up in the air.

Das bestimmende Element der Konstruktion ist eine sich emporschraubende Spirale, die erstaunlicherweise den Eindruck erzeugt, das Gebilde könne sich in die Luft erheben.

Le motif de base de la construction est une spirale ascendante. Assez curieuse dans ce cadre, cette forme donne l'impression de pouvoir s'envoler dans les airs.

The Serpentine Gallery, specialized in temporary exhibitions of contemporary art, has built summer pavilions for eight years with such outstanding architects as Toyo Ito, Oscar Niemeyer, and, in 2006, Rem Koolhaas with Cecil Balmond. Olafur Eliasson collaborated with the Norwegian architect Kjetil Thorsen, of the architectural practice Snøhetta, on the 2007 Pavilion. Made up of a steel structural frame clad in painted plywood and a cantilevered walkway, the pavilion featured a timber ramp that spiraled twice around the periphery, rising from the lawn to a high point, offering visitors a view of Kensington Gardens. As Eliasson and Thorsen describe it, "Based on the principle of a winding ramp, the *Serpentine Gallery Pavilion 2007* explores the idea of vertical circulation within a single space. The aim is to reconsider the traditional, single-level pavilion structure by adding a third dimension: height. The vertical movement of visitors in the Pavilion will complement the horizontal circulation in the exhibition spaces at the adjacent Serpentine Gallery." Olafur Eliasson concludes, "The spiraling form is less about form for its own sake and more about how people move within space."

Im Jahr 2000 hat die auf temporäre Ausstellungen zeitgenössischer Kunst spezialisierte Serpentine Gallery begonnen, jedes Jahr von einem namhaften Architekten einen Sommerpavillon errichten zu lassen, so bisher u. a. von Toyo Ito, Oscar Niemeyer und 2006 von Rem Koolhaas und Cecil Balmond. Den Pavillon des Jahres 2007 entwarf Olafur Eliasson in Zusammenarbeit mit dem norwegischen Architekten Kjetil Thorsen vom Architekturbüro Snøhetta. Das Auffälligste an der mit lackiertem Furnierholz verkleideten Stahlrahmenkonstruktion war die hölzerne Rampe, die sich vom Rasen aus zweimal um die Außenseite bis zum höchsten Punkt hinaufschlängelte, von dem aus die Besucher Kensington Gardens überschauen konnten. Eliasson und Thorsen erklären dazu: „Anhand der sich aufwärts windenden Rampe erkundet der *Serpentine Gallery Pavilion 2007* den Gedanken eines vertikalen Bewegungsstroms in einem einzelnen Raum. Dahinter steht die Absicht, die traditionell eingeschossige Pavillonstruktur infrage zu stellen, indem man eine dritte Dimension – die Höhe – hinzufügt. Die vertikale Bewegung der Pavillonbesucher bildet das Gegenstück zum horizontalen Rundgang in den Ausstellungsräumen der benachbarten Serpentine Gallery." Eliasson führt den Gedanken zu Ende: „Bei der Spirale steht weniger die Form um ihrer selbst willen im Vordergrund als die Frage, wie sich Menschen im Raum bewegen."

La Serpentine Gallery, qui est consacrée à des expositions temporaires d'art contemporain, édifie chaque année depuis huit ans un nouveau pavillon d'été confié à des architectes comme Toyo Ito, Oscar Niemeyer et, en 2006, Rem Koolhaas et Cecil Balmond. Olafur Eliasson a collaboré avec l'architecte norvégien Kjetil Thorsen, de l'agence Snøhetta, sur le projet 2007. Doté d'une ossature en acier habillée de panneaux de contreplaqué peint et entourée d'une coursive en porte-à-faux, le pavillon se caractérise par une rampe en bois qui en fait deux fois le tour, s'élevant de la pelouse jusqu'à son sommet pour offrir aux visiteurs une vue sur Kensington Gardens. Pour Eliasson et Thorsen : «Parti de l'idée d'une rampe sinueuse, le *Serpentine Gallery Pavilion 2007* explore le concept de circulation verticale dans un espace unique. L'objectif est de reconsidérer la structure traditionnelle à un seul niveau d'un pavillon pour lui ajouter une troisième dimension : la hauteur. Le mouvement vertical des visiteurs vient en complément de la circulation horizontale dans les espaces d'expositions de la Serpentine Gallery adjacente. » Olafur Eliasson conclut : «La spirale est moins un exercice sur la forme en tant que telle que sur le déplacement des visiteurs dans l'espace. »

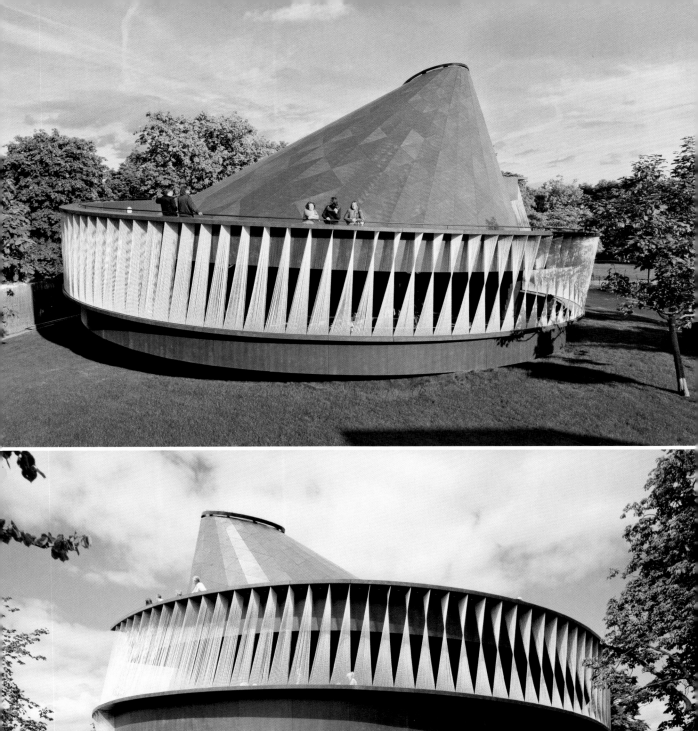

The Serpentine Pavilions, initiated by Julia Peyton-Jones, offer an occasion each summer for the London public to discover one or more of the top names in contemporary architecture and art.

Die von Julia Peyton-Jones initiierten Serpentine Pavilions bieten dem Londoner Publikum jeden Sommer Gelegenheit, herausragende Vertreter der zeitgenössischen Architektur oder Kunst kennenzulernen.

Les Serpentine Pavilions, initiés par Julia Peyton-Jones, offrent chaque été au public londonien l'occasion de découvrir un ou plusieurs grands noms de l'architecture contemporaine et de l'art.

The winding ramp of the building offered visitors views of the gardens, located nearly a couple of kilometers from the Victoria & Albert Museum. The Pavilion is set each year next to the Serpentine Gallery.

Die gewundene Rampe des Bauwerks bot den Besuchern einen Ausblick über den nicht weit vom Victoria & Albert Museum entfernten Park. Der Pavillon wird jedes Jahr neben der Serpentine Gallery errichtet.

Depuis la rampe tournante du bâtiment, les visiteurs bénéficient de vues sur les jardins. Chaque année, est ainsi édifié un pavillon à proximité de la Serpentine Gallery, non loin du Victoria & Albert Museum.

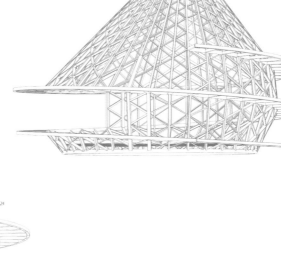

The interior of the structure is essentially constituted of a lecture or concert space. Right, the building of the Serpentine Gallery is visible through the opening.

Der Innenraum der Konstruktion wurde für Vorträge und Konzerte genutzt. Rechts ist durch eine Öffnung das Gebäude der Serpentine Gallery zu sehen.

L'intérieur de la structure se compose essentiellement d'un espace pour concerts et conférences. À droite, le bâtiment de la Serpentine Gallery, visible par l'ouverture.

The oculus of the structure and its web-like roof arch over the main seated area.

Die Dachwölbung über dem Hauptbesucherraum mit netzartiger Struktur und Okulus.

L'oculus de la structure et sa toiture en toile d'araignée situés au-dessus des gradins.

EMERGENT

EMERGENT
6010 Wilshire Boulevard, Suite 303
Los Angeles, CA 90036
USA

Tel: +1 323 938 1475
E-mail: twiscombe@emergentarchitecture.com
Web: www.emergentarchitecture.com

Born in 1970 in La Jolla, California, Tom Wiscombe founded **EMERGENT**, "a platform for researching the relationship between nature, technology, systems, and architectural form," in 1999. Educated at the UCLA (M. Arch.) and UC Berkeley, Wiscombe has taught design and technology at SCI-Arc, UCLA, UC Berkeley, and the University of Applied Arts in Vienna. Tom Wiscombe was Chief Designer and Project Partner at Coop Himmelb(l)au for over 10 years. He was in charge of various realized projects, including the Dresden UFA Cinema Palace, completed in 1998, the Akron Art Museum (page 116), BMW Welt in Munich (page 124), and the Lyon Musée des Confluences (Lyon, France, 2001–10). In 2003, EMERGENT won the competition for the P.S.1/MoMA Urban Beach project, and the New York Engineering Excellence Platinum Award for 2004. According to Greg Lynn, this project "set a new standard for architectural sophistication at that venue." EMERGENT was also awarded the Architectural League of New York Young Architects Award for 2004. EMERGENT won second place in the competition for the Seoul Performing Arts Center in 2005 and was a finalist in the Czech National Library competition in 2007 (published here).

Tom Wiscombe, geboren 1970 im kalifornischen La Jolla, gründete **EMERGENT** im Jahr 1999 als „Plattform zur Erforschung der Beziehung zwischen Natur, Technik, Systemen und architektonischen Formen". Nach seiner Ausbildung an der University of California Los Angeles (Master of Architecture) und der University of California Berkeley arbeitete er als Dozent an diesen Hochschulen sowie an der Universität für Angewandte Kunst Wien und dem Southern California Institute of Architecture. Als Chefdesigner und Projektpartner war Wiscombe mehr als zehn Jahre lang für Coop Himmelb(l)au tätig. Unter Wiscombes Verantwortung entstanden diverse Projekte wie das UFA-Multiplexkino in Dresden (1998), das Akron Art Museum in Ohio (S. 116), die BMW Welt in München (S. 124) und das Musée des Confluences in Lyon (2001–10). 2003 gewann EMERGENT den Architekturwettbewerb für das Projekt MoMA Urban Beach „P.S. 1", das 2004 mit dem New York Engineering Excellence Platinum Award ausgezeichnet wurde. Laut Greg Lynn stellt das Projekt „den architektonischen Standard des Ortes auf ein neues Niveau". Daneben erhielt EMERGENT den Young Architects Award 2004 der Architectural League of New York. Im Wettbewerb für ein Zentrum für darstellende Künste in Seoul 2005 belegte der Entwurf von EMERGENT den zweiten Platz, 2007 kam das Büro mit seinem nachfolgend vorgestellten Vorschlag in die Endrunde des Wettbewerbs um die Tschechische Nationalbibliothek.

Né en 1970 à La Jolla, Californie, Tom Wiscombe a fondé **EMERGENT**, « une plateforme de recherche sur les relations entre la nature, la technologie, les systèmes et la forme », en 1999. Après des études à UCLA (M. Arch.) et UC Berkeley, il a enseigné la conception et la technologie à SCI-Arc, UCLA, UC Berkeley, et à l'université des Arts appliqués de Vienne. Wiscombe a été concepteur principal et associé chargé de projets chez Coop Himmelb(l)au pendant plus de dix ans. Il a été responsable, entre autres, du complexe de salles de cinéma UFA de Dresde, achevé en 1998, de l'Akron Art Museum (page 116), du BMW Welt à Munich (page 124), et du futur musée des Confluences de Lyon (2001–10). En 2003, EMERGENT a remporté le concours pour le projet P.S. 1/MoMA Urban Beach et un New York Engineering Excellence Platinum Award en 2004. Selon Greg Lynn, ce projet « établit un nouveau standard de sophistication architecturale ». EMERGENT a également reçu l'Architectural League of New York Young Architects Award 2004. L'agence est arrivée seconde au concours pour le Centre des arts du spectacle de Séoul en 2005, et a été finaliste à celui de la Bibliothèque nationale tchèque en 2007 (publié ici).

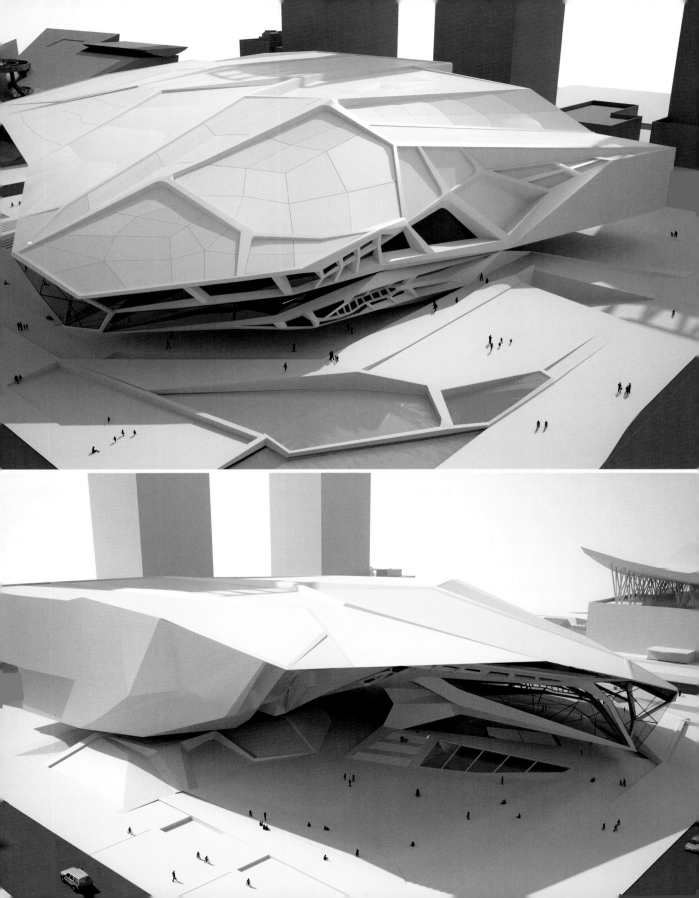

SHENZHEN MUSEUM OF CONTEMPORARY ART

Shenzhen, China, 2007

*Floor area: 28 000 m². Client: Shenzhen Municipal Government.
Cost: not disclosed. Design Team: Tom Wiscombe, Kevin Regaldo, Chris Eskew, Gabriel Huerta,
Sebastian Hiemisch*

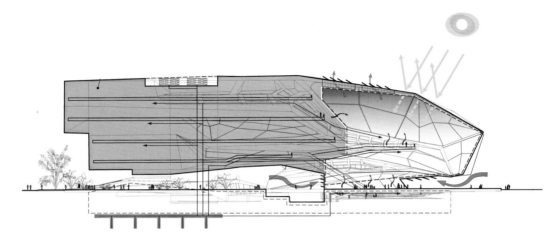

Tom Wiscombe writes, "This proposal creates a world-class institution that is characterized both by its response to its local environment and by its formal and structural elegance." He links the design to traditional Chinese courtyard spaces, although this is certainly architecture for a new city like Shenzhen. Integrating the planned Museum of Contemporary Art and exhibition spaces in a unified project, the proposal of EMERGENT has an essentially L-shaped design with loftlike display areas, and a garden plaza in the void created by the plan. A roof over this space offers shade while creating "an urban microclimate." A "crystalline foyer" links the Garden Plaza to the exhibition areas. The architect explains, "The design is based on structural morphologies found in nature, both in terms of their aesthetic and performative characteristics. Specifically, lilypads were examined for their biomathematical logic, which includes a network of deep veins that support their wide diameters. Although lilypads float naturally on water, their overall stability is determined by the depth, number, and distribution of these veins. The building structure similarly spreads over architectural surfaces according to force flows, driven by a rule-based system of branching and computational subdivision. Ultimately, the morphology of veining and structural surface relief can be understood as a semi-monocoque construction. The semi-monocoque, often found in aerospace and automobile construction, is based on the skin as structure, but utilizes stiffening ribs and bending members as needed to keep the strength-to-weight ratio optimized. The variable, composite sensibility of semi-monocoque construction offers an alternative to dogmatic frame and skin alternatives."

Tom Wiscombe schreibt zum Entwurf des Museums für zeitgenössische Kunst in Shenzhen: „Das Konzept sieht eine Weltklasse-Institution vor, die sich sowohl durch die Einbettung in ihre direkte Umgebung als auch durch die Eleganz ihrer Form und Struktur auszeichnet." Wiscombe berücksichtigt bei seinem Entwurf zwar auch die traditionelle chinesische Innenhofgestaltung, dennoch passt die Architektur ausgezeichnet in eine neue Großstadt wie Shenzhen. Der von EMERGENT vorgelegte Entwurf kombiniert das geplante Museum und weitere Ausstellungsbereiche sowie loftartige Schauflächen in einem Bau mit L-förmigem Grundriss, dessen Freiraum als begrünter Platz gestaltet werden soll. Ein darüber angebrachtes Dach spendet Schatten und sorgt für ein „urbanes Mikroklima". Ein „kristallartiges Foyer" verbindet den Grünbereich mit den Ausstellungsflächen. Der Architekt erklärt ferner: „Der Entwurf orientiert sich sowohl hinsichtlich seiner ästhetischen als auch seiner funktionellen Eigenschaften an Formen, die sich in der Natur finden lassen. Vor allem Seerosenblätter wurden mit Blick auf ihre biomathematische Struktur untersucht, zu der ein Netz aus kräftigen Adern gehört, das die breiten Blätter stabilisiert. Die Gesamtstabilität von Seerosen, wird, obwohl sie auf der Wasseroberfläche schwimmen, von der Anzahl, Stärke und Verteilung der Adern bestimmt. Auf ähnliche Weise verteilt sich in der Gebäudestruktur der Kräftefluss über architektonische Flächen, denen ein klar geregeltes Verzweigungssystem mit einer genau berechneten Unterteilung zugrunde liegt. Letztlich kann man sich die Adernstruktur und die Entlastung der Gebäudeflächen als eine Halbschalenkonstruktion vorstellen, wie man sie häufig im Flugzeug- und Autobau antrifft. Dabei wird die Struktur von der Hülle vorgegeben, die mithilfe von Versteifungselementen und Biegeteilen das gewünschte Verhältnis von Festigkeit und Gewicht erhält. Die variable, anpassungsfähige Sensibilität einer Halbschalenkonstruktion bietet eine Alternative zu dogmatischen Lösungen aus Tragwerk und Hülle."

Tom Wiscombe écrit : « Cette proposition donne naissance à une institution de niveau international qui se caractérise à la fois par sa réponse à son environnement local et son élégance formelle et structurelle. » Il fait le lien avec la conception traditionnelle des maisons à cour chinoises, même si l'architecture de ce musée est réellement celle d'une ville nouvelle comme Shenzhen. Intégrant le musée d'Art contemporain et les espaces d'expositions en un projet unique, EMERGENT a proposé une disposition en « L » à vastes zones d'expositions d'esprit loft et une place jardin occupant le vide créé par le plan. Au-dessus de cet espace, une toiture apporte de l'ombre et crée un « microclimat urbain ». Un « hall d'accueil cristallin » relie le jardin aux salles d'expositions. Selon l'architecte : « Le projet repose sur les morphologies structurelles à l'esthétique et la performances issue de la nature. Plus spécifiquement, nous avons étudié les nénuphars pour leur logique biomathématique. Leur réseau de veines en profondeur leur permet de soutenir leur grand diamètre. S'ils flottent naturellement sur l'eau, leur stabilité d'ensemble est déterminée par la profondeur, le nombre et la distribution de ces veines. La structure du bâtiment s'étend de la même façon sur les surfaces architecturales selon des axes de force, à partir d'un système de branchements et de divisions calculés. Au final, cette morphologie de veines et de surface structurelle peut se comparer à une construction semi-monocoque. Cette structure, que l'on trouve souvent dans l'aéronautique ou l'automobile, consiste en une peau faisant office de structure, mais utilise des raidisseurs et des poutres de flexion pour conserver l'optimisation du ratio résistance/poids. La sensibilité variable et composite de la construction semi-monocoque est une alternative à la construction classique par ossature et peau. »

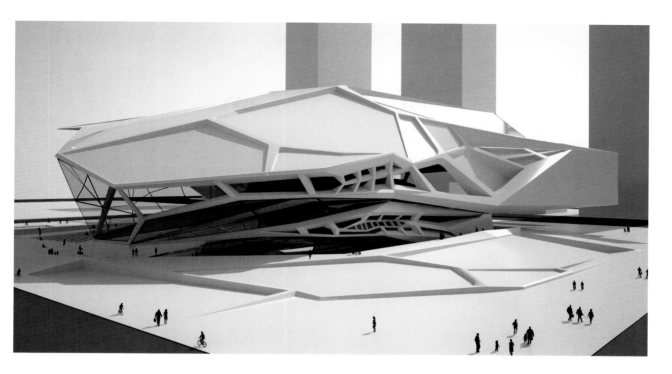

The webbed, angular structure recalls that Tom Wiscombe was a Chief Designer and Project Partner with the firm Coop Himmelb(l)au, but here he goes even further in imagining a break with architectural traditions.

Die winkelreiche gewebeartige Struktur verweist auf Wiscombes Arbeit als Chefdesigner und Projektpartner von Coop Himmelb(l)au, wobei er mit diesem Entwurf die Architekturtraditionen sogar noch stärker infrage stellt.

Ces formes anguleuses rappellent que Tom Wiscombe a été concepteur en chef et partenaire responsable de projets chez Coop Himmelb(l)au. Ici, il va encore plus loin dans la rupture avec les traditions architecturales.

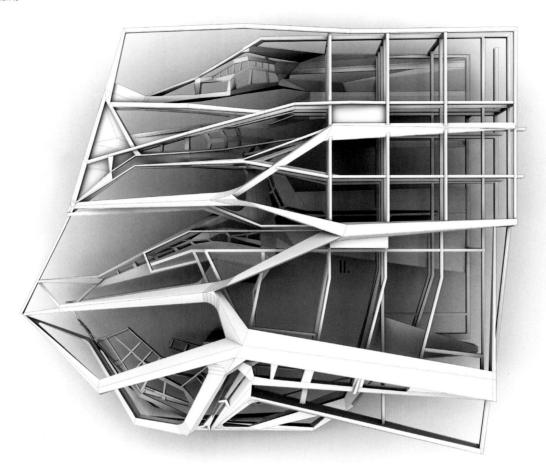

Unlike some "virtual" designs, Wiscombe's drawings for the Shenzhen Museum of Contemporary Art demonstrate a full knowledge of structure and construction.

Im Gegensatz zu vielen anderen „virtuellen" Entwürfen, lassen Wiscombes Zeichnungen für das Shenzhen Museum of Contemporary Art auf hervorragende Kenntnisse in Sachen Statik und Konstruktion schließen.

À la différence de certains projets « virtuels », les dessins de Wiscombe pour le musée d'Art contemporain de Shenzen démontrent une parfaite connaissance des problèmes de structure et de construction.

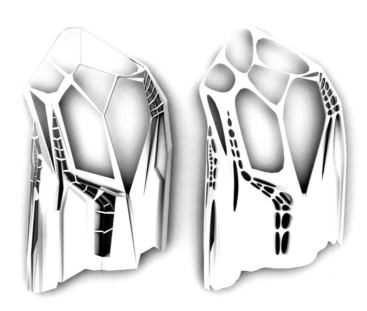

Renderings by EMERGENT show a fractured landscape that undoubtedly owes something to "deconstructivist" influences reinterpreted for today's computer-driven architecture.

Die Darstellungen von EMERGENT zeigen eine fragmentierte Landschaft mit „dekonstruktivistischen" Einflüssen, die hier auf der Basis neuester computergestützter Entwurfsmethoden neu interpretiert werden.

Les simulations d'EMERGENT montrent des perspectives fracturées, non sans rapport avec les influences « déconstructivistes » que l'architecture actuelle réinterprète avec l'aide de l'ordinateur.

NATIONAL LIBRARY OF THE CZECH REPUBLIC

Prague, Czech Republic, 2006–07

*Floor area: 50 000 m². Client: National Library of the Czech Republic. Cost: not disclosed.
Design Team: Tom Wiscombe, Kevin Regaldo, John Hoffman, Alina Grobe, Joshua Sprinkling, Chris Eskew,
Jordan Kanter, Elizabeth Pritchett, Haan Chau, Tim Sola. Engineer: Arup LA*

Tom Wiscombe explains, "This proposal for the National Library of the Czech Republic is based on radical contextualism, where the new building relates simultaneously to its local environment and to the larger urban context of Prague. The project sets into motion a dynamic relation between Prague's old city, the urban topography, and Prague Castle, opening up a dialog with the cultural and political history of the city. The project is intended to become an important landmark for the Czech Republic in the league of similar undertakings in Paris and other world capitals. The building is composed of four components—the Box, the Library Landscape, the National Archive, and the Mountain. Together, these elements constitute a simultaneously public and private building, a simultaneously microcontextual and macrocontextual building." The architects define the Box as the maximum buildable area of the site (100 x 118 m). The actual volume, 13.5 meters high, is lifted off the ground, creating the entry and the Library Landscape. This area contains the General and Reference Services, and the Open Stacks with Study Areas. Located above any potential flood level in the 60-meter-high crystalline Mountain, the National Archive is described as the "heart of the design." The Mountain, according to the architect, "Creates a visual connection with the cultural landscape of the city, establishing an urban triangle connecting the city center, Prague Castle, and the new National Library."

„Unser Vorschlag für die Nationalbibliothek der Tschechischen Republik", führt Tom Wiscombe aus, „beruht auf einem radikalen Kontextualismus, bei dem das neue Gebäude zu seiner unmittelbaren Umgebung und zugleich zum weiteren städtischen Umfeld Prags in Beziehung tritt. Das Projekt setzt eine dynamische Beziehung zwischen der Prager Altstadt, der Stadttopografie und der Prager Burg in Gang und eröffnet so einen Dialog mit der kulturellen und historischen Geschichte der Stadt. Als Nationalbibliothek soll es in einer Reihe mit vergleichbaren Unternehmungen in Paris und anderen Weltstädten stehen und zu einem bedeutenden Wahrzeichen der Tschechischen Republik werden. Vier Komponenten machen das Gebäude aus – die Box, die Bibliothekslandschaft, das Nationalarchiv und der Berg. Gemeinsam bilden diese Elemente ein zugleich öffentliches wie privates, zugleich mikro- und makrokontextuelles Gebäude." Unter der Box verstehen die Architekten die maximal bebaubare Fläche des Grundstücks (100 x 118 m). Zwischen dem eigentlichen Gebäudekörper mit einer Höhe von 13,5 m und der Erde besteht ein Zwischenraum, der den Eingang und die Bibliothekslandschaft aufnimmt. Diese Bibliothekslandschaft umfasst den Haupt- und Informationsbereich sowie die offenen Magazine mit den Lesebereichen. Das Nationalarchiv, weit oberhalb jeder denkbaren Hochwassermarke im 60 m hohen „Kristallberg" untergebracht, wird als „Herzstück des Entwurfs" bezeichnet. Der Berg, so der Architekt, „schafft eine sichtbare Verbindung zur kulturellen Landschaft der Stadt und lässt ein urbanes Dreieck aus Stadtzentrum, Prager Burg und der neuen Nationalbibliothek entstehen".

Pour Tom Wiscombe : « Cette proposition pour la Bibliothèque nationale de la Republic tchèque s'appuie sur une recherche radicale de contextualité dans laquelle le nouveau bâtiment entre simultanément en rapport avec son environnement local et le contexte urbain plus vaste de Prague. Le projet anime une relation dynamique entre la vieille ville, la topographie urbaine et le château de Prague, ouvrant ainsi un dialogue avec l'histoire culturelle et politique de la ville. Il doit devenir l'un des grands monuments de la République tchèque, dans l'esprit des entreprises similaires menées à Paris et dans d'autres capitales mondiales. Le bâtiment se compose de quatre éléments : la Boîte, la bibliothèque paysagée, les Archives nationales et la Montagne. Ensemble, ils forment ce bâtiment qui est à la fois public et privé, micro et macrocontextuel. » L'architecte définit la Boîte comme l'empreinte maximum constructible du terrain (100 x 118 m). Son volume de 13,5 m de haut est surélevé du sol pour laisser place à l'entrée et à la Bibliothèque paysagée. Elle contient les services généraux et de référence, les réserves et les zones d'étude. Implantées loin au-dessus de tout risque d'inondation dans la « Montagne » cristalline de 60 mètres de haut, les Archives nationales sont décrites comme « le cœur du projet ». « Cette Montagne, décrit l'architecte, est en lien visuel avec le paysage culturel de la ville, elle crée un triangle entre le centre-ville, le château et la Bibliothèque nationale. »

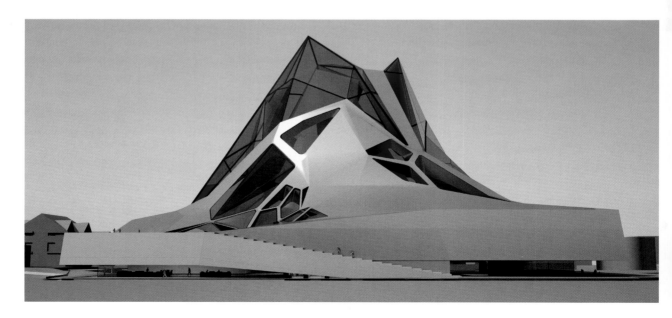

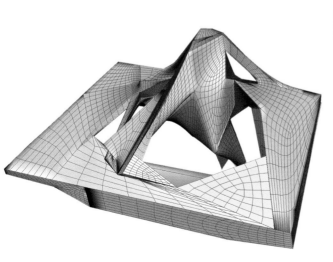

The basic form of the Library recalls a quasi-natural or organic formation, while remaining decidedly non-figurative.

Die Grundform der Bibliothek erinnert an quasi natürliche oder organische Formen, bleibt jedoch dezidiert ungegenständlich.

La forme de la bibliothèque rappelle une formation organique ou presque naturelle, tout en demeurant absolument non figurative.

A rendering (above) shows the Library
(above, far right) standing out against
a somewhat synthetic version of the
skyline of Prague. Left, a bird's-eye
view of the building.

Die obige Computergrafik zeigt rechts
hinten die Bibliothek vor einer abs-
trahierten Version der Prager Silhouette; links die Bibliothek aus der
Vogelperspektive.

La perspective ci-dessus montre la
bibliothèque (au fond, à droite) qui
s'élève au loin dans une vision assez
synthétisée du panorama urbain de
Prague. À gauche, une vue aérienne
du bâtiment.

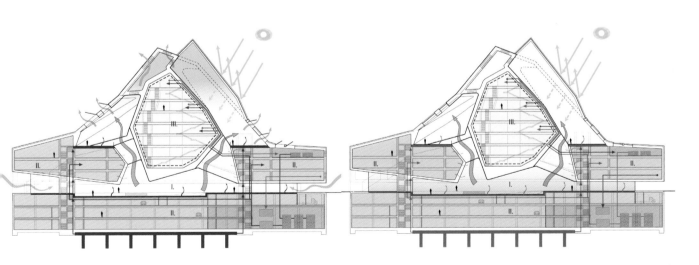

The sections show convection currents within the mountain-like volume of the Library. The use of red in the renderings invites a comparison to a volcano.

Die Querschnitte zeigen die Luftzirkulation innerhalb des bergartigen Baukörpers der Bibliothek. Der rote Farbton in den Darstellungen legt den Vergleich mit einem Vulkan nahe.

Les coupes montrent les courants de convection à l'intérieur du volume « montagneux » de la bibliothèque. L'utilisation du rouge renforce la comparaison avec un volcan.

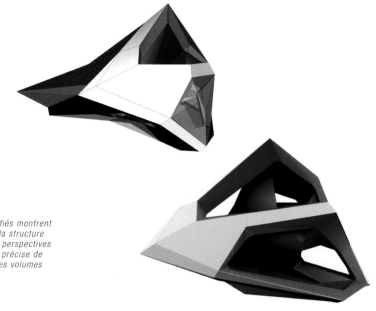

A series of simplified drawings shows
the basic forms of the main structure, while renderings to the right
give a clear impression of the spectacular interior spaces.

Die stilisierten Grafiken geben die
Grundformen der Hauptstruktur
wieder, während die Darstellungen
auf der rechten Seite einen klaren
Eindruck von den spektakulären
Innenräumen vermitteln.

Quelques dessins simplifiés montrent
les formes basiques de la structure
principale. À droite, des perspectives
donnant une impression précise de
l'aspect spectaculaire des volumes
intérieurs.

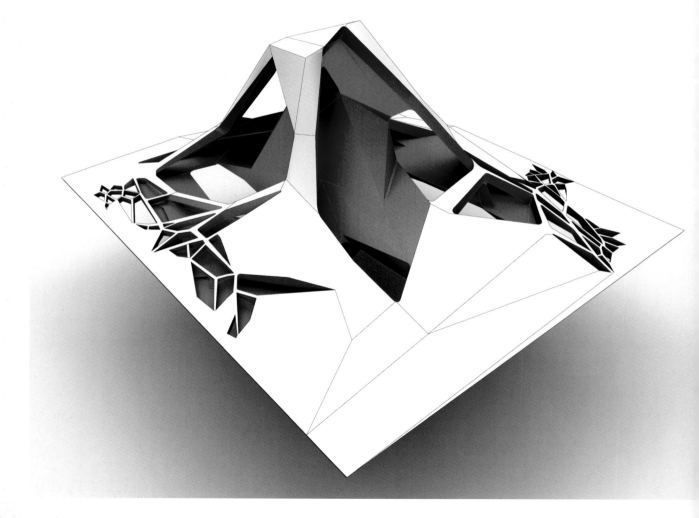

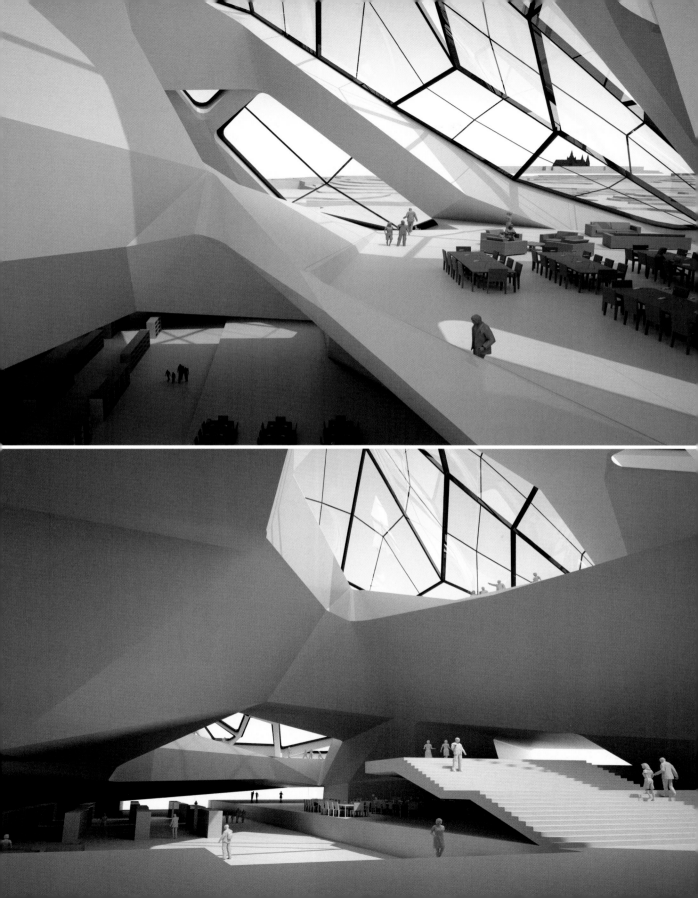

KSP ENGEL UND ZIMMERMANN

KSP Engel und Zimmermann Architekten
Mandelnstr. 6
38100 Braunschweig
Germany

Tel: +49 531 680 13-0
Fax: +49 531 680 13-38
E-mail: info@ksp-architekten.de
Web: www.ksp-architekten.de

Jürgen Engel was born in 1954. He studied at the Technische Universität of Braunschweig, the ETH in Zurich, the Rheinisch-Westfälische Technische Hochschule in Aachen (1974–80), and at MIT (1980–82). He worked as Head of the office of O.M. Ungers in Frankfurt (1986–89), before creating the KSP Partnership in 1990. Michael Zimmermann, born in 1956, also studied at the Technische Universität of Braunschweig (1977–84), before working with Gerkan, Marg + Partner in Hamburg. Since 1998, he has been the co-President of **KSP ENGEL UND ZIMMERMANN**, with Jürgen Engel. Their firm currently has approximately 250 employees (210 architects) and seven branch offices. They average approximately 500 million euros a year in construction costs. Aside from more traditional architectural work, the firm offers general contract management, urban design, consulting, and product development. They have completed the Dorma Headquarters in Ennepetal (2001–04); Philips Headquarters in Hamburg (2002–05); the WestendDuo in Frankfurt am Main (2001–06); and the Bergen-Belsen Documentation and Information Center (Celle, 2005–07, published here), all in Germany. In September 2007, they won the competition for Vietnam's National Museum of History (Tu Liem, Hanoi, 2008–), and, in January 2008, they won the competition for the Grand Mosque in Algiers. The National Library of China opened in September 2008 (Beijing, 2003–08).

Jürgen Engel, geboren 1954, studierte an der Technischen Universität Braunschweig, der ETH in Zürich, der Rheinisch-Westfälischen Technischen Hochschule Aachen (1974–80) und am Massachusetts Institute of Technology (1980–82). Von 1986 bis 1989 war Engel Büroleiter bei O.M. Ungers in Frankfurt, im Anschluss war er 1990 Mitgründer von KSP. Michael Zimmermann, geboren 1956, studierte ebenfalls an der Technischen Universität Braunschweig (1977–84), bevor er für Gerkan, Marg + Partner in Hamburg arbeitete. Seit 1998 führt Zimmermann mit Jürgen Engel die gemeinsame Firma. Gegenwärtig beschäftigt das Unternehmen 250 Mitarbeiter (davon 210 Architekten) in sieben Niederlassungen und übernimmt pro Jahr Aufträge, deren Baukostenvolumen sich auf insgesamt rund 500 Millionen Euro belaufen. Neben den traditionelleren Aufgaben der Gebäudeplanung bietet das Büro auch allgemeine baubegleitende Dienstleistungen, Stadtplanung, Consulting und Produktdesign an. Von Engel und Zimmermann stammen die Zentrale der Firma Dorma in Ennepetal (2001–04), der Philips-Standort Hamburg (2002–05), das WestendDuo in Frankfurt am Main (2001–06) und das hier vorgestellte Dokumentations- und Informationszentrum für die Gedenkstätte Bergen-Belsen (Kreis Celle, 2005–07). Im September 2007 gewannen **KSP ENGEL UND ZIMMERMANN** den Wettbewerb für das vietnamesische Historische Nationalmuseum (Tu Liem, Hanoi, seit 2008), im Januar 2008 belegte ihr Vorschlag den ersten Platz im Wettbewerb für die Große Moschee in Algier. Die Chinesische Nationalbibliothek wurde im September 2008 eröffnet (Peking, 2003–08).

Jürgen Engel est né en 1954. Il a étudié à la Technische Universität de Braunschweig, à l'ETH de Zurich, à la Rheinisch-Westfälische Technische Hochschule à Aachen (1974–80) et au MIT (1980–82). Il a dirigé l'agence de O.M. Ungers à Francfort (1986–89), avant de créer KSP Partnership en 1990. Michael Zimmermann, né en 1956, a également étudié à la Technische Universität de Braunschweig (1977–84) avant de collaborer avec Gerkan, Marg + Partner à Hambourg. Depuis 1998, il est coprésident d'**KSP ENGEL UND ZIMMERMANN** avec Jürgen Engel. Leur agence compte actuellement environ 250 collaborateurs (210 architectes) et sept agences filiales. Ils réalisent un chiffre de travaux engagés d'environ 500 millions d'euros chaque année. En dehors des interventions classiques d'architecture, l'agence propose celles de gestion de chantiers, d'urbanisme, de consultance et de développement de produits. Elle a réalisé le siège social de Dorma à Ennepetal (2001–04) ; le siège de Philips à Hambourg (2002–05) ; le WestendDuo à Francfort (2001–06) et le centre de documentation et d'informations de Bergen-Belsen (Celle, 2005–07, publié ici), tous en Allemagne. En septembre 2007, elle a remporté le concours pour le musée national d'Histoire du Vietnam (Tu Liem, Hanoi, 2008–) et, en janvier 2008, celui de la Grande mosquée d'Alger. La Bibliothèque nationale de Chine a ouvert ses portes en septembre 2008 (Pékin, 2003–08).

BERGEN-BELSEN DOCUMENTATION AND INFORMATION CENTER

Celle, Germany, 2005–07

Floor area: 3300 m². Client: Lower Saxony Monument Foundation. Cost: € 9 million.
Team: Ulrich Gremmelspacher, Michael Reiff, Konstanze Beelitz, Henner Winkelmüller, Hermann Timpe, Alexander Gelhorn, Volker Ziro.
Landscape Architect: sinai. Faust.Schroll.Schwarz, Berlin. Exhibition Design: Hans Dieter Schaal, Attenweiler.
Structural Engineering: Wetzel & von Seht, Hamburg

The unadorned concrete of the structure contrasts with a band of sober windows. Set low in the cantilevered volume seen opposite, these windows do little to alleviate a willful impression of heaviness.

Ein nüchternes Fensterband kontrastiert mit dem schmucklosen Beton des Bauwerks. Die in dem auskragenden Gebäudeteil weit unten angebrachten Fenster (Abbildung rechts) bieten kaum einen Ausgleich zu dem gewünschten Eindruck der Schwere.

Le béton nu du bâtiment contraste avec le sobre bandeau des fenêtres. Ouvertes en partie basse du volume en porte-à-faux (page de droite), ces baies n'allègent qu'à peine l'impression voulue de lourdeur.

Bergen-Belsen was a Nazi concentration and prisoner-of-war camp, southwest of the town of Bergen near Celle, where more than 70 000 people, including Anne Frank, lost their lives. The new Documentation and Information Center is a two-story building, 18 meters wide and 200 meters long, lying on the lines of the former country road leading from Celle to Hörste. The architects write that the building, "stringently structured in terms of function, lies like a dynamically extended walk-in sculpture in the Heidewald forest on the edge of the former concentration camp. Its extraordinary cubature, the radical limitation to just a few monochrome materials, the lack of any detailed ornamentation, as well as the physical presence of the large shape with minimalist recesses and openings, merge into a powerful, meaningful piece of architecture." The design is conceived in terms of two paths: one, leading through the building, rises gently through the exhibition areas leading to a broad window that marks the front of the building. The second route, called the "stony path," leads through the length of the structure without any entry. Past a central courtyard, visitors are confronted with high concrete walls where the path opens to the actual grounds of the camp. The edge of the building is markedly cantilevered over the ground, beginning at the boundary of the former camp, as the architects explain, "out of respect for this place," because the former grounds of the camp are today a cemetery.

Im Konzentrationslager Bergen-Belsen, südwestlich von Bergen in der Nähe des niedersächsischen Celle, kamen mehr als 70 000 Menschen ums Leben, unter ihnen auch Anne Frank. Das zweigeschossige, 200 m lange und 18 m breite Gebäude des Dokumentations- und Informationszentrums zeichnet den Verlauf der einstigen Landstraße von Celle nach Hörste nach. Die Architekten erläutern den Gebäudeaufbau wie folgt: „Der streng funktional gegliederte Bau liegt wie eine dynamisch gestreckte, begehbare Skulptur inmitten des Heidewaldes am Rand des ehemaligen Konzentrationslagers. Seine außergewöhnliche Kubatur, die radikale Beschränkung auf wenige, monochrome Materialien, der Verzicht auf besondere Detailausbildungen sowie die physische Präsenz der großen Form mit minimalistischen Einschnitten und Öffnungen verdichten sich zu einer kraftvollen, aussagestarken Architektur." Der Bau erschließt sich über zwei Wege: Der eine führt sacht ansteigend in das Gebäude hinein und durch die Ausstellungsbereiche bis zu einem großen Fenster an der Stirnseite. Der andere, so genannte steinerne Weg leitet die Besucher quer durch den Bau hindurch, ohne ins Gebäudeinnere hineinzuführen. Hinter einem zentralen Hof werden die Besucher mit hohen Betonwänden konfrontiert, wo der Pfad auf das ehemalige Lagergelände führt. An dieser Stelle, die die ehemalige Lagergrenze markiert, kragt das Gebäude über dem Boden vor, „aus Respekt vor dem Ort", wie die Architekten erklären. Heute befindet sich hier ein Friedhof.

Bergen-Belsen fut un camp de concentration nazi, au sud-ouest de la ville de Bergen près de Celle. Plus de 70 000 personnes, dont Anne Frank, y trouvèrent la mort. Le bâtiment de deux niveaux, 18 mètres de large et 200 mètres de long est implanté sur l'ancienne route menant de Celle à Hörste. Les architectes décrivent ainsi leur projet : « Rigoureusement structuré en termes de fonctions, il se développe comme une sculpture pénétrable dynamique au milieu de la forêt d'Heidewald, à la limite de l'ancien camp de concentration. Son extraordinaire volume, sa limitation radicale à simplement quelques matériaux monochromes, l'absence de tout détail ornemental ainsi que la présence physique de cette grande forme aux retraits et ouvertures minimalistes, donnent naissance à une œuvre architecturale puissante et significative. » La conception repose sur deux cheminements : l'un, traversant le bâtiment, passe par les salles d'expositions pour aboutir à une grande baie donnant sur le camp, l'autre, appelé « le chemin pierreux » conduit les visiteurs à marcher le long du Centre, sans y entrer. Au-delà de la cour centrale, ils sont confrontés à de hauts murs de béton avant d'arriver au camp lui-même. L'extrémité du bâtiment décrit un grand porte-à-faux pour ne pas toucher à la limite du camp « par respect du lieu » car l'ancien camp est aujourd'hui considéré comme un cimetière.

The powerful axial design of the "stony path" that leads past the building and into the former camp grounds heightens the understanding that this location was the theater of events that should never occur again.

Die imposante axiale Anlage des „steinernen Wegs", der bis auf den ehemaligen Lagerplatz führt, vermittelt eindringlich, dass man sich an dem einstigen Schauplatz von Geschehnissen befindet, die sich niemals wiederholen dürfen.

L'axe puissant tracé par le « chemin pierreux », qui longe le bâtiment pour conduire à l'ancien camp, contribue à l'évocation du lieu qui fut le théâtre d'événements qui ne doivent jamais se reproduire.

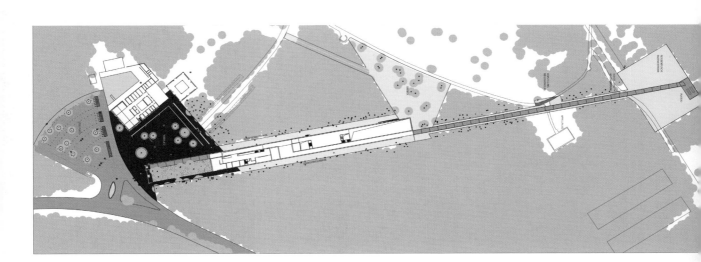

The very sober design of the building is continued in the interiors—dark metal, glass, and concrete dominate the palette of materials.

Der äußerst sachliche Charakter des Gebäudes setzt sich im Innenbereich fort – dunkles Metall, Glas und Beton dominieren die Materialpalette.

La très sobre conception du bâtiment se retrouve à l'intérieur. Le métal sombre, le verre et le béton dominent la palette des matériaux.

FAM ARQUITECTURA

FAM Arquitectura y Urbanismo SLP
C/Duque de Fernán Núñez N2/P5/02
28012 Madrid
Spain

Tel/Fax: +34 91 369 06 77
E-mail: correo@estudiofam.com
Web: www.estudiofam.com

Esaú Acosta Pérez received his diploma from the ETSA of Madrid. He started his career collaborating with AMP Arquitectos in Tenerife in 1999. Subsequently, he worked with Mariano Bayón, Rafael Beneytez, and, in 2004, with Jean Nouvel on the extension of the Reina Sofía National Museum in Madrid. Mauro Gil-Fournier Esquerra also graduated from the ETSA, Madrid. In 2002, he worked with Mariano Bayón, and then, in 2002–04, with the architect Rafael Beneytez. Miguel Jaenicke Fontao also graduated from the ETSA, Madrid, and then attended IIT, the Illinois Institute of Technology. He worked in the Chicago office of Skidmore, Owen & Merrill LLP (SOM), and then the Lamela office in Madrid. He also collaborated with DISC-0 Architecture on the winning project for the Tsunami memorial in Phuket, Thailand. Raquel Buj García worked on the development of residential projects in Spanish cities after attending the ETSA, Madrid. Pedro Colón de Carvajal Salís lived in Paris in 2001 after studying in Madrid, attended the Architecture School at Paris-Belleville, and worked for Jean Nouvel. This group created **FAM ARQUITECTURA** in Madrid in 2002. Their work includes prize-winning projects for a Cultural Center in La Laguna (Tenerife, 2005); the Baronia d'Entenç Wine Cellar (Tarragona, 2006); the March 11 Memorial for the Victims (Madrid, 2005–07, published here); a housing, sports, and cultural complex in Madrid (2007); the CICCM International Madrid Convention Center (Madrid, 2007), all in Spain; and their design for the Spanish Pavilion for Expo '10 (Shanghai, China, 2007).

Esaú Acosta Pérez begann seine Laufbahn 1999, nach dem Abschluss an der Escuela técnica superior de arquitectura de Madrid (ETSAM), bei dem auf Teneriffa ansässigen Büro AMP Arquitectos. Danach arbeitete er für Mariano Bayón und für Rafael Beneytez sowie 2004 für Jean Nouvel am Erweiterungsbau des Museums Reina Sofía in Madrid. Mauro Gil-Fournier Esquerra, ebenfalls Absolvent der ETSAM, arbeitete 2002 für Mariano Bayón und von 2002 bis 2004 mit dem Architekten Rafael Beneytez. Miguel Jaenicke Fontao schloss ebenfalls ein Studium an der ETSAM ab, um anschließend seine Ausbildung am Illinois Institute of Technology zu vertiefen. Er arbeitete in der Chicagoer Niederlassung von Skidmore, Owen & Merrill LLP (SOM) und dann im Architekturbüro Lamela in Madrid. Darüber hinaus war er an dem von DISC-0 Architecture konzipierten Siegerentwurf für das Denkmal für die Tsunami-Opfer im thailändischen Phuket beteiligt. Raquel Buj García war nach ihrem Studium an der ETSAM an der Entwicklung von Wohnhausprojekten in verschiedenen spanischen Städten beteiligt. Pedro Colón de Carvajal Salís studierte zunächst in Spanien, lebte dann 2001 in Paris, wo er die École d'architecture de Paris-Belleville besuchte und für Jean Nouvel arbeitete. 2002 schlossen sich die Genannten in Madrid zu **FAM ARQUITECTURA** zusammen. Zu ihren Arbeiten gehören preisgekrönte Projekte für ein Kulturzentrum in La Laguna (Teneriffa, 2005), das Weinlokal Baronia d'Entenç in Tarragona (Spanien, 2006), das hier vorgestellte Denkmal für die Opfer des Anschlags vom 11. März 2004 in Madrid (2005–07), ein Wohn-, Sport- und Kulturzentrum in Madrid (2007), das internationale Kongresszentrum CICCM in Madrid (2007) sowie der Entwurf für den spanischen Pavillon zur Expo '10 in Shanghai (China, 2007).

Esaú Acosta Perez est diplômé de l'ETSA de Madrid (ETSAM). Il a débuté sa carrière chez AMP Arquitectos à Ténérife en 1999. Par la suite, il a travaillé avec Mariano Bayón, Rafael Beneytez et, en 2004, avec Jean Nouvel sur l'extension du musée national Reina Sofía à Madrid. Mauro Gil-Fournier Esquerra, également diplômé de l'ETSAM, a travaillé en 2002 avec Mariano Bayón puis, en 2002–04, avec Rafael Beneytez. Miguel Jaenicke Fontao, également diplômé de l'ETSAM, a étudié à l'IIT, Illinois Institute of Technology. Il a travaillé dans les bureaux de Chicago de Skidmore, Owen & Merrill LLP (SOM), puis dans l'agence Lamela à Madrid. Il a également collaboré avec DISC-0 Architecture sur le projet gagnant du mémorial du Tsunami à Phuket, Thaïlande. Raquel Buj García, diplômée de l'ETSAM, a travaillé au développement de projets résidentiels dans diverses villes espagnoles. Pedro Colón de Carvajal Salís, après avoir étudié à Madrid est venu à Paris en 2001 à l'École d'architecture de Paris-Belleville et a travaillé pour Jean Nouvel. Ce groupe a créé **FAM ARQUITECTURA** à Madrid in 2002. Parmi leurs réalisations : un projet primé pour un Centre culturel à La Laguna (Ténérife, 2005) ; le chai Baronia d'Entenç (Tarragona, 2006) ; le Mémorial aux victimes de l'attentat du 11 mars 2004 (Madrid, 2005–07, publié ici) ; un complexe culturel et sportif, à Madrid (2007) ; le Centre international de congrès CICCM de Madrid (Madrid, 2007), tous en Espagne, et un projet pour le Pavillon espagnol à Expo '10 (Shanghai, Chine, 2007).

MARCH 11 MEMORIAL FOR THE VICTIMS

Madrid, Spain, 2005–07

Floor area: 1088 m², with 497 m² room below grade.
Client: Madrid City Council and the Spanish Public Works Ministry. Cost: €6 million

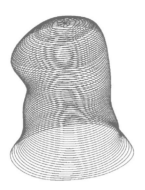

FAM won the competition to design the memorial to the victims of the March 11, 2004, Madrid train bombings. Located near Atocha Station in the center of the Spanish capital, the Memorial is an 11-meter-high, oval, molded glass-block structure without any steel structural elements. A 10-meter ETFE (Ethylene Tetrafluoroethylene) membrane on the inside of the glass shell is engraved with messages from citizens concerning the tragedy. Intended to symbolize "a shimmer of hope," the monument includes a "blue room" below grade with a capacity for up to 200 people that can be accessed directly from the station. The color of this room suffuses the tower at night, creating "an ethereal glow." The design of the visible element of the Memorial consists of approximately 15 000 glass blocks, each weighing 8.4 kilograms, that were assembled using only a transparent adhesive, an innovative construction method. The top of the monument is made of five glass beams supporting 12 glass plates, and the entire structure was made to withstand the strong winds that occasionally blow in the area. The simplicity and elegance of this structure is a testimony to the fact that it is still possible to design memorials that appeal to a wide audience and convey a strong message—in this case amplified by an innovative design.

FAM gewann den Wettbewerb für den Entwurf des Denkmals zur Erinnerung an die Opfer der Madrider Zuganschläge vom 11. März 2004. Das Monument befindet sich unmittelbar neben dem Bahnhof Atocha im Zentrum der spanischen Hauptstadt und besteht oberirdisch aus einem 11 m hohen, ovalen Glashohlkörper, der ganz ohne tragende Stahlelemente auskommt. Darin eingesetzt ist eine 10 m hohe Membran aus ETFE (Ethylen-Tetrafluorethylen), auf der Botschaften eingetragen sind, in denen sich spanische Bürger mit der Tragödie auseinandersetzen. Unterhalb des Monuments, das einen „Schimmer der Hoffnung" symbolisieren soll, befindet sich ein unterirdischer, blauer Raum mit Platz für bis zu 200 Menschen, der direkt von der Bahnstation aus zugänglich ist. Nachts strahlt die Farbe des Raums in den oberirdischen Körper hinauf und sorgt für ein „ätherisches Leuchten". Der oberirdische Teil des Denkmals besteht aus rund 15 000 Glasblöcken von je 8,4 kg Gewicht, die allein von einem durchsichtigen Klebstoff – eine neuartige Konstruktionsmethode – zusammengehalten werden. Die Oberseite besteht aus fünf gläsernen Balken, auf denen wiederum zwölf Glasplatten ruhen. Ungeachtet seiner Transparenz ist das Gebilde so stabil, dass in der Gegend mitunter starke Wind ihm nichts anhaben kann. Die Schlichtheit und Eleganz der Konstruktion beweisen, dass man immer noch Denkmale entwerfen kann, die eine eindringliche Botschaft transportieren und viele Menschen ansprechen – in diesem Fall noch verstärkt durch ein innovatives Design.

FAM a remporté le concours pour la conception du Mémorial aux victimes de l'attentat du 11 mars 2004 à Madrid. Situé en face de la gare d'Atocha, au centre de la capitale espagnole, ce mémorial est une structure ovale de 11 mètres de haut ayant nécessité environ 15 000 pavés de verre moulé de 8,4 kilos chacun, sans aucun élément porteur en acier, assemblés à l'aide d'adhésif transparent selon une nouvelle méthode de construction. À l'intérieur de cette coque de verre sont reproduits, sur une membrane de 10 mètres en ETFE (tétrafluoréthylène d'éthylène), des messages envoyés par des citoyens après la tragédie. Voulant symboliser « une vibration d'espoir », le monument comprend également une « salle bleue » en sous-sol d'une capacité de 200 personnes à laquelle on peut accéder directement de la gare. La nuit, sa couleur se diffuse dans la partie extérieure créant « une lueur éthérée ». La couverture se compose de cinq « rayons » de verre soutenant 12 panneaux du même matériau. La structure est conçue pour résister aux vents qui soufflent parfois sur ce quartier de Madrid. La simplicité et l'élégance de cette structure montre qu'il est encore possible de concevoir des monuments innovants de ce type, qui parlent à un vaste public et véhiculent un message puissant.

Computer-generated drawings (above) show what was imagined as a flexible form for the part of the Memorial that emerges above the earth.

Die obigen am Computer entstandenen Grafiken zeigen, wie die flexible Form des oberirdischen Denkmalteils aussehen sollte.

Des dessins générés par ordinateur (ci-dessus) montrent comment a été imaginée la flexibilité de la partie émergente du mémorial.

Above, visitors in the main space
below the rising glass structure, and,
below, an aerial view of the Memorial
in front of Atocha Station.

Besucher im Hauptraum unter der
aufragenden Glaskonstruktion (oben),
eine Luftaufnahme des Denkmals vor
dem Bahnhof Atocha (unten).

Les visiteurs de l'espace principal
sous la structure de verre (ci-dessus)
et une vue aérienne du monument
devant la gare d'Atocha (ci-dessous).

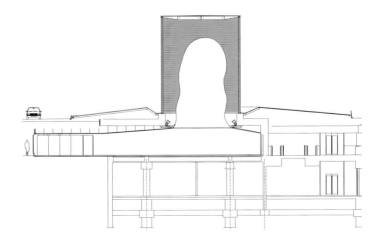

FOSTER AND PARTNERS

Foster and Partners
Riverside / 22 Hester Road / London SW11 4AN / UK

Tel: +44 20 77 38 04 55 / Fax: +44 20 77 38 11 07
E-mail: enquiries@fosterandpartners.com / Web: www.fosterandpartners.com

Born in Manchester, UK, in 1935, **NORMAN FOSTER** studied Architecture and City Planning at Manchester University (1961). He was awarded a Henry Fellowship to Yale University, where he received his M.Arch degree and met Richard Rogers, with whom he created Team 4. He received the RIBA Gold Medal for Architecture (1983) and was knighted in 1990. The American Institute of Architects granted him their Gold Medal for Architecture in 1994. Lord Norman Foster has notably built: the IBM Pilot Head Office (Cosham, UK, 1970–71); the Sainsbury Center for Visual Arts and Crescent Wing, University of East Anglia (Norwich, UK, 1976–77; 1989–91); the Hong Kong and Shanghai Banking Corporation Headquarters (Hong Kong, 1981–86); London's third airport, Stansted (1987–91); the Faculty of Law at the University of Cambridge (Cambridge, UK, 1993–95); and the Commerzbank Headquarters, Frankfurt (Germany, 1994–97). Recent projects include: the airport at Chek Lap Kok (Hong Kong, 1995–98); the new German Parliament, Reichstag (Berlin, Germany, 1995–99); the British Museum Redevelopment (London, 1997–2000); Millennium Bridge (London, 1996–2002); Greater London Authority (1998–2002); the Petronas University of Technology (Seri Iskandar, Malaysia, 1998–2004); the Millau Viaduct (Millau, France, 1993–2005); Wembley Stadium (London, 1996–2006); and Beijing Airport (China, 2003–08). Current work includes the Aldar Central Market Towers (Abu Dhabi, UAE, 2006–10); and the 78-story 200 Greenwich Street Tower (World Trade Center, New York, 2006–12), together with the Russia Tower (2006–) and the Crystal Island (2006–) projects in Moscow, Russia, both published here.

NORMAN FOSTER, geboren 1935 in Manchester, studierte bis 1961 Architektur und Stadtplanung an der Manchester University. An der Yale University, von der er ein Henry Fellowship erhielt, schloss Foster seine Studien mit dem Master of Architecture ab. Dort lernte er auch Richard Rogers kennen, mit dem er unter dem Namen Team 4 firmierte. 1983 wurde Foster die britische Royal Gold Medal for Architecture verliehen, 1994 erhielt er die Gold Medal for Architecture des American Institute of Architects. 1990 wurde er in den Adelsstand erhoben, seit 1999 darf er sich Lord nennen. Einige seiner herausragenden Bauten sind das IBM Pilot Head Office in Cosham (1970–71), das Sainsbury Centre for Visual Arts und der Crescent Wing der University of East Anglia (Norwich, 1976–77; 1989–91), alle in Großbritannien, der Sitz der Hong Kong and Shanghai Bank in Hongkong (1981–86), Londons dritter Flughafen, Stansted (1987–91), die juristische Fakultät der University of Cambridge (1993–95) und die Commerzbank-Zentrale in Frankfurt am Main (1994–97). In den vergangenen zehn Jahren entstanden der Internationale Flughafen Chek Lap Kok von Hongkong (1995–97), der Umbau des Berliner Reichstagsgebäudes (1995–99), die Modernisierung des British Museum in London (1997–2000), die Londoner Millenium Bridge (1996–2002), das Verwaltungsgebäude für Großlondon (1998–2002), die Technische Universität Petronas im malaysischen Seri Iskandar (1998–2004), die Viaduc-de-Millau-Brücke in Frankreich (1993–2005), das neue Londoner Wembley-Stadion (1996–2006) und der Internationale Flughafen Peking (2003–08). Derzeit werden die Aldar Central Market Towers in Abu Dhabi (VAE, 2006–10) und das 78-geschossige Hochhaus in der 200 Greenwich Street in New York, das so genannte World Trade Center 2 (2006–12), sowie die beiden hier vorgestellten Moskauer Projekte Russia Tower und Crystal Island (beide seit 2006) verwirklicht.

Né à Manchester en 1935, **NORMAN FOSTER** a étudié l'architecture et l'urbanisme à Manchester University (1961). Il a bénéficié d'une Henry Fellowship pour Yale University, où il a passé son M. Arch, et rencontré Richard Rogers avec lequel il a créé l'agence Team 4. Il a reçu la RIBA Gold Medal for Architecture en 1983 et a été anobli en 1990. L'American Institute of Architects lui a accordé sa Médaille d'or en 1994. Lord Norman Foster a construit en particulier : le siège pilote d'IBM (Cosham, G.-B., 1970–71) ; le Sainsbury Center for Visual Arts and Crescent Wing, University of East Anglia (Norwich, G.-B., 1976–77 / 1989–91) ; le siège de la Hong Kong and Shanghai Banking Corporation (Hong Kong, 1981–86) ; Standsted, troisième aéroport de Londres (1987–91) ; la faculté de droit de l'université de Cambridge (Cambridge, G.-B., 1993–95) et le siège de la Commerzbank à Francfort (Allemagne, 1994–97). Parmi ses récents projets : l'aéroport de Chek Lap Kok (Hong Kong, 1995–98) ; le nouveau Parlement allemand au Reichstag (Berlin, Allemagne, 1995–99) ; les nouveaux aménagements du British Museum (Londres, 1997–2000) ; le Millennium Bridge (Londres, 1996–2002) ; l'immeuble de la Greater Londres Authority (1998–2002) ; Petronas University of Technology (Seri Iskandar, Malaisie, 1998–2004) ; le viaduc de Millau (Millau, France, 1993–2005) ; le Wembley Stadium (Londres, 1996–2006), et l'aéroport de Pékin (Chine, 2003–08). Actuellement son agence travaille sur les projets des Aldar Central Market Towers (Abu Dhabi, EAU, 2006–10), sur la tour du 200 Greenwich Street et ses 78 niveaux (World Trade Center, New York, 2006–12), enfin sur les projets de la Russia Tower (2006 –) et Crystal Island (2006 –), à Moscou (Russia), tous deux publiés ici.

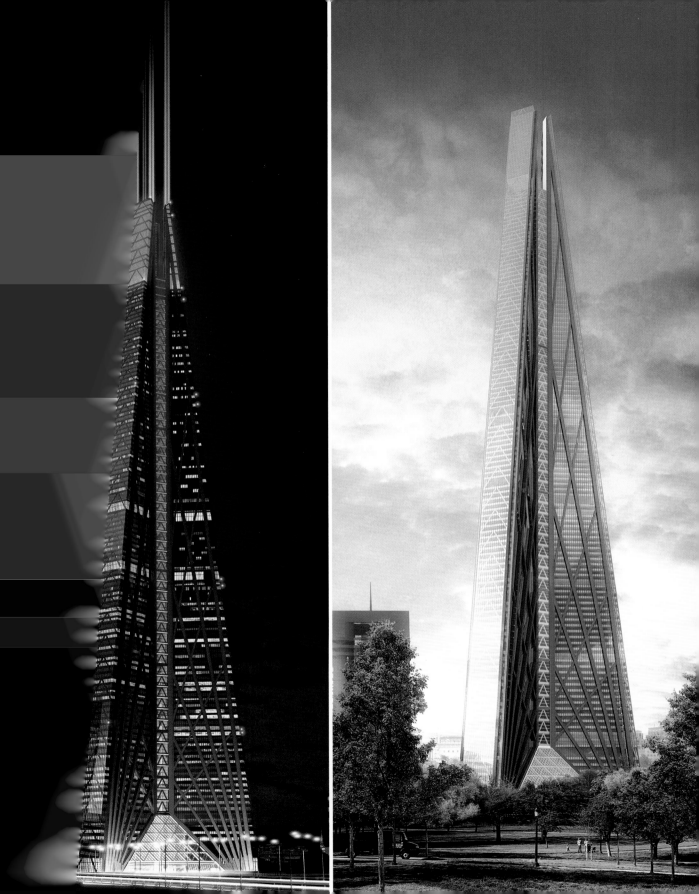

RUSSIA TOWER

Moscow, Russia, 2006–

*Site area: 21 935 m². Floor area: 565 000 m². Height: 600 m.
Client: STT Group. Cost: not disclosed*

Located 5.5 kilometers from the Red Square, this project—including offices, a hotel, shopping, leisure, and residences, with private gardens, public spaces, and an observation deck—is described as a "mixed-use, super-dense, vertical city for 25 000 people." Rising to a total height of 600 meters, with 118 floors above ground, the building is slated to become the tallest naturally ventilated tower in the world, and the tallest building in Europe. As is often the case with Foster's projects, great attention has been paid to the environmental aspects of this project, with energy recycling systems capable of reducing heating demand by 20 percent. Rainwater and snow harvesting will reduce the fresh water demand for the building's toilets by 30 percent as compared to more traditional structures. Given the extreme cold that Moscow faces in winter, triple glazing is used to create a "low-energy façade." The plan of the tower is triangular, with three arms meeting in a central green spire, and creating a pyramidal form. The site is well connected to the Moscow underground system and parking for 2900 vehicles is provided for. The smaller, upper floors of the structure are reserved for residential and hotel spaces, with retail space and offices below. The architects emphasize that the thin floor plates of the tower "maximize daylight penetration and views, providing large, flexible column-free office spaces." Sky gardens "draw in natural ventilation and provide key circulation and social space."

Die Architekten des Rossija-Turms, der, 5,5 km vom Roten Platz entfernt, Büroflächen, ein Hotel, Geschäfte, Freizeiteinrichtungen, Apartments mit Privatgärten, öffentliche Räume und eine Aussichtsplattform umfassen wird, beschreiben ihr Projekt als eine „multifunktionale, extrem verdichtete, vertikale Stadt für 25 000 Menschen". Mit einer Höhe von 600 m und 118 Stockwerken soll das Gebäude das höchste natürlich belüftete Hochhaus der Welt und zugleich das höchste Bauwerk Europas werden. Wie häufig bei Fosters Projekten wurde auch hier großer Wert auf Umweltaspekte gelegt. Energierecyclingsysteme ermöglichen eine Senkung des Heizbedarfs um 20 %, Schnee und Regenwasser werden aufgefangen und reduzieren den Frischwasserverbrauch der Toilettenanlagen im Vergleich zu herkömmlicheren Gebäuden um 30 %. Zum Schutz gegen die extreme Kälte der Moskauer Winter kommt eine „Niedrigenergiefassade" mit Dreifachverglasung zum Einsatz. Über dem dreieckigen Grundriss erheben sich drei Gebäudeteile, die zu einer begrünten Spitze zusammenlaufen und eine Pyramidenform bilden. Das Grundstück ist gut an das Moskauer Metronetz angeschlossen und besitzt zudem Abstellflächen für 2900 Autos. Die oberen, schmaleren Stockwerke des Gebäudes sind für Wohn- und Hotelflächen reserviert, weiter unten sind Geschäfte und Büros vorgesehen. Zur Wahl der dünnen Geschossplatten erläutern die Architekten, dass sie „den Tageslichteinfall und die Aussichtsmöglichkeiten maximieren und große, säulenfreie und flexibel nutzbare Büroflächen ermöglichen". Über die gesamte Gebäudehöhe verteilen sich schwebende Gärten, die „für ein natürliches Gebäudeklima und Luftzirkulation sorgen und als Treffpunkte dienen".

Situé à 5,5 kilomètres de la place Rouge, ce projet comprenant bureaux, hôtel, centre commercial et de loisirs, jardins privatifs, vastes espaces publics et terrasse d'observation est présenté par l'architecte comme une « ville verticale à usage mixte, très dense, conçue pour 25 000 habitants ». S'élevant à la hauteur de 600 mètres pour 118 étages, cette tour devrait être le plus grand immeuble à ventilation naturelle au monde, et le plus haut d'Europe. Comme c'est souvent le cas chez Foster, une grande attention a été portée aux aspects environnementaux. Des systèmes de recyclage de l'énergie sont par exemple en mesure de diminuer la demande de chauffage de 20 %. L'eau de pluie et la récupération de la neige permettront de réduire les besoins d'eau douce pour les toilettes de 30 % par rapport aux solutions traditionnelles. Pour parer aux températures extrêmes que connaît Moscou en hiver, la façade « basse énergie » est à triple vitrage. Le plan au sol est triangulaire, les trois bras se réunissant en une flèche centrale verte pour créer une forme pyramidale. L'emplacement est bien relié au métro moscovite et les parkings accueilleront 2900 véhicules. Les étages supérieurs, moins grands, sont réservés aux appartements et à l'hôtel, les bureaux et les locaux commerciaux occupant la base de la tour. La minceur des plateaux « optimise la pénétration de la lumière naturelle et les vues, et permet d'offrir aux bureaux de vastes espaces ouverts sans colonnes, facilement adaptables ». Des jardins suspendus « facilitent la ventilation naturelle, jouent un rôle clé dans la circulation et offrent un espace de socialisation ».

Above, an interior rendering of the building gives an impression of its scale while it brings to mind certain utopian or dystopian visions of the future of the city.

Die Computergrafik (oben) vermittelt einen Eindruck der Gebäudedimensionen und lässt an gewisse utopische oder dystopische Visionen der Moskauer Zukunft denken.

Ci-dessus, une perspective intérieure fait comprendre l'échelle de l'immeuble et rappelle en même temps certaines visions utopiques ou dystopiennes du futur de la ville.

To the left, the 600-meter-high Russia Tower dominating the Moscow skyline just over five kilometers from Red Square.

Links der 600 m hohe, in gut 5 km Entfernung vom Roten Platz geplante Rossija-Turm als dominierendes Element in der Moskauer Skyline.

À gauche, à cinq kilomètres de la place Rouge, les 600 mètres de haut de la « Tour de Russie » domineront le panorama urbain moscovite.

CRYSTAL ISLAND

Moscow, Russia, 2006–

Site area: 440 000 m². Floor area: 1.1 million m² (excluding parking).
Height: 450 m. Client: not disclosed. Cost: not disclosed. Consultants: Buro Happold, pha consult, Systematica

The spiraling 450-meter-tall central tower of the Crystal Island complex is less a skyscraper than a city landmark, with more than one million square meters of floor space.

Der sich 450 m hoch emporschrau-bende Turm des Crystal-Island-Komplexes mit mehr als 1 Million m² Geschossfläche ist weniger als Wolkenkratzer denn als Wahrzeichen der Stadt zu verstehen.

La tour centrale en spirale du com-plexe de Crystal Island est moins un gratte-ciel qu'un signal pour une ville qui occupera plus d'un million de mètres carrés.

Including its underground parking areas, the Crystal Island project is slated to cover a total floor area of 2.5 million square meters, making it the world's largest inhabited building. "Conceived as a self-contained city within a city, it contains a rich mix of buildings—including museums, theaters, and cinemas—to ensure that it is a major new destination for the whole of Moscow." The complex will include 900 serviced apartments, a 3000-room hotel, offices, retail spaces, a museum, an IMAX theater, and a school for 500 students, as well as a 360° observation deck positioned 300 meters above ground. Located on the Nagatino Peninsula, just 7.5 kilometers from the Kremlin, the spiraling design will rise from a newly landscaped park that will provide a range of activities throughout the year, including cross-country skiing and ice skating in the winter. As the architects describe the project, "The internal built volumes of over one million square meters assume a staggered formation within the triangulated steel mega frame, extending flush against the sloping faceted glazed outer skin. This terracing creates a series of winter gardens, which form a breathable second layer and thermal buffer for the main building, shielding the interior spaces from Moscow's extreme summer and winter climates. A vertical louver system sheaths the internal façades to ensure privacy for the individual apartments." When the project gained planning approval in January 2008, Norman Foster declared, "Crystal Island is one of the world's most ambitious building projects and it represents a milestone in the 40-year history of the practice. It is the largest single building in the world, creating a year-round destination for Moscow and a sustainable, dynamic new urban quarter. It is a paradigm of compact, mixed-use, sustainable city planning, with an innovative energy strategy and 'smart' skin that buffers against climate extremes."

Rechnet man die unterirdischen Abstellflächen hinzu, wird Crystal Island nach der Fertigstellung eine Gesamtnutzfläche von 2,5 Millionen m² aufweisen, was es zu einem der größten bewohnten Gebäude der Welt macht. „Das Projekt ist als eine Stadt in der Stadt gedacht, die die verschiedensten Gebäude umfasst, einschließlich Museen, Theater und Kinos. Dadurch wird es zu einem neuen Hauptanziehungspunkt für ganz Moskau. Der Komplex umfasst 900 Service-Apartments, ein 3000-Zimmer-Hotel, Geschäfte, ein Museum, ein IMAX-Kino, eine Schule für 500 Schüler sowie in 300 m Höhe eine Aussichtsplattform mit Panoramablick auf die Stadt. Standort des sich spiralförmig in die Höhe windenden Entwurfs ist die 7,5 km vom Kreml entfernte Halbinsel Nagatino mit einem neu angelegten Landschaftspark, der das ganze Jahr hindurch zu Freizeitaktivitäten einlädt, im Winter beispielsweise zum Schlittschuhlaufen und Skilanglauf. Nach der Projektbeschreibung der Architekten „verteilen sich die mehr als 1 Million m² Gebäudefläche auf einzelne, innerhalb des triangulierten Riesenstahlrahmens gestaffelt angeordnete Ebenen, die bündig mit der geneigten, facettiert verglasten Außenhülle abschließen. Durch die terrassenförmige Anordnung ergibt sich eine Reihe von Wintergärten, die als luftreinigende zweite Schicht und zugleich als thermischer Puffer dienen, der die Innenbereiche des Gebäudes gegen das extreme Sommer- und Winterklima Moskaus abschirmt. Zum Schutz der Privatsphäre in den einzelnen Apartments sind die Innenfassaden mit einem System aus vertikalen Lamellen umhüllt." Nach der offiziellen Genehmigung des Projekts im Januar 2008 erklärte Norman Foster: „Crystal Island ist eines der ehrgeizigsten Bauprojekte weltweit und ein Meilenstein in der 40-jährigen Geschichte unseres Büros. Als größtes Einzelgebäude der Welt wird es eine ganzjährige Attraktion für die Stadt Moskau und ein neuer, dynamischer und nachhaltiger urbaner Bezirk sein. Angesichts seines innovativen Energiekonzepts und seiner ‚intelligenten' Hülle stellt es einen neuen Maßstab für die Planung nachhaltiger und vielfältig genutzter städtischer Ballungsräume dar."

Si l'on compte ses parkings, le projet de Crystal Island (L'île de cristal) couvrira 2,5 millions de m² ce qui en fera le plus vaste bâtiment habité du monde. « Conçu comme une ville autonome dans une ville, il se compose d'un généreux mélange de constructions… qui en fera un lieu d'attraction pour le tout Moscou. » Le complexe comprendra 900 appartements, un hôtel de 3000 chambres, des bureaux, des commerces, un musée, une salle IMAX et une école pour 500 étudiants, ainsi qu'une plate-forme d'observation panoramique à 300 mètres au-dessus du sol. Situé sur la péninsule de Nagatino, à 7,5 kilomètres du Kremlin, il s'élèvera dans un nouveau parc aménagé qui offrira lui-même une gamme d'activités de plein air tout au long de l'année, dont des circuits de *cross-country* à ski et un anneau de patinage. Selon la présentation de l'agence : « Le volume interne de plus d'un million de mètres carrés s'élève en formation étagée à l'intérieur d'une mégastructure triangulée en acier, venant à fleur de la peau extérieure facettée en verre. Cette construction en terrasses génère une série de jardins d'hiver qui constituent une seconde strate de protection et une barrière thermique pour le bâtiment principal. Elle protège l'intérieur des conditions climatiques moscovites extrêmes, aussi bien en hiver qu'en été. Un système de persiennes verticales double les façades intérieures pour assurer l'intimité des appartements privés. » À l'obtention du permis de construire en janvier 2008, Norman Foster a déclaré : « Crystal Island est l'un des plus ambitieux projets de construction au monde et représente une étape dans les 40 années d'existence de notre agence. C'est le plus grand immeuble du monde. Il attirera tout au long de l'année les visiteurs et fera apparaître un nouveau quartier placé sous le signe du développement durable. Il représente un paradigme d'urbanisme compact, à usage multiple et respectueux de l'environnement, grâce à une stratégie unique d'économie d'énergie et une peau »intelligente« qui protège des rigueurs du climat. »

TERUNOBU FUJIMORI

Terunobu Fujimori
Professor, Institute of Industrial Science
University of Tokyo
4–6–1 Komaba / Meguro-ku / Tokyo 153–8505/ Japan

Tel: +81 3 5452 6370 / Fax: +81 3 5452 6371
E-mail: tanpopo@iis.u-tokyo.ac.jp

Born in Chino City, Nagano, Japan, in 1946, **TERUNOBU FUJIMORI** attended Tohoku University (1965–71) in Sendai, before receiving his Ph.D. in Architecture from the University of Tokyo (1971–78). He is currently a Professor at the University of Tokyo's Institute of Industrial Science. Although research on often long-forgotten Western-style buildings in Japan from the Meiji period onwards remains his main activity, he is also a practicing architect. "I didn't start designing buildings until my 40s, so the condition I set for myself is that I shouldn't just repeat the same things that my colleagues or professors were doing," he has stated. His first built work was the Jinchokan Moriya Historical Museum (Chino City, Nagano, 1990–91), which won mixed praise for the use of local materials over a reinforced-concrete structure. Other completed projects include the Akino Fuku Art Museum (Hamamatsu, Shizuoka, 1995–97); the Nira House (Leek House, Machida City, Tokyo, 1995–97); the Student Dormitory for Kumamoto Agricultural College (Koshi City, Kumamoto, 1998–2000); the Ichiya-tei (One Night Tea House, Ashigarashimo, Kanagawa, 2003); the Takasugi-an (Too-High Tea House, Chino City, Nagano, 2004), set six meters above the ground like a treehouse; and Chashitsu Tetsu (Teahouse Tetsu, Kiyoharu Shirakaba Museum, Nakamaru, Hokuto City, Yamanashi, 2005, published here), all in Japan. He won the Japan Art Grand Prix (1997) for the Nira House, and the Architectural Institute of Japan Prize for Design (2001) for the Student Dormitory for Kumamoto Agricultural College.

TERUNOBU FUJIMORI, geboren 1946 im japanischen Nagano, besuchte von 1965 bis 1971 die Universität Tohoku in Sendai, anschließend setzte er sein Architekturstudium an der Universität Tokio fort, an der er 1978 promoviert wurde. Derzeit ist Fujimori Professor am Institute of Industrial Science der Universität Tokio. Obgleich er sich nach wie vor hauptsächlich mit der Erforschung oftmals in Vergessenheit geratener japanischer Bauten beschäftigt, die seit der Meiji-Zeit in einem westlich geprägten Stil entstanden sind, ist er auch praktizierender Architekt. „Als ich selbst mit dem Bauen anfing, war ich bereits über 40. Deshalb habe ich mir vorgenommen, nicht bloß das zu wiederholen, was schon meine Kollegen oder andere Professoren machen", sagte Fujimori einmal. Sein erstes realisiertes Projekt war das Historische Museum Jinchokan Moriya (Chino, Nagano, 1990–91), das mit seiner Verwendung traditioneller Materialien über einem Tragwerk aus Stahlbeton auf ein geteiltes Echo stieß. Zu seinen weiteren, allesamt in Japan verwirklichten Projekten gehören das Akino Fuku Kunstmuseum (Hamamatsu, Shizuoka, 1995–97), das Haus Nira (Haus Leek, Machida, Tokio, 1995–97), ein Studentenwohnheim für die landwirtschaftliche Hochschule Kumamoto (Koshi, Kumamoto, 1998–2000), das Teehaus Ichiya-tei (Ashigarashimo, Kanagawa, 2003), das wie ein Baumhaus 6 m über der Erde schwebende Teehaus Takasugi-an (Chino, Nagano, 2004) und das hier vorstellte Chashitsu Tetsu (Teehaus Tetsu, Museum Kiyoharu Shirakaba, Nakamaru, Hokuto, Yamanashi, 2005). Für das Haus Nira erhielt Fujimori 1997 den Großen Preis für japanische Kunst, das Studentenwohnheim der landwirtschaftlichen Hochschule Kumamoto wurde 2001 mit dem Designpreis des Architekturinstituts von Japan ausgezeichnet.

Né à Chino City, Nagano (Japon), en 1946, **TERUNOBU FUJIMORI** a fait ses études à l'université Tohoku (1965–71) à Sendai. Il est Docteur en architecture de l'université de Tokyo (1971–78) et enseigne actuellement à l'institut des sciences et techniques de cette université. Si ses recherches sur les réalisations de style occidental au Japon datant de l'ère Meiji, souvent oubliées, restent sa principale activité, il pratique également l'architecture : « Je n'ai pas commencé à concevoir de construction avant la quarantaine, aussi me suis-je donné comme condition de ne pas répéter ce que mes confrères ou professeurs faisaient. » Son premier projet réalisé a été le musée historique Jinchokan Moriya (Chino, Nagano, 1990–91), diversement apprécié pour son recours à des matériaux locaux sur une structure en béton armé. Parmi ses autres réalisations : le musée d'Art Akino Fuku (Hamamatsu, Shizuoka, 1995–97) ; la maison Nira (maison Leek, Machida, Tokyo, 1995–97) ; un dortoir pour le collège d'agriculture de Kumamoto (Koshi, Kumamoto, 1998–2000) ; Ichiya-tei (One Night Tea House, Ashigarashimo, Kanagawa, 2003) ; Takasugi-an (maison de thé Too-High, Chino City, Nagano 2004), à six mètres au-dessus du sol, comme une maison dans un arbre, et Chashitsu Tetsu (maison de thé Tetsu, musée Kiyoharu Shirakaba, Nakamaru, Hokuto City, Yamanashi, 2005, publié ici), toutes au Japon. Il a remporté le Grand Prix d'art du Japon (1997) pour la maison Nira, et le Prix de conception de l'Institut d'architecture du Japon (2001) pour le dortoir du collège agricole de Kumamoto.

CHASHITSU TETSU
(TEAHOUSE TETSU)

Kiyoharu Shirakaba Museum, Nakamaru, Hokuto City, Yamanashi, Japan, 2005

*Floor area: 6.07 m². Client: Kiyoharu Shirakaba Museum. Cost: not disclosed.
Collaborator: Nobumichi Ohshima (Ohshima Atelier)*

The Teahouse seems to be something out of a myth or legend rather than a functioning architectural space. In fact it is both, while also being related to the history of Japanese architecture.

Das Teehaus wirkt, als entstamme es einem Mythos oder einer Legende und weniger wie ein funktionierender architektonischer Raum. Genau genommen ist es beides und außerdem verknüpft mit der Geschichte der japanischen Architektur.

La maison de thé semble davantage être l'illustration d'un mythe ou d'une légende qu'un espace architectural fonctionnel. Elle est en fait les deux, car elle est fortement liée à l'histoire de l'architecture japonaise.

Perched on a cypress trunk, four meters off the ground, the tiny structure functions according to the rules of the Japanese tea ceremony.

Das auf einen Zypressenstamm aufgesetzte Häuschen ist so angelegt, dass man in ihm eine japanische Teezeremonie abhalten kann.

Perchée sur un tronc de cyprès, à quatre mètres du sol, la petite structure fonctionne selon les règles de la cérémonie japonaise du thé.

"The site is famous for cherry blossom…When I go to see the cherry blossom at night, it is as if I strayed into a dream world," says Terunobu Fujimori, "I did not intend it this way, but it looks as if it were a house for a midget from a fairytale." Approached by the owner of the Yoshii Gallery, Chozo Yoshii, to build a teahouse on the grounds of the Kiyoharu Shirakaba Museum, Fujimori at first proposed a structure that would look down on the cherry trees. This idea was abandoned because of the number of older visitors to the museum, and this curious wooden structure was set at a height of four meters next to a restaurant designed by Yoshio Taniguchi. Fujimori cut down a cypress on the site and used it as the single support for his unusual wood-frame teahouse. In order to give the design the necessary stability to withstand earthquakes or typhoons, the architect allowed the cypress trunk to extend up into the teahouse, "like a backbone," so that both the support and the house will sway together. Unlike traditional teahouses that are more inward looking, this one was designed to view cherry blossom, and Fujimori refers to "the gold tea room that Toyotomi Hideyoshi had Rikyu[1] build for cherry-blossom viewing. The tea room was in a tree and had a crawl-in door with a frame embellished all around in gold leaf."

[1] Toyotomi Hideyoshi (1536–98) was a feudal ruler who unified Japan. Rikyu, or Sen no Rikyu (1522–91), is the historical figure who had the most profound influence on the Japanese tea ceremony.

„Dieser Ort ist berühmt für seine Kirschblüte … Wenn ich mir nachts die Kirschblüte ansehe, habe ich das Gefühl, ich verirre mich in eine Traumwelt", sagt Terunobu Fujimori. „Nicht, dass ich es so geplant hätte, aber es sieht aus wie das Haus eines Zwerges aus einem Märchen." Auf Wunsch Chozo Yoshiis, des Besitzers der Galerie Yoshii, ein Teehaus auf dem Gelände des Kiyoharu Shirakaba Museum zu bauen, schlug Fujimori zunächst eine Konstruktion über den Kronen der Kirschbäume vor. Aus Rücksicht auf ältere Museumsbesucher wurde die Idee jedoch wieder aufgegeben und stattdessen diese Holzkonstruktion in 4 m Höhe errichtet, neben einem Restaurant, dessen Entwurf von Yoshio Taniguchi stammt. Dazu ließ Fujimori die Krone einer Zypresse kappen, deren Stamm die einzige Stütze für das Teehaus bildet. Damit die Konstruktion die bei Erdbeben oder Taifunen nötige Stabilität hat, reicht der Baumstamm „wie ein Rückgrat" in das Teehaus hinein, so dass Stütze und Baumhaus gemeinsam schwingen. Im Gegensatz zu traditionellen Teehäusern, die sich eher auf den Innenraum konzentrieren, sollte dieser Entwurf zur Betrachtung der Kirschblüte einladen. Fujimori verweist auf „das goldene Teezimmer, das Toyotomi Hideyoshi sich zum selben Zweck von Rikyu[1] bauen ließ. Dieses Teezimmer befand sich auf einem Baum und hatte eine kleine Tür, durch die man hineinkriechen musste und deren Rahmen rundherum mit Blattgold geschmückt war."

[1] Toyotomi Hideyoshi (1536–98) war ein Feudalherr, unter dessen Hand Japan vereinigt wurde. Die historische Figur Rikyu oder Sen no Rikyu (1522–91) hatte maßgeblichen Einfluss auf die japanische Teezeremonie.

« Le site est célèbre pour ses cerisiers en fleurs… Lorsque je vais voir les cerisiers la nuit, c'est comme si je me perdais dans un rêve, raconte Terunobu Fujimori, je ne l'ai pas voulu ainsi, mais c'est presque une maison pour nain de conte de fée. » Approché par le propriétaire de la galerie Yoshii, Chozo Yoshii, pour construire une maison de thé dans l'enceinte du musée Kiyoharu Shirakaba, Fujimori proposa initialement une structure qui aurait dominé les cerisiers. Cette idée fut abandonnée du fait du grand nombre de visiteurs âgés du musée, mais la construction finale fut néanmoins implantée à une hauteur de quatre mètres, à proximité d'un restaurant conçu par Yoshio Taniguchi. Fujimori fit couper sur place un cyprès dont il se servit comme support central unique de cette très curieuse maison de thé. Pour assurer la stabilité, la cohésion et la résistance aux tremblements de terre et aux ouragans, l'architecte a fait pénétrer le tronc de l'arbre dans la maison « telle une colonne vertébrale ». À la différence des maisons de thé traditionnelles qui sont davantage tournées sur elles-mêmes, celle-ci a été conçue pour observer les cerisiers en fleurs, et Fujimori se réfère au « salon de thé d'or que Toyotomi Hideyoshi avait fait construire par Rikyu[1] également pour regarder les cerisiers. Il était installé dans un arbre et l'on s'y glissait par une porte basse dont le cadre était doré à la feuille d'or. »

[1] Toyotomi Hideyoshi (1536–98) est un souverain féodal qui unifia le Japon. Rikyu ou Sen no Rikyu (1522–91) est la figure historique qui exerça la plus profonde influence sur la cérémonie du thé.

Inside the teahouse, a generous view of surrounding cherry trees greets visitors. Though it is located in the grounds of a museum, the teahouse seems quite alone in its natural setting (below).

Im Innern des Teehauses empfängt den Besucher eine vorzügliche Aussicht auf die Kirschbäume rings-herum. Obgleich es sich auf dem Grundstück eines Museums befindet, scheint das Teehaus einsam in der Landschaft zu stehen (unten).

À l'intérieur de la maison de thé, une vue généreuse sur les cerisiers qui l'entourent accueille les visiteurs. Bien qu'elle soit située sur le terrain d'un musée, la maison semble com-pletement isolée dans son cadre naturel (en bas).

With natural, stripped tree trunks and an irregular wall and ceiling shape, the teahouse might appear to be quite ancient, and yet it is in many ways very modern in its conception.

Angesichts der geschälten Baumstämme und der unregelmäßigen Wand- und Deckenflächen könnte man das Teehaus für recht alt halten; tatsächlich aber folgt es in vielerlei Hinsicht ganz modernen Überlegungen.

Par ses troncs d'arbres sans écorce, ses murs et son plafond irréguliers, la maison de thé peut sembler assez ancienne, tout en étant, à de nombreux égards, plutôt moderne dans sa conception.

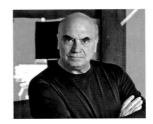

MASSIMILIANO FUKSAS

Massimiliano Fuksas Architetto
Piazza del Monte di Pietà 30
00186 Rome
Italy

Tel: +39 06 68 80 78 71 / Fax: +39 06 68 80 78 72
E-mail: office@fuksas.it
Web: www.fuksas.it

MASSIMILIANO FUKSAS was born in 1944 in Rome. He received his degree in Architecture at Rome's "La Sapienza" University in 1969. He created Granma (1969–88) with Anna Maria Sacconi, and opened an office in Paris in 1989. He won the 1999 Grand Prix d'Architecture in France, and has written the architecture column of the Italian weekly *L'Espresso* since 2000. He was the Director of the 7th Architecture Biennale in Venice (1998–2000). His presence in France was notably marked by the Médiathèque in Rézé (1987–91); the National Engineering School in Brest (ENIB ISAMOR, 1990–92); the Maison des Arts at the Michel de Montaigne University in Bordeaux (1992–95); and the Maximilien-Perret High School in Alfortville near Paris (1995–97). His Cor-ten steel entrance for the caves at Niaux (1988–93) shows, as did the Maison des Arts in Bordeaux, that Fuksas has a sustained interest in contemporary sculpture and art. Other work includes the Twin Tower, a 150-meter-high headquarters for Wienerberger (Vienna, Austria, 1995–2001); the Piazza Mall, an entertainment center, commercial and office complex (Eindhoven, The Netherlands, 1999–2004); and the Ferrari Research Center (Maranello, Italy, 2001–04). More recently, Fuksas has completed the Zénith Strasbourg (Eckbolsheim, Strasbourg, France, 2003–07, published here); and the Armani Ginza Tower (Tokyo, Japan, 2005–07). Upcoming work includes the Peace Center (Haifa, Israel); the Is Molas Golf Resort (Pula, Italy); the Euromed Center (Marseille, France); and the French National Archives (Paris, France).

MASSIMILIANO FUKSAS, geboren 1944 in Rom, erlangte 1969 sein Diplom in Architektur an der Universitá di Roma La Sapienza. Zusammen mit Anna Maria Sacconi gründete er das Büro Granma, das von 1969 bis 1989 bestand. 1989 eröffnete er ein neues Büro in Paris. 1999 gewann Fuksas den französischen Grand Prix d'Architecture. Fuksas war Direktor der 7. Architekturbiennale von Venedig (1998–2000) und schreibt seit 2000 die Architekturkolumne für das italienische Wochenmagazin *L'Espresso*. In Frankreich wurde Fuksas bekannt durch die Médiathèque in Rézé (1987–91), die École Nationale d'Ingénieurs et Institut Scientifique in Brest (ENIB ISAMOR, 1990–92), die Maison des Arts der Université Michel de Montaigne in Bordeaux (1992–95) und das Lycée Maximilien-Perret in Alfortville nahe Paris (1995–97). Wie die Maison des Arts in Bordeaux beweist auch der aus Cor-Ten-Stahl errichtete Eingang für die Höhlen von Niaux (1988–93) Fuksas' beständiges Interesse an zeitgenössischer Bildhauerei und Kunst. Zu seinen weiteren Arbeiten gehören der Vienna Twin Tower, die 150 m hohe Wienerberger-Konzernzentrale in Wien (1995–2001), das Piazza Center, ein Komplex mit Büros, Geschäften und Veranstaltungsbereichen im niederländischen Eindhoven (1999–2004), und das Forschungszentrum von Ferrari im italienischen Maranello (2001–04). In jüngster Zeit entstanden die nachfolgend vorgestellte Konzerthalle Zénith in Eckbolsheim/Straßburg (Frankreich, 2003–07) und das Armani-Hochhaus im Tokioter Ginzaviertel (Japan, 2005–07). In Planung befinden sich das Friedenszentrum im israelischen Haifa, das Golf-Resort Is Molas in Pula (Italien), das Euromed-Zentrum in Marseille (Frankreich) und das französische Nationalarchiv in Paris.

MASSIMILIANO FUKSAS, né en 1944 à Rome est diplômé d'architecture de l'université « La Sapienza » à Rome (1969). Il crée l'agence Granma (1969–88) avec Anna Maria Sacconi et ouvre un bureau à Paris en 1989. En 1999, il remporte le Grand Prix d'Architecture français. Il est l'auteur d'une rubrique d'architecture pour l'hebdomadaire italien *L'Espresso* publiée à partir de 2000. Il a été directeur de la 7e Biennale d'architecture de Venise (1998–2000). Sa présence en France a été marquée par plusieurs réalisations telles que la médiathèque de Rézé (1987–91), l'École nationale des ingénieurs de Brest (ENIB ISAMOR, 1990–92), la Maison des Arts à l'université Michel-de-Montaigne à Bordeaux (1992–95) et le collège Maximilien-Perret à Alfortville près de Paris (1995–97). Son entrée réalisée en acier Corten pour les grottes de Niaux (1988–93) montre, comme la Maison des Arts de Bordeaux, son intérêt soutenu pour l'art et la sculpture contemporains. Parmi ses autres réalisations : la Twin Tower, siège de Wienerberger, de 150 mètres de haut (Vienne, Autriche, 1995–2001) ; le Piazza Mall, centre commercial, de loisirs et de bureaux (Eindhoven, Pays-Bas, 1999–2004) et le centre de recherche Ferrari (Maranello, Italie, 2001–04). Plus récemment, il a achevé le Zénith de Strasbourg (Eckbolsheim, Strasbourg, France, 2003–07, publié ici) et la tour Armani de Ginza (Tokyo, Japon, 2005–07). Il travaille actuellement sur les projets d'un Centre de la Paix (Haïfa, Israël), du golf Is Molas (Pula, Italie), du centre Euromed (Marseille, France et des Archives nationales de France (Pierrefitte-sur-Seine, environs de Paris).

ZÉNITH STRASBOURG

Eckbolsheim, Strasbourg, France, 2003–07

Floor area: 16 564 m².
Client: Communauté urbaine de Strasbourg/SERS – Société d'Aménagement et d'Equipement de la Région de Strasbourg.
Cost: €48 million. Architects: Massimiliano and Doriana Fuksas.
Acoustics: Altia-Acoustique

In October 2003, Massimiliano Fuksas won the international competition for the design of this 10 000-seat (12 000 including standing room) rock concert hall in eastern France. The first Zénith music hall was built in Paris in 1984 and numerous well-known architects, such as Bernard Tschumi (page 496), have participated in the effort. As Fuksas says, "The building is to be understood as a single, unifying, and autonomous sculpture. By layering and rotating the ellipsoid metal façade structure, the design receives a very dynamic character. This is underlined with the translucent textile membrane, which covers the steel frame and creates magnificent light effects." Projections on the outer, orange membrane serve as a large-scale billboard on upcoming events. The Zénith theaters are all based on the same principle of flexibility and clearly defined spaces and functions. This project by Fuksas contributes to the ongoing success of this nationwide French initiative.

Im Oktober 2003 gewann Massimiliano Fuksas den internationalen Architekturwettbewerb für den Entwurf einer Rockkonzerthalle im Elsass, die Platz für 12 000 Besucher haben sollte. Seit 1984 sind bereits mehrere Zénith-Konzerthallen entstanden, die erste davon in Paris; die einzelnen Entwürfe stammen von bekannten Architekten wie Bernard Tschumi (S. 496). Zu seinem Straßburger Beitrag erklärt Fuksas: „Das Gebäude ist als eine einzige, in sich geschlossene autonome Skulptur aufzufassen. Durch die geschichtete und verdrehte elliptische Struktur der Metallfassade erhält der Entwurf einen äußerst dynamischen Charakter. Dieser wird von einer durchscheinenden Stoffmembran unterstützt, die den Stahlrahmen umhüllt und für großartige Lichteffekte sorgt." Projektionen verwandeln die Außenseite der orangefarbenen Membran in eine riesige Ankündigungstafel für kommende Events. Sämtlichen Zénith-Veranstaltungsarenen liegt das gleiche Prinzip zugrunde: klar definierte Räume und Funktionen bei gleichzeitig hoher Flexibilität. Mit seiner Straßburger Konzerthalle trägt Fuksas zu einem in ganz Frankreich erfolgreichen Konzept bei.

Massimiliano Fuksas a remporté le concours international pour cette salle de concerts de rock de 12 000 places en octobre 2003. Le premier Zénith avait été construit à Paris en 1984 et de nombreux architectes connus, dont Bernard Tschumi (page 496), ont participé à ce programme national. Pour Fuksas : « Le bâtiment doit se regarder comme une sculpture unique, autonome, unificatrice. Le plan a pris un caractère très dynamique par la stratification et la rotation de la structure ellipsoïdale de la façade métallique. Cet effet est souligné par une membrane textile translucide qui recouvre l'ossature en acier et crée de superbes effets lumineux. » Des projections sur la membrane orange extérieure font office d'affiches géantes. Les salles Zénith reposent toutes sur le même principe de flexibilité et d'espaces et fonctions clairement définis. Ce projet confirme le succès de cette initiative culturelle française.

Like other signature Zénith projects in France, the Strasbourg building is meant to give a visible signal of its presence to arriving concert-goers.

Wie die anderen Zénith-Hallen in Frankreich soll auch der Straßburger Bau für die ankommenden Konzertbesucher Signalwirkung haben.

Comme d'autres projets de Zénith en France, celui de Strasbourg veut signaler fortement sa présence aux amateurs de concerts.

The sweeping orange-red membrane curves visible inside the structure echo its exterior directly. The simple, open design allows for easy visitor movement.

Die im Gebäudeinnern sichtbare, schwungvolle orange-rote Membranhülle ist das Negativ der Außenseite. Die einfache, offene Konstruktion kommt dem Besucherfluss entgegen.

Les courbes de la membrane rouge-orange, visibles de l'intérieur, rappellent directement l'extérieur. Le plan simple et ouvert permet une circulation aisée des spectateurs.

Intended for a maximum capacity of 12 000 persons, the Zénith meets strict safety requirements, but it does so within the architect's definition of a "single unifying autonomous sculpture."

Da die Zénith-Halle bis zu 12 000 Zuschauer fasst, gelten strenge Sicherheitsbestimmungen. Dennoch präsentiert sie sich, so der Architekt, als eine „einzige, in sich geschlossene autonome Skulptur".

Conçu pour une capacité maximum de 12 000 personnes, le Zénith respecte une réglementation de sécurité très stricte, mais dans le cadre de la définition donnée par l'architecte d'une « sculpture autonome unificatrice et unique ».

The Zénith label calls for flexible space that can be easily subdivided. Above, a view of the actual concert hall and, below, sections showing the seating space.

Die Name Zénith steht für flexible Räume, die sich leicht unterteilen lassen. Oben der Blick in die große Konzerthalle; die Querschnitte unten zeigen die Anordnung der Sitzreihen.

Le label Zénith s'applique à des espaces souples et facilement modulables. Ici, une vue de la salle de concert et, en bas, des coupes montrant l'espace dévolu aux spectateurs.

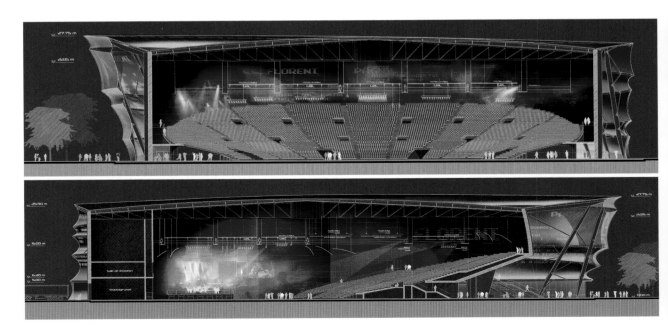

As is the case with other Zénith buildings, Fuksas intentionally gives a somewhat industrial appearance to what is meant to be a big "rough" concert space.

Wie andere Zénith-Bauten hat auch Fuksas' Beitrag nicht zufällig etwas von einem Industriegebäude, damit die äußere Erscheinung einer „ungeschliffenen" Konzertarena entspricht.

Comme pour les autres Zénith, Fuksas a intentionnellement donné un aspect industriel à ce qui est d'abord un espace de concerts jeune et populaire.

ANTÓN GARCÍA-ABRIL & ENSAMBLE STUDIO

Antón García-Abril & Ensamble Studio
c/Cristóbal Bordiú 55, bajos / 28003 Madrid / Spain

Tel: +34 91 541 08 48
E-mail: anton@ensamble.info / Web: www.ensamble.info

ANTÓN GARCÍA-ABRIL was born in Madrid in 1969. He graduated from the ETSA of Madrid (ETSAM) in Architecture and Urbanism in 1995 and went on to receive a doctorate from the same institution in 2000. He is currently a Professor of Architectural Projects at the ETSAM and a visiting critic at Cornell University. García-Abril worked in the office of Santiago Calatrava (1992) and in that of Alberto Campo Baeza (1990–94). He created his first firm in 1995, and his present one, **ENSAMBLE STUDIO**, in 2000. He explains that the name of his firm is derived from a term used in architecture, "assemble," and the musical term "ensemble." "This team," he says, "develops a multidisciplinary working scheme… to carry out the intervention of the architect in the whole process that leads to the artistic work, from the conceptual abstraction to the construction detail." Essentially this means that he has created an in-house contracting firm. Débora Mesa Molina and Javier Cuesta are members of the team. His completed projects include: the Musical Studies Center (Santiago de Compostela, 2002); the Concert Hall and Music School (Medina del Campo, 2003); the Valdés Studio (Madrid, 2004); and the Martemar House (Málaga, 2003–05), all in Spain. Amongst his more recent projects: the Hemeroscopium House (Madrid, 2006); La Casa del Lector Library (Madrid, 2006); the SGAE Central Office (Santiago de Compostela, 2005–07, published here); Berklee SGAE Tower of Music, a vertical campus for contemporary international music education (Valencia, 2008); and the Museum of America (Salamanca, 2008), all in Spain.

ANTÓN GARCÍA-ABRIL, geboren 1969 in Madrid, absolvierte sein Studium im Bereich Architektur und Urbanistik an der Escuela técnica superior de architectura de Madrid (ETSAM), an der er später auch promoviert wurde. Derzeit ist er Dozent am Departamento de proyectos arquitectónicos der ETSAM und Gastdozent an der Cornell University. Von 1990 bis 1994 arbeitete er im Büro von Alberto Campo Baeza und 1992 für Santiago Calatrava. Seine erste eigene Firma gründete er 1995. Den Namen seiner jetzigen, im Jahr 2000 gegründeten Firma **ENSAMBLE STUDIO** erklärt García-Abril als eine Kombination aus dem in der Architektur gebräuchlichen Begriff „assemble" und dem musikalischen „Ensemble". „Das Team", so García-Abril, „entwickelt einen multidisziplinären Arbeitsplan […], der sämtliche Planungen des Architekten umsetzt, aus denen schließlich das fertige Werk hervorgeht, vom abstrakten Konzept bis hin zum einzelnen Baudetail." Im Prinzip hat García-Abril damit also ein hausinternes Vertragsunternehmen geschaffen. Débora Mesa Molina und Javier Cuesta gehören zum Team. Zu den von Ensamble realisierten Projekten gehören die Musikakademie in Santiago de Compostela (2002), die Konzerthalle und Musikschule in Medina del Campo (2003), das Atelier Valdés in Madrid (2004) und die Casa Martemar in Málaga (2003–05). In jüngerer Zeit entstanden die Casa Hemeroscopium (2006) und die Bibliothek der Casa del Lector (2006), beide in Madrid, die Zentrale der Sociedad General de Autores y Editores (SGAE) in Santiago de Compostela (2005–07), die Berklee SGAE Torre de la Música in Valencia (ein Ableger des Berklee College of Music in Boston; 2008), und das Museo de América in Salamanca (2008).

ANTÓN GARCÍA-ABRIL, né à Madrid en 1969, est diplômé en architecture et urbanisme de l'ETSA de Madrid (1995) dont il est également docteur (2000). Il est actuellement professeur en projets architecturaux à l'ETSAM et critique invité à Cornell University. García-Abril a travaillé dans l'agence de Santiago Calatrava (1992) et celle d'Alberto Campo Baeza (1990–94). Il a créé sa première agence en 1995, et l'actuel **ENSAMBLE STUDIO** en 2000. Ce nom vient de la contraction du terme architectural « assembler » et du terme musical « ensemble ». « Cette équipe, dit-il, travaille dans un esprit multidisciplinaire… pour que l'intervention de l'architecte soit menée à bien au cours du processus tout entier qui conduit à une création artistique, de l'abstraction conceptuelle au détail constructif. » Il a donc créé une agence à services intégrés. Débora Mesa Molina et Javier Cuesta font partie de l'équipe. Parmi ses réalisations achevées : un conservatoire de musique (Saint-Jacques-de-Compostelle, 2002) ; une salle de concert et école de musique (Medina del Campo, 2003) ; le studio Valdés (Madrid, 2004) et la maison Martemar (Málaga, 2003–05), tous en Espagne. Parmi ses plus récents projets : la maison Hemeroscopium (Madrid, 2006) ; la bibliothèque de la Casa del Lector (Madrid, 2006) ; le siège de la SGAE (Saint-Jacques-de-Compostelle, 2005–07, publié ici) ; la Torre de la Musica Berklee SGAE (Valence, 2008), un campus pour l'enseignement de la musique contemporaine internationale, et le musée d'Amérique (Salamanque, 2008).

SGAE CENTRAL OFFICE
Santiago de Compostela, Galicia, Spain, 2005–07

*Floor area: 3000 m². Client: SGAE. Cost: not disclosed. Collaborating Architects: Débora Mesa Molina,
Ensamble Studio: José Antonio Millán, Ricardo Sanz, Marina Otero, Elena Pérez,
Helena Serrano, Jorge Consuegra, Andrés Toledo*

The SGAE (General Society of Authors and Publishers) Central Office in Santiago de Compostela is located on the Vista Alegre property, an exceptional site set between a private garden and a public green area, from which the skyline of the historical city can be seen. The project for the development of the area was created by Arata Isozaki and envisaged the construction of a series of buildings with academic purpose, most of them now built. The SGAE Central Office, situated at the western limit of the site, completes the intervention in Vista Alegre and defines its boundaries. According to Antón García-Abril, "The architectural conception of the building incorporates the spirit of the city of Santiago, developing a singular identity and entering into a dialog with the history and memory of the place, as well as a close relationship with contemporary language." The program includes social activities for authors and publishers, but also a wide range of cultural activities open to the public. It is divided into four functional areas distributed on four levels: Distribution, Formation, Public Area, and Management, with access from the garden and the street. Of the unusual rough-stone wall he created, the architect writes, "The great stone wall can be thought of as a monumental sculpture, constructed by the superposition and repetition of prehistoric orders adapted to a Renaissance broken composition." A more discreet glass wall faces the street, allowing views of the spaces within.

Die Zentrale der SGAE (Sociedad General de Autores y Editores) in Santiago de Compostela befindet sich auf dem Gelände von Vista Alegre, einem wunderschön gelegenen Areal zwischen einem privaten Park und einer öffentlichen Grünanlage, von dem aus man die Silhouette der Altstadt betrachten kann. Die Pläne zur Entwicklung des Geländes stammen von Arata Isozaki und sehen eine Reihe von akademischen Gebäuden vor, von denen der größte Teil inzwischen fertiggestellt ist. Der Bau der SGAE-Zentrale am westlichen Ende des Geländes setzt sowohl den planerischen als auch topografischen Schlussstein von Vista Alegre. Antón García-Abril zufolge „verkörpert das architektonische Konzept des Gebäudes den Geist der Stadt Santiago und zeigt einen ganz eigenen Charakter, indem es in einen Dialog mit Geschichte und Andenken des Ortes tritt und zugleich eine enge Beziehung zur zeitgenössischen Formensprache unterhält". Zum Programm des Literaturzentrums gehören Veranstaltungen für Autoren und Verlage, aber auch eine große Bandbreite öffentlicher Kulturveranstaltungen. Vier Funktionsbereiche – Öffentlichkeitsarbeit, Fortbildung, Publikumsbereich und Management – verteilen sich auf ebenso viele Ebenen, die vom Park wie von der Straße aus zugänglich sind. Zum Entwurf der ungewöhnlichen Bruchsteinwand schreibt der Architekt: „Die große Steinmauer lässt sich als eine Monumentalskulptur verstehen, konstruiert aus Über- und Hintereinanderschichtungen nach prähistorischem Muster, die in einer fragmentarischen Renaissance-Komposition aufgehen." Durch eine weniger auffällige Glasfassade auf der Straßenseite kann man von draußen in die Innenräume hineinschauen.

Le siège de la SGAE (Société générale des auteurs et éditeurs) à Saint-Jacques-de-Compostelle est situé sur la propriété de Vista Alegre, site exceptionnel entre un jardin privé et un espace vert public d'où l'on a une vue panoramique sur la cité historique. Le projet d'urbanisation dû à Arata Isozaki prévoyait la construction d'un certain nombre de bâtiments universitaires, la plupart édifiés à ce jour. Le siège de la SGAE se trouve en bordure ouest du terrain et marque ses limites. Pour Antón García-Abril : « La conception architecturale du bâtiment intègre l'esprit de la ville de Saint-Jacques-de-Compostelle en développant son identité singulière et en ouvrant un dialogue avec l'histoire et la mémoire du lieu, tout en maintenant une relation étroite avec un langage contemporain. » Le programme comprend des services pour les auteurs et les éditeurs, mais aussi une gamme étendue d'activités ouvertes au public. Le bâtiment est divisé en quatre zones fonctionnelles réparties sur quatre niveaux : distribution, formation, zone publique et gestion, toutes accessibles du jardin et de la rue. Du grand et curieux mur de pierre, l'architecte précise : « Le grand mur de pierre peut être vu comme une sculpture monumentale, édifiée par la superposition et la répétition d'ordres préhistoriques adaptés à une composition brisée d'esprit Renaissance. » Une façade à mur de verre plus discrète, donnant sur la rue, offre des perspectives sur l'extérieur.

The fractured stone façade has an almost Neolithic appearance—an enigmatic design that recalls the distant past.

Die fragmentierte Steinfassade des enigmatischen Entwurfs erinnert an eine ferne Vergangenheit – sie hat beinahe etwas Jungsteinzeitliches.

La façade fracturée crée une atmosphère presque néolithique à travers un dessin énigmatique qui évoque certainement un lointain passé.

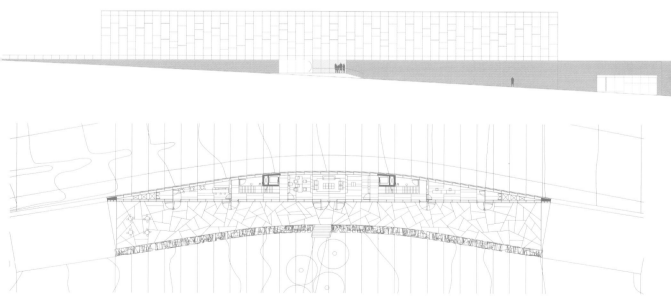

A view of the rear façade and drawings of the building show the contrast between the rough stone areas and the more "machined" glass and metal façades.

Zeichnungen und Ansicht der Rückfassade lassen den Kontrast zwischen den groben, steinernen Abschnitten und den „maschinelleren" Fassaden aus Glas und Metall erkennen.

Une vue de la façade arrière et des croquis du bâtiment montrent le contraste entre les parties en pierre brute et les façades en métal et verre plus « industrialisées ».

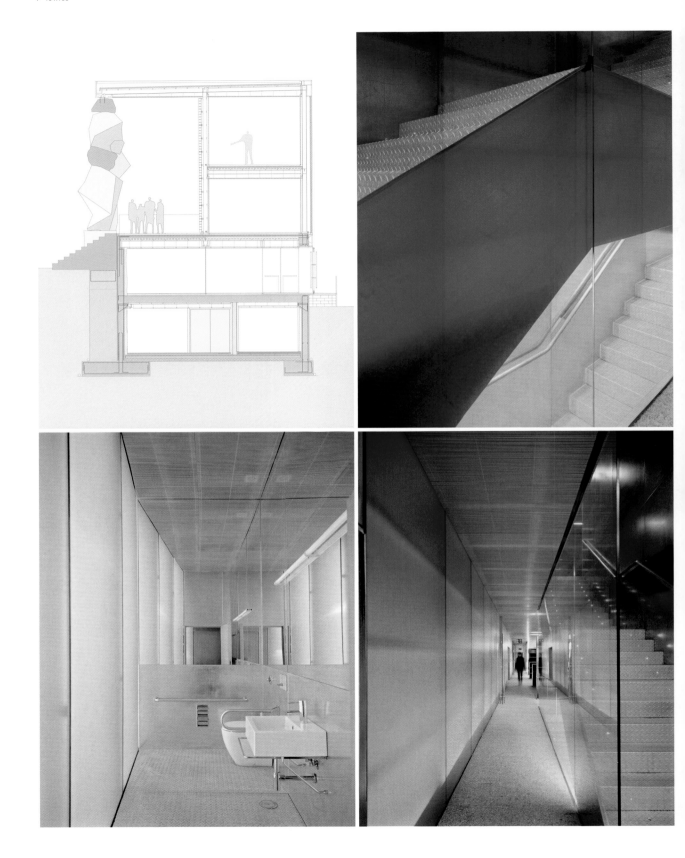

The theatrical aspect of the stone wall is heightened by a play of different-colored lights across its rough surfaces.

Verstärkt wird der dramatische Effekt der Steinmauer durch das verschiedenfarbige Lichtspiel auf ihrer rauen Oberfläche.

L'aspect théâtral de ce mur de pierre est souligné par le jeu des couleurs projetées sur sa surface brute.

DIONISIO GONZÁLEZ

Fiedler Contemporary
Lindenstr. 19
50674 Cologne
Germany

Tel: +49 221 923 08 00
Fax: +49 221 24 96 01
E-mail: info@ulrichfiedler.com
Web: www.ulrichfiedler.com

DIONISIO GONZÁLEZ was born in 1965 in Gijón, Spain. He obtained a Ph.D. in Fine Art from the University of Seville with a dissertation on "The Aesthetics of Horror." He pursued a more academic path than many artists, obtaining research fellowships from the Spanish Ministry of Education and Science (1992–95) and a postgraduate scholarship for artistic creation and research of the Municipal Foundation of Culture, Local Government of Gijón (1994). González lives and works in Seville. His series of altered photographs *Cartografías para a remoçao* and *Arquitetura da sobra: A cidade subexposta* are the result of several years of work in the slums of São Paulo and Rio de Janeiro in Brazil: see the *Favela Series* shot in São Paulo (São Paulo, 2004–07, published here). Dionisio González has received numerous awards, including the Pilar Juncosa Sotheby's Award from the Pilar and Joan Miró Foundation. His most recent exhibitions include his participation in the 2006 Venice Architecture Biennale, Italy, and the solo exhibition held at the Kunstverein in Heidelberg, Germany, in 2007.

DIONISIO GONZÁLEZ, geboren 1965 in Gijón in Asturien/Spanien, promovierte an der Fakultät für bildende Künste der Universidad de Sevilla mit einer Dissertation zur „Ästhetik des Schreckens". Anders als viele seiner Künstlerkollegen konzentrierte González sich stärker auf eine akademische Laufbahn; 1992 bis 1995 erhielt er ein Forschungsstipendium des spanischen Ministeriums für Bildung und Forschung, 1994 ein Postgraduiertenstipendium der städtischen Kulturstiftung von Gijón (1994). González lebt und arbeitet in Sevilla. Seine Serien manipulierter Fotografien „Cartografías para a remoçao" und „Arquitetura da sobra: A cidade subexposta" sind das Ergebnis einer mehrjährigen Arbeit in den Slums von São Paulo und Rio de Janeiro, ebenso wie die in São Paulo aufgenommene Serie „Favela" (São Paulo, 2004–07), die hier vorgestellt wird. Dionisio González erhielt zahlreiche Auszeichnungen, darunter den Pilar Juncosa & Sotheby's Award der Fondació Pilar i Joan Miró. 2006 nahm er an der Architekturbiennale in Venedig teil, 2007 war er mit einer Einzelausstellung im Heidelberger Kunstverein vertreten.

DIONISIO GONZÁLEZ, né en 1965 à Gijón, Espagne, est Docteur en Beaux-Arts de l'université de Séville pour sa thèse sur « L'Esthétique de l'horreur ». Il a poursuivi une carrière plus académique que beaucoup d'artistes grâce à des bourses de recherche du Ministère espagnol de l'éducation et des sciences (1992–95) et une bourse de création artistique et de recherche de la Fondation municipale de la culture de Gijón. Il vit et travaille à Séville. Ses séries de photographies modifiées *Cartografías para a remoçao* and *Arquitetura da sobra : a cidade subexposta* résultent de plusieurs années de recherche sur les taudis de São Paulo et Rio de Janeiro au Brésil, comme la série *Favela* prise à São Paulo (São Paulo, 2004–07, publiée ici). Dionisio González a reçu de nombreuses récompenses dont le Pilar Juncosa Sotheby's Award de la Fondation Pilar et Joan Miró. Plus récemment, il a participé à la Biennale d'architecture de Venise en 2006 et a exposé personnellement à la Kunstverein d'Heidelberg, Allemagne, en 2007.

FAVELA SERIES

São Paulo, São Paulo, Brazil, 2004–07

What might at first appear to be a real photo of stacked slum housing reveals itself to be a complex commentary on such living conditions, but also on contemporary architecture.

Was man zunächst für eine echte Aufnahme gestapelter Slumbehausungen halten könnte, entpuppt sich als ein komplexer Kommentar zu solchen Lebensbedingungen sowie zur zeitgenössischen Architektur.

Ce qui pourrait passer pour la photo réaliste d'un empilement de taudis est en fait un commentaire complexe sur les conditions de vie dans les quartiers défavorisés et l'architecture contemporaine.

Dionisio González spent a great deal of time documenting the *favelas*, or shantytowns, of Brazil's two largest cities. In his exhibitions, the artist presents statements from the Brazilian government recognizing the property ownership of shanty residents, which gives these curious ephemeral structures a legal status. The "Cingapura Project" in São Paulo, for example, aimed to raze the shantytowns in favor of high-rise "Superblock" structures. By altering photos of these areas, the artist attempts to propose an alternative to mass demolition. His work is a kind of partial recycling of reality, an imagined form of urban renewal meant for some of the poorest people in Latin America. Naturally implicit in his altered images, there is a social critique and a willful mixture of the architectural products of plenty (sleek, modern designs) and penury (the *favela*). The images reproduced here were all taken in São Paulo. Where the eye of the spectator might shy away from pictures of slums, there is a curious kind of attraction in these photos, an almost aesthetically pleasing interpretation of misery, improved by the intervention of the artist. Once drawn in, however, the spectator is left attempting to distinguish what is "real" and what has been added by the photographer, an exercise that inevitably leads one to think about architecture itself.

Dionisio González hat in jahrelanger Arbeit die Favelas, die Barackensiedlungen, der beiden größten Städte Brasiliens dokumentiert. Neben Fotografien gehören zu seinen Ausstellungen Erklärungen der brasilianischen Regierung, in denen diese den Anspruch der Barackenbewohner auf Wohneigentum anerkennt und damit den kuriosen, oft wenig dauerhaften Bauten einen offiziellen Rechtsstatus zuerkennt. Das „Cingapura-Projekt" in São Paulo dagegen sah den Abriss der Barackenviertel vor, die dann durch Hochhausbauten, so genannte Superblocks, ersetzt werden sollten. Mit seinen bearbeiteten Favela-Fotografien versucht der Künstler, eine Alternative zum Massenabriss aufzuzeigen. González' Vorgehensweise ist eine Art Teilrecycling der Wirklichkeit, indem er eine andere Form der Stadterneuerung für einige der ärmsten Menschen Lateinamerikas entwirft. Natürlich enthalten die manipulierten Bilder mit ihrer absichtlichen Vermischung von architektonischen Erzeugnissen des Wohlstands (schicke, moderne Designerarchitektur) mit denen des Mangels (den Favelas) auch ein gesellschaftskritisches Moment. Die hier gezeigten Aufnahmen stammen alle aus São Paulo. Während der Betrachter normalerweise vor Bildern aus Slums eher zurückschreckt, erlebt er hier eine seltsame Anziehungskraft, eine beinahe ästhetisch ansprechende Interpretation des Elends, das durch die Einflussnahme des Künstlers abgemildert wird. Steht der Betrachter jedoch einmal in ihrem Bann, muss er selbst herausfinden, was real ist und was der Künstler hinzugefügt hat – eine Aufgabe, die zwangsläufig zu grundsätzlichen Fragen über das Wesen der Architektur führt.

Dionisio Gonzalez a consacré beaucoup de temps à étudier les favelas des deux plus grandes villes du Brésil. Dans ses expositions, il montre des déclarations du gouvernement brésilien reconnaissant les droits de propriété de leurs résidants, ce qui donne à ces structures éphémères un statut légal. Le « projet de Cingapura » à São Paulo, par exemple, devait permettre de raser ces favelas pour construire des « Superblocks » de grande hauteur. En modifiant les photos de ces quartiers, l'artiste tente de proposer une alternative à la démolition massive. Son travail consiste en une sorte de recyclage partiel de la réalité, une forme imaginaire de rénovation urbaine pour certains des plus pauvres des habitants d'Amérique latine. Implicitement, il exprime une critique sociale et un mélange volontaire de productions architecturales symbolisant l'abondance (projets modernes, élégants) et la pénurie (les favelas). Les images reproduites ici ont toutes été prises à São Paulo. Alors que le regard du spectateur se détourne généralement de représentations de taudis, ces photos exercent une curieuse attraction en une interprétation presque esthétique de la misère, modifiée et améliorée par l'intervention de l'artiste. Une fois attiré, le spectateur doit distinguer ce qui est « réel » et ce qui a été ajouté par le photographe, exercice qui fait inévitablement réfléchir à l'architecture.

Each image has bits and pieces of contemporary architecture or such elements as shipping containers (below), inserted into what is otherwise a favela background. A new way of looking at architecture?

Auf allen Fotografien finden sich in der Favelaszenerie kleine Details aus der zeitgenössischen Architektur oder Elemente wie Frachtcontainer (unten) eingefügt. Könnte so ein neuer Umgang mit Architektur aussehen?

Chaque image intègre des touches d'architecture très contemporaine ou des éléments comme des conteneurs (ci-dessous) insérés dans le contexte d'une favela. Une nouvelle façon de regarder l'architecture ?

ZAHA HADID

Zaha Hadid Architects
Studio 9
10 Bowling Green Lane
London EC1R OBQ
UK

Tel: +44 20 72 53 51 47 / Fax: +44 20 72 51 83 22
E-mail: mail@zaha-hadid.com / Web: www.zaha-hadid.com

ZAHA HADID studied architecture at the Architectural Association (AA) in London beginning in 1972 and was awarded the Diploma Prize in 1977. She then became a partner of Rem Koolhaas in the Office for Metropolitan Architecture (OMA) and taught at the AA. She has also taught at Harvard, the University of Chicago, in Hamburg, and at Columbia University in New York. Well-known for her paintings and drawings, she has had a substantial influence, despite having built relatively few buildings. She has completed the Vitra Fire Station (Weil-am-Rhein, Germany, 1990–94); and exhibition designs, such as that for "The Great Utopia" (Solomon R. Guggenheim Museum, New York, 1992). Significant competition entries include her design for the Cardiff Bay Opera House (1994–96); the Habitable Bridge (London, 1996); and the Luxembourg Philharmonic Hall (1997). More recently, Zaha Hadid has entered a phase of active construction with such projects as the Bergisel Ski Jump (Innsbruck, Austria, 2001–02); the Lois & Richard Rosenthal Center for Contemporary Art (Cincinnati, Ohio, 1999–2003); the Phaeno Science Center (Wolfsburg, Germany, 2001–05); the Central Building of the new BMW Assembly Plant in Leipzig (Germany, 2005); and the Nordpark Cable Railway (Innsbruck, Austria, 2004–07, published here). She has recently completed the MAXXI National Center of Contemporary Arts in Rome (Italy, 2008); and is working on the Guangzhou Opera House (Guangzhou, China, 2006–09); and the Sheik Zayed Bridge (Abu Dhabi, UAE, 2005–10). In 2004, Zaha Hadid became the first woman to win the coveted Pritzker Prize.

ZAHA HADID studierte ab 1972 an der Architectural Association (AA) in London und erhielt 1977 den Diploma Prize. Danach war sie zunächst Partnerin von Rem Koolhaas im Office for Metropolitan Architecture (OMA) sowie Dozentin an der AA. Später lehrte Hadid auch in Harvard, an der University of Chicago, an der Columbia University in New York und in Hamburg. Bekannt und zu einer einflussreichen Vertreterin ihrer Zunft wurde sie zunächst vor allem durch ihre Gemälde und Zeichnungen. Ihre Entwürfe dagegen wurden anfangs selten realisiert, etwa das Feuerwehrhaus der Firma Vitra in Weil am Rhein (1990–94) oder das Ausstellungsdesign für „The Great Utopia" im Solomon R. Guggenheim Museum in New York (1992). Zu wichtigen Wettbewerbsbeiträgen Hadids zählen das Cardiff Bay Opera House (1994–96), die Habitable Bridge in London (1996) und die Luxemburger Philharmonie (1997). Vor einigen Jahren begann in Hadids Schaffen eine neue Phase, in der sie eine Reihe von Projekten realisierte, darunter die Bergiselschanze in Innsbruck (2001–02), das Lois & Richard Rosenthal Center for Contemporary Art in Cincinnati, Ohio (1999–2003), das Wolfsburger Wissenschaftsmuseum Phaeno (2001–05), das neue Zentralgebäude für BMW in Leipzig (2005) und die Hungerburgbahn in Innsbruck (2004–07, hier vorgestellt). Zuletzt entstand das MAXXI, das Museo Nazionale delle Arti del XXI secolo in Rom (2008). Derzeit arbeitet die Architektin an dem Opernhaus für die chinesische Stadt Guangzhou (2006–09) und an der Sheik-Zayed-Brücke in Abu Dhabi (VAE, 2005–10). 2004 wurde Zaha Hadid als erste Frau mit dem begehrten Pritzker-Preis ausgezeichnet.

ZAHA HADID a étudié à l'Architectural Association (AA) de Londres de 1972 à 1977, date à laquelle elle a reçu le Diploma Prize. Elle devient ensuite partenaire de Rem Koolhaas, à l'Office for Metropolitan Architecture (OMA) et enseigne à l'AA. Célèbre pour ses peintures et dessins, elle a exercé une réelle influence, même si elle n'a construit que relativement peu pendant longtemps. Parmi ses anciennes réalisations : un poste d'incendie pour Vitra (Weil-am-Rhein, Allemagne, 1990–94), et des projets pour des expositions comme « La Grande Utopie » au musée Solomon R. Guggenheim (New York, 1992). Elle a participé à de nombreux concours dont les plus importants sont le projet de Cardiff Bay Opera House (Pays-de-Galles, 1994–96) ; le Habitable Bridge (Londres, 1996) et la salle de concerts philharmoniques de Luxembourg (1997). Plus récemment, elle est entrée dans une phase active de grands chantiers avec des réalisations comme le tremplin de ski de Bergisel (Innsbruck, Autriche, 2001–02) ; le Lois & Richard Rosenthal Center for Contemporary Art (Cincinnati, Ohio, 1999–2003) ; le musée scientifique Phaeno (Wolfsburg, Allemagne, 2001–05) ; le bâtiment central de la nouvelle usine BMW de Leipzig (2005) et le funiculaire du Nordpark (Innsbruck, Autriche, 2004–07, publié ici). Elle a réalisé récemment le Centre national d'art contemporain de Rome MAXXI (2008), et travaille actuellement sur la réalisation de l'opéra de Guangzhou (Guangzhou, Chine, 2006–09) et du pont Cheikh Zayed (Abu Dhabi, EAU, 2005–10). En 2004, elle a été la première femme à remporter le très convoité Pritzker Prize.

NORDPARK CABLE RAILWAY

Innsbruck, Austria, 2004–07

*Roof surface (all stations inclusive): 2500 m². Client: INKB (Innsbrucker Nordkettenbahnen GmbH), Public Private Partnership.
Cost: not disclosed. Design: Zaha Hadid with Patrik Schumacher.
Project Architect: Thomas Vietzke.
Design Team: Jens Borstelmann, Markus Planteu*

Inaugurated on December 1, 2007, the Nordpark Cable Railway project consists of four new stations and a cable-stayed suspension bridge over the River Inn. The railway runs between the Congress Station in the center of the city, up the Nordkette Mountain to the Hungerburg Station, 288 meters above Innsbruck. Hadid had previously completed the Bergisel Ski Jump in the Austrian city (2001–02). The architect won a 2005 competition for the Nordpark project together with the contractor Strabag. Adapting her designs to the specific locations of each station, Zaha Hadid employed "an overall language of fluidity." According to the architect, "We studied natural phenomena such as glacial moraines and ice movements—as we wanted each station to use the fluid language of natural ice formations, like a frozen stream on the mountainside." Double-curvature glass on top of concrete plinths forms an "artificial landscape." Recently available fabrication methods such as CNC milling and glass thermoforming allowed the use of computer design and production with some techniques borrowed from the automotive industry.

Die am 1. Dezember 2007 neu eingeweihte Nordkettenbahn besteht aus vier neuen Haltestationen und einer Schrägseilbrücke über den Inn. Die Bahn verbindet das Innsbrucker Kongresshaus mit dem Stadtzentrum und führt weiter auf die Nordkette bis zur Hungerburgstation, 288 m oberhalb der Stadt. 2001 bis 2002 war in der Stadt bereits die von Hadid entworfene Bergiselschanze gebaut worden. 2005 gewann die Architektin zusammen mit der österreichischen Firma Strabag den Wettbewerb für das Nordparkprojekt. Hadid entwickelte eine „Formensprache, die sich vor allem durch ihren flüssigen Stil auszeichnet" und an die speziellen örtlichen Gegebenheiten der einzelnen Stationen angepasst ist. Weiter führt sie aus: „Wir haben uns natürliche Phänomene – Gletschermoränen und Eisbewegungen – angeschaut, da die einzelnen Stationen wie natürliche Eisformationen, zum Beispiel wie ein gefrorener Bergbach, gestaltet sein sollten." Gebildet wird die „künstliche Landschaft" von doppelt gebogenem Glas auf Betonsockeln. Um die am Computer entstandenen Entwürfe umzusetzen, kamen erst seit Kurzem gebräuchliche Herstellungsmethoden wie CNC-Zuschnitte und die Thermoverformung von Glas sowie Produktionsverfahren aus der Automobilindustrie zum Einsatz.

Inaugurée le 1er décembre 2007, cette ligne de funiculaire comprend quatre gares et un pont suspendu à haubans sur l'Inn. Elle va de la gare du Congrès en centre-ville à la gare de Hungerburg dans la Nordkette, à 288 mètres au-dessus d'Innsbruck. L'architecte avait précédemment construit le tremplin de ski de Bergisel dans la cité autrichienne (2001–02). Adaptant son style à la spécificité de chaque gare, Zaha Hadid a utilisé «un langage global de fluidité». «Nous avons étudié des phénomènes comme les moraines glaciaires et les mouvements de la glace, car nous voulions que chaque gare parle ce langage fluide des formations glaciaires naturelles, en une sorte de torrent gelé à flanc de montagne.» Une double voûte de verre sur un socle de béton forme un «paysage artificiel». Des systèmes de fabrication récents tels que la découpe CNC ou le thermoformage du verre ont permis d'emprunter des techniques issues de l'industrie automobile.

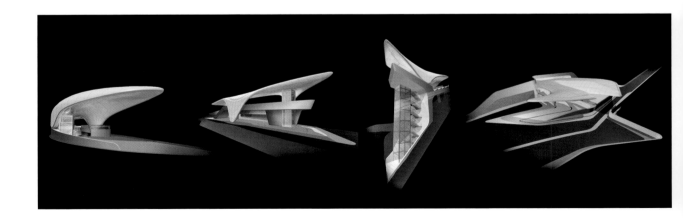

Although Hadid's drawings have evolved over time, in particular with fully computerized design, the spirit of her work is fully visible in the images above.

Wenngleich sich Hadid bei ihren Entwurfszeichnungen zunehmend auf den Computer stützt, ist der besondere Geist ihrer Arbeit in den obigen Abbildungen unverkennbar.

Bien que les dessins d'Hadid aient évolué, en particulier grâce aux logiciels de conception informatiques, l'esprit de ses recherches reste fidèle aux images ci-dessus.

The soaring, curved stations along the Nordpark Cable Railway sit atop rectilinear bases as seen in the section drawing below.

Wie auf der Schnittzeichnung unten zu sehen, sitzen die schwungvoll gebogenen Haltestationen der Nordkettenbahn auf deutlich gradlinigeren Basen auf.

Les formes jaillissantes et incurvées des stations du funiculaire du Nordpark s'appuient sur des socles plus rectilignes, comme le montre la coupe ci-dessous.

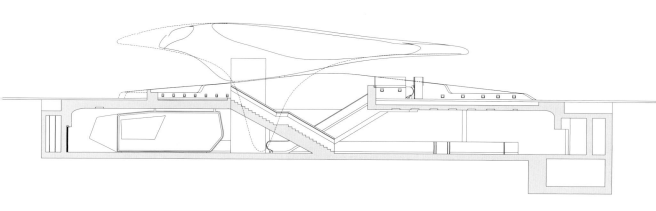

As in much of Hadid's work, the curving lines of the walls blend seamlessly into the ceilings, and run from the
roof to spaces enclosing the escalators (opposite).

Wie bei vielen Arbeiten Hadids gehen
die Kurvenformen der Wände nahtlos
in die Decken über, hier vom Dach
bis hinab zum Rolltreppenbereich
(rechts).

Comme dans beaucoup de réalisations de Hadid, les lignes incurvées
des murs se raccordent sans rupture
aux plafonds et courent du toit aux
volumes des escalators (à droite).

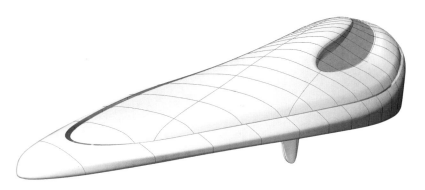

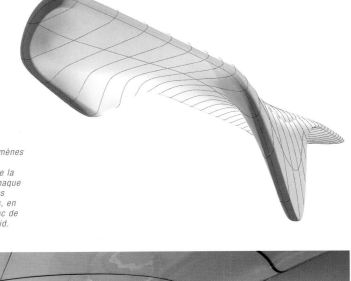

"We studied natural phenomena—such as glacial moraines and ice movements—as we wanted each station to use the fluid language of natural ice formations, like a frozen stream on the mountainside," says Hadid.

„Wir haben uns natürliche Phänomene – Gletschermoränen und Eisbewegungen – angeschaut, da die einzelnen Station wie natürliche Eisformationen, zum Beispiel wie ein gefrorener Bergbach, gestaltet sein sollten", erläutert Hadid.

« Nous avons étudié des phénomènes naturels comme les moraines glaciaires et les mouvements de la glace, car nous voulions que chaque gare parle ce langage fluide des formations glaciaires naturelles, en une sorte de torrent gelé à flanc de montagne », explique Zaha Hadid.

Unlike many rail or cable mountain facilities, the Nordpark system has unique stations, each adapted to its topography and altitude.

Im Gegensatz zu nicht wenigen anderen Berg- oder Seilbahnen sind die Haltestationen im Nordpark alle individuell gestaltet und an ihre jeweilige Umgebung und Höhe angepasst.

À la différence de nombreux funiculaires, le réseau du Nordpark possède des gares toutes différentes, chacune adaptée à sa topographie et à son altitude.

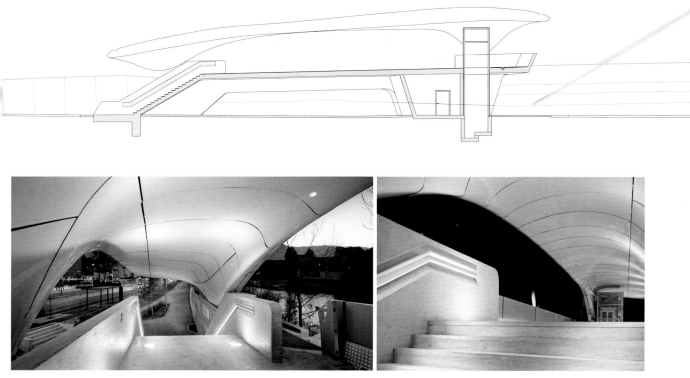

Since the basic technology of the cable car often overwhelms the architecture that surrounds it, Hadid's achievement, creating original, signature forms, is all the more remarkable.

Bedenkt man, dass die technische Seite von Seilbahnen oftmals die zugehörige Architektur in den Hintergrund drängt, sind die originellen, prägnanten Gebilde Hadids umso bemerkenswerter.

La réussite de Zaha Hadid dans la création de formes nouvelles et originales est d'autant plus remarquable que la technologie des funiculaires soumet généralement l'architecture à de puissantes contraintes.

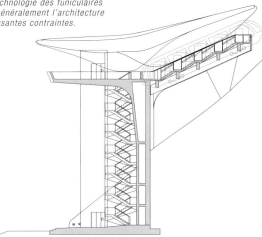

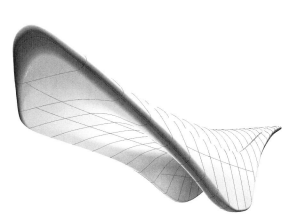

Below, a plan shows the layout of the Nordpark Cable Railway.

Die unten abgebildete Karte zeigt den Verlauf der Nordkettenbahn.

Ci-dessous, un plan du funiculaire du Nordpark.

The sinuous shapes used by Hadid might well appear to be carved from naturally worn ice, and yet there is no such precise metaphor at work here; it is more her own style and the fluidity of her designs that fits into the sites and the project.

Man könnte meinen, die geschmeidigen Formen seien aus dem Eis herausgeschnitzt. Dabei verdanken sie sich weniger einer präzisen Metaphorik als Hadids individuellem Stil, dem typischen Fluss ihrer Entwürfe, der den örtlichen Gegebenheiten von sich aus entgegenkommt.

Les formes sinueuses d'Hadid semblent sculptées dans de la glace, même si la métaphore n'est pas aussi précise. C'est surtout son style personnel et la fluidité des plans qui s'adaptent au site et au projet.

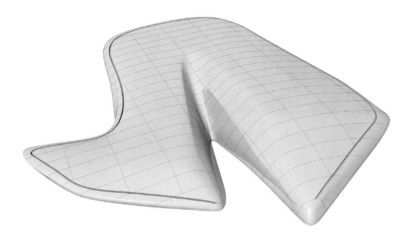

HEATHERWICK STUDIO

Heatherwick Studio
356–364 Gray's Inn Road
London WC1X 8BH
UK

Tel: +44 20 78 33 88 00
Fax: +44 20 78 33 84 00
E-mail: studio@heatherwick.com
Web: www.heatherwick.com

Thomas Heatherwick founded **HEATHERWICK STUDIO** in 1994. The firm deals in architecture, sculpture, urban infrastructure, product design, exhibition design, and "strategic thinking." The team consists of 45 members. Born in London in 1970, Thomas Heatherwick studied Three-Dimensional design at Manchester Metropolitan University, and completed his studies at the Royal College of Art in London. Their work includes the Rolling Bridge (Paddington Basin, London, 2005); Konstam at the Prince Albert restaurant (London, 2006); East Beach Café (Littlehampton, 2005–07, published here); Boiler Suit, Guy's Hospital (London, 2007), all in the UK; and the flagship store of Longchamp on Spring Street (New York, New York, 2006). Current work includes low-cost facilities for 16 start-up arts enterprises for the Aberystwyth Arts Center, at the University of Wales in Aberystwyth, the British Pavilion at Expo '10 in Shanghai, China, and a £80 million retail quarter in Leeds city center.

1994 gründete Thomas Heatherwick das **HEATHERWICK STUDIO**, das sich mit Architektur, Skulptur, städtischer Infrastrukturentwicklung, Produkt- und Ausstellungsdesign sowie „strategischer Planung" befasst. Das Team besteht aus 45 Mitarbeitern. Thomas Heatherwick, geboren 1970 in London, studierte 3-D-Design an der Manchester Metropolitan University und schloss sein Studium am Royal College of Art in London ab. Zu den in Großbritannien realisierten Projekten gehören die Rolling Bridge (Paddington Basin, London, 2005), das Restaurant Konstam at the Prince Albert (London, 2006), das hier vorgestellte East Beach Café (Littlehampton, 2005–07), und Boiler Suit, Guy's Hospital (London, 2007). In New York entstand auf der Spring Street der Flagship Store für Longchamp (2006). Derzeit laufen die Arbeiten an preiswerten Unterkünften für 16 Start-up-Unternehmen am Aberystwyth Arts Centre, das zur University of Wales in Aberystwyth gehört, die Planungen für den britischen Pavillon für die Expo '10 in Shanghai und ein 80-Millionen-Pfund-Projekt für ein Einkaufszentrum in der Innenstadt von Leeds.

Thomas Heatherwick a fondé **HEATHERWICK STUDIO** en 1994. L'agence se consacre à l'architecture, la sculpture, les infrastructures urbaines, le design produit, la conception d'expositions et la « réflexion stratégique ». L'équipe est constituée de 45 collaborateurs. Né à Londres en 1970, Thomas Heatherwick a étudié la conception tridimensionnelle à la Manchester Metropolitan University puis au Royal College of Art à Londres. Parmi les réalisations : le Rolling Bridge (Paddington Basin, Londres, 2005) ; le restaurant Konstam au Prince Albert (Londres, 2006) ; le café East Beach (Littlehampton, 2005–07, publié ici) ; Boiler Suit, Guy's Hospital (Londres, 2007) en Grande-Bretagne, ainsi qu'à l'étranger le magasin amiral Longchamp sur Spring Street (New York, 2006). Actuellement l'agence travaille sur un projet d'installations économiques destinées à 16 jeunes entreprises pour le Aberystwyth Arts Center, à l'université du Pays de Galles située à Aberystwyth, sur le futur Pavillon britannique pour Expo '10 à Shanghai, Chine, et un centre commercial de 80 million de livres sterling dans le centre-ville de Leeds.

EAST BEACH CAFÉ
Littlehampton, West Sussex, UK, 2005–07

Floor area: 205 m². Client: Brownfield Catering.
Cost: not disclosed. Structural Engineer: Adams Kara Taylor. Steelwork: Littlehampton Welding

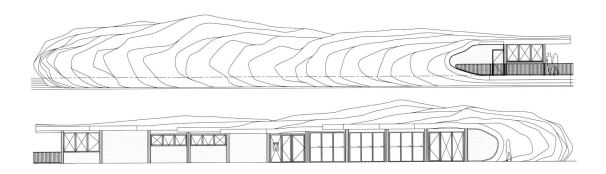

Heatherwick Studio was asked in September 2005 to design a new café, to replace an ice-cream kiosk in the seaside town of Littlehampton. The 40-meter-long café, which seats 60 people inside and 80 outside, is set on a narrow site between the houses of Littlehampton and the sea. Both weather and vandalism posed problems that the studio sought to resolve. As the designers write, "The studio saw its challenge as being to produce a long, thin building without flat, two-dimensional façades. The building is sliced diagonally into ribbons that wrap up and over the building, forming a layered protective shell, open to the sea in front. The opening is filled with glass doors and windows, protected at night by roller shutters concealed within the building's geometry, the 30-centimeter width of the ribbons being the dimension of a shutter mechanism. In contrast to the conventional whitewashed seaside aesthetic, the building is raw and weathered, its structural steel shell finished with an oil-based coating that permits a rustlike patination to develop without affecting structural performance." Made of 34 tons of eight-millimeter-thick mild steel treated with Owatrol Oil, it is intended to appear like a "rusted weatherworn object" on the sea shore. The monocoque steel shell of the building, developed with a 3D computer model, is smooth to the touch, and a surface treatment allows any graffiti to be easily removed. A local firm, Littlehampton Welding, built the steel elements and welded them together on site. Thomas Heatherwick states, "The seaside at Littlehampton has a raw beauty. It isn't fiddly or fuzzy, or about dolphins and anchors, and our building has been designed to fit into this context. Our challenge is to build a functional and durable structure on a tight budget, where you can eat a Mr. Whippy or drink Dom Pérignon."

Im September 2005 erhielt das Heatherwick Studio den Auftrag, in dem Badeort Littlehampton ein neues Café zu entwerfen, das einen Eiskremkiosk ersetzen sollte. Errichtet werden sollte das neue, 40 m lange Lokal, das über 60 Sitzplätze im Innen- und 80 im Außenbereich verfügt, auf einem schmalen Abschnitt zwischen den Häusern von Littlehampton und dem Meer. Zunächst musste sich das Studio mit zwei Problemen auseinandersetzen: dem Wetter und dem Vandalismus. „Die Lösung", so die Designer, „schien uns ein langes, schmales Gebäude ohne flache, zweidimensionale Fassadenflächen sein. Dazu wurde ein Körper diagonal in Scheiben geschnitten, die um und über das eigentliche Gebäude gelegt sind und eine mehrschichtige, zum Meer hin geöffnete Schutzschale bilden. In die Öffnung wurden Glastüren und Fenster eingesetzt, die nachts von Rollläden geschützt sind, deren Dimension genau den 30 cm breiten Scheiben entspricht, wodurch sie sich nahezu unsichtbar in die Gebäudegeometrie einfügen. Im Gegensatz zur üblichen Badeortästhetik mit ihren weiß getünchten Häusern wirkt dieses Gebäude rau und verwittert. Die Stahlhülle wurde mit einer Beschichtung auf Ölgrundlage versehen, die eine rostartige Patina entstehen lässt, ohne sich auf die Stabilität auszuwirken." Das aus 34 t schwerem, 8 mm starkem, mit Owatrolöl behandeltem Stahl bestehende Gebäude sollte aussehen wie irgendein „rostiges, verwittertes Ding", das an der Küste herumliegt. Trotzdem fühlt sich die als 3-D-Modell am Computer entworfene Gebäudeschale ganz glatt an. Graffiti lassen sich dank einer speziellen Oberflächenimprägnierung leicht entfernen. Hergestellt wurden die einzelnen Stahlelemente von der lokalen Firma Littlehampton Welding, die die Teile dann vor Ort zusammenschweißte. Thomas Heatherwick hält fest: „Die Küste von Littlehampton ist von einer rauen Schönheit. Sie hat nichts Lauschig-Beschauliches, man sieht keine Delfine oder Anker. Dem sollte unser Gebäude Rechnung tragen. Unsere Aufgabe bestand darin, mit einem überschaubaren Budget ein funktionales und langlebiges Gebäude zu errichten, in dem man tagsüber Eis essen und abends einen Dom Pérignon trinken kann."

C'est en septembre 2005, qu'Heatherwick Studio a été contacté pour concevoir ce nouveau café en remplacement d'un kiosque de glacier dans la ville balnéaire de Littlehampton. L'établissement de 40 mètres de long qui offre 60 places à l'intérieur et 80 en terrasse, est implanté sur une étroite bande de terre entre le front de mer et la mer. Le temps météorologique et le vandalisme posaient des problèmes que l'agence a cherché à résoudre. Comme elle l'explique : « L'agence s'est assigné une sorte de défi, produire un bâtiment long et étroit sans façades plates, bidimensionnelles. Le bâtiment est tranché diagonalement en rubans qui l'enveloppent, formant une coque protectrice, ouverte du côté de la mer. Cette ouverture est dotée de portes et de baies de verre, protégées la nuit par des volets métalliques dissimulés dans le profil du bâtiment, la largeur de 30 centimètres d'un ruban étant la dimension du mécanisme de ces volets. Contrastant avec l'esthétique habituelle des constructions de plage, le bâtiment s'affirme par un matériau brut et patiné. La coque en acier est recouverte d'un film à base huileuse qui permet le développement d'une patine de couleur rouille sans affecter les performances structurelles. » L'aspect voulu de cette coque de 34 tonnes d'acier doux de huit millimètres d'épaisseur traitée à l'huile Owatrol, est celui d'un « objet rouillé patiné par le temps » déposé sur la côte. La coquille monocoque, mise au point à l'aide d'un modèle informatique en 3D, est de toucher délicat, et un traitement de surface permet de nettoyer aisément les graffitis. Une entreprise locale, Littlehampton Welding, a monté et soudé les éléments d'acier sur place. Pour Thomas Heatherwhite : « La côte de Littlehampton est d'une beauté rude. Elle n'a rien de délicat, ici ni dauphins ni bateaux à l'ancre, et notre bâtiment a été pensé en respectant ce contexte. Notre défi a été de construire une structure durable et fonctionnelle avec un budget restreint, où vous pouvez aussi bien manger un hamburger que boire du Dom Pérignon. »

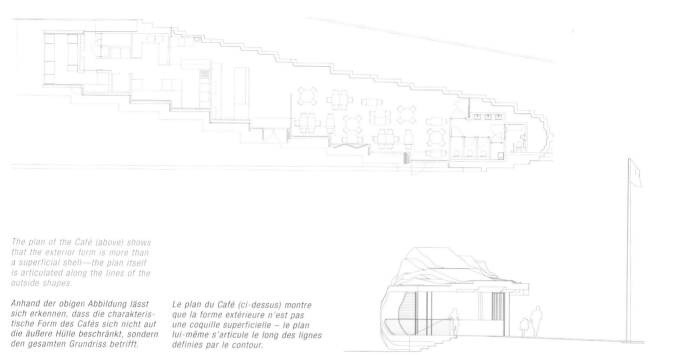

The plan of the Café (above) shows
that the exterior form is more than
a superficial shell—the plan itself
is articulated along the lines of the
outside shapes.

Anhand der obigen Abbildung lässt
sich erkennen, dass die charakteristische Form des Cafés sich nicht auf
die äußere Hülle beschränkt, sondern
den gesamten Grundriss betrifft.

Le plan du Café (ci-dessus) montre
que la forme extérieure n'est pas
une coquille superficielle – le plan
lui-même s'articule le long des lignes
définies par le contour.

HERZOG & DE MEURON

Herzog & de Meuron
Rheinschanze 6 / 4056 Basel / Switzerland

Tel: +41 61 385 57 57 / Fax: +41 61 385 57 58
E-mail: info@herzogdemeuron.com

Jacques Herzog and Pierre de Meuron were both born in Basel in 1950. They received their degrees in architecture from the ETH in Zurich in 1975, and founded their own firm in Basel in 1978, named **HERZOG & DE MEURON** in 1997. Harry Gugger and Christine Binswanger joined the firm in 1991, while Robert Hösl and Ascan Mergenthaler became partners in 2004. Stefan Marbach became a partner in 2006, followed by Wolfgang Hardt, David Koch, and Markus Widner in 2008. Jacques Herzog and Pierre de Meuron won the 2001 Pritzker Prize, and both the RIBA Gold Medal and Praemium Imperiale in 2007. Their built work includes a gallery for a private collection of contemporary art in Munich (Germany, 1991–92); and the Ricola Europe Factory and Storage Building (Mulhouse, France, 1993). They were chosen early in 1995 to design Tate Modern in London, which opened in May 2000. In 2005, Herzog & de Meuron were commissioned again by the Tate to develop a scheme for the completion of the gallery and its surrounding areas due for 2012 completion. More recently, they built the Forum 2004 (Barcelona, Spain, 2002–04); the Allianz Arena (Munich, Germany, 2002–05); the de Young Museum (San Francisco, California, 2002–05); the Walker Art Center Expansion (Minneapolis, Minnesota, 2003–05); and the National Stadium, the Main Stadium for the 2008 Olympic Games in Beijing (China, 2003–08, published here). They have just completed the CaixaForum (Madrid, Spain, 2001–08, also published here). Current work includes the "Vitrahaus," a new building to present Vitra's "Home Collection" in Weil am Rhein (Germany, projected completion 2009); the Elbe Philharmonic Hall in Hamburg (Germany, projected completion 2010); and the Head Office for Roche Basel (projected completion 2011).

Jacques Herzog und sein Partner Pierre de Meuron wurden im selben Jahr, 1950, in Basel geboren und beide studierten an der ETH Zürich, wo sie 1975 ihr Diplom machten. 1978 gründeten sie in Basel ihr Büro, das seit 1997 unter dem Namen **HERZOG & DE MEURON** firmiert. 1991 wurden Harry Gugger und Christine Binswanger Partner, 2004 folgten Robert Hösl und Ascan Mergenthaler, 2006 kam Stefan Marbach dazu, 2008 Wolfgang Hardt, David Koch und Markus Widmer. 2001 wurden Jacques Herzog und Pierre de Meuron mit dem Pritzker-Preis ausgezeichnet, 2007 erhielten sie die Goldmedaille des Royal Institute of British Architects sowie den japanischen Praemium Imperiale. Zu ihren realisierten Projekten gehören ein Ausstellungsbau für eine Privatsammlung zeitgenössischer Kunst in München (1991–92) und das Fabrik- und Lagergebäude der Firma Ricola im französischen Mulhouse (1993). 1995 erhielten sie den Auftrag für den Entwurf der Londoner Tate Modern für zeitgenössische Kunst, die im Mai 2000 eröffnet wurde. 2005 wurden Herzog & de Meuron mit der Konzeptentwicklung zum abschließenden Ausbau des Museums und des dazugehörigen Geländes beauftragt, der bis 2012 umgesetzt werden soll. In jüngerer Zeit entstanden das Forum 2004 in Barcelona (2002–04), die Münchener Allianz Arena (2002–05), das de Young Museum in San Francisco (2002–05), die Erweiterung des Walker Art Center in Minneapolis, Minnesota (2003–05), und das hier vorgestellte Hauptstadion für die Olympischen Spiele 2008 in Peking. Erst kürzlich wurden die Arbeiten am CaixaForum in Madrid abgeschlossen (2001–08, hier vorgestellt). Gegenwärtig in Arbeit sind das Vitrahaus in Weil am Rhein, ein neues Gebäude für die „Home Collection" von Vitra (geplante Fertigstellung 2009), die Elbphilharmonie in Hamburg (geplante Fertigstellung 2010) und die Roche-Zentrale in Basel (geplante Fertigstellung 2011).

Jacques Herzog et Pierre de Meuron, nés à Bâle en 1950, sont diplômés en architecture de l'ETH de Zurich (1975). En 1978, ils fondent, à Bâle, leur agence qui devient en 1997 **HERZOG & DE MEURON**. Harry Gugger et Christine Binswanger les rejoignent en 1991, ainsi que Robert Hösl et Ascan Mergenthaler en 2004, Stefan Marbach en 2006, Wolfgang Hardt, David Koch et Markus Widmer en 2008. Ils ont remporté le Pritzker Prize en 2001, la RIBA Gold Medal ainsi que le Praemium Imperiale en 2007. Parmi leurs premières réalisations : une galerie pour une collection privée d'art contemporain à Munich (Allemagne, 1991–92) et l'usine et entrepôt Ricola Europe (Mulhouse-Brunstatt, France, 1993). Ils ont été sélectionnés en 1995 pour l'aménagement de la Tate Modern, inaugurée en mai 2000. En 2005, Herzog & de Meuron ont reçu une nouvelle commande de la Tate pour la construction d'une nouvelle galerie et de ses aménagements extérieurs, projet qui devrait être achevé en 2012. Plus récemment, ils ont construit le Forum 2004 à Barcelone (2002–04) ; le stade Allianz Arena (Munich, Allemagne, 2002–05) ; le musée de Young (San Francisco, Californie, 2002–05) et l'extension du centre Walker Art (Minneapolis, Minnesota, 2003–05) ; le Stade national, principal stade des jeux Olympiques 2008 de Pékin (publié ici). Ils viennent d'achever le chantier du CaixaForum (Madrid, Espagne, 2001–08, publié ici). Actuellement, ils travaillent entre autres sur un nouveau bâtiment destiné à abriter la « Home Collection » de Vitra à Weil am Rhein (Allemagne, prévu pour 2009) ; sur le hall philharmonique d'Elbe (Hambourg, prévu pour 2010) et sur le siège administratif et financier de Roche à Bâle (prévu pour 2011).

NATIONAL STADIUM

Main Stadium for the 2008 Olympic Games, Beijing, China, 2003–08

Site area: 20.29 ha. Floor area: 258 000 m². Client: National Stadium Co. Ltd., Beijing. Cost: not disclosed.
Project Team Partners: Jacques Herzog, Pierre de Meuron, Stefan Marbach. Project Architects: Linxi Dong (Associate), Mia Hägg (Associate),
Tobias Winkelmann (Associate), Thomas Polster. Artistic Advisor: Ai Wei Wei. Engineering and Sports Architecture: China Architectural
Design & Research Group, Beijing, Ove Arup & Partners Hong Kong Ltd., Arup Sport, London

Herzog & de Meuron were selected for this project subsequent to a 2003 competition organized by the Beijing Municipal Planning Commission. The almost circular design optimizes viewing for the 91 000 seats planned for the Olympic Games. "The bowl superstructure consists of in situ concrete. The primary structure of the roof is independent of the bowl structure and is conceived as a series of steel space frames wrapped around the bowl. The overall depth of the structure is 12 meters. The spaces between the members will be filled with ETFE foil." Façade and structure are identical in this instance, in a form nicknamed by the Chinese the "Bird's Nest". As the architects write, "The spatial effect of the stadium is novel and radical, and yet simple and of an almost archaic immediacy. Its appearance is pure structure." Soccer games and athletic events will be held in the stadium that will be the venue for the opening and closing ceremonies of the 2008 Olympic Games. Set on the Olympic Green designed by Sasaki Associates, the Stadium is also not far from Pei-Zhu's Digital Beijing control and data center for the Games (page 388). The Olympic Stadium, more than any of the other buildings designed for the Chinese capital on the occasion of the 2008 Games, will mark the event in a long-term, symbolic way.

2003 wurden Herzog & de Meuron bei einem Wettbewerb der Pekinger Planungskommission für den Entwurf des chinesischen Nationalstadions ausgewählt. Damit die Zuschauer von allen 91 000 Plätzen aus einen optimalen Blick haben, konzipierten die Architekten einen fast runden Bau. „Die Grundstruktur des Stadions besteht aus Ortbeton. Die Primärkonstruktion des Dachs ist unabhängig vom Betonkessel und besteht aus einem vielfach gegliederten Raumfachwerk aus Stahl, das den Stadionkörper umhüllt. Die Gesamttiefe der Konstruktion beträgt 12 m. Die Zwischenräume zwischen den einzelnen Gliedern werden mit ETFE-Folie ausgefüllt." Fassade und Tragwerk sind in diesem Fall identisch und zeigen eine Form, die die Chinesen „Vogelnest" nennen. „Die Raumwirkung des Stadions ist ungewohnt und radikal, aber dennoch schlicht und von einer beinahe archaischen Unmittelbarkeit. Seine Erscheinung ist reine Struktur." Das Stadion wird den Rahmen für die Eröffnungs- und Abschlussfeierlichkeiten der Olympischen Spiele abgeben und ist Austragungsort für Fußballspiele und Leichtathletikwettkämpfe. Unweit des Stadions befindet sich auf dem von Sasaki Associates entworfenen Olympiagelände auch das Rechenzentrum für die Olympischen Spiele, Digital Beijing, des Studios Pei-Zhu (S. 388). Mehr als jedes andere aus Anlass der Olympischen Spiele in Peking entstandene Bauwerk wird das Nationalstadion ein bleibendes Symbol für die Ereignisse des Sommers 2008 sein.

Herzog & de Meuron ont été choisis pour réaliser ce projet à l'issue d'un concours organisé par la Commission municipale d'urbanisme de Pékin en 2003. Le plan presque circulaire optimise la vision à partir des 91 000 sièges. «La superstructure de la forme en coupe est en béton coulé sur site. La structure primaire indépendante de la couverture enveloppante se compose d'une série de cadres tridimensionnels en acier. L'épaisseur d'ensemble de la structure est de 12 mètres. Les espaces entre les poutres sont remplis par une membrane en ETFE.» Façade et structure sont donc identiques, et prennent cette forme que les Chinois appellent un nid d'oiseau. «L'effet spatial est novateur et radical, mais en même temps simple, presque archaïque dans sa perception immédiate. Son apparence est celle d'une structure pure.» Les matchs de football et les compétitions d'athlétisme mais aussi les cérémonies d'ouverture et de fermeture des Jeux s'y dérouleront. Implanté sur la pelouse olympique dessinée par Sasaki Associates, le stade est également proche du centre informatique des Jeux, «Digital Beijing» (page 388), conçu par Pei-Zhu. Plus que tout autre réalisation conçue pour l'événement 2008, le stade olympique a immédiatement imposé sa forte présence symbolique.

Stadium architecture tends to be relatively repetitive and symmetrical. That is not the case with the new National Stadium in Beijing—it is original and asymmetrical.

Die Architektur von Stadien läuft oft auf relativ repetitive, symmetrische Formen hinaus. Nicht so das neue Nationalstadion in Peking mit seiner originellen, asymmetrischen Gestalt.

L'architecture des stades tend à être relativement répétitive et symétrique. Ce n'est pas le cas du nouveau Stade national de Pékin, sans aucun doute original et asymétrique.

The angled beams of the stadium rise up in a pattern that is not predictable at close quarters, giving a feeling of dynamism to the architecture.

Die schrägen Streben des Stadions erheben sich in einem Muster, das sich nicht einfach in viereckigen Feldern erschöpft, sondern der Architektur eine besondere Dynamik verleiht.

Les poutres inclinées du stade s'élèvent selon un schéma qui semble imprévisible vu de près, conférant une impression de dynamisme.

Though the forms of the architecture are powerful, they open to visitors in a way that gives a sensation of freedom. The structural web that surrounds the actual seating and sports area encloses it, while inviting guests to enter.

Trotz ihrer Robustheit vermitteln die offenen Formen dem Besucher ein Gefühl von Freiheit. Die Gitterkonstruktion umschließt das Gebäude und lädt zugleich die Besucher zum Betreten ein.

Malgré leur puissance, les formes architecturales s'ouvrent aux visiteurs dans un esprit de liberté. Le réseau structurel entoure les gradins et le terrain tout en invitant les spectateurs à entrer.

The roof of the stadium offers protection from sun or rain for most spectators, while opening to the sky above the track and field.

Während das Stadiondach die meisten Zuschauerplätze vor Sonne und Regen schützt, ist es über den Wettkampffeldern geöffnet.

La toiture du stade protège du soleil et de la pluie la plupart des spectateurs, mais ne recouvre ni le terrain ni les pistes d'athlétisme.

The strong and unexpected angles of the structure provide a theatrical envelope for the actual sports areas, heightened at times by the use of colors, such as the red seen here.

Die massiven, ungewöhnlichen Streben des Tragwerks bilden eine dramatisch wirkende Hülle für die eigentlichen Wettkampfbereiche, teilweise noch verstärkt durch die wie hier verwendete rote Farbe.

Les fortes inclinaisons des poutres structurelles, souvent inattendues, offrent un cadre théâtral aux aires de sport, renforcé par moments par des effets de couleur comme le rouge représenté ici.

A webbed ceiling in a foyer space echoes the overall structure of the stadium. Atypical of large sports facilities, the National Stadium is designed carefully at every level.

In der filigran gegliederten Decke im Foyerbereich setzt sich die Gesamt-struktur des Stadions fort. Anders als häufig bei Sportstätten sind sämtliche Bereiche des Nationalstadions sorg-fältig durchgestaltet.

Le plafond du foyer d'accueil fait écho à la structure du stade. À l'in-verse de la plupart des grandes in-stallations sportives, le stade national est conçu avec le plus grand soin jusque dans ses moindres détails.

CAIXAFORUM

Madrid, Spain, 2001–08

Site area: 1934 m² (covered plaza, 650 m²). Floor area: 11 000 m². Client: Obra Social Funacion La Caixa, Madrid;
Caixa d'Estalvis i Pensions de Barcelona, Barcelona. Cost: not disclosed. Associate Architect: Mateu i Bausells Arquitectura, Madrid.
Project Architects: Peter Ferretto (Associate), Carlos Gerhard (Associate), Stefan Marbach (Associate), Benito Blanco (Project Manager).
Green Wall: Herzog & de Meuron in collaboration with Patrick Blanc, Paris

This building accomodates two main galleries with 1720 square meters of exhibition space, a 333-seat auditorium, a cafeteria, a shop, a restaurant, offices, a workshop for conservation and restoration, storage space, and an entrance plaza with a total of 1200 square meters (650 square meters of which are covered). The green wall near the entrance covers an area of 600 square meters and was designed by the architects in collaboration with the noted French botanist and artist Patrick Blanc, who created similar vertical gardens, albeit on a somewhat smaller scale, at the Musée du Quai Branly (architect, Jean Nouvel) and the earlier Fondation Cartier (also by Nouvel), both in Paris. The building faces the Paseo del Prado and the Botanical Garden. The brick walls of the former Mediodía Power Station form the basis of the new building, recalling the conversion—by the same architects—of the Bankside Power Station in London into the Tate Modern. The shell of the former Madrid power station was retained in part because it was classified as being of historic interest. The base of the building was removed, thus allowing for the covered entrance plaza while making the rest of its mass appear to hover above the street. The theater-auditorium is located below grade, as are service areas and parking. The spatially complex top floor contains the restaurant-bar and offices.

Das CaixaForum umfasst zwei Hauptgalerien mit 1720 m² Ausstellungsfläche, einen Vortragssaal mit 333 Sitzplätzen, eine Cafeteria, einen Shop, ein Restaurant, Büros, eine Werkstatt zur Konservierung und Restaurierung, Lagerräume und einen 1200 m² großen Eingangsvorplatz, der gut zur Hälfte überdacht ist. Die Begrünung der 600 m² großen Wandfläche neben dem Eingang entstand in Zusammenarbeit mit dem renommierten französischen Gartenkünstler Patrick Blanc, der ähnliche „vertikale Gärten", wenn auch etwas kleiner, bereits für das Musée du Quai Branly (entworfen von Jean Nouvel) und zuvor für die Fondation Cartier (ebenfalls von Nouvel), beide in Paris, verwirklicht hatte. Das neue CaixaForum liegt nahe dem Paseo del Prado gegenüber dem Botanischen Garten. Die Ziegelwände des früheren Elektrizitätswerks Mediodía bilden die Basis für die neue Konstruktion, womit sie an die ebenfalls von Herzog & de Meuron ausgeführte Umgestaltung der Londoner Bankside Power Station zur Tate Modern erinnert. Während die Architekten die als historisch wertvoll eingestufte Gebäudehülle des ehemaligen Elektrizitätswerks teilweise beibehielten, entfernten sie das Fundament und schufen dadurch den Freiraum für den überdachten Eingangsbereich, über dem die übrige Gebäudemasse zu schweben scheint. Das Auditorium ist unterirdisch angelegt, ebenso die Servicebereiche und eine Parkebene. Im räumlich komplexen Obergeschoss befinden sich Restaurant, Bar und Büros.

Ce nouveau lieu artistique comprend deux galeries d'exposition de 1720 m², un auditorium de 333 places, une cafétéria, une boutique, un restaurant, des bureaux un atelier pour la conservation et la restauration, des réserves et une place devant l'entrée de 1200 m² dont 650 m² couverts. Le mur végétal de 600 m², situé près de cette même entrée, a été conçu par les architectes en collaboration avec le célèbre botaniste et artiste français Patrick Blanc qui a créé des jardins verticaux similaires à Paris, mais à moindre échelle, pour le musée du Quai Branly à Paris ou la Fondation Cartier pour l'art contemporain, tous deux de Jean Nouvel. Le bâtiment fait face au Paseo del Prado et au jardin botanique. Les murs de brique de l'ancienne centrale électrique de Mediodía constituent la base du nouveau bâtiment et rappellent la conversion par les mêmes architectes de la centrale thermique de Bankside à Londres pour la Tate Modern. Ici, la coquille de l'ancienne centrale madrilène a été en partie conservée parce qu'elle était classée monument historique. La base a été supprimée, pour créer la place couverte de l'entrée et le reste de la masse semble en suspension au-dessus de la rue. Le théâtre-auditorium est implanté en sous-sol comme les installations de service et le parking. Le dernier étage contient le bar-restaurant et les bureaux.

Located near the Prado, the CaixaForum combines an old power plant with a fully modern design. Below, left, a "vertical garden" by Patrick Blanc is placed at right angles to the entrance.

Das CaixaForum in der Nähe des Prado ist ein altes Elektrizitätswerk, das ausgesprochen modern erweitert wurde. Die Mauer neben dem Eingang hat Patrick Blanc als „vertikalen Garten" angelegt (unten links).

Situé près du Prado, le CaixaForum associe une ancienne centrale électrique à des interventions contemporaines. En bas à gauche, un jardin vertical de Patrick Blanc est perpendiculaire à l'entrée.

The old brick structure appears to have been lifted off the ground, creating space for a modern entrance.

Der alte Backsteinbau wirkt, als sei er angehoben worden, um einen modernen Eingang einfügen zu können.

L'ancien bâtiment en brique semble s'être soulevé pour laisser place à une entrée moderne.

The upper level of the building and the restaurant are treated with a skin of rusted metal cut in a camouflage pattern to admit light into the building.

Der obere Abschnitt des Gebäudes und das Restaurant wurden mit einer Hülle aus rostig angelaufenem Metall versehen, durch deren eingeschnittenes Tarnmuster Licht ins Innere fällt.

Le niveau supérieur du bâtiment et le restaurant sont habillés d'une peau de métal rouillé découpée selon des motifs de camouflage pour laisser pénétrer la lumière.

Above, a side view of the building;
below, the metal ceiling of the
entrance zone at ground level.

Oben eine Ansicht des Gebäudes von
der Seite, unten die Metalldecke des
Eingangsbereichs im Erdgeschoss.

Ci-dessus, une vue latérale du
bâtiment. Ci-dessous, le plafond en
métal de l'entrée au rez-de-chaussée.

Large underground spaces include an auditorium. Below, the stairway that leads from the ground-level entrance to the ticketing desk and main entrance.

Zu den weitläufigen unterirdischen Räumen gehört auch ein Auditorium. Unten die Treppe, die vom Eingang im Erdgeschoss zur Eintrittskasse und zum Haupteingang führt.

Les vastes espaces en sous-sol comprennent un auditorium. Ci-dessous, l'escalier qui conduit de l'entrée au rez-de-chaussée à l'entrée principale et à la caisse.

Exhibition spaces are treated in a fairly straightforward manner. Left, the main stairway that serves each level of the building. Below, right, the top-level restaurant.

Die Ausstellungsräume sind recht nüchtern gehalten. Links die Haupt-treppe, über die man in die einzelnen Stockwerke gelangt. Unten rechts das Restaurant im Obergeschoss.

Les espaces d'expositions sont trai-tés de façon assez simple. À gauche, l'escalier principal qui dessert tous les niveaux. Ci-dessous à droite, le restaurant situé au dernier étage.

STEVEN HOLL

Steven Holl Architects
450 West 31st Street, 11th floor / New York, NY 10001 / USA

Tel: +1 212 629 7262 / Fax: +1 212 629 7312
E-mail: mail@stevenholl.com / Web: www.stevenholl.com

Born in 1947 in Bremerton, Washington, **STEVEN HOLL** obtained his B.Arch degree from the University of Washington (1970). He studied in Rome and at the Architectural Association in London (1976). He began his career in California and opened his own office in New York in 1976. Holl has taught at the University of Washington, Syracuse University, and, since 1981, at Columbia University. His notable buildings include: the Hybrid Building (Seaside, Florida, 1984–88); the Void Space/Hinged Space, Housing (Nexus World, Fukuoka, Japan, 1989–91); the Stretto House (Dallas, Texas, 1989–92); Makuhari Housing (Chiba, Japan, 1992–97); the Chapel of St. Ignatius, Seattle University (Seattle, Washington, 1994–97); the Kiasma Museum of Contemporary Art (Helsinki, Finland, 1993–98); and an extension to the Cranbrook Institute of Science (Bloomfield Hills, Michigan, 1996–99). Winner of the 1998 Alvar Aalto Medal, Steven Holl's more recent work includes the College of Architecture at Cornell University (Ithaca, New York, 2004); the Turbulence House in New Mexico for the artist Richard Tuttle (2005); the Pratt Institute Higgen Hall Center Wing (Brooklyn, New York, 1997–2005); and an Art and Art History Building for the University of Iowa (Iowa City, Iowa, 1999–2006). He recently won the competition for the Knokke-Heist Casino in Belgium, and completed the Bellevue Art Museum (Bellevue, Washington) and an expansion and renovation of The Nelson-Atkins Museum of Art (Kansas City, Missouri, 2002–07, published here). Current projects include the Linked Hybrid (Beijing, China, 2005–08); the Nanjing Museum of Art and Architecture (China, 2008); the Knut Hamsun Museum (Hamarøy, Norway, 1994–2009); and the Beirut Marina and Town Quay (Beirut, Lebanon, 2009).

STEVEN HOLL, geboren 1947 in Bremerton im US-Bundesstaat Washington, machte 1970 seinen Bachelor of Architecture an der University of Washington. Danach studierte er in Rom und an der Architectural Association in London (1976). Für kurze Zeit war er in Kalifornien tätig, bevor er 1976 sein erstes Büro in New York gründete. Holl war Dozent an der University of Washington und an der Syracuse University, seit 1981 unterrichtet er an der Columbia University. Bedeutende Projekte sind u. a. das Hybrid Building in Seaside, Florida (1984–88), die Wohnanlage Void Space/Hinged Space im japanischen Fukuoka (1989–91), das Stretto House in Dallas, Texas (1989–92), die Makuhari-Wohnanlage in Chiba, Japan (1992–97), die St.-Ignatius-Kapelle auf dem Campus der Seattle University (Washington, 1994–97), das Kiasma Museum für zeitgenössische Kunst in Helsinki (1993–98) und die Erweiterung des Cranbrook Institute of Science in Bloomfield Hills, Michigan (1996–99). 1998 wurde Holl mit der Alvar-Aalto-Medaille ausgezeichnet. Arbeiten aus jüngerer Zeit sind das College of Architecture an der Cornell University in Ithaca, New York (2004), das Turbulence House für den Künstler Richard Tuttle in New Mexico (2005), der Gebäudeflügel des Higgen Hall Center am Pratt Institute in Brooklyn, New York (1997–2005), und ein Institutsgebäude für Kunst und Kunstgeschichte der University of Iowa in Iowa City (1999–2006). Vor Kurzem gewann Holl den Wettbewerb für das Kasino im belgischen Knokke-Heist. Jüngst abgeschlossen wurden die Arbeiten am Bellevue Art Museum in Washington sowie die Erweiterung und Renovierung des Nelson-Atkins Museum of Art in Kansas City, Missouri (2002–07, hier vorgestellt). Zu Holls gegenwärtig laufenden Projekten gehören Linked Hybrid (Peking, 2005–08), das Kunst- und Architekturmuseum in Nanjing (China, 2008), das Knut Hamsun Museum im norwegischen Hamarøy (1994–2009) und eine umfassende Hafen- und Uferbebauung in Beirut (Libanon, 2009).

Né en 1947 à Bremerton, Washington, **STEVEN HOLL** est B. Arch. de l'université de Washington (1970). Il a étudié à Rome et à l'Architectural Association de Londres (1976). Après avoir entamé sa carrière en Californie, il ouvre son agence à New York en 1976. Il a enseigné à l'University of Washington, Syracuse University, et, depuis 1981, à Columbia University. Parmi ses réalisations les plus notables : le Hybrid Building (Seaside, Floride, 1984–88) ; le Void Space/Hinged Space, logements (Nexus World, Fukuoka, Japon, 1989–91) ; la maison Stretto (Dallas, Texas, 1989–92) ; les logements Makuhari (Chiba, Japon, 1992–97) ; la chapelle de St.-Ignatius, Seattle University (Seattle, Washington, 1994–97) ; le musée Kiasma d'art contemporain (Helsinki, Finlande, 1993–98) et l'extension du Cranbrook Institute of Science (Bloomfield Hills, Michigan, 1996–99). Il est titulaire de la médaille Alvar Aalto 1998. Parmi ses réalisations récentes : le College of Architecture de la Cornell University (Ithaca, New York, 2004) ; la maison Turbulence pour l'artiste Richard Tuttle (Nouveau Mexique, 2005) ; le Higgen Hall Center Wing du Pratt Institute (Brooklyn, New York, 1997–2005) et le bâtiment d'art et histoire de l'art pour l'université de l'Iowa (Iowa City, Iowa, 1999–2006). Il a récemment remporté le concours pour le casino de Knokke-Heist en Belgique, et achevé le musée d'Art Bellevue (Bellevue, Washington), ainsi que l'extension et la rénovation du Nelson-Atkins Museum of Art (Kansas City, Missouri, 2002–07, publié ici). Parmi ses projets actuels : le Linked Hybrid (Pékin, Chine, 2005–08) ; le musée d'Art et d'Architecture de Nankin (Chine, 2008) ; le musée Knut Hamsun (Hamarøy, Norvège, 1994–2009) ainsi que la Marina et Town Quay de Beyrouth (Liban, 2009).

THE NELSON-ATKINS MUSEUM OF ART

Bloch Building, Kansas City, Missouri, USA, 2002–07

Floor area: 15 329 m² (addition); 21 739 m² (renovation). Client: The Nelson-Atkins Museum of Art.
Cost: $200 million (expansion and renovation).
Architects: Steven Holl, Chris McVoy

This 256-meter-long addition to the Nelson-Atkins Museum of Art expands the institution by 71 percent. Set in the midst of a 10-hectare sculpture park original-ly designed by Dan Kiley (1989), the Bloch Building was selected by *Time* magazine as the "#1 architectural marvel of 2007." The project received a 2008 Honor Award from the American Institute of Architects. The citation read, "The addition to the Nelson-Atkins Museum of Art places five translucent, rectangular boxes—called 'lens-es'—on the eastern edge of the museum's campus. The new addition engages the existing sculpture garden, transforming the entire museum site into the precinct of the visitor's experience. The expansion of the Nelson-Atkins Museum of Art fuses architecture with landscape to create an experiential architecture that unfolds for visi-tors as it is perceived through each individual's movement through space and time." The glass lenses are in fact the primary natural light sources for the new building. The architect declares: "From the movement through the landscape and threaded between the light openings, exhilarating new experiences of the existing Museum will be formed. Circulation and exhibition merge as one can look from one level to another, from inside to outside. Glass lenses bring different qualities of light to the galleries. The interior of the building, linked with stairways and ramps, encourages a natural flow throughout the long structure, allowing visitors to look from one level to another, from inside to outside." The noted American architecture critic Paul Goldberger wrote, "The building is not just Holl's finest by far, but also one of the best museums of the last generation" (*The New Yorker*, April 30, 2007).

Der 256 m lange Erweiterungsbau für das Nelson-Atkins Museum of Art vergrößert die bisherige Museumsfläche um 71 %. Die Zeitschrift *Time* kürte das Bloch Buil-ding, das auf dem Gelände eines 10 ha großen, 1989 von Dan Kiley entworfenen Skulpturenparks errichtet wurde, zum „größten Architekturwunder des Jahres 2007". Vom American Institute of Architects wurde das Projekt 2008 mit einem der Ehrenpreise ausgezeichnet. In der Begründung hieß es: „Die Ergänzung zum Nelson-Atkins Museum of Art am östlichen Rand des Museumsgeländes besteht aus fünf lichtdurchlässigen, rechteckigen Körpern, die der Architekt als Linsen bezeichnet. Die Einbeziehung des Skulpturenparks macht das gesamte Museumsgrundstück für den Besucher zum Erfahrungsraum. Die Erweiterung des Nelson-Atkins Museum of Art verbindet Architektur und Landschaft zu einer Erlebnisarchitektur, die sich den Besuchern mit jeder Bewegung durch Raum und Zeit eröffnet." Die gläsernen Linsen bilden die Hauptquellen für die natürliche Beleuchtung. Der Architekt kommentiert: „Bewegt man sich durch das Parkgelände und zwischen den Lichtöffnungen hindurch, ergeben sich auch von dem älteren Museumsbau aufregende neue Eindrücke. Durch den freien Blick von einer Etage in die andere und von drinnen nach draußen werden Rundgang und Ausstellung eins. Die Glaslinsen lassen unterschiedliches Licht in die Ausstellungsräume ein. Die Treppen und Rampen, die die Innenräume des Baus durchziehen, sorgen für einen natürlichen Fluss und bieten verschiedenste Blickachsen durch das Gebäude und in den Außenbereich." Der renommierte Architekturkritiker Paul Goldberger schrieb zu Holls Erweiterung: „Das Gebäude ist nicht nur Holls bis dato gelungenstes, sondern überhaupt eines der besten der vergangenen Jahre." (*The New Yorker*, 30. April 2007).

Cette extension longue de 256 mètres du musée d'Art Nelson-Atkins accroît la surface de cette institution de 71 %. Implanté dans un parc de sculptures d'un hec-tare dessiné à l'origine par Dan Kiley (1989), le Bloch Building a été qualifié par le magazine *Time* de « merveille architecturale n°1 pour 2007 ». Le projet a d'ailleurs reçu le Honor Award 2008 de l'American Institut of Architects accompagné du commentaire suivant : « L'extension du musée d'Art Nelson-Atkins dispose cinq boîtes rectan-gulaires translucides, appelée *lentilles*, dans l'angle est du campus du musée. La nouvelle extension s'intègre dans le jardin de sculptures existant et transforme le site du musée tout entier en un lieu d'expérimentations pour le visiteur. Le projet fusionne l'architecture et le paysage pour créer une architecture expérimentale qui se déploie devant le visiteur qui la perçoit au cours de chacun de ses déplacements dans le temps et l'espace. » Les lentilles de verre sont en fait la première source d'éclairage naturel du nouveau bâtiment. Pour Holl : « De passionnantes nouvelles expériences du musée existant se dessinent à l'occasion des déplacements dans le paysage et se tissent lors des passages entre les ouvertures. Circulation et exposition fusionnent dans la vision que l'on peut avoir d'un niveau à l'autre, ou de l'intérieur vers l'extérieur. Les lentilles apportent différentes qualités de lumière aux galeries. L'intérieur du bâtiment, relié par des escaliers et des rampes, génère un flux naturel de déplacements à travers cette longue structure, permettant aux visiteurs de regarder d'un niveau vers l'autre ou de l'intérieur vers l'extérieur. » Le célèbre critique d'ar-chitecture Paul Goldberger a écrit dans le *New Yorker* du 30 avril 2007 : « Ce bâtiment n'est pas seulement le plus raffiné de Holl, c'est, de loin, l'un des musées les plus réussis de la dernière génération. »

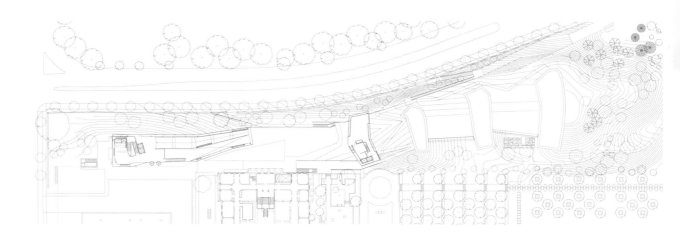

The powerful concrete forms of the old base are opened up and rendered modern through lighting and the addition of ramps and stairways.

Die imposanten Betonformen des alten Bunkers wurden geöffnet und mithilfe von Beleuchtungen und zusätzlichen Rampen und Treppen modernisiert.

Les puissantes formes en béton de l'ancienne base sont aérées et modernisées par l'éclairage et l'ajout de rampes ou d'escaliers.

The vast building retains something of its war-time aura. That said, the architects have recuperated the space as well as its volumes and heaviness allows.

Nach wie vor hat das riesige Bauwerk etwas von seiner kriegsgeschuldeten Imposanz. Angesichts dessen haben die Architekten das Beste aus den Dimensionen des Baus gemacht.

L'immense bâtiment conserve quelque chose de la violence de la guerre. Ceci dit, les architectes ont récupéré au mieux cet espace dans la mesure où le permettaient ses volumes.

Again, lighting and circulation elements added by the architects make the space usable and, indeed, quite interesting. In a time when every square meter is usually the object of careful calculations, here size is no problem.

Der Raum wird durch neu hinzugefügte Beleuchtungen und Treppenelemente nutzbar gemacht und erhält durchaus einen gewissen Reiz. Während heute normalerweise die Kosten für jeden Quadratmeter sorgfältig abgewogen werden, ist Größe hier kein Problem.

Les éléments d'éclairage et de circulation ajoutés par les architectes rendent l'espace utilisable et assez intéressant. À une époque où chaque mètre carré fait l'objet d'une comptabilité précise, la taille n'est pas ici un problème.

MIII ARCHITECTEN

MIII architecten
Generaal Berenschotlaan 211–213
2283 JM Rijswijk
The Netherlands

Tel: +31 70 394 43 49
Fax: +31 70 394 42 34
E-mail: info@m3architecten.com
Web: www.m3architecten.com

MIII ARCHITECTEN is an architectural design firm created in 1990 in Rijswijk, the Netherlands, and headed by Leendert Steijger, Edwin Smit, and Remko van Buren. Leendert Steijger was born in 1961 in Delft. He attended the Faculty of Architecture of the Technische Universiteit of Delft (1981–90). He was Assistant Designer at the architectural office of Hoogstad Weeber en Van Tilburg. He worked as an architect at KOW architects, before co-founding MIII in 1990. Edwin Smit was born in 1963 in Hoorn. He attended the Faculty of Architecture of the Technische Universiteit of Delft (1981–88) and worked in several architectural offices, including Broek & Bakema, before co-founding MIII. Remko van Buren was born in Sittard in 1966. Van Buren attended the Faculty of Architectural Design at the Academy of Art and Design, St. Joost, Breda (1982–87), and gained experience in the office of Morphosis in Santa Monica, before working in the Netherlands (1987–99). He became a partner of MIII in 1999. Their design of the Quantum House gave them the status of pioneers in the area of sustainable building in the Netherlands. Their work includes the Information Center, National Center for Arboriculture (Baarn, 2001–03, published here); 15 houses in Zoetermeer (2005); the Environmental Education Center (Hoorn, 2005); a Waterfront Restaurant (Capelle a/d IJssel, 2007); the Chess Office Building (Haarlem, 2008); and a district police office (Utrecht, 2008). Current projects are for a facility center and hotel at Eindhoven Airport (Eindhoven, 2009); and social housing (The Hague, 2009), all in the Netherlands.

MIII ARCHITECTEN gründeten sich 1990 im niederländischen Rijswijk. Geführt wird das Büro von den Partnern Leendert Steijger, Edwin Smit und Remko van Buren. Leendert Steijger, geboren 1961 in Delft, besuchte von 1981 bis 1990 die Fakultät für Architektur der Technischen Universität Delft. Anschließend war der Assistent-Designer im Architekturbüro Hoogstad Weeber en Van Tilburg. Bevor er 1990 MIII mitgründete, arbeitete er als Architekt bei KOW Architecture. Edwin Smit wurde 1963 in Hoorn geboren. Von 1981 bis 1988 besuchte er ebenfalls die Fakultät für Architektur der Technischen Universität Delft. Bevor er MIII mitgründete, arbeitete er in verschiedenen Architekturbüros, darunter bei Broek & Bakema. Remko van Buren wurde 1966 in Sittard geboren. Van Buren arbeitete nach seinem Besuch der Akademie voor Kunst en Vormgeving St. Joost in Breda (1982–87) ein Zeit lang bei Morphosis in Santa Monica. 1987 bis 1999 ging er verschiedenen Tätigkeiten in den Niederlanden nach, ehe er 1999 als neuer Partner zu MIII stieß. Seit dem Entwurf ihres Quantum Hauses gelten MIII architecten als Pioniere für nachhaltiges Bauen in den Niederlanden. Zu ihren Arbeiten gehören das Informationszentrum des Niederländischen Zentrums für Baumpflege in Baarn (2001–03, hier vorgestellt), eine Ensemble aus 15 Wohnhäusern in Zoetermeer (2005), ein Umweltbildungszentrum in Hoorn (2005), ein Uferrestaurant in Capelle aan den IJssel (2007), das Chess-Bürogebäude in Haarlem (2008) und eine Bezirkspolizeiwache in Utrecht. Derzeit werden ein Funktionsgebäude und ein Hotel am Flughafen von Eindhoven (2009) sowie der Bau von Sozialwohnungen in Den Haag (2009) geplant.

MIII ARCHITECTEN est une agence de conception architecturale créée en 1990 à Rijswijk, Pays-Bas, et dirigée par Leendert Steijger, Edwin Smit et Remko van Buren. Leendert Steijger, né en 1961 à Delft a étudié à la faculté d'architecture de l'Université Polytechnique de Delft (1981–90). Il a été concepteur assistant dans l'agence Hoogstad Weeber en Van Tilburg et travaillé comme architecte chez KOW Architects avant de co-fonder MIII en 1990. Edwin Smit, né in 1963 à Hoorn, a étudié à la faculté d'architecture de la Technische Universiteit de Delft (1981–88) et travaillé dans plusieurs agences, dont Broek & Bakema, avant de cofonder MIII. Remko van Buren est né à Sittard en 1966. Van Buren a étudié à la faculté d'architecture de l'Académie d'art et de design de St-Joost, Breda (1982–87) et travaillé chez Morphosis à Santa Monica, et dans d'autres agences aux Pays-Bas (1987–99). Il est associé de MIII depuis 1999. Leur projet pour la maison Quantum leur a assuré un statut de pionniers de l'architecture écologique aux Pays-Bas. Leurs réalisations comprennent le centre d'information du centre national d'arboriculture (Baarn, 2001–03, publié ici) ; 15 maisons à Zoetermeer (2005) ; le Centre d'éducation environnementale (Hoorn, 2005) ; un restaurant en front de mer (Capelle a/d IJssel, 2007) ; l'immeuble de bureaux Chess (Haarlem, 2008) et un commissariat de police de district (Utrecht, 2008), toutes aux Pays-Bas. Ils travaillent actuellement sur un projet de centre de services et hôtel à l'aéroport d'Eindhoven (2009), et des logements sociaux à La Haye (2009).

INFORMATION CENTER

National Center for Arboriculture, Baarn, The Netherlands, 2001–03

Floor area: 280 m². Client: National Center for Arboriculture.
Cost: € 790 000

The architects imagined this professional information center on the subject of trees as an extension of the tree nursery in which it is located. They explain, "MIII developed a constructive system of rafters and stabilizing arches resulting in a design that is resolved as a frozen movement of a continuum. The construction elements, all made of wood, are positioned in the rhythm of the system. The skin is designed as a fragmented transparency by means of a glass front and a glass roof, thus creating an open volume." The orientation of the building and its various openings toward the sun were carefully studied by the architects, as was the disposition of the structure vis-à-vis points in a grid they established, linking it to nearby roads or other elements of the site. The architects point out that wood construction is a Dutch tradition going back at least 500 years. Their own use of glue-laminated elements and modern glazing techniques certainly updates the wooden building however. The sweeping, open design of the Center, with its strong emphasis on wood and glass, sets this building apart from many other recent examples of Dutch architecture, and yet it appears to be perfectly in tune with the rising interest in more natural and environmentally friendly structures.

Das Informationszentrum für Baumpflege wurde von den Architekten als logische Erweiterung der Baumschule betrachtet, auf deren Gelände es entstehen sollte. „Unser Büro", so die Architekten, „entwickelte ein Konstruktionssystem aus Streben und Stabilisationsbögen, aus dem sich ein Entwurf herauskristallisierte, der den Eindruck eines eingefrorenen Einzelmoments aus einem Bewegungsablauf erweckt. Die einzelnen Bauelemente, alle aus Holz, folgen dem Rhythmus des Systems. Die Hülle wurde auf eine fragmentierte Transparenz hin entworfen: eine Glasfront und ein Glasdach lassen einen offenen Raum entstehen." Die Ausrichtung des Gebäudes und seiner Öffnungen erfolgte zum einen in sorgfältiger Abstimmung mit dem Sonnenlauf, zum anderen nach einem imaginierten Raster, das die Konstruktion in Beziehung zu den in der Nähe vorbeiführenden Straßen und anderen Elementen des Areals setzt. Die Architekten unterstreichen, dass der Holzbau in den Niederlanden auf eine mindestens 500 Jahre alte Tradition verweisen kann – die von ihnen selbst eingesetzten schichtverleimten Elemente und modernen Verglasungstechniken bringen ihn freilich auf einen neuen Stand. Vergleicht man es mit anderen Beispielen junger niederländischer Architektur, so verleiht die schwungvolle, offene Gestalt mit der besonderen Betonung von Holz und Glas dem Gebäude eine Sonderstellung. Mit dem zunehmenden Interesse an natürlicheren und umweltfreundlichen Bauwerken steht es augenscheinlich in bestem Einklang.

Ce centre d'information professionnel sur le thème de l'arbre a été conçu en extension de la pépinière dans laquelle il est situé : « MIII a mis au point un système constructif à base de chevrons et d'arcs de stabilisation qui a abouti à ce dessin évoquant un mouvement gelé dans un continuum. Les éléments constructifs, tous en bois, sont positionnés en fonction du rythme propre de ce système. La peau offre une transparence fragmentée par la façade de verre et le toit de verre, ce qui crée un volume ouvert. » L'orientation du bâtiment et ses diverses ouvertures vers la lumière du soleil ont été soigneusement étudiées par les architectes ainsi que son implantation par rapport à une trame qu'ils ont établie, à laquelle se rattachent les voies de circulations voisines et d'autres éléments du site. L'agence fait remarquer que la construction en bois est une tradition néerlandaise dont l'histoire connue remonte à 500 ans au moins. Cependant l'utilisation d'éléments en bois lamellé-collé et de techniques modernes de vitrage en modernise totalement l'aspect. Ces formes arrondies et ouvertes, comme l'accent mis sur le bois et le verre, distinguent ce projet d'autres exemples récents de l'architecture néerlandaise. Il semble parfaitement dans l'esprit de l'intérêt grandissant pour des constructions plus naturelles et plus écologiques.

The ribbed, shell-like form of the building confers a natural appearance on it, though its basic lines are quite modern.

Die gerippte, muschelartige Form verleiht dem Gebäude ein natürliches Aussehen, wobei seine grundlegenden Züge doch sehr modern sind.

La forme de coque nervurée du bâtiment lui confère un aspect naturel, bien que ses lignes soient fondamentalement assez modernes.

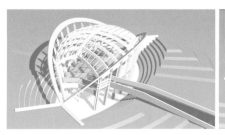
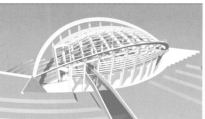
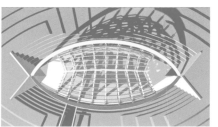

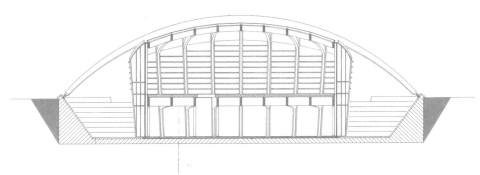

P 334.335

MADA S.P.A.M.

MADA s.p.a.m.
No. 2, Lane 134, Xinle Road
Xuhui District
Shanghai 200031
China

Tel: +86 21 5404 1166 / Fax: +86 21 5404 6646
E-mail: office@madaspam.com / Web: www.madaspam.com

Ma Qingyun graduated from Tsinghua University in China with a degree in Civil Engineering and Architecture in 1988. He worked briefly in a government historic preservation and urban planning office, before attending the Graduate School of Fine Arts at the University of Pennsylvania. He obtained his M.Arch there in 1991. He became a certified architect in the state of Ohio in 1996 and worked in the office of KPF in New York (1991–95). He then established **MADA S.P.A.M.** (for strategy, planning, architecture, and media). Ma has taught at Harvard, Columbia, Pennsylvania, the ETH in Zurich, the Berlage Institute in Amsterdam, and Berlin's Technische Universität. He coordinated the first book by Rem Koolhaas and the Harvard Project on Cities, entitled *Great Leap Forward* (Taschen 2001). Ma Qingyun is presently the Dean of the School of Architecture at the University of Southern California, Los Angeles. The firm's projects include the Ningbo Culture Center (Ningbo, 2000); their own offices in Shanghai (2003–04); Father's House (Xian, 2004); Chunshen Floating Street (Shanghai, 2005); the Xian TV Media Center (2005); Ningbo Y-Town (Ningbo, 2001–06); and the Comprehensive Office Building, Zhujiajiao Administration Center (Quingpu, Shanghai, 2004–06, published here), all in China. As Ma writes, "We see architecture as a process that selects and configures material, technology, and finance. We see it as a construct of ideas as well as products. We also see it as a form of knowledge gained through experiment and readjustment."

Ma Qingyun schloss 1988 sein Studium an der Universität Tsinghua in China mit einem Diplom in Architektur und Bauingenieurwesen ab. Nach kurzer Beschäftigung bei einem staatlichen Büro für Stadtplanung und Denkmalpflege besuchte er die Graduate School of Fine Arts an der University of Pennsylvania, wo er 1991 seinen Master of Architecture erwarb. Von 1991 bis 1995 arbeitete er im Büro von Kohn Pedersen Fox Architects in New York, 1996 erhielt er im Bundesstaat Ohio seine Zulassung als Architekt. Im Anschluss gründete er **MADA S.P.A.M.** (als Abkürzung für „strategy, planning, architecture, and media"). Daneben war Ma als Dozent an den Universitäten Harvard, Columbia und Pennsylvania sowie an der ETH Zürich, am Berlage Institute in Amsterdam und an der TU Berlin tätig. Ferner koordinierte er die Arbeit an der ersten Buchpublikation von Rem Koolhaas und der Harvard Design School über Städte mit dem Titel *Great Leap Forward* (Taschen 2001). Gegenwärtig ist Ma Dekan der School of Architecture an der University of Southern California in Los Angeles. Zu den Projekten seiner Firma gehören das Kulturzentrum von Ningbo (2000), die eigenen Büros in Shanghai (2003–04), Father's House in Xi'an (2004), Chunshen Floating Street in Shanghai (2005), das Fernseh- und Medienzentrum Xian (2005), Y-Town in Ningbo (2001–06) und die hier vorgestellte Behördenzentrale von Zhujiajiao (Quingpu, Shanghai, 2004–06), alle in China. Laut Ma versteht das Büro „Architektur als einen Prozess, bei dem Materialien, Technologien und Finanzierung ausgewählt und zusammengeführt werden. Architektur als Konstruktion sowohl von Ideen als auch von Produkten. Darüber hinaus verstehen wir unter Architektur eine Form von Wissen, das man durch stetes Ausprobieren und Neuanpassen erlangt."

Ma Qingyun est diplômé d'ingénierie civile et d'architecture de l'université de Tsinghua en Chine (1988). Il a brièvement travaillé dans une agence gouvernementale de conservation historique et d'urbanisme avant d'étudier à la Graduate School of Fine Arts, université de Pennsylvanie, où il a obtenu un M. Arch. en 1991. Il est devenu architecte certifié de l'état de l'Ohio en 1996 et a travaillé pour l'agence KPF à New York (1991–95). Il a ensuite créé **MADA S.P.A.M.** (s.p.a.m. pour stratégie, programmation, architecture, et médias). Il a enseigné à Harvard, Columbia, Pennsylvanie, à l'ETH à Zurich, à l'institut Berlage à Amsterdam et à la Technische Universität de Berlin. Il a coordonné le premier livre de Rem Koolhaas et du Harvard Project on Cities, intitulé *Great Leap Forward* (Taschen, 2001). Ma Qingyun est actuellement doyen de l'école d'architecture de l'université de Californie du Sud, Los Angeles. Parmi les réalisations de l'agence : le centre culturel de Ningbo (Ningbo, 2000) ; ses bureaux à Shanghaï (2003–04) ; la maison du Père (Xian, 2004) ; Chunshen Floating Street (Shanghaï, 2005) ; le TV Media Center de Xian (2005) ; Ningbo Y-Town (Ningbo, 2001–06) et l'immeuble de bureaux Comprehensive, centre administratif de Zhujiajiao (Quingpu, Shanghaï, 2004–06, publié ici), le tout en Chine. Ma explique : « Nous voyons l'architecture comme un processus qui sélectionne et configure matériaux, technologies et financement. Nous la voyons autant comme une construction d'idées que de produits. Pour nous, c'est aussi une forme de connaissance que nous acquérons par l'expérimentation et le réajustement. »

COMPREHENSIVE OFFICE BUILDING

Zhujiajiao Administration Center, Quingpu, Shanghai, China, 2004–06

*Site area: 40 500 m². Floor area: 20 598 m². Client: Zhujiajiao Invest Development Co. Ltd. Cost: not disclosed.
Team: Ma Qingyun, Sunny Zhanhui Chen, Rong Huang*

Quingpu is located approximately one hour's drive west of Shanghai, an area where MADA s.p.a.m. also built the Qio Zi Wan Shopping District and the Thumb Island Community Center. The local government asked the architects to design a new government complex, of which the so-called Comprehensive Office Building is the main project. The architects explain: "Its characteristic Jiangnan architectural form makes it also an emotionally accessible government center to the local workers. The project combined traditional gardens with modern architectural concepts: the plan is compact and orderly; it utilizes natural lighting, ventilation and makes complete use of the surrounding courtyard landscape." The building is 12 meters high and occupies three stories. As is the case in a number of other projects lead by Ma Qingyun, the materials used here—bricks, concrete, and patterned brick—are quite austere. One of the most striking elements in the large complex is a round pavilion situated near the water. Extensive use of wood was made in the complex. Here, the architects write, in almost poetic terms, "The wooden curtain wall follows the construction procedure for classical Chinese checkered windows. The wooden shutters in the curtain wall are made visible by the light that leaks in through the windows."

Quingpu liegt rund eine Stunde Autofahrt westlich von Shanghai. Hier hat MADA s.p.a.m bereits den Einkaufsdistrikt Qio Zi Wan und das Gemeindezentrum von Thumb Island gebaut. Auf Anfrage der Lokalverwaltung entwarf das Büro einen neuen Verwaltungskomplex, mit dem so genannten Bürogroßbau als Hauptprojekt. Zum Entwurf erklären die Architekten: „Durch seine für die Architektur in Jiangnan charakteristische Gestalt finden die örtlichen Angestellten leicht einen emotionalen Zugang zu dem Gebäude. Das Projekt kombiniert traditionelle Gärten mit einem modernen architektonischen Konzept: Der Grundriss zeigt eine kompakte, regelmäßige Aufteilung, Beleuchtung und Belüftung erfolgen auf natürlichem Weg und der Bau fügt sich vorzüglich in die Umgebung mit ihren Hofgebäuden ein." Das Gebäude ist 12 m hoch und hat drei Geschosse. Wie bei einer Reihe weiterer Projekte unter Leitung von Ma Qingyun kamen auch hier recht einfache Materialien zum Einsatz – Ziegel, Beton und gemusterte Backsteine. Eines der auffälligsten Elemente des großangelegten Komplexes ist ein runder Pavillon in Wassernähe. Eine herausragende Rolle spielt in der gesamten Anlage die Verwendung von Holz. Hierzu führen die Architekten aus: „Die hölzerne Vorhangfassade folgt der baulichen Anordnung klassischer schachbrettartiger chinesischer Fenster. Sickert Licht hindurch, werden die in die Wand eingelassenen Holzblenden sichtbar."

Quingpu se trouve à une heure de voiture environ de Shanghaï, région où MADA s.p.a.m. a également réalisé le quartier commercial de Qio Zi Wan et le centre communal de Thumb Island. L'administration locale avait demandé aux architectes de concevoir un nouveau complexe administratif dont cet immeuble est le composant principal. Les architectes expliquent : « Sa forme architecturale caractéristique de la région du Jiangnan facilite l'appropriation de ce centre administratif par les travailleurs locaux. Le projet combine des jardins traditionnels à des concepts architecturaux modernes : le plan compact et ordonné utilise l'éclairage et la ventilation naturels et tire le meilleur parti de l'environnement de la cour paysagée. » Le bâtiment de trois niveaux mesure 12 mètres de haut. Comme souvent dans d'autres projets de Ma Qingyun, les matériaux utilisés – brique, béton et brique à motif – sont assez austères. L'un des éléments les plus frappants de ce vaste complexe est un pavillon circulaire au bord de l'eau. Le bois est largement utilisé sur l'ensemble du complexe, ce que l'architecte décrit en termes presque poétiques : « Le mur-rideau en bois suit le mode de construction des fenêtres chinoises classiques. Les volets de bois dans le mur-rideau sont rendus visibles par la lumière qui filtre à travers les fenêtres. »

The emergence of contemporary Chinese architecture on the world scene is related to changes in local laws that allowed individuals like Ma Qingyun of MADA s.p.a.m. to create their own practice.

Der Einzug zeitgenössischer chinesischer Architektur auf die internationale Bühne hat mit der Änderung gesetzlicher Regelungen zu tun, die es Einzelpersonen wie Ma Qingyun von MADA s.p.a.m. erlaubten, eigene Büros zu eröffnen.

L'émergence de l'architecture chinoise contemporaine sur la scène mondiale est liée à des changements législatifs qui ont permis à des individus comme Ma Qingyun de MADA s.p.a.m. de créer leur propre agence.

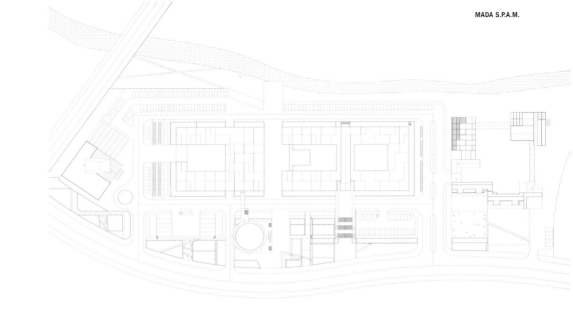

The unexpected and usually rather austere forms of MADA s.p.a.m. confer a strong originality even in the context of an office building.

Die ungewöhnlichen und häufig recht kargen Formen von MADA s.p.a.m. sind ausgesprochen originell, selbst wenn es sich um ein Bürogebäude handelt.

Les formes surprenantes et généralement assez austères de MADA s.p.a.m. confèrent une certaine originalité à ce projet, même dans le contexte de la problématique d'un immeuble de bureaux.

Generous openings usually shielded by wooden shutters characterize the design, which makes allusion to "classical Chinese checkered windows."

Charakteristisch für den Entwurf sind großzügige Gebäudeöffnungen, die in der Regel mit Holzläden verschlossen werden und auf „klassische schachbrettartige chinesische Fenster" Bezug nehmen.

Les généreuses ouvertures, généralement protégées par des volets de bois qui font allusion aux « fenêtres chinoises classiques », sont caractéristiques de ce projet.

PAULO MENDES DA ROCHA

Paulo Mendes da Rocha
Rua Bento Freitas 306 – 5º/51
CEP: 01220–000, São Paulo, SP
Brazil

Tel: +55 11 3259 3175
E-mail: pmr@sti.com.br

PAULO ARCHIAS MENDES DA ROCHA was born in 1928 in the city of Vitória, capital of the state of Espírito Santo, in Brazil. He completed his studies at the Mackenzie Architecture School in 1954. Paulo Mendes da Rocha was the 2006 winner of the Pritzker Prize. His first project outside Brazil was the Brazilian Pavilion for the International Expo in Osaka (Japan, 1970). One of his best-known projects is the Brazilian Museum of Sculpture (São Paulo, 1987–92). His Patriarch Plaza and Viaduct do Cha (São Paulo, 1992), with its great, curving wing canopy, is one of the more visible architectural monuments of Brazil's largest city. He has also done interesting renovation work, such as at the State Museum of São Paulo (1993). Other significant works include the Paulistano Club Gymnasium (São Paulo, 1957–61); the Clubhouse of the Jockey Club of Goiás (1963); the Beach Club in Guarujá (1963); a House in Butantã (1964); the Masetti Residence (São Paulo, 1970); a Hotel in Poxoréu (1971); the Jardim Calux School (São Bernardo do Campo, 1972); the Keiralla Sarhan Office Building (São Paulo, 1984–88); and the Jaraguá Apartment Building (São Paulo, 1984–88), all in Brazil. His more recent work includes a master plan for Vigo University in Spain; the Sesc 24 de Maio Building in the center of São Paulo; the Leme Gallery (São Paulo, 2004); Our Lady of the Conception Chapel (Recife, Pernambuco, 2004–06, published here); the Museum and Theater at the Enseada do Suá, Vitória (Espírito Santo, 2007); and the Central Mill Park, Piracicaba (São Paulo, 2007), all in Brazil unless stated otherwise.

PAULO ARCHIAS MENDES DA ROCHA wurde 1928 in Vitória, der Hauptstadt des brasilianischen Bundesstaates Espírito Santo geboren. 1954 schloss er seine Ausbildung an der Universidade Presbiteriana Mackenzie ab. Im Jahr 2006 wurde Mendes da Rocha mit dem Pritzker-Preis ausgezeichnet. Sein erstes Projekt außerhalb Brasiliens war der brasilianische Pavillon für die Expo '70 im japanischen Osaka. Eines seiner bekanntesten Projekte ist das Brasilianische Skulpturenmuseum in São Paulo (1987–92). Die von ihm neugestaltete Praça do Patriarca und das Viaduto do Chá (São Paulo, 1992) mit seinem großen, geschwungenen Kragdach gehören zu den hervorstechenden architektonischen Monumenten der größten Stadt Brasiliens. Von Mendes da Rocha stammt auch die reizvolle Umgestaltung des Staatsmuseums in São Paulo (1993). Zu seinen weiteren bedeutenden Werken zählen der Clube Atlético Paulistano in São Paulo (1957–61), das Vereinshaus des Jóquei Clube von Goiás (1963), ein Beachclub in Guarujá (1963), ein Wohnhaus in Butantã (1964), das Haus Masetti in São Paulo (1970), ein Hotel in Poxoréu (1971), die Jardim-Calux-Schule in São Bernardo do Campo (1972), das Bürogebäude Keiralla Sarhan (São Paulo, 1984–88) und das Apartmentgebäude Jaraguá (São Paulo, 1984–88). In jüngerer Zeit entwarf Mendes da Rocha den Masterplan für die Universidad de Vigo in Spanien. Ferner entstanden in Brasilien das Gebäude Sesc 24 de Maio im Zentrum von São Paulo, die Galerie Leme in São Paulo (2004), die hier vorgestellte Capela de Nossa Senhora da Conceição in Recife (Pernambuco, 2004–06), das Museum und Theater an der Enseada do Suá in Vitória (Espírito Santo, 2007) und der Parque do Engenho Central in Piracicaba (São Paulo, 2007).

PAULO ARCHIAS MENDES DA ROCHA est né en 1928 à Vitória, capitale de l'État de l'Espírito Santo, au Brésil. Il a achevé ses études à l'école d'architecture Mackenzie en 1954. En 2006, il a remporté le Pritzker Prize. Son premier projet hors du Brésil a été le pavillon brésilien de l'Expo '70 d'Osaka au Japon. L'une de ses œuvres les plus connues est le musée brésilien de la Sculpture (São Paulo, 1987–92). Sa Praça do Patriarca et le Viaduto do Chá (São Paulo, 1992), au vaste auvent en aile incurvée est l'un des monuments les plus remarquables de la grande cité brésilienne. Il a également réalisé d'intéressantes interventions de rénovation comme le Musée d'État de São Paulo (1993). Parmi ses autres réalisations importantes : le Paulistano Club Gymnasium (São Paulo, 1957–61) ; le clubhouse du Jockey Club de Goiás (1963) ; le Beach Club de Guarujá (1963) ; une maison à Butantã (1964) ; la résidence Masetti (São Paulo, 1970) ; un hôtel à Poxoréu (1971) ; l'école du Jardim Calux (São Bernardo do Campo, 1972) ; l'immeuble de bureaux Keiralla Sarhan (São Paulo, 1984–88) et l'immeuble résidentiel Jaraguá (São Paulo, 1984–88), tous au Brésil. Il a récemment conçu le plan directeur de l'université de Vigo (Espagne) ; l'immeuble Sesc 24 de Maio au centre de São Paulo et la galerie Leme (São Paulo, 2004) ; la chapelle de Notre-Dame-de-la-Conception (Recife, Pernambuco, 2004–06, publiée ici) ; le musée et théâtre de l'Enseada do Suá (Vitória, Espírito Santo ; 2007) ; et le parc Central Mill (Piracicaba, São Paulo, 2007).

OUR LADY OF THE CONCEPTION CHAPEL

Recife, Pernambuco, Brazil, 2004–06

Site area: 1300 m². Floor area: 300 m². Client: Francisco Brennand. Cost: not disclosed.
Architects: Paulo Mendes da Rocha, Eduardo Colonelli

Working on a 19th-century ruin on the grounds of the Brennand Ceramics factory, between the forest and a bank of the Capibaribe River, 16 kilometers from Recife, the architect added a new concrete slab roof and two columns, covering the restored walls. A transparent glass casing encloses the old stone walls but remains detached both from these surfaces and from the new concrete slab roof. An underground sacristy, a choir chancel overlooking the nave, and a baptistery on the side opposite the main entrance complete this design. As the architect writes, "The small construction is enlarged by the transparencies, reflections, and refractions that stream through the old door and window frames. Fragments of the original terrace arches form an external line that hedges the building." Mendes da Rocha is best known for his powerful concrete buildings, and although such elements as the concrete slab roof over the church do show his style, there is a delicate and successful integration of the new and the old in this project. Above all, the final result is very much of the present, even if it does integrate elements from the past.

Auf dem Gelände der Keramikfabrik Brennand, 16 km von Recife entfernt zwischen einem Waldstück und dem Ufer des Capibaribe gelegen, widmete Mendes da Rocha sich der Neunutzung einer Ruinenanlage aus dem 19. Jahrhundert: Er restaurierte die alten Mauern und ergänzte sie um zwei Betonsäulen und ein darauf ruhendes Betonflachdach. Eine gläserne Hülle umschließt die alten Ziegelmauern, ist jedoch weder mit den Wänden noch mit dem neuen Dach direkt verbunden. Eine unterirdische Sakristei, eine erhöhte Chorkanzel, von der man das Schiff überblicken kann, und ein seitlich positioniertes Taufbecken gegenüber dem Haupteingang vervollständigen die Komposition. Wie der Architekt schreibt, „wird das eigentlich kleine Bauwerk durch die freien Durchblicke und die Spiegelungen und Brechungen des Lichts, das durch die alten Tür- und Fensterrahmen einfällt, vergrößert. Fragmente der ursprünglichen Arkaden auf den Terrassen bilden eine externe Begrenzung." Während Mendes da Rocha ansonsten vor allem für seine mächtigen Betonbauten bekannt ist, ein Stil, der zum Beispiel auch bei dem Betondach aufscheint, zeigt die Kapelle eine subtile und gelungene Verbindung von Altem und Neuem. Trotz der Einbeziehung von Elementen aus der Vergangenheit steht das Ergebnis ganz in der Gegenwart.

Sur les ruines de l'usine de céramiques Brennand, entre la forêt et le fleuve Capibaribe à 16 km de Recife, l'architecte a protégé les murs restaurés du bâtiment par une dalle de béton soutenue par deux colonnes. Un coffrage en verre transparent double ces anciens murs de pierre, mais reste détaché à la fois de leur surface et de la toiture. Une sacristie en sous-sol, une tribune de chœur à balustrade dominant la nef et un baptistère sur le côté de l'entrée principale complètent la composition. Pour l'architecte : « Cette petite construction s'agrandit par les transparences, les reflets et les réflexions qui se multiplient à travers la vieille porte et les fenêtres. Des fragments des arcs de la terrasse d'origine forment un axe extérieur qui borde le bâtiment. » Mendes da Rocha est surtout connu pour les formes puissantes de ses réalisations en béton. Si le toit témoigne bien ici de son style, on trouve également une intégration délicate et réussie du nouveau et de l'ancien. Par-dessus tout, le résultat final est très actuel, même s'il intègre des éléments du passé.

Reusing elements of an existing building, Mendes da Rocha nonetheless imposes a modern appearance on the chapel with such gestures as the concrete slab roof.

Obleich Mendes da Rocha Teile eines älteren Gebäudes in seinen Kapellenbau einbindet, verleiht er ihm mithilfe von Elementen wie dem Betonflachdach ein modernes Erscheinungsbild.

Réutilisant des éléments du bâtiment original, Mendes da Rocha n'en a pas moins imposé à cette chapelle une apparence contemporaine par des gestes architecturaux visibles, comme le toit en dalle de béton.

The old stone walls of the 19th-century building are encased in glass, while the concrete roof allows for an open span space inside the chapel.

Zwischen die alten Ziegelmauern aus dem 19. Jahrhundert wurde ein gläserner Rahmen eingesetzt, durch den ein offener Innenraum unter dem Betondach entsteht.

Les anciens murs de pierre du XIXᵉ siècle sont enchâssés dans des panneaux de verre, tandis que la toiture en béton a permis d'aménager l'intérieur de la chapelle en plan ouvert.

CORINNA MENN

Corinna Menn
Gäuggelistr. 1
7000 Chur
Switzerland

Tel: +41 81 250 58 30
Fax: +41 81 250 58 69
E-mail: info@corinnamenn.ch
Web: www.corinnamenn.ch

CORINNA MENN was born in 1974 in Chur, Switzerland. She studied at the ETH in Zurich and the GSD at Harvard (1994–2000). She worked during this period as a trainee in the office of Hans Kollhoff in Berlin (1996–97), before obtaining her M.Arch from the ETH (2000). She worked as a junior architect in the office of Herzog & de Meuron in Basel (2001–02), before opening her own office in Zurich in 2002. She has had the present office in Chur since 2006. She has designed a Home for Handicapped Persons (Scharans, 2002–06); renovated a school in Splügen (2004–07); and completed the Conn Viewing Platform (Flims, 2005–06, published here), all in Switzerland. She also worked on a master plan for the Gaoqian Ecological Village (Dongqian Lake Town, Ningbo City, China, 2002–03, with Mayeux, Urban Design, Boston, and Park, Landscape Design, Rotterdam). She is presently building Row Housing in Tamins (Switzerland, 2006–08) and designing villas for the Faqra ski resort (Lebanon, 2008–10).

CORINNA MENN wurde 1974 im schweizerischen Chur geboren. Von 1994 bis 2000 studierte sie an der ETH in Zürich und an der Graduate School of Design in Harvard. Von 1996 bis 1997 arbeitete sie als Praktikantin im Büro von Hans Kollhoff in Berlin. 2000 erwarb sie ihr Diplom als Architektin an der ETH Zürich. Von 2001 bis 2002 war sie als Projektarchitektin bei Herzog & de Meuron in Basel beschäftigt und noch 2002 eröffnete sie ihr eigenes Büro in Zürich, das seit 2006 in Chur ansässig ist. Zu ihren realisierten Entwürfen gehören ein Behindertenheim in Scharans (2002–06), eine Schulhaussanierung in Splügen (2004–07) sowie die hier vorgestellte Aussichtsplattform Conn (Flims, 2005–06), alle in der Schweiz. Daneben war sie am Masterplan für das chinesische Ökodorf Gaoqian beteiligt (Dongqian, Ningbo, 2002–03, zusammen mit Mayeux, Urban Design, Boston, und Park, Landscape Design, Rotterdam). Gegenwärtig ist Menn mit dem Bau von Reihenhäusern im schweizerischen Tamins (2006–08) und dem Entwurf von Villen für das Ski-Resort in Faqra (Libanon, 2008–10) beschäftigt.

CORINNA MENN, née en 1974 à Chur, Suisse, a étudié à l'ETH de Zurich et à la GSD d'Harvard (1994–2000). Elle a été stagiaire dans l'agence de Hans Kollhoff à Berlin (1996–97), avant d'obtenir son M. Arch. de l'ETH (2000). Elle été architecte junior chez Herzog & de Meuron à Bâle (2001–02), avant d'ouvrir sa propre agence à Zurich en 2002. Son bureau est situé à Chur, depuis 2006. Elle a conçu un foyer pour personnes handicapées (Scharans, 2002–06); rénové une école à Splügen (2004–07) et construit la plate-forme d'observation de Conn (Flims, 2005–06, publiée ici), le tout en Suisse. Elle a également travaillé sur les plans du village écologique de Gaoqian (Dongqian, Ningbo, Chine, 2002–03, avec Mayeux, Urban Design, Boston, et Park, Landscape Design, Rotterdam). Elle construit actuellement un ensemble de logements en rangée à Tamins (Suisse, 2006–08) et conçoit differentes villas pour la station de ski de Faqra (Liban, 2008–10).

CONN VIEWING PLATFORM

Flims, Switzerland, 2005–06

Floor area: 19.5 m². Client: Municipality of Flims.
Cost: €250 000. Collaborator: Tamara Prader

The topographic map to the right shows the highly irregular contours of the site. The wing-like shape marks the location of the viewing platform.

Die topografische Karte rechts lässt die großen Höhenunterschiede des Gebiets erkennen. Die flügelförmige Markierung zeigt den Standort der Aussichtsplattform an.

Une carte topographique (à droite) montre les contours très irréguliers du terrain. Le contour en aile marque l'implantation du belvédère.

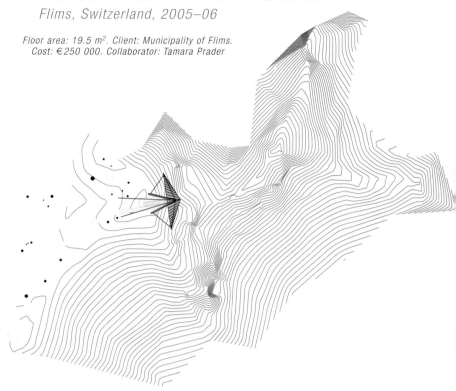

Corinna Menn won an invited competition for this project in 2005. As she says, "The visible relation and the building impact on nature were important aspects for the jury to judge the projects. I took the basic decision that the structure should be placed on the level of the forest and not in the slope of the canyon. My proposal has an impact on the ground only on four points and is reversible without leaving scars on the natural setting." The platform is located above an impressive canyon called the Ruinaulta, formed over the 10 000 years since one of the most significant landslides in the Alps covered part of the Rhine Valley. Ruinaulta is on the Vorderrhein, just upstream from its confluence with the Hinterrhein at Reichenau, and is accessible only from very few points—amongst them the location of the platform. The architect states, "Without touching the site, the structure is based on the exact topographical borderline of the canyon. Rising through the pines, the wooden triangle of the platform hangs from the top and leans forward. Like a swallow, it glides over the precipice. The structure of the viewing platform is a precise geometric structure. The main elements—pylon and platform—are triangles. The connection of the supports by ropes again form triangles. The minimal use of materials and the simple construction express the pure transmission of power and the tension of the spatial figure." Aside from ropes, the essential materials of the platform are steel and local larch wood.

Im Jahr 2005 gewann Corinna Menn die Ausschreibung für den Entwurf dieser Aussichtsplattform. Die Architektin erläutert: „Wichtige Aspekte für die Jury waren der sichtbare Bezug zur und die Auswirkung auf die Natur. Eine grundsätzliche Entscheidung bestand darin, die Konstruktion auf Höhe des Waldes anstatt in das Gefälle der Schlucht hinein zu bauen. Mein Vorschlag ist nur an vier Stellen mit dem Boden verbunden und lässt sich wieder abbauen, ohne Spuren in der Natur zu hinterlassen." Die Aussichtsplattform überblickt die Ruinaulta, eine imposante Schlucht des Vorderrheins in der Nähe der Hinterrheinmündung bei Reichenau. Entstanden ist die Ruinaulta in der Folge eines gewaltigen Bergsturzes in den Alpen, der vor 10 000 Jahren einen Teil des Vorderrheintals verschüttete. Die Schlucht ist nur über wenige Punkte zugänglich, einer davon ist der Standort der Plattform. Die Architektin führt aus: „An der äußersten Kante im Wald verankert, ragt die Aussichtsplattform zwischen die Föhren und neigt sich über den Schluchtraum. Einem Mauersegler gleich schwebt sie über dem Abgrund. Die Struktur der Plattform bildet eine exakte geometrische Figur. Die Hauptelemente – die Mastkonstruktion und die Aussichtsfläche – sind dreieckig und auch die Verbindungen von Stützen und Tragseilen bilden eine Dreiecksform. Durch den minimalen Materialaufwand und den einfachen Aufbau kommen die herrschenden Kräfteverhältnisse und die Spannung der räumlichen Figur zum Ausdruck." Abgesehen von den Seilen wurden als wesentliche Baumaterialen Stahl und aus der Gegend stammendes Lärchenholz gewählt.

Corinna Menn a remporté cette commande à l'issue d'un concours en 2005. Selon elle : « La relation visible entre l'impact du bâti et la nature ont été des critères importants du jury. J'ai décidé que la structure devait se trouver au niveau de la forêt et non dans la pente du canyon. Ma proposition n'exerce un impact sur le sol qu'en quatre points. Elle est réversible, ne laissera pas de cicatrices sur le cadre naturel. » La plate-forme est suspendue au-dessus d'un impressionnant canyon appelé Ruinaulta, formé il y a plus de 10 000 ans lorsqu'un énorme glissement de terrain des Alpes recouvrit partiellement la vallée du Rhin. Le site se trouve sur le Vorderrhein, en amont du confluent du Hinterrhein à Reichenau et n'est accessible que de quelques endroits. « Sans porter atteinte au site, la structure est implantée à la limite topographique exacte de la crête du canyon. S'élevant à travers les sapins, le triangle de bois qui la constitue est suspendu par le haut et se projette vers l'avant. Comme une hirondelle, il s'envole au-dessus du précipice. La structure est une construction géométrique d'une grande précision. Les éléments principaux – pylône et plate-forme – sont des triangles. La connexion avec les supports se fait par des câbles également triangulés. L'utilisation minimaliste des matériaux et la simplicité de construction expriment la transmission de la force et la tension de cette figure spatiale. » En dehors des câbles, les matériaux de base sont l'acier et le mélèze local.

The site is spectacular and rugged,
allowing visitors to view an almost
unspoiled natural setting.

Der spektakuläre, wilde Standort
bietet Besuchern eine weite Aussicht
über eine nahezu unberührte Land-
schaftskulisse.

Le site spectaculaire et sauvage
permet aux visiteurs d'observer un
cadre naturel pratiquement inviolé.

The very light design of the platform
makes its impact on the natural
setting as unobtrusive as possible,
but it also lends an almost airborne
elegance to the architecture.

Dank der ausgesprochen leichten
Konstruktion, die ihr eine beinahe
schwerelose Eleganz verleiht, fällt
die Plattform in der Natur kaum auf.

La conception légère de la plateforme
a limité au maximum son impact sur
le cadre naturel, mais confère à cette
architecture une élégance presque
aérienne.

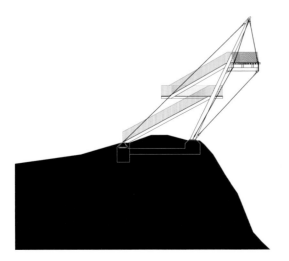

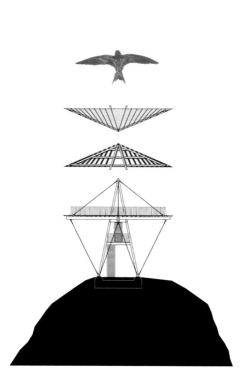

MERKX+GIROD ARCHITECTEN

Merkx+Girod Architecten
Gietersstraat 23 / 1015 HB Amsterdam / The Netherlands

Tel: +31 20 523 00 52 / Fax: +31 20 620 13 29
E-mail: arch@merkx-girod.nl / Web: www.merkx-girod.nl

In 1985, Evelyne Merkx set up her own interior design studio. She started working with architect Patrice Girod in 1990, and in 1996 they founded the firm of **MERKX+GIROD ARCHITECTEN**, for both architecture and interior design. Merkx+Girod has its own materials and model studio, where research and development on form, materials, color, and skin is carried out. Merkx+Girod designs interiors for privately owned buildings, as well as complete strategies for large and complex interiors of public buildings, in which the logistical and functional requirements are integrated into a coherent spatial vision. Its projects include restaurants, museums, department stores, shops, private residences, offices, and public buildings. Merkx+Girod now employs a staff of 34 people in Amsterdam. Evelyne Merkx was born in 1947 in Heerlen. She worked as a project leader with the advertising agency of the Bijenkorf Department Stores (1968–73), and studied Interior Design at the Rietveld Academy, Amsterdam (1979–84). Patrice Girod was born in 1937 in Strasbourg. He studied architecture at the Technische Universiteit of Delft (1957–63), before forming Cahen and Girod Architects (1962–66), Cahen Girod and Groeneveld Architects (1966–70), and Girod and Groeneveld Architects (1970–90). Aside from the Selexyz bookstores—such as the award-winning example published here (Selexyz Dominicanen Bookstore, Maastricht, 2005–07)—the pair worked on the interior design of the HEMA and Bijenkorf department stores (1995–2003) and on the master plan for the renovation of the Concertgebouw Amsterdam (1995–). They completed the interior of the Ernst & Young headquarters in Amsterdam (2008).They are currently working on the renovation and extension of the Dutch Council of State in the Hague (phase 1: 2008).

Evelyne Merkx gründete 1985 ein Büro für Innenarchitektur. Einige Jahre später begann ihre Zusammenarbeit mit Patrice Girod, mit dem sie 1996 die Firma **MERKX+GIROD ARCHITECTEN** gründete, die im Bereich Architektur und Innenarchitektur tätig ist. Zu Merkx+Girod gehört eine eigene Material- und Modellwerkstatt, die sich mit der Entwicklung von Werkstoffen, Formen, Farben und Oberflächenbeschichtungen befasst. Merkx+Girod führen sowohl Innenraumgestaltungen für Privatgebäude aus als auch umfassende Planungen für große, komplexe öffentliche Gebäude, bei denen logistische und funktionale Erfordernisse in einem stimmigen Raumkonzept zusammengeführt werden. Zu ihren Projekten gehören Restaurants, Museen, Kaufhäuser, Einzelhandelsgeschäfte, Privathäuser, Büros und öffentliche Einrichtungen. In ihrem Amsterdamer Büro beschäftigen Merkx+Girod gegenwärtig 34 Mitarbeiter. Evelyne Merkx, geboren 1947 in Heerlen, arbeitete von 1968 bis 1973 als Projektleiterin einer Werbeagentur für die Warenhauskette Bijenkorf und studierte von 1979 bis 1984 Innenarchitektur an der Rietveld Academie in Amsterdam. Patrice Girod, geboren 1937 in Straßburg, studierte von 1957 bis 1963 Architektur an der Technischen Universität Delft. Anschließend gehörte er den Architektengemeinschaften Cahen und Girod (1962–66), Cahen, Girod und Groeneveld (1966–70) sowie Girod und Groeneveld (1970–90) an. Neben ihren Selexyz-Buchhandlungen – darunter die preisgekrönte Filiale in Maastricht (Boekwinkel Selexyz Dominicanen, 2005–07, hier vorgestellt) – entwickelte das Duo Interieurs für die Kaufhausketten HEMA und Bijenkorf (1995–2003) sowie den Masterplan zur Renovierung des Concertgebouw Amsterdam (seit 1995). 2008 wurde die Inneneinrichtung der Ernst & Young Zentrale in Amsterdam fertiggestellt. Gegenwärtig sind Merkx+Girod mit der Renovierung und Erweiterung des niederländischen Staatsrats in Den Haag (Phase 1: 2008) beschäftigt.

C'est en 1985 que Evelyne Merkx a ouvert son agence d'architecture intérieure. Elle avait commencé à travailler avec l'architecte Patrice Girod en 1990, et, en 1996, ils ont fondé ensemble l'agence **MERKX+GIROD ARCHITECTEN**, spécialisée en architecture et architecture d'intérieur. Ils possèdent leur propre atelier de matériaux et de maquettes où ils font des recherches et développent des solutions de formes, de matériaux, de couleurs, d'enveloppes. Merkx+Girod conçoit aussi bien des aménagements intérieurs pour des résidences privées que des stratégies complètes pour de grands bâtiments publics dans lesquels les contraintes logistiques et fonctionnelles sont intégrées dans une vision spatiale cohérente. Ils ont réalisé des restaurants, des musées, des grands magasins, des boutiques, des résidences privées, des bureaux et des bâtiments publics. Merkx+Girod emploie 34 collaborateurs à Amsterdam. Evelyne Merkx, née en 1947 à Heerlen, a travaillé comme chef de projet pour l'agence de publicité du grand magasin Bijenkorf (1968–73), et étudié architecture intérieure à l'Académie Rietveld, Amsterdam (1979–84). Patrice Girod, né en 1937 à Strasbourg, a étudié l'architecture à la Technische Universiteit de Delft (1957–63) avant de créer successivement les agences Cahen and Girod Architects (1962–66), Cahen Girod and Groeneveld Architects (1966–70) ainsi que Girod and Groeneveld Architects (1970–90). En dehors des librairies Selexyz, dont un exemple primé est publié ici (Librairie Selexyz Dominicanen, Maastricht, 2005–07), le couple est intervenu sur les aménagements intérieurs des grands magasins HEMA et Bijenkorf (1995–2003), ainsi que sur le plan directeur de la rénovation du Concertgebouw (Amsterdam, 1995–). Ils ont également achevé l'intérieur du siège de Ernst & Young à Amsterdam (2008). Actuellement, ils travaillent sur la rénovation et l'extension du Conseil d'État à La Haye (Pays-Bas, phase 1 : 2008).

SELEXYZ DOMINICANEN BOOKSTORE

Maastricht, The Netherlands, 2005–07

Floor area: 1200 m². Client: Boekhandels Groep Nederland. Cost: not disclosed.
Team: Evelyne Merkx, Patrice Girod, Bert de Munnik, Abbie Steinhauser, Pim Houben, Josje Kuiper,
Ramon Wijsman, Ruben Bus. Restoration: Satijnplus architecten

Though it might seem unusual to turn a former church into a bookshop, this was the task asked of the architects by the Dutch booksellers Selexyz. The former Dominican church of Maastricht, originally part of a larger complex, was in fact no longer used for its original purpose after the French occupation of the region beginning in 1794. Subsequent to 1910, the building served as a city archive, but it was also used for car shows, flower exhibitions, and boxing matches. This was the third commission carried out by the architects for the Boekhandels Groep Nederland and the Selexyz brand. The client needed 1200 square meters of commercial space, while the floor of the church apparently offered only 750 square meters. The architects devised a monumental walk-in bookcase rising several levels on one side of the church, leaving the other side open to take advantage of the spatial qualities of the structure. Over 20 models were made by the architects before they found the correct solution for this unusual walk-up sales and display area. The structure they used does not actually touch the architecture of the church, in honor of the original function of the building. The architects seem to take some pleasure in explaining that "the former altar now houses the 'Coffeelovers' café with a large central reading table shaped as a cross." This table and other furniture for the cafeteria were designed by Merkx+Girod. The annual "Lensvelt de Architect" Dutch interior design prize for 2007 was awarded to Merkx+Girod Architecten for their design of this Maastricht bookshop.

Es mag etwas ungewöhnlich erscheinen, eine ehemalige Kirche in einen Buchladen zu verwandeln, doch genau darum waren Merkx+Girod von der Buchhandelskette Selexyz gebeten worden. Die frühere Dominikanerkirche von Maastricht, ursprünglich Teil einer größeren Anlage, diente bereits seit 1794, dem Beginn der damaligen französischen Besatzung der Region, nicht mehr ihrer eigentlichen Bestimmung. Nach 1910 wurde sie als Stadtarchiv, aber auch für Autoausstellungen, Blumenschauen und Boxkämpfe genutzt. Die Umnutzung war der dritte Auftrag, den Merkx+Girod für die zur Boekhandels Groep Nederland gehörende Kette Selexyz ausführten. Eine Herausforderung war die von den Auftraggebern gewünschte Ladenfläche von 1200 m², denn die Grundfläche der Kirche betrug nur 750 m². Daher konstruierten die Architekten für die eine Seite des Kirchenschiffs ein überdimensioniertes, begehbares Buchregal mit mehreren übereinanderliegenden Ebenen, während die andere Seite frei bleiben und die besonderen räumlichen Gegebenheiten des Bauwerks direkt in das Ladenkonzept integrieren sollte. Die Architekten bauten mehr als 20 verschiedene Modelle, bevor sie die beste Lösung für den ungewöhnlichen Präsentations- und Verkaufsbereich fanden. Aus Achtung vor der ursprünglichen Funktion des Gebäudes wurde die Regalkonstruktion frei in den Raum gestellt, ohne die Kirchenarchitektur direkt zu berühren. Die Architekten scheinen mit einigem Vergnügen darauf hinzuweisen, dass sich „in dem früheren Altarraum heute ein Coffeelovers-Café befindet, mit einem großen Lesetisch in Form eines Kreuzes in der Mitte". Der Tisch und weitere Einrichtungsgegenstände wurden ebenfalls von Merkx+Girod entworfen. 2007 erhielten die Architekten für ihre Gestaltung der Maastrichter Buchhandlung den jährlich vergebenen Lensvelt de Architect Interieurprijs.

S'il est rare de transformer une ancienne église en librairie, ce fut cependant la tâche assignée aux deux architectes par la chaîne de librairies néerlandaise Selexyz. L'ancienne église des Dominicains de Maastricht faisait à l'origine partie d'un ensemble plus vaste, mais elle n'était plus utilisée depuis l'occupation française en 1794. Après 1910, le bâtiment servit d'archives municipales mais aussi à des expositions de voitures, manifestations florales et matchs de boxe. Ce projet est la troisième commande confiée aux architectes par le Boekhandels Groep Nederland et la marque Selexyz. Le client avait besoin de 1200 m² pour la vente alors que l'église ne mesurait que 750 m² au sol. L'idée principale consiste en la création d'une bibliothèque monumentale d'où l'on peut évoluer sur plusieurs niveaux occupant un côté de l'église et laissant le reste du volume ouvert pour bénéficier des qualités spatiales du lieu. Plus de 20 maquettes ont été réalisées par les architectes avant de trouver la solution la plus adaptée à cet endroit original. La structure qu'ils ont dessinée n'entre jamais en contact avec l'architecture de l'église, une façon de rendre hommage à sa fonction originelle. L'agence semble prendre plaisir à expliquer que « l'ancien autel accueille maintenant le café Coffeelover's qui possède une grande table de lecture en forme de croix ». Cette table et d'autres meubles de la cafétéria ont été dessinés par l'agence. Pour cette réalisation, Mekx+Girod a reçu le prix d'architecture intérieure Lensvelt de Architect 2007.

The bookshop is inserted into the existing walls of the church in a regular manner, as seen on the floor plan to the right.

Wie auf dem Grundrissplan zu erkennen, wurden die Einrichtungselemente des Buchladens regelmäßig verteilt in den Kirchenraum eingepasst.

La librairie a été insérée entre les murs d'une église, dans l'axe de la nef, comme le montre le plan au sol, à droite.

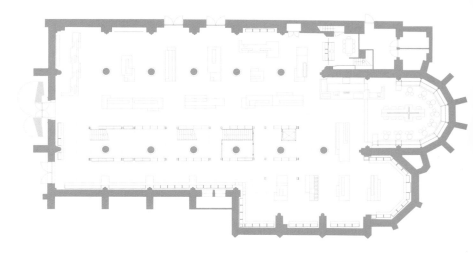

There is a strong contrast between the old columns of the church and the lighter shelving introduced by the architects.

Die von den Architekten eingefügten filigranen Regale bilden einen deutlichen Kontrast zu den alten Säulen.

Un puissant contraste s'est créé entre les piliers anciens et les rayonnages assez légers introduits par les architectes.

Although the original purpose of the church had nothing to do with the sale of books and coffee, the lighting of the interior plays on the religious purpose of the building.

Obgleich die ursprüngliche Bestimmung des Gebäudes nichts mit dem Verkauf von Büchern und Kaffee zu tun hatte, lässt sich die religiöse Atmosphäre mithilfe der Interieurbeleuchtung gezielt nutzen.

L'éclairage intérieur joue sur la nature religieuse passée du bâtiment, même si les boissons et les livres n'en faisaient pas partie.

The linearity of the original nave is accented by the long book shelves, making it seem as though religion and book sales might have more to do with each other than first suspected.

Die langen Buchreihen heben die Flucht des Kirchenschiffes hervor und vermitteln den Anschein, dass Religion und der Verkauf von Büchern mehr miteinander zu haben könnten, als man zunächst annehmen möchte.

La linéarité de la nef ancienne est accentuée par les longs rayonnages, créant des liens entre la religion et les livres plus étroits que l'on ne pouvait s'y attendre au premier abord.

JOSÉ RAFAEL MONEO

José Rafael Moneo
Cinca, 5
28002 Madrid
Spain

Tel: +34 91 564 22 57
Fax: +34 91 563 52 17
E-mail: r.moneo@rafaelmoneo.com

JOSÉ RAFAEL MONEO was born in Tudela, Navarra, Spain, in 1937. He graduated from the ETSA in Madrid in 1961. The following year, he went to work with Jørn Utzon in Denmark. Moneo has taught extensively at the ETSA in Madrid and Barcelona. He was chairman of the Department of Architecture at the GSD at Harvard from 1985 to 1990. He won the 1995 Pritzker Prize, and the 2003 RIBA Gold Medal. His work includes the National Museum of Roman Art, Mérida (1980–86); the San Pablo Airport Terminal in Seville (1989–91), built for Expo '92; the Atocha railway station in Madrid (1991); the Miró Foundation in Palma (1992); the interior architecture of the Thyssen-Bornemisza Collection in Madrid (1992); the Davis Museum at Wellesley College (Wellesley, Massachusetts, 1993); the Potsdamer Platz Hotel and Office Building (Berlin, Germany, 1993–98); the Murcia Town Hall (Murcia, 1995–98); and the Cathredral of Our Lady of the Angels (Los Angeles, California, 2000–02), all in Spain unless stated otherwise. He has also worked on the Souks in Beirut; the Laboratory for Interface and Engineering at Harvard; the Student Center for the Rhode Island School of Design (Providence, Rhode Island); and the Northwest Science Building at Columbia University in New York. Recent work in Spain includes the Art and Nature Center, Beulas Foundation (Huesca, 1996–2005); apartments in Calle Tres Cruces, Sabadell (with José Antonio Martínez Lapeña and Elías Torres, 2000–05); an extension for the Bank of Spain (Madrid, 2001–06); and an extension of the Prado Museum (Madrid, 2001–07, published here).

JOSÉ RAFAEL MONEO, geboren 1937 in Tudela in der spanischen Region Navarra, schloss 1961 sein Studium an der Escuela técnica superior de arquitectura de Madrid (ETSAM) ab. Im darauffolgenden Jahr ging er nach Dänemark, wo er mit Jørn Utzon zusammenarbeitete. Moneo war einige Jahre als Dozent an der ETSAM und in Barcelona beschäftigt. Von 1985 bis 1990 war er Leiter des Department of Architecture der Graduate School of Design in Harvard. 1995 erhielt er den Pritzker-Preis, 2003 die Goldmedaille des Royal Institute of British Architects. Zu seinen Bauten gehören das Nationalmuseum für römische Kunst in Mérida (1980–86), der Terminal des für die Expo '92 gebauten Flughafens San Pablo in Sevilla (1989–91), der Bahnhof Atocha in Madrid (1991), die Stiftung Pilar und Joan Miró in Palma (1992), die Innengestaltung des Villahermosa-Palasts für die Thyssen-Bornemisza-Sammlung in Madrid (1992), das Davis Museum am Wellesley College (Wellesley, Massachusetts, 1993), ein Hotel- und Bürogebäude am Potsdamer Platz in Berlin (1993–98), das Rathaus von Murcia (Spanien, 1995–98) und die Cathedral of Our Lady of the Angels in Los Angeles (2000–02). Ferner arbeitete er in den Beiruter Souks, am Laboratory for Interface and Engineering in Harvard, am Studentenzentrum der Rhode Island School of Design (Providence) und dem Northwest Science Building der Columbia University in New York. Zu seinen jüngsten in Spanien realisierten Projekten gehören das Centro de Arte y Naturaleza der Fundación Beulas im aragonischen Huesca (1996–2005), die Apartmentgebäude in der Calle Tres Cruces im katalanischen Sabadell (zusammen mit José Antonio Martínez Lapeña und Elías Torres, 2000–05), eine Erweiterung für die Banco Central de España in Madrid (2001–06) und ein Erweiterungsbau für den Prado (Madrid, 2001–07, hier vorgestellt).

JOSÉ RAFAEL MONEO est né à Tudela, Navarre, Espagne, en 1937. Diplômé de l'ETSA à Madrid en 1961. il part ensuite travailler chez Jørn Utzon au Danemark, en 1962. Moneo a beaucoup enseigné à l'ETSA à Madrid et Barcelone. Il a présidé le département d'architecture de la GSD à Harvard de 1985 à 1990 et remporté le Pritzker Prize 1995, ainsi que la médaille d'or du RIBA en 2003. Parmi ses réalisations : le musée national d'Art roman de Mérida (1980–86) ; le terminal de l'aéroport San Pablo à Séville (1989–91) pour Expo '92 ; la gare d'Atocha à Madrid (1991) ; la Fondation Miró à Palma (1992) ; l'architecture intérieure de la Collection Thyssen-Bornemisza à Madrid (1992) ; le Davis Museum du Wellesley College (Wellesley, Massachusetts, 1993) ; un hôtel et immeuble de bureaux à Potsdamer Platz (Berlin, Allemagne, 1993–98) ; l'hôtel de ville de Murcie (1995–98) et la cathédrale Notre-Dame-des-Anges (Los Angeles, Californie, 2000–02). Il a également réalisé les nouveaux *souks* de Beyrouth ; le Laboratoire for Interface and Engineering d'Harvard ; le Student Center de la Rhode Island School of Design (Providence, Rhode Island) et le Northwest Science Building de la Columbia University à New York. Parmi ses récentes interventions en Espagne : le Centre Art et Nature, Foundation Beulas (Huesca, 1996–2005) ; des appartements à Calle Tres Cruces, Sabadell (avec José Antonio Martínez Lapeña et Elías Torres, 2000–05) ; une extension de la Banco Central de España (Madrid, 2001–06) et celle du Musée du Prado, publiée ici (Madrid, 2001–07).

PRADO MUSEUM EXTENSION

Madrid, Spain, 2001–07

Floor area: 22 040 m². Client: Spanish Ministry of Culture. Cost: € 106 314 349

A 1995 competition to extend the Prado drew 700 entries but failed for lack of space. Space was eventually found to the rear of the museum, on a plot owned by the monastery of San Jerónimo el Real. Part of this land was occupied by a listed 16th-century cloister. A second competition, won by Rafael Moneo in October of 1998, stipulated that the cloister had to be included in the new building. As Rafael Moneo writes, "The winning project called for the reopening of the Velázquez Entrance in the portico facing the Paseo del Prado, enabling the ascending spatial sequence which culminates in the cloister." Moneo dismantled the cloister so that a new structure could be built in the place of the existing platform originally erected to compensate for the slope in the site. The cloister was rebuilt on top of the new building, with parts of the architect's design rising up to enclose the cloister on two sides. From the street, only Moneo's new brick-faced structure is visible. Temporary exhibition galleries are placed below the cloister, and offices of various kinds around it. Moneo concludes, "The new building and the garden terrace help to consolidate the urban profile in Casado de Alisal as well as Ruiz de Alarcón Streets. Naturally, the garden terrace on top of the oblique space is open to the public. The entire area behind the Prado ends up covered in a blanket of green which is a good spot from which to contemplate the nearby Botanical Garden. The complex geometry of the terrace has been divided into parterres enclosed with stone benches, and their paths lead unavoidably to the apse of Villanueva, obviously without being able to reach it, yet highlighting what was the crux not only of this project, but of most of the other interventions realized over the years in the history of the Museum."

1995 wurden bei einem Wettbewerb für eine Erweiterung des Prado 700 Vorschläge eingereicht, von denen jedoch aufgrund von Platzmangel keiner realisiert wurde. Schließlich fand sich auf der Rückseite des bestehenden Gebäudes doch noch ein verwendbares kleines Grundstück, das dem Kloster San Jerónimo el Real gehörte. Auf einem Teil dieses Geländes befand sich allerdings ein geschützter Kreuzgang aus dem 16. Jahrhundert. Bei einem zweiten Wettbewerb, aus dem im Oktober 1998 Rafael Moneo als Sieger hervorging, gab es die Vorgabe, den Kreuzgang in den Neubau mit einzubeziehen. „Der ausgewählte Vorschlag sah vor, dass das zum Paseo del Prado hin gelegene Velázquez-Portal wieder geöffnet werden und dadurch eine aufsteigende Raumabfolge zustande kommen sollte, die ihren höchsten Punkt in dem Kreuzgang findet." Moneo zerlegte den Kreuzgang in Einzelteile, so dass der Neubau auf einer bereits bestehenden Plattform, die dem Gefälleausgleich des Geländes dient, angelegt werden konnte. Der Kreuzgang wurde dann auf einer neu errichteten Basis wieder zusammengesetzt, auf der sich weitere von Moneo neu entworfene Gebäudepartien erheben, die den Kreuzgang auf zwei Seiten umschließen. Von der Straßenseite aus ist nur Moneos Neukonstruktion mit ihrer Ziegelfassade zu sehen. Unterhalb des Kreuzgangs wurden Ausstellungsräume für temporäre Ausstellungen angelegt, darum herum verschiedene Büros. Moneo führt aus: „Der Neubau und die Gartenterrasse tragen dazu bei, ein geschlossenes urbanes Profil zur Calle de Casado de Alisal und zur Calle de Ruiz de Alarcón herzustellen. Der gesamte Bereich hinter dem Prado wird von einer begrünten Fläche überdeckt, von der aus man gut in den nahegelegenen Botanischen Garten hinüberschauen kann. Selbstverständlich ist die auf dem abgestuften Raum angelegte Gartenterrasse für das Publikum frei zugänglich. Die komplexe geometrische Form der Terrasse wurde in mehrere von Steinbänken umsäumte Felder unterteilt, deren Wege geradewegs zu Villanuevas Apsis zu führen scheinen, ohne dass sie diese freilich erreichen können – dafür lenken sie die Aufmerksamkeit darauf, worin die Problematik nicht nur dieses Projekts, sondern schon der meisten früheren Eingriffe bestand, die in der Geschichte des Prado vorgenommen wurden."

En 1995, un premier concours pour la modernisation du Prado avait été organisé. Il avait attiré 700 participants, mais avait échoué par manque d'espace. Celui-ci fut finalement trouvé à l'arrière du musée : un terrain propriété du monastère de San Jerómino el Real, dont une partie était occupée par un cloître du XVIe siècle. Le nouveau concours, remporté par Rafael Moneo en octobre 1998 stipulait que ce cloître devait être intégré au nouveau bâtiment. Comme l'explique Moneo : « Notre projet proposait la réouverture de l'entrée Velázquez située sous le portique face au Paseo del Prado, ce qui permettait de créer une séquence spatiale ascendante culminant dans le cloître. » Moneo a démantelé le cloître pour qu'une nouvelle construction puisse être édifiée à l'emplacement de la plate-forme érigée à l'origine pour compenser la pente du terrain. Il fut reconstruit au sommet du nouveau bâtiment, dont une partie l'encadre sur deux côtés. De la rue, seul est visible une façade de brique. Les galeries des expositions temporaires sont disposées sous le cloître, entourées de divers bureaux. Rafael Moneo indique pour conclure : « Le nouveau bâtiment et le jardin en terrasse contribuent à renforcer le profil urbain sur les rues Casado de Alisal et Ruiz de Alarcón. Naturellement le jardin en terrasse situé en haut de l'espace en oblique est ouvert au public. Toute la zone derrière le Prado est recouverte de verdure et offre un endroit intéressant d'où contempler le jardin botanique voisin. La géométrie complexe de la terrasse divise celle-ci en parterres délimités par des bancs de pierre, et des allées conduisent inévitablement vers l'abside de Villanueva, sans pouvoir l'atteindre comme on le voit à l'évidence, mais en mettant en valeur ce qui était le point capital non seulement de ce projet mais aussi de la plupart des autres interventions réalisées au cours de l'histoire du musée. »

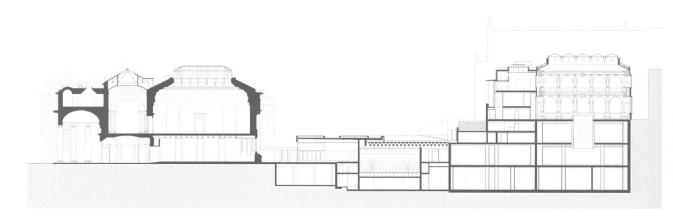

The extension by Moneo opens out from the back of the old building, which is linked to the new structure by a spacious concourse.

Moneos Erweiterungsbau schließt sich an die Rückseite des alten Museums an, mit dem er über einen weiten freien Platz verbunden ist.

L'extension de Moneo part de l'arrière des bâtiments anciens auxquels elle est connectée par un hall spacieux.

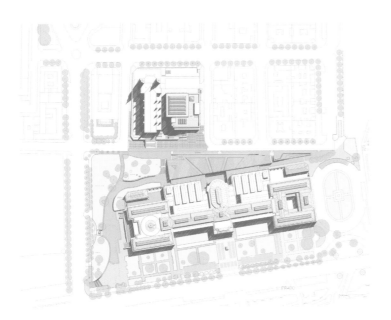

The connecting passage (left) and
the generous entry area for the new
building (above) employ a number of
different types of cladding as well as
a "Pompeian" red paint on one wall.

Im Verbindungskorridor (links) und
dem großzügigen Eingangsbereich
des Neubaus sind eine Reihe verschiedener Verkleidungsmaterialen
sowie auf einer der Wände ein
„pompejanisches" Rot zum Einsatz
gekommen.

Le couloir de connexion (à gauche) et
le généreux hall d'entrée du nouveau
bâtiment utilisent différents types de
parement dont une peinture rouge
pompéien pour un mur.

MORPHOSIS

Morphosis
2041 Colorado Avenue
Santa Monica, CA 90404
USA

Tel: +1 310 453 2247
Fax: +1 310 829 3270
E-mail: studio@morphosis.net
Web: www.morphosis.net

MORPHOSIS principal Thom Mayne, born in Connecticut in 1944, received his B.Arch in 1968 from the University of Southern California, Los Angeles, and his M.Arch degree from Harvard in 1978. He created Morphosis in 1979 with Michael Rotondi, who left to create his own firm, RoTo. He has taught at UCLA, Harvard, Yale, and SCI-Arc, of which he was a founding Board Member. Thom Mayne was the winner of the 2005 Pritzker Prize. Some of the main buildings by Morphosis are the Lawrence House (Hermosa Beach, California, 1981); the Kate Mantilini Restaurant (Beverly Hills, California, 1986); the Cedars Sinai Comprehensive Cancer Care Center (Beverly Hills, California, 1987); the Crawford Residence (Montecito, 1987–92); the Yuzen Vintage Car Museum (project, West Hollywood, 1992); the Blades Residence (Santa Barbara, California, 1992–97); and the International Elementary School (Long Beach, California, 1997–99). More recent work includes the San Francisco Federal Building; the University of Cincinnati Student Recreation Center (Cincinnati, Ohio, 1999–2005); the NOAA Satellite Operation Facility in Suitland (Maryland, 2001–05); a proposal for the 2012 Olympics in New York City made prior to the selection of London; the Hypo Alpe-Adria Bank Headquarters (Udine, Italy, 2004–06, published here); and the Phare Tower (Paris, France, 2006–12).

Thom Mayne, der führende Kopf von **MORPHOSIS**, wurde 1944 in Connecticut, Ohio, geboren. 1968 erwarb er den Bachelor of Architecture an der University of Southern California in Los Angeles, 1978 den Master of Architecture an der Harvard University. 1979 gründete er Morphosis, gemeinsam mit Michael Rotondi, der die Firma später verließ und sein eigenes Büro, RoTo, eröffnete. Mayne unterrichtete an der University of California in Los Angeles, in Harvard und Yale sowie am Southern California Institute of Architecture, zu dessen Gründungsmitgliedern er gehörte. 2005 erhielt er den Pritzker-Preis. Zu den wichtigsten Bauten von Morphosis gehören das Lawrence House in Hermosa Beach (Kalifornien, 1981), das Kate Mantilini Restaurant in Beverly Hills (Kalifornien, 1986), das Krebszentrum Cedars Sinai in Beverly Hills (Kalifornien, 1987), die Crawford Residence in Montecito (Kalifornien, 1987–92), das Oldtimermuseum Yuzen (Projekt, West Hollywood, 1992), die Blades Residence in Santa Barbara (Kalifornien, 1992–97) und die Internationale Grundschule in Long Beach (Kalifornien, 1997–99). In jüngerer Zeit entstanden u. a. das San Francisco Federal Building, das Student Recreation Center in Cincinnati (Ohio, 1999–2005), das Satellitenbetriebszentrum der National Oceanic and Atmospheric Administration in Suitland (Maryland, 2001–05), ein Entwurf für die Olympischen Spiele 2012 in New York (bevor London als Austragungsort feststand), die Zentrale der Hypo Alpe-Adria Bank im italienischen Udine (2004–06, hier vorgestellt) und der Tour Phare in Paris (2006–12).

Le dirigeant de **MORPHOSIS**, Thom Mayne, né dans le Connecticut en 1944, est B. Arch. de l'USC (1968) et M. Arch. d'Harvard (1978). Il crée Morphosis en 1979 avec Michael Rotondi, qui crée par la suite sa propre agence, RoTo. Il a enseigné à UCLA, Harvard, Yale, et SCI-Arc dont il est un des fondateurs. Thom Mayne a reçu le Pritzker Prize en 2006. Parmi les principales réalisations de Morphosis : Lawrence House (Hermosa Beach, Californie, 1981) ; le restaurant Kate Mantilini (Beverly Hills, Californie, 1986) ; le Cedars Sinai Comprehensive Cancer Care Center (Beverly Hills, Californie, 1987) ; la Crawford Residence (Montecito, Californie, 1987–92) ; le Yuzen Vintage Car Museum (projet, West Hollywood, 1992) ; la Blades Residence (Santa Barbara, Californie, 1992–97) et l'International Elementary School de Long Beach (Californie, 1997–99). Plus récemment, il a réalisé le San Francisco Federal Building ; le Student Recreation Center de l'université de Cincinnati (Ohio, 1999–2005) ; le NOAA Satellite Operation Facility (Suitland, Maryland, 2001–05) ; une proposition pour les jeux Olympiques 2012 à New York faite avant la sélection de Londres ; le siège de la banque Hypo Alpe-Adria (Udine, Italie, 2004–06, publié ici) et la tour Phare (Paris-La-Défense, 2006–12).

HYPO ALPE-ADRIA BANK HEADQUARTERS

Udine, Italy, 2004–06

Site area: 10.5 ha. Floor area: 9520 m². Client: Hypo Alpe-Adria Bank. Cost: not disclosed.
Architects: Morphosis; with Local Architect: Gri e Zucchi (Udine).
Team: Thom Mayne (Principal), Tim Christ (Project Manager). Project Team: Chandler Ahrens, Linda Chung,
Graham Ferrier, Rolando Mendoza, Marty Summers, Ted Kane, Ben Damron, Paul Gonzales,
Natalia Traverso Caruana, Chris Warren

This seven-story cast-in-place concrete building, with unitized curtain wall and metal panel skin system with passive and active sun shading, forms a landscape of structures with a 1290-square-meter archive, municipal swimming pool, auditorium, kindergarten, and a bank branch, as well as offices. The pool and fitness center are located at the western edge of the site, forming an integrated complex of buildings and outdoor spaces. A strict 14-meter width was established for the structure, allowing for "a very efficient space planning layout. The other advantages of the narrow floor plate," say the architects, "include ample access to natural daylight and the benefits of cross ventilation through operable windows." Within the main part of the building, an open central core crossed by stairs and a bridge admits natural overhead light. Each office has an exterior view and operable windows. The building is intended to have an "iconic presence"—achieved in part by the unusual 14-degree inclination of the structure toward the south. This offset allows the upper floors to shade the lower ones in the summer.

Dieses siebengeschossige Gebäude wurde in Ortbetonbauweise errichtet und mit einem modularen System aus Vorhangwänden und Metallplatten versehen, das einen passiven und aktiven Sonnenschutz bietet. Der Bau besteht aus einer ganzen Reihe einzelner Einrichtungen. Dazu gehören ein 1290 m² großes Archiv, ein öffentliches Schwimmbad, ein Kongresszentrum, ein Kindergarten, eine Bankfiliale und natürlich Büros. Das Schwimmbad und ein Fitnessstudio befinden sich auf dem westlichen Abschnitt des Geländes und bilden ein Ensemble aus Gebäuden und Außenbereichen. Für die gesamte Konstruktion wurde eine feste Breite von 14 m vorgegeben, die „auf eine sehr effektive Raumaufteilung ausgelegt ist. Weitere Vorteile der schmalen Geschossplatten", so die Architekten, „sind die reichliche Versorgung mit Tageslicht und die Möglichkeit, durch zu öffnende Fenster für geregelten Durchzug zu sorgen." Ein offenes Zentrum innerhalb des Gebäudehauptteils, das von einer Brücke und Treppen durchquert wird, lässt natürliches Licht von oben ein. Jedes Büro bietet einen Ausblick nach draußen und individuell bedienbare Fenster. Die beabsichtigte „zeichenhafte Präsenz" erhält das Gebäude u. a. dank der ungewöhnlichen, nach Süden weisenden Neigung von 14 Grad, dank derer die oberen Geschosse die unteren im Sommer beschatten.

Cet immeuble de béton coulé en place haut de sept niveaux et doté d'une façade à système de mur-rideau et peau en panneaux métalliques à protection solaire active et passive forme un paysage de constructions qui comprend le siège de la banque, des bureaux, 1290 m² d'archives, une piscine municipale, un auditorium et un jardin d'enfants. La piscine et le club de gymnastique sont implantés à l'extrémité ouest du site qui forme un ensemble intégré de bâtiments et d'espaces en plein air. La largeur de 14 mètres du bâtiment permet « une planification très efficace de l'espace. Les autres avantages de ces plans étroits », dit l'architecte, « résident dans l'accès généreux à la lumière naturelle et aux bénéfices de la ventilation croisée grâce à des fenêtres ouvrables. » À l'intérieur de la partie principale de l'immeuble, un noyau central ouvert, zébré d'escaliers et d'une passerelle reçoit la lumière du jour par une verrière zénithale. Chaque bureau jouit d'une vue sur l'extérieur et de fenêtres ouvrables. L'immeuble cultive évidemment une « présence iconique » à laquelle contribue fortement son inclinaison à 14° vers le sud, ce qui permet aux étages supérieurs d'abriter du soleil estival les niveaux inférieurs.

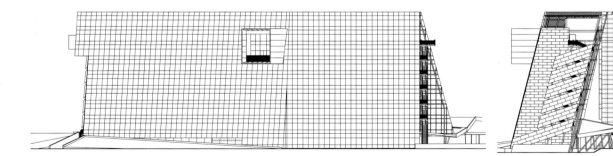

The inclination of the building and its articulated surfaces give it an otherworldly appearance, particularly when seen from the adjacent green field (right).

Die Neigung und die gegliederten Fassaden verleihen dem Gebäude eine irreale Wirkung, insbesondere von dem angrenzenden Feld aus betrachtet (rechts).

L'inclinaison du bâtiment et ses surfaces articulées lui donnent une apparence irréelle, en particulier lorsqu'il est vu des champs voisins (à droite).

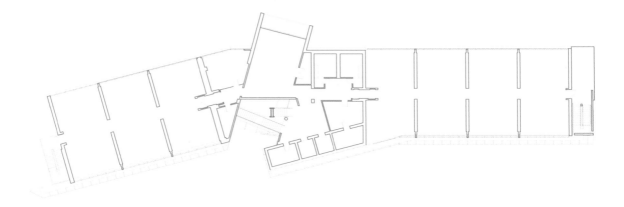

Complex breaks and shifts in surfaces and volumes characterize this building as much as they do other buildings by Morphosis.

Wie bei zahlreichen anderen Bauten von Morphosis zeichnen sich auch hier die Gebäudeabschnitte und Oberflächen durch komplexe Verschiebungen und Lücken aus.

Les ruptures et les glissements complexes entre les surfaces et les volumes qui caractérisent ce bâtiment rappellent d'autres réalisations de Morphosis.

The angled and undulating façade
lends an appearance of movement
to the building at night (opposite).

Nachts lässt die verwinkelt gewellte
Fassade das Gebäude wirken, als
bewege es sich (rechts).

La nuit, la façade penchée et ondulée
confère au bâtiment une impression
de mouvement (à droite).

A canopy with round openings and
angled struts connects parts of the
complex on the exterior.

À l'extérieur, un passage couvert,
ponctué d'ouvertures circulaires et
soutenu par des colonnes inclinées,
relie différentes parties du bâtiment.

Im Außenbereich sind Teile des Komplexes durch eine Überdachung mit
runden Öffnungen und angewinkelten
Stützen miteinander verbunden.

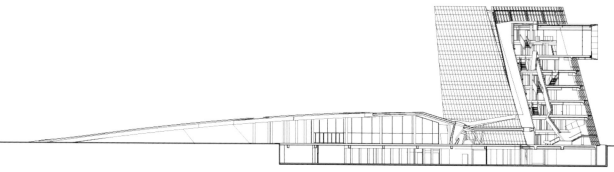

MVRDV

MVRDV
Dunantstraat 10
3024 BC Rotterdam
The Netherlands

Tel: +31 10 477 28 60
Fax: +31 10 477 36 27
E-mail: office@mvrdv.nl
Web: www.mvrdv.nl

MVRDV was created in 1991 by Winy Maas, Jacob van Rijs, and Nathalie de Vries. The name of the firm is made up of the initials of the surnames of the partners. Born in 1959 in Schijndel, Maas, like his two partners, studied at the Technische Universiteit of Delft. Jacob van Rijs was born in Amsterdam in 1964, and Nathalie de Vries in Appingedam in 1964. Both Maas and van Rijs worked for OMA. Maas and de Vries worked in the office of Ben van Berkel, before founding MVRDV, and Nathalie de Vries also worked with Mecanoo in Delft. Their work includes the RVU Building in Hilversum (1994–97); the Double House in Utrecht (1995–97); as well as WoZoCo, 100 apartments for elderly people (Amsterdam-Osdorp, 1997); and the Villa VPRO (Hilversum, 1997), all in the Netherlands. The architects designed the spectacular Dutch Pavilion at Expo 2000 in Hanover. Their plan for a temporary pavilion that would have completely engulfed the Serpentine Gallery in London was delayed for technical reasons in 2004. MVRDV have also worked on urban development schemes such as their "Shadow City Bergen Op Zoom" project (1993); the master plan for Parklane Airport (Eindhoven); and the master plan for Subdivision 10 in Ypenburg (The Hague). Recent work includes the GYRE Building (Shibuya-ku, Tokyo, Japan, 2006–07, published here); their Celosia Housing (Madrid, Spain, 2001–08); Westerdokseiland housing (Amsterdam, The Netherlands, under construction); and the Torre Huerta (Valencia, Spain, 2007–10).

Der Name des 1991 entstandenen Büros **MVRDV** setzt sich zusammen aus den Nachnamensinitialen seiner Gründer Winy Maas, Jacob van Rijs und Nathalie de Vries. Maas wurde 1959 in Schijndel geboren, van Rijs 1964 in Amsterdam, Nathalie de Vries 1964 in Appingedam; alle drei studierten an der Technischen Universität Delft. Van Rijs und Maas arbeiteten eine Zeit lang für Rem Koolhaas' OMA, mit de Vries war Maas vor der Gründung von MVRDV im Büro von Ben van Berkel tätig. Nathalie de Vries arbeitete u. a. auch für Mecanoo in Delft. Zu den von MVRDV entworfenen Bauten gehören das RVU-Gebäude in Hilversum (1994–97), das Doppelhaus in Utrecht (1995–97), die Seniorenwohnanlage WoZoCo (Woonzorgcomplex) mit 100 Apartments in Amsterdam-Osdorp (1997) und die Villa VPRO (Hilversum, 1997); außerdem entwarfen MVRDV den spektakulären niederländischen Pavillon für die Expo 2000 in Hannover. Die geplante Gestaltung eines temporären Pavillons für die Serpentine Gallery in London, der diese komplett umschlingen sollte, wurde 2004 aus technischen Gründen verschoben. MVRDV erstellten auch diverse Stadtentwicklungskonzepte, etwa das Projekt Shadow City Bergen Op Zoom (1993), den Masterplan für den Flughafen Parklane in Eindhoven und den Masterplan für die Wohnsiedlung Waterwijk-Ypenburg (Den Haag). Zu ihren jüngeren Projekten gehören das hier vorgestellte GYRE-Gebäude in Shibuya-ku, Tokio (2006–07), die Wohnanlage Celosia in Madrid (2001–08), die Wohnanlage Westerdokseiland in Amsterdam (im Bau befindlich) und die Torre Huerta im spanischen Valencia (2007–10).

L'agence **MVRDV** a été créée en 1991 par Winy Maas, Jacob van Rijs et Nathalie de Vries. Son sigle est composé des initiales de noms de famille des associés. Né en 1959 à Schijndel, Maas, comme ses deux partenaires, elle a étudié à la Technische Universiteit de Delft. Jacob van Rijs est né à Amsterdam en 1964, et Nathalie de Vries à Appingedam en 1964. Maas et van Rijs ont tous les deux travaillé pour OMA ; Maas et de Vries ont travaillé ensemble dans l'agence de Ben van Berkel, avant de fonder MVRDV. Nathalie de Vries a également travaillé pour Mecanoo à Delft. Parmi leurs réalisations : l'immeuble RVU à Hilversum (1994–97) ; la Double House à Utrecht (1995–97) ; WoZoCo, 100 appartements pour personnes âgées (Amsterdam-Osdorp, 1997) et la villa VPRO (Hilversum, 1997), tous aux Pays-Bas. Ils ont conçu le spectaculaire pavillon néerlandais à Expo 2000 à Hanovre. Leur plan de pavillon temporaire pour la Serpentine Gallery à Londres aurait entièrement entouré celle-ci, mais il a été annulé pour des raisons techniques (2004). MVRDV est également intervenu sur des projets d'urbanisme tel que le projet « Shadow City Bergen Op Zoom » (1993) ; le plan directeur de l'aéroport Parklane (Eindhoven), et le plan directeur de la Subdivision 10 à Ypenburg. Récemment, ils ont réalisé l'immeuble GYRE (Shibuya-ku, Tokyo, Japon, 2006–07, publié ici) ; les logements Celosia à Madrid (Espagne, 2001–08) ; les logements Westerdokseiland (Amsterdam, Pays-Bas, en construction) et la Torre Huerta (Valencia, Espagne, 2007–10).

GYRE BUILDING

Shibuya-ku, Tokyo, Japan, 2006–07

*Site area: 1769 m². Floor area: 8950 m². Client: Takenaka Corporation, Tokyo.
Cost: not disclosed. Architects: MVRDV, Takenaka Corporation*

This five-story, 30-meter-high building is intended for the use of a number of prestigious retail brands such as Chanel. It is located in the prestigious Omotesando area of the Japanese capital, near buildings by Toyo Ito and SANAA, and up the street from others by Tadao Ando and Herzog & de Meuron. "They are the architectural equivalent of supermodels," say the architects. "But, like supermodels, their beauty can be intimidating. Can a new building compete and make a statement? Can a new building strive to be more than merely decorative?" The response of MVRDV, apparently inspired by such earlier works in the area as Fumihiko Maki's Spiral Building (1985), was conceived as a series of five stacked boxes with an open atrium. Each floor is rotated slightly, creating a sense of movement in the architecture, but, above all, terraces and outdoor (i.e. vertical) circulation patterns. Maki's Spiral, used by several tenants, also encouraged vertical movement within the building, rendering the upper floors more attractive than they might otherwise have been. The architects compare their proximity to the sleek, shimmering Dior Building (SANAA) as a case of "beauty and the beast." So much for the supermodels, but the "beast" is attractive nonetheless, rising in its rather Dutch austerity from the fashionable sidewalk of Omotesando.

Das GYRE-Gebäude ist ein fünfgeschossiges, 30 m hohes Geschäftshaus, zu dessen Mietern renommierte Marken wie Chanel gehören. Es befindet sich auf Tokios edler Einkaufsmeile Omotesando, in nächster Nachbarschaft zu Gebäuden von Toyo Ito und SANAA sowie Tadao Ando und Herzog & de Meuron. „Diese Bauten sind die architektonischen Gegenstücke zu Supermodels", stellen die Architekten fest. „Aber wie bei Supermodels kann ihre Schönheit etwas Einschüchterndes haben. Kann ein neues Gebäude mithalten, kann es sich behaupten? Kann es ihm gelingen, mehr als nur dekorativ zu sein?" MVRDVs Antwort, offenbar nicht unbeeinflusst von früheren in der Gegend entstandenen Projekten wie Fumihiko Makis Spiralgebäude (1985), besteht aus fünf übereinandergestapelten Quadern sowie einem offenen Atrium. Die einzelnen Geschosse sind leicht zueinander verschoben und erzeugen so den Eindruck einer bewegten Gesamtarchitektur; vor allem aber entstehen Terrassen und um das Gebäude herum- und hinaufführende Außengänge. Auch bei Makis – von mehreren Mietern genutzter – Spirale spielt die vertikale Bewegung durch das Gebäude eine besondere Rolle: Dadurch erhielten die oberen Stockwerke eine größere Attraktivität, als es ansonsten wohl der Fall gewesen wäre. Die räumliche Nähe ihres eigenen Gebäudes zu dem schlanken, glänzenden Dior-Gebäude von SANAA vergleichen die Architekten mit dem Verhältnis zwischen „der Schönen und dem Biest". Soviel zu den Supermodels, dennoch kann man dem „Biest", wie es sich in seiner recht niederländischen Klarheit auf dem Pflaster des Omotesando erhebt, nicht seine Attraktivität absprechen.

Ce bâtiment de 30 mètres de haut et de cinq niveaux a été conçu pour accueillir un certain nombre de marques de luxe, dont Chanel. Il est situé dans le prestigieux quartier de la capitale japonaise appelé Omotesando près d'immeubles signés Toyo Ito, SANAA, Tadao Ando ou Herzog & de Meuron. « Ce sont les équivalents architecturaux des supermodèles, expliquent les architectes, mais, comme les supermodèles, leur beauté peut être intimidante. » Comment un nouveau bâtiment peut-il entrer dans cette compétition et affirmer son discours ? Peut-il être plus que simplement décoratif ? La réponse de MVRDV, apparemment inspirée de réalisations antérieures dans le même quartier comme le Spiral Building de Fumihiko Maki (1985), a été cet empilement de cinq boîtes et un atrium ouvert. Chaque niveau est en légère rotation par rapport à un axe central, ce qui génère une impression de mouvement, qui se ressent par-dessus tout dans les terrasses et les circulations verticales. Le Spiral Building de Maki encourageait également le mouvement vertical, ce qui rendait les étages supérieurs plus attirants qu'ils ne l'auraient été autrement. Sur la proximité de l'immeuble GYRE du scintillant immeuble Dior de SANAA, les architectes évoquent une vision de « la belle et la bête ». Les supermodèles apprécieront, mais la présumée « bête » est néanmoins séduisante dans son austérité assez hollandaise qui se singularise sur les élégants trottoirs d'Omotesando.

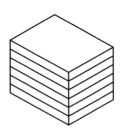  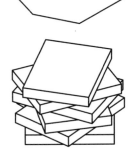 

Drawings (above) show the irregular stacking pattern that inspired the design seen in its completed form to the right.

Die obigen Zeichnungen zeigen die Vorlage aus übereinandergestapelten Quadern für das rechts in realisierter Form abgebildete Gebäude.

Les dessins ci-dessus montrent la disposition irrégulière de l'empilement qui a inspiré le projet, vu sous sa forme finale à droite.

In its Omotesando setting, the building stands out even as compared with
other structures designed by some
of the most famous architects of the
moment—definitely a positive point
for retailers.

Das Gebäude am Omotesando-Boule-
vard hebt sich sogar von den in der
Nachbarschaft von weltberühmten
zeitgenössischen Architekten entworfenen Bauten ab – für gewerbliche
Mieter in jedem Fall ein Pluspunkt.

L'immeuble se remarque, même
dans ce quartier d'Omotesando où
se dressent les réalisations de quel-
ques-uns des architectes les plus
célèbres du monde : c'est un point
définitivement positif pour le commerce.

MANFREDI NICOLETTI

Studio Nicoletti
Via di San Simone 75
00186 Rome
Italy

Tel: +39 06 6880 5903
Fax: +39 06 6892 394
E-mail: studio.nicoletti@libero.it
Web: www.manfredinicoletti.com

MANFREDI NICOLETTI, born in Rieti, Italy, in 1930, graduated from Rome's "La Sapienza" University, and earned his M.Arch at MIT (1955), before obtaining his Ph.D. in Urban Design at Rome University. He worked in the offices of Walter Gropius, Minorou Yamasaki, and P. L. Nervi, before opening his own office in Rome, in 1960. He is a Professor at Rome's "La Sapienza" University and Vice President of the International Academy of Architecture. In 2004, Giulia Falconi and Luca Nicoletti joined his office as partners of Studio Nicoletti Associati. Recent work includes the Palermo Sport Palace (Palermo, 1995–2001); Scientific Greenhouse for Tropical Butterflies, Catania University (Catania, 1999–2002); the G8 Conference Center, Chamber of Deputies' Annex, Palazzo Marini (Rome, 2000–02), all in Italy; the Millennium Park (Abuja, Nigeria, 2003–04); the New Arezzo Hall of Justice (Arezzo, Italy, 2001–07, published here); and the Astana Kazakhstan State Auditorium (Astana, Kazakhstan, 2003–07). Current work includes the Nigeria National Complex, City Hall, Cultural Center, and Millennium Tower (2006–09, Abuja, Nigeria).

MANFREDI NICOLETTI, geboren 1930 im italienischen Rieti, studierte an der Università di Roma La Sapienza und erwarb am Massachusetts Institute of Technology seinen Master of Architecture, gefolgt von einem Doktortitel im Bereich Städtebau von der Universität Rom. Bevor er sich 1960 in Rom selbstständig machte, arbeitete Nicoletti in den Büros von Walter Gropius, Minorou Yamasaki und Pier Luigi Nervi. Nicoletti ist Professor an der Università di Roma La Sapienza und Vizepräsident der International Academy of Architecture. Seit 2004 firmiert er gemeinsam mit Giulia Falconi und Luca Nicoletti als Studio Nicoletti Associati. In jüngerer Zeit entstanden der Palazzo dello Sport in Palermo (1995–2001), ein Schmetterlings-Troparium für die Università di Catania (1999–2002), ein G8-Konferenzzentrum als Anbau zur Abgeordnetenkammer im Palazzo Marini in Rom (2000–02), der Millenium Park im nigerianischen Abuja (2003–04), der hier vorgestellte Nuovo Palazzo di Giustizia in Arezzo (2001–07) und das Staatsauditorium in der kasachischen Hauptstadt Astana (2003–07). Derzeit entsteht u. a. der Nigeria National Complex in Abuja, zu dem Verwaltungsgebäude, ein Kulturzentrum und der Millennium Tower gehören (2006–09).

MANFREDI NICOLETTI né à Rieti, Italie, en 1930, est diplômé de l'université La Sapienza de Rome, M. Arch. du MIT (1955) et docteur en urbanisme de l'université de Rome. Il a travaillé dans les agences de Walter Gropius, Minorou Yamasaki et P. L. Nervi, avant d'ouvrir sa propre agence à Rome en 1960. Il est professeur à « La Sapienza » et vice-président de l'Académie internationale d'architecture. En 2004, Giulia Falconi et Luca Nicoletti sont devenus associés du studio Nicoletti Associati. Parmi leurs récentes réalisations : le palais des sports de Palerme (Palerme, 1995–2001) ; une serre pour l'étude des papillons tropicaux à l'université de Catane (1999–2002) ; le centre de conférences du G8, annexe de la Chambre des députés, Palazzo Marini (Rome, 2000–02), toutes en Italie ; le Millennium Park (Abuja, Nigeria, 2003–04) ; le nouveau palais de justice d'Arezzo (Arezzo, Italie, 2001–07, publié ici) et l'auditorium d'État du Kazakhstan (Astana, Kazakhstan, 2003–07). Ils travaillent actuellement sur le projet du Nigeria National Complex : hôtel de ville, centre culturel et tour Millennium (Abuja, Nigeria, 2006–09).

NEW AREZZO HALL OF JUSTICE

Arezzo, Italy, 2001–07

Floor area: 15 000 m². Client: Comune di Arezzo. Cost: €13.253 million.
With: F. Pagliano Tajani. Collaborators: L. Campagna, A. Senesi, F. Pedri, D. De Santis.

Arezzo is located about 80 kilometers southeast of Florence. It is known for the frescoes that Piero della Francesca painted in the church of San Francesco di Arezzo. The new Hall of Justice is set close to the Medici Fortress (Fortezza Medicea), designed by Antonio da Sangallo the Younger and built in 1538–60. The new building houses the courtrooms and is linked to a neoclassical building, once a large hospital, due to be restored and used for offices and archives. The architect explains the surprising exterior of this building, "An undulating transparent sunscreen façade of stainless steel is shaped according to a geometrically warped geometry which is characteristic of the skin of many living organisms, including leaves. Those complex curvilinear forms were built using only rectilinear elements. Thus, a silver bioclimatic 'foliage' protects the interior spaces with luminous shadows and blends with the park without clashing with the nearby neoclassical architectural elements." In the interior, the polished black granite floor contrasts with the greenish glazed envelope and a horizontal acoustic grey panel ceiling separated by narrow layers of vertical maple. The three-level-high entrance hall receives overhead light from the roof and is dominated by the vertical elevator case, clad like the floor in polished black granite panels.

Die toskanische Stadt Arezzo liegt rund 80 km südöstlich von Florenz und ist bekannt für die Freskenmalereien Piero della Francescas in der Basilica di San Francesco. Der Neue Justizpalast liegt nahe der Medici-Festung (Fortezza Medicea), die zwischen 1538 und 1560 nach den Entwürfen von Antonio da Sangallo gebaut wurde. Der Neubau beherbergt die Gerichtssäle und ist mit einem großen neoklassizistischen Gebäude verbunden, ein ehemaliges Krankenhaus, in dem nach seiner Renovierung Büros und Archive untergebracht werden. Zum ungewöhnlichen Äußeren seines Gebäudes erläutert der Architekt: „Die Formgebung der gewellten durchsichtigen Sonnenblendenfassade aus Edelstahl orientiert sich an geometrisch gebogenen Formen, wie sie für viele lebende Organismen, etwa auch Blätter, charakteristisch sind. Die komplexen Kurvenformen wurden ausschließlich aus geraden Elementen zusammengesetzt. Auf diese Weise wirft ein silbernes bioklimatisches ‚Blattwerk' seinen schützenden Schatten auf die Innenräume und fügt sich harmonisch in den Park ein, ohne sich mit den Elementen der benachbarten neoklassizistischen Architektur zu beißen." Im Inneren kontrastiert ein polierter schwarzer Granitboden mit der grünlich verglasten Außenhülle und einer horizontalen grauen Schallschutzplatte an der Decke. Die Eingangshalle in dreifacher Geschosshöhe empfängt durch das Dach natürliches Licht und wird von einem vertikalen Aufzugsschacht dominiert, der wie der Boden mit poliertem schwarzen Granit verkleidet ist.

À 80 kilomètres au sud-est de Florence, Arezzo est célèbre pour les fresques peintes par Piero della Francesca dans l'église San Francesco. Le nouveau palais de justice se trouve à proximité de la forteresse Médicis (Fortezza Medicea), construite en 1538–60 par Antonio da Sangallo le Jeune. Le nouveau bâtiment abrite des salles de tribunal. Il est relié à un immeuble néoclassique, ancien grand hôpital qui doit être restauré et transformé en bureaux et archives. L'architecte explique ainsi l'aspect surprenant du nouveau palais : « La façade en acier inoxydable formant un écran solaire ondulé tire sa force d'une géométrie d'enveloppement que l'on retrouve dans la peau de nombreux organismes vivants, y compris les feuilles. Ces formes curvilignes complexes ne font appel qu'à des composants rectilignes. Ce »feuillage« bioclimatique argenté protège les volumes intérieurs d'ombres transparentes, et se fond dans l'environnement du parc sans se heurter aux éléments architecturaux néoclassiques voisins. » À l'intérieur, les sols en granit noir poli contrastent avec l'enveloppe vitrée verdâtre et un panneau acoustique horizontal gris au plafond, séparés par de fines strates verticales d'érable. Le hall d'entrée sur trois niveaux de haut est éclairé par une verrière zénithale et dominé par la cage d'ascenseur, habillée, comme le sol, de panneaux de granit noir poli.

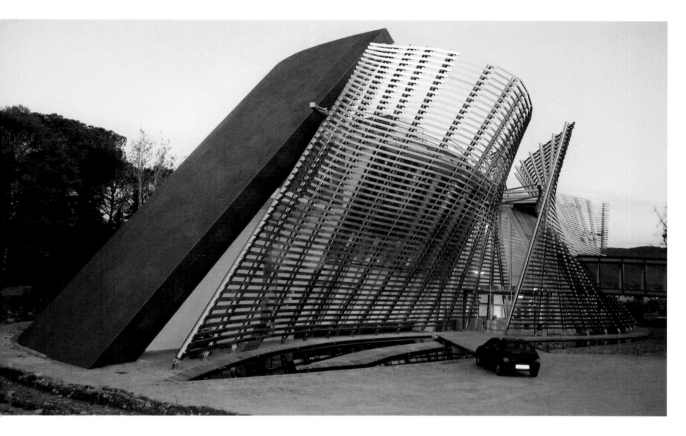

The angled screen of the main façade characterizes the architecture, whose overall plan is ovoid.

Die verwinkelte Blende der Hauptfassade ist das bestimmende Merkmal des Gebäudes, das in einer ovalen Grundform angelegt ist.

L'écran incliné de la façade principale caractérise ce projet, dont le plan au sol est de forme ovoïde.

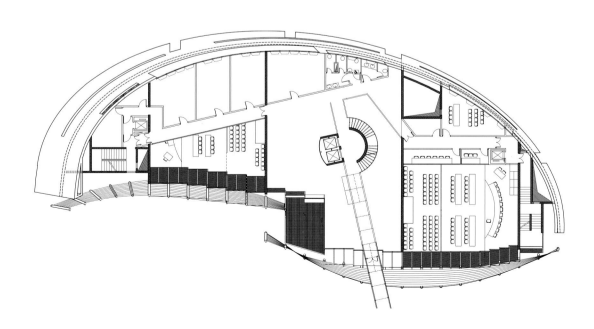

VALERIO OLGIATI

Valerio Olgiati
Via Nova
7017 Flims
Switzerland

Tel: +41 81 650 33 11
Fax: +41 81 650 33 12
E-mail: mail@olgiati.net

VALERIO OLGIATI was born in Chur in 1958. He studied Architecture at the ETH in Zurich. In 1986, he created his own architectural office in Zurich. From 1993 to 1995, he worked in collaboration with Frank Escher in Los Angeles. Escher is a specialist in the work of the architect John Lautner (1911–94). In 1994, Olgiati was Visiting Professor at the Hochschule für Technik in Stuttgart and since 1998 he taught at the ETH and has been a Guest Lecturer at the Architectural Association (AA) in London. Since 2001, he has been a full Professor at the Accademia di Architettura at the Università della Svizzera Italiana in Mendrisio. He has built a number of private homes and participated in competitions such as that for the National Palace Museum (Taiwan, 2004, finalist), and the Learning Center of the EPFL, in Lausanne. Two of his recent projects, the Peak Gornergrat and the University of Lucerne—both in Switzerland—were 2003 competition-winning entries. He has recently completed Atelier Bardill (Scharans, Switzerland, 2006–07, published here).

VALERIO OLGIATI wurde 1958 im schweizerischen Chur geboren. Nach einem Architekturstudium an der ETH Zürich gründete er 1986 hier sein eigenes Architekturbüro. Von 1993 bis 1995 arbeitete er in Los Angeles mit Frank Escher zusammen, einem Spezialisten für die Arbeiten John Lautners (1911–94). 1994 war Olgiati Gastdozent an der Hochschule für Technik in Stuttgart und ab 1998 an der ETH Zürich sowie bei der Architectural Association in London. Seit 2001 hat er einen Lehrstuhl an der Accademia di Architettura der Università della Svizzera Italiana in Mendrisio. Olgiati hat eine Reihe von Privathäusern gebaut sowie an Wettbewerben wie dem für das Nationale Palastmuseum im taiwanesischen Taipeh (2004, Endrunde) oder das Learning Center der École Polytechnique Fédérale de Lausanne teilgenommen. Zwei seiner Projekte jüngeren Datums, die Universität Luzern und ein Gebäude am Schweizer Gornergrat, haben 2003 bei Wettbewerben den ersten Platz belegt. Vor Kurzem wurde das hier vorgestellte Atelier Bardill in schweizerischen Scharans fertiggestellt (2006–07).

VALERIO OLGIATI, né à Chur in 1958, a étudié l'architecture à l'ETH de Zurich. En 1986, il ouvre son agence à Zurich. De 1993 à 1995 il collabore avec Frank Escher à Los Angeles, spécialiste de l'œuvre de l'architecte John Lautner (1911–94). En 1994, Olgiati est professeur invité à la Hochschule für Technik à Stuttgart et, depuis 1998, il enseigne à l'ETH et comme conférencier invité à l'Architectural Association de Londres. Depuis 2001, il est professeur titulaire à l'Accademia di Architettura de l'Universita della Svizzera Italiana à Mendrisio. Il a réalisé un certain nombre de résidences privées et participé à des concours comme celui du National Palace Museum (Taiwan, 2004, finaliste) et le centre d'apprentissage de l'EPFL à Lausanne. Deux de ses projets récents, le Pic du Gornergrat et l'université de Lucerne – tous deux en Suisse – ont été remportés en 2003 à l'issue d'un concours. Il a récemment achevé l'atelier Bardill (Scharans, Suisse, 2006–07, publié ici).

ATELIER BARDILL

Scharans, Switzerland, 2006–07

Floor area: 70 m² (atelier); 65 m² (garage, storage, technical). Client: Linard Bardill. Cost: not disclosed.
Collaborators: Project Managers: Nathan Ghiringhelli, Nikolai Müller, Mario Beeli. Construction Supervisor: Linard Bardill.
Structural Engineer: Patrick Gartmann, Conzett, Bronzini, Gartmann AG, Chur

Scharans is an old town with a population of about 800 people located in the Graubünden region of Switzerland. This private atelier, for the musician and poet Linard Bardill, replaces an old barn in the protected center of the town. Building permission was granted by local authorities on the condition that the new structure would be the same color as the barn. Indeed, Olgiati's design also assumes the shape of the former barn, with its rather blank austerity. Rather than old wood, however, it is made of red poured-in-place concrete, steel, and copper. The only variations in the surface of the concrete are due to the wood of the casting forms and to a repeated, irregular low-relief pinwheel pattern that is typical of local decorative designs. A courtyard with a large oval opening to the sky allows the architecture to attain "greatness and clearness in contrast to the arbitrary geometry of its external appearance and to the small-scale environment of the village." Despite its austerity and simplicity, this building is both surprising and challenging in the sense that it is located in the heart of an old Swiss village.

Scharans ist eine alte Gemeinde mit rund 800 Einwohnern im Schweizer Kanton Graubünden. Im geschützten Dorfkern, am früheren Standort eines alten Stalls, baute Olgiati ein Atelier für den Dichter und Musiker Linard Bardill. Die Baugenehmigung war von der Gemeindeverwaltung unter der Bedingung erteilt worden, dass die neue Konstruktion die gleiche Farbe wie die alte haben müsse. Zwar übernahm Olgiati in seinem karg-nüchternen Entwurf die Form des Stalls, anstelle von altem Holz verwendete er jedoch rot gefärbten Ortbeton, Stahl und Kupfer. Dass die Oberflächenstruktur des Betons nicht durchgängig glatt ist, liegt zum einen an den Spuren, die die Holzschalungen hinterlassen haben, zum anderen an den unregelmäßig verteilten Flachrelief-Rosetten, deren Muster sich in der Region häufig als Dekor findet. Durch einen Innenhof mit einer ovalen Öffnung zum Himmel erhält die Architektur „eine Größe und Klarheit, die einen Gegensatz zu der willkürlichen Geometrie ihrer äußeren Erscheinung und der überschaubaren dörflichen Umgebung bildet." Trotz seiner kargen Schlichtheit und der Tatsache, dass er sich im Herzen eines alten Schweizer Dorfes befindet, ist Olgiatis Bau so ungewöhnlich wie herausfordernd.

Scharans est un ancien village de 800 habitants environ situé dans le canton des Grisons (Graubünden). L'atelier conçu pour le musicien et poète Linard Bardill occupe l'emplacement d'une vieille grange dans le centre classé du village. Le permis de construire a été accordé à condition que la nouvelle structure conserve la couleur de l'ancienne. Le projet d'Olgiati reprend la forme de la grange dans sa sévère austérité, mais au lieu du bois, il a utilisé le béton coulé en place teinté rouge, acier et cuivre. Les seuls effets de surface du béton sont dus au bois des coffrages et à un motif répétitif irrégulier d'étoile en bas-relief, typique de la région. Une cour qui ouvre sur le ciel par une grande ouverture ovale permet à l'architecture d'atteindre « une grandeur et une clarté qui contraste avec la géométrie arbitraire de son aspect extérieur et à l'environnement à petite échelle du village ». Malgré cette austérité et cette simplicité, ce petit bâtiment est à la fois surprenant et provocant par sa position au cœur même d'un vieux village suisse.

The Atelier Bardill stands out against its old-village setting and yet it is very much inspired by local designs, even if the concrete employed is less than traditional. Opposite, a plan and elevation of the building.

Das Atelier Bardill sticht zwar aus der Kulisse des alten Dorfes heraus, dennoch orientiert es sich – wenngleich der verwendete Beton alles andere als traditionell ist – deutlich an lokalen Bautraditionen. Rechts: Grundriss und Aufriss des Gebäudes.

L'atelier Bardill se détache par rapport à son cadre de village ancien, tout en étant très inspiré par les formes vernaculaires locales, même si le béton est un matériau moins que traditionnel. À droite, plan et coupe du projet.

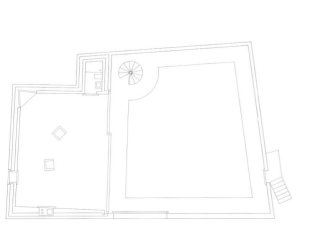

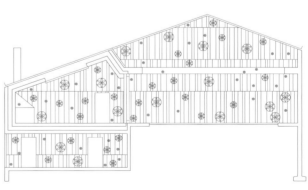

STUDIO PEI-ZHU

Studio Pei-Zhu
B-413 Tianhai Business Center
No.107 N Dongsi Street
Beijing 100007
China

Tel: +86 10 6401 6657
Fax: +86 10 6403 8967
E-mail: office@studiozp.com

PEI-ZHU was born in Beijing in 1962. He received his M.Arch degree from Tsinghua University, China, and his Master of Architecture and Urban Design degree from the UC Berkeley. He has worked with the large American firm RTKL Associates, and as an Associate Professor at Tsinghua University. He is the principal architect and founder of Studio Pei-Zhu and, prior to opening this office in 2005 in Beijing, he was a founding partner and design principal of URBANUS (2001–04). Tong Wu was born in Beijing in 1968. She attended Tsinghua University, and holds a Master's degree in Design. Prior to becoming a principal and co-founder of Studio Pei-Zhu in 2005, she was the art director of the publication *Art and Design*. Studio Pei-Zhu's portfolio includes many significant projects, such as The Guggenheim Art Pavilion at Abu Dhabi, the Guggenheim Museum in Beijing, the Yue Minjun Art Museum, Cai Guoqiang's Beijing Studio, Blur Hotel, and Digital Beijing, a project for the Beijing Olympics in 2008 (published here). Major accolades include *Architectural Record*'s Design Vanguard in 2007, and the 2006 China Award.

PEI-ZHU, geboren 1962 in Peking, erwarb sein Architekturdiplom an der Universität Tsinghua in China und anschließend den Master of Architecture and Urban Design an der University of California in Berkeley. Er arbeitete für die weltweit tätige amerikanische Architekturfirma RTKL Associates und als außerordentlicher Professor an der Universität Tsinghua. Heute ist er leitender Architekt des von ihm 2005 in Peking gegründeten Studio Pei-Zhu, zuvor war er Gründungspartner und Leiter des Designbereichs von URBANUS (2001–04). Tong Wu, geboren 1968 in Peking, besuchte die Universität Tsinghua und besitzt einen Masterabschluss in Design. Bevor sie 2005 das Studio Pei-Zhu mitgründete, das sie heute auch leitet, war sie als Art Director für die Publikation *Art and Design* tätig. Das Portfolio von Studio Pei-Zhu umfasst zahlreiche bedeutende Projekte wie etwa den Guggenheim Art Pavillon in Abu Dhabi, das Guggenheim Museum in Peking, ein dem Künstler Yue Minjun gewidmetes Museum in Qing Cheng Shan (Sichuan), das Pekinger Studio von Cai Guo-Qiang, das Blur Hotel in Peking und das hier vorgestellte Digital Beijing für die Olympischen Spiele 2008 in Peking. Zu ihren wichtigen Auszeichnungen gehören die Aufnahme in den Design Vanguard 2007 von *Architectural Record* und der China Award 2006.

PEI-ZHU, né à Pékin en 1962, est M. Arch. de l'université de Tsinghua en Chine, M. Arch. et titulaire d'un diplôme de Urban Design de UC Berkeley. Il a travaillé dans la grande agence américaine RTKL Associates, et comme professeur associé à l'université de Tsinghua. Il a fondé en 2005 le Studio Pei-Zhu qu'il dirige à Pékin, mais avait précédemment créé l'agence URBANUS (2001–04). Tong Wu, née à Pékin en 1968, a étudié à l'université de Tsinghua et a obtenu un mastère en design. Avant de devenir co-fondatrice et directrice du studio Pei-Zhu en 2005, elle a été directrice artistique de la publication *Art and Design*. Parmi les réalisations de l'agence figurent de nombreux projets significatifs comme le Guggenheim Art Pavilion à Abu Dhabi, le Guggenheim Museum à Pékin, le musée d'Art Yue Minjun, le studio de Cai Guoqiang à Pékin, le Blur Hotel, et Digital Beijing, projet pour les jeux Olympiques 2008, publié ici. Ils ont reçu diverses distinctions dont le Design Vanguard d'*Architectural Record* en 2007 et le China Award 2006.

DIGITAL BEIJING

Control Center for the 2008 Olympics, Beijing, China, 2005–08

*Floor area: 76 000 m². Client: People's Government of Beijing Municipality. Cost: not disclosed.
Architect: Studio Pei-Zhu, URBANUS. Project Designers: Pei-Zhu, Tong Wu, Hui Wang.
Project Team: Liu Wentian, Li Chuen, Lin Lin, Tian Qi*

The massive, apparently windowless volume of the Digital Beijing building, has openings that recall the lines of computer chips.

Die Zwischenräume des wuchtigen, scheinbar fensterlosen Gebäudekörpers des Rechenzentrums erinnern an die Streifen auf Computerchips.

Le volume massif, clos de l'immeuble Digital Beijing présente en fait des ouvertures qui rappellent des circuits de composants électroniques.

Located opposite Herzog & de Meuron's Olympic Stadium on the Olympic Green, Digital Beijing was designed by Pei-Zhu and his former firm URBANUS as the control and data center for the 2008 Olympic Games. Subsequently, the building is due to be used as a "virtual museum and exhibition center for digital products." The architect describes this large and imposing reinforced-concrete and steel-frame building as being an exploration of the impact of electronics on architecture. More specifically, he writes, "The concept for Digital Beijing was developed through reconsideration and reflection on the role of contemporary architecture in the information era. Resembling that omnipresent symbol, the bar code, the building emerges from a serene water surface. The façade itself is detailed to resemble an integrated circuit board. The abstracted mass of the building, reflecting the simple repetition of 0 and 1 in its alternation between void and solid, recreates on a monumental scale the microscopic underpinnings of life in the digital age to form a potent symbol of the Digital Olympics and the Digital Era. In the future, it is expected that the building will be constantly under renovation as it evolves to keep pace with technology."

Das von Pei-Zhu und seiner früheren Firma URBANUS konzipierte Digital-Beijing-Gebäude auf dem Olympiagelände gegenüber dem Stadion von Herzog & de Meuron beherbergt das Rechen- und Kontrollzentrum für die Olympischen Spiele 2008. Danach soll es als „virtuelles Museum und Ausstellungszentrum für digitale Erzeugnisse" dienen. Der Architekt beschreibt den großen, imposanten Stahlbetonbau mit Stahltragwerk als einen Entwurf, der den Einfluss der elektronischen Welt auf die Architektur untersucht. Detaillierter heißt es: „Das Konzept für Digital Beijing ist entstanden aus umfassenden Überlegungen zur Rolle der zeitgenössischen Architektur im Informationszeitalter. Von der Schmalseite betrachtet ähnelt das Gebäude, das sich über einer ruhigen Wasserfläche erhebt, dem omnipräsenten Symbol des Strichkodes. Die Fassadenelemente der Längsseite erzeugen den Eindruck, als sei eine riesige Platine integriert. Mit dem Wechsel von Gebäudeabschnitten und freien Zwischenräumen verweist der abstrakte Baukörper auf die simple Wiederholung von 0 und 1. So wird er zu einem überdimensionalen Abbild der mikroskopischen Abläufe, die das Leben im digitalen Zeitalter unterfüttern, und damit zu einem überzeugenden Symbol für die digitale Olympiade und die digitale Ära. Für die Zukunft ist zu erwarten, dass das Gebäude parallel zur technologischen Fortentwicklung permanent umgestaltet wird."

Face au stade olympique d'Herzog & de Meuron et sur la pelouse olympique, Digital Beijing a été conçu par Pei-Zhu et son ancienne agence URBANUS. C'est le centre informatique de contrôle des Jeux de 2008. Par la suite, le bâtiment sera aménagé en « musée virtuel et centre d'expositions pour produits numériques ». L'architecte présente ce vaste et imposant ensemble en béton armé à ossature d'acier comme une exploration de l'impact de l'électronique sur l'architecture. Plus spécifiquement, il précise : « Le concept de Digital Beijing a été mis au point à l'issue de recherches et de réflexions sur le rôle de l'architecture contemporaine à l'ère de l'information. Évoquant le symbole omniprésent du code-barres, l'immeuble émerge d'un plan d'eau serein. Sa façade ressemble à un circuit imprimé et sa masse abstraite, reflétant la répétition binaire de 0 et 1 dans son alternance de pleins et de vides, recrée à une échelle monumentale l'univers microscopique de la vie à l'ère numérique, pour offrir un puissant symbole des jeux Olympiques et de cette époque placée sous le signe de l'informatique. Dans l'avenir, il est prévu que l'immeuble soit en rénovation permanente pour évoluer en phase avec la technologie. »

Austere like much interesting recent Chinese architecture, the building has a basically rectilinear plan with unexpected angled linear openings on the main façades.

Ähnlich karg wie ein Großteil der interessanteren chinesischen Architektur jüngeren Datums, ist das Gebäude von geraden Linien bestimmt. Überraschend sind die Einschnitte in den Hauptfassaden.

Austère, à l'instar de l'architecture contemporaine chinoise la plus intéressante, l'immeuble présente un plan rectangulaire, animé par les ouvertures en ligne brisée de ses façades principales.

Interior spaces with some colored elements continue the impression of austerity given by the main exterior façades.

In den Innenräumen, die einige farbige Elemente beinhalten, führen den von den Außenfassaden vermittelten Eindruck der Kargheit fort.

Les volumes intérieurs, ponctués de quelques éléments colorés, déclinent l'impression d'austérité donnée par les façades.

RENZO PIANO

Renzo Piano Building Workshop
34 rue des Archives / 75004 Paris / France
Tel: +33 1 42 78 00 82 / Fax: +33 1 42 78 01 98
Via Rubens 29 / 16158 Genoa / Italy
Tel: +39 010 61 711 / Fax: +39 010 61 71 350

E-mail: info@rpbw.com
Web: www.rpbw.com

RENZO PIANO was born in 1937 in Genoa, Italy. He studied at the University of Florence and at the Polytechnic Institute of Milan (1964). He formed his own practice (Studio Piano) in 1965, then associated with Richard Rogers (Piano & Rogers, 1971–78). Piano completed the Centre Pompidou in Paris in 1977. From 1978 to 1980, he worked with Peter Rice (Piano & Rice Associates). He created the Renzo Piano Building Workshop in 1981 in Genoa and Paris. Piano received the RIBA Gold Medal in 1989. His built work includes: the Menil Collection Museum (Houston, Texas, 1981–86); the 1988–90 extension for the IRCAM (Paris, France); the Kansai International Airport Terminal (Osaka, Japan, 1988–94); the Beyeler Foundation (Riehen, Basel, Switzerland, 1991–97); the Jean-Marie Tjibaou Cultural Center (New Caledonia, 1991–98); the reconstruction of a section of Potsdamer Platz (Berlin, Germany, 1992–2000); the Maison Hermès (Tokyo, Japan, 1998–2001); the Rome Auditorium (Rome, Italy, 1994–2002); the conversion of the Lingotto Factory Complex (Turin, Italy, 1983–2003); the Padre Pio Pilgrimage Church (San Giovanni Rotondo, Foggia, Italy, 1991–2004); the renovation and expansion of the Morgan Library (New York, New York, 2000–06); the New York Times Building (New York, 2005–07, published here); and the renovation and enlargement of the Los Angeles County Museum of Art (California, 2006–08). Current work includes the Woodruff Arts Center Expansion (Atlanta, Georgia); the London Bridge Tower (London, UK); and the California Academy of Sciences (San Francisco, California).

RENZO PIANO wurde 1937 in Genua geboren. Nach seinem 1964 abgeschlossenen Studium an der Università degli Studi di Firenze und am Politecnico di Milano eröffnete er 1965 das Studio Piano. Von 1971 bis 1978 firmierte er als Piano & Rogers mit Richard Rogers, mit dem er das 1977 eröffnete Centre Pompidou entwarf. Von 1978 bis 1980 arbeitete er mit Peter Rice zusammen (Piano & Rice Associates). 1981 rief er den Renzo Piano Building Workshop ins Leben, der seinen Sitz in Genua und Paris nahm. 1989 wurde Piano mit der Goldmedaille des Royal Institute of British Architects ausgezeichnet. Zu seinen realisierten Projekten gehören das Museum der Menil Collection in Houston, Texas (1981–86), die Erweiterung des Pariser Institut de Recherche et Coordination Acoustique/Musique (IRCAM) in Paris (1988–90), der Terminal des Internationalen Flughafens Kansai in Osaka (1988–94), das Museum der Fondation Beyeler in Riehen bei Basel (1991–97), das Centre Culturel Tjibaou auf Neukaledonien (1991–98), der Masterplan des Daimler-Quartiers und das dazugehörige debis-Haus am Potsdamer Platz in Berlin (1992–2000), die Maison Hermès in Tokio (1998–2001), das Auditorium Parco della Musica in Rom (1994–2001), der Umbau der Lingotto-Fabrik in Turin (1983–2003), die Chiesa di Padre Pio in San Giovanni Rotondo in der italienischen Provinz Foggia (1991–2004), die Renovierung und Erweiterung der Morgan Library in New York (2000–06), das New York Times Building in New York (2005–07, hier vorgestellt) und die Renovierung und Erweiterung des Los Angeles County Museum of Art in Los Angeles (2006–08). Derzeit in Arbeit sind die Erweiterung des Woodruff Arts Center in Atlanta, Georgia, der London Bridge Tower und die California Academy of Sciences in San Francisco.

RENZO PIANO est né en 1937 à Gêne, Italie, et a étudié à l'université de Florence et au Politecnico de Milan (1964). Il crée son agence, Studio Piano, en 1965, puis s'associe à Richard Rogers (Piano & Rogers, 1971–78). Ils achèvent le Centre Pompidou à Paris en 1977. De 1978 à 1980, il collabore avec Peter Rice (Piano & Rice Associates). Il fonde le Renzo Piano Building Workshop en 1981 à Gênes et Paris. Il a reçu la médaille d'or du RIBA en 1989 et le Pritzker Prize en 1998. Parmi ses réalisations : le musée de la Menil Collection (Houston, Texas, 1981–86) ; l'extension de l'IRCAM, Paris (1988–90) ; le terminal de l'aéroport international de l'aéroport du Kansai (Osaka, Japon, 1988–94) ; le musée de la fondation Beyeler (Riehen, Bâle, Suisse, 1991–97) ; le centre culturel Jean-Marie Tjibaou (Nouvelle-Calédonie, 1991–98) ; la reconstruction d'une partie de Potsdamer Platz (Berlin, 1992–2000) ; la Maison Hermès, Tokyo (1998–2001) ; l'auditorium de Rome (1994–2002) ; la conversion de l'usine du Lingotto (Turin, Italie, 1983–2003) ; l'église de pèlerinage Padre Pio (San Giovanni Rotondo, Foggia, Italie, 1991–2004) ; la rénovation et l'agrandissement de la Morgan Library (New York, 2000–06) ; le New York Times Building (New York, 2005–07, publiée ici) et la rénovation et l'agrandissement du Los Angeles County Museum of Art (Californie, 2006–08). Parmi ses projets actuels : l'extension du Woodruff Arts Center (Atlanta, Georgie) ; la London Bridge Tower (Londres) et la California Academy of Sciences (San Francisco, Californie).

THE NEW YORK TIMES BUILDING

New York, New York, USA, 2005–07

*Site area: 7432 m². Floor area: 143 048 m². Client: The New York Times Company/Forest City Ratner Company.
Cost: not disclosed. Architects: Renzo Piano Building Workshop Architects
in collaboration with FXFowle Architects, P.C. (New York)*

Renzo Piano declares, "The New York Times Building, at 8th Avenue and Times Square, has a very strong urban presence. The building is designed to be part of the street where it is placed. On the ground floor is a garden and an auditorium. In a way this approach may be more European than American." Chosen over Norman Foster, Frank Gehry, and Cesar Pelli, Piano's design for the 52-story building is intended to be as open and transparent as possible, symbolizing the relationship of the newspaper to the city. The façades employ a combination of clear-glass curtain walls and a scrim of white ceramic tubes hanging 61 centimeters outside the glass. Acting as a sunscreen, the tubes obviate the need for tinted or fritted glass. Underway in 2000, and reconfirmed after the attacks on the World Trade Center, the New York Times Building is seen as a sign of confidence and commitment to the city, and part of the general redevelopment of the Times Square area. The newspaper occupies the lower half of the structure while a real-estate development firm, Forest City Ratner, is commercializing the rest of the space. The six-story base of the tower includes an atrium for shops and restaurants and an auditorium for lectures. A roof garden is protected by extensions of the glass curtain wall above the actual building height. Because of its considerable height, central location, and vocation, the New York Times Building is one of the most prestigious commissions to be given to a foreign architect in recent years in Manhattan. Given, too, the post-September 11 mood, the inauguration of the Tower in 2007 is to be seen in some ways as a new beginning for the city.

Renzo Piano erklärt zu seinem Entwurf: „Das an der 8th Avenue und am Times Square gelegene New York Times Building zeichnet sich durch einen ausgesprochen urbanen Charakter aus. Das Gebäude ist so konzipiert, dass es sich optimal in seine direkte Umgebung einfügt. Im Erdgeschoss befinden sich ein Atrium und ein Auditorium. In gewisser Weise ist dieser Ansatz eher europäisch als amerikanisch." Der Entwurf für das 52-geschossige Bauwerk, mit dem Piano sich im Wettbewerb gegen Norman Foster, Frank Gehry und Cesar Pelli durchsetzte, sollte so offen und transparent wie möglich sein und die Beziehung der *New York Times* zu ihrer Stadt symbolisieren. Die Fassadengestaltung wird von einer Kombination aus durchsichtigen Glasvorhangfassaden sowie Blenden aus weißen Keramikröhren bestimmt, die im Abstand von 61 cm vor dem Glas angebracht sind. Diese Röhren fungieren als Sonnenschutz, so dass auf getöntes Glas oder Sinterglas verzichtet werden konnte. Die Anschläge auf das World Trade Center konnten den seit 2000 laufenden Planungen für das New York Times Building keinen Abbruch tun, im Gegenteil: Pianos Bau, Teil der umfassenden Neugestaltung der Gegend um den Times Square, galt und gilt als ein Zeichen der Zuversicht und als Bekenntnis zur Stadt New York. Die Zeitung selbst belegt die untere Hälfte des Gebäudes, die übrige Fläche wird von der Immobiliengesellschaft Forest City Ratner verwaltet. Die sechsgeschossige Basis des Hochhauses enthält einen Lichthof mit Geschäften und Restaurants sowie einen Veranstaltungssaal. Die Ausläufer der gläsernen Vorhangfassade, die über die eigentliche Gebäudehöhe hinausragen, schützen einen Dachgarten. Angesichts seiner stattlichen Höhe, des zentralen Standorts und seiner Bestimmung ist der Auftrag zum Entwurf des New York Times Building einer der prestigeträchtigsten, die in den vergangenen Jahren in Manhattan an einen ausländischen Architekten vergeben wurden. Bedenkt man außerdem die Stimmungslage nach dem 11. September 2001, so ist das New York Times Building in mehrerlei Hinsicht als Neuanfang für die ganze Stadt zu verstehen.

Commentant cette tour, Renzo Piano a déclaré : « Le New York Times Building, situé à l'angle de 8th Avenue et de Times Square, possède une très forte présence urbaine. Il a été conçu pour faire réellement partie de la rue sur laquelle il s'élève. Au rez-de-chaussée se trouvent un jardin et un auditorium. À sa manière, cette approche est peut-être plus européenne qu'américaine. » Choisi devant Norman Foster, Frank Gehry et Cesar Pelli, le projet de Piano pour cette tour de 52 niveaux se voulait aussi ouvert et transparent que possible, afin de symboliser la relation entre le journal et sa ville. Les façades utilisent une combinaison de murs-rideaux en verre clair et d'une trame de tubes de céramique suspendue à 61 cm à l'extérieur du mur de verre. Servant d'écran solaire, ces tubes éliminent la nécessité de verre teinté ou fritté. Immeuble dont le projet fut lancé en 2000 et confirmé après les événements du 11 septembre 2001, il est considéré comme un signe de confiance et d'engagement de la ville et fait partie du programme de rénovation de la zone de Times Square. Le quotidien occupe la moitié inférieure du bâtiment, et un groupe de promotion, Forest City Ratner, commercialise le reste. Les six premiers niveaux comprennent un atrium entouré de boutiques et de restaurants et un auditorium. Le jardin en toiture est protégé par des extensions du mur-rideau de verre qui dépassent la hauteur de la structure proprement dite. Du fait de sa hauteur considérable, de sa situation centrale et de sa vocation, le New York Times Building est l'une des plus prestigieuses commandes jamais accordées récemment à un architecte étranger à Manhattan. L'inauguration de cette tour en 2007 participe d'une nouvelle atmosphère, post-11 septembre, qui marque un nouveau départ pour la ville.

The New York Times Building stands out from its Times Square setting because of its size, but also because of its façade treatments.

Nicht nur aufgrund seiner Größe sticht das New York Times Building aus den Gebäuden am Times Square heraus, sondern auch aufgrund seiner Fassadengestaltung.

Le New York Times Building se distingue par rapport au cadre architectural de Times Square par sa taille, mais aussi par le traitement de ses façades.

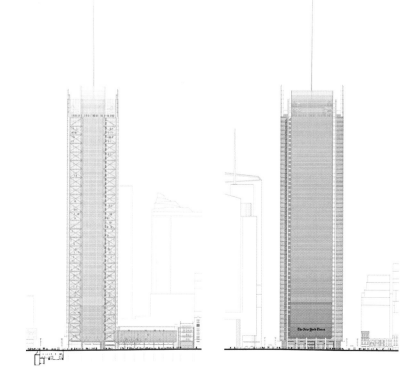

An interior garden recalls that wood is the source of the newsprint used by the New York Times. An openness and warmth typical of Piano can be seen in the images on this page.

Die Bäume im Innenhof erinnern daran, woher das für die Herstellung der New York Times benötigte Papier kommt. Die vorliegenden Abbildungen geben die für Piano typische Offenheit und Wärme wieder.

Un jardin intérieur rappelle que le bois est à la base de la fabrication du journal. Un sentiment d'ouverture et de chaleur, typiques des réalisations de Renzo Piano, transparaît dans ces images.

Open floors for the editorial team underline the sense of common purpose that animates the newspaper. Below, the central garden in different lights.

Offene Etagenflächen in den Redaktionen unterstreichen den Eindruck der Arbeit im öffentlichen Interesse, der das Blatt sich verschrieben fühlt. Unten der zentral angelegte Garten zu unterschiedlichen Tageszeiten.

Les plateaux ouverts des équipes éditoriales correspondent à l'esprit de travail en commun qui anime le quotidien. Ci-dessous : le jardin central vu sous différents éclairages.

An open, bright employee dining area with a stairway leading to an upper level.

Ein heller, offener Speiseraum für die Angestellten mit Treppenaufgang zu einer zweiten Ebene.

Un restaurant d'entreprise, ouvert et lumineux, et l'escalier qui conduit au niveau supérieur.

A corner of the dining area seen from the top of the stairway. Below, a meeting room and seating area.

Eine Ecke des Speisesaals, von der Treppe aus gesehen. Unten ein Konferenzraum und ein Sitzbereich.

Un angle du restaurant vu du sommet de l'escalier. Ci-dessous une salle de réunion et une salle d'attente.

PTW ARCHITECTS

PTW Architects
Level 17, 9 Castlereagh Street
Sydney, NSW 2000
Australia

Tel: +61 2 9232 5877
Fax: +61 2 9221 4139
E-mail: info@ptw.com.au
Web: www.ptw.com.au

PTW ARCHITECTS has offices in Shanghai, Beijing, Hangzhou, Hanoi, Ho Chi Minh City, and Auckland, and works extensively in the Middle East. John Blimon, a principal director of PTW Architects, joined the firm in 1982. He has been particularly active in developing the work of the firm in China, Japan, and Vietnam. Blimon has served as President of the Royal Australian Institute of Architects (NSW) Chapter and as Vice President of Cranbrook School. Aside from the Watercube (Beijing, China, 2003–08, published here), Blimon has also worked recently on the Huangpu Sports and Business Center (Shanghai, China (2005–06); the main Olympic Village in Beijing (China, 2004–07); the FPT Headquarters in Hanoi (Vietnam, 2005–07); and the Kokura Tower project (Kyushu, Japan, 2005–08).

Das australische Architekturbüro **PTW ARCHITECTS** besitzt Niederlassungen in Shanghai, Peking, Hangzhou, Hanoi, Ho-Chi-Minh-Stadt und Auckland und führt auch im Nahen Osten zahlreiche Projekte durch. John Blimon, einer der Direktoren von PTW, gehört der Firma seit 1982 an. Seine Hauptbetätigungsfelder liegen in China, Japan und Vietnam. Blimon war Präsident des Royal Australian Institute of Architects (NSW) und Vizepräsident der Cranbrook School. Neben dem hier vorgestellten Watercube in Peking (2003–08) war Blimon in jüngster Zeit auch für das dortige Olympische Hauptdorf zuständig (2004–07) sowie für das Sport- und Businesszentrum Huangpu in Shanghai (2005–06), die FPT-Zentrale in Hanoi (2005–07) und das Kokura-Turm-Projekt im japanischen Kyushu (2005–08).

PTW ARCHITECTS possède des bureaux à Shanghaï, Pékin, Hangzhou, Hanoï, Ho Chi Minh-Ville et Auckland, et travaille beaucoup au Moyen-Orient. John Blimon, associé et directeur de PTW, a rejoint l'agence en 1982. Il a particulièrement développé sa présence en Chine, au Japon et au Vietnam. Blimon a été président de la Royal Australian Institute of Architects (NSW) et vice-président de la Cranbrook School. En dehors du Watercube (Pékin, 2003–08, publié ici), il est également intervenu sur le centre d'affaires et de sports de Huangpu (Shanghaï, Chine, 2005–06) ; le Village olympique principal à Pékin (2004–07) ; le siège de FPT à Hanoï (Vietnam, 2005–07) et le projet de la tour Kokura à Kyushu (Japon, 2005–08).

THE WATERCUBE

National Swimming Center, Beijing, China, 2003–08

Floor area: 80 000 m². Total seats: 17 000. Client: People's Government of Beijing Municipality, Beijing State Asset Management. Cost: $140 million. Team: John Bilmon, Tristram Carfre, Richard Zhou. Partner: China State Construction Engineering Corporation

 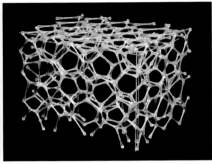 

The most visible part of the Water-cube structure is based on the geometry and appearance of soap bubbles.

Der augenscheinlichste Teil der Watercube-Architektur basiert auf der geometrischen Anordnung und dem Erscheinungsbild von Seifenblasen.

La partie la plus visible de la structure du Watercube repose sur une géométrie précise qui crée cet aspect de bulles de savon.

In July 2003, the consortium of PTW, Ove Arup Pty Ltd., the CSCEC (China State Construction and Engineering Corporation), and the CSCEC Shenzhen Design Institute (CSCEC+DESIGN) won the international design competition for the National Swimming Center for the 2008 Beijing Olympics, one of 18 sports facilities built for the Games. Set near the Olympic Stadium (page 224), the rectilinear structure, which is 31 meters high with a further 11 meters below grade, is intended to harmonize with the round forms of the Herzog & de Meuron structure. Andrew Frost, a director of PTW, explains, "Our 'Watercube' concept is a simple and concise square form that ultimately uses the water bubble theory to create the structure and building cladding, and which makes the design so unique. It appears random and playful like a natural system, yet is mathematically very rigorous and repetitious. The transparency of water, with the mystery of the bubble system, engages those both inside and outside the structure to consider their own experiences with water." The building is essentially a steel space frame with a skin made of pillows made of ETFE (Ethylene Tetrafluoroethylene), designed to react specifically to lighting and projection. The "random, organic appearance" of the cladding based on the natural formation of soap bubbles called on research Professors Denis Weaire and Robert Phelan (Weaire-Phelan Structure). The building was formally opened on January 28, 2008.

Im Juli 2003 gewann das Konsortium aus PTW, Ove Arup Pty Ltd., CSCEC (China State Construction and Engineering Corporation) und CSCEC Shenzhen Design Institute (CSCEC+DESIGN) den internationalen Wettbewerb zum Entwurf des Nationalen Schwimmzentrums für die Olympischen Spiele 2008 in Peking, eine von 18 für die Spiele geplanten Sportstätten. Der unweit des Olympiastadions (Seite 224) errichtete Kubus, der 31 m hoch aufragt und sich zusätzlich 11 m tief in den Boden erstreckt, sollte mit der runden Form von Herzog & de Meurons Bauwerk harmonieren. Andrew Frost, einer der Leiter von PTW, erläutert: „Das Konzept für unseren ‚Watercube' sah eine einfache, prägnante Rechteckform vor, bei der die Wasserblasentheorie sowohl die Grundstruktur als auch die Verkleidung des Gebäudes bestimmen sollte, die den Entwurf so ungewöhnlich macht. Obwohl es zufällig und spielerisch wie ein natürliches System wirkt, folgt das Konzept einem mathematisch strengen Wiederholungsmuster. Die Transparenz des Wassers in Verbindung mit dem geheimnisvollen Blasensystem hält die Besucher innerhalb und außerhalb des Gebäudes dazu an, über ihr eigenes Verhältnis zum Wasser nachzudenken." Die Konstruktion besteht im Wesentlichen aus einem Stahlrahmen mit einer Hülle aus ETFE-Kissen (Ethylen-Tetrafluorethylen), die speziell im Hinblick auf die Beleuchtung und die Projektionen entwickelt wurden. Die „zufällige und organische" Erscheinung der Gebäudeverkleidung basiert auf den Forschungsarbeiten von Denis Weaire und Robert Phelan zur natürlichen Anordnung von Seifenblasen (Weaire-Phelan-Struktur). Am 28. Januar 2008 wurde das Gebäude offiziell eröffnet.

C'est en juillet 2003 que le consortium formé par PTW, Ove Arup Pty Ltd., la CSCEC (China State Construction and Engineering Corporation) et le CSCEC Shenzhen Design Institute (CSCEC+DESIGN) a remporté le concours international pour le Centre national de natation des jeux Olympiques 2008 à Pékin, l'une des 18 installations sportives édifiées pour les Jeux. Voisine du stade olympique (page 224), cette construction rectiligne de 31 m au-dessus du sol et 11 m en sous-sol, a cherché à s'harmoniser avec les formes arrondies du stade d'Herzog & de Meuron. Andrew Frost, directeur du projet pour PTW, explique : « Le concept de notre »Watercube« (cube d'eau) est simple. Il s'agit d'une forme carrée compacte, mais à laquelle l'application de la théorie de la bulle d'eau dans sa structure et l'habillage de ses façades donne un caractère exceptionnel. Ce stade nautique est d'aspect aléatoire et ludique, à la manière d'un système naturel, alors qu'il est mathématiquement rigoureux et basé sur un principe de répétition. La transparence de l'eau et les mystères du système de la formation des bulles font participer les passants et les spectateurs à une expérience de l'eau. » Le bâtiment est à la base une structure tridimensionnelle en acier dont la peau est composée de « coussins » en ETFE (tétrafluoroéthylène d'éthylène), conçus pour réagir à des éclairages et des projections. L'aspect « aléatoire et organique » de cet habillage repose sur la formation naturelle des bulles de savon décrite dans les recherches des professeurs Denis Weaire et Robert Phelan (Weaire-Phelan Structure). Le bâtiment a été inauguré le 28 janvier 2008.

The thin white base of the building is dominated by the blue bubble design that forms the essential volume of the architecture.

Die schmale, weiße Basis des Water-cube wird von dem Blasendesign überragt, das den größten Teil des Gebäudevolumens ausmacht.

Le mince socle blanc du bâtiment est dominé par les parois en bulles bleues qui constituent l'essentiel du volume.

The bubble forms of the exterior also make an appearance above the main swimming hall, and in other spaces where natural light is admitted.

Die Blasenformen, die die Außenseite bestimmen, tauchen ebenfalls über der Schwimmhalle und an anderen Stellen auf, an denen natürliches Licht einfallen soll.

Les bulles de l'extérieur se retrouvent également au-dessus du bassin principal et dans d'autres espaces naturellement éclairés.

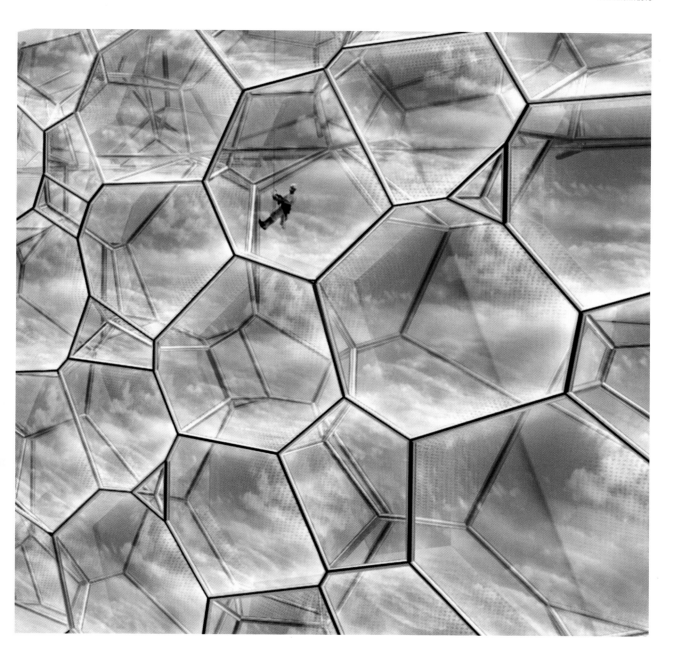

The basic, irregular forms of the building's skin are light and translucid enough to glow from within at night.

Die Gebäudehülle mit ihrem unregelmäßigen Grundmuster ist so dünn und lichtdurchlässig gestaltet, dass sie nachts von innen heraus leuchtet.

Les formes simples et irrégulières de la peau du bâtiment sont légères et translucides pour être éclairées de l'intérieur pendant la nuit.

At night the bubbles give off a blue
glow that makes the building readily
identifiable from a distance.

Nachts schimmern die Blasen in
einem bläulichen Licht, durch das der
Bau schon von Weitem erkennbar ist.

La nuit, les bulles génèrent une lueur
bleuâtre qui rend la construction
identifiable de loin.

The transparency of the skin makes the architecture seem even lighter in the dark than it does in daylight. Right, with the National Stadium (see page 224) in the background.

Die Durchsichtigkeit der Hülle lässt die Architektur im Dunkeln noch luftiger als bei Tageslicht erscheinen. Rechts ist im Hintergrund das Nationalstadion (siehe S. 224) zu erkennen.

La transparence de la peau rend cette architecture d'apparence encore plus légère dans l'obscurité que le jour. À droite : vue du bâtiment et du Stade national (voir page 224) dans le fond à droite.

STUDIO ARNE QUINZE

Studio Arne Quinze BVBA
Walle 113a
8500 Kortrijk
Belgium

Tel: +32 56 240 590
Fax: +32 56 240 599
E-mail: info@studioarnequinze.tv
Web: www.studioarnequinze.tv / www.arnequinze.tv

Born in 1971, Arne Quinze is the founder and artistic director of the Belgian design firm **STUDIO ARNE QUINZE**. While most biographies of architects or designers tend to emphasize their university degrees, Quinze's CV on his Web site reads in part, "Lacking a sterling education and shaped by the street life of his youth, Arne Quinze hung out with a motorcycle gang." Perhaps because he is self-taught, Arne Quinze seems to see no reason why design, architecture, and art cannot coexist and be created by the same person. His Primary Pouf (1999) was a commercial and aesthetic success, selling 15 000 pieces annually. Studio Arne Quinze were the designers of casual seating for the Koolhaas/OMA Seattle Central Library (Washington, 2004); a lounge and breakfast room for the Fox Hotel in Copenhagen (Denmark, 2005); furniture for the Stylesuite shop by Wiel Arets (Maastricht, The Netherlands, 2005); the Lime Bar (Puerto Banúz, Spain, 2005); the renovation of a pharmacy in Oudenaarde (Belgium, 2006); and the installation *Uchronia: Message out of the Future* at the Burning Man Festival (Black Rock City, Black Rock Desert, Nevada, 2006, published here). They opened their large atelier and shop, Gallery 113, in Kortrijk (Belgium) in 2007. His 8000-square-meter wood installation Cityscape, in Brussels (Belgium), was due to stay in place for one year (2007–08).

Arne Quinze, geboren 1971, ist der Begründer und künstlerische Leiter der belgischen Designfirma **STUDIO ARNE QUINZE**. Während die meisten Architekten oder Designer in ihren Lebensläufen gerne ihre akademischen Abschlüsse hervorheben, hat Quinze, wie es in einem Abschnitt seines Lebenslaufs heißt, „keine vernünftige Ausbildung genossen, sondern wurde in seiner Jugend vom Leben auf der Straße geprägt und war Teil einer Motorradgang". Vielleicht ist das Autodidaktische auch der Grund, weshalb Arne Quinze es nicht einsieht, warum Design, Architektur und Kunst nicht einträchtig nebeneinander existieren und von ein und derselben Person geschaffen werden sollen. Sein Hocker Primary Pouf (1999) war ein kommerzieller und designkünstlerischer Erfolg und wird jährlich 15000-mal verkauft. Studio Arne Quinze haben bequeme Sitzmöbel für die Seattle Central Library (Washington, 2004) von Koolhaas/OMA sowie ein Frühstücks- und Loungezimmer für das Hotel Fox in Kopenhagen (Dänemark, 2005), das Mobiliar für den Stylesuite-Shop in Maastricht von Wiel Arets (Niederlande, 2005) und die Lime Bar im spanischen Puerto Banús (2005) entworfen, ferner eine Apotheke im belgischen Oudenaarde renoviert (2006) und die hier vorgestellte Installation „Uchronia: Message out of the Future" für das Burning Man Festival (Black Rock City, Black Rock Desert, Nevada, 2006) konzipiert. 2007 eröffneten sie im belgischen Kortrijk ein großes Atelier mit angeschlossenem Geschäft, die Gallery 113. In Brüssel war ein Jahr lang (2007–08) ihre 8000 m² große Holzinstallation „Cityscape" aufgestellt.

Né en 1971, Arne Quinze est le fondateur et directeur artistique de l'agence belge de design **STUDIO ARNE QUINZE**. Si la plupart des biographies d'architectes et de designers mettent en général l'accent sur les diplômes universitaires, le CV de Quinze publié sur son site Internet diffère : « Sans éducation brillante, formé par la rue pendant sa jeunesse, Arne Quinze a traîné avec une bande de motards… » Peut-être du fait de cette formation autodidacte, il ne voit pas pourquoi le design, l'architecture et l'art ne pourraient coexister et être créés par la même personne. Son Primary Pouf (1999) a été un succès esthétique et commercial puisqu'il en vend chaque année 15 000 pièces. Studio Arne Quinze a dessiné les sièges de la Bibliothèque centrale de Seattle de Koolhaas/OMA (Washington, 2004) ; un salon et salle de petit-déjeuner pour le Fox Hotel à Copenhague (Danemark, 2005) ; du mobilier pour la boutique Stylesuite de Wiel Arets (Maastricht, Pays-Bas, 2005) ; le Lime Bar (Puerto Banúz, Espagne, 2005) ; la rénovation d'une pharmacie à Oudenaarde (Belgique, 2006) et l'installation *Uchronia : Message out of the Future* pour le Burning Man Festival (Black Rock City, Black Rock Desert, Nevada, 2006, publié ici). L'agence a ouvert un grand atelier-boutique, Gallery 113, à Courtrai (Belgique) en 2007. À Bruxelles, *Cityscape*, leur installation en bois de 8000 m² devrait rester en place pendant une année (2007–08).

UCHRONIA: MESSAGE OUT OF THE FUTURE

Burning Man Festival, Black Rock City, Black Rock Desert, Nevada, USA, 2006

Floor area: 2000 m². Client/Art Director: Jan Kriekels, CEO of Jaga. Cost: €260 000.
Joint venture with Jaga. Project Architect: Fréderic van Dooren

Burning Man is a six-day annual festival that takes place in Black Rock City, an ephemeral town in the Black Rock Desert 150 kilometers northeast of Reno. The event is described by organizers as an experiment in community, radical self-expression, and radical self-reliance, and takes its name from the ritual burning of a large wooden effigy on the sixth day. In 2007, 47 366 people participated in the festival. For the 2006 event, Arne Quinze used 150 kilometers of wooden planks, one, two and three meters long, assembled over a period of three weeks, with a team of 25 people to create a sculpture 60 by 30 meters and 15 meters high. Intended for the "final burn" or apotheosis of the festival, this sculpture was designed to be destroyed. Studio Arne Quinze had already created similarly inspired sculptures albeit on a smaller scale at the 100 % Design London and Design Post Cologne fairs. Quinze created another large-scale wooden sculpture in a similar vein in 2007–08 in Brussels (*Cityscape*). For each of the 150 kilometers of wood used in the Nevada installation, the artists planted a tree in Belgium, using ashes from Nevada as fertilizer. "In this way," they say, "we have brought Burning Man to the other side of the world. Unused wood was donated to Habitat for Humanity in Reno." Called *Message out of the Future*, the installation included a large sound system, and nightly dance parties were held in it until it was burnt. The installation was funded by the Belgian radiator manufacturer Jaga and its CEO Jan Kriekels acting as Art Director.

Einmal im Jahr findet in Black Rock City, einer für kurze Zeit errichteten Stadt in der Black-Rock-Wüste von Nevada, 150 km nordöstlich von Reno, das sechstägige Burning Man Festival statt. Die Organisatoren beschreiben das Ereignis als ein Experiment, bei dem es um Gemeinschaft, radikale Selbstentfaltung und radikale Autarkie geht. Seinen Namen trägt das Festival aufgrund des Rituals, jedes Jahr am sechsten Festivaltag ein großes hölzernes Bildnis zu verbrennen. 2007 nahmen 47 366 Menschen an dem Festival teil. Für das Ereignis im Jahr 2006 trugen Arne Quinze und ein 25-köpfiges Team drei Wochen lang Holzbalken von je 1, 2 oder 3 m Länge zusammen – hintereinandergelegt eine Strecke von 150 km –, um eine 60 m lange, 30 m breite und 15 m hohe Skulptur zu bauen. Dieses Gebilde war von vornherein dafür bestimmt, das „finale Feuer", die Apotheose des Festivals abzugeben und zerstört zu werden. Schon früher hatten Studio Arne Quinze ähnliche Skulpturen gebaut, wenn auch in kleinerem Maßstab, etwa für die Messen „100 % Design London" und „Design Post Cologne". Eine ähnliche großformatige Holzskulptur („Cityscape") schuf Quinze für die Stadt Brüssel, wo diese von 2007 bis 2008 aufgestellt wurde. Für jeden einzelnen der Holzbalken der Skulptur pflanzten die Künstler in Belgien einen Baum, wobei sie die beim Burning Man Festival übriggebliebene Asche als Dünger verwenden. „Auf diese Weise", sagen sie, „haben wir den Burning Man auf die andere Seite der Erde gebracht. Nicht zum Einsatz gekommenes Holz haben wir an das Habitat for Humanity in Reno verschenkt." Zu „Message out of the Future" gehörte ein großes Soundsystem und nachts wurde sie zur Party-Location. Gesponsert wurde die Installation von dem belgischen Heizungshersteller Jaga und dessen Geschäftsführer Jan Kriekels, der die Rolle des Artdirectors übernahm.

Burning Man est un festival qui se déroule chaque année durant six jours à Black Rock City, ville éphémère édifiée dans le Black Rock Desert à 150 km au nord-est de Reno. Il est décrit comme une « expérimentation de vie communautaire, d'expression radicale et individualiste radicale » qui tire son nom de la destruction rituelle par le feu d'une grande effigie de bois lors de la clôture de la fête. En 2007, 47 366 personnes y ont participé. Pour l'édition 2006, Arne Quinze a créé une sculpture de 60 m de long, 30 m de large et 15 m de haut, assemblée par une équipe de 25 personnes qui a utilisé 150 km de planches de bois d'une longueur de un, deux et trois mètres. Conçue pour l'apothéose finale, elle a été conçue pour être brûlée. Studio Arne Quinze a déjà créé des sculptures d'inspiration similaire, bien qu'à plus petite échelle, pour les foires 100 % Design London et Design Post Cologne. Quinze a également imaginé une autre sculpture en bois de la même veine à Bruxelles : *Cityscape* (2007–08). Pour chacun des 150 km de planches utilisées dans le Nevada, les artistes ont planté un arbre en Belgique et utilisé les cendres de la construction brûlée à Black Rock comme engrais. « De cette façon, disent-il, nous avons transporté le *Burning Man* à l'autre bout du monde. Le bois non utilisé a été offert à Habitat for Humanity à Reno. » Intitulée *Message out of the Future*, l'installation de Black Rock intégrait un système sonore et des soirées se sont tenues toute la nuit devant ce bûcher. L'installation a été financée par le fabricant de radiateurs belge Jaga dont le CIO Jan Kriekels est intervenu comme directeur artistique.

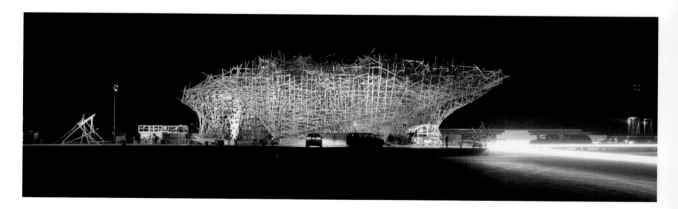

The almost random, nest-like accumulation of wood that formed the Uchronia installation, seen at night (above), and under construction (right).

Die wie nach dem Zufallsprinzip aus Holzbalken zusammengesetzte, vogelnestartige Uchronia-Installation bei Nacht (oben) und bei Tag (rechts).

Une accumulation presque aléatoire d'éléments en bois donne sa forme de nid à Uchronia, vu la nuit (ci-dessus) et en construction (page de droite).

The completed structure in daylight and at night. Decidedly fragile and light in its appearance, the installation is designed unlike almost any other building, to burn.

Die fertige Konstruktion bei Tageslicht und in der Nacht. Die ausgesprochen leicht und fragil wirkende Installation war von vornherein dazu bestimmt, verbrannt zu werden.

La structure achevée, de jour et de nuit. Fait rare, d'apparence légère et fragile, elle a été spécialement conçue et construite pour être brûlée.

Below, pictures of the burning installation; at the end reduced to cinders.

Unten, Fotos der Installation in Flammen und am Ende in Asche.

Ci-dessous, des images de l'installation en feu, puis en cendres.

RCR ARQUITECTES

RCR Aranda Pigem Vilalta Arquitectes
Passeig Blay, 34, 2n
17800 Olot (Girona)
Spain

Tel: +34 972 26 91 05
Fax: +34 972 26 75 58
E-mail: rcr@rcrarquitectes.es
Web: www.rcrarquitectes.es

Rafael Aranda, Carme Pigem, and Ramon Vilalta completed their studies in Architecture at the ETSA, Vallès, in 1987, and the following year created their own studio, **RCR ARQUITECTES**, in Olot, the Spanish city where they were born. Since 1989, they have been Consultant Architects for the Natural Park in the Volcanic Zone of La Garrotxa. They have taught urbanism (1989–2001, Vilalta) and studio projects (1992–2003, Pigem) at ETSAV. Pigem was a Guest Lecturer at the Department of Architecture at the ETH in Zurich. They have won a number of competitions ranging from a Lighthouse in Punta Aldea (Chile) in 1988 to the Crematorium of Hofheide (Belgium), and most recently the very ambitious project for The Edge in Dubai (UAE, 2008–, published here). Built work includes the M-Lidia House (Montagut, Girona, 2001–02); Els Colors Kindergarten (Manlleu, Barcelona, 2003–04); the surprising Rough Rock Park (Les Preses, Girona, 2003–04); pavilions in Les Cols Restaurant (Olot, Girona, 2004–05); and the Library and Center for the Elderly (Barcelona, 2005–07), all in Spain.

Rafael Aranda, Carme Pigem und Ramon Vilalta schlossen 1987 ihr Architekturstudium an der Escola Tècnica Superior d'Arquitectura del Vallès (ETSAV) ab und gründeten im darauffolgenden Jahr in ihrer spanischen Heimatstadt Olot das Büro **RCR ARQUITECTES**. Seit 1989 fungieren sie als beratende Architekten für den Naturschutzpark La Garrotxa, ein Vulkangebiet in Katalonien. Vilalta war von 1989 bis 2001 Dozent für Urbanistik an der ETSAV, Pigem führte dort Studioprojekte durch und war außerdem Gastdozentin am Department Architektur der ETH Zürich. RCR gewannen diverse Architekturwettbewerbe für so unterschiedliche Bauten wie einen Leuchtturm im chilenischen Punta Aldea (1988), ein Krematorium im belgischen Hofheide oder vor Kurzem für das Großprojekt „The Edge" in Dubai (VAE, seit 2008, hier vorgestellt). Zu ihren realisierten Bauten gehören die Casa M-Lidia in Montagut, Girona, in Katalonien (2001–02), der Kindergarten Els Colors in Manlleu, Barcelona (2003–04), der außergewöhnliche Park La Piedra Tosca in Les Preses, Girona (2003–04), die Pavillons im Restaurant Les Cols in Olot, Girona (2004–05) und eine Bibliothek und ein Seniorenzentrum in Barcelona (2005–07).

Rafael Aranda, Carme Pigem et Ramon Vilalta ont terminé leurs études d'architecture à l'ETSA à Vallès en 1987 et ont créé leur agence, **RCR ARQUITECTES**, l'année suivante à Olot, leur ville natale espagnole. Depuis 1989, ils sont architectes consultants pour le Parc naturel de la zone volcanique de La Garrotxa. Ils ont enseigné l'urbanisme (1989–2001, Vilalta) et le design (1992–2003, Pigem) à l'ETSA de Vallès. Pigem a été conférencier invité au département d'architecture de l'ETH à Zurich. Ils ont remporté un certain nombre de concours comme celui du phare de Punta Aldea (Chili, 1988) ou le crématorium d'Hofheide (Belgique) et, plus récemment, le très ambitieux projet The Edge à Dubai (EAU, 2008–, publié ici). Parmi leurs réalisations : la maison M-Lidia (Montagut, Gérone, 2001–02) ; le jardin d'enfants Els Colors (Manlleu, Barcelona, 2003–04) ; le surprenant Parc de Piedra Tosca (Les Preses, Gérone, 2003–04) ; des pavillons pour le Restaurant Les Cols (Olot, Gérone, 2004–05) et une bibliothèque et centre pour personnes âgées (Barcelone, 2005-07), toutes en Espagne.

THE EDGE

Business Bay, Dubai, United Arab Emirates, 2008–

*Total floor area: 343 990 m^2 including 134 550 m^2 (offices), 42 200 m^2 (residential), 38 270 m^2 (commercial), 128 970 m^2 (parking).
Client: The Edge Management LLC, Al Mojil Investment Ltd. Cost: €600 million. Collaboration: Coussée & Goris Architecten.
Team: RCR: A. Schmidt, J. Puigcorbé, N. Baldayo, T. Ferreira de Oliveira, A. Sabença, G. Szücs, K. Fujii, D. Delarue, C. Kuczynski,
S. Piecha, A. Paulicelli, M. Cottone; Coussée & Goris: E. Verstraete, F. De Bruyn, E. Subirah*

RCR were selected after a limited competition, including other architects such as SANAA of Japan, to build a very large complex at the limits of the new Business Bay development district in Dubai. The client, Al Mojil Investment, posed an unusual question to the participating architect: what would the "knowledge worker" need in order to live and work in Dubai? The response was partially contained in the instructions to the architects—combining office space, residential, and retail facilities; in short, everything one might need to live without ever leaving the complex. The unusual proposal of RCR consisted in a series of five tapering towers, planted in a "floating carpet"—or raised platform that would contain a hotel or residential spaces. The towers penetrate the elevated platform and are anchored in the parking levels that will be covered by a landscaping scheme that is in the development phase with the Beirut designer Vladimir Djurovic. Forming an impressive presence quite literally at "the edge" of Dubai's current development zone, the RCR project should be visible from a considerable distance, despite the rising forest of towers nearby, including the record-breaking Burj Dubai complex.

Bei einem beschränkten Wettbewerb – an dem u. a. das japanische Büro SANAA beteiligt war – für den Bau eines Großkomplexes am Rand des neu entstehenden Business-Bay-Bezirks in Dubai fiel die Wahl auf RCR Arquitectes. Der Auslober, Al Mojil Investment, hatte eine ungewöhnliche Frage an die teilnehmenden Architekten gerichtet: Was benötigt ein „Wissensarbeiter", um in Dubai zu leben und zu arbeiten? Die Antwort war teilweise bereits in den Vorgaben an die Architekten enthalten – es waren Büroräumlichkeiten, Wohnbereiche und Einkaufsmöglichkeiten zu kombinieren, kurz gesagt: alles, was es überhaupt zum Leben bedarf, so dass man die Anlage gar nicht zu verlassen bräuchte. Der außergewöhnliche Vorschlag von RCR besteht aus einem Ensemble von fünf sich verjüngenden Hochhäusern, aufgesetzt auf einen „fliegenden Teppich" – eine erhöht angelegte Plattform, die ein Hotel oder Wohnbereiche enthalten soll. Die Türme sind durch die erhöhte Plattform hindurch geführt und in unterirdischen Parkebenen verankert. Diese sollen von einer Grünanlage abgedeckt werden, die derzeit in Zusammenarbeit mit dem Beiruter Landschaftsarchitekten Vladimir Djurovic entworfen wird. Die imposante Erscheinung des RCR-Projekts, das am Rand – also im wörtlichen Sinne „at the edge" – von Dubais gegenwärtiger Neubauzone entstehen soll, dürfte künftig auch aus beträchtlicher Entfernung noch zu sehen sein – trotz des in der Umgebung entstehenden Hochhauswaldes, zu dem auch der alle Rekorde brechende Komplex Burj Dubai gehört.

L'agence RCR a été sélectionnée à l'issue d'un concours sur invitation comprenant entre autres l'agence japonaise SANAA, pour construire ce très vaste complexe aux limites du nouveau quartier en développement de Business Bay à Dubaï. Le client, Al Mojil Investment, avait posé une question inhabituelle aux participants: « Quels seront les besoins des »travailleurs de la connaissance« qui voudront venir vivre et travailler à Dubaï? » La réponse figurait en partie dans les instructions aux architectes: combiner bureaux, appartements et commerces, en bref tout ce que l'on peut espérer trouver sans jamais avoir à quitter le complexe. La proposition originale de RCR consiste en une série de tours effilées, érigées sur « un tapis flottant » ou dalle surélevée, qui contiendra un hôtel ou des logements. Les tours seront ancrées dans les niveaux des parkings recouverts d'aménagements paysagers, en cours de réalisation, par le designer de Beyrouth Vladimir Djurovic. Par son impressionnante présence littéralement « à la limite » (the edge) de la zone actuelle de développement de Dubaï, le projet RCR sera visible d'une distance considérable malgré la forte présence de tours à proximité, dont le complexe de Burj Dubaï qui bat tous les records.

Above, a sketch of the design with its five irregular, cup-like forms. Opposite, renderings of interior volumes show a dark ambiance with high ceilings and an irregular placement of structural elements.

Eine Skizze des Entwurfs (oben) mit seinen fünf becherartigen Gebilden. Die Renderings der Innenräume zeigen ein abgedunkeltes Ambiente mit hohen Decken und unregelmäßig angeordneten Konstruktionselementen.

Un croquis du projet (ci-dessus) aux cinq volumes en forme de coupes. Les perspectives des intérieurs montrent une ambiance sombre, de très hauts plafonds et une disposition irrégulière des éléments structurels.

An aerial view and a site plan show the volumes added by Holl at right angles to the original building, and in contrast with its stony Neoclassical façades.

Das Luftbild und der Lageplan links lassen die orthogonale Anordnung der neu hinzugekommenen Gebäude und deren Kontrast zu den neoklassizistischen Steinfassaden des alten Museums erkennen.

Une vue aérienne et un plan du site montent les volumes ajoutés perpendiculairement par Steven Holl au bâtiment de pierre d'origine. Ils contrastent avec le style néoclassique de celui-ci.

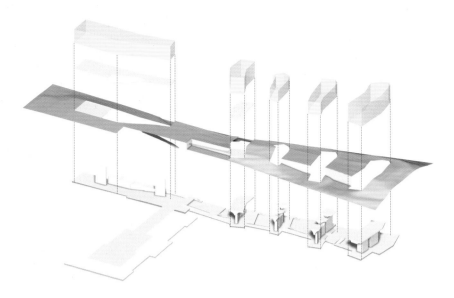

Inserted into a continuous band, the emerging volumes glow in the darkness, as seen below and opposite.

Die Gebäudekörper bilden ein fortlaufendes Band, dessen einzelne Glieder, wie unten und rechts zu sehen, im Dunkeln hell leuchten.

Ci-dessous et à droite : les nouvelles constructions insérées forment un bandeau continu, qui brille dans la nuit.

Holl's use of light and his poetic conception of the architectural volumes find their first expression in his watercolors, like the annotated painting to the right.

Holls Überlegungen zur Lichtgestaltung und die poetische Konzeption seiner Bauten finden ihren ersten Ausdruck in Form von Aquarellen wie dem rechts.

L'utilisation de la lumière et la conception poétique des volumes architecturaux a trouvé sa première expression dans des aquarelles de Holl, comme celle de droite, annotée de sa main.

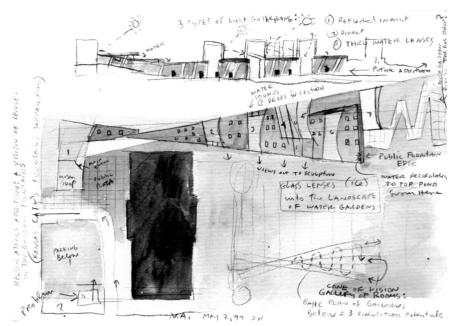

Holl creates a topography around the buildings with pathways for the sculpture garden that wander between them.

Holl gestaltet das umliegende Gelände mit Pfaden, die zwischen den Gebäuden hindurch und in den Skulpturenpark führen.

Steven Holl a crée une topographie autour des bâtiments. Les allées du jardin des sculptures se glissent entre eux.

The remarkable and unexpected illuminated façades of the extension designed by Steven Holl glow from within, making them appear like sculptural art objects at night.

Die eindrucksvolle Komplettbeleuchtung der Fassaden lassen die Gebäude durch das Glühen, das aus ihrem Innern zu dringen scheint, nachts wie skulpturale Kunstobjekte wirken.

Caractérisé par une luminescence qui émane de l'intérieur, l'éclairage des façades, complet et remarquable, transforme l'extension de Steven Holl en véritable objet sculptural.

Ramps and openings articulate and animate the interior spaces in ways seen in previous designs by Steven Holl.

Wie schon bei früheren Entwürfen Holls gliedern Rampen und Öffnungen die Innenräume und geben ihnen eine besondere Dynamik.

Des rampes et des ouvertures articulent et animent les espaces intérieurs d'une façon déjà observée dans des projets antérieurs de Steven Holl.

Steven Holl has long been interested in the effects of light in his architecture—both direct natural light and more nuanced indirect light, often with effects of color.

Bereits seit langem beschäftigt sich Holl in seinen Entwürfen mit der Wirkung von Licht, sowohl von natürlichem als auch von nuancierterem, indirekten Licht, oft auch kombiniert mit Farbeffekten.

Steven Holl s'est longtemps intéressé aux effets de la lumière dans son architecture, que ce soit la lumière naturelle diurne ou des éclairages indirects plus nuancés, qui cultivent souvent les effets de couleur.

HOLZER KOBLER ARCHITEKTUREN

Holzer Kobler Architekturen
Ankerstr. 3 / 8004 Zurich / Switzerland

Tel: +41 44 240 52 00 / Fax: +41 44 240 52 02
E-mail: mail@holzerkobler.ch / Web: www.holzerkobler.ch

HOLZER KOBLER ARCHITEKTUREN was founded in January 2004 by Barbara Holzer and Tristan Kobler. The company is the result of the fusion of their two former offices: d-case (Holzer) and Morphing Systems (Kobler). The two architects have been working together since 2001. The company has 25 employees (architects and designers). Barbara Holzer was born in 1966 in Zurich, studied at the ETH in Zurich (1986–92), and has worked as an architect and exhibition designer in Switzerland and Germany. In 1999, she created her own firm (d-case), concentrating on interior and exhibition design. Since 1994, she has worked for Studio Daniel Libeskind on different international projects, focusing on museum buildings and exhibition design. Tristan Kobler studied at the ETH (1981–87), and has designed and realized more than 70 exhibitions in a cultural and commercial context. In 1999, he created his own office (Morphing Systems) and realized several buildings and exhibitions in Switzerland and abroad. The work of Barbara Holzer and Tristan Kobler "concentrates on the interaction between architecture, exhibition, and media design." Holzer Kobler Architekturen offers services in all planning phases, from the idea, concept, and design, to construction documents, site supervision, and project management. They worked on one of the Arteplages for Expo '02 (Yverdon-les-Bains, Switzerland, 2002). They have also modified and redesigned the Schönbühl Shopping Center (Lucerne, Switzerland, 2006); completed the Arche Nebra Visitors' Center (Wangen, Germany, 2005–07, published here); and are working on the "Freizeit- und Einkaufszentrum EbiSquare," a leisure and shopping center, also in Lucerne.

HOLZER UND KOBLER ARCHITEKTUREN wurde im Januar 2004 von Barbara Holzer und Tristan Kobler gegründet, als Zusammenschluss ihrer vorherigen Büros d-case (Holzer) und Morphing Systems (Kobler). An gemeinsamen Projekten arbeiten die beiden Architekten seit 2001. Ihr jetziges Büro beschäftigt 25 Architekten und Designer. Barbara Holzer wurde 1966 in Zürich geboren, wo sie von 1986 bis 1992 an der ETH studierte. Danach arbeitete sie als freischaffende Architektin und Ausstellungsdesignerin in Deutschland und der Schweiz. Seit 1994 ist sie zudem an internationalen Projekten mit Schwerpunkt Ausstellungen und Museumsbauten des Büros von Daniel Libeskind beteiligt. 1999 gründete sie die Firma d-case, die sich ebenfalls auf Ausstellungs- und Innendesign konzentrierte. Tristan Kobler studierte von 1981 bis 1987 an der ETH und hat mehr als 70 Ausstellungen sowohl im kulturellen als auch kommerziellen Bereich gestaltet. 1999 gründete er das Büro Morphing Systems, mit dem er u. a. in der Schweiz zahlreiche Bauten und Ausstellungsprojekte realisierte. Barbara Holzers und Tristan Koblers Arbeit „ist auf das Zusammenspiel von Architektur, Ausstellungs- und Mediengestaltung ausgerichtet". Mit Holzer Kobler Architekturen betreuen sie Projekte durch sämtliche Entstehungsphasen von der Idee über Konzeption und Gestaltung bis zur Umsetzung und Projektleitung. Sie waren u. a. maßgeblich an einer der Arteplages für die Schweizerische Landesausstellung Expo '02 (Yverdon-les-Bains, 2002) beteiligt. Weiterhin waren sie für den Umbau und die Neugestaltung des Shoppingcenters Schönbühl in Luzern (2006) verantwortlich und für den Entwurf des hier vorgestellten Besucherzentrums Arche Nebra im sachsen-anhaltinischen Wangen (2005–07). Derzeit arbeiten sie an der Realisierung des Luzerner Freizeit- und Erlebniszentrums EbiSquare.

L'agence **HOLZER KOBLER ARCHITEKTUREN** a été fondée en 2004 par Barbara Holzer et Tristan Kobler. Elle résulte de la fusion de leurs deux agences précédentes : d-case (Holzer) et Morphing Systems (Kobler). Les deux architectes travaillent ensemble depuis 2001. Ils emploient 25 collaborateurs (architectes et designers). Barbara Holzer, née en 1966 à Zurich, a étudié à l'ETH de Zurich (1986–92), et a travaillé comme architecte et scénographe en Suisse et en Allemagne. En 1999, elle a créé l'agence d-case, dédiée à l'architecture intérieure et à la conception d'expositions. En 1994, elle a travaillé pour le Studio Daniel Libeskind sur différents projets internationaux, en particulier de musées et d'expositions. Tristan Kobler a étudié à l'ETH (1981–87) et conçu et réalisé plus de 70 expositions culturelles et commerciales. En 1999, il a créé son agence Morphing Systems et mené à bien plusieurs projets d'architecture et expositions en Suisse et à l'étranger. Barbara Holzer et Tristan Kobler se « concentrent sur les interactions entre architecture, expositions, et projets médiatiques ». Holzer Kobler Architekturen propose des services de conception, de l'idée aux plans techniques de construction, en passant par la supervision de chantier et la gestion de projet. Ils sont intervenus sur l'une des Arteplages pour Expo '02 (Yverdon-les-Bains, Suisse, 2002). Ils ont transformé le centre commercial Schönbühl (Lucerne, Suisse, 2006) ; ont achevé le centre d'accueil des visiteurs Arche Nebra (Wangen, Allemagne, 2005–07, publié ici) et travaillent actuellement sur le projet de centre commercial et de loisirs EbiSquare, également à Lucerne.

ARCHE NEBRA VISITORS' CENTER

Wangen, Germany, 2005–07

Site area: 3550 m². Floor area: 2100 m²; 260 m² (tower). Client: Kreisverwaltung des Burgenlandkreises, Saxony-Anhalt.
Cost: €5.48 million. Collaborators: Kai Hellat, Nadine Jerchau, Annett Landsmann, Roland Lehnen,
Volker Mau, Klaus Romberg, Gabriele Zipf

The Nebra Sky Disk is a Bronze Age object (c. 1600 B.C.) that may have served as an astronomical instrument. It was discovered by robbers at a site near Nebra, Saxony-Anhalt, in Germany in 1999. Although there was initially some suspicion that it was a forgery, the Disk has now been accepted as one of the most significant archeological discoveries of the 20th century in Germany. The Arche Nebra Visitors' Center consists of a 60-meter-long, archlike main building inspired by the golden solar boat on the object, which appears to float above the ground, and a 35-meter-high observation tower. The base of the main building is meant to have the appearance of an "archaic" object rising up out of the earth. The tower marks the place of discovery of the Disk and is intended to resemble the needle of an enormous sundial. Architecturally speaking, the Center is interesting because of the strongly tilted or cantilevered forms of the observation tower and the main building. The actual object is not kept at the Visitors' Center but at the Landesmuseum für Vorgeschichte (State Museum of Prehistory) in Halle. The Visitors' Center is described as an "infotainment" facility, with a planetarium, courses for children on the Bronze Age, and presentations relating to the development of the region, from the first signs of life in the Stone Age to the medieval period.

Die Himmelsscheibe von Nebra ist eine Metallplatte aus der Bronzezeit (um 1600 v. Chr.), die offenbar als astronomisches Instrument benutzt wurde. Gefunden wurde sie von Raubgräbern im Jahr 1999 auf einem Gelände in der Nähe von Nebra in Sachsen-Anhalt. Nach anfänglichem Verdacht, es könne sich um eine Fälschung handeln, gilt die Scheibe heute als einer der bedeutendsten archäologischen Funde, die in Deutschland im 20. Jahrhundert gemacht wurden. Das Besucherzentrum Arche Nebra besteht aus einem 35 m hohen Aussichtsturm und einem 60 m langen Hauptgebäude, dessen Name und Form sich von der auf der Scheibe abgebildeten Sonnenbarke ableiten, die über der Erde zu schweben scheint. Die Basis des Hauptgebäudes soll den Anschein eines „archaischen" Objekts unterstützen, das von der Erde aufsteigt. Der Turm ist auf den Fundort der Scheibe ausgerichtet und fungiert darüber hinaus aus als Zeiger einer riesigen Sonnenuhr. Architektonisch reizvoll ist das Besucherzentrum wegen der stark auskragenden Form des Hauptgebäudes und der Neigung des Turms. Die Himmelsscheibe selbst ist nicht in dem Besucherzentrum zu sehen, sondern im Landesmuseum für Vorgeschichte in Halle/Saale. Die Arche Nebra versteht sich als Infotainment-Einrichtung und bietet seinen Besuchern ein Planetarium, Kurse über die Bronzezeit für Kinder und Vorträge zur Entwicklung der Region von den ersten menschlichen Spuren in der Steinzeit bis zum Mittelalter.

Le disque de Nebra est un objet datant de l'âge du bronze (vers 1600 av. J.-C.) qui a pu servir d'instrument d'astronomie. Il a été découvert par des pilleurs dans un site près de Nebra (Saxony-Anhalt, Allemagne) en 1999. Si certains ont pensé au départ qu'il s'agissait d'un faux, il est considéré aujourd'hui comme l'une des plus importantes découvertes archéologiques du XXᵉ siècle en Allemagne. Le centre d'accueil des visiteurs Arche Nebra se compose d'un bâtiment principal de 60 mètres de long en forme d'arche, inspiré de la barque solaire dorée figurant sur le disque, qui semble flotter au-dessus du sol, et d'une tour d'observation de 35 mètres de haut. Le socle du bâtiment a une apparence d'objet « archaïque » sorti du sol. La tour marque l'endroit où a été découvert le disque et ressemble à un énorme gnomon. Ce centre est architecturalement intéressant par ses formes puissantes inclinées en porte-à-faux. Le célèbre objet n'est pas conservé à cet endroit, mais au Landesmuseum für Vorgeschichte (musée de la Préhistoire) de Halle. Le centre d'accueil des visiteurs est décrit comme un équipement d'*infotainment*: planétarium, leçons sur l'âge du bronze pour les enfants, présentations sur le développement de la région de l'apparition de la vie à l'âge de pierre jusqu'à l'époque médiévale.

The slightly angled upper volume of the Visitors' Center sits at the top of a hill and, particularly at night, appears to be lifting off from its base.

Der leicht gebogene obere Abschnitt des Besucherzentrums, das auf einer Hügelkuppe liegt, scheint – insbesondere nachts – von seiner Basis abzuheben.

Le volume supérieur, légèrement concave, du centre d'accueil des visiteurs est implanté au sommet de la colline et semble soulevé de sa base, particulièrement la nuit.

The strong cantilever of the upper volume lends a certain drama to the architecture, suspended somewhere between the earth and the heavens represented on the Nebra Sky Disk.

Die ausgeprägte Auskragung des oberen Gebäudeteils verleiht der Architektur eine gewisse Dramatik, mit der sie wie die Sonnenbarke der Himmelsscheibe zwischen Himmel und Erde schwebt.

Le puissant porte-à-faux du volume supérieur crée une certaine tension dramatique. Il semble suspendu entre la terre et le ciel, symboliquement représentés sur le disque de Nebra.

Although the actual Nebra Sky Disk is not exhibited in the Visitors' Center, the latter is located near the site where the object was discovered, as the architecture and the display make clear.

Im Besucherzentrum ist die echte Himmelsscheibe von Nebra zwar nicht zu sehen, es befindet sich jedoch ganz in der Nähe von ihrem Fundort, auf den die Architektur und die Ausstellung direkten Bezug nehmen.

Bien que le vrai disque de Nebra ne soit pas exposé dans le centre des visiteurs, celui-ci se trouve à proximité du lieu de sa découverte, ce que traduisent clairement l'architecture et l'exposition.

The main building is complemented by a 35-meter-high observation tower (right) that marks the site of the discovery of the Disk. Below, a section of the main building.

Ergänzt wird das Hauptgebäude durch einen 35 Meter hohen Aussichtsturm (rechts), der auf den Fundort der Scheibe ausgerichtet ist. Unten eine Schnittdarstellung des Hauptgebäudes.

Le bâtiment principal est complété par une tour d'observation de 35 mètres de haut (à droite) qui signale le site de la découverte du disque. Ci-dessous, une coupe du bâtiment principal.

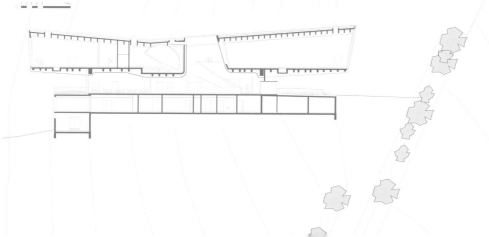

The interior of the building reflects
the elegant yet largely enigmatic
design of the Nebra Sky Disk itself.

Die Innenräume des Gebäudes zeigen
eine ähnlich elegante und zugleich
enigmatische Gestaltung wie die
Himmelscheibe selbst.

L'intérieur du bâtiment reflète le
dessin élégant, mais en grande partie
énigmatique, du disque de Nebra.

The exhibition design with its furniture and objects was also the responsibility of Holzer Kobler.

Für das Ausstellungsdesign samt Möbeln und Objekten zeichnen ebenfalls Holzer Kobler verantwortlich.

La conception de l'exposition, de son mobilier et de ses objets, a également été confiée à Holzer Kobler.

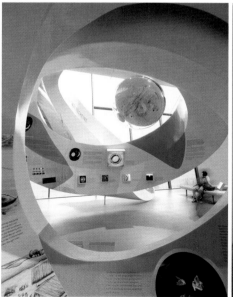

JUNYA ISHIGAMI

junya.ishigami+associates
1–2–6–5F Suido
Bunkyo-ku
Tokyo 112–0005
Japan

Tel: +81 3 5840 9199
Fax: +81 3 5840 9299
E-mail: contact@jnyi.jp
Web: http://jnyi.jp

JUNYA ISHIGAMI was born in Kanagawa, Japan, in 1974. He studied at the Tokyo National University of Fine Arts and Music in the Architecture Department, graduating in 2000. He worked in the office of Kazuyo Sejima & Associates (now SANAA) from 2000 to 2004, establishing Junya Ishigami + Associates in 2004. Given his age, his list of projects is not long, but he has designed a number of tables, including one 10 meters long and 3 millimeters thick made of pre-stressed steel (Table), and a project for the Hotel Kaiyo and housing (2007). Aside from the facility for the Kanagawa Institute of Technology (2007–08, published here), he has designed a New York store for the fashion personality Yohji Yamamoto (2008). He participated in the 2008 Venice Architecture Biennale (Japanese pavilion). Despite his limited number of completed works, with the project published here, Junya Ishigami has emerged as one of the more significant young Japanese architects.

JUNYA ISHIGAMI wurde 1974 im japanischen Kanagawa geboren. 2000 schloss er sein Studium an der Tokyo National University of Fine Arts and Music im Fachbereich Architektur ab. Von 2000 bis 2004 arbeitete er im Büro von Kazuyo Sejima & Associates (heute SANAA), anschließend gründete er Junya Ishigami + Associates. Angesichts seines Alters ist Ishigamis Werkverzeichnis noch überschaubar; bislang gehören dazu mehrere Tische, darunter ein 10 m langer aus vorgespanntem Stahl, und ein Projekt für das Hotel Kaiyo und ein Wohnkomplex (2007). Neben der hier vorgestellten Anlage für das Kanagawa Institute of Technology (2007–08) entwarf Ishigami ein Ladengeschäft für den Modeschöpfer Yohji Yamamoto in New York (2008). 2008 nahm er an der Architekturbiennale in Venedig teil (japanischer Pavillon). Auch wenn erst wenige Arbeiten Junya Ishigamis realisiert wurden, zeigt er sich mit dem nachfolgend präsentierten Projekt bereits als einer der bemerkenswerteren jungen Architekten Japans.

JUNYA ISHIGAMI, né en 1974 à Kanagawa au Japon, a étudié au département d'architecture de la Tokyo National University of Fine Arts and Music, dont il est sorti diplômé en 2000. Il a travaillé avec l'agence de Kazuyo Sejima & Associates (aujourd'hui SANAA) de 2000 à 2004, et a créé l'agence Junya Ishigami + Associates en 2004. Son jeune âge explique que sa liste de réalisations ne soit pas très longue, mais il a dessiné un certain nombre de tables dont une de 10 m de long et 3 mm d'épaisseur, en acier précontraint (Table), et un projet pour l'Hotel Kaiyo et des logements (2007). En dehors des installations pour le Kanagawa Institute of Technology (2007–08), publié ici, il a conçu le magasin de New York du couturier japonais Yohji Yamamoto (2008). Il a participé à la Biennale d'architecture de Venise en 2008 (pavillon japonais). Malgré ce nombre limité de projets achevés, Ishigami apparaît, à travers le projet publié dans ces pages, comme l'un des plus prometteurs jeunes architectes japonais.

FACILITY

Kanagawa Institute of Technology, Kanagawa, Japan, 2007–08

Floor area: 1989 m². Client: Kanagawa Institute of Technology.
Cost: not disclosed. Collaboration: Konishi Structural Engineers, Environmental Engineering

The simple design of Facility is rendered more visually arresting by reflections and the irregular placement of the support columns.

Reflektionen und die unregelmäßige Anordnung der Stützpfeiler machen das erstaunlich simple Design der „Facility" optisch noch faszinierender.

Le projet simple de « Facility » est rendu encore plus intéressant par les reflets et la disposition irrégulière des colonnes de soutien.

This unusual, single-story building is simply called "Facility." It is intended for "making things"—which may range from wooden furniture to robots. Measuring 46 by 47 meters, it is essentially a concrete platform encased in glass. Strip skylights in the ceiling bring overhead natural light into the structure. There are no interior partitions, but the thin steel columns that support the roof at irregular intervals form a kind of forest evoked in photographs that reflect neighboring trees in the façade. The reflective capacity of the façade, something used in somewhat analogous ways in the round 21st Century Museum of Contemporary Art (SANAA, Kanazawa, Ishikawa, 2002–04) incites Ishigami to say, "I want to make spaces with very ambiguous borderlines, not a universal space like Mies." Specially conceived software was used to design the columns so that they could be different while still supporting the roof in an appropriate way. The potted plants and wooden furniture that have taken up residence in the building are less a contradiction of its pure, evanescent lines than they are a confirmation of the fundamental ambiguity described by Junya Ishigami.

Ishigamis ungewöhnliches eingeschossiges Gebäude trägt den simplen Namen „Facility", Anlage, und soll schlicht ein Ort sein, „an dem man etwas herstellen kann" – was ebenso gut Holzmöbel wie Roboter sein können. Es hat eine Grundfläche von 46 x 47 m und besteht im Wesentlichen aus einer Betonplattform, auf der ein gläserne Hülle steht. Fensterbänder im Dach sorgen für natürliches Oberlicht. Statt durch Wände unterteilt, ist der Innenraum durch dünne, unregelmäßig angeordnete Stahlstützen gegliedert, auf denen das Dach ruht. Von außen betrachtet formieren sich die Säulen in Verbindung mit den sich in der Fassade spiegelnden Bäumen des Außenbereichs zu einer Art Wäldchen. Zur Spiegelwirkung der Fassade, die darin in gewisser Hinsicht der Verglasung des 21st Century Museum of Contemporary Art von SANAA (Kanazawa, Ishikawa, 2002–04) ähnelt, erklärt Ishigami: „Ich möchte Räume mit uneindeutigen Abgrenzungen schaffen, keine universellen Räume wie die von Mies van der Rohe." Damit die Säulen unregelmäßig postiert werden konnten und trotzdem das Dach tragen, kam eine eigens entwickelte Software zum Einsatz. Die Topfpflanzen und Holzmöbel, die in dem Gebäude ihren Platz gefunden haben, sind weniger ein Widerspruch zu dessen feinen, klaren Linien als eine Bestätigung der grundsätzlichen Uneindeutigkeit, von der Junya Ishigami spricht.

Ce curieux bâtiment d'un seul niveau est simplement appelé « Facility ». Sa fonction est de contribuer à « faire des choses », ce qui peut aller du mobilier en bois à des robots. Mesurant 46 m x 47 m, il est essentiellement constitué d'une plate-forme en béton enclose de verre. Des bandeaux de verrières en plafond fournissent un éclairage zénithal dans la totalité du bâtiment. On ne trouve pas de cloisonnements intérieurs, mais de minces colonnes d'acier qui soutiennent le toit à intervalles irréguliers, en formant une sorte de forêt évoquée dans les photographies qui montrent un reflet des arbres avoisinants sur la façade. De cette capacité de réflexion de la façade, phénomène utilisé de façon assez analogue dans le 21st Century Museum of Contemporary Art de SANAA (Kanazawa, Ishikawa, 2002–04), Ishigami a déclaré : « Je souhaite faire des espaces aux limites très ambiguës, pas un espace universel comme Mies. » Un logiciel spécialement conçu a été utilisé pour le dessin des colonnes, afin qu'elles puissent être différentes tout en supportant la toiture de manière adéquate. Les plantes en pots et le mobilier de bois installés dans le bâtiment sont moins une contradiction avec ses lignes pures et évanescentes qu'une confirmation de la recherche d'ambiguïté fondamentale décrite par l'architecte.

Built next to a row of cherry trees, the box-like architectural volume is open on all sides with full-height glazing and long strip windows in the ceiling.

Der neben einer Kirschbaumallee errichtete kastenförmige Baukörper ist durch die seitenwandhohe Verglasung und lange Fensterbänder in der Decke zu allen Seiten hin geöffnet.

Édifié près d'une rangée de cerisiers, le volume architectural en forme de boîte est ouvert de tous côtés par un vitrage toute hauteur et de longs bandeaux de fenêtres au plafond.

In an interesting echo of the origins of Modernism, the building appears to sit on the earth very lightly, but its use of light and space is decidedly contemporary.

Nur ganz leicht scheint das Gebäude auf dem Boden aufzusitzen und wirkt damit wie ein reizvolles Echo der frühen Moderne, während die Licht- und Raumnutzung höchst zeitgemäß ist.

Se référant aux origines du modernisme, le bâtiment semble délicatement posé sur le sol, tandis que son utilisation de la lumière et de l'espace reste résolument contemporaine.

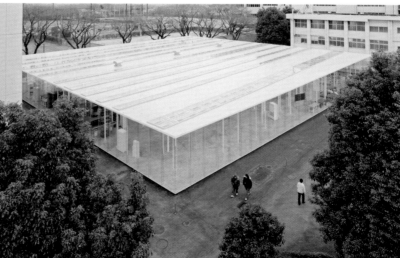

The white-on-white effect of the empty space is rendered more complex and unexpected by the placement of wooden furniture and plants that have since filled the building.

Der Weiß-in-Weiß-Effekt des anfänglich leeren Raumes ist nach dem Einzug von Holzmöbeln und Pflanzen in das Gebäude noch komplexer und verblüffender geworden.

L'effet blanc sur blanc donné par l'espace vide est rendu encore plus complexe et surprenant par la disposition du mobilier de bois et des plantes qui emplissent maintenant le bâtiment.

TOYO ITO

Toyo Ito & Associates, Architects
1–19–4 Shibuya
Shibuya-ku
Tokyo 150–0002
Japan

Tel: +81 3 3409 5822
Fax: +81 3 3409 5969

Born in 1941 in Seoul, Korea, **TOYO ITO** graduated from the University of Tokyo in 1965 and worked in the office of Kiyonori Kikutake until 1969. He created his own office, Urban Robot (URBOT), in Tokyo in 1971, changing its name to Toyo Ito & Associates, Architects, in 1979. His completed work includes the Silver Hut Residence (Tokyo, 1984); Tower of the Winds (Yokohama, Kanagawa, 1986); a Public Kindergarten (Eckenheim, Frankfurt, Germany, 1988–93); the Yatsushiro Municipal Museum (Yatsushiro, Kumamoto, 1989–91); and the Elderly People's Home (1992–94) and Fire Station (1992–95), both located in the same city on the island of Kyushu, all in Japan unless stated otherwise. He participated in the Planning and Urban Design for Shanghai Lujiazui Central Area in 1992. Other projects include his Dome in Odate (Odate, 1993–97); the Nagaoka Lyric Hall (Nagaoka, Niigata, 1993–96); and the Ota-ku Resort Complex (Tobu-cho, Chiisagata-gun, Nagano, 1995–98), all in Japan. One of his most successful and widely published projects, the Sendai Médiathèque, was completed in 2001. He designed a temporary pavilion for the Serpentine Gallery in London (2002). He was awarded the Golden Lion for Lifetime Achievement at the architecture exhibition "Next" at the Venice Biennale the same year. More recently, he has completed Tod's Omotesando Building (Shibuya-ku, Tokyo, 2002–04); the Island City Central Park Grin Grin (Fukuoka, Fukuoka, 2002–05); the Meiso no Mori Municipal Funeral Hall (Kakamigahara, Gifu, 2004–06); the Tama Art University New Library (Hachioji City, Tokyo, 2004–07, published here); and the Mikimoto Ginza 2 in Tokyo, all in Japan.

TOYO ITO, geboren 1941 in Seoul, Korea, schloss 1965 sein Studium an der Universität Tokio ab und arbeitete bis 1969 im Büro von Kiyonori Kikutake. 1971 gründete er in Tokio sein eigenes Architekturbüro Urban Robot (URBOT), das seit 1979 unter dem Namen Toyo Ito & Associates, Architects firmiert. Zu Itos Bauten gehören das Wohnhaus Silver Hut in Tokio (1984), der Turm der Winde in Yokohama, Kanagawa (Japan, 1986), eine Kindertagesstätte in Frankfurt-Eckenheim (1988–93), das städtische Museum in Yatsushiro (Kumamoto, Japan, 1989–91) sowie ein Seniorenwohnheim (1992–94) und eine Feuerwache (1992–95) auf der japanischen Insel Kyushu. 1992 nahm Ito an der internationalen Konferenz zur Planung und Entwicklung des Areals um das Shanghai Lujiazui Center in Shanghai teil. Von Ito stammen ferner der Dome in Odate (Japan, 1993–97), die Lyric Hall in Nagaoka (Niigata, Japan, 1993–96) und die Ferienanlage Ota-ku in Tobu-cho, Chiisagata-gun (Nagano, Japan, 1995–98). Eines seiner bekanntesten und meistgepriesenen Werke ist die 2001 fertiggestellte Mediathek im japanischen Sendai. 2002 entwarf Ito den Pavillon für die Serpentine Gallery in London. Im selben Jahr wurde er bei der Architekturausstellung „Next" auf der Biennale in Venedig mit dem Goldenen Löwen für sein Lebenswerk ausgezeichnet. In den vergangenen Jahren entstanden das Omotesando-Gebäude für die Firma Tod's in Shibuya-ku (Tokio, 2002–04), der Zentralpark Grin Grin auf Island City in Fukuoka (Japan, 2002–05), die städtische Trauerhalle Meiso no Mori in Kakamigahara, Gifu (Japan, 2004–06), die neue Bibliothek der Kunsthochschule Tama in Hachioji, Tokio (2004–07, hier vorgestellt), und das Mikimoto-Gebäude in Tokio.

Né en 1941 à Séoul, Corée, **TOYO ITO** est diplômé de l'université de Tokyo en 1965 puis travaille pour l'agence de Kiyonori Kikutake jusqu'en 1969. Il crée sa propre agence, Urban Robot (URBOT) en 1971, qui prend le nom de Toyo Ito & Associates, Architects en 1979. Parmi ses réalisations : la maison Silver Hut (Tokyo, 1984) ; la tour des Vents (Yokohama, Kanagawa, 1986) ; un jardin d'enfants (Eckenheim, Francfort, Allemagne, 1988–93) ; le Musée municipal de Yatsushiro (Kumamoto,1989–91) ; une maison de retraite (1992–94) et une caserne de pompiers, dans une ville de l'île de Kyushu. Il a participé au concours international d'urbanisme de la zone de Lujiazui à Shanghaï en 1992. Parmi ses récents projets : le Dome à Odate (Japon, 1993–97) ; la salle de concerts lyriques de Nagaoka (Niigata, Japon, 1993–96) et le complexe touristique Ota-ku (Tobu-Cho, Chiisagata-gun, Nagano, 1995–98). Une de ses réalisations les plus réussies et la plus médiatisée est la médiathèque de Sendai (1998–2001). Il a conçu un des pavillons temporaires de la Serpentine Gallery à Londres en 2002 et a reçu cette même année le Lion d'or pour sa carrière lors de l'exposition d'architecture « Next » à la biennale de Venise. Plus récemment, il a achevé l'immeuble Tod's d'Omotesando (Shibuya-ku, Tokyo, 2002–04) ; le Island City Central Park Grin Grin (Fukuoka, 2002–05) ; le funérarium municipal Meiso no Mori (Kakamigahara, Gifu, 2004–06) ; la nouvelle bibliothèque de l'université d'Art Tama (Hachioji, Tokyo, 2004–07, publiée ici) et l'immeuble Mikimoto Ginza 2 à Tokyo, tous au Japon.

TAMA ART UNIVERSITY NEW LIBRARY

Hachioji City, Tokyo, Japan, 2004–07

Site area: 159 184 m². Floor area: 5639 m². Client: Tama Art University. Cost: not disclosed.
Design Team: Toyo Ito, Takeo Higashi, Hideyuki Nakayama, Yoshitaka Ihara.
Associate Architect: Kajima Design. Furniture Design: Fujie Kazuko Atelier

To the right, a floor plan shows that two façades of the building are curved and two are straight, with a rather irregular interior arrangement.

Wie auf dem Geschossgrundriss rechts zu erkennen, besitzt das Gebäude zwei gekrümmte Fassaden und einen verhältnismäßig unregelmäßig gegliederten Innenraum.

À droite, le plan au sol montre que deux des façades sont incurvées, deux autres rectilignes, et la composition interne relativement irrégulière.

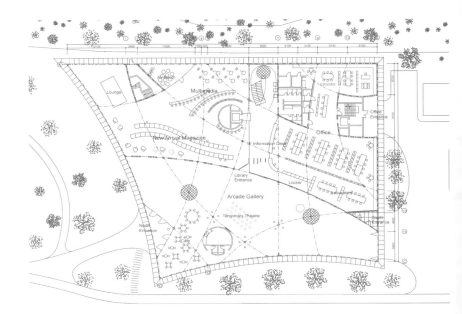

This two-story steel and concrete structure has a maximum height of 13.1 meters. The concrete is finished with a hydrophilic silicon resin. As Toyo Ito explains, "Initially we proposed to place the entire volume of the library underground to achieve a space resembling a cave. However, for various reasons, we found that the proposal was impossible. Although we started designing the volume above the ground, we still tried to build a subterranean space on the ground. We designed a continuous domelike space by subtracting volumes from the 'subterranean space above the ground.' We trimmed down more volumes and it became a structural system of a series of domes and arches." A sloping floor follows the natural inclination of the site, thus more clearly integrating the architecture into the landscape. Toyo Ito concludes, "In this way, spatial continuity is maintained between the inside and the outside space. This spatial concept will give freedom and richness to the architecture, receiving the natural energy that rises up from the earth and transforming it into an architectural order."

Der zweigeschossige Stahlbetonbau, dessen Betonoberfläche mit wasserbindendem Silikonharz beschichtet ist, misst an seiner höchsten Stelle 13,10 m. Zur Konstruktion erläutert Ito: „Ursprünglich hatten wir vorgeschlagen, den gesamten Bau unter die Erde zu verlegen und so einen höhlenähnlichen Raum zu schaffen. Wir mussten allerdings feststellen, dass dieser Vorschlag aus verschiedenen Gründen nicht umzusetzen war. Obwohl wir daraufhin einen oberirdischen Bau planten, versuchten wir, ihn trotzdem wie eine unterirdische Konstruktion anzulegen – nur eben über der Erde. Indem wir einzelne Raumeinheiten aus dieser ‚unterirdischen Konstruktion über der Erde' entfernten, entwickelten wir einen durchgehenden kuppelartigen Raum. Durch den Verzicht auf noch weitere Räume ergab sich schließlich ein Konstruktionssystem mit einer Abfolge von Kuppeln und Bögen." Um die Architektur zusätzlich in die Landschaft zu integrieren, fällt dem Gefälle des Grundstücks entsprechend auch der Fußboden leicht ab. „Auf diese Weise", erläutert Ito, „bleibt die räumliche Kontinuität zwischen Innen- und Außenraum gewahrt. Indem das Raumkonzept die natürliche, der Erde entspringende Energie aufnimmt und sie in eine architektonische Ordnung überführt, gewinnt die Konstruktion eine besondere Freiheit und Ausdruckskraft."

Ce bâtiment de deux niveaux en acier et béton mesure 13,1 m de haut en son point le plus élevé. Le béton est recouvert d'une résine de silicone hydrophile. Comme l'explique Toyo Ito : « Initialement, nous avons proposé d'implanter la totalité du volume de la bibliothèque en sous-sol pour obtenir un espace comparable à celui d'une caverne. Mais pour diverses raisons, nous avons découvert que c'était impossible. Bien que nous ayons commencé à concevoir le volume en surface, nous avons cependant essayé de conserver une impression d'espace souterrain. Nous avons conçu un espace sous coupoles en soustrayant des volumes de »l'espace souterrain au-dessus du sol«. Nous avons aussi supprimé des colonnes pour aboutir à un système structurel composé d'une succession de coupoles et d'arcs. » Le sol incliné suit la pente naturelle du site pour intégrer encore davantage l'architecture au paysage. Toyo Ito conclut : « De cette façon, la continuité spatiale entre l'intérieur et l'extérieur est maintenue. Ce concept spatial apportera liberté et richesse à l'architecture, qui bénéficiera de l'énergie naturelle montant de la terre pour la transformer en un ordre architectural. »

The high, light arched openings of the building are irregular in width, which animates the façades.

Die hohen gebogenen Öffnungen haben unterschiedliche Breite und bringen so Bewegung in die Fassade.

Les grandes ouvertures légèrement arquées sont de largeurs variées, ce qui anime les façades.

The high arches of the interior echo the window openings, and curves also dominate the library.

Die hohen Bögen im Gebäudeinneren nehmen die Form der Fensteröffnungen auf, und auch die Bibliothek wird von Rundungen dominiert.

Les grands arcs intérieurs rappellent les ouvertures. Les lignes courbes dominent également la bibliothèque.

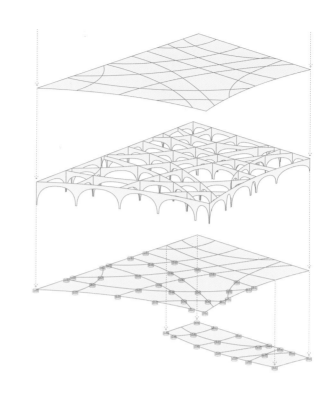

The tree-like design contrasts with the very smooth, flat façade detail seen above.

Die baumartige Konstruktion bildet einen Kontrast zu dem oben abgebildeten, ausgesprochen glatten, flachen Fassadenausschnitt.

La composition en arborescence contraste avec le détail de façade lisse et plate (ci-dessus).

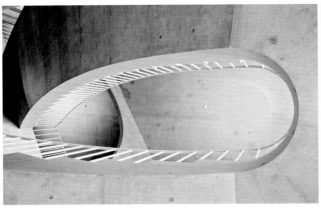

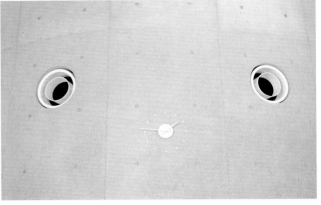

The irregular openings in the building give it an organic appearance that corresponds to Toyo Ito's long-held view that it is the task of architects to create a new, "artificial" nature.

Durch die unregelmäßigen Öffnungen erhält das Gebäude ein organisches Aussehen, das Toyo Itos seit langem vertretenen Anspruch entspricht, Architekten müssten eine neue „künstliche" Natur erschaffen.

Les ouvertures irrégulières confèrent au bâtiment une apparence organique, qui correspond à l'idée défendue par Toyo Ito selon laquelle la tâche des architectes est de créer une nouvelle nature « artificielle ».

Interior spaces are airy and light, conducive to study. The architect was, of course, involved in the interior design and the choice of book shelves and furniture.

Die hellen, freundlichen Innenräume sind bestens zum Lernen geeignet. Auch an der Interieurgestaltung bis hin zur Auswahl der Bücherregale und der Möbel war der Architekt natürlich beteiligt.

Aérés et légers, les espaces intérieurs incitent à l'étude. L'architecte a bien sûr participé aux aménagements intérieurs et au choix des rayonnages et du mobilier.

JAKOB+MACFARLANE

Jakob+MacFarlane SARL d'Architecture
13-15 rue des Petites Écuries
75010 Paris
France

Tel: +33 1 44 79 05 72
Fax: +33 1 48 00 97 93
E-mail: info@jakobmacfarlane.com
Web: www.jakobmacfarlane.com

DOMINIQUE JAKOB was born in 1966 and holds a degree in Art History from the Université de Paris I (1990) and a degree in Architecture from the École d'Architecture Paris-Villemin (1991). She has taught at the École Spéciale d'Architecture (1998–99) and at the École d'Architecture Paris-Villemin (1994–2000). Born in New Zealand in 1961, **BRENDAN MACFARLANE** received his B.Arch at SCI-Arc (1984), and his M.Arch degree at the Harvard GSD (1990). He has taught at the Paris La Villette architecture school (1995–96), at the Bartlett School of Architecture in London (1996–98), at the École Spéciale d'Architecture in Paris (1998–99), and more recently at Havard (2007). From 1995 to 1997, MacFarlane was an architecture critic at the Architectural Association (AA) in London. Both Jakob and MacFarlane started their careers in the office of Morphosis in Santa Monica. They founded their own agency in 1992 in Paris and were also co-founders with Emanuelle Marin-Trottin and David Trottin of Periphériques (1996–98). Their main projects include the T House (La-Garenne-Colombes, 1994, 1998); the Georges Restaurant (Centre Georges Pompidou, Paris, 1999–2000); the restructuring of the Maxime Gorki Theater (Petit-Quevilly, 1999–2000); and the Renault International Communication Center (Boulogne, 2004), all in France. They are currently working on the FRAC Centre (Orléans); the Herold housing complex in Paris; the transformation of Parisian docks into a center and school of fashion (2007–08, published here); and another dock project, the Docks Quai Rimbaud (Lyon), all in France.

DOMINIQUE JAKOB, geboren 1966 in Paris, schloss 1990 ihr Kunstgeschichtsstudium an der Université de Paris 1 ab und erwarb 1991 ihr Architekturdiplom an der École d'Architecture Paris-Villemin. Von 1998 bis 1999 lehrte sie an der École Spéciale d'Architecture und von 1994 bis 2000 an der École d'Architecture Paris-Villemin. **BRENDAN MACFARLANE** wurde 1961 in Neuseeland geboren. 1984 erlangte er seinen Bachelor of Architecture am Southern California Institute óf Architecture, 1990 folgte der Master of Architecture an der Harvard Graduate School of Design. MacFarlane war Dozent an der École Nationale Supérieure d'Architecture de Paris-La Villette (1995–96), an der Bartlett School of Architecture in London (1996–98), an der Pariser École Spéciale d'Architecture (1998–99) und in Harvard (2007). Von 1995 bis 1997 war MacFarlane als Architekturkritiker für die Architectural Association in London tätig. Sowohl Jakob als auch MacFarlane begannen ihre Laufbahn bei Morphosis in Santa Monica. 1992 riefen sie ihr eigenes Büro in Paris ins Leben. Daneben gründeten sie gemeinsam mit Emanuelle Marin-Trottin und David Trottin den Verein Periphériques (1996–98). Zu ihren wichtigsten Projekten gehören – alle in Frankreich – die Maison T in La-Garenne-Colombes (1994, 1998), das Restaurant Georges im Pariser Centre Georges Pompidou (1999–2000), der Umbau des Maxim-Gorki-Theaters in Petit-Quevilly (1999–2000) und das Centre de Communication Renault in Paris-Boulogne (2004). Gegenwärtig arbeiten Jakob+MacFarlane am FRAC Centre in Orléans, der Wohnanlage Herold in Paris, der Umwandlung eines Pariser Lagerhauses an der Seine in die Cité de la Mode et du Design (2007–08, hier vorgestellt) sowie den Pavillons Quai Rimbaud in Lyon.

DOMINIQUE JAKOB, née en 1966, est diplômée d'histoire de l'art de l'université Paris I (1990) et d'architecture de l'école d'architecture Paris-Villemin (1991). Elle a enseigné à l'École spéciale d'architecture (1998–99) et à l'école d'architecture Paris-Villemin (1994–2000). Né en Nouvelle-Zélande en 1961, **BRENDAN MACFARLANE** est B. Arch. de SCI-Arc (1984), et M. Arch. de Harvard Graduate School of Design (1990). Il a enseigné à l'école d'architecture de Paris-La Villette (1995–96), à la Bartlett School of Architecture de Londres (1996–98), à l'École spéciale d'architecture à Paris (1998–99) et plus récemment à Harvard (2007). De 1995 à 1997, il a été critique de projets à l'Architectural Association de Londres. Tous deux ont débuté leur carrière chez Morphosis à Santa Monica. Ils ont fondé leur agence à Paris en 1992 et ont aussi été cofondateurs avec Emanuelle Marin-Trottin et David Trottin de l'agence Périphériques (1996–98). Parmi leurs principaux projets : la maison T (La-Garenne-Colombes, France, 1994, 1998) ; le restaurant Georges (Centre Georges-Pompidou, Paris, 1999–2000) ; la restructuration du théâtre Maxime-Gorki (Petit-Quevilly, France, 1999–2000) et le centre international de communication de Renault (Boulogne, France, 2004). Ils travaillent actuellement sur le FRAC Centre d'Orléans ; l'ensemble de logements Herold à Paris ; la transformation d'un dock au bord de la Seine à Paris en Cité de la mode et du design (2007–08, publié ici) et des docks du quai Rimbaud à Lyon.

CITY OF FASHION AND DESIGN

Paris, France, 2007–08

Floor area: 14 500 m². Client: ICADE (Caisse des Dépôts et des Consignations).
Cost: not disclosed

Located on the quai d'Austerlitz in the 13th arrondissement of Paris, opposite the Gare de Lyon and the Ministry of Finance at Bercy, this project aims to transform a 1907 industrial warehouse building made of concrete into a state-of-the-art showplace of fashion and design. Using a new lightweight glass-construction system called "plug-over," the architects sought to modernize the building with forms inspired by the Seine River and its walkways. The program is a mix centered on the themes of design and fashion, including exhibition spaces, a French fashion institute, music producers, bookshops, cafés, and a restaurant. A panoramic rooftop terrace and a purpose-designed exterior lighting system ensure that the new facility attracts attention at night as well as during the day. This project is part of the willful development of the areas (Seine Rive Gauche) around the French National Library, designed some years ago by Dominique Perrault. After their very visible Georges Restaurant on top of the Centre Pompidou, Dominique Jakob and Brendan MacFarlane have now made their imprint on Paris in an even more surprising way with this snaking green landmark of a building.

Am Quai d'Austerlitz im 13. Pariser Arrondissement, gegenüber dem Gare de Lyon und dem Finanzministerium Bercy, verwandeln Jakob+MacFarlane ein altes Lagerhaus, einen Betonbau aus dem Jahr 1907, in ein hypermodernes Forum für Mode und Design. Mithilfe eines neuartigen, „plug-over" genannten leichten Konstruktionssystems verleihen die Architekten dem Gebäude ein modernes, von der Seine und ihren Uferwegen inspiriertes gläsernes Äußeres. Der gesamte Komplex wird sich künftig um das Thema Mode und Design drehen und das Institut Français de la Mode, Musikstudios, Buchläden, Cafés und ein Restaurant beherbergen. Eine Panoramaterrasse auf dem Dach und eine speziell entwickelte Außenbeleuchtung machen die neue Institution tags wie nachts zu einem Anziehungspunkt. Das Projekt ist Teil der ehrgeizigen Entwicklungspläne für die Rive Gauche, der Gegend rund um die in den 1990er-Jahren nach den Plänen von Dominique Perrault entstandenen Bibliothèque Nationale de France. Ist schon Jakob+MacFarlanes Restaurant Georges auf dem Dach des Centre Pompidou eine weithin sichtbare Attraktion, bereichert das Duo die französische Kapitale nun mit ihrem froschgrünen Modeforum um eine noch auffälligere Landmarke.

Situé quai d'Austerlitz dans le XIIIᵉ arrondissement de Paris, face à la gare de Lyon et au ministère des finances de Bercy, ce projet consiste en la transformation d'entrepôts industriels en béton datant de 1907 en lieu d'avant-garde consacré à la mode et au design. Mettant en œuvre un nouveau système de construction légère en verre appelé « plug-over », les architectes ont souhaité moderniser le bâtiment par des formes inspirées de la Seine et de ses berges. Ce programme multiple est centré sur les thèmes du design et de la mode et comprend des espaces d'expositions, l'Institut français de la mode, des bureaux de producteurs de musique, des librairies, des cafés et un restaurant. Une terrasse supérieure panoramique et un système d'éclairage extérieur attireront l'attention aussi bien de jour que de nuit. Ce projet fait partie du plan de rénovation de la rive gauche dans le quartier de la Bibliothèque nationale de France conçue il y a quelques années par Dominique Perrault. Après la réalisation de leur très spectaculaire restaurant, le Georges, au sommet du Centre Pompidou, Dominique Jakob et Brendan MacFarlane, à travers cette longiligne forme serpentine de couleur vert acide, posent leur marque sur Paris de manière encore plus surprenante.

Sitting on the Seine River, opposite the Gare de Lyon, the new City of Fashion and Design stands out boldly from neighboring architecture.

Die Cité de la Mode et du Design, direkt an der Seine und gegenüber dem Gare de Lyon, setzt sich kühn von der umliegenden Architektur ab.

Au bord de la Seine, face à la gare de Lyon, la nouvelle Cité de la mode et du design se démarque audacieusement des architectures voisines.

The wood-decked roof of the Center offers spectacular views of the river and city, while also providing the location of a new Apple Store. Ramps run along the river-side façade.

Das holzgedeckte Dach des Zentrums bietet eine spektakuläre Aussicht auf Fluss und Stadt und fungiert zugleich als Location für einen neuen Apple Store. Auf der flussseitigen Fassade verlaufen Rampen.

Les terrasses en bois de la Cité offrent des vues spectaculaires sur la Seine et la ville. On y trouvera un Apple Store. Des rampes courent le long de la façade côté fleuve.

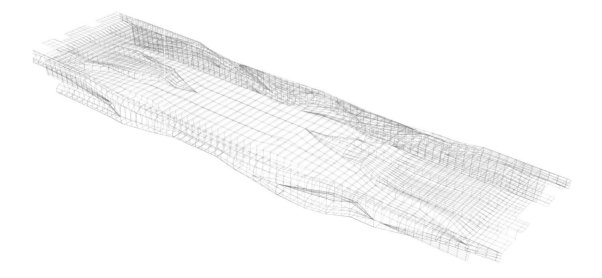

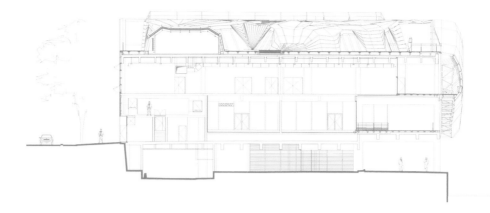

A cross-section of the old warehouse shows that the architects have essentially reused the existing space, while adding the snaking green-metal ramps to its Seine-side façade.

Ein Querschnitt des alten Lagerhauses zeigt, dass die Architekten den vorhandenen Raum in ihre Planung mit einbezogen und zusätzlich grüne Metallaufgänge an der Fassade auf der Seineseite emporschlängeln ließen.

Une coupe des anciens entrepôts montre que les architectes ont essentiellement réutilisé des volumes existants et ajouté les rampes de métal laqué vert qui serpentent sur les façades côté Seine.

JENSEN & SKODVIN ARKITEKTKONTOR

Jensen & Skodvin Arkitektkontor AS
Fredensborgveien 11
0177 Oslo
Norway

Tel: +47 22 99 48 99
Fax: +47 22 99 48 88
E-mail: office@jsa.no
Web: www.jsa.no

JENSEN & SKODVIN ARKITEKTKONTOR was established in 1995 by Jan Olav Jensen and Børre Skodvin. The firm currently has nine architects. Born in 1959, Olav Jensen received his degree from the Oslo School of Architecture in 1985. He has been a Professor at the Oslo School of Design and Architecture since 2004. He was the Kenzo Tange Visiting Critic at Harvard University (1998) and won a 1998 Aga Khan Award for Architecture for the Lepers' Hospital, in Chopda Taluka, India. Børre Skodvin was born in 1960 and received his degree from the Oslo School of Architecture in 1988. He has been a teacher at the Oslo School of Design and Architecture since 1998. They built the Storo Metro Station (Oslo, 2003); the Headquarters and Exhibition Space for the Norwegian Design Council (Oslo, 2004); the Sinsen Metro Station (Oslo, 2005); a Multipurpose City Block (Oslo, 2005); the Tautra Maria Convent (Tautra Island, 2004–06, published here); and the Thermal Bath, Therapy Center and Hotel (Bad Gleichenberg, Austria, 2005–07). Recently, they have worked on the Gudbrandsjuvet tourist project: viewing platforms and bridges (Gudbrandsjuvet, 2008); a Service Center and Landscape Hotel at the same location (2008); and the Giørtz Summer House (Valldal, 2008), all in Norway unless stated otherwise. Ongoing work includes a plan for a new town in south Oslo (2005–15).

JENSEN & SKODVIN ARKITEKTKONTOR wurde 1995 von Jan Olav Jensen und Børre Skodvin gegründet. Gegenwärtig gehören neun Architekten zu dem Büro. Olav Jensen, geboren 1959, machte 1985 seinen Abschluss an der Schule für Architektur in Oslo, an der er seit 2004 unterrichtet. 1998 hatte er die Kenzo-Tange-Gastprofessur an der Harvard University inne, im selben Jahr wurde er für sein Leprakrankenhaus im indischen Chopda Taluka mit einem Aga-Khan-Preis für Architektur ausgezeichnet. Der 1960 geborene Børre Skodvin schloss 1988 sein Studium an der Schule für Architektur in Oslo ab. Seit 1998 ist er dort Dozent. Zu ihren in Oslo realisierten Projekten gehören die Metrostation Storo (2003), das Norwegische Zentrum für Design und Architektur (2004), die Metrostation Sinsen (2005) und ein Mehr-zweckgebäude (2005). Auf der norwegischen Insel Tautra bauten sie das hier vorgestellte Marienkloster Tautra (2004–06) und im österreichischen Bad Gleichenberg ein Ensemble aus Therme, Kurhaus und Hotel (2005–07). In jüngster Vergangenheit entstanden in Norwegen die Aussichtsterrassen und Brücken für das Tourismusprojekt Gudbrandsjuvet samt Besucherzentrum und Hotel (2008) sowie das Sommerhaus Giørtz in Valldal (2008). Seit einiger Zeit sind Jensen & Skodvin zudem mit den Pla-nungen für einen neuen Stadtteil im Süden von Oslo (2005–15) beschäftigt.

L'agence **JENSEN & SKODVIN ARKITEKTKONTOR** a été fondée en 1995 par Jan Olav Jensen et Børre Skodvin. Elle emploie actuellement neuf architectes. Né in 1959, Olav Jensen est diplômé de l'école d'architecture d'Oslo (1985). Il y enseigne depuis 2004. Il a été le critique invité de Kenzo Tange à Harvard University (1998) et a remporté le Prix d'architecture Aga Khan 1998 pour un hôpital pour lépreux à Chopda Taluka (Inde). Børre Skodvin, né en 1960 est diplômé de l'école d'architectu-re d'Oslo (1988). Il y enseigne depuis 1998. Ils ont construit ensemble : la station de métro de Storo (Oslo, 2003) ; le siège et centre d'expositions du Conseil norvégien du design (Oslo, 2004) ; la station de métro de Sinsen (Oslo, 2005) ; un immeuble multifonction (Oslo, 2005) ; le couvent Maria de Tautra (Île de Tautra, 2004–06, publié ici) et un centre thermal et hôtel (Bad Gleichenberg, Autriche, 2005–07). Récemment, ils ont travaillé sur le projet touristique de Gudbrandsjuvet : plates-formes d'observation et ponts (Gudbrandsjuvet, 2008) ; un centre de services et un hôtel sur le même site (2008) ; la maison d'été Giørtz (Valldal, 2008), le plan d'une ville nouvelle au sud d'Oslo (2005–15), tous en Norvège.

TAUTRA MARIA CONVENT

Tautra Island, Norway, 2004–06

Floor area: 2000 m². Client: Cistercian nuns, Mississippi Abbey. Cost: € 6 million.
Project Architects: Jan Olav Jensen, Børre Skodvin, Siri Moseng, Torstein Koch, Kaja Poulsen,
Torunn Golberg, Martin Draleke, AnneLise Bjerkan. Landscape Architects: the nuns

This structure is situated on Tautra Island in the Trondheimsfjord, a 130-kilometer-long inlet of the Norwegian Sea, in the central west part of the country. It is a new monastery for 18 Cistercian nuns, including a small church and the production facilities required for the nuns to make a living. Only ruins remained of a Cistercian monastery founded on the island 800 years ago. "One of our first ideas," say the architects, "was to create a low building with a series of gardens, giving light and creating a sense of privacy and exclusion, while at the same time opening up for some of the spectacular views across the fjord, as, for instance, in the refectory (the dining hall), where the nuns all sit at the same side of the table, like in Da Vinci's *Last Supper*, looking silently through the glass wall toward the sea and the mountains on the other side." By analyzing the daily routine of the nuns, the architects were able to eliminate approximately 30 percent of the original program, most notably by removing corridors. The final plan consists of a system of different-sized rooms connected in the corners and with seven gardens between them. The architects conclude, "The nuns have been very active clients and have planned the landscaping and fencing around the convent and inside the seven gardens themselves, with the help of professionals from the local congregation."

Das Marienkloster Tautra befindet sich auf der gleichnamigen Insel im 130 km langen Trondheimsfjord in Mittelnorwegen. Die neue Anlage wird von 18 Zisterzienserinnen genutzt und umfasst eine kleine Kirche sowie eine Reihe von Werkstätten, in denen die Schwestern ihren Lebensunterhalt besorgen. Von dem vor 800 Jahren auf der Insel gegründeten Zisterzienserkloster sind heute nur noch Ruinen vorhanden. „Gleich zu Anfang hatten wir die Idee", so die Architekten, „ein niedriges Gebäude mit einer Reihe von Gärten zu entwerfen, das einen Charakter von Intimität und Abgeschiedenheit haben, aber zugleich von verschiedenen Punkten aus eine spektakuläre Aussicht über den Fjord eröffnen sollte, etwa vom Refektorium (dem Speisesaal) aus. Bei den Mahlzeiten sitzen die Nonnen nebeneinander an einer Seite der Tafel, wie in Leonardo da Vincis ‚Letztem Abendmahl', und können durch die Glaswand still auf das Wasser und die sich auf der anderen Seite erhebenden Berge hinausschauen." Indem sich die Architekten ein genaues Bild vom Tagesablauf der Schwestern machten, konnten sie die ursprünglichen Planungen um ein knappes Drittel straffen, vor allem durch das Weglassen der Flure. Der endgültige Entwurf besteht aus einem System von verschieden großen und an ihren Ecken miteinander verbundenen Räumen, zwischen denen sieben Gärten angelegt sind. Die Architekten vergessen nicht darauf hinzuweisen, dass ihre „Auftraggeberinnen sich intensiv an den Planungen beteiligt haben. Unterstützt von professionellen Kräften aus der Gemeinde, übernahmen die Schwestern die Gestaltung der Gärten und des Außenbereichs und entwarfen die Umzäunung des Klosters."

Ce bâtiment se trouve sur l'île de Tautra dans le fjord de Trondheim (130 km de long), au centre de sa côte ouest. Il s'agit d'un nouveau monastère conçu pour 18 sœurs cisterciennes comprenant une petite église et les équipements nécessaires à une existence en partie autarcique. Il ne restait sur le site que les ruines d'un monastère cistercien fondé 80 ans plus tôt. «Une de nos premières idées, expliquent les architectes, a été de créer un bâtiment bas et une succession de jardins pour apporter de la lumière et donner un sentiment d'intimité et de vie à l'écart, tout en prévoyant des perspectives spectaculaires sur le fjord, comme, par exemple, dans le réfectoire. Les religieuses sont toutes assises du même côté de la table, comme dans la *Cène* de Vinci, et regardent en silence à travers le mur de verre la mer et les montagnes. » En analysant le rituel quotidien des nones, les architectes ont pu éliminer environ 30 % du programme initial, en particulier en supprimant des couloirs. Le plan définitif se compose d'un système de salles de dimensions diverses réunies par leurs angles et séparées par sept jardins. «Les sœurs ont été des clientes très actives et se sont chargées des jardins et des barrières autour du couvent et dans les jardins avec l'aide d'artisans de la communauté locale. »

The Convent benefits from an exceptional natural setting. Its somewhat irregular appearance allows it to blend in with its environment, while providing a modern home and place of contemplation and worship.

Das Kloster liegt inmitten einer außerordentlichen Naturkulisse. Dank seiner irgendwie „ungeordneten" Erscheinung fügt es sich ganz in die Landschaft ein und erweist sich zugleich als moderne Lebensstätte und Ort der Andacht.

Le couvent bénéficie d'un cadre naturel exceptionnel. Son plan, légèrement irrégulier, lui permet de se fondre dans son environnement, tout en remplissant ses fonctions liturgiques et de logement modernes.

A light, glazed wooden design permits of nature and the inner courtyards. Though largely rectilinear, the architecture achieves an "organic" presence in this location.

Durch die Verglasung der hellen Holzkonstruktion kann man in die Innenhöfe und die Natur hinausblicken. Obgleich fast vollständig rechtwinklig angelegt, besitzt die Architektur eine passende „organische" Anmutung.

La construction légère en bois offre des vues sur la nature et les cours intérieures. Bien qu'en grande partie rectiligne, l'architecture n'en évoque pas moins une présence organique.

Above, the dining area of the nuns enables them to sit side by side, looking out at the natural setting. This communion with nature is visible elsewhere in the Convent as well.

Im Speiseraum sitzen die Schwestern nebeneinander und schauen von der Tafel hinaus in die Natur. Auch an anderen Stellen des Klosters wurde auf die Gemeinschaft mit der Natur Wert gelegt.

Ci-dessus, le réfectoire des nonnes. Elles sont assises côte à côte, face au paysage. Cette communion avec la nature est également visible dans d'autres parties du couvent.

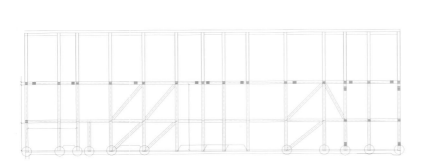

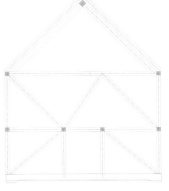

The largest open space within the Convent is this 200-square-meter chapel with its webbed wooden roof, open to natural light.

Der größte offene Raum des Klosters ist die 200 m² große Kapelle mit ihrem vielfach verstrebten Holzdach, durch das natürliches Licht herein-fällt.

Le plus vaste espace ouvert du couvent est cette chapelle de 200 m² à la charpente complexe, mais ouverte sur le ciel.

CARLOS JIMENEZ

Carlos Jimenez Studio
1116 Willard Street
Houston, TX 77006
USA

Tel: +1 713 520 7248
Fax: +1 713 520 1186
E-mail: office@carlosjimenezstudio.com
Web: www.carlosjimenezstudio.com

CARLOS JIMENEZ was born in San José, Costa Rica, in 1959 and moved to the United States in 1974. He graduated from the University of Houston's School of Architecture in 1981, and established his own office in Houston in 1982. He has served as a Visiting Professor at Rice University, Texas A&M University, SCI-Arc, UCLA, the University of Texas at Arlington, the University of Navarra (Pamplona, Spain), Harvard GSD, Tulane University, UC Berkeley, and at the University of Oregon. He is a tenured Professor at Rice University School of Architecture (2000). He served as a jury member of the Pritzker Architecture Prize (2000–08). His projects include the Jimenez Studio (Houston, Texas, 1983–2007); the Houston Fine Art Press (Houston, Texas, 1985–87); the Central Administration and Junior School, Museum of Fine Arts Houston (Houston, Texas, 1991–94); the Jimenez House (Houston, Texas, 1994–2007); the Spencer Art Studio Building, Williams College (Williamstown, Massachusetts, 1994); the Peeler Art Center, Depauw University (Greencastle, Indiana, 1997–2002); the Whatley Library (Austin, Texas, 1999–2002); the Crowley House (Marfa, Texas, 2000–04); the Rice University Library Service Center (2002–05) and Data Center (Houston, Texas, 2006–07, both published here); the Tyler School of Art, Temple University (Philadelphia, Pennsylvania, 2004–08); and the Evry Housing Tower (Evry, France, 2006–09).

CARLOS JIMENEZ wurde 1959 in San José, Costa Rica, geboren. 1974 ging er in die Vereinigten Staaten, wo er 1981 seinen Abschluss an der School of Architecture der University of Houston machte. Im darauffolgenden Jahr gründete er sein eigenes Büro in Houston. Jimenez unterrichtete als Gastprofessor an der Rice University, der A&M University Texas, am Southern California Institute of Architecture, an der University of California in Los Angeles, der University of Texas in Arlington, der Graduate School of Design in Harvard, der Tulane University, der University of California in Berkeley, der University of Oregon sowie in Spanien an der Universidad de Navarra in Pamplona. Seit 2000 ist er Lehrstuhlinhaber an der School of Architecture der Rice University. Von 2000 bis 2008 war Jimenez Mitglied der Vergabejury für den Pritzker-Preis. Zu seinen Projekten gehören sein eigenes Büro (1983–2007), die Fine Art Press (1985–87), die Junior School und die Zentralverwaltung des Museum of Fine Arts (1991–94) sowie sein eigenes Wohnhaus (1994–2007), alle in Houston, Texas. Ferner entwarf er das Spencer Art Studio Building des Williams College (Williamstown, Massachusetts, 1994), das Peeler Art Center der Depauw University (Greencastle, Indiana, 1997–2002), die Whatley Library (Austin, Texas, 1999–2002), das Crowley House (Marfa, Texas, 2000–04), das Servicezentrum der Bibliothek (2002–05) und das Datenzentrum der Rice University (Houston, Texas, 2006–07), beide hier vorgestellt, sowie die Tyler School of Art der Temple University (Philadelphia, Pennsylvania, 2004–08) und ein Wohnhochhaus im französischen Evry (2006–09).

CARLOS JIMENEZ, né en 1959 à San José, Costa Rica, est arrivé aux États-Unis en 1974. Diplômé de l'école d'architecture de la Houston University en 1981, il crée son agence dans cette même ville en 1982. Il a été professeur invité à Rice University, Texas A&M University, SCI-Arc, UCLA, Texas University à Arlington, l'université de Navarre (Pamplona, Espagne), Harvard Graduate School of Design, Tulane University, UC Berkeley, et Oregon University. Il est professeur titulaire à la Rice University School of Architecture (2000). Il a été membre du jury du Pritzker Prize (2000–08). Parmi ses projets : le Studio Jimenez (Houston, Texas, 1983–2007) ; la Houston Fine Art Press (Houston, Texas, 1985–87) ; la Central Administration and Junior School, Museum of Fine Arts, Houston (Texas, 1991–94) ; la maison Jimenez (Houston, Texas, 1994–2007) ; le Spencer Art Studio Building, Williams College (Williamstown, Massachusetts, 1994) ; le Peeler Art Center, université Depauw (Greencastle, Indiana, 1997–2002) ; la Bibliothèque Whatley (Austin, Texas, 1999–2002) ; la maison Crowley (Marfa, Texas, 2000–04) ; le Rice University Library Service Center (2002–05) et le Data Center (Houston, Texas, 2006–07), tous deux publiés ici ; la Tyler School of Art, Temple University (Philadelphie, Pennsylvanie, 2004–08) et une tour de logements à Évry (France, 2006–09).

RICE LIBRARY SERVICE CENTER (2002–05)
RICE DATA CENTER (2006–07)

Rice University South Campus Master Plan, Houston, Texas, USA

Floor area: 1700 m² (Library Service Center); 2359 m² (Data Center).
Client: Rice University. Cost: not disclosed. Associate Architects: Kendall Heaton, PGAL Architects

A 13-hectare trapezoidal site, located eight kilometers south of Rice University's main complex, was planned as a campus annex catering primarily to storage needs and non-academic programs for the university. One half of this plan includes storage buildings and parking areas. The Rice Library Service Center (RLSC) is located here and was the first structure built on the property. The second building added to the site was the Rice Data Center (RDC). Carlos Jimenez designed both of these structures. He explains, "The RLSC is a high-density book-storage facility with an anticipated capacity of 1.75 to 2.0 million volumes. Its key purpose is to serve Fondren Library—Rice University's central library. The off-site book depository improves and expands Fondren Library by providing ample storage and newer, more efficient filing and archiving systems." The RLSC consists of two distinct parts: a two-story office and processing area and a three-story open volume with the book-storage vault containing rows of modular shelving. The vault has a carefully controlled environment for storing rarely used or fragile materials. The RDC is a warehouse that consolidates all of Rice's data needs in one facility. Both buildings feature a tilt-up concrete wall system, in part because of their required opacity. They are both painted in bright fluorescent greens.

Ausgangspunkt für diese Projekt war ein 13 ha großes, trapezförmiges Grundstück, das 8 km südlich des Hauptkomplexes der Rice University entfernt als Campuserweiterung zur Materiallagerung und für andere nichtakademische Aufgaben der Universität dienen sollte. Die ersten Bauten auf dem Grundstück, das zur Hälfte Lagergebäude und Parkflächen aufnehmen sollte, waren das Servicezentrum der Bibliothek (Rice Library Service Center – RLSC) und das Datenzentrum (Rice Data Center – RDC) nach den Entwürfen von Carlos Jimenez. „Beim RLSC", erläutert der Architekt, „handelt es sich um ein Buchmagazin mit der außerordentlichen Aufnahmekapazität von 1,75 bis 2 Millionen Bänden, das vor allem die Fondren Library, die zentrale Universitätsbibliothek, entlasten soll. Das Außenmagazin mit seinen umfassenden Lagermöglichkeiten stellt nicht nur eine Erweiterung, sondern dank neuer, effizienterer Archivierungs- und Verwaltungssysteme auch eine Verbesserung der Fondren Library dar." Das RLSC besteht aus zwei unterschiedlichen Teilen: einem zweigeschossigen Büro- und EDV-Bereich sowie einem dreigeschossigen Gebäudeabschnitt, in dem sich das mit Modulregalen ausgestattete Magazin befindet. Damit es sich auch für selten genutzte oder empfindliche Dokumente eignet, ist das Magazin sorgfältig klimatisiert. Das RDC ist ein Lagergebäude, in dem das gesamte von der Universität benötigte Datenmaterial an einem einzigen Ort zusammengeführt wird. Beide Bauten wurden mit Fertigbetonwänden errichtet, auch um die nötige Abgeschlossenheit zu gewährleisten, und beide haben einen leuchtend grünen Anstrich erhalten.

Ce terrain trapézoïdal de 13 hectares situé à huit kilomètres au sud du complexe principal de Rice University est consacré aux programmes non académiques et aux entrepôts de l'université. La moitié de la surface est affectée à ces bâtiments d'entreposage et à des parkings. Le Rice Library Service Center (RLSC) a été la première construction édifiée, suivie du Rice Data Center (RDC). Carlos Jimenez, auteur de ces deux projets, explique : « Le RLSC est une installation de stockage de haute densité de livres dont la capacité prévue est de 1,75 à 2 millions de volumes. Sa fonction est complémentaire de celle de la Fondren Library, la bibliothèque centrale de Rice. Il améliore et développe Fondren en offrant de nouvelles capacités de stockage et des systèmes de classement et d'archivage plus efficaces. » Le RLSC est divisé en deux parties distinctes : un bâtiment de deux niveaux pour les bureaux et les opérations d'une part, un volume ouvert de trois niveaux pour le stockage des livres équipés de rayonnages modulaires d'autre part. L'atmosphère est soigneusement climatisée pour assurer une meilleure conservation des matériaux fragiles et des ouvrages peu utilisés. Le RDC est un entrepôt qui regroupe toutes les installations informatiques en un lieu unique. Les deux constructions font appel au même système de murs aveugles mis en place par relèvement, en partie parce qu'il assure la protection nécessaire de la lumière. Toutes deux sont peintes dans des couleurs de vert lumineux fluorescent.

The orthogonal lines of the buildings, rendered as simple as possible, are intended to stand out with their bright color.

Durch den leuchtenden Farbton stechen die orthogonalen Linien der so schlicht wie möglich gehaltenen Gebäude hervor.

Les lignes orthogonales des bâtiments, aussi simples que possible, se singularisent par leur couleur vive.

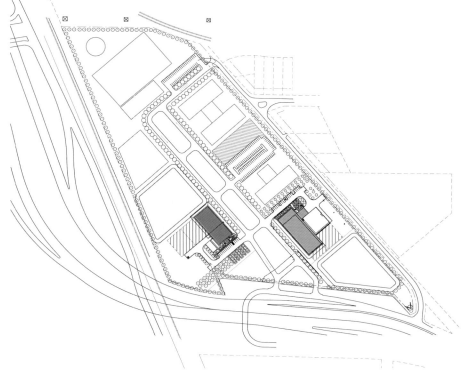

A site plan (left) shows the proximity of the buildings, both of which are visible in the image above.

Der Lageplan links zeigt die auch auf dem obigen Foto zu erkennende direkte Nachbarschaft der Gebäude.

Le plan à gauche, montre la proximité des bâtiments, tous deux visibles sur l'image ci-dessus.

Carlos Jimenez has implemented the program of these structures in a highly organized and rigorous manner, creating a strong modern presence where much more ordinary buildings might have been expected.

Aufgrund von Carlos Jimenez' wohlorganisierter, strenger Programmatik geben die Gebäude rundum ein überzeugendes modernes Bild ab, wo man sonst wohl weitaus gewöhnlichere Bauten erwartet.

Carlos Jimenez a exécuté ces deux constructions de façon organisée et rigoureuse. Elles confèrent une présence très contemporaine à des bâtiments qui auraient pu se contenter d'une approche plus banale.

KENGO KUMA

Kengo Kuma & Associates
2–24–8 BY-CUBE 2–4F Minamiaoyama
Minato-ku
Tokyo 107–0062
Japan

Tel: +81 3 3401 7721 / Fax: +81 3 3401 7778
E-mail: kuma@ba2.so-net.ne.jp / Web: www.kkaa.co.jp

Born in 1954 in Kanagawa, Japan, **KENGO KUMA** graduated in 1979 from the University of Tokyo with an M.Arch degree. In 1985–86, he received an Asian Cultural Council Fellowship Grant and was a Visiting Scholar at Columbia University. In 1987, he established the Spatial Design Studio, and in 1991 he created Kengo Kuma & Associates. His work includes the Gunma Toyota Car Show Room (Maebashi, 1989); the Maiton Resort Complex (Phuket, Thailand); Rustic, Office Building (Tokyo); Doric, Office Building (Tokyo); M2, Headquarters for Mazda New Design Team (Tokyo), all in 1991; the Kinjo Golf Club, Club House (Okayama, 1992); the Karuizawa Resort Hotel (Karuizawa, 1993); the Kiro-san Observatory (Ehime, 1994); the Atami Guest House, Guest House for Bandai Corp (Atami, 1992–95); the Japanese Pavilion for the Venice Biennale (Venice, Italy, 1995); the Tomioka Lakewood Golf Club House (Tomioka, 1993–96); and the Toyoma Noh-Theater (Miyagi, 1995–96), all in Japan unless stated otherwise. He has also completed the Stone Museum (Nasu, Tochigi, 2000); a Museum of Ando Hiroshige (Batou, Nasu-gun, Tochigi, 2000); the Great (Bamboo) Wall Guest House (Beijing, China, 2002); One Omotesando (Tokyo, 2003); LVMH Osaka (Osaka, 2004); the Nagasaki Prefecture Art Museum (Nagasaki, 2005); the Fukusaki Hanging Garden (Osaka, 2005); and the Zhongtai Box, Z58 Building (Shanghai, China, 2003–06), all in Japan unless stated otherwise. Recent work includes the Suntory Museum of Art (Tokyo Midtown, Minato-ku, Tokyo, 2004–07, published here); the Tobata C Block Project (Kitakyushu, Fukuoka, 2005–07); and the Steel House (Bunkyo-ku, Tokyo, 2005–07), all in Japan.

KENGO KUMA, geboren 1954 im japanischen Kanagawa, schloss 1979 sein Studium an der Universität Tokio mit dem Master of Architecture ab. Von 1985 bis 1986 besuchte er mit einem Stipendium des Asian Cultural Council als Gastwissenschaftler die Columbia University. 1987 gründete Kuma das Spatial Design Studio und 1991 das Büro Kengo Kuma & Associates in Tokio. Zu seinen Bauten gehören der Gunma Toyota Car Showroom in Maebashi, Japan (1989), die Ferienanlage Maiton in Phuket, Thailand, sowie die Bürogebäude Rustic und Doric und die M2 genannte Zentrale der Designabteilung von Mazda, letztere alle 1991 in Tokio fertiggestellt. Ferner entwarf er das Klubhaus des Kinjo Golf Club in Okayama (1992), das Ferienhotel Karuizawa (Karuizawa, 1993), das Observatorium Kiro-san in Ehime (1994), das Gästehaus für die Firma Bandai in Atami (1992–95), das Klubhaus des Lakewood Golf Club in Tomioka (1993–96) und das No-Theater Toyoma in Kome, Miyagi (1995–96), alle in Japan, sowie den japanischen Pavillon für die Biennale 1995 in Venedig. Außerdem stammen von Kengo Kuma das Steinmuseum in Nasu, Tochigi (2000), ein Museum für Ando Hiroshige in Batou, Nasu-gun, Tochigi (2000), das Gästehaus Great (Bamboo) Wall bei Peking (2002), die Büro- und Geschäftsgebäude One Omotesando in Tokio (2003), die Niederlassung von Moët Hennessy-Louis Vuitton in Osaka (2004), das Kunstmuseum der japanischen Präfektur Nagasaki (2005), die Hängenden Gärten von Fukusaki in Osaka (2005) und das Zhongtai-Gebäude Z58 in Shanghai, China (2003–06). In jüngster Zeit entstanden das hier vorgestellte Suntory-Kunstmuseum in Minato-ku, Tokio (2004–07), das Projekt Tobata C Block in Kitakyushu, Fukuoka (2005–07), und das Stahlhaus in Bunkyo-ku, Tokio (2005–07).

Né en 1954 à Kanagawa, Japon, **KENGO KUMA** est diplômé M. Arch de l'université de Tokyo (1979). En 1985–86, il bénéficie d'une bourse de l'Asian Cultural Council et devient chercheur invité à Columbia University. En 1987, il crée le studio Spatial Design, et en 1991, Kengo Kuma & Associates. Parmi ses réalisations : le Car Show Room Toyota de Gunma (Maebashi, Japon, 1989) ; le Maiton Resort Complex (Phuket, Thaïlande, 1991) ; l'immeuble de bureaux Rustic (Tokyo, 1991) ; l'immeuble de bureaux Doric (Tokyo, 1991) ; M2, siège du département de design de Mazda (Tokyo, 1991) ; le club house du Kinjo Golf Club (Okayama, 1992) ; le Karuizawa Resort Hotel (Karuizawa, 1993) ; l'observatoire Kiro-san (Ehime, 1994) ; l'Atami Guest House pour Bandaï Corp (Atami, 1992–95) ; le pavillon japonais pour la Biennale de Venise (1995) ; le club house du Tomioka Lakewood Golf Club (Tomioka, 1993–96) et le théâtre Nô Toyoma (Miyagi, 1995–96). Il a également réalisé le musée de la Pierre (Nasu, Togishi, 2000) ; un musée consacré à Ando Hiroshige (Batou, Nasu-gun, Tochigi, 2000) ; la Great (Bamboo) Wall Guest House (Pékin, Chine, 2002) ; l'immeuble One Omotesando (Tokyo, 2003) ; l'immeuble LVMH Osaka (2004) ; le musée d'Art de la préfecture de Nagasaki (2005) ; le jardin suspendu de Fukusaki (Osaka, 2005) et la Zhongtai Box, immeuble Z58 (Shanghaï, Chine, 2003–06). Plus récemment se sont ajoutés le musée d'Art Suntory (Tokyo Midtown, Minato-ku, Tokyo, 2004–07, publié ici), le projet Tobata C Block (Kitakyushu, Fukuoka, 2005–07) et la Steel House (Bunkyo-ku, Tokyo, 2005–07).

SUNTORY MUSEUM OF ART

Minato-ku, Tokyo, Japan, 2004–07

Floor area: 4663 m².
Client: Suntory Limited, RP, Special Purpose Company, and nine other companies.
Cost: not disclosed. Architects: Kengo Kuma & Associates: Kengo Kuma, Toshio Yada, Eishi Sakamoto.
Nikken Sekkei Ltd.: Masashi Tatsumi, Makoto Ochiai, Fujio Kawazoe, Daisuke Shirai

Like Tadao Ando's 21_21 Design Sight (page 78), this project is part of the 10-hectare Tokyo Midtown development, near the Roppongi district in Tokyo, developed by Nikken Sekkei on the site of the former Self-Defense Agency of Japan in Tokyo Midtown. Kengo Kuma explains that this museum was designed like a Japanese-style room in the city. He says, "A 'Japanese-style room' is a comfortable space where people are able to relax on tatami mats that are laid on the floor, and, among the Japanese traditions, is the most relaxing and relieving environment. In the background lies the phenomenon of the transforming of the city indoors. Communication and transportation technology have destroyed the distance that had existed among objects, and have transfigured the entire city into a massive 'indoor' house." Visitors enter the six-story building, with its top three floors devoted to the Suntory Museum, from the shopping mall of the Tokyo Midtown complex. It is clad on the exterior with vertical, white ceramic louver panels. Reinforcing the ceramic panels with aluminum extrusions, the architect succeeded in giving them very fine edges. Wooden floors are made from recycled Suntory whisky barrels, while slatted screens made of paulownia wood based on the traditional Japanese *muso-koshi* soften the light and view of the greenery in the neighboring park.

Wie Tadao Andos 21_21 Design Sight (S. 78) ist Kengo Kumas Suntory-Kunstmuseum Teil des 10 ha großen Tokyo-Midtown-Areals unweit des Tokioter Bezirks Roppongi, das von dem Architekturbüro Nikken Sekkei auf dem Gelände der ehemaligen japanischen Verteidigungsbehörde entwickelt wird. Zum Konzept seines Museumsbaus erklärt Kengo Kuma, dass er einem Raum im klassischen japanischen Stil ähneln sollte, der sich mitten in der Stadt befindet. „Ein solcher Raum", so Kuma, „ist ein bequemer Ort, an dem die Menschen sich auf den ausgelegten Tatami-Matten entspannen können – von allen japanischen Traditionen diejenige, bei der man am besten zur Ruhe kommt und sich sammeln kann. Dahinter steht das Phänomen, dass die Stadt immer mehr ins Innere der Häuser dringt. Kommunikations- und Transporttechnologien haben die Distanz zerstört, die früher zwischen den Dingen herrschte, und die ganze Stadt zu einem einzigen ‚Hausinneren' gemacht." Für Besucher ist das sechsgeschossige Gebäude, dessen obere drei Etagen dem Museum gewidmet sind, vom Einkaufszentrum des Tokyo-Midtown-Komplexes aus zu betreten. Die Außenseite des Gebäudes ist mit vertikalen Lamellen aus weißer Keramik verkleidet, die der Architekt mithilfe stranggepresster Aluminiumverstärkungen äußerst schmal gestalten konnte. Für die Holzböden wurden recycelte Suntory-Whiskeyfässer verwendet, die Blendleisten aus Paulownienholz nach Art des traditionellen japanischen „muso-koshi" dämpfen das Licht und legen sich vor die Aussicht auf das Grün des benachbarten Parks.

Comme le 21_21 Design Sight de Tadao Ando (page 78), ce projet fait partie de l'opération de rénovation urbaine de Tokyo Midtown occupant dix hectares près du quartier de Roppongi, développé par Likken Sekkei sur le site de l'ancienne Agence japonaise de défense située en plein centre de la capitale. Kengo Kuma explique que le concept de ce musée était celui d'une pièce d'esprit japonais en pleine ville : « Une pièce d'esprit japonais est un espace confortable où l'on peut se détendre sur des tatamis posés au sol et, parmi toutes les traditions japonaises, c'est certainement l'environnement le plus reposant. En arrière-plan, figure le phénomène de la transformation de la ville. Les technologies de communication et de transport ont détruit les distances qui existaient entre les objets et ont transfiguré la ville entière en une énorme maison »intérieure« . » Les visiteurs entrent dans cet immeuble de six niveaux, dont les trois derniers sont consacrés au musée lui-même, par le centre commercial du complexe de Tokyo Midtown. Le bâtiment est habillé à l'extérieur de persiennes verticales en céramique blanche renforcées d'extrusions d'aluminium auxquelles l'architecte a réussi à donner des rebords extrêmement fins. Les sols en bois sont faits de douves de barriques de whisky Suntory recyclées, tandis que des écrans en paulownia inspirés des *muso-koshi* traditionnels japonais adoucissent l'éclairage naturel et filtrent la vue sur la verdure du parc avoisinant.

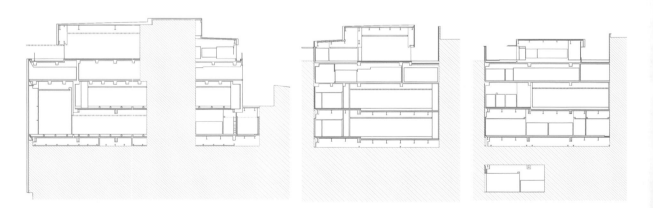

A part of the much larger Tokyo Midtown complex, the Suntory Museum of Art stands apart with its elegant vertical strip façade.

Das Suntory Museum unterscheidet sich von den übrigen Bauten des Tokyo-Midtown-Komplexes durch seine elegante Lamellenfassade.

Appartenant au vaste complexe de Tokyo Midtown, le musée d'Art Suntory se distingue par son élégante façade à bandes verticales.

Kengo Kuma masters the creation of
interior spaces and interior volumes
that correspond to a certain Japanese tradition of lightness and light,
while remaining fully modern in the
most international sense of the term.

Kengo Kuma gelingt es, seine Innenräume und -bereiche in die Nachfolge
bestimmter japanischer Traditionen
zu stellen, die sich mit Licht und
Leichtigkeit befassen, und sie gleichzeitig im international gebräuchlichen
Sinne des Begriffs hoch modern zu
gestalten.

Kengo Kuma maîtrise la création des
espaces et volumes intérieurs qui
correspondent à une certaine tradition de légèreté et de lumière, tout
en restant pleinement moderne au
sens le plus international du terme.

Exhibition areas contrast with the light public spaces and, indeed, with the white façade of the structure, creating intimate, warm volumes.

Die warmen, intimen Räume des Ausstellungsbereichs kontrastieren mit den hellen Besucherbereichen sowie mit der weißen Gebäudefassade.

Les zones d'expositions contrastent avec les espaces publics et la façade blanche du bâtiment, pour créer des espaces intimes et chaleureux.

The vertical bands used to shade
windows again recall Japanese tradition, albeit in a mode that creates no
impression of historicism or pastiche.

Die vertikalen Streifen, die die Fenster beschirmen, verweisen auf die
japanische Tradition, ohne dabei einen
Eindruck von Historismus oder Pastiche zu erwecken.

Les bandes verticales, utilisées pour
protéger l'intérieur du soleil, rappellent une tradition japonaise, mais
sans laisser la moindre impression
d'historicisme ou de pastiche.

LASSILA HIRVILAMMI ARCHITECTS

Lassila Hirvilammi Architects Ltd.
Hakalankatu 10 B
60100 Seinäjoki
Finland

Tel/Fax: +358 6 4141 225
E-mail: info@lh-ark.fi
Web: www.lh-ark.fi

LASSILA HIRVILAMMI was founded in Oulu, Finland, in 2001 as Lassila Mannberg Architects. In 2004, the office moved to Seinäjoki, a small town located in southern Ostrobothnia known for the Library, Lakeuden Risti Church, and Central Administrative buildings designed by Alvar Aalto. The office works on a variety of different projects, including churches, office buildings, housing, private residences, interior design, and renovations. The principal is Anssi Lassila, born in 1973; Teemu Hirvilammi was born in 1974. Their work includes the Kärsämäki Church (Kärsämäki, 1999–2004, published here) and the Klaukkala Church and Parish Center (Klaukkala, 2005). They are currently working on the Frami D-Block, a 7000-square-meter extension to the Seinäjoki Technology Center Frami (a joint venture with architects Lahdelma Mahlamäki Ltd., 2005–); the Maakunta-aukio housing and commercial building (Seinäjoki, 2005–); and the Kuokkala Church (a joint venture with Luonti Ltd., Jyväskylä, 2006–), all in Finland.

2001 gründete sich im finnischen Oulu das Architekturbüro Lassila Mannberg Architects, aus dem später **LASSILA HIRVILAMMI** hervorgegangen ist. 2004 zog das Büro nach Seinäjoki, einer kleinen Stadt im südlichen Ostbottnien, die durch ihre von Alvar Aalto entworfenen Gebäude – eine Bibliothek, die Kirche Lakeuden Risti und städtische Verwaltungsgebäude – bekannt geworden ist. Das Büro wird von Anssi Lassila, geboren 1973, geführt; Teemu Hirvilammi wurde 1974 geboren. Zusammen arbeiten sie an einer Vielzahl unterschiedlicher Projekte, darunter Kirchen, Bürogebäude, Wohnanlagen und Privathäuser sowie Innendesign und Renovierungen. Neben der hier vorgestellten neuen Kirche von Kärsämäki (1999–2004) gehören auch eine Kirche und das Gemeindezentrum in Klaukkula (2005) zu ihren Bauten. Derzeit arbeiten Lassila und Hirvilammi am Frami Block D, einer 7000 m² großen Erweiterung des Technologiezentrums Frami in Seinäjoki (in Zusammenarbeit mit dem Architekturbüro Lahdelma Mahlamäki Ltd., seit 2005), an dem Wohn- und Geschäftshaus Maakunta-aukio in Seinäjoki (seit 2005) und an der Kuokkala-Kirche in Jyväskylä (in Zusammenarbeit mit Luonti Ltd., 2006).

L'agence **LASSILA HIRVILAMMI** a été fondée en 2001 à Oulu, en Finlande, sous la dénomination initiale de Lassila Mannberg Architects. En 2004, elle s'est installée à Seinäjoki, petite ville du Sud de l'Ostrobothnie connue pour sa bibliothèque, l'église de Lakeuden Risti et les bâtiments de l'administration centrale conçus par Alvar Aalto. L'agence travaille sur des projets variés : églises, immeubles de bureaux, logements, résidences privées, architecture intérieure et rénovation. L'agence est dirigée par Anssi Lassila, né en 1973 ; Teemu Hirvilammi est né en 1974. Parmi leurs réalisations, toutes en Finlande : l'église de Kärsämäki (1999–2004, publiée ici) et l'église et centre paroissial de Klaukkala (2005). Ils travaillent actuellement sur le projet de Frami D-Block, une extension de 7000 m² du centre de technologie Frami de Seinäjoki (en collaboration avec les architectes Lahdelma Mahlamäki Ltd., 2005–) ; l'immeuble de logements et de commerces Maakunta-aukio (Seinäjoki, 2005–) et l'église de Kuokkala (en collaboration avec Luonti Ltd., Jyväskylä, 2006–).

KÄRSÄMÄKI CHURCH

Kärsämäki, Finland, 1999–2004

Floor area: 200 m².
Client: Parish of Kärsämäki. Cost: €1 million

The first church in the parish of Kärsämäki was completed in 1765 and demolished in 1841. In 1998, the municipality decided to rebuild the old church, without any clear idea of the original appearance of the building. So it was decided, instead, to create a modern building using traditional 18th-century methods, and the project of Lassila Hirvilammi was chosen through a competition. The building has two essential elements, a log "core" and a black, tarred and shingle-clad "cloak." The architects have tried "to generate an atmosphere of archaic simplicity and optimal weather resistance." Vestibules, a vestry, and a storeroom are housed in the space between the "cloak" and the church itself. There is no fixed seating in the church and even the altar is movable. There is no electricity or heating in the church either, and lighting during the day is through a skylight, whereas candle lanterns light the space at night. The hand-sawn logs used for the frame were cut in forests owned by the parish and transported partly with the aid of horses. The notched corner joints were carved with axes, handsaws, and chisels. The 50 000 shingles used for roofing and cladding were made of hand-split aspen dipped in tar, just as the 70 000 nails used in the process were hand-forged. Though the goal was to use old methods, the net result is both beautiful and ecologically responsible.

Die 1765 gebaute erste Kirche der Gemeinde Kärsämäki wurde im Jahr 1841 abgerissen. 1998 entschied die Gemeindeverwaltung, die alte Kirche wiederauferstehen zu lassen, allerdings ohne eine genaue Vorstellung davon zu haben, wie das Original genau ausgesehen hat. Daher entschloss man sich, mithilfe traditioneller Baumethoden aus dem 18. Jahrhundert ein neues Gebäude zu errichten. Der über einen Wettbewerb ausgewählte Vorschlag von Lassila Hirvilammi sah zwei wesentliche Bestandteile vor, einen „Kern" aus Holz und eine schwarz geteerte Schindelverkleidung als „Mantel". Dabei haben die Architekten versucht, „eine Atmosphäre von archaischer Einfachheit bei gleichzeitig optimaler Wetterfestigkeit zu erzeugen". Zwischen dem „Mantel" und dem eigentlichen Kirchenraum wurden ein Vestibül, eine Sakristei und ein Lagerraum eingesetzt. Im Kirchenraum verzichtete man auf fest installierte Sitzbänke, sogar der Altar lässt sich verschieben. Auch Elektrizität und Heizung gibt es nicht, die Raumbeleuchtung erfolgt tagsüber durch ein Oberlicht und abends mit Kerzenlicht. Die handgesägten Baumstämme für das Tragwerk wurden in gemeindeeigenen Forsten geschlagen und teilweise mithilfe von Pferden transportiert. Die genuteten Verbindungseckpunkte der Planken wurden mit Äxten, Handsägen und Beiteln zurechtgearbeitet. Für die Dachdeckung wurden 50 000 Schindeln per Hand aus Espenholz gespleißt und mit Teer überzogen und auch die insgesamt 70 000 verwendeten Nägel sind allesamt handgeschmiedet. Ging es zunächst darum, auf alte Baumethoden zurückzugreifen, ist das Gesamtergebnis nun ebenso reizvoll wie umweltbewusst.

La première église de la paroisse de Kärsämäki a été édifiée en 1765 et démolie en 1841. En 1998, la municipalité décida de la reconstruire sans idée précise de l'apparence initiale de l'édifice. On opta pour une construction à l'aide des méthodes traditionnelles du XVIIIe siècle et le projet de Lassila Hirvilammi a été choisi à l'issue d'un concours. Les architectes ont essayé de « susciter une atmosphère de simplicité archaïque et de résistance optimale au passage du temps. » Les vestibules, un vestiaire et une salle de rangement occupent l'espace entre le « manteau » et l'église elle-même. Aucun siège n'est fixe et l'autel lui-même est mobile. L'église n'est ni électrifiée ni chauffée. L'éclairage diurne est assuré par une verrière tandis que des lanternes à chandelles sont utilisées la nuit. Les poutres en bois juste scié qui ont servi à l'ossature proviennent des forêts de la paroisse et ont été en partie transportées à l'aide de chevaux. Les jointures d'angles en encoche ont été travaillées à l'aide de haches, de scies manuelles et de ciseaux. Les 50 000 shingles de la toiture et de parement sont en peuplier fendu à la main, et goudronnés. Les 70 000 clous ont été forgés à la main. Si le but était surtout d'utiliser des méthodes anciennes, le résultat est à la fois superbe et écologique.

The simple shingle siding of the church corresponds to its bucolic natural setting.

Die Außenwandverkleidung der Kirche aus Schindeln passt gut zu ihrem idyllischen Standort in der Natur.

Le parement en simples shingles de l'église répond à son cadre naturel bucolique.

The interior, as simple as and clad
in wood like the exterior, offers a
soaring space with light coming from
openings in the roof.

Das Kircheninnere, ebenso schlicht
und wie die Außenseite vollständig
mit Holz verschalt, bildet einen hoch
aufragenden Raum, der sein Licht
durch Öffnungen im Dach erhält.

L'intérieur, aussi simple que l'extérieur et également habillé de bois,
n'en offre pas moins un volume
élancé. La lumière vient d'ouvertures
pratiquées dans la toiture.

The plan of the church is made up of squares, as can be seen from the drawings below.

Wie in den unteren Zeichnungen zu sehen, setzt sich der Grundriss der Kirche aus mehreren Quadraten zusammen.

Le plan de l'église se compose de carrés comme le montrent les dessins ci-dessous.

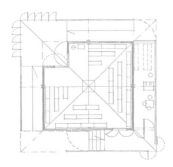
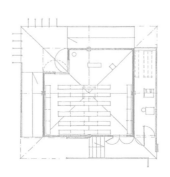
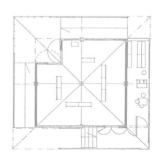

La Purificadora Boutique Hotel

LEGORRETA + LEGORRETA

Legorreta + Legorreta
Palacio de Versalles 285-A / Lomas de Reforma
Mexico City 11930 / Mexico

Tel: +52 55 5251 9698 ext 133 / Fax: +52 55 5251 9698 ext 120
E-mail: info@lmasl.com.mx / Web: www.legorretalegorreta.com

Legorreta Arquitectos was founded in 1963 by Ricardo Legorreta, Noe Castro, and Carlos Vargas. They made their early reputation with such works as the Camino Real Hotels (Mexico City, 1966–68; Cancun, 1973–75, etc.). They started working in the United States in the 1980s, completing such buildings as the San Antonio Public Library (San Antonio, Texas, 1993–95). In 2000, the firm changed its name to **LEGORRETA + LEGORRETA**; currently it employs 50 to 60 people. Despite their international reputation, the firm insists on its base in Mexican vernacular architecture. Ricardo Legorreta was born in 1931 in Mexico City. He obtained his degree in Architecture from the Universidad Nacional Autónoma de Mexico (1948–52) and worked from 1948 to 1960 with José Villagran García. He won the AIA Gold Medal in 2000. Victor Legorreta was born in 1966 in Mexico City and obtained his degree in Architecture from the Universidad Iberoamericana in Mexico (1990). He became a Partner and Lead Designer at Legorreta Arquitectos in 1991, positions he holds in the current firm. Other principals of the firm are Miguel Almaraz, Adriana Ciklik and Carlos Vargas. Recent work includes the Texas A&M Engineering College (Doha, Qatar, 2004–07); the Hotel Camino Real Monterrey (Monterrey, Mexico, 2004–07); the Labyrinth of Science and the Arts (San Luis Potosí, Mexico, 2005–08); and La Purificadora Boutique Hotel (Puebla, Mexico, 2006–07, published here). Current work includes the School of Foreign Service (Doha, Qatar, 2007–); the College of Business and Computer Science (Doha, Qatar, 2005–08); and the Fort Worth Museum of Science and History (Fort Worth, Texas, 2007–09).

1963 gründeten Ricardo Legorreta, Noe Castro und Carlos Vargas Legorreta Arquitectos, das sich mit seinen Entwürfen etwa für die Camino Real Hotels (u. a. Mexiko-Stadt, 1966–68; Cancun, 1973–75) rasch einen Namen machte. In den 1980er-Jahren begann das Büro Projekte in den Vereinigten Staaten umzusetzen, darunter Gebäu-de wie die Public Library von San Antonio (Texas, 1993–95). Im Jahr 2000 benannte sich das Büro in **LEGORRETA + LEGORRETA** um. Die Firma beschäftigt gegenwärtig zwischen 50 und 60 Mitarbeiter. Ungeachtet ihres internationalen Ansehens hält die Firma an der traditionellen mexikanischen Architektur als Ausgangspunkt für ihre Arbeit fest. Ricardo Legorreta wurde 1931 in Mexiko-Stadt geboren, wo er sein Architekturstudium an der Universidad Nacional Autónoma de Mexico (1948–52) abschloss und von 1948 bis 1960 bei José Villagran García arbeitete. 2000 wurde Ricardo Legorreta mit der Goldmedaille des American Institute of Architects ausgezeichnet. Sein 1966 ebenfalls in Mexiko-Stadt geborener Sohn Victor Legorreta schloss sein Architekturstudium 1990 ebendort an der Universidad Iberoamericana ab. Seit 1991 ist Victor gleich-berechtigter Partner sowie Leitender Designer von Legorreta Arquitectos bzw. jetzt Legorreta + Legorreta. Die weiteren führenden Köpfe der Firma sind Miguel Almaraz, Adriana Ciklik und Carlos Vargas. Zu ihren jüngeren Bauten gehören das Texas A&M Engineering College in Doha, Katar (2004–07), das Camino Real Hotel in Monterrey (Mexiko, 2004–07), das Museum Laberinto de la Ciencia y las Artes im mexikanischen San Luis Potosí (2005–08) und das hier vorgestellte Boutique-Hotel La Purificadora im mexikanischen Puebla (2006–07). Gegenwärtig arbeiten Legorreta + Legorreta an einer Schule für den diplomatischen Dienst (seit 2007) und einem Hochschulbau für Wirtschaft und Informatik in Doha, Katar (2005–08), sowie dem Fort Worth Museum of Science and History (Fort Worth, Texas, 2007–09).

Legorreta Arquitectos a été créé en 1963 par Ricardo Legorreta, Noe Castro et Carlos Vargas. Ils se sont faits initialement connaître par des réalisations comme les Camino Real Hotels (Mexico, 1966–68 ; Cancun, 1973–75 ; etc.). Ils ont commencé à travailler aux États-Unis dans les années 1980 et réalisé des projets comme la bibliothèque publique San Antonio (San Antonio, Texas, 1993–95). En 2000, l'agence a pris le nom de **LEGORRETA + LEGORRETA**, et emploie actuellement de 50 à 60 collaborateurs. Malgré sa réputation internationale, elle attache beaucoup d'importance à la base de son inspiration : l'architecture vernaculaire mexicaine. Ricardo Legorreta, né en 1931 à Mexico, est diplômé d'architecture de l'Universidad Nacional Autónoma de Mexico (1948–52) et a travaillé de 1948 à 1960 avec José Villagran García. Il a remporté la médaille d'or de l'American Institute of Architects (AIA) en 2000. Victor Legorreta, né en 1966 à Mexico, est diplômé d'architecture de l'Univer-sidad Iberoamericana de Mexico (1990). Il est devenu associé et responsable de la conception de Legorreta Arquitectos en 1991, position qu'il occupe toujours dans l'agence actuelle. Les autres associés de l'agence sont Miguel Almaraz, Adriana Ciklik et Carlos Vargas. Parmi leurs réalisations récentes : le Texas A&M Engineering College (Doha, Qatar, 2004–07) ; l'Hotel Camino Real (Monterrey, Mexique, 2004–07) ; le Labyrinthe de la Science et des Arts (San Luis Potosí, Mexique, 2005–08) et l'hôtel-boutique La Purificadora (Puebla, Mexique, 2006–07, publié ici). Ils travaillent actuellement sur l'École des relations extérieures (Doha, Qatar, 2007–) ; le Collège des affaires et des sciences de l'informatique (Doha, Qatar, 2005–08) et le Fort Worth Museum of Science and History (Fort Worth, Texas, 2007–09).

LA PURIFICADORA BOUTIQUE HOTEL

Puebla, Mexico, 2006–07

Floor area: 3000 m². Client: Plus Arrendamientos. Cost: not disclosed. Architects: Ricardo Legorreta, Victor Legorreta.
Associate Architect: Pablo Serrano Rafael Monjaraz Arquitectos. Art: Laureana Toledo

This project won a 2008 AIA Honor Award in the Interior Design category. The jury's comments read, "This project seamlessly weaves together indoor and outdoor living spaces, existing and new buildings, historic and contemporary materials, and traditional and modern lifestyles to create a relaxed and rejuvenated hotel by breathing new life and purpose into a historic water purification plant. Great respect was shown to the existing facility, intervening as required to support its new program." Located in the Paseo San Francisco Master Plan area, next to the Iglesia de San Francisco, the building is a registered landmark. The 19th-century structure was formerly an ice factory and water purification and bottling facility. The name "La Purificadora" is related to this former function of the new hotel, which includes 26 rooms, a reception area and shop, restaurant-bar, patio, assorted meeting or event rooms, and a 30-meter-long pool. The architects explain, "The project consists of a large lateral patio that is surrounded by an L-shape building on each level: on the ground floor, working as a living room, it is a prolongation of the height of the restaurant-bar and the reception-shop; on the second and third floors it is an empty space that separates the circulation from the rooms; and on the fourth floor it limits the amenities zone. The patio is partially covered by a rooftop. The façades have been given the same treatment as the old buildings, extending plaster and stone to their full height." Designed for the hotelier Carlos Couturier, La Purificadora does not have the bright colors often associated with the work of Legorreta; instead, old wood, onyx, or even found elements such as glass fragments are frequent materials.

Das Boutique-Hotel La Purificadora wurde 2008 vom American Institute of Architects mit einem Honor Award in der Kategorie Interior Design ausgezeichnet. In ihrer Begründung schrieb die Jury: „Die Architekten haben einer historischen Wasseraufbereitungsanlage neues Leben eingehaucht und ihr eine ganz neue Bestimmung gegeben. Auf gelungene Weise wurden Innen- und Außenwohnräume, bereits bestehende und neue Gebäudeteile, historische und zeitgenössische Materialien, traditioneller und moderner Stil nahtlos miteinander verknüpft, um ein junges, legeres Hotelgebäude zu schaffen. Dabei gingen die Architekten mit großer Rücksicht gegenüber der bestehenden Anlage vor, in die sie gerade so stark eingriffen, wie es für die neue Programmatik des Gebäudes notwendig war." Das Gebäude befindet sich auf dem Masterplanareal des Paseo San Francisco, in direkter Nachbarschaft zur Iglesia de San Francisco, und hat den Status einer offiziellen Sehenswürdigkeit. Der Name „La Purificadora" verweist auf die frühere Funktion des aus dem 19. Jahrhundert stammenden Gebäudes, das als Eisfabrik und Anlage zur Wasseraufbereitung und Flaschenabfüllung diente. Das heutige Hotel umfasst 26 Zimmer, einen Empfangsbereich nebst Laden, ein Restaurant mit Bar, einen Patio, verschiedene Tagungs- bzw. Veranstaltungsräume und einen 30 m langen Swimmingpool. In der Erläuterung der Architekten heißt es: „Das Projekt besteht aus einem großen Patio, der von einem mehrgeschossigen, L-förmigen Gebäude umbaut ist: Auf der untersten Ebene, deren Höhe mit der des Restaurants und des Rezeptionsladens übereinstimmt, dient er als Aufenthaltsbereich, auf der zweiten und dritten Ebene gibt es einen Freiraum, der die Gänge von den Zimmern abtrennt, und auf der vierten Ebene grenzt er den Freizeitbereich ab. Ein Teil des Patios ist von einem Dach überdeckt. Die Fassaden wurden wie bei den alten Gebäuden auf der gesamten Höhe mit Steinputz versehen." Das für den Hotelier Carlos Couturier entworfene La Purificadora zeigt nicht die kräftigen Farbtöne, die man häufig mit Legorreta assoziiert; stattdessen stehen Materialien wie altes Holz, Onyx und sogar gefundene Teile wie Glasscherben im Vordergrund.

Cette réalisation a remporté un AIA Honor Award en 2008 dans la catégorie architecture intérieure. Pour le jury: « Ce projet fusionne dans un continuum les espaces de vie intérieurs et extérieurs, existants ou construits à neuf, les matériaux historiques et contemporains, les styles de vie modernes et traditionnels pour créer un hôtel décontracté en insufflant dans cette usine de purification d'eau une vie et des objectifs fonctionnels nouveaux. Le plus grand respect a été porté aux installations existantes, les interventions se faisant au bénéfice du programme. » Situé dans la zone du plan directeur du Paseo San Francisco, près de l'église San Francisco, le bâtiment présentait une valeur historique. Le nom de « La Purificadora » renvoie à l'ancienne fonction de ces constructions du XIXᵉ siècle, ancienne usine d'embouteillage, de purification d'eau et de fabrication de glace. Le nouvel hôtel compte 26 chambres, un hall de réception et une boutique, un bar-restaurant, un patio, des salles de réunions ou pour événements et une piscine de 30 m de long. Selon les architectes: « Le projet consiste en un important patio disposé latéralement et entouré à chaque niveau par le bâtiment en L: au rez-de-chaussée, il constitue un séjour en prolongation du bar-restaurant et de la zone de réception-boutique. Aux second et troisième niveaux, un espace vide sépare les circulations des chambres. Et au quatrième niveau, il marque la fin des aménagements. Ce patio est en partie couvert par une toiture. Les façades ont reçu le même traitement que les vestiges de l'ancienne usine, plâtre et pierre sur toute la hauteur. » Conçu pour l'hôtelier Carlos Couturier, la Purificadora ne présente pas les couleurs vives généralement associées aux interventions de Legorreta, qui a préféré ici l'usage des vieux bois, de l'onyx et même d'éléments trouvés comme des fragments de verre.

A generous opening and a large flight of stairs stand next to outdoor, yet covered, seating areas.

Der Sitzbereich auf der überdachten Terrasse, deren Außenseite über einer breiten Treppe weit geöffnet ist.

La généreuse ouverture et la grande volée d'escaliers sont dehors, mais toujours proches des salons.

Numerous elements of the original building were restored and used in the new hotel, but modern windows and openings make it clear that this was more than a restoration.

Zahlreiche Elemente des ursprünglichen Gebäudes wurden wiederhergestellt und für das Hotel genutzt, doch die modernen Fenster und Öffnungen unterstreichen, dass es sich nicht um eine bloße Restaurierung handelt.

De nombreux éléments du bâtiment d'origine ont été restaurés et utilisés dans le nouvel hôtel, mais les fenêtres et les ouvertures modernes signalent clairement qu'il s'agit de plus qu'une simple restauration.

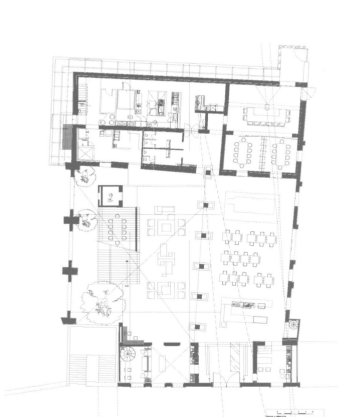

A combination of the relative rough-
ness of the original industrial building and the more refined approach
of a boutique hotel, La Purificadora is
unusual for architects like Legorreta
+ Legorreta.

Die Robustheit eines ehemaligen
Industriebaus mit dem subtileren
Anspruch eines Boutique Hotels zu
kombinieren, macht das Purificadora
zu einem ungewöhnlichen Projekt
für ein Architekturbüro wie Legorreta
+ Legorreta.

Combinaison de la brutalité relative
d'un bâtiment industriel ancien et
du raffinement d'un hôtel-boutique,
la Purificadora est une réalisation
inhabituelle pour une agence comme
Legorreta + Legorreta.

DANIEL LIBESKIND

Studio Daniel Libeskind, Architect LLC
2 Rector Street, 19th Floor / New York, NY 10006 / USA

Tel: +1 212 497 9154 / Fax: +1 212 285 2130
E-mail: info@daniel-libeskind.com / Web: www.daniel-libeskind.com

Born in Poland in 1946 and a US citizen since 1965, **DANIEL LIBESKIND** studied music in Israel and in New York before taking up architecture at the Cooper Union in New York (B.Arch, 1970). He received a postgraduate degree in the History and Theory of Architecture (School of Comparative Studies, Essex University, UK, 1972). He has taught at Harvard, Yale, Hanover, Graz, Hamburg, and UCLA. His work includes the Jewish Museum in Berlin (1989–2001), which is an extension of the Berlin Museum, and numerous proposals, such as his 1997 plan to build an extension of the Victoria & Albert Museum in London, and his prize-winning scheme for the Bremen Philharmonic Hall, 1995. Like Zaha Hadid, Libeskind has had a considerable influence through his theory and his proposals, and more recently with his built work. The city museum of Osnabrück in Germany, the Felix Nussbaum Haus, was inaugurated in 1998. In 2002, the Imperial War Museum North in Manchester, UK, opened to the public. The Danish Jewish Museum was completed in 2004; his extension of the Denver Art Museum in 2006; and that of Toronto's Royal Ontario Museum (published here) in 2007. Libeskind's 2003 victory in the complex competition to redesign the World Trade Center site in New York placed him at the forefront of contemporary architecture. Current work includes a residential high-rise in Warsaw, Poland; the New Center for Arts and Culture (Boston, Massachusetts); Editoriale Bresciana Tower (Brescia, Italy); and the Ørestad Downtown Masterplan Site (Ørestad, Denmark). In 2004, Libeskind was appointed the first Cultural Ambassador for Architecture by the US Department of State, as part of the Culture Connect Program.

DANIEL LIBESKIND, 1946 in Polen geboren und seit 1965 US-amerikanischer Staatsbürger, studierte zunächst in Israel und New York Musik, bevor er ein Architekturstudium an der Cooper Union in New York aufnahm (Bachelor of Architecture 1970). 1972 promovierte er in Architekturgeschichte und -theorie an der School of Comparative Studies der Essex University in Großbritannien. Lehraufträge führten Libeskind an die Universitäten Harvard, Yale, Hannover, Graz und Hamburg sowie an die University of California in Los Angeles. Zu Libeskinds Arbeiten gehören das Jüdische Museum in Berlin (1989–2001), eine Erweiterung des ehemaligen Berlin-Museums, zahlreiche Wettbewerbsbeiträge wie etwa sein Erweiterungskonzept für das Victoria & Albert Museum in London sowie der preisgekrönte Entwurf für die Philharmonie Bremen (1995). Ähnlich wie bei Zaha Hadid verdankte sich Libeskinds Einfluss anfangs eher seinen theoretischen Ansätzen und Wettbewerbsbeiträgen und erst in jüngerer Zeit seinen realisierten Projekten. Eines der ersten war das 1998 eröffnete Felix-Nussbaum-Haus in Osnabrück. 2002 öffnete das Imperial War Museum North in Manchester seine Pforten. 2004 wurde das Museum für jüdische Geschichte in Kopenhagen fertiggestellt, 2006 der Erweiterungsbau für das Denver Art Museum und 2007 der hier vorgestellte für das Royal Ontario Museum in Toronto. Mit seinem Beitrag für die Neugestaltung des World-Trade-Center-Geländes in Manhattan, mit dem er 2003 aus einem schwierigen Wettbewerb als Sieger hervorgegangen war, stellte er sich in die vorderste Reihe zeitgenössischer Architekten. Zu Libeskinds derzeit laufenden Projekten gehören ein Wohnhochhaus in Warschau, das New Center for Arts and Culture in Boston, Massachusetts, das Editoriale-Bresciana-Hochhaus im italienischen Brescia und der Masterplan für den Bezirk Ørestad in Kopenhagen. 2004 wurde Libeskind vom US-Außenministerium im Rahmen des Culture Connect Program zum ersten Kulturbotschafter für Architektur ernannt.

Né en Pologne in 1946 et citoyen américain depuis 1965, **DANIEL LIBESKIND** étudie la musique en Israël et à New York avant d'opter pour l'architecture à la Cooper Union à New York (B. Arch., 1970). Il est diplômé d'études supérieures en histoire et théorie de l'architecture (School of Comparative Studies, Essex University, G.-B., 1972) et a enseigné à Harvard, Yale, Hanovre, Graz, Hambourg et UCLA. Son œuvre comprend le Musée juif de Berlin (1989–2001), extension du Musée de Berlin, et de nombreuses propositions comme son plan de 1997 pour une extension du Victoria & Albert Museum de Londres, ou son projet primé pour la salle philharmonique de Brême, 1995. Comme Zaha Hadid, Libeskind a exercé une influence considérable à travers ses recherches théoriques et ses propositions, et seulement plus récemment grâce à ses réalisations. Le musée municipal d'Osnabrück en Allemagne, la Felix Nussbaum Haus, a été inauguré en 1998 et, en 2002, son Imperial War Museum North à Manchester, G.-B., a été ouvert au public. Le Musée juif danois a été achevé en 2004 ; son extension du musée d'Art de Denver en 2006 et celle du Royal Ontario Museum de Toronto (publiée ici) en 2007. En 2003, gagner le concours complexe pour le site du World Trade Center à New York l'a placé au premier rang des grands créateurs contemporains. Parmi ses travaux actuels ; un immeuble résidentiel de grande hauteur (Varsovie, Pologne) ; le New Center for Arts and Culture (Boston, Massachusetts) ; la tour de l'Editoriale Bresciana (Brescia, Italie) et le plan directeur du centre d'Ørestad (Ørestad, Danemark). En 2004, il a été nommé le premier « Ambassadeur culturel pour l'architecture » par le département d'État américain, dans le cadre du programme Culture Connect.

ROYAL ONTARIO MUSEUM EXTENSION

Toronto, Canada, 2002–07

Floor area: 18 600 m². Client: Royal Ontario Museum. Cost: not disclosed.
Joint venture with B+H Architects. Landscape Architect: Quinn Design Associates

The so-called Renaissance ROM (Royal Ontario Museum) project entailed the renovation of 10 galleries in an existing historical building and the creation of an extension, called the Michael Lee-Chin Crystal, to the museum. The extension provides 9290 square meters of new exhibition space, as well as a new entrance and lobby, a retail shop, and three restaurants. It is called the "Crystal" because it is made up of five intersecting volumes. The void created by the meeting of two of the "crystals" is an atrium called the Spirit House, rising from the ground to the fourth floor. The intersecting spaces of the Michael Lee-Chin Crystal create atriums at different levels, affording views into galleries and other spaces within the Museum. One large atrium, known as the Gloria Hyacinth Chen Court, separates the new construction from the ROM's existing heritage building and provides a nearly complete view of the restored heritage façades. The Crystal is clad in champagne-colored anodized aluminum extrusions, with 20 percent of its surface devoted to glazing. Daniel Libeskind declares, "This building tells a unique and a particular story which crystallizes the ROM's programmatic content and the singularity of the site. The Crystal transforms the character of the ROM into an inspired atmosphere dedicated to the resurgence of the Museum as the dynamic center of Toronto."

Dieses als ROM-Renaissance (ROM für Royal Ontario Museum) bezeichnete Projekt umfasste zum einen die Renovierung von zehn Ausstellungsräumen des historischen Museums und zum anderen einen Erweiterungsbau, den so genannten Michael Lee-Chin Crystal. Durch den Neubau entstanden 9290 m² zusätzliche Ausstellungsfläche sowie ein neuer Eingang samt Foyer, ein Museumsladen und drei Restaurants. Der Name „Crystal" erklärt sich aus fünf, sich überschneidenden Baukörpern. Ein zwischen zwei „Kristallen" frei gebliebener Zwischenraum bildet einen Innenhof, der auf den Namen Spirit House getauft wurde und sich vom Boden bis zum vierten Geschoss erstreckt. An den jeweiligen Überschneidungskanten des Michael Lee-Chin Crystal sind in unterschiedlichen Höhen weitere Atrien entstanden, von denen aus man in einzelne Ausstellungsgalerien und andere Räume des Museums hineinblicken kann. Ein größeres Atrium, der Gloria Hyacinth Chen Court, teilt den Neubau vom ursprünglichen ROM-Gebäude ab und bietet fast eine Komplettansicht der restaurierten alten Fassaden. 80 % der Oberfläche des Erweiterungsbaus sind mit champagnerfarbenen Platten aus eloxiertem Aluminium verkleidet, der Rest ist verglast. Daniel Libeskind über sein Projekt: „Das Gebäude erzählt eine besondere, eine einzigartige Geschichte, die sich in dem programmatischen Gehalt und der Einmaligkeit des Ortes kristallisiert. Der Crystal verleiht dem ROM eine aufregende Atmosphäre, die das Museum wieder als ein dynamisches Zentrum Torontos aufleben lässt."

Le projet Renaissance ROM (pour Royal Ontario Museum) comprenait la rénovation de dix galeries du bâtiment historique existant et la création d'une extension, le Michael Lee-Chin Crystal. Cette dernière regroupe 9290 m² de salles d'expositions, une entrée et un hall d'accueil nouveaux, une boutique et trois restaurants. Elle est appelée «Crystal» pour sa forme composée de cinq volumes s'entrecoupant. Le vide créé par la rencontre de deux «cristaux» est un atrium appelé Spirit House de quatre niveaux de haut. Les intersections créent ainsi des atriums à différents niveaux, ce qui génère des vues perspectives entre les galeries et les autres volumes. Un grand atrium, le Gloria Hyacinth Chen Court, sépare les nouvelles constructions du bâtiment historique classé du ROM et offre une vue presque intégrale des façades anciennes restaurées. Le Crystal est paré d'extrusions en aluminium anodisé de couleur champagne et 20 % de la surface sont vitrés. Libeskind a déclaré : «Ce bâtiment raconte une histoire spécifique qui cristallise le contenu programmatique du ROM et la singularité du terrain. Le Crystal transforme le caractère du ROM pour créer une atmosphère inspirée, dédiée à la résurgence du musée, élément dynamique du centre de Toronto. »

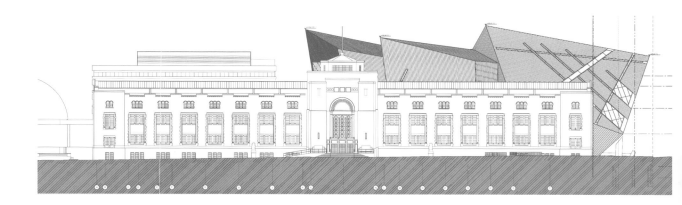

Seen in an elevation drawing showing the main façade of the old building, Libeskind's extension is by comparison exuberantly dynamic.

Der Aufriss der Hauptfassade des alten Gebäudes zeigt im direkten Vergleich die außerordentliche Dynamik von Libeskinds Erweiterungsbau.

Sur le dessin d'élévation de la façade principale de l'ancien bâtiment, l'extension de Libeskind semble d'un dynamisme exubérant.

The angled, crystalline forms of the
extension seem to emerge directly
from the earth, or to be pressed
into it.

*Die verwinkelte Kristallform des Neu-
baus wirkt, als käme er direkt aus der
Erde oder sei in sie hineingedrückt
worden.*

*Les formes inclinées et cristallines
de l'extension semblent émerger
du sol, ou s'être écrasées sur lui.*

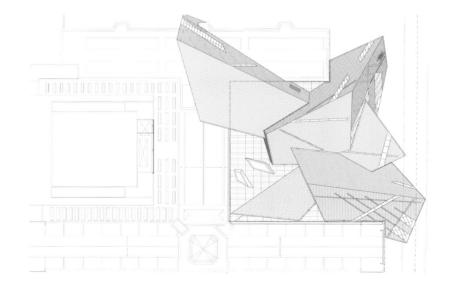

Angled and unexpected in its config-urations, the interior space translates the exterior form and is compatible with it.

Die äußere Gestalt findet im Inneren des Gebäudes ihre Fortsetzung in ebenso ungewöhnlich verwinkelten Raumformen.

Dans ses configurations inclinées et surprenantes, l'espace intérieur reprend et exprime les formes extérieures.

LIN FINN GEIPEL + GIULIA ANDI

LIN Finn Geipel + Giulia Andi Architects Urbanists
Helmholtzstr. 2–9
10587 Berlin
Germany
Tel: +49 30 39 800 900
Fax: +49 30 39 800 909

54 rue du Vertbois
75003 Paris
France
Tel: +33 1 46 94 61 57
Fax: +33 1 46 94 67 67

E-mail: office@lin-a.com / Web: www.lin-a.com

FINN GEIPEL was born in 1958 in Stuttgart. He received his diploma in Architecture in his native city in 1984. He worked with Bernd Hoge and Jochen Hunger in the firm Labfac Stuttgart from 1983 to 1987, and in the period 1987–2001 with Nicholas Michelin in Labfac Paris. Since 2000, he has been the head of the Laboratory for Integrative Architecture (LIA) at the Technische Universität of Berlin. He established **LIN** in Berlin and Paris with **GIULIA ANDI** in 2001. Giulia Andi was born in 1972 in Rome, where she studied Architecture, obtaining her diploma in 2001. She has been the manager of LIN offices in Berlin and Paris since 2001. They participated in competitions for the urban transformation of the railway site Zentrale Bahnflächen in Munich (Germany, 2001–03); the School of Architecture in Nantes (France, 2003); and the Cœur d'Orly Airport district in Paris (France, 2007). Their work includes a house for the Kleyer Family (Oldenburg, Germany, 2002–03); the exhibition space at Pavillon de l'Arsenal in Paris (France, 2003); Alvéole 14, Submarine Base Rehabilitation (Saint-Nazaire, France, 2005–07, published here); and the nearly completed Saint-Étienne's Cité du Design, a center for the exhibition and study of design in Saint-Étienne (France, 2004–09).

FINN GEIPEL wurde 1958 in Stuttgart geboren. 1984 schloss er dort sein Architekturstudium ab. Von 1983 bis 1987 leitete er mit Bernd Hoge und Jochen Hunger das Büro Labfac Stuttgart, von 1987 bis 2001 arbeitete er mit Nicholas Michelin für Labfac Paris. Seit 2000 leitet er das Labor für Integrative Architektur (LIA) an der Technischen Universität Berlin. Gemeinsam mit **GIULIA ANDI** gründete Geipel im Jahr 2001 das Büro **LIN**. Andi wurde 1972 in Rom geboren, wo sie 2001 ihr Architekturdiplom erwarb. Seit 2001 ist Andi Leiterin der LIN-Niederlassungen in Berlin und Paris. Das Büro nahm an verschiedenen Wettbewerben für die Umnutzung von Industrieflächen teil, u. a. für die Zentralen Bahnflächen in München (2001–02), die École d'Architecture in Nantes (2003) und das neue Viertel Cœur d'Orly am Flughafen Orly in Paris (2007). Zu ihren realisierten Projekten gehören das Haus Kleyer in Oldenburg (2002–03), die Ausstellungsfläche des Pavillon de l'Arsenal in Paris (2003); der Alvéole 14 genannte Teilumbau eines U-Boot-Bunkers im französischen Saint-Nazaire (2005–07, hier vorgestellt) und die fast fertiggestellte Cité du Design im französischen Saint-Étienne (2004–09), ein Ausbildungs- und Ausstellungszentrum für den Designbereich.

FINN GEIPEL, né en 1958 à Stuttgart, a fait ses études d'architecture dans sa ville natale (diplômé en architecture en 1984). Il travaille avec Bernd Hoge et Jochen Hunger dans l'agence Labfac à Stuttgart de 1983 à 1987, puis, de 1987 à 2001, avec Nicholas Michelin à Labfac Paris. Depuis 2000, il dirige le Laboratory for Integrative Architecture (LIA) à la Technische Universität de Berlin. Il fonde **LIN** à Berlin et Paris avec **GIULIA ANDI** en 2001. Giulia Andi est née en 1972 à Rome, où elle a étudié l'architecture (diplômée en 2001). Elle est directrice des bureaux de LIN à Berlin et Paris depuis 2001. Ils ont participé à des concours pour le développement urbain et paysager sur des anciens sites ferroviaires à Munich (Allemagne, 2001–03) ; l'école d'architecture de Nantes (2003) et le nouveau quartier Cœur d'Orly à Paris (2007). Parmi leurs réalisations : une maison pour la famille Kleyer (Oldenburg, Allemagne, 2002–03) ; l'espace d'exposition au Pavillon de l'Arsenal à Paris (2003) ; Alvéole 14, transformation d'une base de sous-marins (Saint-Nazaire, France, 2005–07, publiée ici) ; et la Cité du design à Saint-Étienne, centre d'étude et d'exposition sur le design à Saint-Étienne (France, 2004–09).

ALVÉOLE 14

Submarine Base Rehabilitation, Quartier Ville Port, Saint-Nazaire, France, 2005–07

Floor area: 3300 m² (Alvéole 14); 2270 m² (public space). Client: City of Saint-Nazaire.
Cost: €5.9 million (Alvéole 14); €1.2 million (public space).
Team: Hans-Michael Földeak (Project Manager), David Letellier, Philip Rieseberg, Simon-Martin Schultze,
Marie Taveau, Cécile Grelier, Annabelle Munsch, Philip Hegnauer, Amélie Poncety, Aurélie Berhault,
Thomas Kupke, Nacera Mahi, Marc Dujon, Timo Foerster

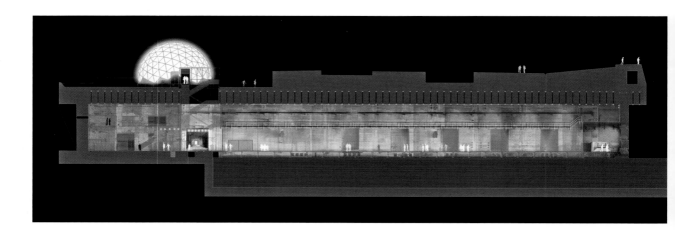

This project involved the transformation of a former submarine base in the French port city of Saint-Nazaire into a public space for contemporary art and music. Built between 1941 and 1943 by the German Navy, the structure is 295 meters long by 130 meters wide and up to 19 meters high. There were originally 14 submarine cells (called alvéoles in French), each of which has a basin 11 meters high by 117 meters long. These cells were connected by internal tracks used for the transportation of machine parts. Eighty-five percent of the city of Saint-Nazaire was destroyed by bombing raids beginning in 1942, but the submarine base remained virtually unscathed. Although rebuilding began in 1949, the mass of the submarine base made it a sort of barrier between the city center and the harbor, hence this project and others, destined to give new life to the enormous facility. For reasons of cost (and aesthetics) the intervention involved "minimal interference" with the existing building. There are two essential elements in the new design. The hall for the international center for emerging art forms (Lieu international des Formes Emergentes, or LiFE) is a former submarine basin that forms a "monospace" that can be opened to the harbor through a large retractable gate. The VIP venue for contemporary music occupies a former bunker volume—a simple cubic space enclosed by a steel frame with space for 600 spectators. A "light carpet" runs along former tracks and links the volumes. A staircase leads to the roof, where a geodesic radar dome recovered from Berlin's Tempelhof Airport "serves as a think tank for art and music projects."

„Alvéole 14" bezeichnet einen Veranstaltungsort für zeitgenössische Kunst und Musik in der französischen Hafenstadt Saint-Nazaire, der durch den Teilumbau eines früheren U-Boot-Bunkers entstanden ist. Der zwischen 1941 und 1943 von der deutschen Kriegsmarine errichtete Bunker ist 295 m lang, 130 m breit und an einzelnen Stellen bis zu 19 m hoch. Ursprünglich existierten 14 einzelne U-Boot-Zellen (französisch alvéoles) mit je einem Becken von 11 m Tiefe und 117 m Länge. Die einzelnen Zellen waren durch Schienen miteinander verbunden, über die Maschinenteile transportiert wurden. Während die Stadt Saint-Nazaire durch die 1942 einsetzenden Bombenangriffe zu 85 % zerstört wurde, blieb der U-Boot-Bunker praktisch unversehrt. Zwar begann 1949 der Wiederaufbau der Stadt, die massive U-Boot-Basis verblieb jedoch als eine Art Barriere zwischen dem Stadtzentrum und dem Hafen. „Alvéole 14" und weitere Projekte sollen die riesige Anlage zu neuem Leben erwecken. Aus Kostengründen (sowie aufgrund ästhetischer Erwägungen) beschränkte sich die Umnutzung auf „minimale Eingriffe" in die bestehende Struktur. Die Neugestaltung besteht im Wesentlichen aus zwei Elementen: zum einen dem Saal für junge Kunstformen (Lieu international des Formes Emergentes – LiFE), entstanden aus einem der ehemaligen U-Boot-Becken, das nun einen „Monospace" bildet, der sich über ein großes Schiebetor zum Hafen hin öffnen lässt; zum anderen einem VIP-Bereich für zeitgenössische Musik in einem ehemaligen Bunkerraum, ein einfacher, von einem Stahlrahmen umschlossener Raumkubus, der Platz für 600 Besucher bietet. Entlang der ehemaligen Gleise verläuft ein interner, überdachter „Lichtteppich", der die einzelnen Raumeinheiten des Bauwerks verbindet. Über eine Treppe gelangt man auf das Dach, wo eine vom Berliner Flughafen Tempelhof stammende geodätische Radarkuppel als „Thinktank für Kunst- und Musikprojekte" dient.

Ce projet portait sur la transformation d'une ancienne base de sous-marins du port de Saint-Nazaire, dans l'Ouest de la France, en espace public pour l'art contemporain et la musique. Construite entre 1941 et 1943 par la marine allemande, cette structure mesure 295 mètres de long par 130 de large et 19 de haut. Elle abritait à l'origine 14 quais pour sous-marins appelés «alvéoles», chacune constituée d'un bassin de 11 mètres de haut sur 117 mètres de long. Ces cellules étaient reliées par des rails, utilisés pour le transport des pièces mécaniques. 85 % de la ville de Saint-Nazaire ont été détruits par les raids aériens qui ont débuté en 1942, mais cette base resta intacte. La reconstruction de la ville ait débuté en 1949, la masse de béton de la base formait toujours une sorte de barrière entre le centre-ville et le port, d'où l'idée de ce projet et de quelques autres destinés à redonner vie à ces énormes installations. Pour des raisons de coût et d'esthétique, l'intervention ne devait entraîner que des «interférences minimales». Le projet comprend essentiellement deux éléments. Le hall du «Lieu international des formes d'art émergentes» (LiFE) est une ancienne alvéole formant un «mono-espace» qui peut s'ouvrir sur le port par une énorme porte en accordéon. Le VIP, lieu pour la musique contemporaine, occupe un ancien bunker, simple volume cubique qui peut accueillir 600 auditeurs. Un «tapis lumineux» court le long des rails et relie les volumes. Un escalier mène jusqu'au toit, où un dôme géodésique pour radars, récupéré à l'aéroport berlinois de Tempelhof, sert de «lieu de réflexion pour des projets artistiques et musicaux».

The geodesic dome recovered from Berlin's Tempelhof Airport is an unexpected touch on the roof of the former submarine base, glowing from within at night.

Durch ihre nach außen dringende Beleuchtung wird die Radarkuppel auf dem Dach des früheren U-Boot-Bunkers, die vom Berliner Flughafen Tempelhof stammt, zu einem außergewöhnlichen nächtlichen Blickfang.

Éclairé de l'intérieur pendant la nuit, le dôme géodésique qui a été récupéré de l'aéroport berlinois de Tempelhof apporte une touche inattendue à la couverture de l'ancienne base sous-marine.

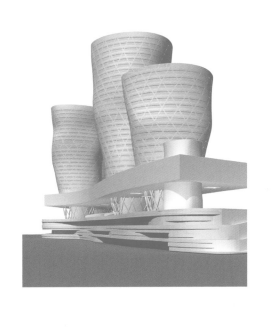
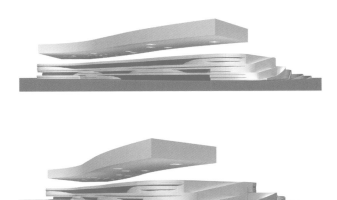

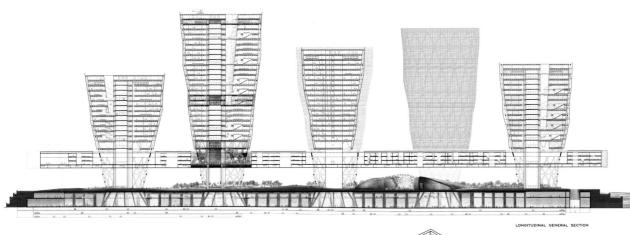

LONGITUDINAL GENERAL SECTION

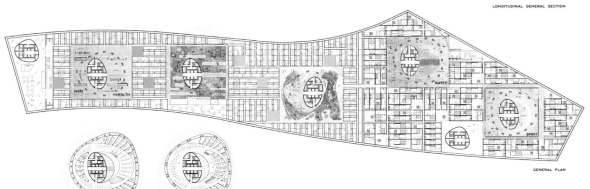

GENERAL PLAN

HIGHER LEVEL CLUSTER TYPE   LOWER LEVEL CLUSTER TYPE

PLANS, LONGITUDINAL SECTION   0   20M

Left, a section and a plan show the complexity and size of the complex. The towers are lifted up off the desert floor, allowing room for a landscaped area above the underground parking zones.

Der Querschnitt und der Grundriss auf der linken Seite lassen die Größe und Komplexität der Anlage erkennen. Durch den Abstand zwischen den Hochhäusern und dem Wüstenboden entsteht Raum für eine Grünanlage über unterirdischen Parkebenen.

À gauche, coupe et plan montrant la complexité et les dimensions de l'ensemble. Les tours sont comme suspendues au-dessus du désert, permettant l'aménagement d'une zone paysagée par-dessus des parkings souterrains.

Four renderings (right) show interior spaces in this multi-use complex intended for almost every phase of the day-to-day life of its occupants or visitors.

Vier Computergrafiken (rechts) des Mehrzweckkomplexes, in dem Bewohner oder Besucher praktisch sämtliche Phasen des Tages verbringen sollen.

Quatre perspectives (à droite) montrent les volumes intérieurs de ce complexe polyvalent destiné à répondre pratiquement à toutes les heures de la vie quotidienne de ses occupants ou visiteurs.

ROJKIND ARQUITECTOS

Rojkind Arquitectos
Campos Eliseos # 432
Colonia Polanco
Mexico City 11560
Mexico

Tel: +52 55 5280 8396
Fax: +52 55 5280 8021
E-mail: michel@rojkindarquitectos.com
Web: www.rojkindarquitectos.com

MICHEL ROJKIND was born in 1969 in Mexico City, where he studied Architecture and Urban Planning at the Universidad Iberoamericana. After working on his own for several years, he teamed up with Isaac Broid and Miquel Adria to establish Adria+Broid+Rojkind (1998–2002). In 2002, he established his own firm in Mexico City. With Arturo Ortiz, Derek Dellekamp, and Tatiana Bilbao, Michel Rojkind co-founded the non-profit MXDF Urban Research Center (2004). The main goal of MXDF is to intervene in specific areas, modifying the production of urban space in Mexico through the systematic study of social, political, environmental, global, and cultural conditions. In order to achieve this, MXDF has been collaborating with several universities in Mexico, Studio Basel, ETH in Zurich, and MIT in Boston. Rojkind's built work includes the F2 House (Mexico City, 2001); the Tlaxcala 190 Apartment Building (Colonia Condesa, Mexico City, 2002); the Mexico City National Videotheque (Mexico City, 2002); Falcon Headquarters (San Angel, Mexico City, 2004); Boska Bar (Mexico City, 2004); the Nestlé Auditorium (Toluca, 2007); and the Nestlé Chocolate Museum (Phase I) (Toluca, Mexico City, 2007, published here), all in Mexico. Work in progress includes the renovation of the Hotel Del Angel (Mexico City, 2007–); and of the San Francisco Hotel (Mexico City, 2007–).

MICHEL ROJKIND wurde 1969 in Mexiko-Stadt geboren, wo er später Architektur und Stadtplanung an der Universidad Iberoamericana studierte. Nach einigen Jahren, in denen er allein arbeitete, tat Rojkind sich mit Isaac Broid und Miquel Adria zusammen (Adria+Broid+Rojkind, 1998–2002). 2002 gründete er seine derzeitige Firma in Mexiko-Stadt. 2004 rief er gemeinsam mit Arturo Ortiz, Derek Dellekamp und Tatiana Bilbao das Nonprofitzentrum MXDF für Stadtforschung ins Leben. MXDF sieht seine Hauptaufgabe darin, in bestimmten urbanen Gebieten aktiv einzugreifen, das heißt, durch systematische Forschungsarbeit zu sozialen, politischen, umwelt-technischen, globalen und kulturellen Verhältnissen Einfluss auf die Entstehung neuer städtischer Räume zu nehmen. Zu diesem Zweck arbeitet MXDF mit verschiede-nen Universitäten in Mexiko sowie mit Studio Basel, der ETH Zürich und dem MIT in Boston zusammen. Zu Rojkinds realisierten Bauten gehören die Casa F2 (Mexiko-Stadt, 2001), das Apartmentgebäude Tlaxcala 190 (Colonia Condesa, Mexiko-Stadt, 2002), die Videoteca Nacional Educativa (Mexiko-Stadt, 2002), die Falcon-Zentrale (San Angel, Mexiko-Stadt, 2004), die Boska-Bar (Mexiko-Stadt, 2004), das Nestlé Auditorium und das hier vorgestellte Nestlé Schokoladenmuseum (Phase I), beide in Toluca (Mexiko-Stadt, 2007). Derzeit arbeitet der Architekt u. a. an der Umgestaltung des Hotels Del Angel (seit 2007) und des Hotels San Francisco (seit 2007), beide in Mexiko-Stadt.

MICHEL ROJKIND, né en 1969 à Mexico, a étudié l'architecture et l'urbanisme à l'Universidad Iberoamericana. Après avoir travaillé seul pendant plusieurs années, il s'est associé à Isaac Broid et Miquel Adria pour créer Adria+Broid+Rojkind (1998–2002). En 2002, il a fondé sa propre agence à Mexico. Avec Arturo Ortiz, Derek Dellekamp, et Tatiana Bilbao, Michel Rojkind est cofondateur du Centre de recherches urbaines MXDF (2004), une association à but non-lucratif dont le principal objectif est d'intervenir dans des régions spécifiques et de modifier la production d'espace urbain au Mexique par l'étude systématique des conditions sociales, politiques, environnementales, globales et culturelles. Dans cet esprit, MXDF collabore avec plusieurs universités mexicaines, Studio Basel, l'ETH à Zurich et le MIT à Boston. Parmi ses réalisations : la maison F2 (Mexico, 2001) ; l'immeuble d'appartements Tlaxcala 190 (Colonia Condesa, Mexico, 2002) ; la vidéothèque nationale de Mexico (Mexico, 2002) ; le siège de Falcon (San Angel, Mexico, 2004) ; le Boska Bar (Mexico, 2004) ; l'auditorium Nestlé (Toluca, 2007) et le musée du chocolat Nestlé, phase I (Toluca, Mexico, 2007, publié ici). Parmi ses réalisations en cours : la rénovation de l'Hotel Del Angel (Mexico, 2007–) et du San Francisco Hotel (Mexico, 2007–).

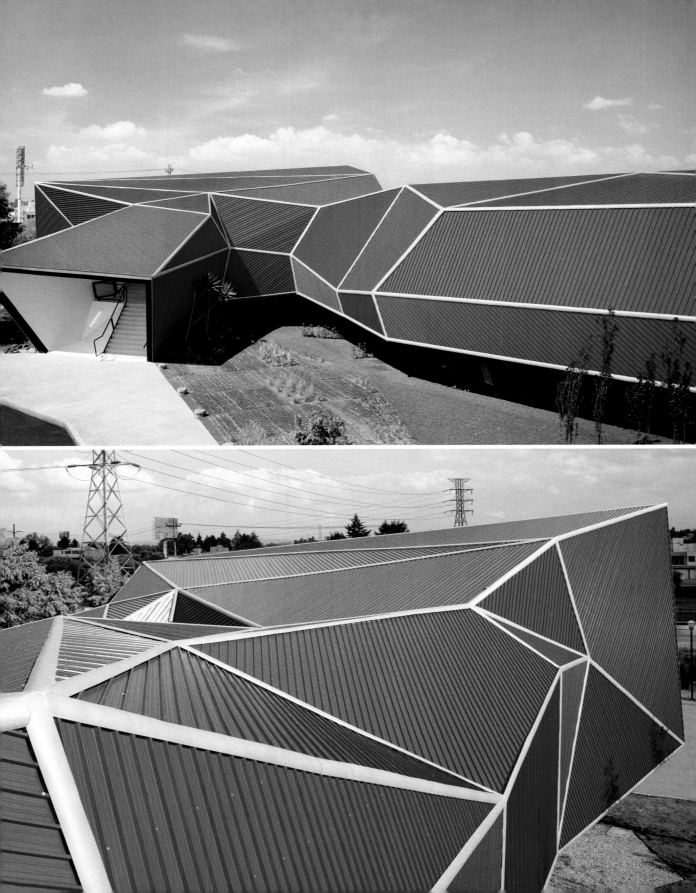

NESTLÉ CHOCOLATE MUSEUM (PHASE I)

Toluca, Mexico City, Mexico, 2007

Floor area: 550 m². Client: Nestlé Mexico. Cost: not disclosed.
Project Team: Agustin Pereyra, Mauricio Garcia-Noriega, Moritz Melchert, Juan Carlos Vidals,
Paulina Goycoolea, Daniel Dusoswa, Matthew Lohden

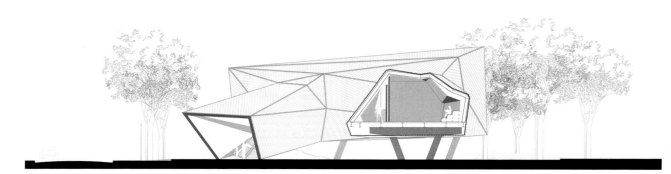

The extremely rapid design and construction schedule for the building certainly did not keep it from being original and very visible.

Dem extrem kurzen Entwurfs- und Bauzeitplan zum Trotz ist ein originelles und nicht zu übersehendes Gebäude entstanden.

Le calendrier extrêmement serré de la conception et de la réalisation du projet n'a pas empêché celui-ci d'être original et très visible.

The architect suggested that Nestlé create the first chocolate museum in Mexico, with a project that would generate a 300-meter-long façade along the Paseo Tollocan highway that could act as an image for the neighboring factory. Given that children would form a large part of the audience, the building is described as "playful yet striking." The first phase of this project, a reception area, auditorium, and shop, was carried forward in an amazing two and a half months from design to completion, working three eight-hour shifts a day. This schedule was imposed by the fact that the firm had committed itself to open a new visitors' center designed by another architect at a specific date. One advantage of this system was that the client was not able to request changes in the plans, which were built as the architect drew them. Rojkind describes his concept of the museum as "a playful folding red shape that resembles something for kids, an origami-shaped bird, or maybe a spaceship…" Rojkind used a red frequently employed by Nestlé to clad the structure in corrugated aluminum, set on a "folded" steel structure elevated off the ground on concrete columns. Inside, pour-in-place concrete floors are finished in white resin. A large window looks out toward the highway and will eventually link to the museum imagined by Rojkind.

Angeregt durch den Vorschlag des Architekten entschloss sich die Firma Nestlé, das erste Schokoladenmuseum Mexikos zu bauen. Dazu sollte eine 300 m lange Fassade parallel zum Paseo Tollocan gehören, die auf die angrenzende Fabrik hinweisen würde. Da unter den Besuchern viele Kinder sein dürften, sollte das Gebäude „verspielt, aber auch überzeugend" sein. In der ersten Phase des Projekts wurden in dem erstaunlich kurzen Zeitraum von nur zweieinhalb Monaten – in drei Achtstundenschichten täglich – ein Empfangsbereich, ein Veranstaltungssaal und ein Museumsladen realisiert. Der enge Zeitplan kam durch das Datum zustande, an dem die Firma ein von einem anderen Architekten entworfenes neues Besucherzentrum eröffnen wollte. Ein Vorteil des raschen Ablaufs bestand darin, dass die Auftraggeber keine Änderungen an den Bauplänen mehr verlangen konnten, da diese quasi gleichzeitig mit der Ausführung entstanden. Rojkind beschreibt den Entwurf des Museumsbaus als eine „verspielt verknickte rote Form, die an irgendein Kinderspielzeug erinnert, an einen Origami-Vogel vielleicht oder ein Raumschiff…" Die auf Betonpfeilern aufgeständerte „gefaltete" Stahlkonstruktion verkleidete der Architekt mit gewellten Aluminiumplatten in einem häufig von Nestlé verwendeten roten Farbton. Die Ortbetonböden im Innenbereich sind mit einer weißen Harzbeschichtung versehen. Eine große Glasfront weist zur Straße hin und soll künftig die Verbindung zu dem von Rojkind geplanten Museum herstellen.

L'architecte a proposé à Nestlé de créer le premier musée du chocolat au Mexique, un projet caractérisé par une façade de 300 m de long sur le Paseo Tollocan qui annonce la présence de la chocolaterie Nestlé. Comme les enfants forment une grande partie des visiteurs attendus, la construction est « ludique mais surprenante à la fois ». La première phase – réception, auditorium et boutique – a été réalisée dans le délai étonnamment court de deux mois et demi, de la conception à l'achèvement des travaux, grâce à des équipes travaillant 24 heures sur 24. Ce calendrier était imposé par Nestlé qui s'était engagé à ouvrir un nouveau centre d'accueil de visiteurs conçu par un autre architecte à une date précise. Un des avantages de cette situation est que le client n'a pas pu demander de modifications des plans qui ont donc été réalisés tels que l'architecte les a dessinés. Rojkind décrit le concept de ce musée comme « une forme pliée ludique et rouge qui ressemble à quelque chose qui serait destiné aux enfants, à un oiseau en origami, ou peut-être à un vaisseau spatial… » L'architecte s'est servi d'un rouge fréquemment utilisé par Nestlé pour habiller sa structure de tôle d'aluminium ondulée posée sur une structure en acier « pliée », et surélevée par rapport au sol sur des colonnes de béton. À l'intérieur, les sols en béton coulé en place sont recouverts de résine blanche. Une grand baie donne sur la voie rapide et sera éventuellement reliée au musée imaginé par Rojkind.

The snaking form of the structure is
lifted off the ground, contributing to
an impression of potential movement
and dynamism.

Der Abstand zum Boden trägt zu dem
Eindruck bei, die dynamisch geschlän-
gelte Gestalt des Baus könnte sich
möglicherweise bewegen.

La forme serpentine de la construction semble être en suspension
au-dessus du sol, ce qui contribue à
donner une impression de mouvement
potentiel ou de dynamisme.

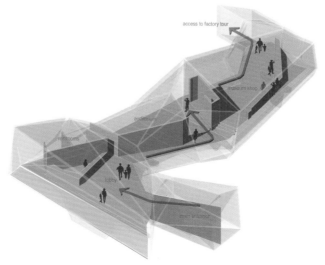

The bright red of the exterior gives way to a white interior, accessed through the large opening with a stairway seen above.

Dem leuchtenden Rot der Außenseite steht ein weißer Innenbereich gegenüber, der durch eine breite Öffnung über eine Treppe zu betreten ist (oben).

À l'intérieur, le rouge vif des façades fait place à un univers intégralement blanc, auquel on accède par un escalier traversant une grande ouverture.

The white interior assumes a part of the planar, faceted aspect of the exterior, but resolves itself into spaces that are easy to use for the client.

Das weiße Interieur übernimmt einen Teil der facettierten Ebenen der Außenseite, geht dann aber in Räume über, die auf die Bedürfnisse des Auftraggebers abgestimmt sind.

L'intérieur blanc reprend en partie l'aspect facetté et planaire de l'extérieur, mais en s'articulant en espaces faciles à utiliser par le client.

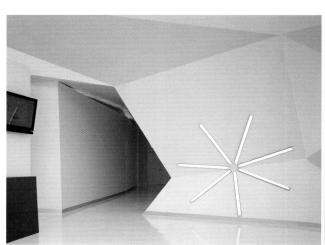

MARC ROLINET

Rolinet et associés
9 rue Pierre Villey
75007 Paris
France

Tel: +33 1 44 42 01 10
Fax: +33 1 44 42 01 20
E-mail: rolinet@rolinet.fr
Web: www.rolinet.fr

Born in Montbeliard, France, in 1956, **MARC ROLINET** earned a Master's degree in Urbanism from the prestigious École des Ponts et Chaussées in 1980 and created his own architectural office the following year. Rolinet has built a large number of housing projects in Paris, Marseille, and Cergy-Pontoise, including the prestigious Gros Caillou complex on the rue de l'Université in Paris (2001). He also has considerable experience in the area of office buildings and, more unexepectedly, religious structures. He has completed several projects for the Protestant Deaconesses de Reuilly, such as the chapel published here, as well as churches in Paris, Villeneuve-le-Roi, and Montreuil in the Paris area. Despite the ease with which he works on a large scale, Marc Rolinet has also designed a number of individual homes. He is currently working on housing and office projects in Montpellier (France), Lisbon (Portugal), Saint-Étienne (France), and Grimentz (Switzerland). Having opened an office in Geneva in 2006, he is also active in the area near the borders of France and Switzerland, such as the French city of Annemasse, where he was selected as architect of the large ZAC Chablais-Gare district.

MARC ROLINET, geboren 1956 im französischen Montbeliard, erwarb 1980 das Masterdiplom in Stadtplanung an der renommierten École des Ponts et Chaussées. Im darauffolgenden Jahr gründete er ein Architekturbüro in Paris. Rolinet hat eine große Zahl von Wohnbauprojekten in Paris, Marseille und Cergy-Pontoise realisiert, darunter die bekannte Anlage Gros Caillou in der Rue de l'Université in Paris (2001). Ferner verfügt er über weitreichende Erfahrungen mit dem Bau von Bürogebäuden sowie – etwas ungewöhnlicher – von religiösen Bauten. Rolinet hat mehrere Projekte für die protestantische Gemeinschaft der Diakonissen von Reuilly verwirklicht, darunter die hier vorgestellte Kapelle, sowie Kirchenbauten in Paris, Villeneuve-le-Roi und Montreuil. Neben seiner souveränen Gestaltung von Großbauten entwarf Rolinet auch eine Reihe von Privathäusern. Derzeit arbeitet er an Wohnbau- und Büroprojekten in Montpellier, Lissabon und Saint-Étienne sowie im schweizerischen Grimentz. Seit der Eröffnung eines Büros in Genf im Jahr 2006 ist er auch in der schweizerisch-französischen Grenzregion aktiv, etwa in dem französischen Ort Annemasse, wo er für die Entwicklung des Stadterneuerungsgebiets Chablais-Gare ausgewählt wurde.

Né à Montbéliard, France, en 1956, **MARC ROLINET** est diplômé d'urbanisme de la prestigieuse École nationale des Ponts et Chaussées (1980) et a créé son agence d'architecture l'année suivante. Il a construit un grand nombre de logements à Paris, Marseille et Cergy-Pontoise, dont le luxueux complexe du Gros Caillou, rue de l'Université à Paris (2001). Il possède également une expérience considérable des immeubles de bureaux et, de façon plus inattendue, des édifices religieux. Il a réalisé plusieurs projets pour les Diaconesses de Reuilly, dont la chapelle publiée ici, et des églises à Paris, Villeneuve-le-Roi et Montreuil en banlieue parisienne. Très à l'aise dans les réalisations à grande échelle, il a également conçu un certain nombre de résidences individuelles. Il travaille actuellement sur des projets de logements et de bureaux à Montpellier, Lisbonne (Portugal), Saint-Étienne et Grimentz (Suisse). Après avoir ouvert un bureau à Genève en 2006, il est très actif dans la région frontalière entre la Suisse et la France, à Annemasse en particulier, ville pour laquelle il a été nommé architecte de la ZAC Chablais-Gare.

CHAPEL OF THE DEACONESSES OF REUILLY

Versailles, France, 2004–07

Site area: 40 156 m². Floor area: 620 m².
Client: Diaconesses of Reuilly. Cost: €2.2 million

The almost strictly triangular plan makes space for the irregular wooden oval that forms the inner sanctum, or chapel itself.

Der dreieckige Grundriss bietet Raum für eine in etwa ovale Schale aus Kiefernholz, die die eigentliche Kapelle bildet.

Le plan quasiment triangulaire ménage la place de l'espace ovale irrégulier qui constitue le sanctuaire proprement dit.

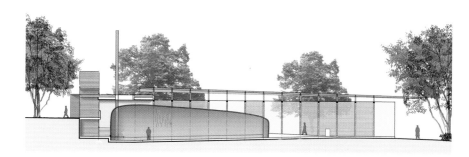

The Community of the Protestant Deaconnesses of Reuilly was founded in Versailles in 1841. There are approximately 80 nuns associated with this order. Rolinet had completed a 450-square-meter activity center for the nuns on the same site in 2002 (L'Arbresle, 2001–02). The same sense of austerity coupled with modernity that was visible in the earlier project is also apparent in the newer Chapel, which is made essentially of concrete, glass, galvanized steel, and pine. Within a triangular glass envelope, the architect has placed what he calls a shell made of slats of pine that admit some light, while creating an essentially enclosed place of worship. While he chooses to refer to a nutshell in describing the interior, wooden design of the chapel proper, it is apparent that there is also a reference to the boat hull, which can be associated with Christian symbols, ranging from the bark of Saint Peter through architectural and artistic references to the Bible. "Then he got into the boat and his disciples followed him. Without warning, a furious storm came up on the lake, so that the waves swept over the boat. But Jesus was sleeping. The disciples went and woke him, saying, 'Lord, save us! We're going to drown!' He replied, 'You of little faith, why are you so afraid?' Then he got up and rebuked the winds and the waves, and it was completely calm" (Matthew 8:23–26).

Die Gemeinschaft der Diakonissen von Reuilly ist ein 1841 in Versailles gegründeter protestantischer Orden, dem heute 80 Nonnen angehören. Auf dem Gelände der neuen Kapelle hatte Rolinet für die Schwestern bereits früher ein 450 m² großes Gemeinschaftszentrum (L'Arbresle, 2001–02) gebaut. Die in diesem Bau zum Ausdruck kommende Verbindung von Nüchternheit und Modernität nahm Rolinet in seinem Kapellenneubau wieder auf, der im Wesentlichen aus Beton, Glas, galvanisiertem Stahl und Kiefernholz besteht. In eine dreieckige Hülle aus Glas setzte der Architekt eine – wie er es nennt – Schale aus Kiefernholzleisten ein, durch die einerseits genügend Licht einfällt und die andererseits einen hinreichend geschlossenen Andachtsraum bilden. Wenngleich Rolinet die Gestalt des hölzernen Innenraums der eigentlichen Kapelle mit einer Nussschale vergleicht, ist auch die Ähnlichkeit mit einen Schiffsrumpf nicht zu übersehen. Dieser lässt sich als ein christliches Symbol verstehen, das etwa als Boot des heiligen Petrus oder in zahllosen architektonischen und anderen künstlerischen Bibelreferenzen auftritt. „Er stieg in das Boot und seine Jünger folgten ihm. Plötzlich brach auf dem See ein gewaltiger Sturm los, so dass das Boot von den Wellen überflutet wurde. Jesus aber schlief. Da traten seine Jünger zu ihm und weckten ihn; sie riefen: Herr, rette uns, wir gehen zugrunde! Er sagte zu ihnen: Warum habt Ihr solche Angst, ihr Kleingläubigen? Dann stand er auf, drohte den Winden und dem See und es trat völlige Stille ein" (Matthäus 8,23–26).

La communauté protestante des Diaconesses de Reuilly été fondée à Versailles en 1841. Rolinet a réalisé pour cet Ordre, qui compte environ 80 sœurs, un centre d'activité de 450 m² sur le même site en 2002 (L'Arbresle, 2001–02). Le sentiment d'austérité et de modernité du projet antérieur se retrouve dans cette nouvelle chapelle construite pour l'essentiel en béton, verre, acier galvanisé et bois de pin. À l'intérieur d'une enveloppe de verre triangulaire, l'architecte a implanté ce qu'il appelle une « coque » en lattes de pin qui laissent filtrer un peu de lumière tout en délimitant l'espace clos de la prière. S'il se réfère à une coque de noix pour décrire cet intérieur, il fait également appel, semble-t-il, à la coque du bateau liée à la symbolique chrétienne, avec notamment la barque de saint Pierre, et à des références architecturales et artistiques de la Bible : « Puis il monta dans la barque, suivi de ses disciples. Et voici qu'une grande agitation se fit dans la mer, au point que la barque était couverte par les vagues. Lui cependant dormait. S'étant approchés, les disciples le réveillèrent en disant : Au secours, Seigneur, nous périssons ! Il leur dit : Pourquoi avez-vous peur, gens de peu de foi ? Alors, s'étant levé, il menaça les vents et la mer, et il se fit un grand calme » (Mathieu 8 :23–26).

The outer glass and metal shell of the building is so light it appears almost to dissolve into the wooded background of the site. The wooden strip shell of the chapel (above) is reminiscent of an inverted boat.

Die Hülle des Bauwerks, aus Glas und Metall, wirkt so leicht, dass sie vor dem mit Bäumen bestandenen Gelände zu verschwinden scheint. Die aus Holzleisten bestehende Hülle der Kapelle (oben) erinnert an einen auf den Kopf gestellten Bootsrumpf.

coquille de verre et de métal qui constitue l'édifice semble si légère qu'elle se dissout pratiquement dans le contexte boisé du site. La coque de bois de la chapelle (ci-dessus) évoque un bateau inversé.

The lattice-work interior of the chapel shell allows some light to enter. Aside from the cross, the interior has no fixed elements.

Durch das Gitterwerk dringt schwaches Licht in den Innenraum. Abgesehen von dem Kreuz lassen sich sämtliche Gegenstände bewegen.

L'intérieur de la chapelle en lattis de bois laisse entrer une certaine quantité de lumière naturelle. Hormi la croix, aucun élément n'est fixe.

The Deaconesses of Reuilly were firm in their desire to keep the interior of the chapel as simple as possible, with only folding wooden chairs and a minimal altar.

Die Diakonissen von Reuilly bestanden darauf, den Kapelleninnenraum so schlicht wie möglich zu belassen und ihn nur mit hölzernen Klappstühlen und einem kleinen Altar auszustatten.

Les Diaconesses de Reuilly souhaitaient vivement une chapelle aussi simple que possible, uniquement équipée d'un autel minimaliste et de chaises pliantes.

HANS-JÖRG RUCH

Hans-Jörg Ruch
Via Brattas 2
7500 St. Moritz
Switzerland

Tel: +41 81 837 32 40
Fax: +41 81 837 32 50
E-mail: info@ruch-arch.ch
Web: www.ruch-arch.ch

HANS-JÖRG RUCH was born in 1946 and received his diploma in Architecture from the ETH in Zurich in 1971. He received his Master's from the Rensselaer Polytechnic Institute (Troy, New York, 1973) with a thesis entitled, "Towards an Architecture of Tourism." From 1974 to 1977, he worked in the office of Obrist und Partner, St. Moritz, and then created a partnership with Urs Hüsler (Ruch + Hüsler, Architekten, St. Moritz, 1977–88). He created his present firm in 1989. Widely traveled, Ruch has nonetheless made his career largely in the Engadine region of Switzerland, specializing in the renovation of the area's rich patrimony of old stone and wood houses. His delicate and knowing touch on these buildings provides an interesting answer to the question of how to modernize structures that date, in some cases, from medieval times. Since working on the Chesa Madalena in Zuoz (2001–02, published here), he has completed numerous projects, including a number of guest rooms in the Hotel Castell (Zuoz, 2004, renovation project, undertaken with UNStudio, page 504); the Not Vital House (Tschlin, 2004); the Badrutt's Palace Hotel (St. Moritz, south façade renovation, 2005); the Palace Gallery opposite the Badrutt's Palace Hotel (St. Moritz, 2002); the Chesa Albertini (Zuoz, 2006); and the reconstruction and enlargement of the Chamanna da Tschierva for the Swiss Alpine Club (St. Moritz, 2007), all in Switzerland.

HANS-JÖRG RUCH, geboren 1946, erwarb 1971 sein Architekturdiplom an der ETH Zürich. Anschließend absolvierte er ein Masterstudium am Rensselaer Polytechnic Institute in Troy, New York (1973), das er mit einer Arbeit zum Thema „Towards an Architecture of Tourism" abschloss. Von 1974 bis 1977 arbeitete er bei Obrist und Partner in St. Moritz, danach bildete er eine Ateliergemeinschaft mit Urs Hüsler (Ruch + Hüsler Architekten, St. Moritz, 1977–88). Seine heutige Firma gründete er 1989. Ungeachtet seiner vielen Reisen konzentriert sich Ruchs wesentliches Schaffen auf das Engadin, wobei der Schwerpunkt auf der Renovierung alter Stein- und Holzhäuser liegt, die dort in reicher Zahl zu finden sind. Ruchs einfühlsamer und kenntnisreicher Umgang mit diesen Häusern zeigt interessante Wege auf, wie sich Bauten modernisieren lassen, die mitunter noch aus dem Mittelalter stammen. Nach seiner Arbeit an der Chesa Madalena in Zuoz (2001–02, hier vorgestellt), hat Ruch noch zahlreiche weitere Projekte in der Schweiz abgeschlossen, darunter mehrere Zimmer des Hotel Castell in Zuoz (2004, ein gemeinsam mit UNStudio durchgeführtes Renovierungsprojekt, Seite 504), das Haus Not Vital in Tschlin (2004), Badrutt's Palace Hotel in St. Moritz (2005, Restaurierung der Südfassade), die Palace Galerie gegenüber des Badrutt's Palace Hotel (St. Moritz, 2002), die Chesa Albertini in Zuoz (2006) und die Erweiterung der Chamanna da Tschierva des Schweizer Alpenclub (St. Moritz, 2002).

HANS-JÖRG RUCH, né en 1946, est diplômé en architecture de l'ETH à Zurich (1971). Il reçoit son mastère du Rensselaer Polytechnic Institute (Troy, New York, 1973) pour un mémoire intitulé : « Vers une architecture du tourisme ». De 1974 à 1977, il travaille pour l'agence Obrist und Partner, St. Moritz, puis s'associe avec Urs Hüsler (Ruch + Hüsler, Architekten, St. Moritz, 1977–88). Il a créé son agence actuelle en 1989. S'il voyage beaucoup, il a néanmoins accompli sa carrière en grande partie en Engadine (Suisse), où il s'est spécialisé dans la rénovation du riche patrimoine local de maisons de pierre et de bois anciennes. Son approche délicate et informée de ces constructions est une intéressante réponse à la question de la modernisation d'un bâti datant, dans certains cas, de l'époque médiévale. Depuis son intervention sur la Chesa Madalena à Zuoz (2001–02, publiée ici), il a achevé de nombreux projets dont plusieurs chambres de l'Hotel Castell (Zuoz, 2004, rénovation, avec UNStudio, page 504) ; la maison Not Vital (Tschlin, 2004) ; le Badrutt's Palace Hotel (St. Moritz, rénovation de la façade sud, 2005) ; la galerie Palace situé en face de ce dernier (St. Moritz, 2002) ; la Chesa Albertini (Zuoz, 2006) et l'élargissement de la Chamanna da Tschierva de club alpin suisse (St. Moritz, 2002), tous en Suisse.

CHESA MADALENA

Zuoz, Switzerland, 2001–02

Floor area: 900 m². Client: Ruedi Tschudi. Cost: not disclosed.
Collaborator: Peter Lacher

No other village in the Graubünden region has as many medieval buildings as Zuoz, a small town located near St. Moritz. In recent decades, a number of hidden towers that had been enclosed in other structures were discovered in Zuoz. The results of dendrochronological examinations prove that these towers were built in the 14th century and that they survived the fire on June 6, 1499, during the Swabian War thanks to their thick walls. The tower in today's Chesa Madalena is 10 meters by 10 meters and, at approximately 16 meters in height, it is the tallest surviving tower. The original upper part of the roof is no longer extant: when the present roof was put on, roughly a hundred years ago, the old roof was dismantled and adapted to suit the new shape. In the uppermost part of the tower, charred wood from the original tier of beams was found walled in. When it underwent dendrochronological analysis, the date of felling (1304) was pinpointed. The building was used as a farm structure until 1999. After consulting the Office for the Preservation of Historic Buildings, local authorities permitted the removal of parts of the building without historic significance in the first phase. Thus, the old tower could be laid bare and a limited number of essential new structures could be planned. The desired minimal room layout meant that most of the new empty space, created by eliminating historically insignificant building structures, could be retained. Again it was possible to leave the former stables and hayloft and the tower roof space empty. Now used as a contemporary art gallery, the irregular old spaces and marks of history left by Ruch in the building clash in no way with his own modern additions and readily accept the art itself.

In keinem anderen Ort Graubündens finden sich so viele mittelalterliche Gebäude wie in Zuoz, einer kleinen Gemeinde nicht weit von St. Moritz. In den vergangenen Jahrzehnten wurden hier zahlreiche alte Wohntürme entdeckt, die von neueren Bauwerken eingeschlossen sind. Dendrochronologische Untersuchungen ergaben, dass die Türme dank ihrer dicken Wände den im Schwabenkrieg ausgebrochenen großen Brand vom 6. Juni 1499 überstanden haben und auf das 14. Jahrhundert zurückgehen. Das Exemplar in der heutigen Chesa Madalena, mit einer Grundfläche von 10 x 10 m und einer Höhe von ca. 16 m, ist der höchste der erhaltenen Türme. Nicht mehr vorhanden ist der obere Teil des Dachs; als man vor etwa 100 Jahren das gegenwärtige Dach aufsetzte, wurde das alte abgetragen und der neuen Form angepasst. Im oberen Teil des Turms fanden sich jedoch noch eingemauerte, verkohlte Holzreste der originalen Balkendecke. Als Fällungsdatum stellte die dendrochronologische Analyse das Jahr 1304 fest. Bis 1999 diente das Gebäude landwirtschaftlichen Zwecken. Nach Beratung mit dem Büro für Denkmalpflege erlaubten die örtlichen Behörden, in einer ersten Arbeitsphase historisch unbedeutende Teile des Gebäudes zu entfernen. So wurden der alte Turm freigelegt sowie einige wenige neue Strukturen eingeplant. Da ohnehin nur eine minimale Raumaufteilung gewünscht war, wurde der durch die Eliminierung historisch unbedeutender Baubestandteile neu gewonnene leere Raum beibehalten. Ebenso wurden die früheren Stallungen, der Heuboden und das Dachgeschoss des Turms leer belassen. Die unregelmäßigen alten Räume und die von Ruch nicht getilgten Spuren der Geschichte stehen der heutigen Nutzung des Gebäudes als Galerie für zeitgenössische Kunst nicht im Weg, sondern bieten einen äußerst passenden Rahmen für die Kunstwerke.

Aucun autre village des Grisons ne possède autant de constructions médiévales que Zuoz, près de St. Moritz. Au cours des dernières décennies, plusieurs tours cachées, alors englobées dans d'autres structures, y ont été découvertes. Les examens dendrochronologiques montrent qu'elles datent du XIVe siècle et ont survécu grâce à l'épaisseur de leurs murs à l'incendie survenu en 1499, au cours de la guerre de Souabe. La tour de la Chesa Madalena mesure 10 m x 10 m, et environ 16 m de haut. Elle est la plus élevée de celles subsistant dans le village. La partie supérieure du toit a disparu, démantelée et adaptée, pour laisser place, il y a un siècle, à une nouvelle couverture. Dans la partie la plus élevée, des vestiges de bois calciné de la charpente originale ont été trouvés dans les murs. L'analyse dendrochronologique a montré que l'arbre avait été coupé en 1304. Le bâtiment avait servi de ferme jusqu'en 1999. Après avoir consulté le Bureau de préservation des bâtiments historiques, les autorités locales ont autorisé la suppression de certaines parties sans intérêt historique. Ainsi la vieille tour pouvait réapparaître et la construction d'extensions essentielles au projet devenait possible. Les nouveaux espaces pouvaient ainsi répondre au plan souhaité. On a pu ainsi conserver les anciennes étables et le grenier à foin, ainsi que le volume sous le toit. Actuellement transformés en galerie d'art, les anciens volumes irréguliers et les marques de l'histoire conservés par Ruch dans le bâtiment s'accordent sans heurts à ses propres interventions et s'adaptent aisément aux œuvres exposées.

The Chesa Madalena has been subtly modernized, revealing aspects of the original structure that had long been hidden, while creating spaces well suited to contemporary art.

Bei der umsichtigen Modernisierung der Chesa Madalena wurden Teile des ursprünglichen Bauwerks freigelegt und ein geeigneter Ausstellungsort für zeitgenössische Kunst geschaffen.

La Chesa Madalena a été subtilement modernisée, et révèle des caractéristiques de la construction originale, tout en créant un espace adapté à l'exposition d'art contemporain.

SANAA/KAZUYO SEJIMA + RYUE NISHIZAWA

SANAA/Kazuyo Sejima + Ryue Nishizawa
7–A Shinagawa-Soko / 2–2–35 Higashi-Shinagawa / Shinagawa-ku / Tokyo–140 / Japan
E-mail: sanaa@sanaa.co.jp

Born in Ibaraki Prefecture in 1956, Kazuyo Sejima received her M.Arch degree from the Japan Women's University in 1981 and went to work in the office of Toyo Ito the same year. She established Kazuyo Sejima and Associates in Tokyo in 1987. She has been a Visiting Lecturer at the Japan Women's University and at Waseda University since 1994. Ryue Nishizawa was born in Tokyo in 1966, and graduated from the National University in Yokohama in 1990. He began working with Sejima the same year, and the pair created the new firm **SANAA/KAZUYO SEJIMA + RYUE NISHIZAWA** in 1995. He has been a Visiting Professor at the Harvard GSD and at the National University in Yokohama. The built work of Kazuyo Sejima includes the Saishunkan Seiyaku Women's Dormitory (Kumamoto, 1990–91); the Pachinko Parlor I (Hitachi, Ibaraki, 1992–93); the Pachinko Parlor II (Nakamachi, Ibaraki, 1993); the Villa in the Forest (Tateshina, Nagano, 1993–94); the Chofu Station Police Box (Tokyo, 1993–94); and the Pachinko Parlor III (Hitachi, Ibaraki, 1995), all in Japan. The work of SANAA includes the 21st Century Museum of Contemporary Art (Kanazawa, Ishikawa, 2002–04); the Moriyama House (Tokyo, Japan, 2002–05); the Glass Pavilion of the Toledo Museum of Art (Toledo, Ohio, 2003–06); De Kunstlinie, the Theater and Cultural Center (Almere, The Netherlands, 2004–07, published here); an extension of the Valencia Institute of Modern Art (IVAM, Valencia, Spain, under construction); and a building for the New Museum of Contemporary Art (New York, 2005–07, also published here). Kazuyo Sejima and Ryue Nishizawa won the competitions to design the Learning Center of the EPFL in Lausanne, Switzerland, and the new building of the Louvre, in Lens, France.

Kazuyo Sejima, geboren 1956 in der japanischen Präfektur Ibaraki, erlangte 1981 ihren Masterabschluss an der Japanischen Frauenuniversität und begann im selben Jahr, im Büro von Toyo Ito zu arbeiten. 1987 gründete sie in Tokio das Büro Kazuyo Sejima and Associates. Seit 1994 hält sie Gastvorlesungen an der Japanischen Frauenuniversität und an der Waseda-Universität. Ryue Nishizawa wurde 1966 in Tokio geboren. 1990 schloss er sein Studium an der japanischen Nationaluniversität in Yokohama ab und begann mit Sejima zusammenzuarbeiten. 1995 gründete das Duo die Firma **SANAA/KAZUYO SEJIMA + RYUE NISHIZAWA**. Nishizawa war Gastprofessor an der Graduate School of Design in Harvard und an der japanischen Nationaluniversität Yokohama. Zu Kazuyo Sejimas in Japan realisierten Arbeiten gehören u. a. das Frauenwohnheim Saishunkan Seiyaku in Kumamoto (1990–91), die Pachinko-Halle I in Hitachi, Ibaraki (1992–93), die Pachinko-Halle II in Nakamachi, Ibaraki (1993), eine Waldvilla in Tateshina, Nagano (1993–94), die Polizeistation Chofu in Tokio (1993–94) und die Pachinko-Halle III in Hitachi, Ibaraki (1993–94). Von SANAA stammen das Museum für zeitgenössische Kunst des 21. Jahrhunderts in Kanazawa, Ishikawa (2002–04), das Haus Moriyama in Tokio (2002–05), der Glaspavillon des Toledo Museum of Art, Ohio (2003–06), das hier vorgestellte Theater und Kulturzentrum „De Kunstlinie" im niederländischen Almere (2004–07), eine Erweiterung des Instituto Valenciano de Arte Moderno (IVAM, im Bau) im spanischen Valencia und ein Gebäude für das New Museum of Contemporary Art in New York (2005–07, ebenfalls hier vorgestellt). Bei den Wettbewerben für den Entwurf des Learning Center der École Polytechnique Fédérale de Lausanne in der Schweiz sowie für den Entwurf des Louvre-Ablegers im französischen Lens belegten Kazuyo Sejima und Ryue Nishizawa jeweils den ersten Platz.

Née dans la préfecture d'Ibaraki en 1956, Kazuyo Sejima obtient son M. Arch. de l'Université féminine du Japon en 1981 et est engagée par Toyo Ito la même année. Elle crée l'agence Kazuyo Sejima and Associates à Tokyo en 1987. Elle est chargée de cours invitée à l'Université féminine et à l'université de Waseda depuis 1994. Ryue Nishizawa, né à Tokyo en 1966, est diplômé de l'Université nationale de Yokohama (1990). Il a commencé à travailler avec Sejima la même année avant qu'ils fondent ensemble **SANAA/KAZUYO SEJIMA + RYUE NISHIZAWA** en 1995. Il a été professeur invité à la Harvard Graduate School of Design et à l'Université nationale de Yokohama. Les réalisations de Kazuyo Sejima comprennent le dortoir pour jeunes filles Saishunkan Seiyaku (Kumamoto, 1990–91); Pachinko Parlor I (Hitachi, Ibaraki, 1992–93); Pachinko Parlor II (Nakamachi, Ibaraki, 1993); une villa en forêt (Tateshina, Nagano, 1993–94); le poste de police de Chofu (Tokyo, 1993–94) et Pachinko Parlor III (Hitachi Ibaraki, 1995), toutes au Japon. Parmi les références de SANAA: le musée d'Art contemporain du XXIe siècle (Kanazawa, Ishikawa, 2002–04); la maison Moriyama (Tokyo, 2002–05); le pavillon de verre du Toledo Museum of Art (Toledo, Ohio, 2003–06); De Kunstlinie, un théâtre et centre culturel à Almere (Pays-Bas, 2004–07, publié ici); une extension de l'Institut d'art moderne de Valence (IVAM, Espagne, en construction) et un immeuble pour le New Museum of Contemporary Art à New York (2005–07, également publié dans ces pages). Kazuyo Sejima et Ryue Nishizawa ont remporté les concours pour le centre d'enseignement de l'EPFL à Lausanne, Suisse, et les nouvelles installations du Louvre à Lens, France.

DE KUNSTLINIE

Theater and Cultural Center, Almere, The Netherlands, 2004–07

*Site area: 15 354 m². Floor area: 19 085 m². Client: City of Almere, Dienst Stadscentrum.
Cost: €40 million (including €6 million of theater equipment). Architects: SANAA/Kazuyo Sejima + Ryue Nishizawa,
Yoshitaka Tanase, Go Kuwata, Jonas Elding, Yoritaka Hayashi.
Design Collaboration: Adviesbureau voor Bouwtechniek bv*

The master plan for the new town of Almere, located east of Amsterdam, was drawn up by the Rotterdam firm of Rem Koolhaas, OMA. SANAA was selected to design the city's theater and cultural community center on the lake that faces the new center. The architects say, "We sought a plan without hierarchy, a very public building where everything from circulation to classrooms is given the same spatial treatment. Circulating through the building is like passing through a series of rooms, and, despite an apparent uniformity in plan, the sprawling main floor renders specific characteristics in different areas depending on their relationship with the water at the perimeter. In this plan there is no difference between structure and partition. The main structural system is made up of flat steel bars, acting as columns inside what appear to be normal partition walls." The steel frame and reinforced-concrete structure includes seven stories and a basement.

Almere ist ein östlich von Amsterdam neu angelegter Ort, dessen Masterplan von Rem Kohlhaas' Rotterdamer Office for Metropolitan Architecture stammt. SANAA wurde für den Entwurf eines städtischen Theaters und Kulturzentrums ausgewählt, das direkt an einen See angrenzen soll. Sejima und Nishizawa führen dazu aus: „Wir haben uns um eine hierarchiefreie Grundaufteilung bemüht, um ein öffentliches Gebäude, in dem alle Räume, von den Gängen bis hin zu den Unterrichtsräumen, auf die gleiche Weise behandelt werden. Man bewegt sich durch das Gebäude wie durch eine Abfolge von einzelnen Räumen. Trotz der erkennbar einheitlichen Grundrissgestaltung weist das weite Hauptgeschoss jedoch in seinen einzelnen Abschnitten unterschiedliche Merkmale auf, je nachdem, in welchem Verhältnis diese sich zu dem Gewässer im angrenzenden Außenbereich befinden. Dabei wird nicht zwischen tragenden Elementen und Zwischenwänden unterschieden. Das Hauptprinzip der Konstruktion sind flache Stahlstäbe, die sich als Stützen in den scheinbar gewöhnlichen Trennwänden befinden." Der Stahlrahmen- und Stahlbetonbau umfasst sieben Geschosse und einen Keller.

Le plan directeur de la ville nouvelle d'Almere, située à l'est d'Amsterdam, a été établi par l'agence rotterdamoise de Rem Koolhaas, OMA. SANAA a été sélectionné pour concevoir son théâtre et un centre culturel sur le lac, face au nouveau centre. Selon les architectes : « Nous avons cherché à créer un plan sans hiérarchie, un bâtiment très public où tout, des circulations aux salles de classe, reçoit le même traitement spatial. Circuler dans le bâtiment se compare au franchissement d'une succession de pièces, et, malgré l'apparente uniformité de plan, le niveau principal présente des caractéristiques spécifiques dans ses différentes zones en fonction de leur relation avec l'eau présente en périmétrie. Ce plan ne fait pas de différences entre structure et partitions. Le système structurel principal se compose de barreaux plats en acier qui font office de colonnes prises dans ce qui semble être des cloisonnements classiques. » L'ossature en acier et la structure en béton armé se développent sur sept niveaux et un sous-sol.

SANAA masters extremely simple forms whose skin glows in the light, giving much more presence to the architecture than a more complex façade might have done.

SANAA verstehen es, extrem schlichte Formen zu gestalten, deren Oberflächen im Hellen leuchten, wodurch die Architektur eine weitaus stärkere Präsenz erhält als es bei einer komplexeren Fassade der Fall wäre.

SANAA maîtrise les formes extrêmement simples dont la peau s'illumine sous la lumière, ce qui donne une présence beaucoup plus forte à l'architecture qu'une façade plus complexe n'aurait pu le faire.

The composition is decidedly geometric with some variations on the repetitive placement of cladding elements and doors or windows.

Die Komposition ist streng geometrisch angelegt. Eine wenige Variationen finden sich in der repetitiven Anordnung von Verkleidungselementen und Türen oder Fenstern.

La composition est résolument géométrique avec juste quelques variations sur l'implantation répétitive d'éléments d'habillage, de portes et de fenêtres.

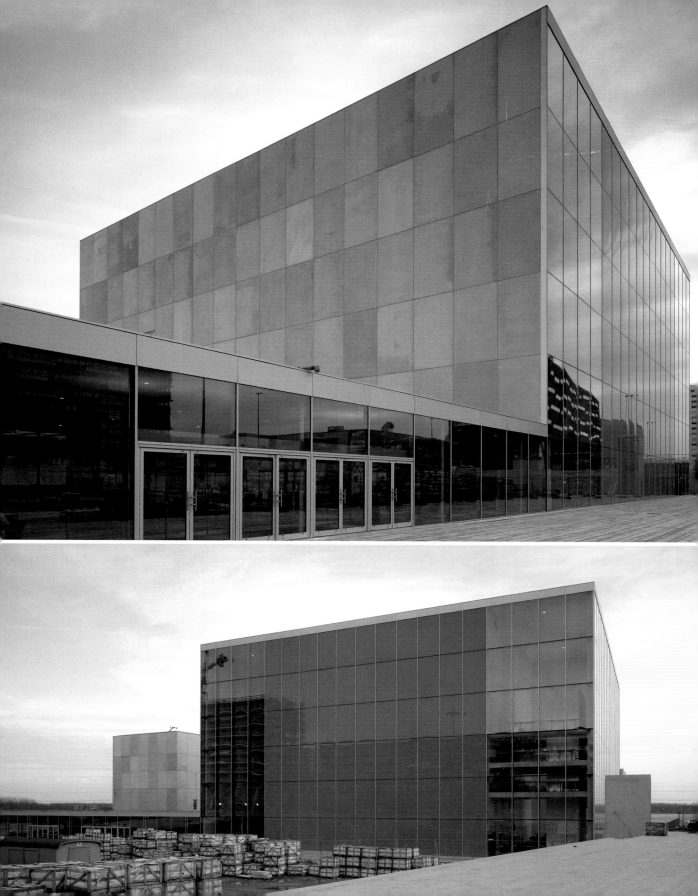

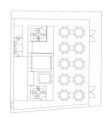

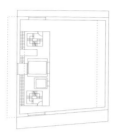
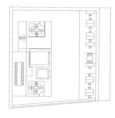

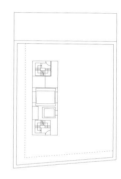

Interior spaces, such as the one to the left, continue the glowing minimalism seen in the exteriors of the building—light and fully open spaces are the rule. Above, floor plans for each level of the building.

In den Innenräumen wie dem links abgebildeten setzt sich der leuchtende Minimalismus der Außenseiten des Gebäudes fort; helle, offene Räume sind die Regel. Oben die jeweilige Raumanordnung in den einzelnen Geschossen.

Les volumes intérieurs, comme celui ci-contre, cultivent le minimalisme brillant observé à l'extérieur : les espaces lumineux et pleinement ouverts sont la règle. Au-dessus, le plan au sol de chaque étage du bâtiment.

Some curvilinear elements, such as a
spiral staircase, are introduced inside
the building, where extreme simplicity
remains the guiding principle.

Im Innern des Gebäudes, das von
extremer Schlichtheit bestimmt ist,
finden sich nur wenige nicht gerad-
linige Elemente, so etwa die Treppen-
spirale.

Certains éléments curvilignes, comme
cet escalier en spirale, ont été introduits, mais une extrême simplicité
reste le principe directeur.

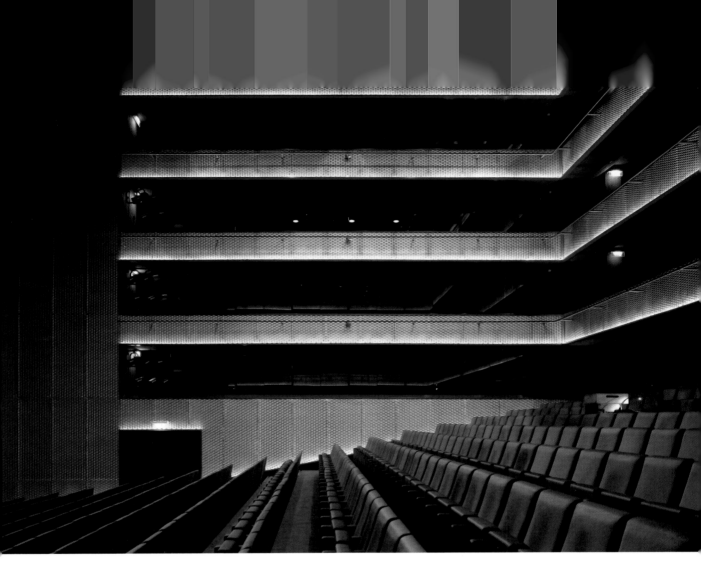

The main theater is dark, in marked contrast to the exterior or the other, white interior spaces. Right, a view outside through high windows.

Der dunkle Hauptsaal des Theaters bildet einen ausgeprägten Kontrast zur Außenseite des Gebäudes und den übrigen weißen Innenräumen. Rechts der Blick durch hohe Fenster nach draußen.

La salle de théâtre principale est de couleur sombre, en contraste marqué avec l'extérieur ou le reste des volumes intérieurs traités en blanc. À droite, une vue de l'extérieur prise à travers des fenêtres.

NEW MUSEUM OF CONTEMPORARY ART

New York, New York, USA, 2005–07

*Floor area: 3948 m². Client: Zubatkin Owner Representation, New York City.
Cost: not disclosed. Principals in Charge: Kazuyo Sejima, Ryue Nishizawa. Project Architects: Florian Idenburg,
Toshihiro Oki, Jonas Elding, Koji Yoshida, Hiroaki Katagiri, Javier Haddad, Erika Hidaka.
Associate Architect: Gensler, New York City*

The stacked, irregular form of the
New Museum stands out against
the otherwise old-fashioned architecture of the Bowery area of lower
Manhattan.

Die unregelmäßige Stapelform des
New Museum hebt sich deutlich von
den übrigen, älteren Gebäuden der
Gegend um die Bowery in Lower
Manhattan ab.

L'empilement de forme irrégulière
du New Museum se détache de
l'architecture démodée du quartier
du Bowery, dans le bas de Manhatan.

Making use of setbacks, the building allows space for light to come into gallery floors and for views of Manhattan.

Durch die Einrückungen entstehen Lichtöffnungen für die Ausstellungsetagen sowie Außerterrassen, von denen man Manhattan überblickt.

Les retraits permettent d'éclairer les galeries et d'offrir des vues sur Manhattan.

Located on the Bowery, a Lower East Side avenue that has recently undergone a process of gentrification, the New Museum is one of the most remarkable new buildings to rise in Manhattan in a number of years. Consisting essentially of a series of apparently blank, randomly stacked boxes, the structure in fact represents an intelligent and economical solution to problems posed by the narrow site (21 m wide x 34 m deep for a height of 52 m). By displacing the boxes that form the essentially neutral and high gallery spaces, the architects managed to bring light in where it was desired and to create outdoor terraces. Their aluminum cladding material gives the structure a constantly changing shimmer that certainly sets it apart from more staid neighbors. The building has eight floors above grade and two below. The gallery floors vary in area between 316 (3rd floor) and 427 square meters (2nd floor). Furthermore, the building includes a lobby gallery, café, shop, and theater. An Education Center and a seventh-floor event space round out the public areas, though the building also has 325 square meters of office space. The exterior of the building is finished in expanded aluminum mesh, with a bright anodized finish. In public areas inside the building, the architects have employed polished concrete floors, drywall, and metal mesh ceilings, with exposed ceilings in the galleries. The New Museum architectural initiative is "the centerpiece of a $64 million capital project that included construction of the new building, expansion of the Museum's endowment, and other costs related to planned growth."

Das neue Museum in der Lower East Side auf der Bowery, die in letzter Zeit sozial aufgewertet wird, ist eines der meistbeachteten Gebäude jüngeren Datums in Manhattan. Dem Anschein nach ein Ensemble von fensterlosen, zufällig gestapelten Kästen, stellt der Bau in Wirklichkeit eine intelligente, ökonomische Lösung für das kleine Grundstück dar (21 x 34 m Grundfläche für eine mögliche Höhe von 52 m). Durch ein Verschieben der Kästen, in denen die naturgemäß neutralen, hohen Ausstellungsräume untergebracht sind, konnten die Architekten auf die Innenbereiche abgestimmte Lichtöffnungen und zugleich Außenterrassen schaffen. Die Aluminiumverkleidungen sorgen für einen permanent changierenden Schimmer, durch den sich die Konstruktion deutlich von ihren gesetzteren Nachbarbauten abhebt. Das Gebäude hat acht Ober- und zwei Untergeschosse. Die Ausstellungsräume befinden sich auf der zweiten, dritten und vierten Ebene, deren Grundflächen zwischen 316 m² (dritte Ebene) und 427 m² (zweite Ebene) variieren. Außerdem umfasst das Gebäude eine Foyergalerie, ein Café, einen Museumsshop und ein Theater. Ein Education Center und ein Veranstaltungsbereich auf der siebten Ebene vervollständigen den öffentlichen Bereich; außerdem verfügt das Gebäude über 325 m² Bürofläche. Die Außenseite des Museums ist mit einem groben Geflecht aus hellem eloxiertem Aluminium verkleidet. Die öffentlichen Innenbereiche statteten die Architekten mit polierten Betonböden, Trockenmauerwerk und Decken mit Metallgeflecht aus; die Decken der Galerieräume blieben nackt. Die Initiative zum Bau des Museums ist „das Herzstück eines 64 Millionen Dollar teuren Projekts, das außerdem die finanzielle Ausstattung des Museums vergrößert sowie zusätzliche Budgets für eine geplante Erweiterung umfasst."

Situé en bordure du Bowery, une avenue du Lower East Side qui connaît depuis peu un processus d'embourgeoisement, le New Museum est l'une des plus remarquables constructions apparues à Manhattan depuis plusieurs années. Essentiellement composée d'une série de boîtes apparemment aveugles et empilées au hasard, cette structure de 52 m de haut représente en fait une solution intelligente et économique aux problèmes posés par l'étroitesse du terrain (21 m x 34 m). En déplaçant légèrement ces boîtes qui constituent des volumes neutres à grande hauteur de plafond, les architectes ont réussi à faire entrer l'éclairage naturel là où il était souhaité et créer des terrasses. Le parement en aluminium, qui fait vibrer visuellement l'ensemble en permanence, le distingue fortement de ses voisins plus sages. Le musée se développe sur sept niveaux au-dessus du rez-de-chaussée et deux en sous-sol. Les surfaces des galeries varient de 316 m² (3e niveau) à 427 m² (2e niveau). Par ailleurs, les installations comprennent une galerie d'entrée, un café, une boutique et un auditorium. Un centre éducatif et un espace pour événements situés au septième niveau complètent les espaces publics ainsi que 325 m² de bureaux. Les façades extérieures sont recouvertes d'un treillis d'aluminium déployé à finition anodisée brillante. Dans les zones publiques intérieures, on trouve des sols en béton poli, des murs à sec et des plafonds en treillis métalliques, et, dans les galeries, des plafonds en verrière. « Cette création est le composant essentiel d'un projet de 64 millions de dollars qui comprend la construction du nouveau bâtiment, l'extension de la fondation du musée, et d'autres dépenses pour la croissance des activités. »

Although interior space does give the same type of minimalist impression that is typical of the work of SANAA, the client wanted basic empty boxes for flexibility of display.

Zwar zeigen die Innenräume einen für SANAA typischen minimalistischen Ausdruck, hier geht er indes auf den Auftraggeber zurück, der die leeren, viereckigen Räume für eine flexible Ausstellungsgestaltung verlangte.

Si les espaces intérieurs n'ont pas vraiment la teinte minimaliste caractéristique des autres réalisations de SANAA, ils répondent à une demande du client qui voulait des « boîtes » vides d'utilisation souple.

The high galleries can be easily subdivided and are well designed for the display of contemporary art.

Die hohen Ausstellungsräume lassen sich ohne großen Aufwand unterteilen und eignen sich bestens, um zeitgenössische Kunst zu zeigen.

Les galeries hautes de plafond peuvent se subdiviser aisément et sont conçues pour la présentation d'œuvres d'art contemporain.

THOMAS SCHÜTTE

Thomas Schütte
Frith Street Gallery
17–18 Golden Square
London W1F 9JJ
UK

E-mail: info@frithstreetgallery.com

THOMAS SCHÜTTE was born in Oldenburg, Germany, in 1954 and studied under painter Gerhard Richter at the Düsseldorf Kunstakademie (1973–81). He has had personal exhibitions at the Dia Center for the Arts in New York (1999–2000); the Sammlung Goetz in Munich (2001); the Kunstmuseum Winterthur (Switzerland, 2003); the Musée de Grenoble (France); and the K21 in Düsseldorf (Germany, 2004). He participated in Documenta 8 (1987), Documenta 9 (1992), and Documenta 10 (1997) in Kassel, as well as at the Venice Biennale in 2005, where he was awarded the Golden Lion. His work is extremely varied, ranging from architectural models of imaginary buildings, photographs, steel figures that look like robots to ceramic urns. Thomas Schütte says, "Fundamentally my works are almost always in the nature of a proposal... they exist in the form of models." On the occasion of the Dia exhibition in New York, Lynne Cooke wrote, "Décor and scenographic and architectural models formed the vocabulary of Schütte's first works. Vehicles for thought rather than action, they limned a history of the reconstruction and reconstitution of the built environment in the postwar years, and, on occasion, proposed alternatives. Miniaturized worlds that are predicated on a kind of displaced placelessness, they inscribe a restless nomadism that rigorously eschews the settled and established" (Lynne Cooke, "In Medias Res," www.diabeacon.org/exhibs/schutte/inmediares/essay.html).

THOMAS SCHÜTTE wurde 1954 in Oldenburg geboren. Von 1973 bis 1981 studierte er bei Gerhard Richter an der Düsseldorfer Kunstakademie. Einzelausstellungen hatte er u. a. im Dia Center for the Arts in New York (1999–2000), in der Sammlung Goetz (München, 2001), im Kunstmuseum Winterthur (Schweiz, 2003), im Musée de Grenoble (Frankreich) und in der Kunstsammlung K21 in Düsseldorf (2004). 1987, 1992 und 1997 nahm Schütte an der documenta 8, 9 bzw. 10 in Kassel teil sowie 2005 an der Biennale in Venedig, wo er mit dem Goldenen Löwen ausgezeichnet wurde. Sein Werk ist höchst vielseitig und erstreckt sich von Architekturmodellen für imaginäre Gebäude über Fotografien bis hin zu Stahlplastiken, die wie Keramikurnen oder Roboter aussehen. Schütte erklärt zu seiner Arbeit: „Im Grunde genommen sind meine Arbeiten ihrem Wesen nach fast immer Vorschläge ... sie existieren in der Form von Modellen." Anlässlich der Ausstellung im New Yorker Dia Center schrieb Lynne Cook: „Die Formensprache von Schüttes ersten Arbeiten war von Dekor und von szenografischen und architektonischen Modellen bestimmt. Eher als Gedanken- denn als Handlungsträger schilderten sie eine Geschichte der Rekonstruktion und Rekonstitution der gebauten Umwelt in der Nachkriegszeit; gelegentlich schlugen sie auch Alternativen vor. Als Miniaturwelten, die auf einer Art dislozierter Ortlosigkeit beruhen, beschreiben sie ein ruheloses Nomadentum, das das Gesetzte und Etablierte streng vermeidet" (Lynne Cooke, „In Medias Res", www.diabeacon.org/exhibs/schutte/inmediares/essay.html).

THOMAS SCHÜTTE, né à Oldenburg, Allemagne, en 1954, a étudié auprès du peintre Gerhard Richter à la Kunstakademie à Düsseldorf (1973–81). Il a exposé personnellement au Dia Center for the Arts à New York (1999–2000) ; Sammlung Goetz (Munich, 2001) ; Kunstmuseum Winterthur (Suisse, 2003) ; musée de Grenoble (France) ; et K21 à Düsseldorf (Allemagne, 2004). Il a participé aux Documenta 8 (1987), 9 (1992) et 10 (1997) à Kassel et à la Biennale de Venise de 2005 où il a reçu le Lion d'Or. Son œuvre, extrêmement variée, va de maquettes architecturales, à des constructions imaginaires, en passant par des photographies, des figures en acier qui ressemblent à des robots et même des urnes en céramique. Schütte explique : « Fondamentalement, mes œuvres sont presque toujours de la nature de la proposition... elles existent sous forme de maquettes. » À l'occasion de l'exposition au Dia à New York, Lynne Cooke a écrit : « Décors et maquettes architecturales et scénographiques formaient le vocabulaire des premières œuvres de Schütte. Véhicules d'une pensée plutôt que d'une action, elles dessinaient une histoire de la reconstruction et de la reconstitution de l'environnement réalisée dans les années de l'après-guerre, et, à l'occasion, proposaient des alternatives. Mondes miniaturisés fondés sur une sorte de localisation déplacée, elles déterminent un nomadisme sans fin qui renonce rigoureusement à tout ce qui est posé et établi » (Lynne Cooke, « In Medias Res, » www.diabeacon.org/exhibs/schutte/inmediares/essay.html).

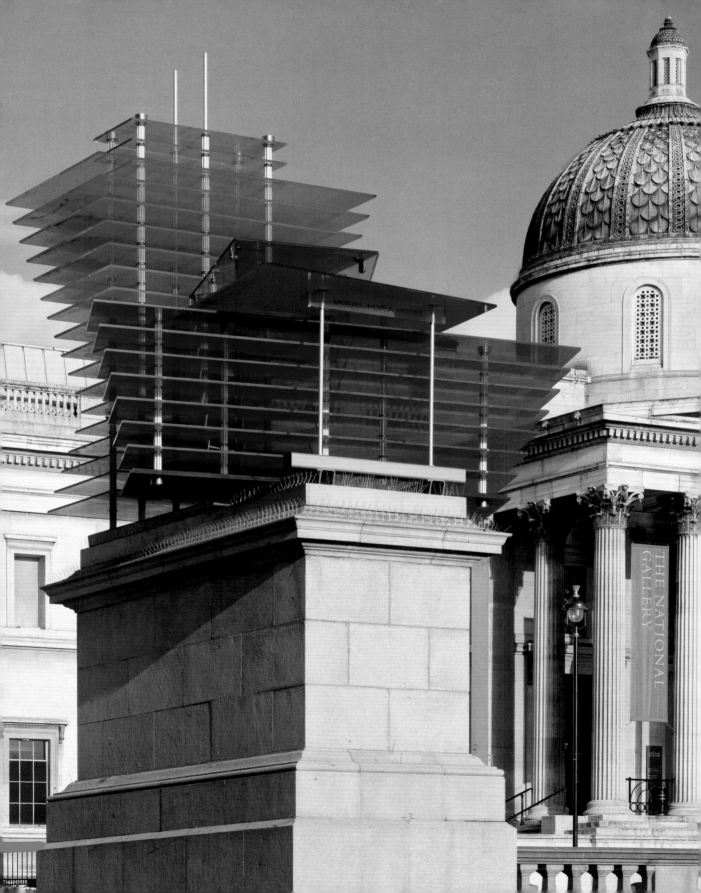

MODEL FOR A HOTEL

Fourth Plinth, Trafalgar Square, London, UK, 2007–08

The Fourth Plinth, located in the northwest corner of Trafalgar Square, was designed by Sir Charles Barry in 1841 and intended for a statue of King William IV, but the plinth remained empty until 1999, when the Royal Society of Arts began to commission works by contemporary artists intended for brief display on the stone base. The first of these was Mark Wallinger's *Ecce Homo* (1999). It was followed by sculptures by Bill Woodrow (2000), Rachel Whiteread (2001), and Mark Quinn (2005). When Thomas Schütte's proposal for the Fourth Plinth in London's Trafalgar Square was first unveiled in 2003, it carried the name "Hotel for the Birds". His varied work includes a series of architectural models for imaginary buildings, the first of which was completed in 1980. This 21-level structure is made of specially engineered red, yellow, and blue laminated glass. Though it weighs eight tons, the sculpture almost seems to disappear under certain angles, only to sharply affirm its colors and angles from other perspectives. Asked about the work by *The Guardian* daily newspaper (November 8, 2007), Schütte stated, "I make these things because I want to see them. The reason to make them is because they are not there. Certainly, the problem of architecture is not in glamorous buildings like the World Trade Center; the real issue is the living city, low-cost housing, parks, and so on."

Die so genannte Fourth Plinth (der Vierte Sockel) in der nordwestlichen Ecke des Londoner Trafalgar Square wurde 1841 von Sir Charles Barry entworfen. Ursprünglich sollte der Sockel mit einer Statue des britischen Königs Wilhelm IV. geschmückt werden, blieb jedoch bis in die Gegenwart leer. Erst seitdem die Royal Society of Arts entsprechende Aufträge an zeitgenössische Künstler vergibt, dient der Sockel regelmäßig der Präsentation von Kunstobjekten. Als erstes Werk wurde 1999 Mark Wallingers „Ecce Homo" (1999) gezeigt; es folgten Skulpturen von Bill Woodrow (2000), Rachel Whiteread (2001) und Mark Quinn (2005). Als Thomas Schütte seinen Vorschlag für die Fourth Plinth 2003 erstmals vorstellte, trug das Werk noch den Namen „Hotel for the Birds". Zu Schüttes vielfältigem künstlerischem Werk gehören seit 1980 auch verschiedene Serien von Architekturmodellen für imaginäre Gebäude. Die Konstruktion „Model for a Hotel" besteht aus speziell hergestellten rot, gelb und blau laminierten Glasscheiben, die in 21 Ebenen übereinander angeordnet sind. Obwohl sie fast 8 t wiegt, scheint die Skulptur aus manchen Blickwinkeln betrachtet zu verschwinden, während ihre Farben und Kanten aus anderer Perspektive umso deutlicher hervortreten. Von der Tageszeitung *The Guardian* zu seiner Arbeit befragt (8. November 2007), erklärte Schütte: „Ich stelle diese Dinge her, weil ich sie sehen möchte. Der Grund, sie zu machen, ist einfach der, dass sie noch nicht existieren. Das Problem der Architektur sind gewiss nicht die glamourösen Gebäude wie das World Trade Center; die wirkliche Herausforderung sind lebendige Städte, erschwingliche Wohnungen, Grünanlagen und so weiter."

The Fourth Plinth (le quatrième socle), situé à l'angle nord-ouest de Trafalgar Square, a été dessiné par Sir Charles Barry en 1841 pour une statue du roi William IV, mais resta vide jusqu'en 1999, date à laquelle la Royal Society of Arts décida de commander à des artistes contemporains des œuvres qui seraient brièvement exposées. La première œuvre fut le *Ecce Homo* (1999) de Mark Wallinger, suivie de sculptures par Bill Woodrow (2000), Rachel Whiteread (2001) and Mark Quinn (2005). Lorsque la proposition de Thomas Schütte fut dévoilée en 2003, elle portait le nom d'*Hotel for the Birds (hôtel pour les oiseaux)*. Son travail hétéroclite comprend une série de maquettes d'architecture pour des constructions imaginaires, dont la première fut achevée en 1980. La pièce de 21 niveaux de Trafalgar Square est en verre laminé bleu, rouge et jaune, spécialement usiné. Bien qu'elle pèse huit tonnes, elle semble pratiquement disparaître quand on la regarde sous certains angles, mais affirme puissamment ses formes anguleuses et ses couleurs sous d'autres. Interrogé par le quotidien le *Guardian* (8 novembre 2007), Schütte a déclaré : « Je fabrique ces choses parce que j'ai envie de les voir. La raison pour les faire est qu'elles n'existent pas. Il est certain que le problème de l'architecture n'est pas ces constructions séduisantes comme le World Trade Center, le vrai enjeu est la ville, les logements économiques, les parcs, etc. »

Standing in front of the National Gallery of Art on Trafalgar Square, the Fourth Plinth offers an unparalleled exposure for the artists selected to place a work there.

Die Fourth Plinth vor der National Gallery of Art auf dem Trafalgar Square garantiert ausgewählten Künstlern maximale Aufmerksamkeit für ihre hier aufgestellten Arbeiten.

Face à la National Gallery sur Trafalgar Square, la Fourth Plinth offre aux artistes sélectionnés une qualité d'exposition incomparable.

SCOPE CLEAVER

Scope Cleaver
SCDA (60, 128, 24)
"Second Life" www.secondlife.com
E-mail: scope.cleaver@gmail.com / Web: www.scopecleaver.com

It is safe to say that **SCOPE CLEAVER** is the first "virtual" architect to be featured in the pages of the *Architecture Now!* series. He has practiced (extensively) in "Second Life" (www.secondlife.com). Scope Cleaver entered "Second Life" in January 2006. He describes his work there as "fantastic shapes that push the limits of virtual building while retaining realistic structural components." He began his career as a freelance designer and architect in September 2006, with the Virtual Incident Command Simulations (VICS) Conference Center. He was first recognized for his design for the Telus store, which was completed in August 2006. Subsequent designs include MagDenon (August 2006, private residence); UrbanWolf Studio (October 2006); Inside This World Offices (November 2006); Autodesk Island (November 2006, with Keystone Bouchard); Great Northern Way Campus (November 2006); KZero Offices (December 2006); the Charlotte Bartlett House (February 2007); the Center Stage for the Global Condo Center (March 2007); 9th Club (May 2007); the Princeton University Gallery of the Arts (June 2007, published here); SCDA (June 2007, company headquarters); Alexander Beach for Princeton University (November 2007); Virtual Estonia (December 2007); and the Evolutions Museum (December 2007). His prefabricated buildings include the Camber House (released October 2006); the Okim series (released October 2006); the Nawstriv Convolution building series (released July 2007); and several sets of furniture, including EdgeCrow and ITWO. Current projects include Aeolia (for Princeton University, with Aldo Manutio Abruzzo, due to open 2008); and the Umberto Giano House (due to open 2009). All of these buildings can be found on "Second Life."

Von **SCOPE CLEAVER** darf man mit Fug und Recht sagen, dass er der erste „virtuelle" Architekt ist, der in *Architecture Now!* vorgestellt wird. Seit Januar 2006 ist Cleaver Mitglied in der virtuellen Welt von „Second Life" (www.secondlife.com), in der er eine äußerst rege Bautätigkeit entwickelt hat. Seine Arbeiten beschreibt er als „fantastische Formen, die sämtliche Möglichkeiten des virtuellen Bauens ausschöpfen, gleichzeitig aber realistische Konstruktionskomponenten beibehalten." Cleaver begann seine Karriere im September 2006 als freischaffender Architekt und Designer mit dem Konferenzzentrum Virtual Incident Command Simulations (VICS). Erste Aufmerksamkeit erlangte er mit seinem Entwurf für den im August 2006 fertiggestellten Telus Store. Es folgten u. a. die Entwürfe für die Privatresidenz MagDenon (August 2006), das UrbanWolf Studio (October 2006), die Inside This World Offices (November 2006), das Autodesk Island (November 2006, zusammen mit Keystone Bouchard), der Great Northern Way Campus (November 2006), die KZero Offices (Dezember 2006), das Charlotte Bartlett House (Februar 2007), das Podium für das Global Condo Center (März 2007), der 9th Club (Mai 2007), die Princeton University Gallery of the Arts (Juni 2007, hier vorgestellt), die SCDA-Firmenzentrale (Juni 2007), der Alexander Beach für die Princeton University (November 2007), das Virtual Estonia (December 2007) und das Evolutions Museum (December 2007). Zu seinen „Fertighäusern" gehören das Camber House (zugänglich seit Oktober 2006), die Okim-Serie (zugänglich seit Oktober 2006) und das Gebäudeensemble Nawstriv Convolution (zugänglich seit Juli 2007). Darüber hinaus entwarf Cleaver Möbelserien wie EdgeCrow und ITWO. Zu seinen laufenden Projekten gehören das Aeolia-Gebäude für die Princeton University (zusammen mit Aldo Manutio Abruzzo, geplante Eröffnung 2008) und das Umberto Giano House (geplante Eröffnung 2009). Ale Projekte können auf „Second Life" besichtigt werden.

On peut certainement dire que **SCOPE CLEAVER** est le premier architecte « virtuel » à faire vraiment une entrée dans la collection *Architecture Now !*. À partir de janvier 2006, il est beaucoup intervenu sur « Second Life » (www.secondlife.com). Il y décrit son travail comme « des formes fantastiques qui repoussent les limites des constructions virtuelles, tout en conservant des composants structurels réalistes. » Il a entamé sa carrière comme designer et architecte indépendant en septembre 2006, par son Virtual Incident Command Simulations Conference Center (VICS). Il a été remarqué au départ pour le magasin Telus, achevé en août 2006. Parmi ses projets ultérieurs : MagDenon (août 2006, résidence privée) ; UrbanWolf Studio (octobre 2006) ; bureaux Inside This World (novembre 2006) ; Autodesk Island (novembre 2006, avec Keystone Bouchard) ; Great Northern Way Campus (novembre 2006) ; bureaux KZero (décembre 2006) ; la maison Charlotte Bartlett (février 2007) ; la scène centrale du Global Condo Center (mars 2007) ; 9th Club (mai 2007) ; la Princeton University Gallery of the Arts (juin 2007, publiée ici) ; SCDA (juin 2007, siège de société) ; Alexander Beach, pour Princeton University (novembre 2007) ; Virtual Estonia (décembre 2007) et le musée des Évolutions (décembre 2007). Parmi ses propositions de constructions préfabriquées : la maison Camber (proposée en octobre 2006) ; la série Okim (octobre 2006) ; la série Nawstriv Convolution Building (juillet 2007) et plusieurs ensembles de mobilier dont EdgeCrow et ITWO. Parmi ses projets actuels : Aeolia (pour Princeton University, avec Aldo Manutio Abruzzo, qui ouvrira en 2008) et la maison Umberto Giano (2009). Tous ces projets peuvent être retrouvés sur « Second Life ».

PRINCETON UNIVERSITY GALLERY OF THE ARTS

Princeton University (120, 204, 24), "Second Life," 2007

*Floor area: 2200 m². Client: Princeton University. Cost: not applicable.
Project Manager: Persis Trilling*

 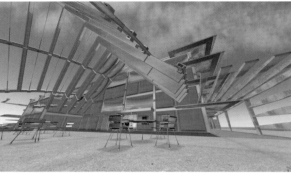

Though the lightness imagined in these renderings might not be possible in reality, Scope Cleaver bases his designs on feasible architecture.

Auch wenn Scope Cleavers Entwürfe in der Realität möglicherweise nicht die in seinen Renderings entworfene Leichtigkeit haben können, zeigen sie doch eine mögliche Architektur.

Bien que la légèreté imaginée dans ces perspectives ne soit peut-être pas possible dans la réalité, Scope Cleaver travaille ses projets architecturaux pour qu'ils soient réalisables.

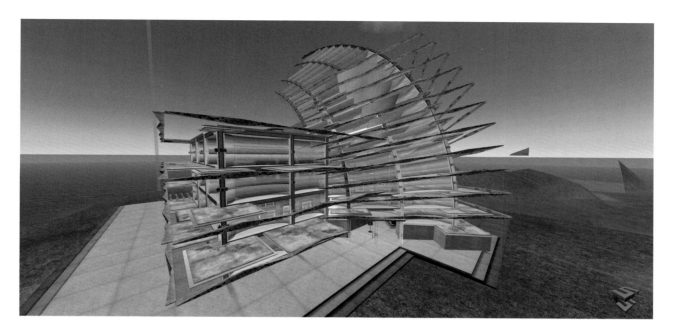

Essentially computer renderings like those that many architects create, these works have the advantage of being fully interactive—participants in "Second Life" can walk through them or engage in events.

Cleavers Arbeiten – im Prinzip nichts anderes als jene Renderings, wie sie von Architekten entworfen werden – sind vollständig interaktiv nutzbar. In „Second Life" kann man durch die Gebäude hindurchgehen oder an Veranstaltungen teilnehmen.

Traités en images de synthèse utilisées par de nombreux architectes, ces projets ont l'avantage d'être intégralement interactifs. Les habitués de « Second Life » peuvent s'y promener ou participer aux manifestations organisées dans ces cadres.

The Princeton University Gallery of the Arts on the virtual campus of Princeton in "Second Life" is the first in a series of commissioned architectural works by Scope Cleaver. The building was designed to house and display works of art created by members of the actual campus community. As the designer explains, "The Gallery is distinguished by its irregular profile, a soaring superstructure that supports and defines the light-filled interior. The carapace-like framework of the building is formed of similarly shaped structural elements repeated on a precise rotation." This feature and the rich textures that define the building's components are characteristic of Cleaver's work. "A highly articulated system of tensioning cables and connecting cubes tie the superstructure together; curved and tinted glazing adds visual interest to the building, and the composition, taken as a whole, achieves a sense of architectonic integrity through the clear expression of structure, function, and visual drama." The virtual gallery is entered via a two-story atrium. The gallery fittings, glass cases, and display panels that showcase artworks were also designed by Cleaver. The interest of this project may lie as much with the client, Princeton University, as with the specific design. The fact that a prestigious institution should be commissioning virtual architecture in "Second Life" says a great deal about the evolution of attitudes toward computer-driven environments and their relation to the "real" world.

Die Princeton University Gallery of the Arts auf dem virtuellen Princeton-Campus in „Second Life" war das erste von weiteren Bauwerken, für die Scope Cleaver einen Designauftrag erhielt. Gedacht war das Gebäude als Ausstellungs- und Aufbewahrungsort für Kunstwerke, die von Mitgliedern der Campusgemeinschaft geschaffen werden. Wie der Designer erklärt, zeichnet sich die Galerie „durch ihr ungewöhnliches Profil aus: eine aufsteigende Überbaukonstruktion, die den lichtdurchfluteten Innenbereich trägt und umgrenzt. Der rückenstachelartige Gebäuderahmen besteht aus einzelnen, ähnlich geformten Strukturelementen in einer präzisen Aufeinanderfolge." Dieses Merkmal im Verbund mit weiteren einfallsreichen baubestimmenden Komponenten sind charakteristisch für Cleavers Arbeiten. „Ein äußerst exakt gegliedertes System aus Spannkabeln und Verbindungsröhren hält den Überbau zusammen; gebogene und getönte Verglasungen erhöhen den visuellen Reiz des Gebäudes. Insgesamt gesehen erzielt die Komposition durch ihren klaren Ausdruck von Struktur, Funktion und visueller Spannung ein Bild hoher architektonischer Integrität." Die virtuelle Galerie ist über ein zweigeschossiges Atrium zu betreten. Die Ausstattung der Ausstellungsräume, die Vitrinen und Stellwände wurden ebenfalls von Cleaver entworfen. Das Interessante an diesem Projekt ist nicht nur der Entwurf selbst, sondern auch der Auftraggeber, die Princeton University. Die Tatsache, dass eine renommierte Institution einen Designauftrag für ein virtuelles Gebäude in „Second Life" vergibt, sagt einiges darüber aus, wie weit sich unsere Haltung gegenüber computergesteuerten Umgebungen und deren Verhältnis zur „realen" Welt inzwischen entwickelt hat.

The Princeton University Gallery of the Arts du campus virtuel de Princeton sur « Second Life » est la première de plusieurs commandes architecturales passées par l'université à Scope Cleaver. Le « bâtiment » a été conçu pour accueillir et présenter des œuvres d'art créées par des étudiants du campus, bien réel celui-ci. Comme l'explique le créateur : « La Galerie se distingue par son profil irrégulier dont la superstructure en expansion soutient et définit le volume intérieur baigné de lumière. L'ossature, en forme de carapace, est constituée d'éléments structurels de forme semblable qui se répètent selon un angle de rotation précis. » Cet aspect comme les riches textures qui personnalisent les composants du bâtiment sont caractéristiques du travail de Cleaver. « Un système très articulé de câbles en tension et de cubes de connexion maintient l'ensemble. Des éléments vitrés teintés et incurvés enrichissent l'intérêt visuel du projet, et la composition, dans sa globalité, atteint un niveau élevé d'intégrité architectonique par l'expression claire de la structure, de la fonction et du spectacle visuel. » Un atrium construit sur deux niveaux donne l'accès à cette galerie virtuelle. Les équipements de présentation, les vitrines et les panneaux de présentation ont également été conçus par Cleaver. L'intérêt de ce projet tient autant au client, l'Université de Princeton, qu'à sa conception. Le fait qu'une prestigieuse institution passe commande à un architecte virtuel sur « Second Life » en dit long sur l'évolution des attitudes envers les environnements numériques et leur relation au monde « réel ».

Although the architect is not constrained by precise materials as much as he would be for a "real" design, surfaces and spaces are rendered in a realistic way, inviting visit and movement through the spaces.

Obgleich der Architekt hinsichtlich der Materialwahl weniger gebunden ist als bei „realen" Entwürfen, hat er die Oberflächen und Räume realistisch und im wahrsten Sinne einladend gestaltet.

Si l'architecte ne subit pas les contraintes des matériaux imposées par le monde « réel », les surfaces et les volumes sont rendus de façon réaliste et invitent à parcourir les espaces.

ÁLVARO SIZA VIEIRA

Álvaro Siza Arquitecto, Lda
Rua do Aleixo 53 2
4150–043 Porto
Portugal

Tel: +351 22 616 72 70
Fax: +351 22 616 72 79
E-mail: siza@mail.telepac.pt

Born in Matosinhos, Portugal, in 1933, **ÁLVARO SIZA** studied at the University of Porto School of Architecture (1949–55). He created his own practice in 1954, and worked with Fernando Tavora from 1955 to 1958. He has been a Professor of Construction at the University of Porto since 1976. He received the European Community's Mies van der Rohe Prize in 1988 and the Pritzker Prize in 1992. He has built a large number of small-scale projects in Portugal, and has worked on the restructuring of the Chiado (Lisbon, Portugal, 1989–); the Meteorology Center (Barcelona, Spain, 1989–92); the Vitra Furniture Factory (Weil am Rhein, Germany, 1991–94); the Porto School of Architecture (Porto University, Portugal, 1986–95); and the University of Aveiro Library (Aveiro, Portugal, 1988–95). More recent projects include the Portuguese Pavilion for the Expo '98 in Lisbon; the Serralves Foundation (Porto, 1998); and the Adega Mayor Winery, Argamassas Estate – Campo Maior (2005–06, published here), all in Portugal. He designed the 2005 Serpentine Pavilion (Kensington Gardens, London) with Eduardo Souto de Moura. His Museum for the Iberê Camargo Foundation in Porto Alegre, Brazil, opened in 2008 (published here).

ÁLVARO SIZA, geboren 1933 im portugiesischen Matosinhos, studierte von 1949 bis 1955 an der Fakultät für Architektur der Universität Porto. 1954 gründete er ein eigenes Büro und arbeitete von 1955 bis 1958 mit Fernando Tavora zusammen. Seit 1976 lehrt Siza als Professor für Bauwesen an der Universität Porto. 1988 bekam er den Mies-van-der-Rohe-Preis der Europäischen Gemeinschaft verliehen, 1992 erhielt er den Pritzker-Preis. In Portugal hat Siza zahlreiche kleinere Bauten ausgeführt, seit 1989 arbeitet er zudem am Wiederaufbau des Lissabonner Chiado-Viertels. Hervorzuhebende Gebäude sind daneben das Meteorologische Zentrum in Barcelona (1989–92), eine Fabrikhalle für Vitra in Weil am Rhein (1991–94), die Architekturfakultät der Universität Porto (1986–95) und die Bibliothek der Universität Aveiro (1988–95). In jüngerer Zeit entstanden der portugiesische Pavillon für die Expo '98 in Lissabon, die Stiftung Serralves in Porto (1998) und die hier vorgestellte Weinkellerei Adega Mayor in Herdade das Argamassas, Campo Maior (Portugal, 2005–06). Gemeinsam mit Eduardo Souto de Moura entwarf Siza den Serpentine Pavilion des Jahres 2005 in den Londoner Kensington Gardens. 2008 wurde im brasilianischen Porto Alegre sein Museum für die Stiftung Iberê Camargo eröffnet (ebenfalls hier vorgestellt).

Né à Matosinhos, Portugal, en 1933, **ÁLVARO SIZA** a étudié à l'École d'architecture de l'université de Porto (1949–55). Il a créé son agence en 1954 et travaillé avec Fernando Tavora de 1955 à 1958. Il est professeur de construction à l'université de Porto depuis 1976. Il a reçu le prix Mies van der Rohe de la Communauté européenne en 1988 et le Pritzker Prize en 1992. Il a réalisé un grand nombre de projets à petite échelle au Portugal, et a travaillé sur la restructuration du quartier du Chiado (Lisbonne, Portugal, 1989–) ; le Centre de météorologie (Barcelone, Espagne, 1989–92) ; l'usine de meubles Vitra (Weil am Rhein, Allemagne, 1991–94) ; l'École d'architecture de Porto (Université de Porto, Portugal, 1986–95) et la bibliothèque de l'université d'Aveiro (Aveiro, Portugal, 1988–95). Parmi ses plus récents projets : le pavillon portugais pour la Foire mondiale de Lisbonne de 1998 ; la Fondation Serralves (Porto, 1998), et le chais Adega Mayor (domaine d'Argamassas, Campo Maior, 2005–06, publié ici), tous au Portugal. Il a dessiné le pavillon 2005 de la Serpentine Gallery (Kensington Gardens, Londres) en collaboration avec Eduardo Souto de Moura. Son musée pour la fondation Iberê Camargo, à Porto Alegre, au Brésil, a ouvert en 2008 (publié ici).

ADEGA MAYOR WINERY

Argamassas Estate – Campo Maior, Portugal, 2005–06

Site area: 5543 m². Floor area: 4262 m². Client: SEATUR, Sociedade Empreendedora de Agricultura e Turismo, S.A. Cost: €3 million.
Principal in Charge: Avelino Silva. Collaborator: Rita Amaral

The purity and simplicity of the architecture of Álvaro Siza appear to be reaching new heights with this winery, isolated in its vineyard setting.

Die Einfachheit und Reinheit von Sizas Architektur scheinen mit seinem Weingut, das einsam inmitten seines Anbaugebiets liegt, ein noch höheres Niveau als bisher erreicht zu haben.

La pureté et la simplicité de l'architecture d'Álvaro Siza semblent atteindre de nouveaux sommets dans ce chais isolé au milieu des vignes.

This reinforced-concrete building, with 45-centimeter load-bearing walls clad on the exterior with plastered and whitewashed brick, was designed to serve as a facility for the production and storage of wine. Álvaro Siza acted as architect for the building, but also as the landscape architect for the site. The more vertical of the two main volumes, at the southwestern end, contains the main entrance protected by a pergola. The entrance volume contains a reception hall, offices, a quality-control lab, a store, and worker showers and cloakrooms. The second floor is intended for tourists and the promotion of the vineyard's wine. The production requirements of the structure imposed a certain number of loading and unloading constraints that are part of the design. The interior walls of the production zone are in exposed concrete and the floors are coated with epoxy resin. In the remaining areas the walls and ceilings are plastered and the floors finished with Riga wood. The interior and exterior window and door casings are in enameled wood, with the exception of the production zone doors, which are made of stainless-steel plates. Álvaro Siza wrote of the site and of the project, "The building appears in a place that is already in strong contrast to the extensive plain and is not used as a cultivation zone. Reutilizing an existing path, the impact to the site, in terms of creating access, is kept to a minimum."

Sizas Stahlbetonbau mit seinen 45 cm dicken tragenden Wänden, die außen mit verputzten, weißgetünchten Ziegeln verkleidet sind, dient der Herstellung und Lagerung von Wein. Siza war in diesem Fall aber nicht nur Gebäudearchitekt, sondern zeichnete auch für die Landschaftsgestaltung verantwortlich. Der langgestreckte Teil der beiden Hauptgebäude enthält auf der südöstlichen Seite den Haupteingang, der durch eine Pergola geschützt ist. Dahinter liegen eine Empfangshalle, Büroräume, ein Labor zur Qualitätskontrolle, ein Verkaufsbereich sowie Umkleideräume und Duschen für die Arbeiter. Im darüberliegenden Geschoss werden Besucher empfangen und Werbeveranstaltungen des Weinguts durchgeführt. Die Erfordernisse einer solchen Produktionsanlage brachten bestimmte erschwerende, aber auch wegweisende Zwänge mit sich, die dementsprechend in dem Entwurf eingeflossen sind. Die Oberflächen der Betoninnenwände im Produktionsbereich blieben unbehandelt, die Böden wurden mit Epoxidharz versiegelt. In den übrigen Bereichen wurden Wände und Decken verputzt und auf den Böden wurde Rigaholz verlegt. Innen wie außen bestehen die Tür- und Fensterrahmen aus lackiertem Holz, mit Ausnahme der Türen im Produktionsbereich, die aus Edelstahlplatten angefertigt sind. Álvaro Siza schrieb über das Projekt und das Gelände: „Das Gebäude befindet sich augenscheinlich an einem Standort, der schon als solcher einen starken Kontrast zu der weiten, unkultivierten Ebene bildet. Durch die Wiedernutzung eines alten Weges blieben, was die Zufahrt angeht, die Auswirkungen auf das Gelände auf ein Minimum reduziert."

Ce bâtiment à murs porteurs de 45 centimètres d'épaisseur en béton armé, plâtré sur leur face extérieure, et en briques chaulées, est le chais de production et de vieillissement du Domaine viticole d'Argamassas. Álvaro Siza a été à la fois l'architecte et le paysagiste du projet. Le volume le plus élevé, à l'extrémité sud-ouest, contient l'entrée principale que protège une pergola. Le volume d'entrée comprend un hall de réception, des bureaux, un laboratoire de contrôle qualité, ainsi que des vestiaires et des douches pour le personnel. L'étage est réservé aux visiteurs et à la promotion des vins du domaine. Un certain nombre de contraintes de charge et de décharge imposées par le système de production ont exercé une influence sur le projet. La face interne des murs de la zone de production est en béton brut et les sols sont recouverts d'une résine époxy. Ailleurs, les murs et les plafonds sont plâtrés et les sols parquetés de bois Riga. Les huisseries sont en bois peint, à l'exception de celles de la zone de production qui sont en acier inoxydable. Álvaro Siza a écrit sur le site et le projet : « Le bâtiment apparaît dans un lieu qui contraste déjà fortement avec la grande plaine et qui n'était pas cultivé. En réutilisant un chemin existant, l'impact sur le site, en terme d'accès, est maintenu au minimum. »

A sketch (above) by Siza shows the building in a form that can be readily identified next to a photo of the completed building, seen in other images from a distance on its site.

Eine von Siza angefertigte Skizze (oben) zeigt eine Gebäudeperspektive, die sich auf den Fotos in fertiggestellter Form wiederfindet.

Un croquis de Siza (ci-dessus) représente le bâtiment sous sa forme future, comme le montrent les autres images.

A pool extends the space of the architecture and reflects its pure, modern forms.

Ein Bassin erweitert den Raum der Architektur und spiegelt ihre reinen, modernen Formen.

Un bassin étend l'espace architectural et reflète ses formes pures et modernes.

The axial linearity of the architecture appears to connect the building to the land but also to the sky in these images. The plan (below left) is basically rectangular.

Auf den Abbildungen wirkt die axiale Linearität der Architektur, als sei das Gebäude sowohl mit der Erde als auch mit dem Himmel verbunden. Unten links der im Wesentlichen rechteckige Grundriss.

Dans ces images, la linéarité axiale de l'architecture semble connecter le bâtiment au terrain, mais également au ciel. Le plan (ci-dessous à gauche) est essentiellement rectangulaire.

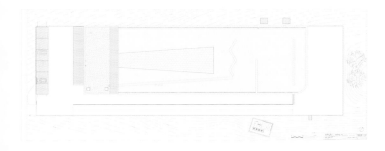

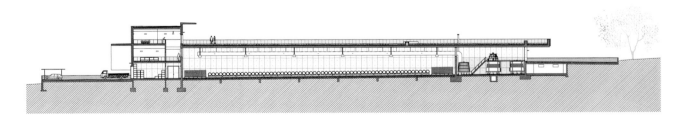

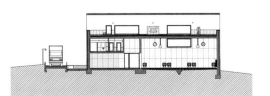

The design, perhaps simpler than many others by Siza, allows for direct communication with the flat natural setting (left). interiors allow for some relative darkness.

Sizas Entwurf, vielleicht noch schlichter als die meisten seiner Projekte, steht in engem Zusammenspiel mit seiner natürlichen flachen Umgebung. Die Innenräume sind relativ dunkel.

Le projet, peut-être plus simple que beaucoup d'autres de Siza, favorise la communication directe avec le paysage plat (à gauche). Les intérieurs sont relativement sombres.

IBERÊ CAMARGO FOUNDATION

Porto Alegre, Rio Grande do Sul, Brazil, 1998–2008

Floor area: 960.38 m². Client: Iberê Camargo Foundation.
Cost: not disclosed. Principals in Charge: Bárbara Rangel, Pedro Polónia

Designed beginning in 1998, this new museum has been described as the "masterpiece" of Álvaro Siza. It received a Golden Lion Award at the 2002 Venice Architecture Biennale. It is located in Porto Alegre, one of the largest cities in Brazil, and capital of the state of Rio Grande do Sul. This building, set between Padre Cacique Avenue and a cliff, is intended for the exhibition of the Foundation's collection of 4000 works by local artist Iberê Camargo, and for housing archives, a library and video library, bookstore, café, and small auditorium, but also administrative offices, and artists' workshops. The main volume of the structure appears to be carved out of the cliff, assuming an undulating form on the north and east, with orthogonal walls on the south and west. An atrium, surrounded by exhibition galleries, marks the entrance. No distinction is made between the temporary and permanent exhibition areas that can be opened into the atrium, space with four-meter-high movable panels. There is natural overhead light available on the top floor, and the other galleries can receive light from the atrium depending on the positioning of the dividing panels. External ramps and a terrace at the lowest level define the exterior form, together with the undulating wall, and allow for visitors to have the carefully selected views of the natural scenery that Siza has always favored.

Álvaro Sizas neues Museum, an dem der Architekt von 1998 an gearbeitet hat, wurde als sein „Meisterstück" bezeichnet. 2002 erhielt es den Goldenen Löwen der Architekturbiennale von Venedig. Das Gebäude befindet sich im brasilianischen Porto Alegre, einer der größten Städte des Landes und zugleich Hauptstadt des Bundesstaates Rio Grande do Sul, wo es zwischen der Avenida Padre Cacique und einer Klippe angelegt wurde. Zusätzlich zu der Sammlung der Fundação Iberê Camargo, die 4000 Werke des aus der Region stammenden Künstlers umfasst, soll das Museum Archive, eine Bibliothek, eine Videothek, einen Buchladen, ein Café und einen kleinen Vortragssaal umfassen, aber auch Raum für Verwaltungsbüros und Künstlerwerkstätten bieten. Der Hauptteil des Gebäudes wirkt wie aus der Klippe herausgeschnitten und hat auf seiner Nord- und Ostseite eine gewellte Form, während die Außenmauern auf der südlichen und westlichen Seite rechtwinklig sind. Den Eingangsbereich bildet ein von Ausstellungsgalerien umfasstes Atrium. Die Räume für Sonderschauen sind nicht von den Sälen mit den Dauerausstellungen abgetrennt, die sich mithilfe von beweglichen, 4 m hohen Wandelementen zum Atrium hin öffnen lassen. Im Obergeschoss fällt natürliches Licht durch die Decke ein, die übrigen Ausstellungsräume werden je nach Ausrichtung der Trennwände über das Atrium mit Licht versorgt. Die außerhalb des Gebäudes verlaufenden Rampen und eine Terrasse auf der untersten Ebene bestimmen im Verbund mit der gewellten Fassade die äußere Gestalt des Museums und bieten Besuchern sorgfältig ausgewählte Ausblicke in die Naturkulisse, der Siza von jeher besondere Bedeutung beimisst.

Conçu début 1998, ce nouveau musée a pu être qualifié de « chef d'œuvre » d'Álvaro Siza. Il a reçu un Lion d'or à la Biennale d'architecture de Venise en 2002. Situé à Porto Alegre, l'une des plus grandes villes du Brésil et capitale de l'État du Rio Grande do Sul, il est implanté entre l'avenue Padre Cacique et une falaise. Il regroupe une collection de 4000 œuvres de l'artiste local Iberê Camargo, des archives, une bibliothèque, une vidéothèque, une librairie, un café, un petit auditorium, des bureaux administratifs et des ateliers d'artiste. Le volume principal, de forme ondulée au nord et à l'est et orthogonale au sud et à l'ouest, semble sculpté dans la falaise. L'entrée est suivie d'un atrium entouré de galeries d'exposition. Aucune distinction n'est faite entre les espaces d'expositions temporaires ou permanente qui ouvrent sur cet atrium par des panneaux mobiles de quatre mètre de haut. Le niveau supérieur est éclairé zénithalement et les autres galeries reçoivent la lumière de l'atrium en fonction de la position de ces panneaux de partition. Au niveau inférieur, des rampes externes et une terrasse participent à la définition de la forme extérieure et permettent aux visiteurs de bénéficier de vues choisies sur le paysage naturel que Siza privilégie toujours.

More complex than the Adega Mayor Winery, the Iberê Camargo Foundation profits from its insertion into a cliff side near the sea. Sketches by Siza show its undulating form on two sides.

Komplexer als das Weingut Adega Mayor ist die Fundação Iberê Camargo, die von ihrem Standort auf einem felsigen Abhang am Meer profitiert. Sizas Zeichnungen zeigen die auf zwei Seiten gewellte Gebäudeform.

Plus complexe que le chais Adega Mayor, la Fondation Iberê Camargo met à profit son implantation contre une falaise au bord de la mer. Les croquis de Siza montrent l'ondulation des formes sur deux côtés.

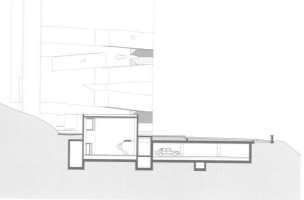

Interiors display the kind of relative complexity seen in earlier work by Siza, but here the mastery of space and light achieves a new high point for the architect.

Die Innenräume erweisen sich analog zu früheren Arbeiten Sizas als verhältnismäßig komplex; hinsichtlich der Raum- und Lichtgestaltung übertrifft er seine bisherigen Leistungen eindeutig.

Les espaces intérieurs affichent la relative complexité d'œuvres antérieures de Siza. La maîtrise de l'espace et de la lumière atteignent ici un nouveau sommet dans la carrière de l'architecte.

Windows and openings frame natural views—another frequent technique of Álvaro Siza, here made almost into an art form.

Fenster und Gebäudeöffnungen bilden gerahmte Ausblicke in die Natur – ein häufig von Álvaro Siza eingesetztes Stilmittel, das hier beinahe zur Kunstform erhoben wird.

Les fenêtres et les ouvertures cadrent des perspectives sur la nature, autre technique fréquente chez Álvaro Siza, dont il a pratiquement fait une forme d'art.

Siza has an innate sense of form
and light that sets him apart in the
company of other contemporary
architects. He is a master of a very
personal form of Modernism.

Siza hat einen untrüglichen Sinn für
Licht und Form, der ihn von anderen
zeitgenössischen Architekten unterscheidet. Seine Meisterschaft besteht
in einer sehr persönlichen Form
moderner Architektur.

Siza possède un sens inné de la
forme et de la lumière qui le place
à part parmi ses confrères. Il est
le maître d'une approche très
personnelle du modernisme.

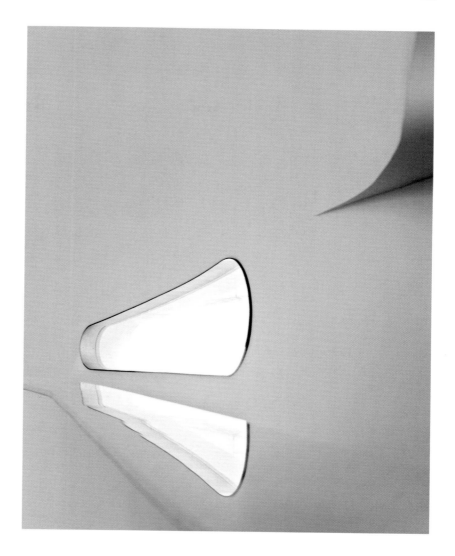

SNØHETTA

Snøhetta AS
Skur 39, Vippetangen
0150 Oslo
Norway

Tel: +47 24 15 60 60 / Fax: +47 24 15 60 61
E-mail: post@snoarc.no / Web: www.snoarc.no

SNØHETTA is a mountain in central Norway. It is a central theme in early Viking sagas and is the mythical home of Valhalla. Henrik Ibsen developed the story of *Peer Gynt* around Snøhetta, which gave its name to the architectural practice founded in 1987 in Oslo. Directed by Craig Dykers, Christoph Kapeller, and Kjetil Trædal Thorsen, Snøhetta has a staff of 13 architects, seven landscape architects, and two interior designers. Aside from the Alexandria Library completed in 2002, Snøhetta won an anonymous, open international competition for the New National Opera House in Oslo, which opened in April 2008 (published here). Other work by the firm includes the Lillehammer Art Museum, the centerpiece cultural building for the 1994 Winter Olympics; the Skistua School (Skistua, Narvik, 1998); the Karmøy Fishing Museum (Karmøy, 1999); the Hamar Town Hall (Hamar, 2000); and the Petter Dass Museum (Alstadhaug, Sandnessjøen kommune, Nordland fylke, 2001–07), all in Norway. Kjetil Thorsen of Snøhetta designed the 2007 Serpentine Pavilion with Olafur Eliasson (page 138). The firm has been working for some time on the WTC Cultural Center (New York) and they are due to complete the National Academy of the Arts in Bergen, Norway, in 2009. Snøhetta was selected in 2007 to create an iconic gateway building for the new capital city of Ras Al-Khaimah in the United Arab Emirates. This 300 000-square-meter complex will contain a congress center, exhibition halls, a shopping center, a five-star+ hotel, a five-star Hotel, and a four-star hotel.

SNØHETTA ist der Name eines Bergs in Mittelnorwegen, der eine zentrale Rolle in frühen Wikingersagen spielt und auch der Standort der sagenhaften Walhall sein soll. Auch in Henrik Ibsens „Peer Gynt" hat der Berg eine Bedeutung, dem das 1987 in Oslo gegründete Architekturbüro seinen Namen verdankt. Snøhetta wird geleitet von Craig Dykers, Christoph Kapeller sowie Kjetil Trædal Thorsen und beschäftigt dreizehn Architekten, sieben Landschaftsarchitekten und zwei Innenarchitekten. Neben dem Wettbewerb für den Entwurf der – 2002 fertiggestellten – neuen Bibliothek von Alexandria erhielt Snøhetta auch den Zuschlag für den Entwurf der hier vorgestellten Neuen Nationaloper in Oslo, die im April 2008 eröffnet wurde. Zu Snøhettas weiteren Arbeiten gehören u. a. das Kunstmuseum Lillehammer als zentrales Kulturgebäude für die Olympischen Winterspiele 1994, die Skistua-Schule in Narvik (1998), das Fischereimuseum in Karmøy (1999), die Stadthalle von Hamar (2000) und das Petter Dass Museum in Alstadhaug, Sandnessjøen, Nordland fylke (2001–07), alle in Norwegen. Kjetil Thorsen entwarf gemeinsam mit Olafur Eliasson den Serpentine Pavilion des Jahres 2007 (S. 138). Seit einiger Zeit plant das Büro das World Trade Center Cultural Center in New York, daneben ist für 2009 die Fertigstellung der Nationalen Kunstakademie in Bergen geplant. 2007 erhielt Snøhetta den Zuschlag für den Entwurf eines symbolträchtigen Gebäudekomplexes an der Einfallstraße in die neue Hauptstadt des Emirats Ra's al-Chaima. Zu der 300 000 m² Nutzfläche umfassenden Anlage werden ein Tagungszentrum, Ausstellungssäle, ein Einkaufszentrum sowie ein Vier-, ein Fünf- und ein Fünfsterneplushotel gehören.

SNØHETTA est une montagne mythique du centre de la Norvège, représentant un lieu que l'on retrouve dans les premières sagas vikings, laquelle abriterait Valhalla. Henrik Ibsen l'a mise en scène dans *Peer Gynt*. C'est aujourd'hui également le nom d'une agence d'architecture fondée en 1987 à Oslo. Dirigée par Craig Dykers, Christoph Kapeller et Kjetil Trædal Thorsen, Snøhetta emploie 13 architectes, sept architectes paysagistes et deux architectes d'intérieur. En dehors de la bibliothèque d'Alexandrie achevée en 2002, l'agence a remporté un concours international ouvert, anonyme, pour le nouvel opéra d'Oslo (publié ici), qui a été inauguré en avril 2008. Parmi ses autres réalisations : le musée d'Art de Lillehammer, principal équipement culturel des jeux Olympiques d'hiver 1994 ; l'école de Skistua (Narvik, 1998) ; le musée de la Pêche de Karmøy (1999) ; l'hôtel-de-ville de Hamar (2000) et le musée Petter Dass (Alstadhaug, Sandnessjøen kommune, Nordland fylke, 2001–07), toutes en Norvège. Kjetil Thorsen a conçu, en collaboration avec Olafur Eliasson, le pavillon 2007 de la Serpentine Gallery (Londres, page 138). L'agence travaille sur le projet du WTC Cultural Center (New York) et terminera l'Académie nationale des arts de Bergen, Norvège, en 2009. Snøhetta a été sélectionné en 2007 pour créer un immeuble porte d'entrée monumentale pour la nouvelle capitale de l'émirat de Ras Al-Khaimah (EAU). Ce complexe de 300 000 m² contiendra un centre de congrès, des halls d'exposition, un centre commercial et trois hôtels de luxe.

OSLO OPERA HOUSE

Oslo, Norway, 2003–08

*Gross floor area: 38 500 m². Client: Ministry of Church and Cultural Affairs.
Cost: €500 million*

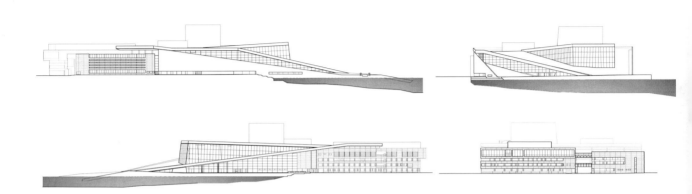

The new Oslo Opera House was inaugurated by the King of Norway on April 12, 2008, and is described by the architects as the "largest single cultural-political initiative in contemporary Norway." In 1999, the Norwegian National Assembly decided to build the Opera House at Bjørvika, facing the Oslo fjord. The building was intended to be the foundation for the urban redevelopment of this area of the capital. The architects further explain, "The government wished that the Opera House be a monumental building which would mark Norway as a cultural nation as well as highlighting the social and cultural importance of the Norwegian Opera & Ballet. The building should be a landmark insofar as its architecture, construction, use of materials and technical solutions" are concerned. The facility features a main 1360-seat performance auditorium and a smaller, flexible auditorium with 400 seats. The main auditorium is laid out in a "classical horseshoe form." The large foyer is "characterized by its simple use of materials and minimal details." Ample back-of-the-house space is provided on four floors plus a basement for rehearsal rooms, changing rooms, offices, workshops, and storage areas. Clad in white Carrara marble, the "roofscape," an area that is open to the public, "describes the building's monumental character," again according to the architects. They go on to say that the "horizontal and sloping plane of the roof provides the Opera with an unusually dramatic expression, quite different from the surrounding buildings." Given that the Oslo Opera was previously housed in a converted movie theater, this new facility, located near the central station and the stock exchange in an area slated for redevelopment by 2018, may well achieve the government's admitted goal of making it the number one tourist attraction in Oslo.

Das am 12. April 2008 vom norwegischen König eingeweihte neue Osloer Opernhaus wird von seinen Entwerfern als „die größte einzelne kulturpolitische Initiative im heutigen Norwegen" beschrieben. 1999 hatte das norwegische Parlament den Bau den Opernhauses beschlossen, das im Hafenareal Bjørvika am Rand des Oslofjords entstehen und einen ersten Schritt zur Sanierung dieses Bezirks darstellen sollte. Wie die Architekten weiter ausführen, „hatte die Regierung den Wunsch, es solle sich bei dem Opernhaus um ein eindrucksvolles Gebäude handeln, das sowohl das Land Norwegen als Kulturnation als auch die soziokulturelle Bedeutung des Norske Opera & Ballett zur Geltung bringt. Das Gebäude sollte hinsichtlich Architektur und Bauweise, der verwendeten Materialien und technischen Lösungen ein Meilenstein werden." Das Gebäude hat einen Hauptzuschauersaal mit 1360 Sitzplätzen und ein kleineren, variablen Saal für 400 Gäste. Der Hauptsaal ist in einer „klassischen Hufeisenform" angelegt. Das weitläufige Foyer „zeichnet sich durch die Verwendung schlichter Materialien und minimale Details aus". Der rückwärtige Teil des Gebäudes bietet reichhaltigen Platz für Proberäume, Umkleiden, Büros, Werkstätten und Lagerbereiche. Die mit weißem Carrara-Marmor verkleidete „Dachlandschaft" ist der Öffentlichkeit frei zugänglich und veranschaulicht, so die Architekten, den „eindrucksvollen Charakter des Gebäudes [...] Die schräg-horizontale Dachfläche verleiht dem Opernhaus einen außergewöhnlich spannungsreichen Ausdruck, der sich deutlich von den umliegenden Bauten abhebt." Bedenkt man zudem, dass die Osloer Oper zuvor ihr Domizil in einem umgebauten Kino hatte, dürfte das neue Haus – in Bahnhofs- und Börsennähe in einem der Planung nach bis 2018 runderneuerten Viertel – das von der Regierung ausgegebene Ziel, zur größten Touristenattraktion Oslos zu werden, unschwer erreichen.

Le nouvel opéra d'Oslo a été inauguré par le roi de Norvège le 12 avril 2008. Il est présenté par les architectes comme « la plus importante initiative culturo-politique de la Norvège contemporaine. » En 1999, l'Assemblée nationale a décidé d'édifier cet opéra à Bjørvika, face au fjord d'Oslo. Le bâtiment devait être le point de départ de la rénovation urbaine de ce quartier de la capitale. « Le gouvernement souhaitait que l'opéra soit une réalisation monumentale qui souligne le rôle culturel de la Norvège et mette en valeur l'importance de l'opéra et du ballet norvégiens dans la culture nationale. Le bâtiment devait donc être un événement tant en termes d'architecture que de construction, de solutions techniques et de matériaux. » L'opéra contient une salle principale de 1360 places et un auditorium plus petit et d'aménagement plus flexible de 400 places. La grande salle est en « forme classique de fer à cheval ». Le vaste foyer se « caractérise par l'utilisation simple des matériaux et le minimum de détails d'ornement ». De vastes locaux sont prévus pour les salles de répétition, les loges des artistes, les bureaux, les ateliers et les réserves sur cinq niveaux, dont un en sous-sol. Paré de marbre blanc de Carrare, le *roofscape* est une terrasse en toiture ouverte au public qui, selon les architectes, « précise le caractère monumental du bâtiment ». Les architectes affirment encore : « Les plans horizontaux et inclinés du toit confèrent à l'opéra une expression spectaculaire surprenante, assez différente de celle des immeubles avoisinants. » L'opéra antérieur était auparavant installé dans un ancien cinéma. Ces nouvelles installations proches de la gare centrale et de la bourse, dans un quartier qui sera entièrement rénové vers 2018, a des chances de remplir l'objectif du gouvernement norvégien d'en faire la principale attraction touristique de la capitale.

The wedge-like shape of the Opera rises up from the water's edge, creating a dramatic, modern form.

Die keilförmige Oper erhebt sich in unmittelbarer Wassernähe und gibt ein spannungsreich-modernes Bild ab.

La masse en coin de l'opéra s'élève du bord de l'eau en une forme spectaculaire et moderne.

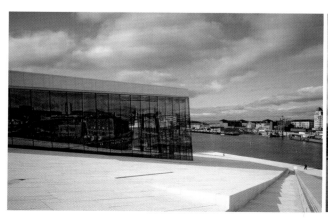

Despite its large dimensions, the building has a strong yet discreet presence that honors its architects.

Löblicherweise haben die Architekten dem Gebäude trotz seiner Größe eine zwar starke, doch zugleich zurückhaltende Präsenz verliehen.

Malgré ses vastes dimensions, le bâtiment possède une présence à la fois forte et discrète à porter au crédit de ses architectes.

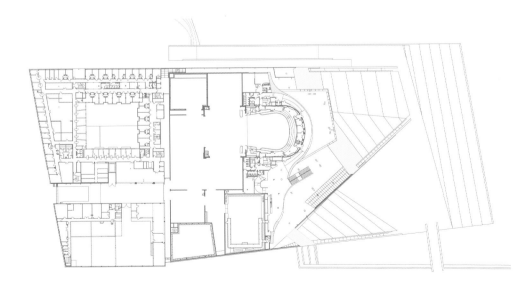

The interior design echoes the modest yet very present architectural design of the exterior volumes. Details are mastered at all levels, making this a memorable building.

Im Innern setzt sich die bescheidene, aber eindringliche Gestaltung der äußeren Gebäudeform fort. Sämtliche Details wurden vorbildlich gehandhabt und lassen ein eindrucksvolles Gebäude entstehen.

La conception intérieure fait écho aux principes architecturaux mis en œuvre à l'extérieur. Les détails maîtrisés à tous les niveaux en font une remarquable réalisation.

TONKIN LIU

Tonkin Liu Ltd.
24 Rosebery Avenue
London EC1R 4SX
UK

Tel: +44 20 78 37 62 55
Fax: +44 20 78 37 62 77
E-mail: mail@tonkinliu.co.uk
Web: www.tonkinliu.co.uk

Mike Tonkin was born in 1969 in the UK. He received his Architecture degrees from the Metropolitan University of Leeds (B.Arch, 1983) and from the Royal College of Art in London (M.A., 1986). He has been a Unit Master at the Architectural Association (AA) in London, and worked for Branson Coates (London, 1986–87) and Eva Jiricna Architects (London, 1987–88), before creating **TONKIN LIU** in 1999. Anna Liu was born in Taiwan in 1965. She received her M.Arch from Columbia University in New York (1994). She has also been a Unit Master at the AA, and has worked with Rocco Design (1994–97) and with Arup Associates, on the Manchester Stadium (UK, 1998–99). The pair met in Hong Kong, where Mike Tonkin directed Tonkin Design. Their projects since 2006 include a Roof Garden Apartment (London, 2006); the Singing Ringing Tree (Burnley, 2005–06, published here); the Promenade of Light, Old Street (London, 2006); the EC1 Music Project (recording studios for children and young people, 2007); the refurbishment of the Alan Cristea Gallery (London, 2007); the London Festival of Architecture Fresh Flower Pavilion (London, 2008); and the Future Flower, Widnes Waterfront (2008), all in the UK.

Mike Tonkin, geboren 1969 in Großbritannien, erlangte 1983 seinen Bachelor of Architecture an der Metropolitan University of Leeds und 1986 seinen Master of Architecture am Royal College of Art in London. Tonkin war Fachdozent an der Architectural Association (AA) in London und hatte vor der Gründung von **TONKIN LIU** im Jahr 1999 u. a. bei Branson Coates (London, 1986–87) und bei Eva Jiricna Architects (London, 1987–88) gearbeitet. Anna Liu, geboren 1965 in Taiwan, erhielt ihren Master of Architecture 1994 an der Columbia University in New York. Liu war ebenfalls Fachdozentin an der AA. Von 1994 bis 1997 arbeitete sie bei Rocco Design, von 1998 bis 1999 wirkte sie für Arup Associates bei der Entstehung des Stadions von Manchester (1998–99) mit. Kennengelernt hat sich das Architektenduo in Hongkong, wo Mike Tonkin das Büro Tonkin Design leitete. Folgende Projekte haben sie seit 2006 verwirklicht: ein Dachgarten-Apartment in London (2006), den hier vorgestellten „Singing Ringing Tree" im englischen Burnley (2005–06), die Promenade of Light in der Londoner Old Street (2006), das EC1 Music Project, Aufnahmestudios für Kinder und Jugendliche (2007), die Renovierung der Alan Cristea Gallery in London (2007), den Fresh Flower Pavilion für das London Festival of Architecture (2008) und die Future Flower an der Uferpromenade von Widnes im englischen Cheshire (2008).

Mike Tonkin, né en 1969 en Grande-Bretagne, est diplômé en architecture de la Metropolitan University de Leeds (B. Arch., 1983) et du Royal College of Art de Londres (M.A., 1986). Il a été responsable d'unité à l'Architectural Association (AA) de Londres, et a travaillé pour Branson Coates (Londres, 1986–87) et Eva Jiricna Architects (Londres, 1987–88), avant de créer l'agence **TONKIN LIU** en 1999. Anna Liu, née à Taiwan en 1965, est M. Arch. de Columbia University de New York (1994). Elle a également été responsable d'unité à l'AA, et a travaillé pour Rocco Design (1994–97) et Arup Associates sur le projet du stade de Manchester (G.-B., 1998–99). Le couple s'est rencontré à Hong Kong où Mike Tonkin dirigeait Tonkin Design. Depuis 2006, ils ont réalisé en Grande-Bretagne : un appartement terrasse-jardin (Londres, 2006) ; le *Singing Ringing Tree* (Burnley, 2005–06, publié ici) ; la Promenade of Light sur Old Street (Londres, 2006) ; l'EC1 Music Project (studios d'enregistrement pour enfants et jeunes, 2007) ; la rénovation de la galerie Alan Cristea (Londres, 2007) ; le Fresh Flower Pavilion pour le London Festival of Architecture (Londres, 2008) et le Future Flower (Widnes Waterfront, 2008), l'ensemble des réalisations en Grande-Bretagne.

SINGING RINGING TREE

Crown Point, Burnley, UK, 2005–06

*Dimensions: 6.2 x 3.5 x 3.8 m (canopy). Client: Mid-Pennine Arts and Burnley Borough Council.
Cost: € 93 871. Team: Tonkin Liu, Jane Wernick Associates, Mike Smith Studio*

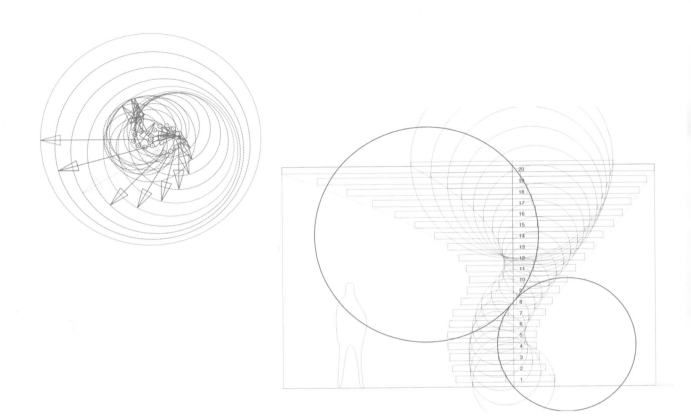

Singing Ringing Tree is a musical sculpture composed of stacked galvanized steel pipes of varying lengths. It is located on top of a hill near Burnley, in the Pennines, Lancashire. This work is part of the Panopticons project of the East Lancashire Environmental Arts Network (ELEAN), intended to create a series of "all-seeing structures" for high-point sites in the Lancashire hills. The goal of the Panopticons project is to explore the "value of art's role in regeneration." Inspired by trees, the stacked pipes of *Singing Ringing Tree* emit a low frequency "song" in the wind. The asymmetrical stacking of the pipes and their varying length produce a range of different musical chords depending on wind conditions. *Singing Ringing Tree* was named winner of a 2007 National Award for architectural excellence at the Royal Institute of British Architects (RIBA). It can be viewed at youtube: www.youtube.com/watch?v=_rhuFGvXARA.

„Singing Ringing Tree" ist eine Klangskulptur aus übereinandergesetzten galvanisierten Stahlröhren von unterschiedlicher Länge, die auf einem Hügel in den Pennines in der Nähe der Stadt Burnley, Lancashire, aufgestellt wurde. Die Arbeit ist Teil des Projekts Panopticons des East Lancashire Environmental Arts Network (ELEAN), das sich zur Aufgabe gesetzt hat, bestimmte höhergelegene Standorte in den Lancashire Hills mit weithin sichtbaren Installationen zu versehen. Das Projekt will erkunden, „welche Bedeutung Kunstwerke in Erholungsgebieten spielen können". Die gestapelten Röhren des „Singing Ringing Tree", zu dessen Gestalt sich die Designer von rauschenden Bäumen anregen ließen, stoßen bei Wind einen tief tönenden „Gesang" aus. Durch die asymmetrische Schichtung der Röhren und deren ungleiche Länge kommen je nach Windverhältnissen unterschiedliche Akkorde zustande. Der „Singing Ringing Tree" wurde vom Royal Institute of British Architects mit einem National Award for architectural excellence des Jahres 2007 ausgezeichnet. Im Internet ist eine Videoaufnahme zu sehen (und zu hören): www.youtube.com/watch?v=_rhuFGvXARA.

Singing Ringing Tree est une sculpture musicale en tuyaux d'acier galvanisé de différentes longueurs empilés. Elle est installée au sommet d'une colline près de Burnley dans les Pennines (Lancashire). Elle fait partie du projet Panopticons de l'East Lancashire Environmental Arts Network (ELEAN), qui se propose de créer des « structures à vue panoramique » sur les points les plus élevés des collines de la région. L'objectif de ce programme est d'explorer la « valeur du rôle de l'art dans la régénération ». Inspiré par les arbres, les tuyaux empilés émettent un « chant » basse fréquence dans le vent qui fait l'objet de variation qui sont dues à la relation entre l'assymétrie et les longueurs variées des tuyaux et la force et la position du vent. *Singing Ringing Tree* a remporté le prix national d'excellence 2007 du Royal Institute of British Architects (RIBA). Il peut être contemplé sur internet : www.youtube.com/watch?v=_rhuFGvXARA.

It is surely debatable as to whether the Singing Ringing Tree is a work of art more than of architecture. Its movement and use of sound make it an unusual work, realized by architects in a sculptural format.

Sicherlich lässt sich darüber streiten, ob der „Singing Ringing Tree" eher Kunst oder Architektur ist. Seine dynamische Form und die Einbeziehung von Klang machen ihn zu einem außergewöhnlichen Werk, geschaffen von Architekten in Form einer Skulptur.

On peut certainement se demander si le Singing Ringing Tree est plus une œuvre d'art que d'architecture. Sa dynamique et l'utilisation du son en font une œuvre curieuse réalisée par des architectes qui ont maîtrisé la forme sculpturale.

BERNARD TSCHUMI

Bernard Tschumi Architects
227 West 17th Street
New York, NY 10011
USA

Tel: +1 212 807 6340
Fax: +1 212 242 3693
E-mail: nyc@tschumi.com
Web: www.tschumi.com

BERNARD TSCHUMI was born in Lausanne, Switzerland, in 1944. He studied in Paris and at the ETH in Zurich. He taught at the Architectural Association (AA), London (1970–79), and at Princeton (1976–80). He was the Dean of the Graduate School of Architecture, Planning and Preservation of Columbia University in New York from 1988 to 2003. He opened his own office, Bernard Tschumi Architects (Paris, New York), in 1981. Major projects include: the Parc de la Villette (Paris, France, 1982–95); the Second Prize in the Kansai International Airport Competition (1988); the Video Gallery (Groningen, The Netherlands, 1990); Le Fresnoy National Studio for Contemporary Arts (Tourcoing, France, 1991–97); the Lerner Student Center, Columbia University (New York, 1994–98); the School of Architecture (Marne-la-Vallée, France, 1994–98); and the Interface Flon railroad station (Lausanne, Switzerland, 1988–2001). Recent work includes the Vacheron-Constantin Headquarters (Geneva, 2004); the Linder Athletic Center at the University of Cincinnati (Cincinnati, Ohio, 2006); the Zénith Concert Hall (Limoges, France, 2005–07, published here); and BLUE, a 17-story residential tower on the Lower East Side (New York, 2008). Among the firm's current projects are the New Acropolis Museum (Athens, Greece); and a museum and interpretive center at the Parc Archéologique d'Alésia (Alésia, France). Currently in design development are the West Diaoyutai Hotel and Residence in Beijing (China); and the Grote Markstraat mixed-use center (The Hague, The Netherlands).

BERNARD TSCHUMI, geboren 1944 in Lausanne in der Schweiz, studierte in Paris und an der ETH Zürich. Von 1970 bis 1979 lehrte er an der Architectural Association in London und von 1976 bis 1980 in Princeton. Von 1988 bis 2003 war Tschumi Dekan der Graduate School of Architecture, Planning and Preservation der Columbia University in New York. 1981 eröffnete er das Büro Bernard Tschumi Architects mit Niederlassungen in Paris und New York. Zu seinen wichtigsten Projekten gehören der Parc de la Villette in Paris (1982–95), ein Wettbewerbsbeitrag für den Internationalen Flughafen Kansai, Japan (1988), eine Videogalerie im niederländischen Groningen (1990), das staatliche Zentrum für zeitgenössische Kunst Le Fresnoy in Tourcoing, Frankreich (1991–97), das Lerner Student Center der Columbia University in New York (1994–98), die École d'architecture im französischen Marne-la-Vallée (1994–98) und der Bahnhof Interface Flon in Lausanne (1988–2001). In jüngerer Zeit entstanden die Vacheron-Constantin-Zentrale in Genf (2004), das Linder Athletic Center der University of Cincinnati (2006), die hier vorgestellte Zénith-Konzerthalle in Limoges (2005–07) und ein 17-geschossiges Wohnhochhaus namens BLUE in der New Yorker Lower East Side (2008). Derzeit in Ausführung sind das neue Akropolis-Museum in Athen und ein Museum und Informationszentrum für den Parc Archéologique d'Alésia. In der Planungsphase befinden sich das West Diaoyutai Hotel and Residence in Peking und der Mehrzweckkomplex Grote Markstraat in Den Haag.

BERNARD TSCHUMI, né à Lausanne, Suisse, en 1944, a étudié à Paris et à l'ETH de Zurich. Il a enseigné à l'Architectural Association de Londres (1970–79) et à Princeton (1976–80). Il a été doyen de la Graduate School of Architecture, Planning and Preservation de Columbia University à New York de 1988 à 2003, et a ouvert son agence, Bernard Tschumi Architects (Paris, New York), en 1981. Parmi ses interventions majeures : le Parc de la Villette (Paris, France, 1982–95) ; le second prix au concours pour l'aéroport international du Kansai (Osaka, 1988) ; la Video Gallery (Groningen, Pays-Bas, 1990) ; Le Studio national d'Art contemporain du Fresnoy (Tourcoing, France, 1991–97) ; le Lerner Student Center, Columbia University (New York, 1994–98) ; l'École d'architecture de Marne-la-Vallée (France, 1994–98) et la gare d'échanges ferroviaires de Lausanne (Suisse, 1988–2001). Plus récemment, il a réalisé le siège de Vacheron-Constantin (Genève, 2004) ; le Linder Athletic Center (University of Cincinnati, 2006) ; le Zénith de Limoges (France, 2005–07, publiée ici) et BLUE, une tour d'appartements de 17 étages dans le Lower East Side à New York (2008). Actuellement, l'agence travaille sur le nouveau musée de l'Acropole (Athènes) ; un musée et centre d'interprétation pour le Parc archéologique d'Alésia (France) ; l'Hôtel et Residence de Diaoyuta Ouest à Pékin (Chine) et le centre polyvalent de Grote Markstraat (La Haye, Pays-Bas).

ZÉNITH CONCERT HALL

Limoges, France, 2005–07

*Site area: 6 ha. Floor area: 8500 m². Client: Community of Limoges.
Cost: $36.6 million. Partners in Charge: Bernard Tschumi, Véronique Descharrières.
Project Architects: Jean Jacques Hubert, Antoinne Santiard, Joël Rutten. Site Architects: Atelier 4.
Landscape Architects: Michel Desvigne with Sol Paysage*

The curving façade of the Zénith,
together with its somewhat angled
placement in the site, make it stand
out clearly from the nearby road.

Dank seiner gerundeten Fassaden ist
das Zénith, zumal es etwas schräg
auf dem Gelände steht, von der Straße aus kaum zu übersehen.

Vus de la route, les façades
incurvées du Zénith et son léger
déhanchement par rapport au site.

Bernard Tschumi is at ease with the combination of industrial scale and interesting design required for the Zénith theaters, as these images demonstrate.

Wie die Abbildungen demonstrieren, weiß Bernard Tschumi spannendes Design, wie es zu einer Zénith-Halle gehört, gekonnt mit den Dimensionen einer Industriearchitektur in Einklang zu bringen.

Bernard Tschumi est à l'aise dans la combinaison de l'échelle industrielle et de concepts originaux caractéris- tiques des projets Zénith, comme le montrent ces images.

UNSTUDIO

UNStudio/Van Berkel & Bos
Stadhouderskade 113 / 1070 AJ Amsterdam / The Netherlands

Tel: +31 20 570 20 40 / Fax: +31 20 570 20 41
E-mail: info@unstudio.com / Web: www.unstudio.com

Ben van Berkel was born in Utrecht in 1957, and studied at the Rietveld Academy in Amsterdam and at the Architectural Association (AA) in London, receiving the AA Diploma with honors in 1987. After working briefly in the office of Santiago Calatrava in 1988, he set up his practice in Amsterdam with Caroline Bos, Van Berkel & Bos Architectural Bureau, **UNSTUDIO** since 1998. He has been a Visiting Professor at Columbia and a visiting critic at Harvard (1994). He was a Diploma Unit Master at the AA (1994–95). As well as the Erasmus Bridge in Rotterdam (inaugurated in 1996), UNSTUDIO has built the Karbouw and ACOM office buildings (1989–93), and the REMU Electricity Station (1989–93), all in Amersfoort; and housing projects and the Aedes East Gallery for Kristin Feireiss in Berlin, Germany. More recent projects include an extension for the Rijksmuseum Twente (Enschede, 1992–96); the Möbius House (Naarden, 1993–98); Het Valkhof Museum (Nijmegen, 1998); and the NMR Laboratory (Utrecht, 2000), all in the Netherlands; a Switching Station (Innsbruck, Austria, 1998–2001); an Electricity Station (Innsbruck, Austria, 2002); Hotel Castell (Zuoz, Switzerland, 2001–04, published here); VilLA NM (Upstate New York, 2000–06); the Mercedes-Benz Museum (Stuttgart, Germany, 2003–06); the Theater Agora (Lelystad, The Netherlands, 2004–07, published here); the Arnhem Station (The Netherlands, 1986–2008); and a Music Facility (Graz, Austria, 1998–2008). UNStudio was also a participant in the competition for the new World Trade Center in New York, in collaboration with Foreign Office Architects, Greg Lynn FORM, Imaginary Forces, Kevin Kennon and Reiser + Umemoto, RUR under the name of United Architects.

Ben van Berkel, geboren 1957 in Utrecht, studierte an der Rietveld Academie in Amsterdam sowie der Architectural Association (AA) in London, wo er 1987 sein Diplom mit Auszeichnung erwarb. Nach kurzer Tätigkeit bei Santiago Calatrava gründete er 1988 zusammen mit Caroline Bos das Büro Van Berkel & Bos Architectural Bureau in Amsterdam, 1998 umbenannt in **UNSTUDIO**. 1994 war er Gastprofessor an der Columbia University und Gastkritiker in Harvard, 1994 bis 1995 lehrte er als Diploma Unit Master an der AA. Neben der 1996 eröffneten Erasmusbrücke in Rotterdam führte das Architekturbüro UNSTUDIO im niederländischen Amersfoort die Bürogebäude Karbouw und ACOM (1989–93) und ein REMU-Umspannwerk (1989–93) aus, in Berlin gestalteten sie Wohngebäude und die Galerie Aedes East für Kristin Feireiss. Ferner realisierten sie in den Niederlanden die Erweiterung des Rijksmuseum Twente in Enschede (1992–96), das Möbius-Haus in Naarden (1993–98), das Museum Het Valkhof in Nimwegen (1998) und ein NMR-Labor in Utrecht (2000). In Innsbruck führten sie eine Schaltanlage (1998–2001) und ein Umspannwerk (2002) aus. Zu den jüngeren UNStudio-Projekten gehören das Hotel Castell im schweizerischen Zuoz (2001–04, hier präsentiert), die VilLA NM im US-Bundesstaat New York (2000–06), das Mercedes-Benz Museum in Stuttgart (2003–06), das hier vorgestellte Agora Theater im niederländischen Lelystad (2004–07), der Bahnhof Arnheim (1986–2008) und ein Musiktheater in Graz (1998–2008). In Kooperation mit anderen Architekturbüros (Foreign Office Architects, Greg Lynn FORM, Imaginary Forces, Kevin Kennon und Reiser + Umemoto, RUR) beteiligte sich UNStudio unter dem gemeinsamen Namen United Architects an dem Wettbewerb für das neue World Trade Center in New York.

Ben van Berkel, né à Utrecht en 1957, étudie à l'Académie Rietveld d'Amsterdam ainsi qu'à l'Architectural Association de Londres dont il sort diplômé avec mention en 1987. Après avoir brièvement travaillé pour Santiago Calatrava en 1988, il ouvre, en association avec Caroline Bos, son agence à Amsterdam, Van Berkel & Bos Architectural Bureau, **UNSTUDIO** en 1998. Il a été professeur invité à Columbia University, New York, critique invité à Harvard en 1994, et responsable d'unité pour le diplôme de l'AA en 1994–95. En dehors du pont Erasme à Rotterdam (inauguré en 1996), UNSTUDIO a construit les immeubles de bureaux Karbouw et ACOM (1989–93), le poste d'électricité REMU (1989–93), le tout à Amersfoort ainsi que des logements et l'Aedes East Gallery de Kristin Feireiss à Berlin. Parmi leurs projets plus récents : l'extension du Rijksmuseum Twente (Enschede, 1992–96), la maison Möbius (Naarden, 1993–98), le musée Het Valkhof (Nimègue), le laboratoire NMR (Utrecht, 2000), tous aux Pays-Bas ; une gare d'échange (Innsbruck, Autriche, 1998–2001) ; une station électrique (Innsbruck, Autriche, 2002) ; l'Hotel Castel (Zuoz, Suisse, 2001–04, publié ici) ; la VilLa NM (État de New York, 2000–06) ; le musée Mercedes-Benz (Stuttgart, Allemagne, 2003–06)) ; le Théâtre Agora (Lelystad, Pays-Bas, 2004–07, publié ici ; la gare d'Arnhem (Pays-Bas, 1986–2008) et un complexe consacré à la musique (Graz, Autriche,1998–2008). UNStudio a participé au concours pour le World Trade Center à New York, en collaboration avec Foreign Office Architects, Greg Lynn FORM, Imaginary Forces, Kevin Kennon and Reiser + Umemoto, RUR, sous le nom de United Architects.

HOTEL CASTELL

Zuoz, Switzerland, 2001–04

*Site area: 2200 m². Total floor area: 5500 m², including 3000 m² (apartment building); 260 m² (hamam); 700 m² (hotel rooms).
Client: Castell Zuoz AG, Herrliberg. Cost: not disclosed. Team: UNStudio: Ben van Berkel with Olaf Gipser and Pablo Rica,
Sebastian Schaeffer, Andrew Benn, Dag Thies, Eric den Eerzamen, Ron Roos, Claudia Dorner, Martin Kuitert, Marco Hemmerling,
Sophie Valla, Tina Bayerl, Peter Irmscher. Executive Architect: Walter Dietsche AG, Chur*

Located on a beautiful site at an altitude of 1900 meters in the Engadine Valley of Switzerland not far from St. Moritz, the Hotel Castell was added on to the existing early 1912–13 structure partly renovated. The work of UNStudio consisted in adding a new apartment building with 14 luxury residences (Chesa Chastlatsch), a two-story parking structure, a spectacular redesign of the existing hotel basement to create a hamam, the renovation of 25 hotel rooms, the renovation of the hotel reception area, and the creation of a new kitchen and utility area. A number of other architects and artists have intervened on the hotel, including the local architect Hans-Jörg Ruch (page 438), who was responsible for the design of the rooms not handled by UNStudio. A large outdoor wooden terrace and walkway leading to an outdoor sauna were designed and built by the Japanese artist Tadashi Kawamata, while James Turrell has more recently created a *Skyspace* on the grounds of the hotel. Inside, the Red Bar was designed by Zurich architect Gabrielle Hächler and multimedia artist Pipilotti Rist. The atmosphere of cutting-edge architecture, design, and art is completed by a large collection of works by such artists as Roman Signer, Peter Fischli/David Weiss, Carsten Höller, and Martin Kippenberger, on loan from the extensive private collection of principal shareholder Ruedi Bechtler (Walther A. Bechtler Foundation).

In einer herrlichen Lage auf 1900 m Höhe befindet sich im Engadin, nicht weit von St. Moritz, das Hotel Castell – ein 1912/13 errichteter Bau, der vor einiger Zeit teilrenoviert wurde. Dabei entstanden nach den Entwürfen von UNStudio auch ein Zusatzgebäude mit 14 Luxusapartments (die Chesa Chastlatsch) und eine zweigeschossige Parkgarage. Ferner gestalteten die Niederländer das Hoteluntergeschoss neu, das nun einen Hamam enthält, sowie eine neue Küche und einen neuen Haustechnikbereich, außerdem renovierten sie 25 Hotelzimmer und den Rezeptionsbereich. Neben UNStudio waren eine Reihe weiterer Architekten und Künstler an der Hotelerneuerung beteiligt, darunter der in St. Moritz tätige Architekt Hans-Jörg Ruch (S. 438), der die übrigen Zimmer gestaltete. Eine große hölzerne Freiluftterrasse führt über einen Steg zu einer Sauna, entworfen und gebaut von dem japanischen Künstler Tadashi Kawamata. Ebenso befindet sich im Außenbereich ein erst vor Kurzem von James Turrell angelegter „Skyspace". Im Innern des Hotels trifft man auf die von der Züricher Architektin Gabrielle Hächler und der Multimediakünstlerin Pipilotti Rist gestaltete „Rote Bar". Kunstwerke von Roman Signer, Peter Fischli/David Weiss, Carsten Höller und Martin Kippenberger – Leihgaben aus der umfangreichen Privatsammlung des Hauptgesellschafters Ruedi Bechtler (Walther A. Bechtler Stiftung) – machen die Mischung aus herausragender Architektur, Kunst und Design perfekt.

Situé en Engadine sur un site magnifique à 1900 mètres d'altitude, non loin de St. Moritz, l'Hotel Castell actuel est l'aboutissement d'une extension et d'une rénovation partielle du bâtiment ancien, datant de 1912–13. Le travail d'UNStudio a consisté à ajouter un nouveau bâtiment contenant 14 appartements de luxe (Chesa Chastlatsch), créer un parking sur deux niveaux, rénover spectaculairement les sous-sols de l'hôtel existant pour un hammam, restaurer 25 chambres, la salle de réception, une nouvelle cuisine et des installations techniques. Un certain nombre d'autres architectes et artistes sont intervenus sur cet hôtel, dont l'architecte de la région Hans-Jörg Ruch (page 438), responsable du réaménagement des chambres restantes. Une vaste terrasse en bois et un passage couvert conduisant à un sauna extérieur ont été construits par l'artiste japonais Tadashi Kawamata, tandis que James Turrell a plus récemment créé un de ses *Skyspace*, sur le terrain de l'hôtel. À l'intérieur, le Red Bar a été conçu par l'architecte zurichoise Gabrielle Hächler et l'artiste multimédia Pipilotti Rist. L'atmosphère de cette architecture et ces interventions artistiques d'avant-garde sont encore enrichies par l'importante collection d'œuvres d'artistes comme Roman Signer, Peter Fischli/David Weiss, Carsten Höller et Martin Kippenberger, prêtées à partir de sa vaste collection par le principal actionnaire des lieux, Ruedi Bechtler (Fondation Walther A. Bechtler).

Set above the medieval village of Zuoz, the new building by UNStudio stands next to an older, renovated hotel structure.

Der von UNStudio entworfene Neubau wurde neben einem renovierten Hotelgebäude oberhalb des mittelalterlichen Ortes Zuoz errichtet.

Au-dessus du village médiéval de Zuoz, le nouveau bâtiment d'UNStudio est implanté à proximité d'un hôtel ancien qui a été rénové.

The new building, containing apartments, is seen above, next to the
original Hotel Castell building.

Oben der Neubau, in dem sich zusätzliche Apartments befinden, neben
dem alten Gebäude des Hotel Castell.

Le nouveau bâtiment, qui contient
des appartements, non loin de l'Hôtel
Castell de l'origine.

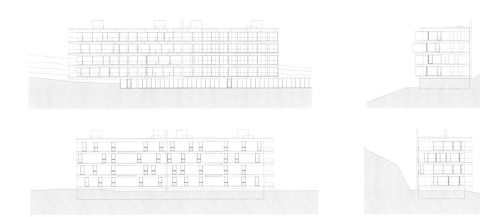

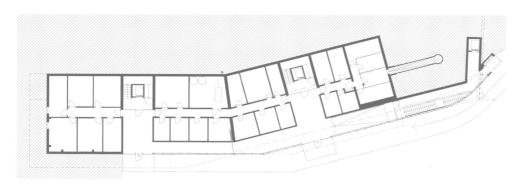

A floor plan of the new building, views
of the façade, and of an inner hall-
way of the building.

*Ein Geschossgrundriss, Ansichten der
Fassade und ein Innenflur des neuen
Gebäudes.*

*Plan au sol du bâtiment neuf, vues
de la façade et d'un passage
intérieur.*

An installation by James Turrell
stands next to the older hotel building. Right, the exterior of the structure
designed by Turrell and, below, two
views of its interior in different light.

Neben dem älteren Hotelgebäude
befindet sich eine Installation von
James Turrell. Rechts eine Außen-
ansicht von Turrells Arbeit, unten
zwei Ansichten des Innenraums bei
unterschiedlicher Beleuchtung.

Une installation de James Turrell
a été aménagée près du bâtiment
ancien. À droite, l'extérieur de la
petite construction dessinée par
Turrell et, ci-dessous, deux vues
intérieures sous différentes lumières.

The hamam in the older Hotel Castell building was designed entirely by UNStudio and is located in the basement level of the hotel. It features relatively small, modern volumes with bright colors.

Der Hamam im Untergeschoss des älteren Hotel Castell wurde komplett von UNStudio entworfen; die verhältnismäßig kleinen Räume zeichnen sich durch eine moderne, farbenfrohe Gestaltung aus.

Le hammam dans l'ancien bâtiment de l'hôtel Castell a été entièrement conçu par UNStudio. Il se trouve dans les sous-sols. Ses volumes contemporains, relativement petits, sont animés de couleurs vives.

To the left, a deck near the outdoor sauna of the hotel was designed, like the main wooden terrace of the older building, by the Japanese artist Tadashi Kawamata.

Die Plattform an der Außensauna des Hotels (links) sowie die hölzerne Hauptterrasse des älteren Gebäudes wurde von dem japanischen Künstler Tadashi Kawamata entworfen.

À gauche, la terrasse du sauna extérieur a été dessinée, comme la principale terrasse de l'ancien bâtiment, par l'artiste japonais Tadashi Kawamata.

THEATER AGORA

Lelystad, The Netherlands, 2004–07

Site area: 2925 m². Floor area: 7000 m². Client: Municipality of Lelystad. Cost: €20 million.
Team: UNStudio: Ben van Berkel with Gerard Loozekoot, Jacques van Wijk, Job Mouwen, Holger Hoffmann, Khoi Tran,
Christian Veddeler, Christian Bergmann, Sabine Habicht, Ramon Hernandez, Ron Roos, Rene Wysk, Claudia Dorner, Markus Berger,
Markus Jacobi, Ken Okonkwo, Jorgen Grahl-Madsen. Executive Architect: B+M, The Hague

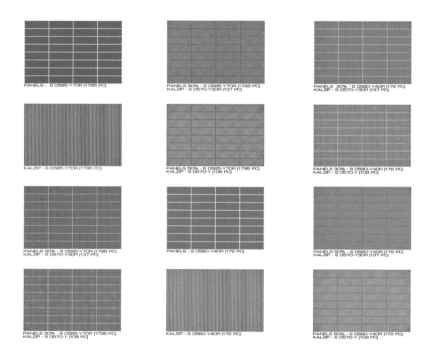

This regional theater, part of the master plan for the town of Lelystad designed by West 8, includes a large theater hall with seating for 725 and a small hall that seats 200. Cultural and social activities are concentrated near the theater, giving it an important position both during the day and at night. This role is, of course, heightened by the colorful, faceted envelope of the building. The reason for this faceting, according to Ben van Berkel, is "to reconstruct the kaleidoscopic experience of the world of the stage, where you can never be sure of what is real and what is not." A vertical foyer penetrates the building and connects the theater and congress spaces on different floors. Color is also present inside, with a snaking pink handrail on the main staircase, changing color as it moves toward the roof. The main theater is entirely red. The architects write, "The typology of the theater has become more and more complex during the years. UNStudio strived to bring the complexity of a multifunctional theater back into a flexible, transparent, and intelligent design. The clear and open organization of the design will serve as a cultural icon for Lelystad."

Das Regionaltheater Agora ist Bestandteil eines von West 8 entworfenen Masterplans für den Ort Lelystad und umfasst einen großen Zuschauersaal mit 725 und einen kleinen mit 200 Sitzplätzen. Zahlreiche Kultur- und Freizeitangebote im näheren Umkreis werten den Theaterstandort tags wie abends zusätzlich auf. Die zentrale Rolle des Hauses wird durch seine bunte, facettierte Gebäudehülle hervorgehoben. Die Motivation für diese Facettierung bestand darin, so Ben van Berkel, „das kaleidoskopische Erlebnisspektrum der Bühnenwelt äußerlich nachzuvollziehen, bei der man nie sicher sein kann, was echt ist und was nicht". Das Foyer zieht sich vertikal durch das Gebäude und verbindet die auf verschiedenen Ebenen liegenden Theater- und Veranstaltungsräume. Auch innen dominieren Farbenspiele, etwa in Form des komplett in Rot gehaltenen Hauptsaals oder eines pinkfarbenen Handlaufs am Haupttreppenaufgang, der auf seinem Weg zum Dach langsam blasser wird. Wie die Architekten schreiben, ist „die Typologie des Theaters im Lauf der Jahre immer komplexer geworden. Diese Komplexität des multifunktionalen Theaters wollten wir in eine flexible, transparente und intelligente Gestaltung überführen. Die klare, offene Aufteilung des Entwurfs macht ihn zu einem kulturellen Wahrzeichen für Lelystad."

Ce théâtre régional, prévu par le plan directeur de la ville de Lelystad conçu par West 8, comprend une grande salle de théâtre de 725 places et une plus petite de 200. Des activités sociales et culturelles sont concentrées à proximité du théâtre, ce qui lui offre une excellente implantation. Son rôle civique est signalé par son enveloppe à facettes de couleur vive. La raison de ces facettes, selon Ben van Berkel, est « de reconstruire l'expérience kaléidoscopique du monde de la scène, où vous ne pouvez jamais être certain de ce qui est réel ou non ». Le foyer vertical pénètre le bâtiment et relie la salle et les espaces de rencontre à différents niveaux. La couleur est également très présente à l'intérieur, comme sur la rampe rose de l'escalier principal, qui change de couleur au fur et à mesure que l'on s'élève. Le théâtre principal est entièrement rouge. Pour les architectes : « La typologie du théâtre est devenue de plus en plus fouillée au cours des années. UNStudio s'est efforcé de ramener la complexité d'un théâtre aux multiples fonctions à une conception souple, transparente et intelligente. L'organisation ouverte et lisible du projet en fera une icône culturelle pour Lelystad. »

The folded planar design of the theater is very much in the current mood of architecture. Ben van Berkel innovates with the bright orange, red, and yellow palette he has chosen for the exterior cladding.

Mit seinen abgekanteten Flächen zeigt der Theaterentwurf eine Architektur ganz auf der Höhe der Zeit. Einen neuen Akzent setzt Ben van Berkel mit der Farbpalette aus leuchtendem Orange, Rot und Gelb für die Außenverkleidung.

La conception en plans repliés du théâtre illustre un des courants actuels de l'architecture. Ben van Berkel innove par sa palette d'orange, de rouge et de jaune vifs qu'il a choisie pour l'habillage extérieur.

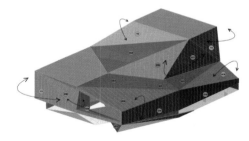

The design of the building, as seen in drawings representing colors and zones, resembles a Japanese origami paper cut-out. The completed structure appears to be almost monolithic in its imposing shape.

Mit den verschiedenen Flächen und Farben erinnern die Entwurfszeichnungen an japanisches Origamipapier. Das fertige Gebäude hat angesichts seiner imposanten Gestalt beinahe etwas Monolithisches.

Le projet, vu à travers des dessins représentant les zones et les couleurs, fait penser à l'origami japonais. La structure achevée paraît presque monolithique dans sa forme imposante.

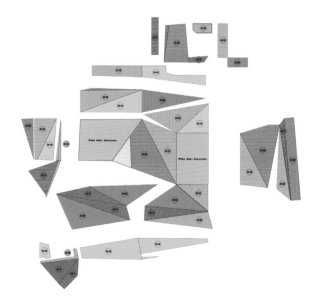

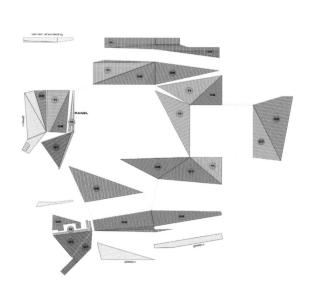

The interiors take up a somewhat more muted yet nonetheless vibrant color scheme. Ben van Berkel is interested in contemporary art, as his use of color in this and other instances demonstrates.

In den Innenräumen kommt ein etwas gedämpfteres, aber nicht weniger spannendes Farbenspiel zum Einsatz. Schaut man sich hier wie bei anderen Projekten Ben van Berkels Umgang mit Farben an, ist sein Interesse für zeitgenössische Kunst unverkennbar.

Les volumes intérieurs sont traités dans une gamme de couleurs un peu plus sobres, mais néanmoins vibrantes. Ben van Berkel s'intéresse à l'art contemporain comme le montre ici, et dans d'autres projets, son recours à la couleur.

The auditorium interior takes up the fractured planar design of the exterior, this time taking into account acoustics, but still using the strong colors of the outside of the building.

Im Innern des Zuschauersaals wird die Gestaltung der Außenseite mit ihren fragmentierten Flächen wieder aufgenommen, freilich unter Berücksichtigung der Akustik, aber in ebenso kräftigen Farben wie außen.

L'intérieur de la salle décline les plans fracturés de l'extérieur en prenant en compte cette fois les contraintes acoustiques, mais toujours en utilisant des couleurs fortes.

URBANUS ARCHITECTURE & DESIGN

URBANUS Architecture & Design, Inc.
Building E-6, 2nd Floor
Huaqiaocheng Dongbu Industrial Zone / Nanshan District
Shenzhen 518053 / China
Tel: +86 755 8609 6345 / Fax: +86 755 8610 6336
E-mail: office@urbanus.com.cn

B302, Sky & Sea Business Plaza, No. 107
Dong Si Bei Da Jie St, Dongcheng District
Beijing 100007 / China
Tel: +86 10 8403 3551 / Fax: +86 10 8403 3561
E-mail: office-bj@urbanus.com.cn / Web: www.urbanus.com.cn

Liu Xiaodu is one of the founding partners of **URBANUS**. Prior to establishing the office, Liu was a project architect and project designer at Design Group Inc. (Columbus, Ohio) and Stang & Newdow Inc. in Atlanta, Georgia. He received his B.Arch degree from Tsinghua University, China, and M.Arch from Miami University, Oxford, Ohio. He gained six years of teaching experience at Tsinghua University. Prior to co-founding URBANUS, Meng Yan was a project architect and designer at Kohn Pedersen Fox Associates PC and Meltzer Mandl Architects in New York; Brown & Bills Architects in Dayton, Ohio; and Yongmao Architects and Engineers in Beijing. Wang Hui, another co-founder of the firm, worked with Gruzen Samton Architects; Gensler; and Gary Edward Handel + Associates. Like his two partners, he was educated at Tsinghua University and Miami University. Their completed works include Diwang Park A (Shenzhen, 2000); the CRL and Constellation Development Sales Office (Beijing, 2003); the OCT Contemporary Art Terminal (Shenzhen, 2004); and Diwang Park B (Shenzhen, 2005), all in China. Current projects include the Shenzhen International Yacht Club (Shenzhen, 2006); the Public Art Plaza (Shenzhen, 2006); the Shanghai Multimedia Valley Office Park (Shanghai, 2007); the Nanyou Shopping Park (Shenzhen, 2007); Digital Beijing (with Studio Pei-Zhu, 2005–08, page 388); and the Dafen Art Museum (Shenzhen, 2006–08, published here), all in China.

Liu Xiaodu ist einer von mehreren Gründungspartnern des Architekturbüros **URBANUS**. Vorher arbeitete Liu als Projektarchitekt und Projektdesigner für Design Group Inc. in Columbus, Ohio, und für Stang & Newdow Inc. in Atlanta, Georgia. Seinen Bachelor of Architecture erwarb Liu an der Universität Tsinghua in China, seinen Master of Architecture an der Miami University in Oxford, Ohio. Liu verfügt über eine sechsjährige Lehrerfahrung an der Universität Tsinghua. Meng Yan war vor der URBANUS-Mitgründung Projektarchitekt für die New Yorker Büros Kohn Pedersen Fox Associates PC und Meltzer Mandl Architects, für Brown & Bills Architects in Dayton, Ohio, und für Yongmao Architects and Engineers in Peking. Wang Hui, der dritte Mitgründer der Firma, arbeitete für Gruzen Samton Architects sowie für Gensler und für Gary Edward Handel + Associates. Wie seine beiden Partner absolvierte Wang sein Studium an der Universität Tsinghua und an der Miami University. Zu ihren realisierten Projekten gehören der Diwang Park A (2000), das CRL and Constellation Development Sales Office in Peking (2003), das OCT-Terminal für zeitgenössische Kunst (2004) und der Diwang Park B (2005), der Internationale Jachtklub Shenzhen (2006), der Public Art Plaza (2006), der Shanghai Multimedia Valley Office Park in Shanghai (2007), der Einkaufspark Nanyou (2007), das Digital Beijing in Peking (mit Studio Pei-Zhu, 2005–08, Seite 388) und das hier vorgestellte Kunstmuseum Dafen (2006–08). Sämtliche genannten Projekte entstanden, sofern nicht anders angegeben, in Shenzhen.

Liu Xiaodu, l'un des associés fondateurs d'**URBANUS**, a été auparavant architecte et concepteur de projets chez Design Group Inc. (Columbus, Ohio) et Stang & Newdow Inc. à Atlanta, Géorgie. Il est B. Arch. de l'université de Tsinghua en Chine et M. Arch. de Miami University à Oxford, Ohio. Il a enseigné pendant six ans à l'université de Tsinghua. Avant d'être cofondateur d'URBANUS, Meng Yan a été architecte de projet et concepteur chez Kohn Pedersen Fox Associates PC ; Meltzer Mandl Architects à New York ; Brown & Bills Architects à Dayton et Yongmao Architects and Engineers à Pékin. Wang Hui, autre cofondateur de l'agence, a travaillé pour Gruzen Samton Architects ; pour Gensler ainsi que pour Gary Edward Handel + Associates. Comme ses deux associés, il a fait ses études à l'université de Tsinghua et à Miami University. Parmi leurs réalisations achevées : Diwang Park A (Shenzhen, 2000) ; CRL and Constellation Development Sales Office (Pékin, 2003) ; OCT terminal d'art contemporain (Shenzhen, 2004) et Diwang Park B (Shenzhen, 2005), toutes en Chine. Parmi leurs projets actuels : le Yacht club international de Shenzhen (Shenzhen, 2006) ; une place aménagée pour des présentations d'art (Shenzhen, 2006) ; le parc de bureaux de la Multimedia Valley de Shanghaï (2007) ; le parc commercial Nanyou (Shenzhen, 2007) ; Digital Beijing (avec Studio Pei-Zhu, 2005–08, page 388) et le musée d'Art de Dafen (Shenzhen, 2006–08, publié ici), le tout en Chine.

DAFEN ART MUSEUM

Dafen Village, Shenzhen, China, 2006–08

Site area: 11 300 m². Floor area: 16 866 m². Cost: €10 million.
Partners in Charge: Liu Xiaodu, Meng Yan. Project Architects: Fu Zhuoheng, Chen Yaoguang

The Dafen Village area is well known in China for its oil painting replica workshops that export to Europe, America, and Asia. What is produced in the area has long been considered to be a "strange mixture of art, bad taste, and commercialism," according to the architects. Their goal has been to reinterpret this image with an innovative approach that seeks to "hybridize" different programs, including oil painting galleries, shops, commercial spaces, and studios. Pathways through the building's public spaces encourage interaction with the community. Their strategy of confronting their project with the typical idea of a museum is actually quite daring, as the architects acknowledge. As they write, "The walls of a traditional museum clearly define the boundary between the art world and the outside world. Its exclusiveness protects the museum's content from the reality of daily life on the outside. But here the name 'museum' can hardly describe the contents of the new building, which will be located in Dafen Village, or at least it contains much more than a typical museum is willing or capable of including. The irony is that in a place unimaginable for a typical art museum, we hope it can host the most avant-garde contemporary art shows, and, at the same time, can include the local new vernacular pop art. It should be a highly mixed building, a hybrid container."

Das Stadtviertel Dafen in Shenzhen ist bekannt für seine Malwerkstätten, in denen berühmte Ölgemälde kopiert werden, um sie ins asiatische Ausland und nach Europa und Amerika zu exportieren. Was in Dafen entsteht, wird, so die Architekten, seit Längerem als „eine verquere Mischung aus Kunst, Kommerz und schlechtem Geschmack" beäugt. URBANUS nahm sich vor, dieses Image zu überarbeiten. Die Architekten entschieden sich für einen innovativen Ansatz, bei dem verschiedene Bereiche inklusive Gemäldegalerien, Geschäfte, Gewerberäume und Ateliers „hybridisiert" werden sollten. Die Wege durch die öffentlichen Räume des Gebäudes ermutigen die Interaktion. Wie die Architekten zugeben, ist die Strategie, ihr Projekt mit der typischen Vorstellung eines Museums zu konfrontieren, eigentlich recht gewagt. „Die Mauern des traditionellen Museums", so schreiben sie, „bilden eine Grenze zwischen der Welt der Kunst und der Außenwelt. Seine Exklusivität schützt den Museumsbestand vor der Realität des alltäglichen Lebens auf der anderen Seite. Hier dagegen lässt sich mit dem Begriff ‚Museum' der Inhalt des neuen Gebäudes in Dafen nur schwerlich umschreiben oder zumindest beinhaltet er hier viel mehr, als das typische Museum willens oder in der Lage ist zu umfassen. Die Ironie besteht darin, dass wir mit einem Ort, der für ein typisches Museum undenkbar wäre, die innovativsten Ausstellungen zeitgenössischer Kunst anzulocken hoffen, einem Ort, der aber ebenso gut Platz für die neue hier entstehende Pop-Art bietet. Dieser Ort sollte also ein Mischgebäude sein, ein hybrider Behälter."

La région du village de Dafen est très connue en Chine pour ses ateliers de copies de peintures à l'huile qui s'exportent vers Europe, l'Amérique et l'Asie. Cette production a longtemps été considérée par les architectes comme « un étrange mélange d'art, de mauvais goût et de commerce ». Leur objectif a été de réinterpréter cette image à travers une approche novatrice qui cherche à « hybrider » différents programmes comprenant des galeries de peinture, des boutiques, des espaces commerciaux et des ateliers. Des passages créés à travers les espaces publics du bâtiment facilitent les interactions. Leur stratégie est en fait assez audacieuse, comme ils le reconnaissent, dans sa confrontation au concept classique de musée : « Les murs d'un musée traditionnel définissent clairement les limites entre le monde de l'art et le monde extérieur. Cette exclusion protège le contenu du musée de la réalité de la vie quotidienne du dehors. Mais, dans ce cas, le terme de musée peut difficilement décrire le contenu de ce nouveau bâtiment situé au cœur du village de Dafen, ou du moins de celui qui contiendra beaucoup plus qu'un musée typique serait prêt à recevoir. L'ironie de la situation est que, dans un lieu inimaginable pour musée d'art typique, nous espérons qu'il accueillera les expositions d'art contemporain les plus avant-gardistes et, en même temps, s'ouvrira au nouveau pop art vernaculaire. Ce devrait être un bâtiment hétéroclite, un conteneur hybride. »

A large square in front of the building serves as a place for local residents to practice early-morning Tai-Chi.

Anwohner nutzen den großen Platz vor dem Museum für ihre frühmorgendlichen Tai-Chi-Übungen.

Une grande place aménagée devant le bâtiment sert à la pratique matinale du Tai-chi par les résidants locaux.

The roof design appears to fit into the juxtaposition of existing buildings, continuing the village-like atmosphere that neighboring towers appear to threaten.

Das Dach scheint sich zwischen die vorhandenen Gebäude einreihen und die dörfliche Atmosphäre fortführen zu wollen, die indes von den umliegenden Hochhäusern bedroht wirkt.

Le dessin du toit semble recouvrir une juxtaposition de constructions existantes, comme pour traduire l'atmosphère de village que les tours environnantes semblent menacer.

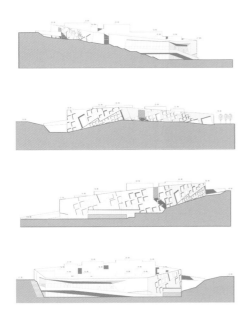

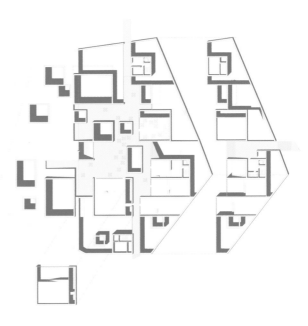

A jumble of real and outlined windows at curious angles again echoes the somewhat chaotic environment of the older residential or gallery buildings in the vicinity.

Ein Durcheinander aus tatsächlichen und angedeuteten Fenstern in seltsamen Winkeln spiegelt die ein wenig chaotische Umgebung aus älteren Wohngebäuden und Galerien in der Nachbarschaft.

Un fouillis de fenêtres réelles ou simplement esquissées, disposées selon des inclinaisons curieuses, rappelle à sa façon l'environnement chaotique des constructions résidentielles ou commerciales du voisinage.

The interiors of the building are functional and generous in size, contrasting somewhat with the jumbled appearance of the outside of the museum.

Die funktionalen, großzügigen Innenräume des Gebäudes bilden einen gewissen Kontrast zu dem etwas ungeordneten Äußeren des Museums.

Les volumes intérieurs sont fonctionnels et de dimensions généreuses, ce qui contraste avec l'aspect assez désordonné de l'extérieur du musée.

PEKKA VAPAAVUORI

Arkkitehtitoimisto Vapaavuori Oy
Itäinen Rantakatu 64
20810 Turku
Finland

Tel: +358 2 250 44 14
Fax: +358 2 250 44 28
E-mail: pekka.vapaavuori@arkva.fi
Web: www.arkva.fi

PEKKA JUHANI VAPAAVUORI was born in 1962 in Turku, Finland. In 1993, he obtained an M.Arch from the Tampere University of Technology, Finland. He created his own office, Arkkitehtitoimisto Pekka Vapaavuori, in 1993. From 1997 to 2002, his office was called Arkkitehdit Arosuo & Vapaavuori Oy, and, since 2000, Arkkitehtitoimisto Vapaavuori Oy/Vapaavuori Architects. He was a member of the Façades Review Board in Turku (2002–05), and was nominated for the Mies van der Rohe Award in 2007. In 1994, he won First Prize in an international architectural competition for the Art Museum of Estonia (Tallinn, Estonia, 2003–06, published here). Among his projects are, in Finland, the Lillberg House (Naantali, 1999); the Härmälä House (Raisio, 2000); the Lehtinen House (Turkus, 2006); and in Estonia, the Sarkop Offices (Tallinn, 2007).

PEKKA JUHANI VAPAAVUORI, geboren 1962 im finnischen Turku, erlangte 1993 sein Architekturdiplom an der Technischen Universität Tampere. 1993 gründete er sein Büro Arkkitehtitoimisto Pekka Vapaavuori, das von 1997 bis 2002 unter dem Namen Arkkitehdit Arosuo & Vapaavuori Oy firmierte und seit 2000 Arkkitehtitoimisto Vapaavuori Oy/Vapaavuori Architects heißt. Von 2002 bis 2005 war er Mitglied der Denkmalschutzbehörde in Turku, 2007 war er für den Mies-van-der-Rohe-Preis nominiert. 1994 gewann Vapaavuori den internationalen Architekturwettbewerb für den Entwurf des hier vorgestellten Kunstmuseums KUMU in der estnischen Hauptstadt Tallinn (2003–06). Zu seinen Projekten gehören das Haus Lillberg in Naantali (1999), das Haus Härmälä in Raisio (2000), Haus Lehtinen in Turku (2006), alle in Finnland, und die Sarkop Büros in Tallinn (2007).

PEKKA JUHANI VAPAAVUORI, né en 1962 à Turku, Finlande est M. Arch. de l'université de technologie de Tampere (Finlande, 1993). Il a créé son agence, Arkkitehtitoimisto Pekka Vapaavuori en 1993. De 1997 à 2002 elle s'appelait Arkkitehdit Arosuo & Vapaavuori Oy, et, depuis 2000, Arkkitehtitoimisto Vapaavuori Oy/ Vapaavuori Architects. Il a été membre du comité de rénovation des façades de Turku (2002–05) et nominé pour le prix Mies van der Rohe en 2007. En 1994, il a remporté le premier prix du concours international pour le musée d'art d'Estonie (Tallinn, Estonie, 2003–06, publié ici). Parmi ses projets : la maison Lillberg (Naantali, 1999), maison Härmälä (Raisio, 2000), la maison Lehtinen (Turku, 2006), toutes en Finlande, et les bureaux Sarkop (Tallinn, Estonie, 2007).

KUMU

Main Building of the Art Museum of Estonia, Tallinn, Estonia, 2003–06

Site area: 32 206 m². Floor area: 23 900 m². Client: Government of Estonia. Cost: not disclosed.
Collaborators: Johan Roman, Miikka Hirsimäki, Pia Sabelström, Marcus Uppmeier, Elina Juureva, Mika Väisänen, Sauli Luttinen

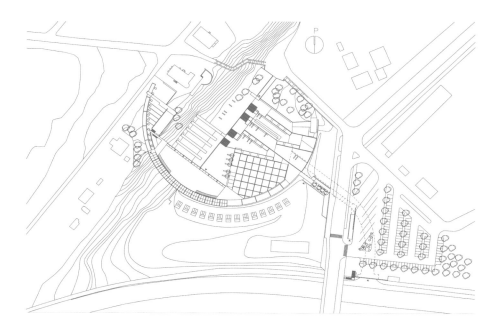

As the site plan (left) shows, the defining form of the museum is semi-circular. The overall disposition of the elements of the design is visible in the aerial photo (bottom, opposite).

Wie auf dem nebenstehenden Lageplan zu erkennen, bildet die Grundform des Museums ein Halbrund. Die Luftaufnahme auf der rechten Seite unten zeigt die Gesamtverteilung der einzelnen Elemente der Museumsanlage.

Comme le montre le plan d'ensemble (à gauche), la forme générale du musée est semi-circulaire. La disposition générale des éléments est visible dans la photo aérienne (page de droite, en bas).

Based on the winning proposal of an international architectural competition held in 1994, preliminary designs were submitted in January 1995, but the project was held up by funding concerns until 1999. The building permit was issued in 2002 and the excavation of 216 000 cubic meters of limestone from the site began in 2003. The site, with its 20-meter-high limestone slope, is situated at the south end of the Kadriorg Park, three kilometers from the center of Tallinn, the Estonian capital. Partly in order to reduce the apparent bulk of this large building, it was inserted into the limestone slope, partially underground. Parking and a bus stop are located at the uppermost level and visitors walk down through a pedestrian tunnel and through an outdoor sculpture garden to the main entrance. A second entrance is located at ground level from the neighboring park. A high lobby divides the museum into two parts and features connecting bridges. The structure has five stories above ground and two basement levels with 5106 square meters of exhibition space. The architect writes, "The design aims at simplicity and clarity. The exhibition halls are simple and unassuming, placing the artwork at center stage. The ascetism of the interior continues in the exterior, which relies on the power of plain geometric forms. The main façade materials are limestone, green-patinated copper, and glass."

Der Entwurf des estnischen Kunstmuseums KUMU basiert auf einem Vorschlag, mit dem der Architekt bereits 1994 als Sieger aus dem entsprechenden Wettbewerb hervorgegangen war. Im Januar 1995 reichte Vapaavuori erste Vorentwürfe ein, doch erst im Jahr 1999 war die Finanzierung gesichert. 2002 schließlich wurde die Baugenehmigung erteilt, im darauffolgenden Jahr begann auf dem vorgesehenen Gelände der Aushub von 216 000 m³ Kalkstein. Das Gelände mit seinem 20 m hohen Kalksteinabhang befindet sich am südlichen Ende des Kadriorg Parks, 3 km außerhalb des Tallinner Stadtzentrums. Um dem großen Gebäude einen Teil seiner Massigkeit zu nehmen, wurde es in die Böschung hineingesetzt und teilweise unterirdisch angelegt. Parkplätze und eine Bushaltestelle liegen am obersten Punkt des Geländes, von dem aus Besucher über einen Fußgängertunnel und einen sich anschließenden Skulpturenpark zum Haupteingang gelangen. Ein zweiter Eingang befindet sich auf der Höhe des angrenzenden Parks. Eine hoch aufragende Eingangshalle unterteilt das Museum in zwei Bereiche und wird von dazwischen verlaufenden Verbindungsbrücken durchzogen. Das Gebäude besitzt fünf oberirdische und zwei Kellergeschosse mit insgesamt 5106 m² Ausstellungsfläche. Der Architekt schreibt: „Der Entwurf zielt auf Einfachheit und Klarheit ab. Die Ausstellungssäle sind schlicht und zurückhaltend, das Kunstwerk steht im Mittelpunkt. Das Asketische des Innenbereichs setzt sich auf der Außenseite fort, die sich auf die Kraft klarer geometrischer Formen verlässt. Die Hauptfassade besteht im Wesentlichen aus Kalkstein, patiniertem Kupfer und Glas."

Inspirés des propositions qui avaient remporté un premier concours international en 1994, les plans préliminaires furent soumis en janvier 1995, mais le projet fut bloqué pour des raisons de financement jusqu'en 1999. Le permis de construire a été délivré en 2002 et le creusement de 216 000 m³ de roche calcaire a débuté sur le site en 2003. Le terrain en dénivelé de 20 mètres est situé à l'angle du parc de Kadriorg, à trois kilomètres du centre de Tallinn, la capitale estonienne. En partie pour réduire sa masse apparente, cette importante construction a été partiellement enterrée dans le sol calcaire. Le parking et l'arrêt de bus sont au niveau le plus élevé et les visiteurs descendent par un tunnel et un jardin de sculptures vers l'entrée principale. Une seconde entrée se trouve au rez-de-chaussée du parc adjacent. Un hall, de grande hauteur, divise le musée en deux sections reliées par des passerelles. La structure compte cinq niveaux et deux en sous-sol représentant 5106 m² d'espaces d'expositions. L'architecte présente ainsi le musée : « Le projet vise à la clarté et à la simplicité. Les salles d'expositions simples et sans prétention placent les œuvres d'art au premier plan. L'ascétisme de cet intérieur se retrouve à l'extérieur qui joue sur la puissance de formes géométriques massives. Les principaux matériaux utilisés pour la façade sont le calcaire, le cuivre patiné vert et le verre. »

Green-patinated copper cladding and sharp angles characterize the exterior of the building.

Charakteristisch für die Außenseite sind scharfe Kanten und Verkleidungen aus grün patiniertem Kupfer.

Les façades extérieures caractérisées par des angles vifs et un habillage en cuivre vert patiné.

The museum, carved into a limestone site, can be approached from above, through an outdoor sculpture garden.

Zum Eingang des Museums, das aus einem Kalksteingrund herausgearbeitet wurde, gelangt man über einen oberhalb angelegten Skulpturenpark.

On peut accéder au musée, creusé dans le calcaire, par le haut à travers un jardin de sculptures.

The architect calls the interiors simple and clear, but they retain a good deal of the theatricality of the exterior of the building.

Der Architekt beschreibt die Innenräume als einfach und klar, aber auch das Theatralische der Außenseite findet sich in ihnen wieder.

L'architecte a dessiné des volumes intérieurs simples et clairs, mais qui conservent en grande partie le caractère théâtral de l'extérieur.

VARIOUS ARCHITECTS

Graft
Heidestr. 50 / 10557 Berlin / Germany
Tel: +49 30 24 04 79 85 / Fax: +49 30 24 04 79 87
E-mail: berlin@graftlab.com / Web: www.graftlab.com

GRAFT was established in Los Angeles in 1998 by Lars Krückeberg and Wolfram Putz. Thomas Willemeit joined the firm in 2001 and opened an office in Berlin, Germany, the same year. In 2005, Gregor Hoheisel, who had been a partner in Los Angeles (2000–01), became a partner of Graft Beijing, founded in 2001. In 2007, Alejandra Lillo became a partner for the firm in Los Angeles. Lars Krückeberg was educated at the Technische Universität of Braunschweig, Germany, as an engineer (1989–96), and at SCI-Arc in Los Angeles (1997–98). Wolfram Putz attended the Technische Universität of Braunschweig (1988–95), the University of Utah, Salt Lake City (1992–93), and SCI-Arc (1996–98). Thomas Willemeit was also educated in Braunschweig (1988–97), and at the Bauhaus Dessau (1991–92), before working in the office of Daniel Libeskind (1998–2001). Taking advantage of their German background combined with US training, Graft declares: "We can see an architecture of new combinations, the grafting of different cultures and styles. The English word graft includes a variety of meanings and multiple readings. It has a particular meaning in the terminology of botany, the grafting of one shoot onto a genetically different host. The positive properties of two genetically different cultures are combined in the new biological hybrid." They have built a studio and house for the actor Brad Pitt in Los Angeles (California, 2000–03); Hotel Q! in Berlin (Germany, 2002–04); and designed a private dental clinic (Berlin, Germany, 2005). They have designed restaurants in the Mirage and Bellagio Casinos in Las Vegas and have worked on several luxury resort hotels in the Caribbean. Working with Brad Pitt and William McDonough + Partners, Graft are the lead architects for the Pink Project and Make It Right initiative in New Orleans (Louisiana, 2007–, published here).

GRAFT wurde 1998 in Los Angeles von Lars Krückeberg und Wolfram Putz ins Leben gerufen. Im Jahr 2001 kam Thomas Willemeit dazu und eröffnete eine Graft-Niederlassung in Berlin. 2005 wurde Gregor Hoheisel, der von 2000 bis 2001 für Graft in Los Angeles gearbeitet hatte, Partner im 2001 gegründeten Ableger Graft Peking. Seit 2007 gehört Alejandra Lillo als Partnerin in Los Angeles zu Graft. Lars Krückeberg absolvierte seine Ausbildung zum Bauingenieur an der Technischen Universität Braunschweig (1989–96) und am Southern California Institute of Architecture (1997–98). Wolfram Putz besuchte zunächst ebenfalls die TU Braunschweig (1988–95) sowie die University of Utah in Salt Lake City (1992–93) und anschließend das Southern California Institute of Architecture (1996–98). Thomas Willemeit studierte ebenfalls in Braunschweig (1988–97) sowie zwischenzeitlich am Bauhaus Dessau (1991–92) und war von 1998 bis 2001 für Daniel Libeskind tätig. Die Kombination aus deutscher Herkunft und Ausbildung in den USA sieht Graft als besonderen Vorteil: „Wir haben eine Architektur im Auge, die die Dinge neu kombiniert, verschiedene Kulturen und Stile ‚veredelt'. Der englische Begriff ‚graft' umfasst ein großes Bedeutungsspektrum und lässt sich ganz verschieden auslegen. Eine spezielle Bedeutung hat er in der Botanik, wo er für das Aufpfropfen eines Triebs auf eine genetisch unterschiedliche Trägerpflanze steht. Die positiven Bestandteile zweier genetisch unterschiedlicher Kulturen werden in einer neuen biologischen Hybridform vereint." Zu Grafts realisierten Projekten gehören ein Wohnhaus in Los Angeles für den Schauspieler Brad Pitt (2000–03), das Hotel Q! in Berlin (2002–04) und eine private Zahnklinik in Berlin (2005). Ferner entwarfen sie Restaurants für die Casinos Mirage und Bellagio in Las Vegas sowie mehrere Luxushotels in der Karibik. Als leitende Architekten führen sie zusammen mit Brad Pitt und William McDonough + Partners in New Orleans das Pink Project und die Initiative „Make It Right" (2007) durch.

GRAFT a été créé à Los Angeles en 1998 par Lars Krückeberg et Wolfram Putz. Thomas Willemeit les a rejoint en 2001 et a ouvert un bureau à Berlin la même année. En 2005, Gregor Hoheisel, qui avait été leur partenaire à Los Angeles (2000–01), est devenu partenaire de Graft à Pékin, fondé en 2001. En 2007, Alejandra Lillo est devenue partenaire de l'agence de Los Angeles. Lars Krückeberg a étudié l'ingénierie à la Technische Universität de Braunschweig, Allemagne (1989–1996) et à SCI-Arc à Los Angeles (1997–98). Wolfram Putz a étudié à la même université (1988–95), à celle de l'Utah à Salt Lake City (1992–93), et à SCI-Arc à Los Angeles (1996–98). Thomas Willemeit, a également étudié à Braunschweig (1988–97) et au Bauhaus Dessau (1991–92) avant de travailler auprès de Daniel Libeskind (1998–2001). En s'appuyant sur leur formation à la fois allemande et américaine, Graft se propose «d'envisager une architecture de combinaisons nouvelles, la greffe de différents styles et cultures. Le terme anglais de *graft* offre une grande variété de sens et de lectures. Il possède un sens particulier en botanique, celui de greffage sur un hôte génétiquement différent. Les propriétés positives de deux cultures génétiquement différentes se combinent alors en un nouvel hybride biologique. » Ils ont construit un atelier et une maison pour l'acteur Brad Pitt à Los Angeles (2000–03) ; l'hôtel Q (Berlin, Allemagne, 2002–04) ; conçu une clinique dentaire privée (Berlin, Allemagne, 2005) ; des restaurants pour les casinos Mirage et Bellagio à Las Vegas et travaillé sur plusieurs projets de complexes hôteliers de luxe dans les Caraïbes. Avec Brad Pitt et William McDonough + Partners, Graft est l'agence principale du Pink Project et de l'initiative de Make It Right à la Nouvelle-Orléans (Louisiane, 2007, publiée ici).

MAKE IT RIGHT/PINK PROJECT

New Orleans, Louisiana, USA, 2007–

Site area: 16 ha. Client: Make It Right/Brad Pitt. Cost: not disclosed. Curator: Brad Pitt/Graft.
Executive Associate at Graft and Executive Producer of the Pink Project: Stefan Beese.
Senior Advisor to Jolie Pitt Foundation and Co-Producer of the Pink Project: Nina Killeen. Founder of Rehage Entertainment
and Co-Producer of the Pink Project: Stephen Rehage. Principal Founder of L'Observatoire International and
Lighting Designer of the Pink Project: Hervé Descottes

The Lower Ninth Ward, long known for its high proportion of resident ownership, was left devastated and homeless in the wake of Hurricane Katrina in August 2005. The Pink Project, the inaugural event for Brad Pitt's "Make It Right" initiative, was intended to focus attention on the Lower Ninth Ward. The organizers called Pink "the virtual city of hope," erecting pink tents where it is hoped 150 homes will be built again. Graft and William McDonough + Partners collaborated with Brad Pitt, Reed Kroloff, and the Lower Ninth Ward Community Coalition to develop a scheme that would eventually call on a total of 13 local, national, and international architects to design low-cost houses for the area. Criteria for the selection were prior interest or involvement in New Orleans, preferably post-Katrina and/or experience with disaster relief, familiarity and interest in sustainability, experience with residential and multi-family housing, proven to be skilled innovators on low-budget projects, experience dealing with structures that have to successfully address water-based or low-lying environment(s), and a clear respect for design quality. Amongst the participating architects are Graft (Berlin), Trahan Architects (Baton Rouge), Kieran Timberlake (Philadelphia), Morphosis (Santa Monica), Pugh + Scarpa (Santa Monica), Adjaye/Associates (London), MVRDV (Rotterdam), and Shigeru Ban (Tokyo). John Williams Architects from New Orleans are serving as executive architects for the project. Brad Pitt unveiled the 13 proposals in December 2007. The average cost of the houses will be $150 000 and the foundation will coordinate interest-free loans. To subsidize construction, Pitt and film producer Steve Bing have promised to match up to $10 million in donations. The pair is also seeking sponsorship of materials or houses via the Web site www.makeitrightnola.org.

Der Bezirk Lower Ninth Ward, früher bekannt für seinen hohen Anteil an Wohneigentum, war nach dem Hurrikan Katrina vom August 2005 ein Ort der Verwüstung und Obdachlosigkeit. Das Pink Project bildete die erste Phase von Brad Pitts „Make-It-Right"-Initiative und sollte die Aufmerksamkeit der Öffentlichkeit auf das Viertel lenken. Das von den Organisatoren als „virtuelle Stadt der Hoffnung" bezeichnete Projekt bestand aus rosafarbenen Zelten, die auf einem Gelände aufgestellt wurden, das man sich als späteres Baugelände für 150 Wohnhäuser vorstellte. Graft und William McDonough + Partners setzten sich mit Brad Pitt, Reed Kroloff und der Lower Ninth Ward Community Coalition zusammen und entwickelten ein Konzept, mit dem sie schließlich 13 sowohl in der Region ansässige und weitere US-amerikanische als auch ausländische Architekten bzw. Architekturbüros aufforderten, kostengünstige Häuser zu entwerfen. Folgende Kriterien hatten die Architekten zu erfüllen: Sie sollten ein schon bestehendes Interesse an oder Engagement in New Orleans, vorzugsweise aus der Zeit vor dem Hurrikan Katrina, und/oder Erfahrung im Bereich der Katastrophenhilfe vorweisen können, mit nachhaltigem Bauen vertraut sein, Erfahrung haben im Bau von Mehrfamilienunterkünften, mit gering budgetierten Projekten, mit dem Bauen in Gewässernähe oder auf Wasserspiegelniveau und natürlich hohen Wert auf anspruchsvolles Design legen. Zu den Projektbeteiligten gehören neben Graft (Berlin) die Büros Trahan Architects (Baton Rouge), Kieran Timberlake (Philadelphia), Morphosis (Santa Monica), Pugh + Scarpa (Santa Monica), Adjaye/Associates (London), MVRDV (Rotterdam) und Shigeru Ban (Tokio). John Williams Architects aus New Orleans fungieren als ausführende Architekten. Im Dezember 2007 stellte Brad Pitt die 13 Entwürfe vor. Die durchschnittlichen Kosten betragen 150 000 Dollar pro Haus, eine Stiftung soll zinsfreie Darlehen koordinieren. Zur Bezuschussung des Projekts haben sich Pitt und der Filmproduzent Steve Bing vorgenommen, Spendengelder in Höhe von 10 Millionen Dollar zu sammeln. Darüber hinaus sprechen sie über die Webseite www.makeitrightnola.org potenzielle Material- oder Häusersponsoren an.

Le quartier du Lower Ninth Ward, longtemps connu pour sa forte proportion de petits propriétaires, a été dévasté par l'ouragan Katrina en août 2005. Le Pink Project, événement inaugural de la matérialisation de l'initiative « Make it Right » de Brad Pitt, avait pour intention de concentrer l'attention sur cette zone sinistrée. Les organisateurs ont parlé d'une « cité de l'espoir » et ont dressé des tentes roses en attendant la reconstruction de 150 maisons. Graft et William McDonough + Partners ont collaboré avec Brad Pitt, Reed Kroloff et la Lower Ninth Ward Community Coalition afin de mettre au point un programme qui fera appel à 13 architectes locaux, nationaux et étrangers pour concevoir des maisons économiques pour ce quartier. Les critères de sélection ont été d'abord l'intérêt et l'engagement pour la Nouvelle-Orléans, de préférence après Katrina, et/ou l'expérience des opérations de sauvetage, l'intérêt pour le développement durable et sa pratique, l'expérience des logements familiaux, la compétence prouvée sur l'innovation dans le domaine des projets à faible budget, l'expérience de la construction sur des zones humides ou inondables et un respect pour la qualité de la conception. Parmi les architectes participants figurent ainsi Graft (Berlin), Trahan Architects (Bâton-Rouge, Louisiana), Kieran Timberlake (Philadelphie), Morphosis (Santa Monica), Pugh + Scarpa (Santa Monica), Adjaye/Associates (Londres), MVRDV (Rotterdam) et Shigeru Ban (Tokyo). John Williams Architects de la Nouvelle-Orléans ont réalisé l'exécution du projet. Brad Pitt a dévoilé les 13 propositions en décembre 2007. Le coût moyen de ces maisons sera de 150 000 dollars et la Fondation créée coordonnera des prêts sans intérêts. Pour financer le projet de construction, Pitt et le producteur de films Steve Bing ont promis de trouver jusqu'à 10 millions de dollars de donations. Ils cherchent également des soutiens pour les matériaux ou les maisons via Internet : www.makeitrightnola.org.

On this page, designs by Graft for
low-cost homes destined to be built
in the Lower Ninth Ward of New
Orleans, devastated by Hurricane
Katrina.

Die Entwürfe auf dieser Seite zeigen
Vorschläge von Graft für kostengüns-
tige Wohnhäuser, die in dem von
Hurricane Katrina verwüsteten Bezirk
Lower Ninth Ward in New Orleans zu
errichten sein sollten.

Sur cette page, des perspectives
de propositions de maisons à bas
coût de Graft, destinées au quartier
du Lower Ninth Ward de la Nouvelle-
Orléans dévasté par la tornade
Katrina.

A house designed by the UK architect
David Adjaye for the Make It Right
project.

Ein von dem britischen Architekten
David Adjaye entworfenes Wohnhaus
für das Make-it-Right-Projekt.

Une maison conçue par l'architecte
britannique David Adjaye pour le
projet Make it Right.

Trey Trahan, an architect from Baton Rouge, Louisiana, made this proposal for the new houses planned for the Lower Ninth Ward in New Orleans.

Dieser Vorschlag für die im Bezirk Lower Ninth Ward in New Orleans neu zu errichtenden Häuser stammt von Trey Trahan, einem Architekten aus Baton Rouge in Louisiana.

Trey Trahan, architecte à Bâton-Rouge en Louisiane, a proposé ce projet pour le quartier du Lower Ninth Ward à la Nouvelle-Orléans.

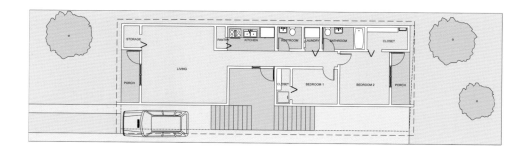

A proposed house designed by the
California architects Pugh + Scarpa.

Ein Vorschlag des kalifornischen
Architekturbüros Pugh + Scarpa.

Une maison proposée par les architectes californiens Pugh + Scarpa.

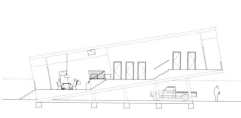

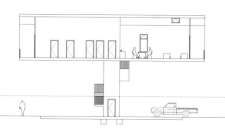

The Dutch firm MVRDV proposed
a tilted structure that includes a
parking spot beneath the front of
the house.

Der Beitrag des niederländischen
Büros MVRDV besteht aus einem zur
Mitte hin geneigten Haus mit Park-
platz unter der Vorderfront.

L'agence néerlandaise MVRDV
a imaginé une maison inclinée qui
comprend un emplacement de
parking sous sa façade avant.

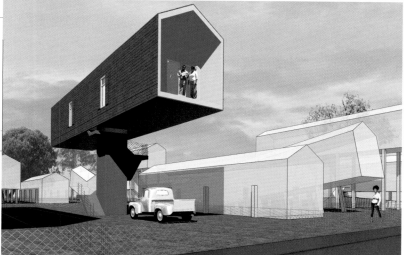

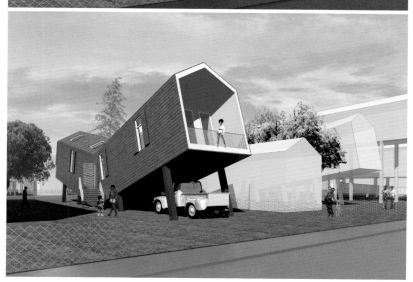

The design by architects Kieran Timberlake essentially proposes to lift the house up off the ground, perhaps protecting it from future flooding.

Der Vorschlag des Architekturbüros Kieran Timberlake sieht einen wesentlichen Abstand zwischen Untergrund und Haus vor, um es vor künftigen Überflutungen zu schützen.

Le projet des architectes Kieran Timberlake propose essentiellement de soulever la maison, peut-être pour la protéger de futures inondations.

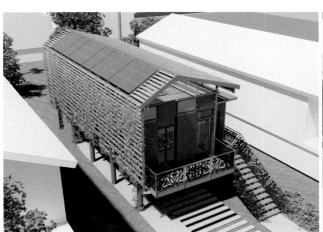

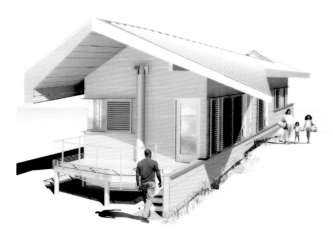

Above, a house that takes local architectural traditions and habits into account, designed by Morphosis from Santa Monica.

Oben ein von Morphosis aus Santa Monica entworfenes Haus, das die Traditionen und Besonderheiten der lokalen Architektur berücksichtigt.

Ci-dessus, une maison qui reprend les traditions et habitudes de l'architecture locale, par Morphosis de Santa Monica.

Below, Shigeru Ban, who has considerable experience in emergency relief housing, made this proposal for the Lower Ninth Ward.

Von Shigeru Ban, der über umfangreiche Erfahrungen mit der Konzeption von Notunterkünften verfügt, stammt der unten abgebildete Vorschlag.

Ci-dessous, Shigeru Ban, qui a une grande expérience de l'habitat d'urgence, a fait cette proposition pour le Lower Ninth Ward.

WANDEL HOEFER LORCH

Wandel Hoefer Lorch Architekten + Stadtplaner
Dolomitenweg 19
66119 Saarbrücken
Germany

Tel: +49 681 92 65 50
Fax: +49 681 926 55 95
E-mail: info@wandel-hoefer-lorch.de
Web: www.wandel-hoefer-lorch.de

Wolfgang **LORCH** was born in 1960 in Nürtingen am Neckar, Germany. He studied Architecture in Darmstadt and at the ETSA, Barcelona. He has taught at the Hochschule für Technik in Stuttgart and at the Technische Universität (TH) of Darmstadt. Andrea **WANDEL** was born in 1963 in Saarbrücken and studied Architecture at the Technische Universität in Kaiserslautern and the TH Darmstadt. Rena **WANDEL-HOEFER** was born in 1959 in Saarbrücken and also studied at the TH Darmstadt. Andreas Hoefer was born in Hamburg and studied in Berlin and at the TH Darmstadt. Their work includes a memorial at the Börneplatz (Frankfurt, 1995–98); a monument at the deportation train station at Berlin-Grunewald; a synagogue in Dresden (2001); and the Hinzert Documentation Center (2003–05), all in Germany. Recent work includes the Ohel-Jakob Synagogue and the Jewish Museum (Munich, Germany, 2003–06, published here) and Tschavtschavadze Avenue (Tbilisi, Republic of Georgia).

Wolfgang **LORCH**, geboren 1960 in Nürtingen am Neckar, studierte Architektur an der Technischen Hochschule Darmstadt (heute Technische Universität) und an der Escola Tècnica Superior d'Arquitectura in Barcelona. Als Dozent war er an der Hochschule für Technik in Stuttgart und an der TH Darmstadt tätig. Andrea **WANDEL** wurde 1963 in Saarbrücken geboren und studierte an der Technischen Universität Kaiserslautern sowie an der TH Darmstadt. Rena **WANDEL-HOEFER**, geboren 1959 in Saarbrücken, studierte ebenfalls an der TH Darmstadt. Der in Hamburg gebürtige Andreas Hoefer studierte in Berlin und ebenfalls an der TH Darmstadt. Zu ihren Arbeiten gehört das Holocaust-Mahnmal auf dem Frankfurter Börneplatz (1995–98), ein Mahnmal am Bahnhof Berlin-Grunewald (von dem aus Deportationszüge abfuhren), die Neue Synagoge Dresden (2001) und das Dokumentationszentrum Hinzert (2003–05). Projekte jüngeren Datums sind die neue Synagoge Ohel Jakob und das angeschlossene Jüdische Kulturzentrum am St.-Jakobs-Platz in München (2003–06, hier vorgestellt) sowie ein Verwaltungs- und Geschäftsbau in der georgischen Hauptstadt Tiflis.

Wolfgang **LORCH**, né en 1960 à Nürtingen am Neckar, Allemagne, a étudié l'architecture à la Technische Universität (TH) Darmstadt et à l'ETSA à Barcelone. Il a enseigné à la Hochschule für Technik à Stuttgart et à la TH de Darmstadt. Andrea **WANDEL**, né en 1963 à Saarebruck, a étudié l'architecture à la Technische Universität de Kaiserslautern et à celle de Darmstadt. Rena **WANDEL-HOEFER**, née en 1959 à Saarebruck, sort également de la TH de Darmstadt. Andreas Hoefer, né à Hambourg, a étudié à Berlin et à la TH de Darmstadt. Parmi leurs réalisations : un mémorial sur la Börneplatz (Francfort, 1995–98) ; un monument dans la gare des trains de déportation de Berlin-Grunewald ; une synagogue à Dresde (2001) et le Centre de documentation Hinzert (2003–05), toutes en Allemagne. Plus récemment, ils ont réalisé la synagogue et le musée juif de la St.-Jakobs-Platz (Munich, Allemagne, 2003–06, publiée ici) et l'avenue Tschavtschavadze (Tbilissi, Géorgie).

OHEL JAKOB SYNAGOGUE

Jewish Center in Munich, St.-Jakobs-Platz, Munich, Germany, 2003–06

Floor area: 1200 m². Client: Israelite Religious Community Munich and Upper Bavaria.
Cost: not disclosed

The actual Synagogue building has a base clad in cleft travertine with a glass and steel cube above.

Das Synagogengebäude besteht aus einem mit Travertin verkleideten Kubus als Unterbau und einem darauf aufsitzenden Kubus aus Glas und Stahl.

Le bâtiment de la synagogue se présente sous la forme d'une base massive parée de travertin clivé, et surmontée d'un cube en verre et acier.

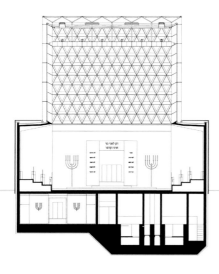

This three-building Synagogue and Community Center contains the chief synagogue of Munich and the Jewish Museum. The architects explain, "Our competition concept was the idea of a natural integration of the Jewish Center into the structure of the city through public space. Its public nature and openness can be experienced in a succession of squares, paths, and passageways between the buildings and in their neighborhood." The main building contains the Synagogue and has a rough travertine base with a glass and steel construction rising from its center. The smallest cube in the composition houses the Jewish Museum of the City of Munich. It has a closed space for exhibitions and a glazed ground floor and polished travertine. The Community Center is a composition of fragmented cubes, containing two floors below grade and six above, with youth and cultural centers, event rooms, dining facilities, a school and daycare area for children, as well as administrative offices.

Das Jüdische Zentrum am St.-Jakobs-Platz besteht aus drei Gebäuden: der neuen Münchener Hauptsynagoge, einem Gemeindehaus und dem Jüdischen Museum München. Die Architekten erklären zu ihrem Wettbewerbsbeitrag: „Unserem Konzept lag die Idee zugrunde, das Jüdische Zentrum durch seine öffentlichen Räume auf ganz selbstverständliche Weise in den Stadtraum einzugliedern. Sein öffentlicher Charakter, seine Offenheit, wird erlebbar durch eine Reihe von Plätzen, Wegen und Durchgängen, die die Gebäude umsäumen und sich in die Nachbarschaft hinein erstrecken." Das Hauptgebäude mit der Synagoge besteht aus einem mit Travertin verkleideten Kubus als Unterbau und einem sich aus dessen Mitte erhebenden zweiten Kubus aus Glas und Stahl. Ein weiterer, freistehender Kubus, der kleinste des Ensembles, beherbergt das Jüdische Museum der Stadt München. Er besteht aus einem verglasten Untergeschoss und einem mit glattem Travertin umkleideten Oberbau; die Ausstellungsflächen befinden sich in den beiden fensterlosen Obergeschossen. Das Gemeindehaus umfasst auf sechs Ober- und zwei Untergeschossen ein Jugend- und Kulturzentrum, einen großen Veranstaltungssaal, ein Restaurant, eine Schule, einen Kindergarten und Verwaltungsbüros.

Ce complexe de trois bâtiments regroupe la principale synagogue de Munich et le musée juif. Selon les architectes : « Notre concept pour ce concours était l'idée d'une intégration naturelle du Musée juif dans la structure urbaine par le biais de l'espace public. Sa nature publique et son ouverture se matérialisent par une succession de places, de cheminements et de passages entre les bâtiments et le quartier. » L'immeuble principal, celui de la synagogue, présente un socle en travertin brut d'où s'élève, au centre, une construction en verre et acier. Le cube le moins grand accueille le Musée juif de la ville de Munich. Il dispose d'un espace fermé pour des expositions, et d'un rez-de-chaussée vitré en travertin poli. Le centre communautaire est une composition de cubes fragmentés de cinq étages et deux niveaux en sous-sol regroupant un centre culturel, un centre pour la jeunesse, des salles pour manifestations, des salles pour restauration, une école, une garderie d'enfants, ainsi que des bureaux administratifs.

The Synagogue is part of a three-building complex—all of which reveal a rather rough exterior treatment. To the right, the interior of the synagogue.

Die Synagoge gehört zu einem Ensemble aus drei Gebäuden, die alle eine relativ grobe äußere Oberflächengestaltung zeigen. Rechts ein Blick ins Innere der Synagoge.

La synagogue fait partie d'un complexe de trois bâtiments, dont chacun présente un traitement extérieur assez brutal. À droite, l'intérieur de la synagogue.

JEAN-MICHEL WILMOTTE

Wilmotte & Associés SA
68 rue du Faubourg Saint-Antoine / 75012 Paris / France
Tel: +33 1 53 02 22 22 / Fax: +33 1 43 44 17 11
E-mail: wilmotte@wilmotte.fr / Web: www.wilmotte.fr

Born in 1948, a graduate of the Camondo school in Paris, **JEAN-MICHEL WILMOTTE** created his own firm in 1975. Although he is best known for his work in interior design, Wilmotte joined the Order of Architects in France in 1993. With approximately 140 employees, his office works on industrial and furniture design, such as the lighting fixtures and benches installed on the Champs-Élysées, but he also participated in the competition for the British Museum, making use of the experience he gathered as architect of the Decorative Arts Department of the Louvre for the Richelieu Wing, completed in 1993. As an architect, Jean-Michel Wilmotte has completed two buildings in Tokyo, the International Executive Office building in the Shinjuku area, and the New No. 3 Arai Building, while he also carried out the furniture design for the Bank of Luxembourg Building, completed by Arquitectonica in 1994. He designed the Gana Art Center (Seoul, South Korea, 1996–98) and a museum for objects given to former French President Jacques Chirac (Sarran, France). Recent work includes the design of a new boutique concept for Cartier (Paris, Milan, New York, Los Angeles, Tokyo, 2000); new showrooms for Chaumet, John Galliano, and Montblanc International; the interior design of the new LVMH Headquarters in Paris; as well as numerous housing, cultural, or rehabilitation projects in France, Italy, and Korea. He recently completed the interior design of the Museum of Islamic Art (architect I. M. Pei, Doha, Qatar, 2003–08). His reputation for cultural facilities has also led him to work on the Ullens Center for Contemporary Art (UCCA, Beijing, China, 2006–07, published here); and the Museum of Jewish Art in Brussels, Belgium, a 4500-square-meter renovation and construction project. Wilmotte is building a 160-meter-high office tower in Baku, Azerbaijan.

JEAN-MICHEL WILMOTTE, geboren 1948, studierte an der École Nissim de Camondo in Paris und gründete 1975 seine eigene Firma. Er ist vor allem durch seine Arbeit als Innenarchitekt bekannt geworden, seit 1993 aber auch Mitglied im französischen Ordre des Architects. Mit seinen rund 140 Mitarbeitern ist Wilmottes Büro vornehmlich in den Bereichen des Industrie- und Möbeldesigns tätig und hat beispielsweise die Beleuchtungskörper und Sitzbänke auf den Champs-Elysées entworfen. Ferner nahm Wilmotte am Wettbewerb für das British Museum teil, wobei er auf seine Erfahrungen als Architekt der 1993 fertiggestellten Abteilung für Angewandte Kunst im Richelieu-Flügel des Louvre zurückgreifen konnte. Von Wilmotte stammen außerdem die Entwürfe für das Mobiliar der Banque de Luxembourg, die 1994 von Arquitectonica umgesetzt wurden. Als Architekt realisierte Wilmotte u. a. das International Executive Office im Tokioter Bezirk Shinjuku sowie das New No. 3 Arai, ebenfalls in Tokio, die Kunstgalerie Gana in Seoul (1996–98) und das Musée Jacques Chirac im französischen Sarran, in dem Geschenke ausgestellt werden, die der ehemalige französische Präsident während seiner Amtszeit erhalten hat. Weiterhin entwarf Wilmotte ein neues Konzept für die Boutiquen von Cartier in Paris, Mailand, New York, Los Angeles und Tokio (2000), neue Showrooms für Chaumet, John Galliano und Montblanc International, das Interieur der neuen Pariser Zentrale von Moët Hennessy-Louis Vuitton und zahlreiche Wohnhausprojekte, Kulturinstitutionen und soziale Einrichtungen in Frankreich, Italien und Korea. In jüngerer Zeit stellte er die Innengestaltung des Museums für Islamische Kunst in Doha im Emirat Katar fertig (2003–08, Architekt I. M. Pei). Seinem Ruf als Architekt von Kultureinrichtungen verdankte er die Aufträge für den Entwurf des hier vorgestellten Ullens Center for Contemporary Art (UCCA) in Peking (2006–07) und des Museums für Jüdische Kunst in Brüssel, für das 2500 m² Gebäudefläche renoviert und umgebaut wurden. Derzeit führt Wilmotte einen 160 m hohen Büroturm in der aserbaidschanischen Hauptstadt Baku aus.

Né en 1948, diplômé de l'École Camondo à Paris, **JEAN-MICHEL WILMOTTE** a créé son agence en 1975. Connu surtout au départ pour ses réalisations d'architecture intérieure, Wilmotte s'est inscrit à l'Ordre des architectes en 1993. Son agence, comptant environ 140 collaborateurs, travaille sur des projets de design industriel et de mobilier, comme les éclairages et bancs des Champs-Elysées, mais a également participé au concours pour le British Museum, mettant à profit son expérience d'architecte du département des arts décoratifs du Louvre dans l'aile Richelieu (1993). En tant qu'architecte, Jean-Michel Wilmotte a réalisé deux immeubles à Tokyo, l'International Executive Office building dans le quartier de Shinjuku, et l'immeuble Arai N° 3, tout en concevant le mobilier de la Banque de Luxembourg d'Arquitectonica (Luxembourg, 1994). Il a réalisé le centre d'art Gana (Séoul, Corée du Sud, 1996–98) et un musée pour les cadeaux reçus par le président Jacques Chirac à Sarran (France). Plus récemment, il a conçu un nouveau concept de magasin pour Cartier (Paris, Milan, New York, Los Angeles, Tokyo, 2000) ; de nouveaux *show-rooms* pour Chaumet, John Galliano, et Montblanc International ; l'architecture intérieure du siège de LVMH à Paris, ainsi que de nombreux immeubles de logements, projets culturels ou de rénovation en France, en Italie et en Corée. Il a récemment achevé les aménagements intérieurs du musée des Arts islamiques (I. M. Pei architecte, Doha, Qatar, 2003–08). Sa réputation de spécialiste des équipements l'a conduit à travailler sur le centre d'art contemporain Ullens/UCCA (Pékin, Chine, 2006–07, publié ici) et le musée d'Art juif à Bruxelles, un projet de rénovation et de construction de 4500 m². L'agence construit également une tour de bureaux de 160 m de haut à Bakou, Azerbaïdjan.

ULLENS CENTER FOR CONTEMPORARY ART (UCCA)

Beijing, China, 2006–07

Floor area: 7500 m². Client: Ullens Center for Contemporary Art. Cost: €5 million.
Project Architects: Emmanuel Brelot with Moochul Shin, Jérôme Peuron, Myun Kim. Site Architect: MADA s.p.a.m. (Shanghai).
Lighting Consultant: MC2

The Guy & Myriam Ullens Foundation was created in Switzerland in 2002, and is an active supporter of the Chinese art world. It sponsors events and exhibitions of Chinese art all over the world, including the Venice Biennale Chinese projects in 2003 and 2005; lends pieces from its collection to museums and art centers around the world; and organizes exhibitions. When the collectors sought a location in China for their activities, they found what was a 1950s Bauhaus-style factory building. It is located in the so-called 798 area in the Dashanzi district of the capital, an area where Chinese contemporary artists have congregated since 2000. The structure is made up of two large naves with ceiling heights rising as high as 9.6 meters. As usual, Wilmotte based his intervention on the intrinsic qualities of the building, removing elements added since its construction. Doorways 7.4 meters high and a 34-meter brick chimney structure the space. In the first area, the entrance, bookshop and cafeteria, an amphitheater, and exhibition galleries of 200 square meters and 280 square meters occupy the ground floor. A documentation area and VIP zone are on the mezzanine level. The second nave has an area of 1950 square meters for performances and exhibitions and was left as free as possible. The natural overhead lighting is diffused along the central axis and is associated with indirect artificial light, creating a homogeneous brightness in the space. The entire installation was conceived to meet the highest international standards for the exhibition of art.

Die 2002 in der Schweiz gegründete Stiftung Guy & Myriam Ullens widmet sich der Förderung der chinesischen Kunstwelt. Die Stiftung sponsert weltweit Events und Ausstellungen chinesischer Kunst – darunter die chinesischen Projekte für die Venedig-Biennalen von 2003 und 2005 –, verleiht Stücke aus ihrer Sammlung an Museen und Kunstzentren in aller Welt und organisiert selbst Ausstellungen. Als die Sammler in China nach einen Standort für ihre Unternehmungen Ausschau hielten, stießen sie auf ein Fabrikgebäude aus den 1950er-Jahren im Bauhausstil. Der Bau befindet sich im so genannten Bezirk 798 im Pekinger Viertel Dashanzi, einer Gegend, in der sich seit 2000 eine lebendige Kunstszene entwickelt hat. Die Fabrik besteht aus zwei großen, nebeneinanderliegenden Hallen mit bis zu 9,60 m hohen Decken. Wie gewohnt konzentrierte Wilmotte sich bei der Umgestaltung auf die ursprünglichen Gebäudequalitäten und entfernte sämtliche Elemente, die seit der Errichtung hinzugekommen waren. Der Gesamtraum wird von 7,40 m hohen Toren und einem 34 m hohen Kamin gegliedert. In der ersten Halle sind im Erdgeschoss der Eingangsbereich, ein Buchladen nebst Cafeteria, ein Vortragssaal sowie eine 200 und eine 280 m² große Ausstellungsfläche untergebracht. Im Zwischengeschoss befinden sich ein Archiv und ein VIP-Bereich. Die zweite Halle mit einer Fläche von 1950 m² ist für Ausstellungen und Performances vorgesehen und so unverstellt wie möglich geblieben. Entlang der Mittelachse fällt durch das Dach Tageslicht ein, das in Verbindung mit indirektem künstlichem Licht dem Raum eine homogene Helligkeit gibt. Die gesamte Einrichtung wurde so angelegt, dass sie höchsten internationalen Standards für Kunstausstellungen entspricht.

La Fondation Guy & Myriam Ullens, créée en Suisse en 2002, soutient activement le monde de l'art chinois. Elle finance des manifestations et des expositions dans le monde entier, y compris les projets chinois pour la Biennale de Venise (2003 et 2005), prête des pièces de ses collections aux musées et centres d'art partout dans le monde et organise elle-même des expositions. Cherchant à s'installer en Chine, elle découvrit une vieille usine datant des années 1950 de style Bauhaus dans le secteur 798 du quartier de Dashanzi de la capitale où de nombreux artistes chinois se sont installés depuis 2000. Le bâtiment se compose de deux grandes nefs dont les plafonds mesurent jusqu'à 9,6 m de haut. Comme à son habitude, Wilmotte s'est appuyé sur les qualités intrinsèques de l'existant, et a supprimé des éléments qui avaient été ajoutés. Des passages de portes de 7,4 m de haut et une cheminée de brique de 34 m structurent l'espace. Au rez-de-chaussée de la première partie sont implantés l'entrée, une librairie, une cafétéria, un amphithéâtre, des galeries d'expositions de 200 et 280 m². Une zone de documentation et une autre réservé aux VIP occupent une mezzanine. La seconde nef, ouverte au maximum, contient une salle de 1950 m² pour des performances ou des expositions. L'éclairage naturel zénithal est diffusé sur l'axe central et complété par un éclairage artificiel indirect qui crée un niveau de luminosité homogène dans tous les volumes. L'installation tout entière répond aux meilleurs standards internationaux de qualité pour les expositions d'art.

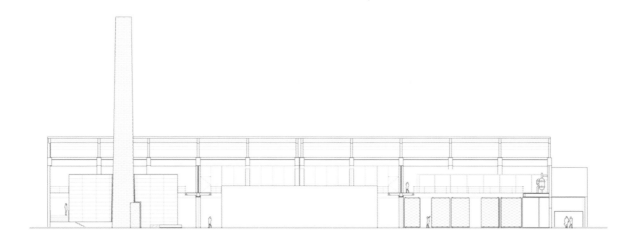

Jean-Michel Wilmotte, a specialist in interior design and architecture, took a large industrial building and converted it into a modern exhibition space for contemporary Chinese art.

Jean-Michel Wilmotte, ein Experte für Architektur und Interieurdesign, machte aus einem großformatigen Industriebau einen modernen Ausstellungsort für zeitgenössische chinesische Kunst.

Jean-Michel Wilmotte, architecte spécialiste d'architecture intérieure a transformé ce vaste bâtiment industriel en espace d'expositions consacré à l'art contemporain chinois.

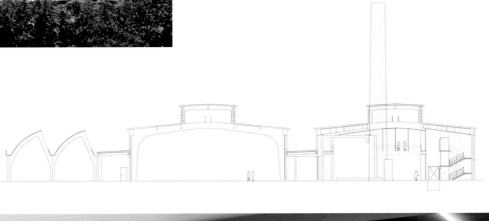

The hallmarks of Wilmotte's design
are clarity and open space, seen
here in the exhibition area (right).
An orthogonal plan in keeping with
the original factory design is imposed
on the new spaces.

Kennzeichnend für Wilmottes Entwurf
sind dessen Klarheit und die offenen
Räume, so etwa in dem rechts abgebildeten Ausstellungsbereich. Die in
die neuen Räume rechtwinklig eingefügten Elemente orientieren sich an
dem ursprünglichen Grundriss.

Les traits caractéristiques du travail
de Wilmotte sont la clarté et les
espaces ouverts, comme on le voit
ici dans une salle d'expositions
(à droite). Le plan orthogonal est
en accord avec le plan d'origine
de l'usine.

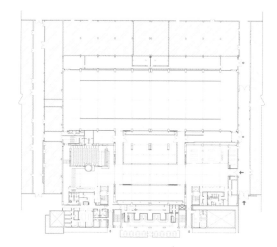

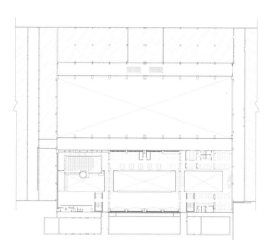

RIKEN YAMAMOTO

Riken Yamamoto & Field Shop
Takamizawa Bldg.7f, 2–7–10 Kitasaiwai
Nishi-Ku
Yokohama 220–0004
Japan

Tel: +81 45 323 6010
Fax: +81 45 323 6012
E-mail: field-shop@riken-yamamoto.co.jp
Web: www.riken-yamamoto.co.jp

RIKEN YAMAMOTO was born in Beijing, China, in 1945. He graduated from the School of Architecture at Nihon University, Japan, in 1968, received his M. A. from the Tokyo National University of Fine Art and Music, Faculty of Architecture, in 1971, and was a research student at the Hara Laboratory, Institute of Industrial Science, University of Tokyo (1971–73), an experience that seems to have influenced his "topological" approach to architecture. In 1973, he established his own office, Riken Yamamoto & Field Shop, in Yokohama. In 2002, he became a Professor at Kogakuin University in Tokyo and a Professor at Yokohama National University, Director of Y-GSA (Yokohama Graduate School of Architecture) from 2007. His recent principal works, all in Japan, are the Saitama Prefectural University (Saitama, 1999); the Future University Hakodate (Hokkaido, 2000); the Hiroshima Nishi Fire Station (Hiroshima, 2000); the ecoms House (2003); the Shinonome Canal Court, Block 1 (2003); the Research Building for the Future University of Hakodate (Hokkaido, 2005); the Yokosuka Museum of Art (Kanagawa, 2004–07, published here); and Fussa City Hall (Tokyo, 2008). Furthermore, he designed Jian Wai SOHO (Beijing, China, 2004); the Gershwin Project (Amsterdam, The Netherlands, 2004–); and the Pangyo Housing (Seongnam, South Korea, 2006–).

RIKEN YAMAMOTO, geboren 1945 in Peking, schloss 1968 sein Studium an der Architekturschule der Universität Nihon in Japan ab und machte 1971 seinen Masterabschluss an der Fakultät für Architektur der Tokioter National-Universität für Bildende Kunst und Musik. Von 1971 bis 1973 arbeitete er als wissenschaftlicher Mitarbeiter im Hara Labor am Institute of Industrial Science der Universität Tokio, eine Erfahrung, die von Einfluss für Yamamotos „topologischen" Architekturansatz gewesen sein dürfte. 1973 gründete er in Yokohama ein eigenes Büro mit Namen Riken Yamamoto & Field Shop. 2002 wurde er Professor an der Universität Kogakuin in Tokio sowie an der National-Universität in Yokohama, seit 2007 ist er Leiter der Graduate School of Architecture in Yokohama. Zu seinen wichtigsten in Japan realisierten Projekten jüngeren Datums gehören die Universität der Präfektur Saitama (1999), die Future University in Hakodate (Hokkaido, 2000), die Feuerwache Hiroshima Nishi in Hiroshima (2000), das ecoms House (2003), der Block 1 der Wohnanlage Shinonome Canal Court in Tokio (2003), ein Forschungsgebäude für die Future University in Hakodate (2005), das hier vorgestellte Kunstmuseum Yokosuka in Kanagawa (2004–07) und das Rathaus von Fussa (Präfektur Tokio, 2008). Außerhalb Japans entstanden etwa in Peking das Wohnquartier Jian Wai SOHO (2004), das Gershwin-Projekt in Amsterdam (2004–) oder die Wohnanlage Pangyo im südkoreanischen Seongnam (2006–).

RIKEN YAMAMOTO, né à Pékin en 1945, est diplômé de l'école d'architecture de l'université Nihon (Japon, 1968) et M. A. de l'Université nationale des Beaux-Arts et de Musique de Tokyo en 1971. Il a été chercheur au laboratoire Hara de l'institut des sciences industrielles de l'université de Tokyo de 1971 à 1973, expérience qui semble avoir influencé son approche « topologique » de l'architecture. En 1973, il crée son agence, Riken Yamamoto & Field Shop, à Yokohama. En 2002, il est nommé professeur à l'université Kogakuin à Tokyo et est professeur à Yokohama National University, directeur de Y-GSA (École supérieure d'architecture de Yokohama) depuis 2007. Parmi ses principales réalisations récentes, toutes au Japon : l'université de préfecture de Saitama (Saitama, 1999), la Future University à Hakodate (Hokkaido, 2000), la station de pompiers Nishi (Hiroshima, 2000) ; ecoms House (2003) ; Shinonome Canal Court, Block 1 (2003) ; le bâtiment de la recherche à l'Université du Futur d'Hakodate (Hokkaido, 2005); le musée d'Art de Yokosuka (Kanagawa, 2004–07, publié ici) et la mairie de Fussa (Tokyo, 2008). À l'étranger, il a réalisé le Jian Wai SOHO (Pékin, 2004) ; le projet Gershwin (Amsterdam, 2004–) ; les logements Pangyo (Seongnam, Corée du Sud, 2006–).

YOKOSUKA MUSEUM OF ART

Yokosuka, Kanagawa, Japan, 2004–07

Site area: 22 000 m². Floor area: 4234 m². Client: Yokosuka City. Cost: not disclosed.
Team: Riken Yamamoto, Kiyoshi Nishikura, Motoki Yasuhara, Tomohiro Tanaka, Shinjiro Tomizawa, Yuki Katsura

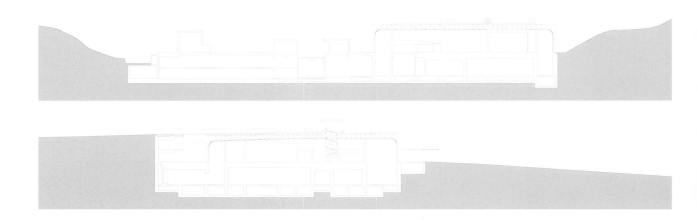

The architect explains the unusual method by which he was selected for this project: "In February of 2002, I was appointed architect of the Yokosuka Art Museum. However, I did not have any architectural idea at that moment as the selection method of the architect was based on a new system called QBS. QBS stands for 'Quality Based Selection,' in other words, it is based on the qualification evaluation method to appoint the architect of the project. Contrary to the typical competition appointing the architect based on the submitted idea, the project architect is decided by looking at the buildings of the candidate and interviewing the clients of those buildings." The concept that evolved was that of a "stay-over type of museum," meaning that visitors would not get bored even if they stayed the whole day. It was decided to make the building as low as possible, to clad it entirely in glass, and to open the ocean side of the building with the main access area. Thin steel plate panels with openings selected according to the outdoor scenery mark the interior. Yamamoto concludes, "Although this museum appears to be a part of the surrounding environment from the exterior and open toward the surroundings, visitors can experience a completely different space once stepping into the interior space." (Riken Yamamoto quoted in *GA Document 98*)

Über das ungewöhnliche Auswahlverfahren, in dem er als Architekt des Kunstmuseums Yokosuka bestimmt wurde, berichtet Yamamoto: „Im Februar 2002 wurde vereinbart, dass ich das Museum konzipieren sollte. Zu dem Zeitpunkt wusste ich allerdings noch gar nicht, wie der Entwurf aussehen sollte, da die Methode zur Auswahl des Architekten auf einem neuen System beruhte, das sich QBS nennt. Die Abkürzung steht für ‚Quality Based Selection' und bedeutet, das zunächst die Qualifikation des möglichen Architekten ausgewertet wird: Im Gegensatz zur sonst üblichen Wettbewerbsform, bei der man den Architekten anhand eines eingereichten Vorschlags auswählt, wird er hier bestimmt, indem man sich die Bauten des Kandidaten anschaut und die Auftraggeber dieser Projekte interviewt." Daraus ergab sich das Konzept eines „Aufenthaltsmuseums", in dem die Besucher einen ganzen Tag verbringen können, ohne sich zu langweilen. Es wurde entschieden, ein möglichst niedriges und komplett verglastes Gebäude zu planen, dessen Hauptzugangsbereich zum Meer hin geöffnet ist. Kennzeichnend für den Innenbereich sind dünne Stahlplatten, die an bestimmten Stellen mit Öffnungen versehen sind, durch die man die Landschaft betrachten kann. Yamamoto hält fest: „Während sich das Museum ganz in seine Umgebung einfügt und zu ihr hin öffnet, erlebt man die Landschaft nach dem Betreten aus dem Innern des Gebäudes heraus als einen völlig anderen Raum." (Riken Yamamoto zitiert in: *GA Document 98*)

L'architecte présente ainsi la méthode peu courante qui lui a permis d'être choisi pour ce projet : « En février 2002, j'ai été nommé architecte du musée d'Art de Yokosuka. Cependant, je n'avais pas la moindre idée architecturale à cette époque puisque la méthode de sélection de l'architecte s'appuyait sur une nouvelle approche appelé QBS. QBS signifie Quality Based Selection (« sélection basée sur la qualité »), en d'autres termes sur une méthode d'évaluation de la qualification… Contrairement aux concours classiques qui désignent un architecte en fonction de l'idée qu'il a soumise, l'architecte du projet est ici choisi pour ses réalisations antérieures et à travers des entretiens avec ses clients. » Le concept, qui a évolué, est parti d'un « type de musée adapté à une visite longue », ce qui signifie que les visiteurs ne doivent pas s'ennuyer, même dans le cas où ils y passent une journée entière. On a décidé de faire un bâtiment aussi bas que possible, de l'habiller entièrement de verre et d'implanter l'accès principal face à l'océan. Dans les minces panneaux d'acier des façades, des ouvertures ont été réalisées en fonction des perspectives qu'elles offrent sur l'extérieur, qui animent l'intérieur… Bien que ce musée semble faire partie de son environnement à l'extérieur et soit ouvert sur celui-ci, les visiteurs qui y pénètrent font à l'intérieur l'expérience d'un espace entièrement différent. » (Riken Yamamoto, *GA Document 98*)

Partially buried into its site, the Yokosuka Museum of Art has a sophisticated, sleek design that contrasts with the site, but also fits into it smoothly.

Das teilweise in den Boden eingelassene Yokosuka Museum mit seinem eleganten, geschmackvollen Design fügt sich sanft in das Gelände ein, bildet aber zugleich auch einen Kontrast zu seiner Umgebung.

Partiellement enterré, le musée d'Art de Yokosuka présente un dessin sophistiqué et lisse qui contraste avec le site, tout en s'y intégrant délicatement.

The clean lines of the building give it a decidedly minimalist appearance, with a mastery of materials and colors rendering spaces and volumes attractive.

Die klaren Linien geben dem Gebäude ein ausgesprochen minimalistisches Aussehen, und durch die meisterhafte Verwendung von Materialien und Farben erhalten die einzelnen Abschnitte eine besondere Attraktivität.

Les lignes nettes du bâtiment lui confèrent une apparence résolument minimaliste. La maîtrise des matériaux et des couleurs rend ces espaces très séduisants.

Where rectilinear design is the rule for the exterior volumes, curving stairs or round openings in galleries and public spaces provide a geometric contrast.

Als geometrischer Kontrast zu dem von rechten Winkeln bestimmten Äußeren finden sich in den Ausstellungsräumen und den sonstigen Besucherbereichen geschwungene Treppen und runde Wandöffnungen.

Si l'orthogonalité est de règle pour les volumes extérieurs, les escaliers incurvés et les ouvertures rondes dans les galeries et les espaces publics apportent un contraste géométrique.

PETER ZUMTHOR

Peter Zumthor
Atelier Zumthor
Süsswinkel 20
7023 Haldenstein
Switzerland

Tel: +41 81 353 28 06
Fax: +41 81 353 30 59

PETER ZUMTHOR was born in 1943 in Basel, Switzerland. In 1958, he worked as an apprentice carpenter. He graduated from the Schule für Gestaltung in Basel in 1963 and then attended the Pratt Institute in New York, studying Architecture and Design. From 1968 to 1977, he worked as an architect for the preservation of historic monuments in the Graubünden region of Switzerland. He served as tutor at the University of Zurich in 1978 and created his own firm in the town of Haldenstein, also in the Graubünden, in 1979. He has taught at SCI-Arc in Santa Monica, the Technische Universität of Munich, Tulane University in New Orleans, and at the Academy of Architecture in Mendrisio, beginning in 1996. His major buildings include the Thermal Baths in Vals (Switzerland, 1996); the Kunsthaus in Bregenz (Austria, 1997); and the Swiss Pavilion at Expo 2000 in Hanover (Germany, 2000). He also built a Single Family House (Graubünden, 1997–2003); and has recently completed the St. Niklaus von Flüe Chapel (Mechernich-Wachendorf, Germany, 2003–07); and the Kolumba Art Museum of the Archdiocese of Cologne (Cologne, Germany, 2003–07), both published here.

PETER ZUMTHOR wurde 1943 in Basel geboren. Nach einer Lehre als Möbelschreiner Ende der 1950er-Jahre besuchte er zunächst die Schule für Gestaltung in Basel (Abschluss 1963) und anschließend das Pratt Institute in New York, wo er Architektur und Design studierte. Von 1968 bis 1977 arbeitete er als Denkmalpfleger für den Kanton Graubünden. 1978 hatte er einen Lehrauftrag an der Universität Zürich, im darauffolgenden Jahr gründete er in Haldenstein in Graubünden ein eigenes Büro. Ab 1996 unterrichtete Zumthor am Southern California Institute of Architecture in Santa Monica, an der Technischen Universität München, an der Tulane University in New Orleans und an der Accademia di Architettura in Mendrisio im Tessin. Zu seinen bedeutendsten Bauten zählen die Therme Vals im gleichnamigen Ort in der Schweiz (1996), das Kunsthaus Bregenz (Österreich, 1997) und der schweizerische Pavillon für die Expo 2000 in Hannover. Ferner hat Zumthor ein Einfamilienhaus in Graubünden (1997–2003) ausgeführt und in jüngster Zeit eine Niklaus von Flüe gewidmete Kapelle in Mechernich-Wachendorf (2003–07) sowie das Diözesanmuseum Kolumba in Köln fertiggestellt (2003–07). Letztere werden hier vorgestellt.

PETER ZUMTHOR, né en 1943 à Bâle, Suisse, travaille d'abord comme apprenti-menuisier (1958). Il est diplômé de la Schule für Gestaltung de Bâle en 1963, puis étudie l'architecture et le design au Pratt Institute à New York. De 1968 à 1977, il est architecte spécialisé dans le patrimoine historique dans le canton des Grisons. Il est tuteur à l'université de Zurich en 1978 et crée sa propre agence à Haldenstein, également dans les Grisons, en 1979. Il a enseigné à SCI-Arc à Santa Monica, à la Technische Universität de Munich, à Tulane University à la Nouvelle-Orléans et à l'Académie d'architecture de Mendrisio, à partir de 1996. Parmi ses réalisations majeures : les Thermes de Vals (Suisse, 1996) ; la Kunsthaus de Bregenz (Autriche, 1997) et le pavillon suisse à Hanovre (Allemagne, 2000). Il a également construit une résidence familiale (Grisons, 1997–2003) et, plus récemment, la chapelle de St. Niklaus von Flüe (Mechernich-Wachendorf, Allemagne, 2003–07) et le musée d'Art Kolumba pour le diocèse de Cologne (Allemagne, 2003–07), tous deux publiés ici.

ST. NIKLAUS VON FLÜE CHAPEL

Mechernich-Wachendorf, Germany, 2003–07

Floor area: not disclosed. Height: 12 m. Client: Trudel, Hermann-Josef Scheidtweiler. Cost: not disclosed.
Collaborators: Rainer Weltschies, Michael Hemmi, Frank Furrer, Pavlina Lucas, Rosa Gonçalves

This chapel is located in the Eifel region of western Germany, not far from Cologne. Built at the same time as the Kolumba Art Museum in Cologne (2003–07, page 566), this unusual chapel, entered through a single triangular metal door, contains a five-cornered, windowless space almost 12 meters high, with an opening to the sky at its summit. It is dedicated to St. Niklaus von Flüe (1417–87), also known as Brother Klaus, a Swiss hermit and ascetic who is the patron saint of Switzerland. A small basin collects water, and a channel directs the water out of the building. The rough, dark texture of the walls was obtained by burning the 112 spruce branches used as formwork selected by the architect. Concrete was poured at the rate of one layer a day for a total of 24 layers before the inner branches or trunks were burnt. The farmer who commissioned the work built it himself with the help of a few neighbors and artisans.

Peter Zumthors Bruder-Klaus-Kapelle in der Eifel im Kreis Euskirchen entstand zwischen 2003 und 2007, im selben Zeitraum wie das Diözesanmuseum Kolumba (S. 566) in Köln. Betritt man die ungewöhnliche Feldkapelle durch ihre dreieckige Stahlpforte, befindet man sich in einem fünfeckigen, knapp 12 m hohen, fensterlosen Raum, der sich an seinem höchsten Punkt zum Himmel hin öffnet. Gewidmet ist die Kapelle dem Einsiedler und Asketen Niklaus von Flüe (1417–87), dem Schutzheiligen der Schweiz. Ein kleines Bassin im Kapelleninnern fängt Wasser auf, das durch einen Abfluss nach außen geleitet wird. Die dunkle, rußige Beschaffenheit der Wände kam durch ein Gerüst aus 112 Fichtenstämmen zustande, das zum Abschluss der Bauausführung abgebrannt wurde. Zuvor wurden um die Schalung herum insgesamt 24 Lagen Beton aufgegossen, eine Schicht pro Tag. Die Kapelle wurde vom Bauherrn selbst – einem Landwirt – mit der Hilfe von Nachbarn und einigen Handwerkern errichtet.

Cette chapelle se trouve dans la région de l'Eifel, dans l'ouest de l'Allemagne, non loin de Cologne. On pénètre dans ce lieu de prière pentagonal inhabituel, édifié au même moment que le musée d'Art Kolumba de Cologne (2003–07, page 566), par une unique porte triangulaire en métal. L'espace sans fenêtres mesure près de 12 mètres de haut sous une verrière zénithale. Le lieu est dédié à St. Niklaus von Flüe (1417–87), également connu sous le nom de frère Klaus, un ermite et ascète suisse, saint patron de la Suisse. Un petit bassin collecte l'eau de pluie et la dirige vers l'extérieur par un canal. La sombre texture brute des murs a été obtenue par le brûlage de 112 planches d'épicéa qui avaient servi au coffrage, toutes sélectionnées par l'architecte. Le béton a été coulé au rythme d'une couche par jour jusqu'à obtenir 24 couches avant que les branches intérieures ou troncs soient brûlées. Le fermier commanditaire de cette chapelle l'a construite lui-même avec l'aide de quelques voisins et artisans.

A simple triangular door leads into the Chapel, isolated in its field setting.

Die einsam auf einem Feld stehende Kapelle ist durch eine einfache, dreieckige Türöffnung zu betreten.

Une simple porte triangulaire donne accès à la chapelle, isolée dans les champs.

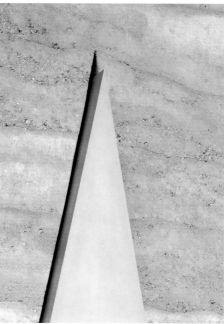

The Chapel stands alone, an enigmatic presence that does not immediately reveal its age. This is a modernity that does not lose sight of the past.

Die Kapelle ist ein geheimnisvoller Solitär, dessen Alter nicht sofort zu erraten ist. Hier trifft man auf eine Modernität, die die Vergangenheit nicht aus dem Blick verloren hat.

La chapelle se détache, retirée, présence énigmatique qui ne révèle pas immédiatement son âge. Sa modernité n'a pas rompu avec le passé.

The interior of the Chapel was black-
ened by burning the formwork used
for the exterior concrete walls. An
ovoid oculus marks the top of the
space and allows natural light in.

Durch das Verbrennen der Holzver-
schalung für die Betonwände erhielt
der Kapellenraum eine schwarze Fär-
bung. Ein ovaler Oculus markiert den
höchsten Punkt und lässt natürliches
Licht einfallen.

L'intérieur de la chapelle est en bois
de coffrage (utilisé pour la construction des murs) dont la surface a été
carbonisée. Tout en haut, un oculus
ovale admet la lumière du jour.

KOLUMBA ART MUSEUM OF THE ARCHDIOCESE OF COLOGNE

Cologne, Germany, 2003–07

Floor area: 3750 m².
Client: Archdiocese of Cologne. Cost: €44.5 million

The strong brick walls of the Museum are marked in their lower part by openings that allow some daylight into an area that contains archeological remains.

Die dicken Ziegelwände des Museums sind in ihrem unteren Bereich mit Öffnungen versehen, durch die Tageslicht in den um archäologische Funde herum angelegten Bereich dringt.

Les puissants murs de brique du musée sont allégés en partie inférieure par un bandeau travaillé qui permet à la lumière naturelle d'éclairer les salles archéologiques.

The building is an intriguing combination of decidedly modern architecture with archeological elements, and even encompasses a modern chapel by another architect.

Das Bauwerk ist eine faszinierende Kombination aus ausgesprochen moderner Architektur und archäologischen Elementen und bindet sogar den modernen Kapellenbau eines anderen Architekten mit ein.

Le bâtiment est une combinaison intrigante d'architecture très actuelle et d'éléments archéologiques. Il va jusqu'à englober une chapelle moderne due à un autre architecte.

Founded in 1853 by the Society for Christian Art, the Kolumba Museum came under the control of the Archdiocese of Cologne in 1989. In 1997, Peter Zumthor won the competition organized to create a new museum on the site of the St. Kolumba church, where a choir pier with a late Gothic sculpture of the Virgin Mary survived bombing in World War II. Gottfried Böhm designed a chapel to contain this relic and later archeological digs revealed Roman, Gothic, and medieval elements beneath the site of the former church. Zumthor designed a high, dark space with concrete and steel columns ringed by open brickwork to contain the archeological remains of the church and earlier traces found on the site. A red wood walkway allows visitors to walk through these remains. The Böhm chapel has been subsumed into the body of the Zumthor building. Very thin bricks form the façade of the new building, which has a blocklike appearance from the outside. An interior courtyard with a few trees occupies what used to be the church cemetery. The galleries of the museum, with 1600 square meters of floor area, were not designed for specific works, and the collections involved span the 2000 years of the history of Christianity. Zumthor's mastery here lies in his treatment of surfaces, materials, and light, creating a subtle and unusual mixture of geometric modernity and an obvious sensitivity not only to the archeological significance of the site, but also to such existing elements as Böhm's chapel.

Das heutige Kunstmuseum Kolumba wurde 1853 vom Christlichen Kunstverein gegründet, 1989 ging es in die Trägerschaft des Erzbistums Köln über. 1997 gewann Peter Zumthor den anonymen Wettbewerb für einen Kirchenneubau, der auf dem Gelände der im Zweiten Weltkrieg zerstörten Pfarrkirche St. Kolumba entstehen sollte. Die Zerstörung überstanden hatte ein Chorpfeiler mit einer spätgotischen Marienskulptur, um den herum 1950 die Kapelle „Madonna in den Trümmern" nach einem Entwurf von Gottfried Böhm errichtet wurde. In den folgenden Jahrzehnten förderten archäologische Grabungen römische, gotische und mittelalterliche Überreste zutage. Zumthor entwarf einen hohen, dunklen Raum aus Beton und Stahlpfeilern, der die Reste der Kirche und die archäologischen Mauerfunde umschließt. Museumsbesucher können über einen roten Steg durch die historischen Bauzeugnisse hindurchwandern. Auch Böhms Kapelle band Zumthor in seinen Entwurf ein. Die Fassade des Museums mit seiner kastenförmigen Außenerscheinung besteht aus ungewöhnlich schmalen Backsteinen. Auf dem einstigen Friedhof wurde ein Innenhof mit einigen Bäumen angelegt. Die Grundrisse der Ausstellungsräume mit einer Gesamtfläche von 1600 m² sind nicht auf eine bestimmte Aufstellung der Kunstwerke ausgerichtet, sondern bieten variablen Platz für einen Museumsbestand mit Stücken aus 2000 Jahren christlicher Geschichte. Zumthor legt in seinem Umgang mit Oberflächen, Materialien und Licht eine besondere Meisterschaft an den Tag. Das Ergebnis ist ein ungewöhnliches und feinsinniges Zusammenspiel aus geometrischer Moderne und unverkennbarem Gespür nicht nur für die archäologische Bedeutung des Orts, sondern auch für vorhandene Elemente wie Böhms Madonnenkapelle.

Fondé en 1853 par la Société pour l'art chrétien, le musée Kolumba a été confié à l'archidiocèse de Cologne en 1989. En 1997, Peter Zumthor a remporté le concours organisé pour construire un nouveau musée sur le site de l'église de Sainte-Colombe, où un pilier de chœur ornée d'une sculpture de la Vierge Marie en style gothique tardif avait survécu aux bombardements. Gottfried Böhm a conçu une chapelle qui contient ce vestige, puis des fouilles archéologiques ont mis à jour des éléments romains, gothiques et médiévaux sous l'ancienne église. Zumthor a conçu un volume haut et sombre à colonnes de béton et acier réunies par un une maçonnerie de brique pour protéger les vestiges archéologiques de l'église et ceux plus anciens trouvés sur place. Un passage en bois rouge permet aux visiteurs de déambuler parmi eux. La chapelle de Böhm a été intégrée dans le corps du nouveau bâtiment qui, de l'extérieur, semble très fermé. La façade de la nouvelle construction est en briques très minces. Une cour intérieure ornée de quelques arbres occupe l'ancien cimetière. Les galeries du musée de 1600 m² n'ont pas été dessinées en fonction des œuvres. La collection couvre 2000 ans de l'histoire du monde chrétien. La maîtrise de Zumthor se révèle ici dans le traitement des surfaces, des matériaux et de la lumière, et dans ce mélange subtil et surprenant de géométrie moderne et de sensibilité, non seulement au sens archéologique du site, mais aussi au regard des éléments existants comme la chapelle de Böhm.

The irregular pattern of openings in the lower wall surfaces breaks any hint of monotony or monumentality.

Dank der unregelmäßigen Muster der Öffnungen in den unteren Wandbereichen kommt weder Monotonie noch Monumentalität auf.

Le motif irrégulier de l'ouverture en bandeau rompt tout effet de monotonie ou de monumentalité.

The complexity of the architecture is naturally increased by the different archeological or historic elements. Zumthor manages, nonetheless, to preserve a unity and an undeniable strength in his intervention.

Die verschiedenen archäologischen oder historischen Elemente steuern natürlich zur Komplexität der Architektur bei. Dennoch gelingt es Zumthor, ein Ergebnis von unbestreitbarer Einheitlichkeit und Intensität vorzulegen.

La complexité de l'architecture est naturellement renforcée par la présence de divers éléments archéologiques et architecturaux. Peter Zumthor a réussi néanmoins à conserver une unité et une force indéniable.

A courtyard with a single visitor typi-
fies the quiet power of the architecture—amply present and yet in no
way obtrusive.

Ein einzelner Besucher im Innenhof
versinnbildlicht die stille Kraft der
Architektur – von imposanter Präsenz
und doch nicht aufdringlich.

Une cour et un visiteur, image
de la puissance tranquille de cette
architecture, fortement présente,
mais à aucun moment écrasante.

INDEX OF ARCHITECTS, BUILDINGS, AND PLACES

CREDITS